A Centenary History of Nottingham

A CENTENARY HISTORY OF
NOTTINGHAM

edited by John Beckett

with Philip Dixon, Adrian Henstock, Colin Griffin and Ken Brand

Phillimore

First published 1997 by Manchester University Press

This edition 2006
PHILLIMORE & CO. LTD
Shopwyke Manor Barn, Chichester, West Sussex, England
www.phillimore.co.uk

ISBN 1-86077-438-5
ISBN 13 978-1-86077-438-6

Typeset in Great Britain
by Northern Phototypesetting Co. Ltd., Bolton

Printed and bound in Great Britain by
CAMBRIDGE UNIVERSITY PRESS

To the people of Nottingham

Contents

List of plates

The majority of the illustrations in this book are from the collection in the Nottinghamshire County Library at Angel Row, Nottingham, and we are grateful to the County Council for permission to reproduce them.

List of figures

List of tables

Centenary History Advisory Board

Mr Tom Huggon (Chairman)

Professor John Beckett (University of Nottingham)

Mr Ken Brand (Nottingham Civic Society)

Mr Philip Dalling (University of Nottingham)

Dr Trevor Foulds (Nottingham City Council)

Dr Colin Griffin (Nottingham Trent University)

Dr Steven Halls (Nottingham City Council)

Mr Adrian Henstock (Nottinghamshire County Council and Thoroton Society)

Councillor Carole Stapleton (Nottingham City Council)

Mr Brian Loughbrough (co-opted)

Mr Bob Martin (Nottingham Society of Engineers)

Mrs Sandra Rose (The Boots Company PLC)

Mr Tim Saunders (T. Bailey Forman Ltd)

Mr Steven Scotney (Nottinghamshire County Council, Education Department)

Professor Hinrich Siefken (University of Nottingham)

Dr Richard Stevens (Nottingham and District Trades Union Council)

Mr Ron Walton (co-opted)

Mr Bob White (Nottingham City Council)

Mr Michael Williams (Nottingham City Council)

Mr Brian Playle (Secretary and Treasurer)

Centenary History sponsors

The Boots Company PLC

National Westminster Bank

Midland Bank

Greater Nottingham TEC

Nottingham Civic Society

Nottingham City Council

Nottinghamshire County Council

University of Nottingham

Nottingham Trent University

Marks & Spencer

Browne Jacobson

The Centenary History of Nottingham Advisory Board is also grateful to the following local companies and organisations who have contributed towards the success of the project: Benjamin Gough Ltd, Hawthornes Printers, CCN Group, T. Bailey Forman Ltd, East Midlands Electricity, Nottingham Building Society, Kodak Ltd, Dowsons, Wilkinsons, Warren & Allen, Banharts, Barton Buses, Commercial Union Assurance, Nottinghamshire Chamber of Commerce, Desa Limited, People's College, and Sherwood Press.

Foreword

It is a sobering thought that people are 'immortal' only as long as they are remembered by anyone still living. A person who has known great-grandparents is rare, and yet everyone feels some interest in the life of the past, and wants to find out what kind of existence the generality of people endured in the city with which they are familiar. Local history serves a human and educational purpose in attempting to satisfy this fundamental curiosity of human nature.

Henry Ford, the car manufacturer, disgracefully said that 'history is bunk', but perhaps someone who made history thought he did not need to understand it, which shows how much less of a human being he was than those who do. History is an attempt to recreate the past and learn its lessons. As a child at school the subject took account mainly of battles and imperial conquests, but I memorised their dates with alacrity, and perused accompanying maps with pleasure, as if such events were the gaudy garments fluttering from a clothes' line, whose gaps I was later to fill by extensive and enjoyable reading.

The more one reads the more one realises that there is much left to learn, especially with history, and with local history most of all, which one goes on reading in an attempt to make sense out of the lives of people who, by their reactions to adversity, reveal that human nature rarely alters. Local history enables us to grasp the reality of their lives, endured against a background of causes and events over which they had little control, though no doubt such conditions were different to those in existence today.

That the raw material of the past consists of ordinary people is a truism, yet it seems a little more true of Nottingham than anywhere else. The idiosyncratic and often turbulent nature of its inhabitants produced a more vivid past than most places. The history of the city also goes beyond the local because of its strategic situation.

Nottingham, the city of my heart, is endlessly fascinating. Previous histories, from Erring and Thoroton through to Emrys Bryson's *Portrait* published in 1974, are treasured and often consulted by me. This new work, edited by John Beckett and others, is important because every age needs to redefine the past from its particular and unique standpoint of the present. Ways of looking at the past change with every generation – or even decade – and a recording of such change is necessarily interesting. This factor is fully taken care of in a volume which will also find a permanent place on my shelf.

Alan Sillitoe, 1996

Preface

Nottingham has no recent municipal history. To coincide with the Coronation, Duncan Gray, City Librarian 1935–53, published a short history of Nottingham. As a single volume covering the city's complete history, it has not subsequently been superseded, although in many areas it is now long out of date.[1] Much new research has been undertaken in the past forty years, and the centenary of the City Charter in 1997 offered an opportunity to prepare a new history of Nottingham, a volume to rank alongside recent studies of other major provincial towns such as Birmingham, Leeds, and Sheffield. The result is this book.

The *Centenary History* project was launched in September 1991 with a ceremony in the Council House as a joint venture between the city, the county, local commerce and industry, and the two Nottingham universities. The project has involved a travelling exhibition focusing on the history of Nottingham, and designed to raise awareness of the city's past, an education pack for use in local schools during the centenary year (1997) and, as a centrepiece, this scholarly history bringing together the results of new and recent research in a single volume.[2] The book has been researched and written by academic and research staff of the two universities, together with a number of historians working in the local community. Although an Advisory Board has controlled the overall project, including financial sponsorship, the editorial team has enjoyed complete independence. This is not a celebratory volume of the older tradition of municipal history, but an attempt to present the history of Nottingham in a scholarly and judicious manner. However, the contributors have been uncomfortably aware over the past five years of how many areas remain to be researched in the future.

I am particularly grateful to the editorial team which has worked to produce this volume. The parameters of the book were originally established in conjunction with Richard Purslow of Manchester University Press in 1992–93, and at a meeting of contributors hosted by Professor Roger Tooze of Nottingham Trent University in April 1994. During the winter of 1994–95 the contributors were able to try out their ideas in a series of public seminars held at the Friends' Meeting House in Nottingham, and we are grateful to the vice-chancellors of the University of Nottingham and Nottingham Trent University for their sponsorship of these events.[3] A further and final opportunity for discussion was held on 1 July 1995, when contributors read papers to a specially invited audience, and received considerable feedback from three rapporteurs: Professor Peter Clark of the Centre for Urban History at the University of Leicester, Professor Martin Daunton of University

College London, and Dr Alan Vince of the City of Lincoln Archaeology Unit. We are grateful to Nottingham Trent University and Browne Jacobson, Solicitors, for sponsoring this event.

The book includes the findings of much new research. We are grateful to the Leverhulme Trust, sponsors of the Nottingham Borough Court Rolls project; to the University of Nottingham for funding the work on probate inventories and apprenticeship records (chapters 7 and 8) as well as for considerable help with cartographical and secretarial costs; to Nottingham Trent University for funding part of the research in chapter 22 and elsewhere in the book; and to the Centenary History Advisory Board for help with research costs. The Better Employment Skills Training Company (BESTCO) kindly helped with our work on oral history, and many of the interviews were conducted by Peter Diamond. Julie O'Neill (chapter 21) is particularly grateful to Nottinghamshire County Leisure Services Department for permission to use extracts from the Oral History Collection at the County Library in Nottingham, and to the Nottingham residents who agreed to be interviewed and permit the use of their taped memories in the *Centenary History*. We are grateful also to Sue Clayton for help with interviews. Jeff Hill (chapter 22) wishes to thank Ken Gibson and Philip Gorski for carrying out archival research; John Giggs (chapter 18) is particularly grateful to Graham Gardner, Paul Hillier, Stuart Robertson, and Amanda Rowley; and Brian Tolley (chapter 23) wishes to thank Ian Ward. Others who have made their expertise available and in so doing saved us from many possible errors include Stephen Best, Alan Booth, Wendy Bowen, Michael Brook, Steph. Mastoris, Brian Playle and John Severn.

We should also like to thank the following for their contributions towards the production of this book: the staff of Nottinghamshire Archives Office, Nottingham University Manuscripts Department, the Local Studies Library of the County Library, Angel Row, the Brewhouse Yard and Castle Museums, and the Nottingham *Evening Post*. John Severn collected the data for figures 15.1 and 15.2, Ben Cowell prepared the graphs, Chris Lewis and David Taylor drew the maps and plans, Ian Brown, Trevor Clayton, and Martine Hamilton-Knight took most of the pictures. Many local people were kind enough to draw our attention to sources which we might otherwise have missed, and others pointed to matters of moment through their participation in the seminar series. Although we cannot thank them individually we are most grateful for their help. The Leisure Services Departments of Nottinghamshire County Council and Nottingham City Council kindly agreed to waive reproduction rights so that we could use some of the best photographs and pictures in their care. Many other individuals are thanked in the endnotes, for their help and advice.

Finally, as editor-in-chief, I have a number of personal thanks to offer. First, to Brian Loughbrough, formerly Director of Leisure Services for Nottingham City Council, who was instrumental in setting up the project; and then to his successor as chairman of the Advisory Board, Tom Huggon, who has been a magnificent supporter throughout, encouraging and cajoling contributors and fending off over-exuberant suggestions from local government officials! Second, to the many local companies and organisations who have sponsored the *Centenary History* project, and perhaps most notably Sandra Rose and The Boots Company PLC (the principal sponsors). Third, to Ken Brand of Nottingham Civic Society, whose unpaid research for the volume was undertaken with a speed, efficiency, and cheerfulness calculated to put the rest of the team to shame, and whose energy in collecting pictures has been astonishing. Finally, to Janice Avery of the History Department at the University of Nottingham, who has cheerfully undertaken a vast amount of administrative work throughout the project and, in the final stages of production, put in more hours than she cares to remember ensuring that the whole manuscript was accurately typed, that endnotes were in the right places, and that the text was complete.

This is not the last word on Nottingham's history, but it has been a collective effort involving many people and many organisations, not least Manchester University Press who have worked with us throughout. For the mistakes that remain the editors and contributors can only apologise and accept full responsibility.

Easter 1996 John Beckett

Notes

1 Duncan Gray, *Nottingham: Settlement to City* (Nottingham, 1953). The British Association volume, K. C. Edwards (ed.), *Nottingham and Its Region* (Nottingham, 1966) was in some ways a replacement for Gray, although it covered a much greater range of subjects and a broader area.

2 A second volume, telling the same story but in a popular format and with many more pictures, will also be published by Manchester University Press during 1997.

3 The seminars were held on 25 October and 23 November 1994, and 26 January, 7 March, 2 May and 8 June 1995.

List of contributors

John Beckett Professor of English Regional History, University of Nottingham

Philip Dixon Senior Lecturer, Department of Archaeology, University of Nottingham, and currently President of the Council for British Archaeology

David Knight Field Archaeologist, Trent and Peak Archaeology Trust

Ron Firman Senior Research Fellow, Department of Archaeology, University of Nottingham

David Roffe historian

Trevor Foulds Documentary Historian, Nottingham City Council, Brewhouse Yard Museum

Pamela Marshall field archaeologist

David Marcombe Senior Lecturer, Department of Continuing Education, University of Nottingham, and Director of the Centre for Local History, University of Nottingham

Adrian Henstock Principal Archivist, Nottinghamshire County Council

Sandra Dunster part-time tutor, University of Nottingham

Stephen Wallwork formerly Reader in Chemistry, University of Nottingham

Martin Bennett Senior Lecturer, Department of International Studies, Nottingham Trent University

Ken Brand local historian and vice-chairman of the Nottingham Civic Society

Geoffrey Oldfield local historian

Stanley Chapman Professor of Business History, Department of History, University of Nottingham

Brian Tolley Senior Lecturer, Department of Education, University of Nottingham

Colin Griffin Reader in History, Department of International Studies, Nottingham Trent University

John Giggs Reader in Geography, Department of Geography, University of Nottingham

Nick Hayes Lecturer in History, Department of International Studies, Nottingham Trent University

Julie O'Neill local historian

Jeff Hill Principal Lecturer in History, Department of International Studies, Nottingham Trent University

Richard Stevens historian

Abbreviations

Anon.	'Copy [by Dr Charles Deering] of a Ms Account of Nottingham [1641]', *Transactions of the Thoroton Society*, 2 (1898), pp. 17–57
Bailey, *Annals*	T. Bailey, *Annals of Nottinghamshire: History of the County of Nottingham including the Borough* (4 vols., Nottingham, 1853)
Barley and Straw	M. W. Barley and F. I. Straw, 'Nottingham', in M.D. Lobel (ed.), *Historic Towns*, I (1969)
BL	British Library
Blackner	J. Blackner, *The History of Nottingham* (Nottingham, 1815)
Brazier, *New Geography*	S. Brazier *et al.*, *A New Geography of Nottingham* (2nd edn Nottingham, 1988)
CClR	*Calendars of the Close Rolls* (PRO)
Church	R. A. Church, *Economic and Social Change in a Midland Town: Victorian Nottingham, 1815–1900* (1966)
CPR	*Calendars of the Patent Rolls* (PRO)
DAJ	*Derbyshire Archaeological Journal*
Date Book	H. Field (ed.), *The Date Book of Remarkable and Memorable Events connected with Nottingham, 850–1884* (Nottingham, 1884)
Deering	C. Deering, *Nottinghamia Vetus Et Nova or an Historical Account of the Ancient and Present State of the Town of Nottingham* (Nottingham, 1751)
DNB	Dictionary of National Biography
Drage, *Castle*	C. Drage, 'Nottingham Castle: a place full Royal', *Transactions of the Thoroton Society*, 93 (1989)
EC	Nottingham City Council, Education Committee
Edwards	K. C. Edwards (ed.), *Nottingham and its Region* (Nottingham, 1966)
EMG	*East Midland Geographer*
EP	*Nottingham Evening Post*
Gawthern, *Diary*	A. Henstock (ed.), *The Diary of Abigail Gawthern of Nottingham 1751–1810* (*Thoroton Society Record Series*, 33, 1980)

Gray, *500 Years*	D. Gray, *Nottingham through 500 Years* (2nd edn, Nottingham, 1960)
Gray, *Settlement*	D. Gray, *Nottingham: Settlement to City* (Nottingham, 1953)
HMC, *Middleton*	Historical Manuscripts Commission, *Report on the Manuscripts of Lord Middleton preserved at Wollaton Hall* (1911)
Iliffe and Baguley	R. Iliffe and W. Baguley, *Victorian Nottingham: a story in pictures* (20 vols., Nottingham, 1970–83)
NAO	Nottinghamshire Archives Office
Newstead I	College of Arms MS 60 (Newstead Priory cartulary of 1286)
Newstead II	V. W. Walker (trans.), and D. Gray (ed.), *Newstead Priory Cartulary, 1344 and other archives* (Nottingham, 1940)
NG	*Nottingham Guardian*
NH	*Nottinghamshire Historian*
NJ	*Nottingham Journal*
NLSL	Nottinghamshire Local Studies Library
NR	*Nottingham Review*
NUMD	Nottingham University Manuscripts Department
Orange	J. Orange, *History and Antiquities of Nottingham* (2 vols., 1840)
Pevsner and Williamson	N. Pevsner and E. Williamson, *The Buildings of England: Nottinghamshire* (2nd edn., 1979)
PR	Pipe Roll Society, Pipe Rolls
PRO	Public Record Office
RBN	W. Stevenson *et al.* (eds.), *Records of the Borough of Nottingham*, I–IX (Nottingham, 1882–1956)
Rufford Charters	C. J. Holdsworth (ed.), *Rufford Charters*, I (*Thoroton Society Record Series*, 24, 1972)
Thomis, *Politics*	M. I. Thomis, *Politics and Society in Nottingham, 1785–1835* (Oxford, 1969)
Thoroton	R. Thoroton, *The Antiquities of Nottinghamshire* (1677)
Thurgarton Cartulary	T. Foulds (ed.), *Thurgarton Priory Cartulary* (Stamford, 1994)
TSRS	*Thoroton Society Record Series*
TTS	*Transactions of the Thoroton Society*
VCH *Nottinghamshire*	Victoria County History, Nottinghamshire, *I (1906), II (1910)*
White	W. White, *History and Directory of the County of Nottinghamshire* (1832, 1844, 1853)
Wylie	W.H. Wylie, *Old and New Nottingham* (1853)

Introduction

John Beckett

Modern Nottingham is a thriving provincial city in the heart of midland England. Home to more than one-quarter of a million people, and a work and shopping area to many more, it sits just to the east of the M1, two hours' drive north of London, close to the centre of England. Visitors tend to come in search of the people's hero Robin Hood and a medieval castle, or to buy the city's famous lace products and stare at its traditionally pretty girls. The city shamelessly uses Robin Hood to attract tourists, and has even considered trying to recreate something of the medieval castle, which was demolished more than 300 years ago. But there is much more to Nottingham than this. For more than 1,000 years people have lived and worked in the town. Over the first 800 years of that period it was a small, compact settlement locked between what is today Parliament Street to the north and Canal Street to the south, and between Chapel Bar to the west and the Ice Stadium to the east. The physically fit could walk the limits in either direction in around ten minutes. And it was also small in size, with 3,000 or at maximum 4,000 people scattered around its streets and narrow lanes. Only in the eighteenth century did it begin to change. Numbers grew, houses were built in profusion, and the town expanded near to bursting point within its medieval boundaries. From the 1850s the bubble was slowly deflated as development took place to the north, to the south, to the west, and in the surrounding villages which in 1877 were incorporated within the town. A city charter followed in 1897, and over the past 100 years the centre has gradually been transformed into a commercial and business area, while the population has moved to new estates in areas brought within the boundaries through twentieth-century extensions, and to suburbs beyond the city limits. Today Nottingham is a thriving city, priding itself on being – in its own view, at least – the 'Queen of the Midlands'. This is its story.

City biographies are recognised as 'essential' by modern urban historians,[1] and this is a study in the modern mode, a critical discussion, not a gilded celebratory account.[2] Yet the biography of a living town must be, like biographies of people who are still alive, an interim statement. Nottingham has no recent or complete history. The earliest published account of the town was by Dr Robert Thoroton in 1677, although the first single-volume history was Charles Deering's *Nottingham*, published posthumously in 1751 and now most useful for its contemporary accounts of events in the town. Deering was followed by John Blackner, James Orange, and a series of brief accounts of the town, written in the typical Victorian style.[3] In the twentieth century there have been a number of histories, many of them drawing on the work of earlier scholars.[4] Brief contributions were made in the post-war years by Professor J. D. Chambers, and the City Librarian Duncan Gray. An important study of the nineteenth-century town was published in 1966 by Roy Church.[5] Although articles and books on different aspects of the city's history have been published in profusion, no recent attempt has been made to bring this research, and new and unpublished research, together to compile a comprehensive account of the city's history. In this book, published to coincide with the centenary of the City Charter, we offer much new evidence relating to the city, culled from archaeological, architectural and documentary sources, and many original interpretations which are set within the wider context of urban issues, including the late medieval crisis, the urban renaissance of the period 1660–1760, and the significance in the more recent period of suburbanisation and class-distinctions.

To try to give some coherence to our biography, we have divided the story loosely into four parts. In a broad sweep, Part I carries us from Neolithic man to the mid-sixteenth century. Nottingham cannot offer the romance of a York or a Lincoln, with their major Viking (in the case of York) and Roman settlements, so the story really begins in 920 when Nottingham became a key centre of royal administration with a regional role throughout the Midlands. Initially a Saxon *burgh* was established on the plateau of St Mary's Hill (the Lace Market area of the modern city), but when William I built a castle several hundred yards to the west in 1067–68 he founded a new borough. This soon grew physically to link up with the Saxon *burh* across the divide between St Mary's Hill and Castle Rock, and to create a built-up area which remained almost unchanged in size until the 1850s. Physically, the town lay over a mile north of the River Trent, on high ground above the floodplain, and until the building of the canal contact between town and river was always difficult and may have impeded its economic development. The Castle, built as a defensive fortress, became a royal palace, but life in the medieval town went on with only occasional interruptions for monarchical visitations. Thanks to the extraordinarily rich material in the (almost unique) series of borough court rolls, chapters 4 and 5 offer a series of remarkable insights into the life of the town in the Middle Ages. Chapter 6 carries the story on to look at how the town changed in the wake of the 1449 Charter of Incorporation and then at its response to the Protestant Reformation.

Although the layout of the town was well established by 1550, and is known in detail from the maps of 1609 and 1610, few physical structures have survived. The most notable exceptions, apart from a handful of domestic buildings and two city-centre public houses, are St Mary's and St Peter's churches. This is partly a consequence of the major rebuilding and refurbishing of the town which is described in Part II. With the introduction of brick as a building material in the early seventeenth century, and allowing for the disruption caused by the civil wars in which – despite the town's fame as the place where Charles I raised his standard in 1642

– Nottingham took the Parliamentarian side, a new townscape began to emerge. Many of the houses surviving in the city centre today date from the great rebuilding of the years after 1660. Perhaps the most notable is the Duke of Newcastle's magnificent Renaissance palace on Castle Rock, which replaced the old medieval castle while adopting (misleadingly for visitors) its name. With improvements to the water supply and to public buildings, by 1750 Nottingham was a fashionable town, even if constraints of space and topography ensured that it was never able to develop the planned promenades and squares of York and Bath. Even so, 'prospects' of the town drawn in the early eighteenth century, and Thomas Sandby's superb marketplace perspectives of the 1740s, can leave no one in any doubt that Nottingham was a splendid place.[6] In the first half of the eighteenth century it was also growing. A major new analysis of population (chapter 8) pinpoints the start of rapid and sustainable growth, which coincided with the early development of hosiery manufacture.

Part III carries the town from Georgian splendour, to Victorian slum, and on to improved Edwardian city. Between the mid-eighteenth century and the 1830s the town grew rapidly, as hosiery and later lace became major occupations. It also grew in upon itself because the open fields which surrounded it remained unenclosed. Houses were built on every conceivable piece of land, and even when the hosiery industry went into prolonged depression after 1815 people continued to crowd into the town, attracted by rapidly expanding opportunities in the lace industry in the 1820s. By 1830 50,000 people were living in the space which had seldom accommodated more than 3,000–4,000 before the late seventeenth century. Many more had flowed out into newly developing industrial villages on the periphery, but in the inner core conditions deteriorated. In the 1830s the reform of the Municipal Corporations, the demands of the newly-formed railway companies to run lines into Nottingham, and the movement of employers to the industrial villages in search of building land, reopened the debate on enclosure. The issue came to a head following a government enquiry in 1844, when Nottingham was shown to have some claim to forming the worst urban slum in England. As a direct result, and in spite of fierce opposition, the open fields were enclosed in the period 1845–67. This was no instant solution to the town's problems, but gradually the centre was redeveloped (particularly with the creation of the Lace Market), the old open fields were covered with houses and factories as the hosiery industry at last came out of recession and followed the lace industry in using powered machinery, and the middle classes retreated into purpose-built suburbs such as the Park Estate. By the closing years of the nineeeteenth century industry was diversifying out of textiles into a range of new interests, including bicycle-making, pharmaceuticals and cigarette manufacture, the problems of public health were being systematically tackled, and the borough extension of 1877 brought within the town boundaries the industrial villages round the periphery. What was already a major provincial town received a city charter as part of the celebrations surrounding Queen Victoria's Diamond Jubilee in 1897. Yet the extent of improvement must not be exaggerated: as late as 1920 an application to extend the borough boundaries was turned down partly on the grounds that

Nottingham had an excessive number of poor-quality houses, mostly dating from the 1820s and earlier.

In the twentieth century, the subject of Part IV, the major development can be summed up as diversification. The rapid population growth which was such a feature of Victorian Nottingham has ceased, leaving the city hardly any larger – in simple numbers – than in 1901. What has changed is the physical shape and form of Nottingham as the old town centre has become the commercial heart of the city. The middle-class movement to the suburbs began in the nineteenth century, but in the twentieth century they have moved further afield – indeed many of them now live in districts outside the town boundaries. Major rehousing programmes have seen the working classes moved from the early nineteenth-century slums during the inter-war years to new council estates, and since the 1970s into new housing within the Meadows and St Ann's, both post-enclosure developments. The large estates are on land brought within the borough boundaries by extensions in 1932 and 1951, so that the city area today is about nine miles from north to south and five-and-a-half miles from east to west. The heart of pre-1850 Nottingham is virtually deserted for residential purposes; instead it is a thriving commercial area, with two vast retail centres (Broad Marsh and Victoria) sitting where once there were notorious slums. The century has seen considerable improvements in public health, although with significant variations depending on area, and in educational provision. Nottingham is still a textile centre, but the largest employer is now Boots (pharmaceuticals) and, as elsewhere, service industries have become the major feature of the employment structure. Nottingham has fostered, and continues to foster its image as 'Queen of the Midlands'.

This is a complex story, and yet we are well aware that in numerous respects we are glossing over broad issues about which we still know far too little. In this sense we are also setting an agenda for future research, particularly perhaps about the twentieth century, where the number of topics is so large that we have been able here to do no more than offer a series of essays. In the process many subjects have been excluded: we have said little about the physical impact of war,[7] town planning,[8] the development of the National Health Service, and the role of the city council in local government and as an employer, to name only a handful. Others, including the modernisation of the twentieth-century city,[9] have perhaps received less than their due share of attention, but a volume of this nature is always going to have difficulty placing the rapid and unprecedented changes which have occurred in the twentieth century into the true perspective of the long view of history. Similarly it has been impossible to do justice to every firm and every organisation whose work goes towards maintaining the economic, professional, cultural and educational fabric of city life. To have even tried to do so would have saddled us with long lists, and those lists would have throttled our search for trends and movement through time.[10]

While recognising these omissions – and the list could be extended by many pages both for the twentieth century and earlier periods – we have tried to reflect changes of interest in the historical agenda. Thirty years ago, when the British Association visited Nottingham, it was thought sufficient to discuss 'leisure' purely in terms of libraries, museums and theatre.[11] Today, with the development of social history, this is seen as inadequate as a description of leisure because it omits popular culture, and both chapters 16 and 22 have been written with these more recent considerations in mind. Yet so vast has been the change in the twentieth century that we can still only touch the surface of the subject: it seems scarcely credible than it is only 120 years since Nottingham people reached the seaside, when the railway line to Skegness was laid in 1873. First came the day trip, then the boarding-house holiday, and then after 1945, the static caravan. Today Spain and Florida are increasingly the holiday spots sought out by working people with more money in their pockets, and a greater awareness of the flat dreariness and inclement weather of the Lincolnshire coastline. Here is a subject worthy of study in itself, but it is one to which we have been able to make only passing reference.

Also reflecting a change in the way we view the past, greater emphasis is now placed by urban historians on the visual understanding of our cities. As H. J. Dyos, the founder of modern British urban history, wrote in 1974, 'the most fundamental obligation of urban history … is to undertake a task no one else will and make plain how the land was built upon in the way that it was'.[12] Or, in the more recent words of his successor as editor of *Urban History*, a town biography should

> enrich the historical awareness of urban communities. Contemporary interest in the heritage industry, in renovation, and in city centre refurbishment result in part from a deepening community-based awareness of local historical and urban culture … urban biographies provide the empirical bedrock for systematic analyses of the processes at work within towns and cities.[13]

The comparative perspective we can adopt must be weaker than that to be found in studies which cover groups of towns – although wherever possible we have drawn attention to relevant comparisons – but at the same time we attempt to investigate, analyse and explain the economic, political, social and cultural processes which go to make up 'the city of Nottingham'. We examine the changing economic foundations, and we look at the way in which these have affected the city's physical shape, its built environment, employment opportunities and its 'urban character'.

H. J. Dyos wrote on one occasion that 'when I think about cities, I think the central purpose to the thing is finding some way to explain how this, outside the window here, came about, and what it means to those experiencing it'.[14] In this book we shall be looking out of the window to try to explain the long history of Nottingham. How did settlement come to this area and then develop on this particular site, and what did it mean to those who were there and who have left a record of the experiences? In describing and explaining the history of Nottingham we hope to open up many vistas, and perhaps even to move beyond some of the stereotypical images of the city. When William Cobbett came to Nottingham in 1830 he wrote that his interest in the town was stirred by the tales of Robin Hood, and rumours of its 'sprightly and beautiful women'.[15] Today Robin Hood remains one of the cornerstones of the city's tourist industry, and as this book was near completion the local BBC radio station *Radio Nottingham* was preparing a series of programmes on pretty girls in the city. Yet there is much more to Nottingham than these stereotypes, and we hope to reveal some of the many colours in the mosaic of the city's long and rich history.

Notes

1 R. Rodger, 'Urban History: prospect and retrospect', *Urban History*, 19 (1992), p. 8. We recognise however, from painful experience (!), that some urban historians may agree with Lynn Hollen Lees that 'these urban biographies have absorbed all too much of urban historians' energies': 'The challenge of political change: urban history in the 1990s', *Urban History*, 21 (1994), p. 9.

2 G. H. Martin and S. McIntyre, *A Bibliography of British and Irish Municipal History* (1972).

3 Thoroton; Deering; Blackner; Orange; Wylie; G. A. Cooke, *Topographical and statistical description of Nottingham* (n.d.); C. Brown, *A History of Nottingham* (1891); W. H. Wylie and J. Potter Briscoe, *A Popular History of Nottingham* (1893). Although some of the nineteenth-century works were rather thin, credit should be given to W. H. Stevenson and his fellow authors who began the series *Records of the Borough of Nottingham*, I–IX (1882–1956), which covers the period to 1900 and has been drawn upon liberally in Parts I to III of this book. For the origins of this series see I, pp. v–viii.

4 E. L. Guilford, *Nottingham* (1920); *The Book of Nottingham* (1926); R. Mellors, *Men of Nottingham and Nottinghamshire* (1924).

5 J. D. Chambers, *Modern Nottingham in the Making* (Nottingham, 1945); *A Century of Nottingham History, 1851–1951* (1952); Gray, *Settlement*; Gray, *500 Years*; Church. The series of illustrated books by Iliffe and Baguley have also added greatly to our knowledge of the nineteenth-century town.

6 For Sandby see plate 23. Perhaps the most magnificent of all is Jan Sieberechts' 'Prospect' of *c.*1700, now in the Nottingham Castle Museum.

7 Nottingham suffered relatively little damage in the two world wars, although there was much disruption to local life, which is touched on in several chapters. See also P. Foster, 'Zeppelins over Nottingham', *NH*, 44 (1990), pp. 23–8; 'The Nottingham Blitz, May 1941', *NH*, 38 (1987), pp. 7–9; C. Hardy and N. Arthur, *Nottingham at War, 1939–45* (1986).

8 For a brief overview see Brazier, *New Geography*, ch. 12.

9 Brazier, *New Geography*; M. Barley and R. Cullen, *Nottingham Now* (Nottingham, 1975); *Nottingham's Heritage* (Nottingham City Planning Department, 1985).

10 It is hoped to pay more attention to individual people and firms in the companion volume to this book.

11 Edwards, pp. 416–27.

12 Editorial in the *Urban History Yearbook*, I (1974), pp. 3–6.

13 R. Rodger, 'Urban History', p. 8.

14 Quoted in R. J. Dennis, *English Industrial Cities of the Nineteenth Century* (Cambridge, 1984), p. 294.

15 William Cobbett, *Rural Rides* (1982 edn), pp. 155–6.

Part I

THE ORIGINS OF NOTTINGHAM AND THE MEDIEVAL TOWN

1

THE ORIGINS OF NOTTINGHAM

Philip Dixon, David Knight and Ron Firman

Topography and geology

Until its Victorian expansion, Nottingham was built wholly and exclusively on or in, but not of, sandstone. This formation was formerly called the Bunter Pebble Beds, and is now known to geologists as the Nottingham Castle Sandstone.[1] It is dissected by shallow valleys and extends, under rising ground, north through Sherwood into the Dukeries area of north Nottinghamshire and beyond. In the city itself, its outcrop is abruptly truncated by a discontinuous line of ancient river cliffs, separated by southward-directed valleys which formerly were occupied by powerfully erosive tributaries of the Trent. The valley in the Park is particularly deeply incised, and its eastern slopes beneath the Ropewalk and the Castle are especially steep. These formed in part a natural boundary to the medieval town.

All four sandstone bluffs, bounded by cliffs (the Park, Castle Rock, Lace Market and Sneinton Hermitage) overlook the important shallow river-crossing now utilised by Trent Bridge. Only the 500 metres of cliffs stretching east from Broad Marsh were capped by a sufficiently large relatively flat area on which a defensible town could be built, and it was here that the late Saxon *burh* was established. To the west, the higher but smaller sandstone spur may have been occupied in prehistoric times, but it seems to have had no other occupants until the building of the Castle in the eleventh century. The later medieval town spread into the intervening valley between the *burh* and the Castle, and also north and north-west towards what is now Parliament Street and Chapel Bar.[2] The topography was the result of the glacial and post-glacial erosion of the sandstone, and affected the choice of sites, defences, and to some extent the street plan and road approaches to the town.

The underlying, 240 million-year-old coarse, pebble, cross-bedded sandstone has a remarkable combination of properties which significantly influenced the town's development and environment. First, it is exceptionally permeable; this ensures not only a guaranteed supply of drinking-water from sufficiently deep wells (perhaps up to thirty metres deep at the Castle),[3] but excellently drained building sites, streets, roads and easily constructed soakaways for effluents – a not unimportant consideration in medieval towns. Second, though the rock is generally weak and friable, its strength increases sufficiently with depth to make the sandstone, at a depth of two to six metres, an almost ideal medium for tunnelling when only hand tools were available. The sub-vertical joints at these depths are widely spaced, about ten metres apart. Thus if roof spans are not excessive, excavations into the rock are self-supporting, and cliffs and buildings could be safely undermined. No doubt it was because of the ease with which the sandstone could be excavated that by 1840 Nottingham had more man-made underground structures for its area than any other British town. Some probably pre-date the Norman Conquest, but most seem to have been excavated before the mid-nineteenth century. The structures included rock houses and probably hermitages in the old river cliffs, malt kilns, public-house cellars, storage vaults and even a tannery. Beyond the town walls sand mines were developed adjacent to the hollow ways along the Derby and Mansfield roads.[4]

Apart from this building sand, and rare instances (as at Bramcote, where the sandstone is cemented with baryte) the Nottingham Castle Sandstone was unsuitable for building. Thus one disadvantage was that almost all building materials, including timber and clay, had to be transported from outlying areas: Wollaton, Trowell and Stanton for well-cemented Coal Measures sandstones; Bulwell for magnesian limestone and lime; and Gedling for the softer, more workable Triassic waterstone. Clay presumably had to be brought either from the Trent or from weathered Mercia Mudstones at Mapperley and Carlton, where later huge quarries for brick were developed. During the Middle Ages stone for special purposes was brought from further afield, including Swarkstone and Mansfield, but it was not until the railway era that substantial quantities were transported more than twenty miles, and then only for prestige buildings.

The great Victorian expansion of Nottingham saw the town expand on the sandstone north into Forest Fields and Hyson Green and west into Radford; north-east across the Clay Field, underlain by Mercia Mudstones, on to the more hilly ground of St Ann's; and south over the wetter lands of the Meadows on the Trent flood plain. Yet even today more than half of the built area of Nottingham is on the Nottingham Castle Formation.

Palaeolithic hunter-gatherers (*c.* 500,000–10,000 BC)

The prehistoric origins of Nottingham are obscure, but evidence from neighbouring areas of the Trent Valley suggests that we should expect a much higher density of prehistoric settlement in the area of the modern city than can at present be demonstrated. Urban and industrial development since the nineteenth century has destroyed without record most of the sites to be expected in this area. Consequently the present distribution of sites and finds in the area of the city can be understood only by looking at the Trent Valley as a whole. Previous archaeological surveys have emphasised the richness of the area's prehistoric archaeological resource, and it seems reasonable to assume that Nottingham must have shared the general pattern.[5]

The earliest settlement of the middle Trent Valley was by small bands of Palaeolithic ('Old Stone Age') hunter-gatherers, represented in the archaeological record by discarded stone artefacts and the waste flakes derived from tool manufacture.[6] Climatic and vegetation conditions, and hence the suitability of the area for settlement, varied significantly during this lengthy period, and changes affected even the appearance of the landscape. Ice sheets periodically penetrated this region during the period between about 500,000 and 130,000 years ago, scouring away *in situ* artefactual and structural traces of human activity: our knowledge of the Lower and Middle Palaeolithic settlement of the area, between about 500,000 and 40,000 years ago, is accordingly at present based upon finds redeposited in glacial outwash or boulder clays. The largest groups of implements have been recorded during gravel extraction, notably in the sand and gravel deposits of the Hilton Terrace at Hilton and Willington, Derbyshire, and from the Beeston Terrace during extraction at the Stoney Street and Tottle Brook gravel pits in Beeston. Many commentators have drawn attention to the small quantity of Lower and Middle Palaeolithic material which has been recorded, by comparison with areas further south, especially the Thames Valley, but it is unclear whether this shows a genuinely low density of human activity, or is due to the smaller number of collectors and the heavy emphasis upon mechanical extraction in the Trent Valley by comparison with the Thames and other areas, where large-scale manual excavations were carried out from the nineteenth century. A few finds have also been recovered from boulder clays laid down by advancing ice sheets, notably at Thorpe in the Glebe, but again the sites from which they derived no longer survive.[7]

Evidence of Upper Palaeolithic activity in the middle Trent Valley is largely restricted to single finds of the late Upper Palaeolithic period, between about 13,000 and 10,000 BC. The most significant discovery is a dense cluster of flintwork recorded during recent fieldwalking of the Floodplain Terrace at Farndon Fields, Newark, which may represent a rare example of an open-air settlement. Some of the flint resembles artefacts of the late Upper Palaeolithic ('Creswellian') phase at the caves of Creswell Crags, about twenty-two miles to the north-west; Farndon Fields could have been a stopping point for some of the wide-ranging hunter-gatherer bands who may have used the caves as temporary shelters during hunting expeditions.[8] This could indicate that parts of the Trent Valley, which would have comprised a shifting network of braided channels over a wide plain, with scant steppe or tundra vegetation on raised areas of sand and gravel, had served as the hunting and gathering grounds for groups ranging widely over territories extending at least to Creswell Crags.

Figure 1.1 The geology of the Nottingham area

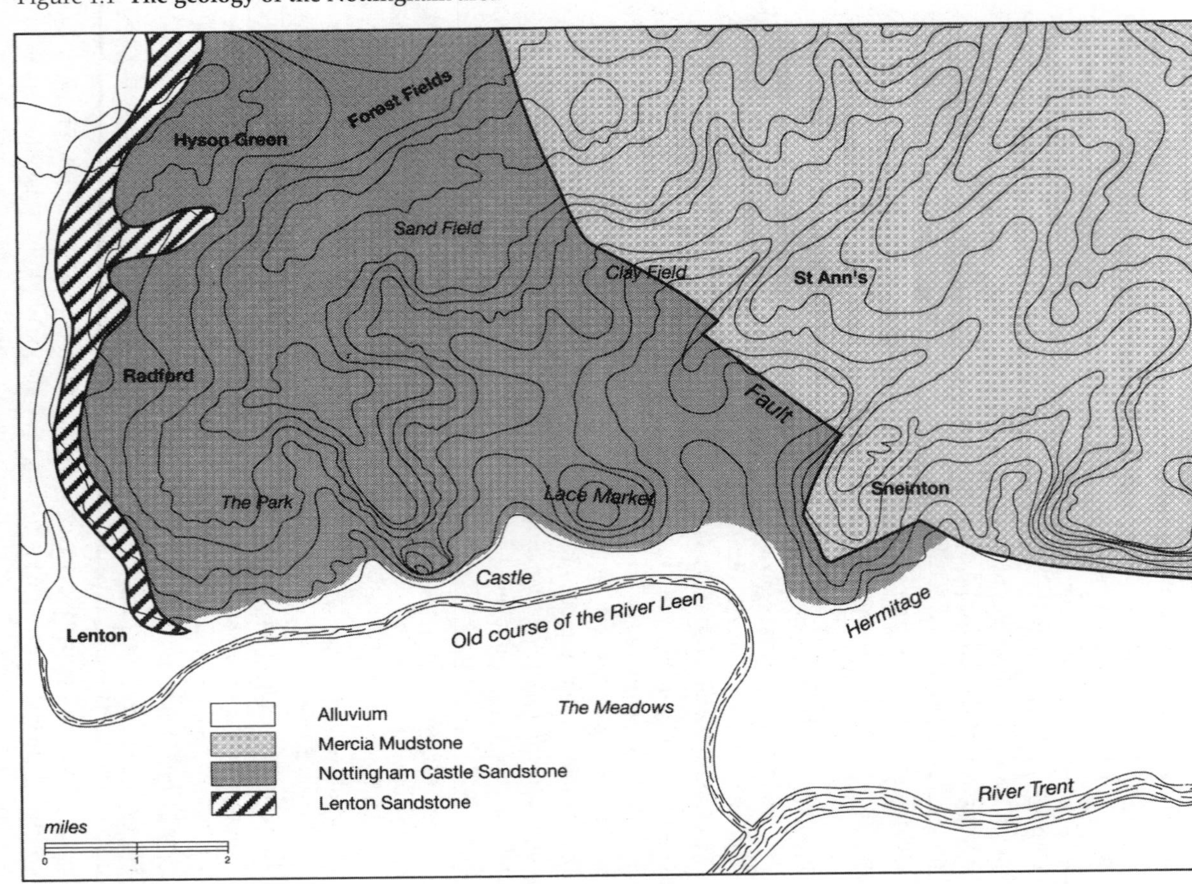

Mesolithic hunter-gatherer communities (*c.*10,000–4,000 BC)

Warming of the climate from about 10,000 BC, and the gradual colonisation of the Trent Valley by mixed woodland, created favourable conditions for post-glacial hunter-gatherer communities. These 'Mesolithic' groups are represented in the archaeological record by single finds or scatters of worked stone, and by rare finds of worked antler.[9] The density of known Mesolithic sites in the region has increased significantly in recent years, mainly as a result of systematic fieldwalking, but structural traces of Mesolithic settlements or specialised activity foci remain elusive. Moreover, although early Mesolithic sites are known in some parts of the Trent Valley, notably at Misterton Carr, Misson and possibly Newton Cliffs, Nottinghamshire, the emphasis in this region is firmly upon sites of the later Mesolithic period.[10] This is a common phenomenon, since late Mesolithic sites have been shown to dominate in all other parts of the country where systematic field surveys have been carried out, suggesting that there were significant differences in the character, density and spatial distribution of sites between the earlier and later Mesolithic. The evidence from the early Mesolithic site at Misterton Carr suggests that in this period the Trent Valley may have been settled by small-scale itinerant hunter-gatherer bands, possibly established to exploit the fish, wildfowl and other resources of the valley bottom. These may have ranged widely on a seasonal basis between the Trent Valley and upland sites of the Pennines and Lincolnshire Wolds, given the presence of Wolds-type flint from the Wolds or the Trent gravels on Pennine sites, and of Peak District chert at Valley sites such as Misterton Carr.[11] The results of fieldwalking in the Trent Valley suggest a significant increase in Late Mesolithic activity, possibly indicating changes in the methods of subsistence during this period.

The Trent floodplain near Nottingham, formed in this period of numerous low sand and gravel islands among interwoven channels, may have provided an attractive habitat, but direct archaeological evidence for Mesolithic settlement in the area occupied by the modern city is sparse. Stone artefacts have been recovered from the outskirts of Nottingham during excavations of later sites such as Gamston and during fieldwalking of the gravel terraces, notably from around Holme Pierrepont, but within modern Nottingham the only evidence consists of a thin scatter of stray lithic finds and occasional finds of flintwork, reported during excavation of later sites, notably at the Castle site. Many more sites may have been destroyed, although on the floodplain some may lie concealed beneath later alluvium. Comparisons may be drawn with the Idle Valley in north Nottinghamshire, where early Mesolithic sites on islands above contemporary marshland were sealed beneath peat as water levels rose during the climatic warming after the Ice Age.[12]

Neolithic agriculturalists (*c*.4,000–2,000 BC)

The Neolithic period saw the gradual transition of the Trent Valley from a hunter-gatherer to a settled agricultural society, and the beginnings of the process of woodland clearance, which by the end of the prehistoric period appears to have transformed it from dense mixed woodland into a predominantly open landscape. The discovery during gravel quarrying at Colwick and Holme Pierrepont of numerous large tree trunks, buried within redeposited gravel, which have been dated by radiocarbon and dendrochronology to the Neolithic and Bronze Age periods, may provide important indirect evidence of woodland clearance. These tree trunks are distributed in broad bands within former courses of the Trent, with their long axes orientated parallel to the direction of flow, and they provide an unusually vivid insight into the pattern of river channels in this area in both the Neolithic and Bronze Age periods. They imply natural bankside erosion of floodplain woodland, accentuated perhaps by woodland clearance and consequent changes in the levels of surface run-off and soil erosion.[13]

The early Neolithic in the region is comparatively poorly represented. By contrast, the later Neolithic is distinguished by a larger number of known settlements, notably at Willington and beneath a Bronze Age barrow at Swarkestone Lowes;[14] and in some parts of the Valley by a remarkable wealth of ceremonial and funerary monuments. However, within the immediate vicinity of Nottingham, evidence for Neolithic activity is restricted mainly to finds of stone artefacts. Particularly noteworthy are occasional stray finds of flint or polished stone axes, the latter manufactured most commonly from igneous rocks, which were probably quarried at production sites in the Great Langdale area of the Lake District or in the Graig Lwyd area of north Wales. Other stray lithic finds of this period have also been recorded, notably an axe-hammer of olivine dolerite from the area of the Victoria Centre and an axe-hammer from Wollaton Park, together with occasional finds of Neolithic and Bronze Age flintwork.[15] As well as surface lithic scatters on the gravel terraces, for example at Gamston and Adbolton, occasional discoveries of early to late Neolithic pottery have been made during gravel extraction in the vicinity of Attenborough and Holme Pierrepont. The contexts of these finds are unknown, but their discovery adds to the accumulating evidence for Neolithic settlement in the immediate vicinity of Nottingham.[16]

The most impressive site of this period in the Nottingham area is an early Neolithic burial monument excavated ahead of gravel quarrying at Great Briggs, Holme Pierrepont.[17] This comprised several intercutting concentric ditches, enclosing an area of about twelve metres in diameter, which had apparently been recut consistently outwards, suggesting progressive enlargement of the monument to a maximum diameter of around fifteen metres internally. The ditches may have enclosed a central mound which could in turn have sealed burials, but excavation of the interior revealed only five shallow pits and a hollow, none certainly associated with burials. Earlier Neolithic pottery and flintwork and two polished stone axe

Figure 1.2 Prehistoric and Romano-British sites

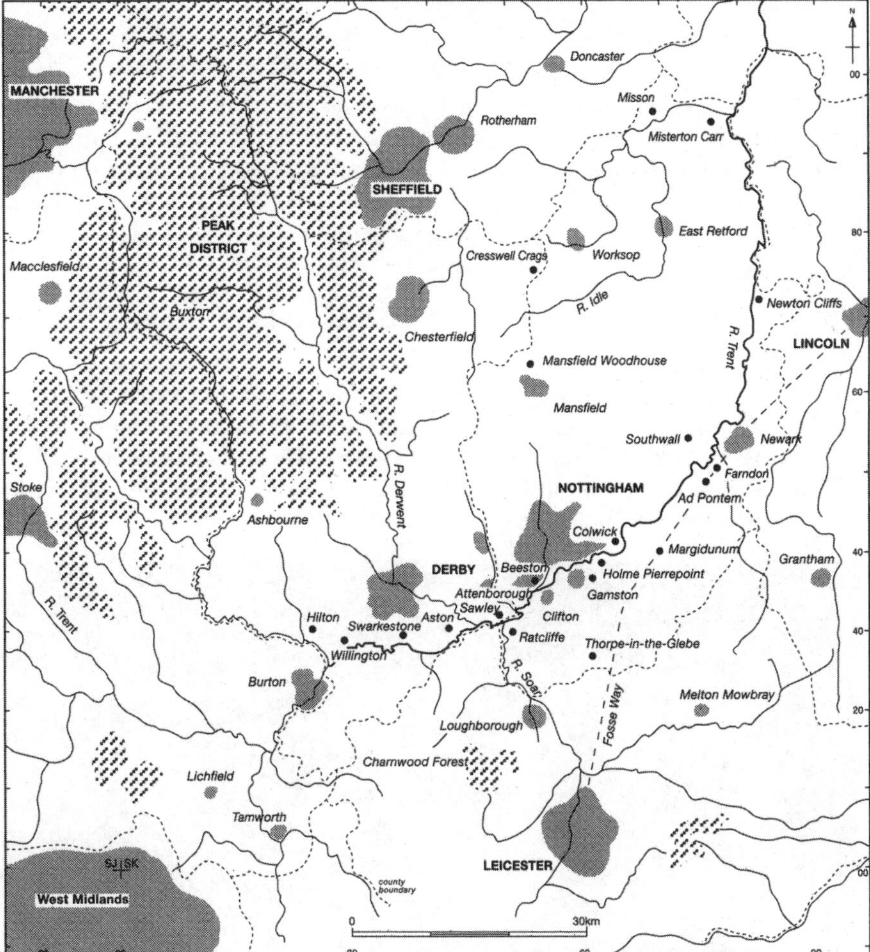

fragments were obtained from the ditches, while the internal features yielded earlier Neolithic sherds and flintwork. Four small pits at a distance from the ring-ditch contained later Neolithic and Bronze Age pottery, possibly derived from domestic activity.

The Bronze Age (*c.*2,000–700 BC)

In contrast to the sparse details of Neolithic activity, the Nottingham area has produced many bronze tools and weapons of the second and earlier first millennia BC, mainly from rivers during dredging, fishing or gravel quarrying. These bronzes are not uniformly distributed, and show variations even within individually quarried areas; clear clusters may be discerned in the vicinity of Attenborough, Clifton/Wilford and Colwick/Holme Pierrepont.[18] The circumstances of deposition of these artefacts remain unclear, but comparisons with similar deposits in other southern British river valleys suggest a wide range of mechanisms, including casual loss, erosion from bankside settlements, votive offerings and funerary deposits. Occasional stray finds of metalwork have also been recovered from the Nottingham area in non-riverine contexts, for example an early Bronze Age flat axe from Edwalton and a middle Bronze Age looped palstave from Bestwood, but interpretation of these is equally problematic.[19]

Plate 1 **Late Bronze Age metalwork at Great Freeman Street**. The collection comprises ten socketed axes, a palstave, a hollow ring and a spear-shaft terminal ('ferrule'). Typological parallels suggest a date of deposition in the final phase of the Late Bronze Age, the late ninth and eighth centuries BC. The broken condition of some of the artefacts could imply that this was a hoard of old implements gathered together by a bronzeworker for recasting

Two discoveries of Bronze Age metalwork merit particular mention. The first is a hoard of late Bronze Age metalwork recovered from Great Freeman Street, discovered during building work in 1860. It was found 'all of a heap' at a depth of 3½ feet in sandy soil. The second collection was recovered during dredging of the Trent near Clifton. A large number of oak stakes, spaced 'about a yard apart', was observed in the river bed, while from the same area were recovered three dug-out canoes, six human skulls and an outstanding collection of middle and late Bronze Age metalwork (including ten socketed spearheads, two rapiers, a dirk, two swords and two knives). This has been interpreted as a Bronze Age 'pile structure – possibly a dwelling', although a direct association between the oak stakes and the bronzes cannot be demonstrated.[20]

Wooden posts or stakes which might derive from comparable waterside sites have been recorded, together with Bronze Age metalwork, from floodplain contexts, notably at Attenborough and Holme Pierrepont, but in no case can a direct association with metalwork be demonstrated. Elsewhere in the Trent Valley, evidence for Bronze Age settlements is gradually accumulating.[21] Of particular interest in connection with sepulchral sites are the 'ring-ditches' which feature prominently in the crop-mark record. These sites, characterised by a circular ditch up to about 30 metres in diameter which in many cases may have enclosed originally an upstanding burial mound, are densely distributed over the gravel terraces, notably around Clifton and Holme Pierrepont. Some of these monuments may originate in the Neolithic period, but on present evidence a Bronze Age date may be suggested for the majority. Two ring-ditches on the outskirts of Nottingham have been shown by excavation to indicate earlier Bronze Age burials. The first of these was sited adjacent to an old channel of the Trent near Clifton. A narrow trench dug across this site in 1969 revealed four cremations inside the enclosed area, two associated with Early Bronze Age pottery; no traces survived of a mound, but this could have been erased by ploughing. The other site was excavated in 1992, in advance of gravel quarrying to the south of Holme Pierrepont Hall. A trench across one of several ring-ditches observed as crop-marks revealed three deposits of cremated bone, in each case associated with Bronze Age pots; two of these vessels, including a complete collared urn, had been inverted, while two cremations were accompanied by a flint knife. Other investigations during quarrying and building work have also uncovered examples of Bronze Age pots associated with cremations, notably at Holme Pierrepont and Bramcote. A Bronze Age 'pygmy cup' found during gravel quarrying at Attenborough, from the same general area as items of Bronze Age metalwork, may also derive from a burial, but no associated bones were recorded.[22]

None of the Bronze Age funerary monuments has preserved traces of associated earthworks, although Derry Mount, within the northern bailey of the Castle, could represent a rare survival of a prehistoric barrow.[23] This mound was levelled in 1781, revealing disarticulated human remains and a dagger, possibly indicative of a prehistoric burial, although the site could date from as late as the Civil War. Bronze Age barrows have occasionally survived as earthworks elsewhere in the Trent Valley,[24] but it would be remarkable if such a monument had stood within the urban core of Nottingham until the 1780s.

The accumulating evidence suggests a fairly high level of Bronze Age activity, including continued woodland clearance.[25] High levels of clearance may in turn have accelerated surface run-off and soil erosion, and hence may have accentuated the uprooting of floodplain woodland which is first documented at Colwick in the Neolithic period.

The Iron Age (*c.*700 BC–AD 43)

Numerous Iron Age settlements have been recorded during excavations in the Trent Valley, including several sites on the gravel terraces at Holme Pierrepont and Gamston. Discoveries suggest a dense pattern of mixed farming settlements in this part of the Trent Valley, each probably occupied by a single family group. Charred plant remains and artefacts associated with cereal processing imply arable agriculture, probably confined to the better drained gravels, while neighbouring floodplain areas would have provided plentiful summer pasture and other wetland resources. Soil conditions have not favoured the preservation of bones, but sufficient survived to imply an interest in animal husbandry. Artefacts from these sites indicate a wide range of craft and industrial activities, including pottery and textile production. At Gamston an extensive exchange network was suggested on the basis of pottery which may have been brought in from Charnwood Forest, salt containers from Cheshire and querns from the Pennines and Charnwood Forest, emphasising the complex social and economic ties which may have linked widely distributed settlements in this period.[26]

Excavations elsewhere in the Trent Valley have also pointed to a high density of Iron Age sites, usually single farmsteads engaged in mixed crop and animal husbandry and a restricted range of craft and industrial activities, with no clear evidence for significant variations in status. It is impossible to establish how many of these places were in contemporary use, but the density suggests a significant expansion of settlement and hence population during this period. Further evidence for significant settlement expansion could be the 'brickwork plan' field systems of the Sherwood Sandstones, immediately north of Nottingham. These rectilinear field systems may have originated in the late Iron Age, and could signify expansion into areas which, due to poor sandy soils, may previously have been judged too marginal for extensive cultivation. Pressure upon better quality land resources in the Trent Valley has been cited as a possible factor in their development, and in the Nottingham area could underlie the trend towards a more organised agricultural landscape implied by the development of a rectilinear boundary system in the late Iron Age at Gamston. Parallels can be drawn with the remarkable pattern of 'coaxial' field systems recorded to the north of Newark, which may also be of the late Iron Age.[27]

Although plentiful evidence for Iron Age occupation has come from excavations on the gravel terraces, signs of activity within the Nottingham area itself are limited. Prehistoric fortifications on the Castle site are possible, but although Iron Age finds have been recovered from this area the character of the activity from which they derive is unknown. Residual Iron Age pottery was found during excavations of the earthwork defences of the middle bailey. In addition, excavations in 1994 within what was once the northern bailey, uncovered a substantial V-shaped ditch, yielding a small quantity of probably Iron Age pottery and sealed by about 0.5m of medieval deposits. Late Iron Age pottery has also been recovered during excavations at Halifax Place, at Fisher Gate (from residual contexts), at Willoughby

House on Low Pavement, and from the fill of a wide and shallow ditch recorded during excavations between Barker Gate and Woolpack Lane. Five small sherds of pottery, possibly of Iron Age date, were obtained mainly from a weathered sand layer beneath a possible Norman bank during excavations of the Town Wall at Cumberland Place. Interpretation of the Iron Age phases of activity at Halifax Place and Fisher Gate is difficult, but both sites preserved several stratigraphically early features incorporating small quantities of late Iron Age pottery which could derive from domestic activity.[28] The Halifax Place site preserved several early pits yielding Iron Age sherds, some only slightly abraded. Although pits for storage or other uses are a common component of Iron Age sites in the Trent Valley, it seems likely that the pits at Halifax Place were dug through Iron Age deposits in the Saxon period. Excavations at Fisher Gate revealed a shallow curving gully and a right-angled length of ditch which could conceivably form the corner of a ditched enclosure; both features had been truncated and were characterised by a heavily leached fill which was not to be found in features elsewhere on the site, and so perhaps was earlier than the rest.[29]

The Trent was almost certainly an important trade route of movement in the Iron Age. Direct archaeological evidence for river transport is provided by three dugout canoes from Holme Pierrepont, one dated by radiocarbon to the later Iron Age. These were buried in gravels as the river migrated across its floodplain, together perhaps with an Iron Age spoked wheel recovered from beneath one of the canoes. The river seems also to have acted as a focus for deposits of metalwork, hence the discovery of early Iron Age swords at Holme Pierrepont, and of rich metalwork from elsewhere along the Trent, most notably the remains of a magnificent bronze shield from the river at Ratcliffe-on-Soar. This recalls the pattern of Bronze Age riverine deposition, and may signify ceremonial or burial activities.[30]

It is still hard to be sure of the density of settlement during the Iron Age within the area of the modern city. It seems clear, however, that Piggott was mistaken in seeing a 'heavily wooded midland plain, where pre-Roman occupation of any kind is likely to have been scanty or transient or both'. Caesar's description of south-eastern Britain as an area where the population was 'exceedingly large, and the ground thickly studded with homesteads'[31] may prove eventually to be a more apt appraisal of the area in the years immediately preceding the Roman Conquest.

The Romans

After the long history of prehistoric settlement burials, and stray finds, the Roman period marks an important hiatus in the pattern of occupation. To the south of the Trent the main transport artery, the Fosse Way, came no closer than ten miles, and the interest of its travellers, hastening north from the tribal capital of Leicester, was in reaching the halt at *Margidunum* near Bingham, and so on to Lincoln, with not even a byway towards Nottingham. The principal crossings of the Trent lay at Thorpe by

East Stoke (*Ad Pontem*) to the north-east, and perhaps Sawley near Derby to the west. The alluvial plains between these places probably continued in occupation without change; this is certainly indicated by excavation at Holme Pierrepont, Shelford and other rural settlements.[32]

Centres with some pretensions were founded on the fringe of the area. To the north, for example, a large and, in detail, little-known country house was built at Mansfield Woodhouse. An even larger villa was built at Southwell, where parts of the building, including mosaics and painted plaster, have been found under the gardens between the Minster School and the Vicars' Court. These were almost certainly estate centres of families who dominated the region. In the case of the Woodhouse villa, there are signs that the large and complex building (which 'must have contrasted sharply with the extreme rusticity of the surrounding hilly countryside') grew slowly from a simple farmstead of round houses in an enclosure similar to those of the Iron Age in the Trent Valley. It suggests the increasing prosperity of a local family during the second and third centuries, and the creation of an estate which collapsed perhaps early in the fourth century. The Southwell villa, in contrast, sat above a small house of the second century, but showed no sign of organic growth: the great courtyard house here was, it seems, a sudden construction of the fourth century, implying the arrival of external wealth. A century later it was in ruins. Elsewhere, even the best of the rural settlements seem to have been no more than simple farmhouses.[33] To the south-west a plaque from Ratcliffe-on-Soar has been claimed to indicate the location of a religious centre. The area of the city itself has yielded little evidence of occupation. The record of stray finds is minimal: a few Roman coins have been reported in Wollaton, Radford, Thorneywood, Basford and the central area of the city, with a small hoard beside the river at Clifton. Pottery and other Roman artefacts have come from Bilborough, Wollaton, and the fields of the deserted village of Keighton (on the campus of the University of Nottingham), but the quantity is inconsiderable. When one considers that the discovery of Roman sherds is the single most common experience of any gardener in almost any part of England, the silence of the evidence from Nottingham is remarkable. Only in Bilborough (Broxtowe), well beyond the area of the city until comparatively recent times, was there any substantial Roman occupation. House building during the construction of the suburban estate here in 1937–38 revealed ditches and traces of settlement in the first century AD. Further work in 1964 confirmed the presence of ditches, but increased the apparent complexity of the layout. This site is likely to have been a fort, occupied perhaps during several phases, but little is known of it, and the construction of the modern housing estate has made further investigation unlikely.[34]

The end of Roman Britain did nothing to remove Nottingham from its obscurity. Cemeteries of a new style indicate the presence of incomers at Newark, Bingham, Cotgrave, Willoughby-on-the-Wolds, Kingston on Soar, and in the ruins of the villa at Southwell.[35] Nothing of the migration period of the fifth to the seventh centuries has yet been identified in the city itself; indeed, the whole region from Nottingham to Doncaster is sparsely represented in comparison with the dense scattering of finds in Eastern Nottinghamshire, Lincolnshire and Leicestershire: that is, the region south and east of the Trent. The lands between the Derwent and the Trent, northwards to the fringe of Hatfield and the Humber plains, are almost devoid of proven occupation.[36] Further to the west, in the vicinity of Burton on Trent, a series of place-names in Wal- (*walh*, a foreigner or Welshman), or Bret- (Briton) suggest the settlements of numbers of Romano-British. They indicate a frontier line between natives and Anglo-Saxons, running north and south in the central Trent Valley, and dividing the British to the west from the English of the newly created Mercia, who may at first have taken their lands to the south of the Trent. The same survival of the British may be true of central and northern Nottinghamshire: elsewhere, too, the historically recorded presence of British kingdoms among the Anglo-Saxons is coupled with a complete absence of recognisable material culture. During the next two centuries other centres (Leicester, Lincoln, *Northworthig* (Derby), Tamworth) flourished,[37] but little or nothing seems to have occurred at Nottingham. However, by the middle of the ninth century the site of the future city had been named, and a settlement of some sort, perhaps even a site of high status, had developed on St Mary's Hill: from this period onwards we can trace with some certainty the development of Nottingham.

Notes

1 T. J. Charsley, T. J. Rathbone and D. J. Lowe, *Nottingham: a Geological Background for Planning and Development* (British Geological Survey, Technical Report, WA/90/1, 1990).

2 Drage, *Castle*, fig. 2, pp. 19–20.

3 *Ibid.*, fig. 20, p. 91.

4 A. C. Waltham, 'The sandstone caves of Nottingham', *Mercian Geologist*, 13 (1992), pp. 5–36; 'The sand mines of Nottingham', *Bulletin of the Peak District Mines Historical Society*, 12 (1994), pp. 1–11.

5 Royal Commission on Historical Monuments, *A Matter of Time* (1960); C. O'Brien, 'Land and settlement in Nottinghamshire and lowland Derbyshire', *East Midland Archaeological Bulletin*, 12 (Supplement, 1978); C. O'Brien, 'Iron Age and Romano-British settlement in the Trent Basin', in B. C. Burnham and H. B. Johnson (eds.), *Invasion and Response: the Case of Roman Britain, 299–313* (Oxford, 1979); Edwards, pp. 177–90; C. Smith, 'The landscape and natural history of Iron Age settlement on the Trent gravels', in B. Cunliffe and T. Rowley (eds.), *Lowland Iron Age Communities in Europe* (Oxford, 1978), pp. 91–102; R. Whimster, *The Emerging Past: Air Photography and the Buried Landscape* (Abingdon, 1989); D. Knight and A. J. Howard, *Archaeology and Alluvium in the Trent Valley: an Archaeological Assessment of the Floodplain and Gravel Terraces* (Nottingham 1995).

6 Edwards, pp. 177–80; O'Brien, 'Land and settlement', pp. 2–3; M. Posnansky, 'The Lower and Middle Palaeolithic industries of the English East Midlands', *Proceedings of the Prehistoric Society*, 29 (1963), pp. 357–94.

7 Knight and Howard, *Archaeology and Alluvium*, pp. 2–4; Posnansky, 'Lower and Middle', especially pp. 361, 378; ex. inf. P. M. Richer, E. Toms.

8 D. Garton, 'A Late Upper Palaeolithic site near Newark, Nottinghamshire', *TTS*, 97 (1993), p. 145; R. D. S. Jenkinson, *Creswell Crags: Late Pleistocene Sites in the East Midlands* (Oxford, 1984).

9 R. M. Jacobi, 'Northern England in the eighth millennium bc: an essay', in P. Mellars (ed.), *The Early Postglacial Settlement of Northern Europe* (1978); T. Manby, 'Some Mesolithic sites in the Peak District and Trent Basin', *DAJ*, 83 (1963), pp. 10–23; Edwards, pp. 177–90; A. Myers, 'The organisation and structural dimensions of hunter–gatherer Lithic technology' (University of Sheffield,

Ph.D. thesis, 1986); O'Brien, 'Land and settlement'; M. Posnansky, 'Some considerations of the Pleistocene chronology and prehistory of part of the East Midlands' (University of Nottingham, Ph.D. thesis, 1956), fig. 27; ex. inf. J. Brown.

10 Knight and Howard, *Archaeology and Alluvium*, p. 75; P. C. Buckland and M. J. Dolby, 'Mesolithic and later material from Misterton Carr, Notts.: an interim report', *TTS*, 77 (1973), pp. 5–33; D. Garton, P. Phillips and D. Henson, 'Newton Cliffs: a flint-working and settlement site in the Trent Valley', in P. Phillips (ed.), *Archaeology and Landscape Studies in North Lincolnshire* (Oxford, 1989), pp. 81–180.

11 Myers, 'Organisation', pp. 354–5, 375–9; Buckland and Dolby, 'Mesolithic'; O'Brien, 'Land and settlement', p. 4.

12 D. Knight, 'Excavations of an Iron Age settlement at Gamston, Nottinghamshire', *TTS*, 96 (1992), p. 23; G. Guilbert, K. Fearn and G. Woodhouse, 'Archaeological evaluation of crop-marks near Holme Pierrepont, Nottinghamshire 1992: an interim report', *TTS*, 98 (1994), p. 19; Nottingham finds: H. Swinnerton, 'The story of early man in Nottinghamshire', *TTS*, 54 (1950), pp. 69–70; Drage, *Castle*, p. 15; Idle Valley: O'Brien, 'Land and settlement', p. 4.

13 C. R. Salisbury, P. J. Whitley, C. D. Litton and J. L. Fox, 'Flandrian courses of the River Trent at Colwick, Nottingham', *Mercian Geologist*, 9 (1984), pp. 189–207; Knight and Howard, *Archaeology and Alluvium*, pp. 25–33.

14 For settlements and burial ceremonial sites: O'Brien, 'Land and settlement', pp. 6–9; Knight and Howard, *Archaeology and Alluvium*, pp. 14–15, 34–5, 76–7; H. M. Wheeler, 'Excavations at Willington, Derbyshire, 1970–72', *DAJ*, 99 (1979), pp. 58–220; E. Greenfield, 'The excavation of Barrow 4 at Swarkeston, Derbyshire', *DAJ*, 80 (1960), pp. 1–48.

15 W. A. Cummins, 'A Graig Lwyd stone axe rough-out from Holme Pierrepont, Nottinghamshire', *TTS*, 82 (1978), pp. 66–8; W. A. Cummins and C. N. Moore, 'Petrological identification of stone implements from Lincolnshire, Nottinghamshire and Rutland', *Proceedings of the Prehistoric Society*, 39 (1973), pp. 219–55; T. H. McK Clough and W. A. Cummins (eds.), *Stone Axe Studies, vol. 2: the Petrology of Prehistoric Stone Implements from the British Isles* (Council for British Archaeology Research Report 67, 1988), pp. 45–8, 198–9; J. Evans, *The Ancient Stone Implements, Weapons and Ornaments of Great Britain* (1897), pp. 202–4.

16 For fieldwalking see Knight, 'Excavations', pp. 74–7; Knight and Howard, *Archaeology and the Alluvium*, pp. 35–6. For pottery ex. inf. A. G. MacCormick; P.M. Vine, 'Analysis of the distribution of selected Neolithic and Bronze Age artifacts in Central England' (University of Nottingham, Ph.D. thesis, 1987), pp. 496, 499.

17 Guilbert *et al.*, 'Archaeological evaluation', p. 22; Knight and Howard, *Archaeology and Alluvium*, fig. 3.13.

18 A. MacCormick, 'Prehistoric bronzes in Nottingham city museums' (unpublished report, Brewhouse Yard Museum, 1992).

19 Bestwood: J. May, 'Some bronze implements from Nottinghamshire', *TTS*, 66 (1962), pp. 15–16; Edwalton: A. W. Macmillan, 'Bronze Age metalwork' (Handlist 1, University of Nottingham Museum, 1976).

20 Great Freeman Street: *Proceedings of the Society of Antiquaries*, 2nd series, 1 (1861), pp. 332–3; Edwards, pp. 177–90; Clifton: C. W. Phillips, 'Some recent finds from the Trent near Nottingham', *Antiquaries Journal*, 21 (1941), pp. 133–43.

21 Attenborough: May, 'Bronze implements', p. 14; Holme Pierrepont: C. B. Burgess and I. Colquhoun, *The Swords of Britain* (Prahistorische Bronzefunde Abteilung IV, Band 5, Munchen, 1988), p. 113; Bronze Age Settlements: Knight, 'Excavations', pp. 23–7, 83; Phase I: Wheeler, 'Excavations'; S. M. Elsdon, 'Iron Age and Roman sites at Red Hill, Ratcliffe-on-Soar, Nottinghamshire', *TTS*, 89 (1982), pp. 14–82.

22 Trent Valley ring-ditches: Whimster, *Emerging Past*, pp. 31, 67; C. Allen, *et al.* 'A Bronze Age burial site at Clifton, Nottinghamshire', *TTS*, 98 (1994), pp. 130–3; Guilbert, *et al.*, 'Archaeological evaluation', pp. 19–23; Neolithic origins of ring ditches: I. Kinnes, *Round Barrows and Ring Ditches in the British Neolithic* (British Museum Occasional Paper, 7, 1979).

23 Drage, *Castle*, p. 15; Notts. Sites and Monuments Record, Site 1062; *Date Book*, p. 136; VCH *Not-*

tinghamshire, I, p. 292.

24 Greenfield, 'The excavation of Barrow 4'; M. Posnansky, 'The Bronze Age round barrow at Swarkeston, Derbyshire', *DAJ*, 75 (1955), pp. 123–39; Round Hill, Twyford, Derbyshire: O'Brien, 'Land and settlement', p. 8.

25 Knight and Howard, *Archaeology and Alluvium*, pp. 14–16.

26 C. O'Brien, 'Iron Age and Romano-British settlement in the Trent Basin', in B. C. Burnham and H. B. Johnson (eds.), *Invasion and Response: the case of Roman Britain, 299–313* (Oxford, 1979); Knight, 'Excavations', pp. 84–5; Smith, 'Iron Age settlement'.

27 D. Garton, 'Dunston's Clump and the brickwork plan field systems at Babworth, Nottinghamshire', *TTS*, 91 (1987), pp. 16–73; D. N. Riley, *Early Landscapes from the Air: Studies of Cropmarks in South Yorkshire and North Nottinghamshire* (Sheffield, 1980); Knight, 'Excavations', pp. 83–4.

28 Drage, *Castle*, pp. 15, 81–3, 110; VCH *Nottinghamshire*, I, pp. 291–2; Notts. Sites and Monuments Record, 01061a (Castle); S. M. Elsdon, *Iron Age Pottery in the East Midlands* (Nottingham, 1993), p. 15; C. S. B. Young, *Discovering Rescue Archaeology in Nottingham* (Nottingham, 1982); M. W. Ponsford, 'Nottingham Town Wall: Park Row excavations 1967', *TTS*, 75 (1971), pp. 5–32; ex. inf. R. Buckley (Leicestershire Archaeology Unit): North Bailey excavations, C. S. B. Young, A. G. MacCormick.

29 G. Young, 'Archaeology in Nottingham: the Halifax Place Excavations', in S. N. Mastoris (ed.), *History in the Making* (Nottingham, 1987).

30 W. A. Cummins and A. J. Rundle, 'The geological environment of the dug-out canoes from Holme Pierrepont, Nottinghamshire', *Mercian Geologist*, 3 (1969), pp. 177–88; A. G. MacCormick *et al.*, 'Three dug-out canoes and a wheel from Holme Pierrepont, Notts.', *TTS* 72 (1968); J. Musty and A. G. MacCormick, 'An early Iron Age wheel from Holme Pierrepont, Notts.', *Antiquaries Journal*, 53 (1973), pp. 275–7; J. Watkin, 'An Iron Age shield from Ratcliffe-on-Soar', *Current Archaeology*, 141 (1994), pp. 336–40; Holme Pierrepont Swords: J. D. Cowen, 'The Hallstatt sword of bronze: on the Continent and in Britain', *Proceedings of the Prehistoric Society*, 33 (1967), p. 444.

31 S. Piggott, 'Native economies and the Roman occupation of north Britain', in I. A. Richmond *et al.*, *Roman and Native in North Britain* (1958), p. 13; *De Bello Gallico*, V, p. 2.

32 A. L. F. Rivet and C. Smith, *The Placenames of Roman Britain* (1979), p. 231; J. Wacher and B. Burham, *The 'Small Towns' of Roman Britain* (1990), pp. 222, 260–4, 272–3; O'Brien, 'Land and settlement'.

33 M. Todd, *The Coritani* (1973), pp. 83–8; *Archaeologia*, IX (1789), p. 199; W. Dickinson, *Antiquities in Nottinghamshire*, I (1801), p. 88; A. M. Y. Baylay, 'Southwell, pavement probably Pre-Norman', *TTS*, 5 (1901), pp. 58–9; C. Daniels, 'Excavations on the site of the Roman Villa at Southwell, 1959', *TTS* 70 (1966), pp. 13–54.

34 Edwards, p. 195; Notts. Sites and Monuments Record; D. F. Mackreth, 'Nottingham, Broxtowe', *East Midland Archaeological Bulletin*, 8 (1965), pp. 30–1.

35 G. Kinsley, *The Anglo-Saxon Cemetery at Millgate, Newark-on-Trent, Nottinghamshire* (Nottingham Archaeological Monographs 2, 1989), pp. 26–8; G. Kinsley, *Broughton Lodge* (Nottingham Archaeological Monographs 4, 1992), pp. 73–4; Daniels, 'Excavations', p. 50; M. W. Barley, 'Notes on the Anglo-Saxon Pottery from Kingston on Soar', *TTS*, 61 (1957), pp. 21–6.

36 S. Neel, 'The Early Saxons in the Middle Trent Valley' (University of Nottingham, Ph.D. thesis, 1995).

37 K. Cameron, 'The meaning and significance of Old English walh in English place-names', *Journal of the English Place Name Society*, 12 (1979–80), pp. 1–53; P. Rahtz, 'The archaeology of West Mercian towns', in A. Dornier (ed.), *Mercian Studies* (Leicester, 1977), pp. 107–30.

2

THE ANGLO-SAXON TOWN AND THE NORMAN CONQUEST

David Roffe

In 868 the Danish army went from Northumbria into Mercia and took up winter quarters at Nottingham. King Burghred of Mercia appealed for help to King Æthelred of Wessex and Alfred his brother, and a large force was dispatched to besiege the Danes within that fortress. No serious battle occurred, and the Mercians made peace with the enemy. After staying a year the Danish army returned to York.

This incident, recorded in a version of the *Anglo-Saxon Chronicle*, and in variant forms in Asser's *Life of Alfred*, and Æthelweard's *Chronicle*, provides the first reference to Nottingham in the historical record.[1] Documentary sources for the history of the next 200 years of settlement are limited. The most comprehensive is the Domesday Survey, dating from the very end of the period considered in this chapter.[2] Compiled by order of William the Conqueror in 1086, it contains a detailed description of the rights of the King and his tenants-in-chief in the borough, along with an account of their pre-Conquest antecedents. Much of the reconstruction of the social and economic topography of Nottingham and its surroundings is derived from its evidence. Before 1086 there are only a handful of references. Nottingham is explicitly noticed in the 918, 920, 942, and 1067 annals of the *Anglo-Saxon Chronicle* and in a charter and estate memorandum of 934 and *c*.973 respectively.[3] These sources provide the framework, albeit incomplete, for an understanding of Nottingham's wider political significance, together with some information about the settlement itself.

The etymology of the place-name Nottingham suggests a long unrecorded history before the ninth century, while the names of surrounding places indicate something of its interaction with neighbouring settlements both before and after 868.[4] Local boundaries also preserve vestiges of the organisation of land at an early period. In Nottinghamshire the territorial division, the wapentake, is a late tenth-century institution: its bounds may therefore be no earlier than the system that brought it into being. By contrast, ecclesiastical boundaries, notably those of parishes, frequently perpetuate the area of earlier estates, for the render of tithe was often divorced from the tenure of land. The churches of Nottingham point at discrete interests and settlement nuclei, and topographical relationships hint at a sequence of development.[5] However, archaeology has provided the most considerable volume of detailed evidence for the early history of the town. Despite the technical problems presented by sandstone rock, sandy soil, underlying caves, massive disturbances caused by centuries of building and rebuilding in the same place, and extensive stripping at various periods, sensitive excavation in the last twenty-five years has brought to light a sequence of occupation and use. Dates are necessarily imprecise through a paucity of stratified artefacts; even those objects which are stratified are rarely closely datable.[6] The history of Nottingham that emerges from these diverse sources is patchy and not always coherent. It is, however, clear that it was not a typical Danelaw borough, and the experience of the settlement was markedly different from that of the major mercantile and industrial centres of Lincoln and Stamford to the east.

The Danish settlement and the English reconquest

Nottingham enters the historical record at a crucial moment in the history of the East Midlands. Bands of ship-borne Danes had raided settlements on the coasts and estuaries of England from the late eighth century, but from the mid-ninth century 'the great army' had begun to overwinter in England and extend its raids inland. Its arrival at Nottingham in 868 represented the first known threat to the heartland of the kingdom of Mercia. The nature of the settlement at this time is more a matter of speculation than fact. Asser records that it was called in British *Tig Guocobauc,* meaning 'cavey house, dwelling of caves'. The name clearly indicates that the soft sandstone was already being excavated for habitation or other use,[7] but it is unclear what it signifies in terms of settlement: the British language could indicate a British community in the vicinity some time before the late ninth century. On the other hand, it may be an invention by Asser based on local knowledge.[8] The name Nottingham itself, in its earliest form *Snotengaham,* is Old English and signifies 'the *ham* of Snot's people'. *Ham* has the root meaning of 'a safe dwelling', and its compounding with the name of a people suggests a territory dependent on a tribal or family group. The extent of the land of the eponymous Snot or his successors can be only dimly perceived. It probably included Sneinton to the east, for its name, *Notintone, Snotinton,* means 'the village of Snot's people'; the settlement is described with Nottingham in Domesday Book, and throughout the Middle Ages St Stephen's Church in Sneinton appears to have been subordinate to St Mary's. Whiston, the northern suburb of Nottingham, with its church of St Michael, was also in its parish and was probably likewise a part of *Snotengaham.* But this is unlikely to be the full extent of the territory. Wider ecclesiastical links between St Mary's and surrounding estates have been obscured by the early grant of all the churches of the area to Lenton Priory on its foundation in the early twelfth century.[9] It is possible that some or all of the land of the King and the Earl in the immediate vicinity of the borough in 1066 – Lenton, Radford, Basford, Arnold, West Bridgford, Wilford, Barton, Clifton – had belonged to Nottingham from an early date.

Estates of this size, and greater, were not unusual in the Middle Saxon period. They functioned as tributary units, the centres to which rents in agricultural produce were brought, but they did not necessarily assume wider responsibilities as regional administrative centres. Nottingham was probably no exception.[10] Its primary attraction to the Danes in 868 is more likely to have been its defensible position. Occupying high ground above the River Trent at the lowest point at which it was easily fordable, it commanded two major routes between Northumbria and Mercia, namely the river and the Great North Road, which did not assume its present course until a bridge was built at Newark in the twelfth century.[11] Nevertheless, there may have been other factors that brought the Danes to Nottingham. The sources portray the Danes as predators on a peaceful realm. In reality, Mercia was far from a united kingdom. King Burghred was the latest representative of a dynasty which had probably first come to power in 757 in the person of Beornred. The dynasty was opposed by a royal line descended from Ceolwulf I (821–23) with equal claims to legitimacy, and which, after the marriage of his daughter Ælfflæd to King Wiglaf's son Wigmund, had a

Plate 2 **Caves**. Nottingham was already known for its caves in 868, and they continued to be excavated and used until the mid-nineteenth century. This photograph, taken on 26 November 1934, shows the rock cellars under The Elephant and Castle on Hounds Gate, an inn considered to date from just after the Commonwealth and demolished in 1935. This lower cellar, of 30 feet by 20 feet by 8 feet high, may have been a cockpit

substantial patrimony in the East Midlands. It was probably this line that came to power in 874 when Burghred was replaced by Ceolwulf II (874–79) as King of Mercia. West Saxon propaganda portrays Ceolwulf as a Danish puppet, calling him 'a foolish king's thegn'.[12] From Ceolwulf's perspective the events of 874 look more like a coup to remove the ruling dynasty in which Danish support was a means to his end. If this is true, an alliance between the Danes and Mercian dissidents may have frustrated the English attempt to threaten the invaders: opposition within Mercia is suggested by Æthelweard's report that Burghred and Æthelred gave the Danes the right to stay in Nottingham in 868.

If there was an alliance between Mercian dissidents and Vikings, it soon proved to be an unequal one. There was no permanent settlement in Nottingham in 868, or in the East Midlands generally. It was not until a decade later that a Danish hegemony was established in Eastern and Northern England. In 877 Mercia was divided, and Danes from East Anglia settled in the East Midlands.[13] The extent and nature of that settlement still remain a matter of debate, but there can be no doubt that Danish warlords took effective control of the main centres of power. Nottingham must have been one of them, although it did not occupy a special position, military or otherwise, at this time. Up to the early tenth century, the whole area of Danish settlement between the Humber and Welland was subordinate to York: Æthelweard records that the Danes of Northumbria were active as far south as the Welland in 894, and according to the *Anglo-Saxon Chronicle* King Edward the Elder of Wessex (899–924) made a raid into Lindsey in the territory of the Danes of the North in 909. York was clearly the main centre of power in the Northern Danelaw and, by implication, there were no independent garrisons elsewhere.[14]

The fortification and manning of boroughs by the Danes south of the Humber was a response to the quickening pace of English reconquest in the early years of the tenth century. The campaign had begun in the reign of King Alfred (871–99), but it made inroads into the heartlands of Danish settlement only in the time of his children, Edward the Elder and his sister, Æthelflæda, Lady of the Mercians (911–18). The first significant success was the defeat of the army of York at Tettenhall in Staffordshire in 910. The battle saw the all-but-complete destruction of the leaders of the northern army, and the Danes of the East Midlands were thereafter forced to look to their own defence. Garrisons are noticed for the first time at Northampton and Leicester in 913, Derby in 917, and Stamford in 918.

Nottingham, well to the rear and of little strategic significance in an English onslaught from the south and the west, seems to have remained subject to York, and probably ungarrisoned, until late in the campaign. In 917 Æthelflæda took Derby by force, but a change in policy appears to have been under way, for in the following year Leicester submitted of its own free will. The reason seems to have been Æthelflæda's negotiations with the Danes of York which, the Mercian Register suggests, had been under way for some time. Both parties found a common cause against Norsemen led by the Dane Ragnald who threatened Northumbria and Mercia from the north-west and Wales, and they were about to sign a treaty when Æthelflæda died in 918.[15]

Her brother Edward the Elder, king of Wessex, was at Stamford when he heard the news and dashed into Mercia to secure Tamworth and accept the allegiance of the Mercians. The kingdom remained unstable, and Edward, apparently picking up the strands of Æthelflæda's policy of *rapprochement*, seems to have reached an accommodation with the northern Danes in order to consolidate his authority. He then went to Nottingham, occupied and repaired the defences, and installed an English and Danish garrison. With his eastern flank secured, he was free to suppress opposition in Mercia and to fortify its northern boundaries by the construction of boroughs at Thelwall in Cheshire and at Manchester.[16]

Plate 3 **Old and New Trent Bridges**. The first bridge, the Hethbethebrigg, dates from 920, and was doubtless a wooden structure. It was strengthened with stone piers by the mid-thirteenth century and thereafter often patched and buttressed. It was nearly destroyed in the severe winter of 1663. In 1867 careful surveys revealed that the foundations of the piers were insecure and the narrow arches restricted the passage of floodwater. A new bridge was commissioned (upper picture) to designs by the borough engineer, Marriott Ogle Tarbotton. It was opened on 25 July 1871, after which the old bridge (lower picture) was taken down. The bridge was doubled in width in 1926

In the following two years political upheavals in the North sabotaged this settlement and inexorably led to the English subjugation of Nottingham. In 919 there was a change of regime at York when Ragnald entered the city with a Norse army and took control of Northumbria. The North no longer shared a common interest with the English, and Edward was forced to take measures to secure the North Midlands from attack. In 920 he returned to Nottingham and built a borough south of the Trent and linked the two forts with a bridge. With a tactic which he had previously used at Buckingham, Hertford, Bedford, and Stamford, he thereby commanded the river crossing and the Great North Road, and dominated passage along the Trent. At the same time he may have consolidated his control of lines of communication in depth by building a borough at Tickhill in the north. His eastern flank again secure, he built a borough at Bakewell. With his northern boundary fortified with a string of strategic fortresses, the whole of the North then came to terms with him.[17] Nottingham, apparently under full English control for the first time, was incorporated into a united kingdom of England south of the Humber.

The reconquest of the East Midlands transformed Nottingham from a backwater with no significant military function into a frontier town and invested it with a regional role which it retained throughout the medieval period. For the first time a formal burghal system was introduced into the East Midlands, and Nottingham became a key centre of royal administration. The only tangible vestige of these developments is the survival of coins minted in Nottingham for King Athelstan (924–39). However, the pattern of tolls in the East Midlands in the later Middle Ages may hint at the territory assigned to the borough. In the thirteenth century the burgesses of Nottingham collected toll in an area bounded by the River Ryton to the north, the Trent to the east, and the county boundary to the south and west. Up to the late twelfth century they seem to have also had a right to the tolls of Derby and Ashbourne.[18] Nottingham's territory would appear to have commanded the Trent Valley from the River Dove, on the western boundary of modern Derbyshire, to the River Ryton in the north and therefore to have encompassed the neighbouring borough of Derby.

The Confederacy of the Five Boroughs and its aftermath

The arrangement proved to be short-lived, for the West Saxon burghal system did not survive much beyond the reign of King Athelstan. In 937 Olaf Guthfrithson, Ragnald's successor, attempted to retake the East Midlands, but was defeated at the unidentified *Brunanburh*. He was more successful after the death of Athelstan in 939, after which he returned to Yorkshire and was accepted by the Danes of York. Almost immediately the Danes of the East Midlands accepted his lordship, and at Leicester in 940 King Edmund (940–46), Edward the Elder's son, ceded to Olaf the boroughs of Stamford, Nottingham, Derby, Leicester, and possibly Lincoln (it remained a part of the Viking kingdom of York until at least 927 and may never have been reconquered by the English), along with their territories.[19] Nottingham submitted to the hegemony of Anglo-Scandinavian Northumbria.

In the event rule from York proved as irksome and as short as the West Saxon yoke, and in 942 Edmund reasserted his authority over the Danes of the East Midlands as far north as the Humber.[20] The instability of the region had seriously threatened the security of the whole kingdom, and in the next twenty years successive kings took measures to consolidate their authority and to ensure the loyalty of its inhabitants. Defences were probably strengthened: there is no documentary record of such works in Nottingham, but Newark (the place-name means 'the new work', that is, 'the new fort') was probably fortified at this time to function as a forward defence for the borough by controlling the lower reaches of the Trent.[21] Until now Newark seems to have been part of Lindsey, but in the reign of Eadwy (955–59) it had its own mint and was subsequently administered from Nottingham. The fortification of boroughs was accompanied by English colonisation. In 942, for example, Edmund granted to Wulfsige Maur, a trusted ally of Mercian descent, a large tract of land in Derbyshire and Staffordshire which effectively controlled the upper Trent Valley. Steps were also taken to limit the influence of the Archbishop of York south of the Humber, notably the revival of the bishopric of Lindsey, although there is no known parallel for Nottinghamshire.[22]

Measures of this kind, although effective in the short term, did nothing to reconcile the Danish population to the English Crown. In the 950s or early 960s a more radical solution was sought. The whole area of the East Midlands was divided into wapentakes, a regional subdivision in the Danelaw which was the equivalent of the hundred elsewhere. New royal courts were set up in each wapentake and charged with the collection of taxes, the maintenance of the King's peace, and the organisation of military service. Previously, the kin had enforced such duties; now for the first time they devolved upon the community, through a network of twelve-carucate hundreds (hundreds of twelve ploughlands), a novel system of organisation for freemen (*frankpledge*) in which groups of villages were mutually responsible for the behaviour of members. Collections of wapentakes were in their turn assigned to boroughs. Nottingham assumed responsibility for the administration of the four wapentakes and four half-wapentakes which subsequently constituted the medieval shire. Individual boroughs were not autonomous: the whole structure was co-ordinated through the Confederacy of the Five Boroughs of Nottingham, Lincoln, Derby, Stamford, and Leicester under the control of an ealdorman, a royal official of noble status, and a king's reeve.[23]

This initiative was not unique: a similar system of local government had already been introduced in southern England and the Mercian Council was resurrected at about the same time.[24] In the northern Danelaw, however, it had a well-defined function in relation to the area. Its immediate purpose was clearly military. York had submitted to the English Crown in 954, but was still hostile and unstable. The hundreds and wapentakes facilitated the raising of a militia to defend the region against its northern neighbour. Furthermore, the founding of the system in the local community seems to have been further intended to foster a sense of identity in the East Midlands by providing a locus of patronage and thereby creating a buffer against Northumbria.[25] It was remarkably successful. Despite the renewal of Danish raids in the reign of Æthelred II Unræd (978–1016), the system continued to function, largely because it recognised the customs of the Danelaw, and the Danes of the area generally remained loyal to the Crown for about fifty years.

Ultimately it proved incapable of coping with overwhelming pressures when the Danes renewed their onslaught in the early years of the eleventh century. In 1013 King Swein of Denmark and his son Cnut invaded, and, after the North had succumbed, the Anglo-Scandinavian population of the area threw in its lot with them.[26] In the reorganisation of local government that was initiated by King Cnut (1016–35), the Five Boroughs were absorbed into a larger earldom of Mercia. The Confederacy ceased to exist, but the reforms of the 950s and 960s lived on in the shires of the East Midlands. Lincoln assumed control of the wapentakes which had formerly looked to Stamford, to form Lincolnshire, and the late tenth-century territories of Derby, Leicester, and Nottingham were constituted as shires. Nottingham retained a dominant position, probably perpetuating a pre-eminent role in the Confederacy. Derbyshire was administered on the King's behalf by the Sheriff of Nottingham, and until 1256 the men of the county met with Nottinghamshire in a moot hall situated close to what is now Friar Lane.[27] Nottingham continued to be the main centre of royal and comital power in the Trent Valley.

The history of the fifty years before the Norman Conquest is obscure, but it was probably dominated by the attempts of rival earls to control the network of shires. The earldoms of the period can be perceived only dimly. The East Midlands may have passed to an earl of the Middle Angles after 1017. By the middle 1050s the region was held by Earl Ralph of Hereford. Subsequently, however, the Earl of Mercia may have assumed control before it was incorporated into Tosti's earldom of Northumbria, probably in 1062. By and large successive earls respected local sensibilities by observing the customs of the Northern Danelaw. In 1065, however, Earl Tosti provoked rebellion in the North and East Midlands by attempting, it was alleged, to introduce novel taxation. The men of Nottingham rose with the rest, and King Edward the Confessor (1041–66) acceded to their demands by appointing Morcar as Earl.[28]

The development of the pre-Conquest borough

Nottingham's regional importance after 920 was largely due to its defensible site. The middle Trent Valley at this point is wide, and was probably marshy throughout the period. A bridge was constructed over the river in 920[29] and a causeway must have been built at the same time. The River Leen, however, fell into the Trent on the Nottingham/Lenton boundary until the mid- to late twelfth century when something like its present channel was cut to provide water for the King's mills,[30] and the rest of the floodplain must therefore have remained impassable. To the north of the marshes a series of sandstone hills dominates the steeply rising ground. The Castle Rock and Standard Hill to the west are by far the most dramatic topographical features of the site today, but there is no evidence that the Castle site was occupied in the late Saxon period. To the east, a shallow valley between Castle Hill and St Mary's Hill became the French Borough, but none of this area is likely to have been occupied before the eleventh century: the district is first noticed as 'the new borough' in 1086. The probable area of this borough can be determined from post-Conquest court records. It was almost exactly coterminous with the small parishes of St Peter and St Nicholas, perhaps indicating a late date for its formation.[31] Indeed, the apparent laying-out of the three axial roads of Hounds Gate, Castle Gate, and Friar Lane in relation to the east gate of the Castle suggests that the Castle and the new borough formed part of the same design.

The English Borough is to be found further to the east on and around St Mary's Hill, with the church from which it takes its name at the summit. This church is first noticed in Domesday Book, and its medieval parish embraced the rest of the territory of Nottingham, including its extensive common fields. The English Borough was clearly an important early nucleus of settlement. Although not as formidable as the site of the Castle, the hill was defensible. To the south the Cliff, until the twelfth century more a steep slope than a precipice,[32] formed a natural barrier, as did to a lesser extent the Beck to the east. The course of a line of defences is suggested by a series of parallel streets to east, west, and north, with Fletcher Gate, Warser Gate, Woolpack Lane, Hollow Stone, and High Pavement forming an intramural road.[33]

Chance finds and a series of rescue excavations have in large part confirmed these topographical observations. No evidence for significant occupation between the Iron Age and the Norman Conquest has come to light in the precincts of the castle and on Standard Hill. Likewise, there is nothing in the archaeological record to indicate extensive Anglo-Saxon settlement in the French Borough. A handful of pre-Conquest pottery sherds have been found close to Bridlesmith Gate just to the west of the pre-Conquest borough. No investigation has been carried out to the east of the Beck, on the hill around Green's Windmill, so that there is no knowledge of any early settlement here. Research has been largely confined to the English Borough and abundant evidence of pre-Conquest occupation has been found. Early activity in the vicinity of Fisher Gate is suggested by the discovery of pagan Saxon pottery in what may have been a ditch, mixed with Romano-British and Iron Age material. This ditch, and another between Woolpack Lane and Barker Gate, could have been part of a small fortified enclosure on the eastern side of St Mary's Hill during the sixth to eighth centuries.[34] A minimal amount of Pagan Saxon pottery found abraded in a ditch in Halifax Place, to the west of St Mary's church, cannot be related to a settlement phase, and Middle Saxon pottery from this site is at present unconnected with actual occupation. Halifax Place is the single most important window into the early use of the interior of the English borough, and for at least two or three hundred years large timber halls, perhaps within their own enclosure, stood here at the top of the hill, immediately to the west of St Mary's Church.[35] The earliest structure on the site was a two-phase timber hall, undated, but perhaps of the eighth century. This was succeeded by a bow-sided hall. The narrowness of the excavation site prevented the examination of the whole of these buildings, but it is likely that the bow-sided hall and its successors were each at least 100 feet long, a size comparable to that of the grandest buildings of the period.[36] In its turn this latter was replaced by a sequence of three similar buildings further to the west, which probably date from the early

Figure 2.1 **The Medieval town**

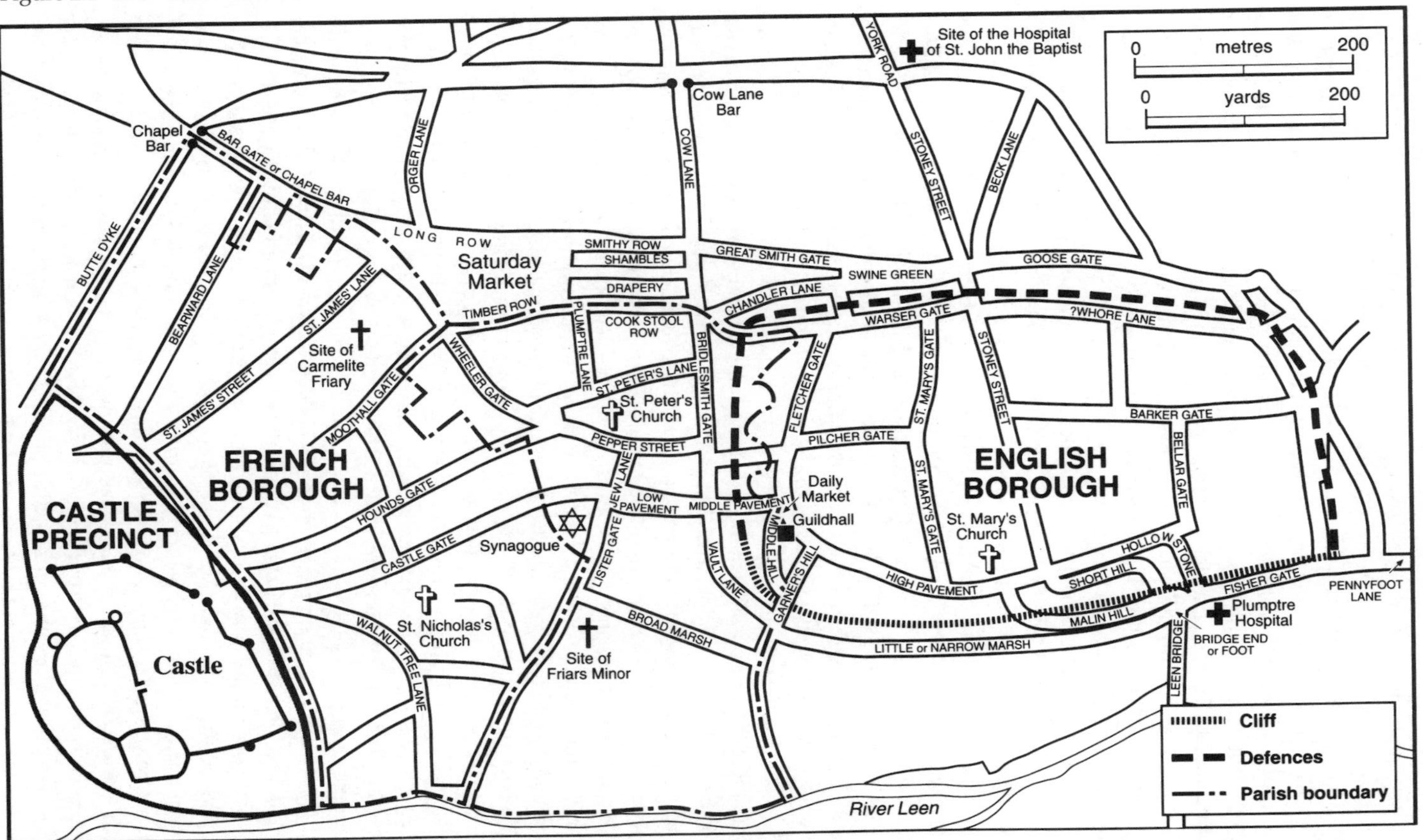

Note: The figure shows the physical location of the French (post-1066) and English (Saxon) boroughs and street-names which can be identified in contemporary documents.

tenth to early eleventh centuries. Stone buildings are found on the site from the late eleventh or twelfth centuries, when two phases of large aisled hall were constructed. All these structures probably faced towards High Pavement which, in the absence of evidence to indicate a central axial road, appears to have been the principal street of the borough in the pre-Conquest period, as it continued to be throughout the Middle Ages.[37] With its proximity to the church, the site has every appearance of being an important early nucleus, which remained the focus of the town. It survived the Conquest to come, significantly, into the hands of William Peveril, who gave the land to his new priory at Lenton. The large halls were replaced by simple small tenement buildings, and the site lost its status.

The suggested line of the English borough's defences has been verified on a number of sites, and two distinct phases have been observed. The first consisted of a ditch some thirty feet wide and at least fifteen feet deep behind which was built a massive timber rampart. This ditch was subsequently recut and the spoil cast up over the remains of the rampart to form a dump bank. It is tempting to identify these phases with the Danish defences of 868 and the repairs of Edward the Elder in 918. However, in the absence of firm archaeological dating, there are historical grounds for rejecting this. Æthelweard specifically states that the Danes were responsible for construction, yet the scale of the timber rampart and ditch suggest public works beyond the resources or the needs of Vikings in time and manpower. Camps built at Repton and possibly Stamford at the same period were more modest in size and construction.[38] The defences within which the Danes were besieged in 868 were almost certainly situated within an as yet undiscovered defensive circuit. The supposed enclosure in the vicinity of St Mary's Church and Halifax Place is a distinct possibility, but other sites, such as Castle Hill or even Sneinton, are not precluded. If Nottingham remained ungarrisoned in the early tenth century, it must have been this small early circuit that Edward the Elder repaired in 918. Only the construction of the borough south of the Trent, together with a bridge, is recorded in 920. However, the works must have implied some reorganisation of the English Borough on St Mary's Hill, and the timber rampart and ditch may have been built at the same time or later. The scale of the fortifications is consistent with the burghal system introduced by Edward. Furthermore, they are of a kind known elsewhere at the period.[39] The remodelling of the defences probably dates from the middle years of the tenth century. The period of Norse ascendancy between 939 and 942 provides a possible context, but the works are likely to postdate the establishment of the Confederacy.

Evidence for the growth of Nottingham before the eleventh century is slight. The borough south of the Trent was to be of ephemeral importance. No trace of the settlement has been found in historical sources after 920, and even the site cannot now be positively identified: it is most likely to have been close to the main road from the south in West Bridgford.[40] Similar fortifications survived in other towns, but do not seem to have retained a distinct identity.[41] In Nottingham such a development was perhaps precluded by the great width of the Trent floodplain, and the settlement seems to have disappeared by 1066, although, perhaps significantly, Clifton, Wilford and West Bridgford were, as a comital estate, closely associated with the borough at that time, and may have formed part of the original West Bridgford territory.

The English Borough probably saw some degree of growth after the remodelling of the defences. A site between Woolpack Lane and Barker Gate produced evidence of stripping of the land up to the intramural road, suggesting clearance for development, before a complex sequence of structures of the late tenth or early eleventh centuries. The properties were widely spaced and the buildings modest in size and construction, possibly indicating a phase of intramural expansion into a previously undeveloped area. Unfortunately, there is no evidence to illuminate the development of the internal streets of the borough, but it would perhaps be surprising if the main outline of the medieval plan had not been established by 1100.

Nottingham in 1066

Domesday Book noted 192 inhabitants in Nottingham on the eve of the Conquest. However, this figure furnishes few clues as to the size of the population, because it relates only to those who were 'of the borough': in other words, those who were primarily responsible for the payment of the farm of £18 to the King. There is no evidence to rank Nottingham demographically with other boroughs in England at this time.[42] Domesday Book is more eloquent on the structure of lordship and society of Nottingham. There were two foci of power in 1066. The first was the English Borough. Most boroughs in 1066 were royal and comital centres, but not exclusively so. There were also numerous fees held by rural thegns and townsmen. The proliferation of churches, a lucrative appurtenance of an estate and a sign of lordship in the eleventh century, indicates communities with a high degree of tenurial heterogeneity and freedom. The Borough of Nottingham was of a different character. Of its 192 inhabitants, 173 were burgesses. They were in the King's soke, that is jurisdiction and lordship, rendering miscellaneous small monetary rents and services in kind known as 'the customs'.[43] As in other boroughs, they had agricultural interests – thirty-eight burgesses held six carucates of land in the fields of Nottingham – but their main occupations were probably in industry and trade. The remaining nineteen inhabitants are described as villeins. As 'villagers' who worked on the land, they may have been tenants of the burgesses or of the King.[44]

Unlike comparable boroughs in the Northern Danelaw, no other classes of inhabitant are recorded and the only other landholdings noticed are the King's demesne lands. King Edward probably held the church of St Mary with three tenements and land in the fields, and an estate of one carucate in Sneinton which belonged to the borough at this time. It is likely that there were many other holders of land in 1066 – the burgesses probably had tenants – but none enjoyed the extensive privileges which characterised tenure in other boroughs. As the appearance of a single royal church suggests, soke was evidently reserved exclusively to the King.[45] Throughout the Middle Ages the custom of the English Borough was Borough English whereby, in the absence of a will, on the death of a burgess land descended to the youngest rather than eldest son. Ultimogeniture, as it was known, was characteristic of 'ancient demesne' in Nottinghamshire, and it would seem that in terms of lordship and tenure the borough was little different from these rural estates.[46]

The King's borough was complemented in 1066 by the second centre of power, a more shadowy but equally substantial estate held by the earl in what subsequently became the French Borough. Domesday Book records that Earl Tosti had one carucate of land in Nottingham. The account indicates that the estate encompassed land to the west of the English Borough, but it was apparently not part of the latter, for the dues of thirteen houses built by the sheriff, Hugh son of Baldric, after the Conquest 'in the new borough' were transferred to the old, a transaction which clearly distinguishes the two. The survey affords no further explicit details of the fee, but much of its structure was preserved in the post-Conquest honour of Peveril. The fee was the caput of the barony, which met in St James's Chapel close to the moot hall in Moothallgate,[47] and it seems likely that the Earl's principal residence was also situated in the estate.

Neither the King's borough nor the Earl's estate existed in isolation. They stood at the centre of a network of royal and comital manors which encircled Nottingham. Arnold and its soke, commanding the northern approaches to Nottingham, were held by Edward the Confessor, and Clifton and its soke, straddling the North Road to the south, were probably controlled by the Earl. With the exception of soke of Toki's manor of Stoke Bardolph in Carlton, Gedling, and Colwick, the rest of the estates in the immediate vicinity of the borough were held by their thegns who were charged with the defence of the borough and shire. Nottingham was the hub of a concentration of royal and comital power that was largely unparalleled in the East Midlands.[48]

The Norman Conquest

This pattern of power aided the smoothness with which Nottingham and Nottinghamshire were conquered and settled by the Normans. After the Battle of Hastings William attempted to rule the country through English officials, but in 1067 he began a campaign of direct rule. In 1068 castles, a Norman innovation, were constructed at Warwick and Nottingham. York was then fortified and further castles were built at Lincoln, Huntingdon, Cambridge, and almost certainly at Stamford.[49] The main centres of population in the East Midlands and the lines of communication with the North were secured, and the area did not rise when Northumbria rebelled in 1069. With control of the borough and the associated administration of the shire, royal estates were seized, and between 1068 and 1086 the lands of Anglo-Saxon lords in Nottinghamshire were taken into the King's hands and distributed to his barons. Of the twenty-nine tenants-in-chief in the county in 1086, only the Archbishop of York and the Abbot of Peterborough could demonstrate continuity of tenure from the pre-Conquest period, and then not in all of their estates.

In and around Nottingham Edward the Confessor's lands and dues passed to William the Conqueror. At the time of the Domesday survey William held the Church of St Mary with its lands, notably 'the priest's croft' in which sixty-five houses were situated along with all the estates in the vicinity that had been held by King Edward, and the lordship of the English Borough. By 1086 the farm had increased from £18 to £30 and the number paying it 120. No earl was appointed after the Conquest, and William also succeeded to the Earl's third penny of the borough and of the shire. The Earl's lands, however, passed to William Peveril, the Constable of the Castle. He was in full possession of the thegnlands around Nottingham in 1086, although many of the thegns remained as his tenants. Domesday Book is silent on the holder of the Earl Tosti's land in Nottingham itself, but they came into William Peveril's hands, because by *c.*1106 he appears to have had free disposal of the estate.[50]

The transfer of lordship was orderly, but the new world of the Norman settlement demanded institutional changes which transformed Nottingham's community. The pre-Conquest provisions for borough defence probably remained in place; it appears that Peveril's English tenants performed much the same services for their land as they had before the Conquest as tenants of the Earl.[51] However, the garrisoning of the Castle required new arrangements. William's barons were granted land in return for service in the feudal army and the guarding of royal castles. Unfortunately, the organisation of guard at Nottingham in the eleventh century, or indeed later, is not known, but both William Peveril and Ralph de Buron held twenty-five 'horsemen's houses' in 1086, which were almost certainly the accommodation for soldiers which they were obliged to provide.[52] A further 101 houses, held by five tenants-in-chief and many in the occupation of merchants in 1086, had probably served a similar function. All were constituted as fees, that is, estates with some degree of judicial and administrative independence from the borough. Those held by Richard Frail and Wulfbert were probably entirely urban: one or the other was represented by the thirteenth-century estate of Gilbert le Gluton in and around Wheeler Gate, which was held in chief in return for acting as a bailiff errant. The remaining five were probably all attached to the tenant-in-chief's principal manor in the county.[53]

The community of the borough

The social and tenurial changes accompanying the Conquest marked the emergence of a truly urban community. It seems unlikely that Nottingham had ever been a Danish borough, and, despite the establishment of an English mint, and presumably market, in or after 920, there is little sign of the development of a flourishing urban economy in the first half of the tenth century. At the same time Lincoln, York, Stamford, and Thetford benefited from access to the wider northern world of the Vikings to become the principal mercantile and industrial centres of England. Nottingham was never of their number. The output of coin was always small compared with that of those in other boroughs of the East Midlands. Evidence for pottery manufacture has been found on Halifax Place, possibly dating from this period, but its wares have not been found elsewhere in the town, and it is likely that it represents a special production for the high status site with which it was associated.[54] Some metalworking was also undertaken, but its scale was again modest. Derby may have been the principal market centre. It was evidently an important economic centre, as its coin production was second to none in the East Midlands at this period, and its administrative subordination to Nottingham may suggest that it was a mercantile suburb of the borough.[55] Nottingham itself was primarily a fortress.

The later tenth and early eleventh centuries probably saw no great change in Nottingham's character. The proliferation of properties, and presumably the development of back lanes and side streets, suggests some increase in population, but this may simply reflect the borough's wider political role. Apart from the courts, the internal workings of the Five Boroughs are unknown, but given Nottingham's pre-eminent status in the Trent valley on the break-up of the Confederacy in the early eleventh century, the organisation's headquarters may have been situated in the borough. At any event the Earldom must have had a considerable establishment there, and it may be at that time, if not before, that the fee held by Earl Tosti in 1065 in what became the French Borough came into being. Likewise, the King's reeve probably had a hall in the English Borough; High Pavement is the most likely site, where the King's hall was situated in the post-Conquest period.[56] Such interests might be expected to foster some degree of growth, but Nottingham remained a military and administrative centre with an essentially command economy.

The concentration of royal and comital thegns around the borough in 1066 reflects this specialist role. The relatively small group of burgesses responsible for the farm of the borough must have been some communal mechanism to collect the dues owed, but there is no sign of the free lawmen who apparently played such an important role in urban life elsewhere in the Danelaw.[57] Customs, with the associated jurisdictions that they implied, were reserved to the King or the Earl, and the life of the community was subservient to the needs of a strategic borough which commanded the north–south routes.

The construction of the Castle in 1067 marks a significant change. Nottingham remained a key centre of power, but the borough ceased to be the main focus of royal interest, and the measures that were taken to garrison and provision the new fortress changed the town's society and economy. The creation of urban fees as the corollary of castle guard introduced a tenurial heterogeneity into the borough that was unprecedented. Probably for the first time rural manors such as Shelford had free access to the market in Nottingham. The garrison's needs produced further changes. The new borough was created (1068–86) between the Castle and the English Borough within the Earl's estate, and the churches of St Nicholas and St Peter were probably founded at about the same time to serve its population.[58] The primary purpose of the new creation was probably to provision the Castle, but advantageous customs were instituted to attract Norman settlers and to foster trade. The French Borough, with its own administration within the honour of Peveril, remained distinct from the English Borough to the east into the late thirteenth century.[59] Nevertheless, Nottingham had begun to assume the social and tenurial character that was common elsewhere. From 1086 it was to take a new course as a community with its own interests and history.

Notes

1 D. Whitelock, D. C. Douglas and S. I. Tucker (eds.), *The Anglo-Saxon Chronicle: a Revised Translation* (1965), p. 146: recorded in the A chronicle; W. H. Stevenson (ed.), *Asser's Life of King Alfred* (Oxford, 1959), pp. 24–5; A. Campbell (ed.), *The Chronicle of Æthelweard* (1962), pp. 36–7.

2 A. Williams and R. W. H. Erskine (eds.), *The Nottinghamshire Domesday* (1990); Abraham Farley (ed.), *Greater Domesday Book* (1783) (hereafter *GDB*), fo. 280.

3 Whitelock *et al.*, *Anglo-Saxon Chronicle*, pp. 67, 71, 148; P. H. Sawyer, *Anglo-Saxon Charters: an Annotated Handlist and Bibliography* (1968), no. 407; A. J. Robertson (ed.), *Anglo-Saxon Charters* (Cambridge, 1956), no. 54.

4 J. E. B. Gover, A. Mawer and F. M. Stenton, *The Place-Names of Nottinghamshire* (Cambridge, 1940).

5 A. Rogers, 'Parish boundaries and urban history: two case studies', *Journal of the British Archaeological Association*, 3rd series, 35 (1972), pp. 46–64; W. Stevenson, 'Topographical and other early notes about Nottingham', TTS, 22 (1918), pp. 51–74; Barley and Straw, p. i.

6 C. S. B. Young, 'Archaeology in Nottingham: the pre-Conquest borough', in S. N. Mastoris (ed.), *History in the Making: Recent Historical Research in Nottingham and Nottinghamshire 1985* (Nottingham, 1986), pp. 1–4; C. S. B. Young, 'Excavations in Nottingham', *TTS*, 74 (1970), pp. 2–3; *TTS*, 75 (1971), pp. 1–2; *TTS*, 76 (1972), pp. 1–3; *TTS*, 78 (1974), pp. 2–3; C. S. B. Young, *Discovering Rescue Archaeology in Nottingham* (Nottingham, 1982); G. Young, 'Archaeology in Nottingham: the Halifax Place Excavation', in S. N. Mastoris (ed.), *History in the Making: Recent Historical Research in Nottingham and Nottinghamshire 1986* (Nottingham, 1987), pp. 1–6.

7 Stevenson (ed.), *Asser*, pp. 24, 230–1; S. Keynes and M. Lapidge (trans.), *Alfred the Great: Asser's Life of King Alfred and other Contemporary Sources* (1983), p. 241; no surviving caves can be dated earlier than the thirteenth century. Excavations were probably continually reworked to suit the needs of the time (A. Hamilton, *Nottingham City of Caves* (Nottingham, n.d.), p. 2). I am grateful to A. G. MacCormick for an overview of recent speleological research in the city.

8 Gover *et al.*, *Place-Names of Nottinghamshire*, p. 174; *GDB*, 280, 282 (where duplicated); BL Loans 29/60, Cartulary of Sir Henry Pierpoint, f.51v. The church or chapel belonged to Lenton Priory, but there is no record of a grant, and it seems likely that the house had it by right of St Mary's; W. H. Stevenson and A. Stapleton, *The Religious Foundations of Old Nottingham* (Nottingham, 1895), I, p. 22; G. Vanderzee (ed.), *Nonarum Inquisitiones* (1807), p. 290; T. Foulds, 'The foundation of Lenton Priory and a reconstruction of its lost Cartulary', TTS, 92 (1988), pp. 32–44.

9 Gover *et al.*, *Place-Names of Nottinghamshire*, p. 13; B. Cox, 'The significance of English place names in *ham* in the Midlands and East Anglia', in K. Cameron (ed.), *Place-Name Evidence for the Anglo-Saxon Invasion and Scandinavian Settlements* (Nottingham, 1975), pp. 71–2, 79.

10 Little is known of the organisation of land in the Middle Saxon period in the Nottingham area. However, it is significant that major battles between Mercia and Northumbria seem to have been fought further to the north, on the Went and Idle, or in Hatfield. For the boundary between the two kingdoms, see M. S. Parker, 'The province of Hatfield', *Northern History*, 28 (1992), pp. 42–69.

11 In both 934 and *c.*973 the *witan* (assembly) met in the borough as the King and his court moved into Yorkshire: Sawyer, *Anglo-Saxon Charters*; Robertson, *Anglo-Saxon Charters*.

12 C. R. Hart, 'The Kingdom of Mercia', in A. Dornier (ed.), *Mercian Studies* (Leicester, 1977), pp. 54–7; A. Williams, A. P. Smyth and D. P. Kirby, *A Biographical Dictionary of Dark Age Britain: England, Scotland and Wales c.500–c.1050* (1991), p. 78; Whitelock *et al.*, *Anglo-Saxon Chronicle*, p. 48.

13 Whitelock *et al.*, *Anglo-Saxon Chronicle*, p. 48.

14 Campbell (ed.), *Æthelweard*, p. 51; D. R. Roffe, 'Nottinghamshire and the North; a Domesday study' (University of Leicester, Ph.D. thesis, 1987), pp. 220–2; Whitelock *et al.*, *Anglo-Saxon Chronicle*, p. 61.

15 Whitelock *et al.*, *Anglo-Saxon Chronicle*, pp. 64–7; F. T. Wainwright, *Scandinavian England* (Chichester, 1975), pp. 317–24.

16 Whitelock *et al.*, *Anglo-Saxon Chronicle*, pp. 61–2, 64, 66–7; C. M. Mahany and D. R. Roffe, 'Stamford: the development of an Anglo-Scandinavian Borough', *Anglo-Norman Studies*, 5 (1982), pp. 206–11. Lindsey, to the east, remained a part of Viking York at this time and probably did so until 927 or 942: D. R. Roffe, 'Introduction to the Lincolnshire Domesday', in A. Williams and G. H. Martin (eds.), *The Lincolnshire Domesday* (1992), p. 40; Wainwright, *Scandinavian England*, p. 324; Roffe, 'Nottinghamshire and the North', pp. 228–9.

17 D. R. Roffe, 'Introduction to the Nottinghamshire Domesday', in Williams and Erskine (eds.), *Nottinghamshire Domesday*, pp. 21–2.

18 C. Blunt, 'The coinage of Athelstan, King of England 924–39', *British Numismatic Journal*, 42 (1974), pp. 44–5; D. R. Roffe, 'The origins of Derbyshire', *DAJ*, 106 (1986), pp. 111–14. The restriction of trade to boroughs was introduced in the early tenth century, but the toll boundaries that the monopoly implied are only recorded in post-Conquest sources. *RBN*, I, pp. 2, 3, 11; BL Additional Charter 47,498; T. D. Hardy (ed.), *Rotuli Chartarum* (1837), p. 138a. To the north the tolls belonged to Blyth/Tickhill: R. T. Timson (ed.), *The Cartulary of Blyth Priory* (*TSRS*, 27–8, 1973), no. 293.

19 A. P. Smyth, *Scandinavian York and Dublin* (Dublin, 1987), II, pp. 7–10, 91–4.

20 Whitelock *et al.*, *Anglo-Saxon Chronicle*, p. 71.

21 Gover *et al.*, *Place-Names of Nottinghamshire*, p. 199; For possible defences see A. G. Kinsley, 'Excavations of the Saxo-Norman town defences at Slaughterhouse Lane, Newark-on-Trent, Nottinghamshire', *TTS*, 97 (1993), pp. 56–8. Further Saxon ditches and an early cemetery were found during excavations at Newark Castle in 1995; ex inf. Philip Dixon.

22 D. R. Roffe, 'Hundreds and wapentakes', in Williams and Martin (eds.), *Lincolnshire Domesday*, pp. 40–1; Sawyer, *Anglo-Saxon Charters*, nos. 479, 484, 1606; Roffe, 'Nottinghamshire and the North', pp. 242–5.

23 Roffe, 'Introduction to the Nottinghamshire Domesday', pp. 17-21; Roffe, 'Origins of Derbyshire', pp. 108–11.

24 A. Williams, '"Princeps Merciorum Gentis": the family, career and connections of Ælfhere, Ealdorman of Mercia, 956–83', *Anglo-Saxon England*, 10 (1984), p. 164; H. R. Loyn, *The Governance of Anglo-Saxon England 500–1087* (1984), p. 142.

25 D. R. Roffe, 'Nottingham and the Five Boroughs', in Mastoris, *History in the Making 1986*, pp. 7–11; Roffe, 'Introduction to the Lincolnshire Domesday', p. 41.

26 Whitelock *et al.*, *Anglo-Saxon Chronicle*, pp. 92–5.

27 Roffe, 'Introduction to the Lincolnshire Domesday', pp. 41–2; D. Crook, 'Moothallgate and the venue of the Nottinghamshire County Court in the thirteenth century', *TTS*, 88 (1984), pp. 99–102; D. Crook, 'The establishment of the Derbyshire County Court, 1256', *DAJ*, 103 (1983), pp. 98–106.

28 A. Williams, 'The King's nephew: the family and career of Ralph, Earl of Hereford', in C. Harper-Bill, C. J. Holdsworth and J. L. Nelson (eds.), *Studies in Medieval History Presented to A. Allen Brown* (Woodbridge, 1989), pp. 327–44; Roffe, 'Nottinghamshire and the North', pp. 256–60; Whitelock *et al.*, *Anglo-Saxon Chronicle*, pp. 137–8; W. E. Kapelle, *The Norman Conquest of the North* (1979), pp. 98–100.

29 Whitelock *et al.*, *Anglo-Saxon Chronicle*, p. 67.

30 T. D. Hardy (ed.), *Rotuli Litterarum Clausarum in Turri Londinensi Asservati*, II (1834), p. 208; H. E. Boulton (ed.), *The Sherwood Forest Book* (*TSRS*, 23, 1967), p. 37; J. Deas and P. M. Barnes (eds.), *The Great Roll of the Pipe for the Third Year of the Reign of King Henry III, Michaelmas 1219*, PR 80 (1976); Newstead I, f. 82r no. 1 indicates that properties originally ran from the Castle Rock down to the Trent. There may, however, have been various streams which ran into the river, and the channels of some or all of these may have been utilised to make the new cut.

31 Whitelock *et al.*, *Anglo-Saxon Chronicle*, p. 148; *GDB*, 280; S. N. Mastoris, 'The boundary between the English and French Boroughs in Mediaeval Nottingham', *TTS*, 81 (1981), pp. 68–74; Rogers, 'Parish boundaries', 51–6.

32 *GDB*, 280; Rogers, 'Parish boundaries', p. 51. Early properties extended down from the Cliff top to Narrow Marsh (Brewhouse Yard Museums, Nottingham Deeds Survey database). At the eastern end of the Cliff, excavation has shown that the vertical face is artificial, due to scarping and cutting: ex. inf. C. S. B. Young.

33 Stevenson, 'Topographical notes about Nottingham', pp. 51–74.

34 Young, 'Archaeology in Nottingham', 1–4. We are grateful to Charles Young for his help in preparing this account, which deviates in many respects from earlier reports, in advance of his own publication of the excavations. We would not however wish necessarily to implicate Mr Young in the conclusions which we have drawn from his data.

35 For a comparable site beside St Peter's Church, Northampton – identified as the palace of the Mercian kings – see J. Williams *et al.*, *Middle Saxon Palaces at Northampton* (Northampton, 1985).

36 P. Rahtz, 'Buildings and rural settlement', in D. M. Wilson (ed.), *The Archaeology of Anglo-Saxon England* (Cambridge, 1976), pp. 49–98, 63–9.

37 No evidence has come to light to indicate that there was a through route between Pilcher Gate and Barker Gate, and it would seem that the intramural road always functioned as the main thoroughfare. Weekday Cross, the market-place of the English Borough, is situated at the west end of High Pavement.

38 Barley and Straw; Campbell (ed.), *Æthelweard*, p. 36; M. Biddle, 'Repton', *Current Archaeology*, 100 (1986), pp. 138–41; Mahany and Roffe, 'Stamford', pp. 203–4. For Danish military practices and the defences that they built at this time, see A. P. Smyth, *Scandinavian Kings in the British Isles 850–880* (Oxford, 1977), pp. 183–5. A Mercian origin for the rampart (that is, eighth or nineth century, pre Viking) has been suggested, but a tenth-century date is more likely: Roffe, 'Nottinghamshire and the North', pp. 216–17.

39 M. Biddle, 'Towns', in Wilson, *Archaeology*, pp. 120–9.

40 Barley and Straw, p. 2. Mickleborough Hill, 'the great borough hill' between West Bridgford and Ruddington, has been suggested as the site (VCH *Nottinghamshire*, I, p. 291n.), as has an earthwork in Wilford: J. Haslam, 'The Second Burh of Nottingham', *Landscape History*, 9 (1987), pp. 45–51.

41 Mahany and Roffe, 'Stamford', p. 206; H. R. Lyon, 'Anglo-Saxon Stamford', in A. Rogers (ed.), *The Making of Stamford* (Leicester, 1965), p. 29.

42 Roffe, 'Introduction to the Nottinghamshire Domesday', pp. 24–5; Borough farms are perhaps the best indicator of relative wealth, but so many factors conditioned the render that comparison becomes meaningless.

43 Roffe, 'Introduction to the Nottinghamshire Domesday', p. 25; F. M. Stenton, *Anglo-Saxon England* (3rd edn, Oxford, 1971), pp. 149–50; P. H. Sawyer, *From Roman Britain to Norman England* (1978), p. 245; Roffe, 'Introduction to the Nottinghamshire Domesday', p. 24.

44 Alternatively, they could have been rural villeins whose land had become incorporated into the borough by 1086. Lenton may have lost land when the Castle was built: cf. Stamford, where the construction of the Castle led to the absorption of a manor in Rutland into the borough: D. R. Roffe and C. M. Mahany, 'Stamford and the Norman Conquest', *Lincolnshire History and Archaeology*, 21 (1986), pp. 5–9.

45 The only possible exceptions are the moneyers. Elsewhere it is clear that their tenements were non-customary, and they probably always had the status of king's thegns; some, indeed, had sake and soke: GDB 171. There is no direct evidence for the Nottingham moneyers, although in 1086 they paid their own farm, suggesting an identity separate from that of the burgesses. In the twelfth and thirteenth centuries their lands were held directly from the King.

46 W. Stevenson, 'Land tenures in Nottinghamshire', in J. P. Briscoe (ed.), *Old Nottinghamshire* (1881), pp. 66–71.

47 Roffe, 'Nottinghamshire and the North', pp. 164–74; D. R. Roffe, 'From thegnage to barony: Sake and Soke, title and tenants-in-chief', *Anglo-Norman Studies*, 12 (1989), pp. 173–4; Williams,

'King's Nephew', pp. 327–40. The honour of Peveril has been cited as a classic example of a post-Conquest castlery: R. Fleming, *Kings and Lords in Conquest England* (Cambridge, 1991), pp. 196–7. In fact, much of the land was held by Englishmen by English terms of tenure. Other arrangements had to be made for the garrisoning of the Castle. Stevenson and Stapleton, *Religious Institutions*, I, p. 50.

48 *GDB*, 281v, 287–88; F. E. Harmer (ed.), *Anglo-Saxon Writs* (Manchester, 1952), no. 119.

49 Whitelock *et al.*, *Anglo-Saxon Chronicle*, p. 148.

50 Foulds, 'Lenton', pp. 42–4.

51 They are said in Domesday Book to 'have [their lands] from', rather than 'hold of' William Peveril. Most were held in various forms of sergeancy, the typical translation of pre-Conquest thegnages, in the later Middle Ages: Roffe, 'From thegnage to barony', pp. 173–4.

52 *GDB*, 280.

53 *The Book of Fees* (1920–31), p. 288; *Curia Regis Rolls* (1922 and in progress), XII, p. 124; *CPR* 1255–58, p. 29; *List of the Inquisitions Ad Quod Damnum Preserved in the Public Record Office* (New York, 1963), p. 94; *Rufford Charters* no. 33; NAO CA 1295, Nottingham Borough Court Enrolments, f.2v; J. Standish (ed.), *Abstracts of the Inquisitions Post Mortem Relating to Nottinghamshire* (*TSRS*, 3–4, 1904–14), II, p. 85.

54 P. Stafford, *The East Midlands in the Early Middle Ages* (Leicester, 1985), pp. 44–53; A. V. Nailor, 'A group of tenth-century pottery from Nottingham', *Medieval Ceramics*, 7 (1983).

55 Whitelock *et al.*, *Anglo-Saxon Chronicle*, pp. 64–5; Roffe, 'An introduction to the Derbyshire Domesday', p. 24; R. A. Hall, 'The Five Boroughs of the Danelaw', *Anglo-Saxon England*, 18 (1989), p. 162.

56 A. J. Robertson (ed.), *The Laws of England from Edmund to Henry I* (Cambridge, 1925), III Æthelred 1, the Wantage Code; CClR 1296–1302, p. 168; 1330–33, p. 433.

57 J. Tait, *The Medieval English Borough: Studies in its Origins and Constitutional History* (Manchester, 1936), pp. 43–4.

58 St. Nicholas's may have been the church of the pre-Conquest earl's fee. Recent excavations within the church produced evidence to suggest that the medieval building on the site was cruciform, perhaps indicating a foundation somewhat more important than a simple urban *eigenkirche* (C. S. B. Young, Nottingham Museums, personal communication).

59 Roffe, 'Nottinghamshire and the North', 171–2.

3

THE ROYAL CASTLE

Pamela Marshall and Trevor Foulds

When William the Conqueror, during his northern campaign of 1067–68, ordered a castle to be built on the steep hill to the west of the English Borough at Nottingham he was following an accepted pattern. Royal castles were placed where they would dominate existing centres of population.[1] Consequently, established administrative foci formed special targets and, since towns very often lay at strategic points in the communications network, two objectives could be achieved simultaneously. While the East Midlands had not joined the Northern earls in rebellion against Norman rule in 1068, Nottingham Castle should be seen as one of a group designed to control both the area and the passage to the north. Another was at Lincoln, where the Ermine Street joined the Fosse Way, and a third might have been sited at Newark, also on the Fosse.[2] Newark and Nottingham were probably comparable in size and prosperity and were both located on river-crossings of the Trent, but Nottingham had certain advantages. The borough held a supremely defensible position, it was already regarded as a fortress and head of its shire, and the Trent Bridge (920) placed it on a major route to Doncaster and York from the Central Midlands. Nottingham was a vital link in any northern campaign.[3]

At the time of the Conquest Lincoln Castle would seem more probably destined to become the principal royal residence of the East Midlands. Lincoln housed an international trading community and population, which probably exceeded 6,000, was already overspilling the Roman boundaries. The old minster or mother church of the county stood within its walls, and by 1072 plans were being implemented to transfer the see from Oxfordshire and to begin work on a prestigious new cathedral. Special treatment of the Castle is indicated by the addition of stone walls before 1100, followed by a fine shell keep, also in stone.[4] Yet a comparison of the subsequent histories of these neighbouring castles is illuminating. Despite Lincoln's economic superiority over Nottingham, pitifully small sums were spent on its castle by the Angevin kings and no expenditure by the Crown is recorded after 1270. By the fourteenth century the Castle was incapable of defence and had been all but relinquished to the earls of Chester. After 1335 it was considered of no use other than to serve as the county court and gaol. By contrast, Nottingham Castle continued to thrive throughout the medieval period and developed into a grandiose royal residence. Money was repeatedly poured into the work of improvement and repair, even in the reign of the notoriously parsimonious Elizabeth I, who spent over £1,000 on restoration. She planned two visits, although neither actually took place.[5]

The origins of the Castle

Nottingham Castle was built on an oustanding natural site at a distance of some 500 metres from the Saxon borough (figure 2.1). The site chose itself: a narrow sandstone crag with steep cliffs formed a natural basis for a fortress. The highest point of the rock, at the southern end, provided a ready-made motte, while a bailey or courtyard was formed to the north on the remaining high ground, defended by a cliff to the east and easily cut off at the northern end by a rampart and ditch. A great arc enclosed the lower ground to the east and north in a further, outer bailey (figure 3.1A),[6] which was capable of housing a division of cavalry. Such large outer baileys were rare in urban castles, where space was normally at a premium. By utilising the rock site, additional land of 250 acres (100 hectares) could be encompassed by the castle, with a park to the west, and the King's meadows, fishponds and mills to the south.[7]

The separation of the Castle from the town departed from the normal pattern of royal urban foundations, where castles were sited on the edge of the built-up area and often intruded into the settlement.[8] At Nottingham the Normans were able to combine an urban castle with the amenities normally available only at the hand-picked virgin sites favoured by barons developing rural estates. In fact the royal officers soon took steps to develop the land between the Castle and the English Borough, and the New, or French, Borough was settled by 1086. The founding of a settlement to provision the Castle, peopled by newcomers, and with an independent administration under the honour of Peveril, could hardly have seemed of direct benefit to the English population. Even the physical orientation of the new borough must have accentuated the division between the two communities, with the three main streets of the French Borough (Castle Gate, Hounds Gate and Friar Lane) converging towards the east gate of the Castle, probably towards a planned market-place.

Little medieval work survives on the site of the Castle today, except for part of the wall of the outer bailey and its truncated gatehouse of mid-thirteenth-century date, all heavily restored during the nineteenth century. The bulk of the castle ruins which survived destruction following the civil wars were swept away in 1674–79 in preparation for the building of a grand palace by the Duke of Newcastle. While excavations have thrown additional light on the medieval Castle, any reconstruction relies heavily on a plan of the upper and middle baileys drawn by John Smythson

Figure 3.1 **The development of the castle defences**

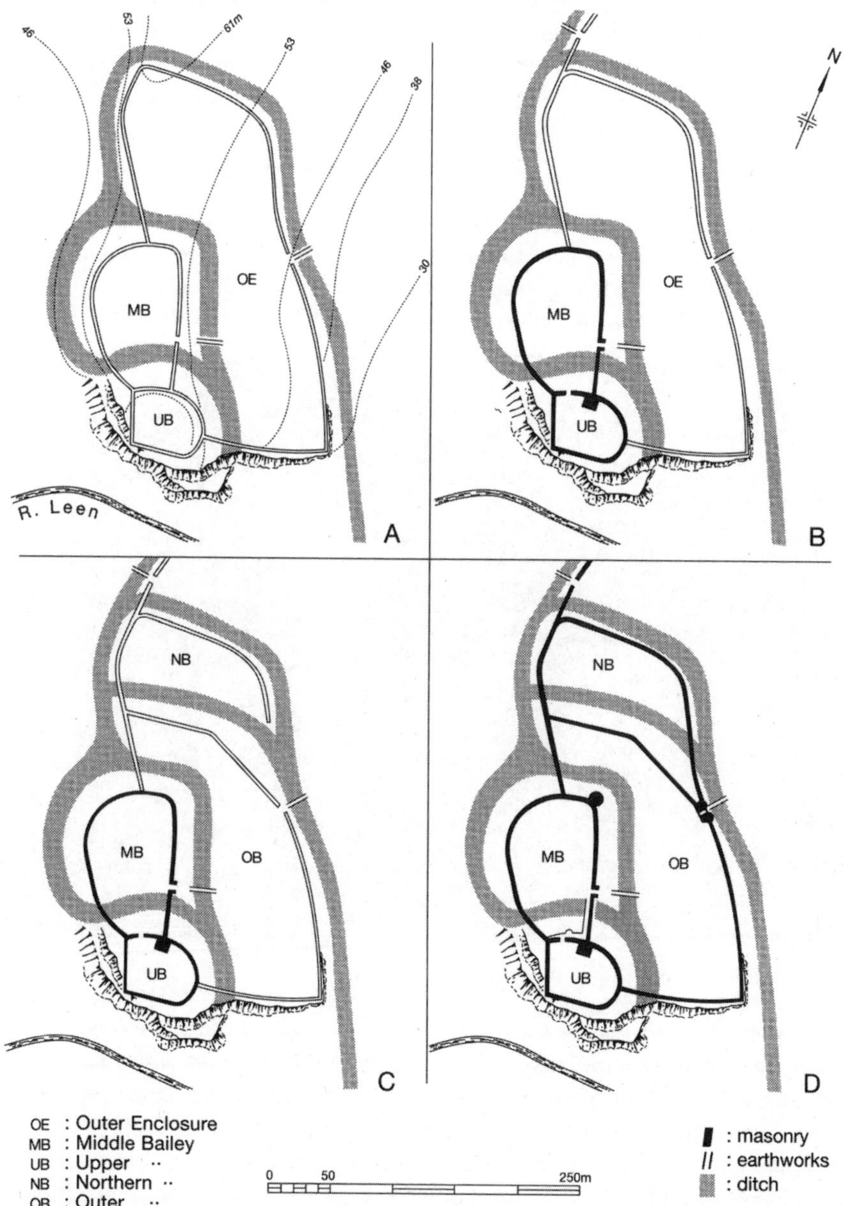

Note: (A) the Castle, late eleventh century, exploiting the natural topography with additional earth ramparts, ditches and timber palisades; (B) mid-twelfth century, with the upper and middle baileys defended in stone; (c) early 13th century, with the outer bailey reduced in size; (D) mid-thirteenth century, with the outer bailey reduced in size; (D) mid-thirteenth century, with some curtain-wall added to outer bailey, and gatehouse. Round tower added to the middle bailey.

in 1617 and on documentary sources.[9] These are sparse for the earliest period of the Castle's history: the Conqueror's Castle has to be reconstructed from later work and by comparison with contemporary sites, with occasional confirmation presented by the excavations. After 1155 the Pipe Rolls of the Exchequer, which recorded the expenditure of succeeding sheriffs on behalf of the King, provide valuable information about royal building projects.[10]

Plate 4 **Plan of Nottingham Castle**. Plan of the buildings in the upper and middle baileys drawn by the architect John Smythson in 1617. As the buildings were destroyed in 1651 and their ruins largely cleared in 1674–79, this plan is the best surviving record of the medieval structure. Excavation has confirmed its general accuracy

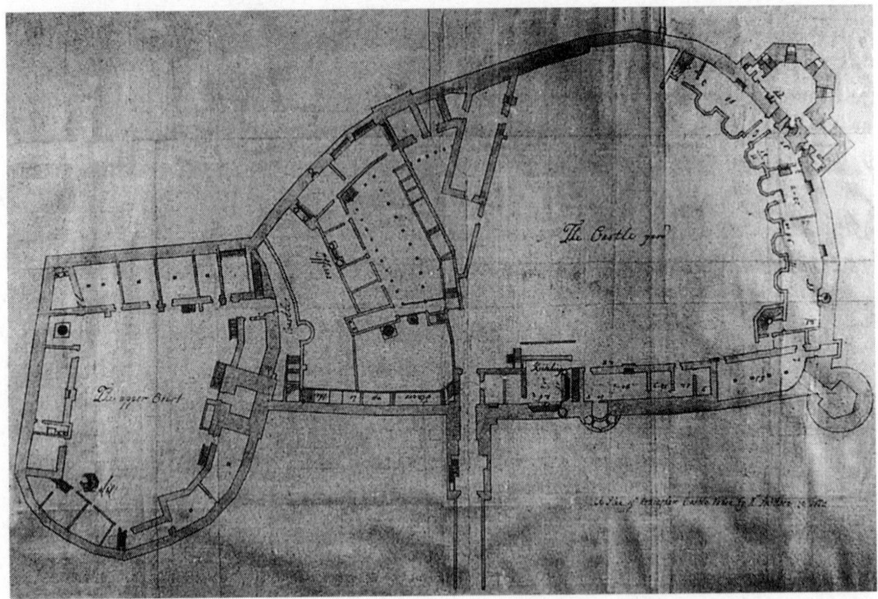

It seems unlikely that the Castle had any work in stone during its earliest Norman phase: each bailey was probably enclosed by an earthen rampart with a timber palisade and, in the absence of a natural cliff, a ditch. The upper bailey stood eight metres above the middle bailey and was separated from it by a ditch. Often called the motte, the upper bailey would have been regarded as the heart or nucleus of the Castle. In its early phase a timber wall probably enclosed some private accommodation, an arrangement copied in stone from the twelfth century. The word 'motte' was sometimes interchangeable with 'donjon', which more usually meant a tower. Both were regarded as signs of lordship.[11] The first stone building within the Castle was probably the small stone tower, about twelve metres square, in the upper ward, shown on Smythson's plan. This is likely to have been built by the second constable, William II

Peveril, before his fall in 1155.[12] A tower, still extant, of a similar scale was built by Henry II at Peveril's confiscated Castle of the Peak at Castleton in Derbyshire, the *caput*, or head, of his honor. In view of the small sum spent by the King on this tower (£135) and its similarity in size and plan to the donjon at Nottingham, it is possible that the tower of Peak had already been started by Peveril.[13] Both towers were small: at Peak the accommodation was particularly limited, providing only one reception room above a storage basement. The building, however, was carefully finished with ashlar facing and external decorative detail. Possibly an extra room was provided at Nottingham by the addition of a further storey, but it would never have been spacious. This type of tower essentially combined a disproportionately modest amount of accommodation within a bold architectural statement. Deliberately sited in order to be visible from long distances, and underlining the lordship which they symbolised, the visual impact of such towers was an essential part of their function, and they should be seen as adjuncts of more extensive domestic apartments.[14]

William I Peveril and his son, William II (1114–55), held the Castle by virtue of a royal grant. However, they held it loyally for the King and this gave them a well-founded sense that the Castle was in many respects their own and, with their lands, conferred on them a superior position in both Nottingham and Nottinghamshire. A number of the sheriffs of Nottinghamshire in the early twelfth century can be identified as Peveril men, and William I Peveril obtained King Henry I's permission to grant the Church of St Mary, a royal church in the English Borough, to the Cluniac priory of Lenton he founded in 1103–14. The other churches in Nottingham were also granted to Lenton Priory which held the castle chapels and took tithes from the Castle's mills and fishponds. Had the close ties between Nottingham and the Peveril family continued, the relationship between the town and the Castle might have developed differently, perhaps along lines similar to other boroughs which had a baronial family in semi-permanent residence.[15] The civil war between King Stephen (1135–54) and the Empress Matilda, the emergence of a regional power struggle centred on Ranulph Earl of Chester, and political misfortune, combined to ensure that no such relationship developed.

In September 1140 Robert of Gloucester attacked Nottingham: he 'suddenly assaulted the town of Nottingham, and finding it unprovided with military defence, commenced sacking it while the citizens on every side fled to the churches'. One of the wealthier citizens was forced to surrender his gold and led his captors into the cellar of his house. He contrived to escape, bolting the doors behind him, and then set fire to the house. The result was a disaster, as fire swept through the town. Many people were arrested and taken to Gloucester. Others, who had taken refuge in the churches, perished as they burned. The reason for the attack is not known unless it was revenge against William II Peveril who had taken part in the 'Battle of the Standard' near Northallerton in 1138 at which Matilda's uncle, King David of Scotland, was defeated. William had hosted the peace treaty between Stephen and David at Nottingham in 1139. At the battle of Lincoln (2 February 1141) William II Peveril and King Stephen were captured. Matilda extorted Nottingham Castle from

William and installed William Painel as her commander. When Nottingham was recaptured by William II Peveril's knights, Matilda's forces were expelled.

In 1154 Henry II peacefully succeeded King Stephen, and the following year he moved to York, where he was met by the men of Nottingham to whom he granted a charter confirming the town's rights and liberties. This may have been a deliberate manoeuvre by the citizens to distance themselves from Peveril, and it was in Henry's interests to have an ally in the town, or at least to ensure its neutrality. Peveril conceded defeat by fleeing to a monastery, and Nottingham, the Castle, and the honor of Peveril, returned to the King. The events of 1140–55 had demonstrated that Nottingham Castle was of strategic significance to the region, and the lesson was not lost on either Henry II, Richard I – who had to besiege the castle in 1194 when it was held against him by supporters of his brother John – or John (1199–1216), who recognised the importance of holding the castle in order to frustrate rebellions in the north and east.[16]

Royal interest renewed

The Peveril family's fall from grace in 1155 marked the beginning of renewed royal interest in the Castle. Events which occurred in 1140 during the civil war between Stephen and Matilda underlined the crucial role played by both Nottingham and its castle in holding the region, and doubtless raised the town in the consciousness of the King. Henry's attention turned to Nottingham in earnest in 1170 as political tension built towards what became the barons' rebellion of 1172–73. He concentrated on updating the fortress, and was probably responsible for replacing the earth and timber defences of the upper and middle wards with stone walls (figure 3.1B).[17] In most places spending tailed off after the crisis had passed and some fortresses appear to have been dropped altogether, but royal expenditure continued at Nottingham. Altogether Henry II spent £1,816 0*s* 3*d*, more than on any other English castle except Dover, which in this period was a special case because it guarded the vulnerable Channel ports. To put this sum into context, the normal cost of maintaining the fabric of a royal castle, including some modest improvement, was about £230 during Henry's reign, and an entire castle was built at Orford for £1,471.[18]

Although the main thrust of Henry's building programme at Nottingham seems to have been motivated by military considerations, he was probably responsible for a treasury as well as some domestic improvements, among them the King's bedchamber, the King's chamber, an almonry in the bailey and a new great hall. The latter was to cause endless problems due to subsidence and, not surprisingly, it had fallen down by the seventeenth century. Henry also spent money on the park and on building a falcon house. While the Angevins were primarily alert to the strategic importance of the Castle, they were not blind to the natural beauty of the site and the immense potential for recreation provided by the park and nearby Sherwood Forest.[19]

The Castle retained its military significance for the remainder of the Angevin period. It was seized twice by Prince John in his attempts to make political capital out of the disaffection which prevailed in England during Richard I's four-year absence at the Third Crusade. Richard returned to England on 13 March 1194 and within twelve days was personally supervising the siege which rapidly brought about the recovery of Nottingham Castle. The repairs which followed were mainly domestic, indicating the scant damage inflicted during the siege, which was in any case of short duration. The domestic improvements made by Henry II seem to have been adequate since, as King, John concentrated his royal works elsewhere.[20] However, Nottingham's defences were maintained and improved, probably under the direction of an engineer named William Baiard.[21] John ordered a tower to be built on the motte, and ten miners were engaged under a Master Pinell to reduce the extent of the outer bailey and build a barbican at the gate (figure 3.1C).[22] The military improvements carried out by the Crown served the Castle well during the baronial unrest which culminated in the invasion by Prince Louis of France in 1216. The Castle formed the headquarters of the King's government north of the Trent and proved to be a formidable bar to Louis's progress. He chose, instead, to attack Lincoln, where his advance was arrested.[23]

The Castle was to perform the role of a military base into the fourteenth century, but the range of its functions was wide. It was used as a place to construct stone-throwing engines, as a weaponry store, and as a base from which a siege train could be sent.[24] On four occasions (1223, 1258, 1260 and 1297) Henry III and Edward I sent letters to the constables of castles they were particularly anxious to have securely held, and Nottingham was one of only five castles to receive a communication on each occasion. Until 1422 the Castle also housed political prisoners and prisoners of war – including David II of Scotland – and occasionally common criminals, although there was a sheriff's court and gaol in the town where the latter were normally confined. For the bulk of its history, the functions of the castle were peaceful. When King John established a system of local treasuries in England, Nottingham Castle was entrusted with one of two northern depositories, the other being at Northampton. The King's two officials were the County Sheriff and the Constable, posts which were not combined at Nottingham. The Sheriff was responsible for carrying out the King's writ and administering justice, while the Constable's duties were more closely tied to the running of the Castle itself, including its maintenance, provisioning and staffing. One of the more mundane duties of the Constable was to ensure the smooth running of the castle mills, and in 1247 he was ordered to supply wheat to the army in Wales.[25]

In 1251, during a visit to the Castle, Henry III ordered that the reduced outer bailey should be encircled in stone and a twin-towered gatehouse be built (figure 3.1D). This was to be almost the last of the military improvements. With the end of the Barons' War of the mid-thirteenth century castles which were not situated on the borders, marches or newly subdued territory gradually began to lose their military significance.[26] For some, like Lincoln, it was to sound their death knell, for without a resident lord the Castle took on the dry function of county gaol and court. At Nottingham the martial front was maintained but inwardly the accent was on comfort: the Castle was converted into a palace. The middle years of Henry III's reign saw the beginning of a general overhaul which is remarkable for the degree of personal involvement shown by the King: plasterwork, decoration, wainscoting, cornicing, the glazing, positioning and style of windows, the subject-matter of wall paintings and painted panels, even fitting his chamber with 'a new and becoming door', were all the subject of Henry's attention. Having ordered a new round tower to be built on the motte, he wrote twice from Gascony concerning its progress, once to remind his household steward about the favoured window arrangement: 'fair windows looking towards the cliff and only one window towards the town'. The work does not always appear to have been carried out promptly or smoothly, and some plans were not implemented, but the intention of the King and his ambition for the building are clear. We may assume that the £2,464 19*s* he spent on the Castle constituted a considerable refit.[27]

In the mid-fourteenth century Edward III initiated another campaign of improvement supervised by his Constable Stephen Romylow. The accommodation in the upper ward was refurbished and new buildings erected in the middle bailey, including a constable's suite. A service complex covered the ditch which once served to protect the approach to the motte. The process of conversion to palace was completed by Edward IV. Between August 1476 and December 1480 expenditure of £3,000 or more on 'the newe buildinge and reparacion of the castell of Nottingham' included a stone great tower of three storeys with an adjoining residential suite, finished in timber by Richard III.[28] This complex finally brought the private state apartments into the more spacious middle bailey from the cramped inner ward, where they had stood since the Conquest.

The celebrated description of the Castle as 'a place full royall' by the poet John Skelton (d. 1529) reflects the impact of Edward IV's work.[29] However, by 1525 the new domestic buildings were in decay, illustrating the constant maintenance demands which the building made upon every monarch. The Tudors increasingly neglected the Castle, although Elizabeth I made an attempt to restore the residence, spending £1,075 13*s* 3¾*d* on repairs. In 1536 the Earl of Rutland put the Castle into a state of readiness to resist the Pilgrimage of Grace, and it played a final military role during the civil wars in the 1640s, although by this time 'the buildings were ruinous and uninhabitable, neither affording room to lodge soldiers nor provisions'.[30]

Royal visitors

The kings of England visited the Castle frequently, but usually for only a few days at a time. Henry II visited seven times between 1155 and 1185, and Henry III visited it thirteen times between 1226 and 1264. Few visits were of any great duration: the longest were those made by Edward II, 15 July–7 August 1317 and 6–31 December 1324. Between 1226 and 1405 three-, five- and seven-year gaps between royal visits were not uncommon, and in the periods 1264–79, 1345–63 and 1363–83, the monarch did not visit.

Plate 5 **Nottingham Castle**. A reconstruction of the Castle *c.*1500 (a model by Philip Dixon and David Taylor). In the centre foreground is the keep, a large rectangular tower which dominated the approach to the upper bailey, and was also known as the *white*, *great*, or *high* tower. In the centre background are the state apartments, with Richard's Tower behind them

These figures indicate that while in its heyday Nottingham Castle was the occasional venue of glittering national events, for most of the time it was empty. Local people were most likely to have contact with the Constable, the King's official of the castle. The appointment in 1308 of the energetic and unscrupulous John de Seagrave upset a number of interests and contributed to local instability. In subsequent years gangs roamed the countryside, protecting those they favoured or who could pay, and attacking or removing unpopular officials. The Folville gang of Ashby Folville (Leicestershire) consisted not of peasants or desperate cut-throats but of country gentry. They were tacitly supported by a number of Nottingham citizens for reasons which are not entirely clear, although in 1322 a Simon Folville was a burgess and Member of Parliament for Nottingham. In these volatile conditions the Mayor of Nottingham, Walter of Thornhill (1312–13), was murdered by his own bailiff, Roger le Orfevre ('the goldsmith'). John de Seagrave imprisoned le Orfevre in the Castle, and a group of townspeople responded by attacking the Castle, breaking its gates, and besieging it for eight days.[31] The exact reasons for the murder and retaliation are unclear, although these events seem to have led directly to Edward II's Charter to the borough (16 March 1314), which increased the burgesses' rights concerning properties within the borough, gave the mayor and bailiffs the right to determine trespasses, and ordered the exclusion of outsiders from juries and inquests. The terms of the Charter were upheld when in 1325 Robert Ingram impleaded Bartholomew of Cotgrave in the court of king's bench for a trespass in Nottingham, and the action and its record were returned to the mayor and bailiffs to determine.[32]

During the early years of Edward III's reign when Edward II's queen, her lover Mortimer, and Edward III spent time at Nottingham, further trouble occurred. Soldiers were attacked in 1328, and in 1329–30 an enquiry was launched into Nottingham's liberties. Local people played no discernible role in the coup which overthrew Queen Isabella and Roger Mortimer when in 1330 the conspirators entered the Castle through the underground passage known as 'Mortimer's Hole'.[33] From the 1330s the Constable was instructed to arrest and detain people notoriously suspected of trespasses against the peace. A member of the Folville gang, Roger Savage, was charged with unspecified crimes in Nottingham. He was arrested in London but escaped. He and John Coterel were traced to High Peak Forest in Derbyshire, but they escaped after being tipped off by their spy Walter Ufton, a coiner of false money. Possibly Ufton was a Nottingham man. A Walter Ufton, Cecilia his wife and their son Roger held property in Fletcher Gate in the 1320s.[34]

Castle and town

It is easy to suppose that the Royal Castle must have had a considerable impact on the economy of the town, but the reality may be rather different. Initially the Castle would have been built by forced labour, although the townsfolk escaped wholesale destruction of their houses, which occurred elsewhere. Subsequently building works were paid for.[35] Materials were available locally and their acquisition must have generated some employment in the region. Timber was brought from Sherwood forest, lead from Haddon in the Peak and stone from Basford, Gedling, Wollaton, Trowell, Swarkestone and Mansfield. Some stone came from 'Hasilbarrow', which may have been in Northamptonshire or Derbyshire. Labourers and artisans were employed on the routine repairs which account for the expenditure of most monarchs, but probably not for the major building programmes of Henry II, Henry III, Edward III and Edward IV. Where master craftsmen are identified in the records they generally appear to have belonged to an elite band employed exclusively on the King's works. The glazing of the King's chapel in 1348 was entrusted to a London man, John of Gedding, and the glass was supplied from London.[36] Of twenty-five carpenters employed in the early fourteenth century, seven came from London and were described as 'the king's carpenters'. The appointment of a local man, William of Bramcote, as master mason was probably no more than coincidence as he had been engaged on the King's works in Scotland. Later in the century some local names are associated with the castle works: John of Mansfield, clerk of the works; Richard of Chesterfield, comptroller; Adam of Holmesfield, master carpenter – but only one, John of Nottingham, master mason, seems to have been from the town. In the late fifteenth century the master of the King's works was Gervase Clifton who was perhaps a local man, and the master mason under Richard III, William Turner,was still living in Nottingham during the reign of Henry VII, although he might simply have decided to retire there. Overall the impact of the castle works in stimulating local employment cannot be seen as either permanent or even regular.[37]

The physical presence of this magnificent building must have aesthetically enhanced the town, but against this must be weighed potential nuisance and hazard, notably the conflagration in 1140. There were also less dramatic occasions. Domesday records that the townspeople were deprived of their fishing rights in the Trent, possibly when a leat was constructed to bring more water to the King's mills, and in the fourteenth century they complained of flooding in Wilford due to interference with the course of the Trent by the keepers of the Castle. In the later medieval period the Castle acquired a reputation for harbouring wrongdoers in the garrison, who thereby escaped retribution for crimes committed in the town.[38]

The regular castle inhabitants were unlikely to have made much impact on town life. The permanent staff would have been small and numbers would swell only during intensive building campaigns and royal visits. On the other hand the Crown occasionally took advantage of the town. In 1289 or 1290 Edward I took the proceeds of the borough murage tolls, which should have been spent on defence of the town, to repair the outer bailey of the Castle. In addition, the local market suffered from pre-emptive buying when the Constable was instructed to accumulate stores and, conversely, he would offload stores which were deteriorating.[39]

On the whole the Castle was always rather detached from the town, and the development of the building into a palace residence may actually have loosened ties with the community. Medieval castles were never permanently occupied by their owners, but frequency of use would recede in proportion to their high rank. A closer relationship between Castle and town was probably envisaged in the late eleventh century when the French Borough was laid out under the constableship of William Peveril. The main streets converging on a possible market-place at the castle gate are typical of castle 'new towns', such as Richmond in Yorkshire or Ludlow in Shropshire. However, Nottingham Castle had no lord regularly in residence, particularly after 1155, and although the Castle found special favour with several monarchs they spent relatively little time in the town. The result is still clear today. The French Borough was probably conceived as an independent foundation laid out, as it were, with is back towards the English Borough. The older English Borough was, of course, likely to exert a pull on the new borough, but despite the distinction between their respective administrations which survived until the late thirteenth century, the interests of the two soon united and the town prospered quite independently of the patronage of the Castle. Consequently the second market-place was sited not, as almost certainly planned, at the castle gates but within a space just to the north of the intersection of the two communities, where it remains to this day. The Royal Castle was a breathtaking example of Medieval secular architecture which provided a superb backdrop to the medieval town of Nottingham. Yet in terms of day-to-day life the lines of their history may be seen as running parallel more often than converging.

Notes

1 N. J. G. Pounds, *The Medieval Castle in England and Wales* (Cambridge, 1990), pp. 57–8: F. Barlow, *The Feudal Kingdom of England 1041–1216* (1988), p. 87; H. M. Colvin, *History of the King's Works*, I (1963), p. 21.

2 J. Earle and C. Plummer (eds.), *Two of the Saxon Chronicles* (Oxford, 1892–99), I, p. 202; Ordericus Vitalis, *Historiae Ecclesiasticae libri tredecim* (ed. A. le Prévost, Paris, 1838–55), II, p. 184. Newark Castle was believed to date from the twelfth century, but an early earthwork castle has recently been discovered by excavation and is hinted at in the documentary sources: P. Marshall and J. Samuels, 'Recent excavations at Newark Castle, Nottinghamshire', *TTS*, 98 (1994), p. 53; P. Marshall and J. Samuels, *Newark Castle Excavations* (forthcoming).

3 Barley and Straw, p. 2; Drage, *Castle*, p. 15.

4 F. Hill, *Medieval Lincoln* (Cambridge, 1948), pp. 35, 54, 65, 72; A Willson, 'Lincoln Castle', *Proceedings of the Archaeological Institute* (1848), p. 285; Colvin, *King's Works*, II, p. 704.

5 R. A. Brown, 'Royal Castle building in England 1154–1216', *English Historical Review*, 60 (1955), p. 59; Colvin, *King's Works*, II, pp. 285, 705.

6 The alternative interpretation, that this bailey was added during the reign of King John, seems less likely.

7 R. A. Brown, 'The Norman Conquest', *Transactions of the Royal Historical Society*, 5th series, 17 (1967), pp. 109–30; D. R. Cook, 'The Norman military revolution in England', *Anglo-Norman Studies*, 2 (1978), pp. 94–102; M. Bennett 'Peace and warfare', *Anglo-Norman Studies*, 11 (1988), pp. 37–57; Pounds, *Medieval Castle*, pp. 7–8; Drage, *Castle*, p. 25.

8 Colvin, *King's Works*, I, p. 24; M. W. Barley, 'Town defences in England and Wales after 1066', in M. W. Barley (ed.), *The Plans and Topography of Medieval Towns in England and Wales* (CBA, Research Report 14, 1976), pp. 51–71.

9 Drage, *Castle*, pp. 75–136.

10 Colvin, *King's Works*, I, p. 51. The Close, Liberate and Misae Rolls occasionally give further information from the reign of King John.

11 J. Shipman, *Excavations at Nottingham General Hospital* (1899); Drage, *Castle*, pp. 25, 81; R. A. Brown, *English Castles* (1976), pp. 17–18.

12 PR 34 Henry II, 110–111 refers to 'planking the tower of Nottingham' at a cost of £2 8*s* 10*d*. This means putting in floorboards or roof sarking and has been taken to mean finishing or repairing the donjon: Drage, *Castle*, p. 39. As no reference is made to any other work on the tower during Henry's reign and, given the time lapse of thirty-two years between the fall of Peveril and the entry, the 'planking' seems more likely to be repair if it refers specifically to the donjon. The term 'tower', however, could equally have been applied to the whole upper bailey, where new buildings at that time had been recently erected.

13 PR 22 Henry II, 90 (1176–77); for details, Colvin, *King's Works*, II, p. 776.

14 In Germany the phrase 'nailing the valley' is used of the distinctive local type of tower called *Bergfrieden*: M. W. Thompson, *The Rise of the Castle* (Cambridge, 1991), p. 23; P. Dixon and P. Marshall, 'The Great Tower at Hedingham Castle: a reassessment', *Fortress*, 18 (1993), pp. 19–22.

15 J. Schofield and A. Vince, *Medieval Towns* (1994), pp. 42–6.

16 T. Foulds, 'The siege of Nottingham castle in 1194', TTS, 95 (1991), pp. 20–8; *Thurgarton Cartulary*, xxxi–xxxviii; T. Foulds, 'The fall of William II Peveril: Nottinghamshire in the reign of Stephen' (unpublished).

17 Brown, 'Royal Castle building', p. 20; Colvin, *King's Works*, I, pp. 51–2; II, p. 756; Pounds, *Medieval Castle*, pp. 77–8; Drage, *Castle*, pp. 84–5.

18 Pounds, *Medieval Castle*, pp. 77–8; Brown, 'Royal Castle building', p. 57; Colvin, *King's Works*, II, pp. 769, 854. Orford Castle was built to check Bigod activity in their home territory.

19 PR 21 Henry II, 29; Colvin, *King's Works*, II, p. 756. The records contain numerous references to remedial work on a defective north wall. Evidence from the excavations suggests that the ground of the middle bailey had been raised, possibly when the Castle was first built, which perhaps resulted in a weak foundation: Drage, *Castle*, p. 83; PR 24 Henry II, 86; 25 Henry II, 80. For a fuller discussion of castles as residences and contemporary appreciation of their aesthetics see Brown, *English Castles*, ch. 8.

20 Foulds, 'Siege', pp. 20–7; PR 6 Richard I, f.80; 7 Richard I, f.15; Brown, 'Royal Castle Building', pp. 60–2.

21 T. D. Hardy (ed.), *Rotuli Litterarum Clausarum in Turri Londinensi Asservati* I (1833), pp. 153, 399b. Unidentified on Smythson's plan, this was probably a 'watch tower' referred to in 1219; Colvin, *King's Works*, II, p. 756.

22 PR 16 John, rot.15; Drage, *Castle*, p. 43; *Rot. Litt. Clause*. I, p. 481b; *CClR* 1227–31, f. 508; *CPR* 1232–47, f. 167.

23 Colvin, *King's Works*, II, p. 757; Barlow, *Feudal Kingdom*, pp. 427–8.

24 PR 16 John, 156: Pounds, *Medieval Castle*, pp. 108, 112, 118: Drage, *Castle*, p. 42; Calendars of Liberate Rolls, 1245–51, f. 234; *CClR* 1322–27, f. 247; Roger of Wendover, RS 84, vol. IV, f. 67.

25 Pounds, *Medieval Castle*, pp. 101, 103; Drage, *Castle*, pp. 60–3; Barlow, *Feudal Kingdom*, p. 406; *CClR*, 1247–51, f. 2.

26 Cal. Lib. Rolls, 1251–60, 11; Pounds, *Medieval Castle*, p. 121.

27 Cal. Lib. Rolls, 1251–60, 9, 11, 17–18: Colvin, *King's Works*, II, pp. 758–60; *CClR* 1242–47, f. 68.

28 Colvin, *King's Works*, II, pp. 762, 765; Drage, *Castle*, p. 52; P. W. Dixon and B. Lott, 'The courtyard and the tower: contexts and symbols in the development of late medieval great houses', *Journal of the British Archaeological Association*, 146 (1993), pp. 93–101; L. Toulmin-Smith (ed.), *Itinerary of John Leland, 1534–43* (1907), I, pp. 95–6.

29 P. Henderson (ed.), *The Complete Poems of John Skelton, Laureate* (1959), p. 2.

30 PRO Special Collections, Rentals and Surveys, 11/12; Colvin, *King's Works*, III, pp. 284–5; J. Hutchinson (ed.), *Lucy Hutchinson: Memoirs of Colonel Hutchinson* (1908), p. 128.

31 *CPR* 1313–17, fos. 62, 314.

32 *RBN*, I, pp. 76–81; NAO CA 1259 m12.

33 A. Cameron, 'William de Amyas and the community of Nottingham, 1308–50', *TTS*, 75 (1971), p. 75; Drage, *Castle*, p. 50.

34 E. L. G. Stones, 'The Folvilles of Ashby Folville, Leicestershire, and their associates in crime 1326–47', *Transactions of the Royal Historical Society*, 5th series, 7 (1957), pp. 117–36; NAO CA 1258b m21; 1261 m14.

35 Pounds, *Medieval Castle*, pp. 208–9. In *c.*1236 compensation was paid for the destruction of one house when the barbican was built: *CPR* 1232–47, f. 167.

36 Colvin, *King's Works*, II, pp. 762, 763, 765.

37 Colvin, *King's Works*, II, pp. 761, 763, 765. Professor Sir James Holt has suggested that there may have been employment opportunities for labourers in support of craftsmen.

38 Drage, *Castle*, pp. 62–3.

39 Colvin, *King's Works*, II, p. 761. Murage grants were permissions to levy tolls on goods entering the town in order to finance town defences; Pounds, *Medieval Castle*, pp. 124, 214; *CClR* 1242–47, fos. 50, 328, 373, 425; Drage, *Castle*, p. 44.

4

THE MEDIEVAL TOWN

Trevor Foulds

To modern eyes, no English medieval town was large, but Nottingham was small even by contemporary standards. Assessing relative status at any given time can only be an approximation, but 137 burgesses were listed in 1327, and 204 in 1341. Estimates for 1377 and 1381 suggest a taxable population of 1,447 and 1,266 respectively.[1] Using tax assessment evidence, a ranking order of towns for their absolute assessed wealth in 1334 would place Nottingham (£371) twenty-sixth in a list of thirty-seven: slightly below Newark (£390), above Derby (£300), but poorer and less populous than Lincoln (£1,000), York (£1,620) and Coventry (£750), towns with which it had a number of connections.[2] Nottingham was important because it was a county town. Here the Sheriff of Nottinghamshire and Derbyshire chiefly resided; much of the legal and financial administration for Sherwood Forest was dealt with in the town; and the judicial functions of the county, the borough and the honor of Peveril were also centred here. On Saturdays Nottingham's market was crowded with people who had come from surrounding villages to sell their produce, and to buy goods and services not available in the country.

Nottingham probably shared in the general expansion of English towns from the late twelfth to the late thirteenth centuries. Archaeologists have noted elements of twelfth-century reorganisation in certain areas and contraction by the mid-fourteenth century. However, given the town's comparative lack of wealth one element seems noteworthy: Nottingham was successful in obtaining rights and privileges which many other towns, often wealthier and more populous, coveted and sometimes fought long campaigns to achieve. The first extant royal charter describing Nottingham's rights and liberties (1155) was obtained from the King in York at a time of regional political crisis. It is addressed to the burgesses of Nottingham obliquely hinting, perhaps, at a sense of common purpose among some of its citizens. By 1241 the burgesses were certainly acting communally by renting pasture in Thorpe-in-the-Glebe, ten miles to the south, and in 1271 they were vigorously defending their rights of pasture against the prior of Shelford in adjacent Basford.[3] From King John, in the early days of his reign, the burgesses achieved the restoration of liberties removed by King Richard; and from Edward I in 1284 they obtained the office of mayor, long before the right was granted to much wealthier towns. During a time of acute stress in the early fourteenth century they obtained significant privileges from Edward II.

Exactly why Nottingham was so successful is not clear. Perhaps the fondness of successive monarchs for the Castle and its amenities, and their awareness of its strategic importance in troubled times, helped to lodge the town in the royal consciousness. The Castle became personally important to the future King John as a young man, and to Henry III as an adolescent. During his brief stay Richard I was impressed by what Nottingham and its surrounding countryside had to offer, and aesthetic considerations about the look of the town and its setting should not be undervalued. Henry III in 1243 reminded William de Cantilupe, Keeper of the Castle, not to forget to make windows in the tower and other chambers in the Castle which were to look towards the river, and one window was to look towards the town.[4]

The urban landscape

The urban landscape is comparatively unstable owing to the varying demands placed upon it. However, despite severe modifications the later medieval town survives in the street-plan. The English Borough straddled the important York road (Stoney Street) and an east–west route. Its street-plan was further determined by its defences. The routes leading out of and around the English Borough became part of the later street-plan.

The chief determinants of the post-Conquest town were the establishment of the Castle (1068), the French Borough and the Saturday Market.[5] These changes were almost certainly reflected in population increase, they stimulated trade, and they were responsible for shifting the town's focus westwards to the valley between the Castle and the English Borough. New houses had been built before 1086, including some in the borough ditch, indicating movement out of the old borough.[6] The location of the daily market in the south-west corner of the English Borough could have been influenced by this westward trend. Although probably incorporating older routes, streets radiated from the Castle to the Saturday Market and to the English Borough (Hounds Gate–Pepper Street). The Castle was connected to the principal southern entrances to the town (Hollowstone, Malin Hill) and to subsidiary entries (Drury Hill, Garners Hill, Middle Hill) by the Castle Gate, Low, Middle and High Pavement route. Apart from development around St Nicholas's Church on higher ground, this route marked Nottingham's southern limits. Beyond were marshy areas into which water and the seasonal stream, the Rowell, drained from the valley containing the Saturday Market.

Many streets were surfaced: Fisher Gate had a metalled road in the twelfth century; the three Pavements were so named because they were paved; and Pepper Street and Cow Lane were surfaced. In 1464 a paver was paid for eighty-six teys (from 'toise', a measure of six 'French feet', about 1.949 metres; therefore in total about 550 feet) of paving in the Marsh, 'Dedelane' and High Pavement, and pavers were supplied with 'cogyls stones', sand and a wheelbarrow.[7] Water was essential and the common well (which has not been located) and its hauling equipment was repaired in 1396. Some tenements had their own well or share of one. Wells were dug in cellars: Alice Lyversege, for her tenement in Long Row, was granted access to a well in Thomas Thurland's adjacent tenement which he had excavated in its cellar. She could take her vessels to it at any time provided she contributed to the repair costs. A vital service was conducted by the waterleaders, who sold large quantities of water in 'bushels' in horse-loads for brewing. The waterleaders were highly organised and could be obstructive if payment was denied or their 'bushels' were damaged. From where they obtained their water is not known, although there was a 'Waterleader Gate', possibly in Broad Marsh, which may indicate that water was drawn from the River Leen after it was diverted to flow around the town in the twelfth century.[8]

The town had a rural character with intra-mural orchards, gardens and other open spaces. In the early fourteenth century gardens were mentioned in most areas and in the defences. They contained vegetables and herbs, while apple, pear and cherry trees were grown in the orchards. There was even a vineyard in Castle Gate in 1376. Sheep and pigs were kept in curtilages and in or near the ditch. Intra-mural granges, probably barns, were mentioned in 1360 in a number of places: near the Saturday Market in Orger Lane, near the ditch, near St Mary's cemetery, opposite St Peter's cemetery, and in Goose Gate.[9] There were corn-drying and malt kilns in Fisher Gate, Barker Gate, Goose Gate and Halifax Place, but it was expected that corn would be ground at the King's mills below the Castle Rock. An attempt in 1401 to set up a horse-mill to circumvent this restriction was rapidly suppressed by the authorities.[10]

Timber-built cottages and a twelfth-century aisled hall have been uncovered on Drury Hill, and timber-framed buildings elsewhere.[10] Evidence for building types is sparse. Thomas Mapperley (mayor 1402–03) remodelled his house re-using old timbers. It was an extensive building containing four halls, a chamber near the gates of the property, three windows in the main hall with passages at either end, and a pantry. The 'halls' probably represented a terrace of separate houses for letting. In 1479 William Hurst, a smith (sheriff 1477–78), expected a timber house eighteen feet wide occupying the length of his 'smith yard', with two bay windows and square windows, to be built for him within ten months at a cost of £6.[11] Stone buildings were uncommon. In the thirteenth century a 'rock' or 'stone house' (*domum petrinam*) next to the daily market was granted to Thurgarton Priory, and there was a stone storeroom (*solarium lapideum*) with a cellar opposite St John's Hospital. The untranslatable *tenementum edificatum* in the 'Woman Market' in 1451 may have been of stone.[12] Some speculative building occurred as Newstead Priory built a new tenement in the daily market in 1333, and the Prior of Lenton stipulated in 1336 that his lessee for a messuage should build a new house.[13] The height of buildings is not known, but many were of more than one storey, with manufacturing and retail facilities. Some were like modern shops at ground level, with living-quarters or storerooms above. Plots could be quite substantial. A messuage in the Saturday Market in 1316 with an oven and two curtilages had a plot of land eighty-one feet long by seventeen feet broad. A curtilage in 'Tanners' Street' (Barker Gate) was 120 feet long in 1335, with the front sixty feet wide, the middle forty-one feet and the end eighteen feet wide.[14] Although the physical dimensions of plots are often known the buildings on them were infrequently described. In 1301 a large property in Great Smith Gate had a great hall with chambers, privy, cellar under the hall with its entry in the court, a leased small house, stable, granary, great barn with two leased curtilages, and gates. A messuage in Castle Gate had its own 'chapel' in 1330, while Vault Lane (Drury Hill) was named after a house constructed over a vault.[15]

The earliest post-Conquest mention of a cellar is in a grant to Newstead Priory of land next to the Castle between the Rock and the River Trent, with the authority to dig the Rock for making a cellar without injury to the house above. Assigning dates, or differentiating a medieval from a later cave, is almost impossible. Many of them have been altered in the past, and archaeological deposits rarely allow a cave to be precisely dated. Judging from the documentary evidence cellars were not inhabited, and many were storerooms or possibly workshops: the temperature was constant, about 10°C, but humidity is quite high, and they were fireproof, ideal conditions for storage. John Wylcokosyn stored his goods in Alice Palmer's cellar in 1336. In Stoney Street a property consisted of a toft divided in two: in one part was a cellar and a kiln with a separate entrance, and the holder could enlarge the cellar in whichever part. There were two cellars below one property in the daily market, and more than one house could be above one cellar. The cellar could be excepted from a property grant. A cottage with a curtilage and a storeroom in Broad Marsh had a cellar below the Rock. In Little (Narrow) Marsh a number of properties had the messuage on the southern part of the road and the cellar on the northern part of the same road 'below the rock'.[16] These were not underneath the property but were cut into the base of the cliff opposite.

It is not known how or by whom excavation was carried out – whether by professional 'cellar-diggers', or by the owner or lessee of the buildings above-ground. Expertise would be required to excavate a cellar and a number of 'medieval' caves have a certain consistency of style which implies specialised craftsmen. Some are distinctive for having a central pillar and sometimes carvings; others are elaborate with kilns, garderobes and water-supply. In Barker Gate a cellar created for a high-status thirteenth-century building had settings in the rock floor to support the timber superstructure. This is the only one of its kind to indicate a possible style of excavation in association with buildings above. 'Severns', a fourteenth-century timber building, was provided with increased footings to prevent it from collapsing into the caves already underneath. In addition, there were 'common caves' belonging to the town in 1411, at the ends of St James's Street and Bearward Lane. Others were outside the town walls.[17]

The town defences

Before the first half of the twelfth century there seems to have been no attempt to link the defences of the Castle and the English Borough to protect the post-Conquest French Borough in the valley between the two. There is no documentary evidence for any twelfth-century defences. The town ditch on the north is mentioned in deeds from before the mid-thirteenth century, and the ditch towards St John's hospital was described as 'new' in a series of mid-thirteenth-century conveyances to Thurgarton Priory. The first grant of murage, the right to collect a levy towards the costs of building a town wall, was made in May 1267. The bars, or at least Chapel Bar (named 1285–1317), were in existence before the wall: Bartholomew of Bargate witnessed a deed between 1230 and 1239 and Benedict 'atte Gate' witnessed another between 1236 and 1248. The other bars are not mentioned until later: Cow Bar (North Bar) at the north end of Cow Lane in 1336 and Swine Bar at the north end of Beck Lane in 1408. Only two gates, both in poor repair, were mentioned in 1512.[18]

The town wall was built in stages of varying quality by separate gangs of workmen. Near St John's Hospital it was completed relatively quickly since the series of Thurgarton Priory deeds ends with a description of the property as 'on [next] the wall'. Late thirteenth-century deeds still referred to the ditch at Bar Gate (Chapel Bar). The wall east of Chapel Bar is not mentioned until 1336. Between the wall and the boundaries of tenements was a road the breadth of one cart, and in 1355 there was a gap of sixteen feet between the defences and the northern edge of a tenement extending from Long Row. By 1360 the wall had progressed east of Cow Bar since a property had Great Smith Gate as its southern frontage and the wall as its northern boundary. Another deed, for a property fronting Great Smith Gate with Cow Lane on the west, referred to the ditch as its northern boundary. Similarly, in deeds for the period 1315–1596 for properties extending northwards from Long Row only one (in 1490) stated that it was bounded on the north by the town wall.[19] The others continued to define the ditch as the northern boundary, although archaeologists found sections of the wall here during the building of an underpass in front of the Theatre Royal.

The documentary evidence for the town wall is confusing. Eastwards beyond Cow Lane Bar there is no evidence for the wall, but only for the ditch: the imprecise terminology thus makes it uncertain if an actual wall ever existed along this eastern arc. There is no evidence at all for a southern wall: here the cliff and the River Leen seem to have acted as the sole defences to the town. The purpose of a postern gate at the top of Vault Lane was probably to check and monitor traffic, and it was not part of any defences. In the early sixteenth century much of the wall 'was down', and by the eighteenth century nothing remained above ground.[20]

Plate 6 **Town wall**. The demolition of buildings and the excavation of foundations on the eastern side of Park Row in April 1964 revealed lower sections of the thirteenth-century town wall. The ditch beyond the wall, known as Butt Dykes, was filled and Park Row set out upon it in 1797. This section of the town wall may be seen, stylised, on Speed's 1610 map, although Leland noted as early as 1540 that 'much of the waul is now down'. Part of the main Co-operative buildings on Parliament Street can be seen, top right

Outside the walls

There is little evidence for ribbon development or for any suburbs. Gardens, buildings and a 'grange' lay beyond Cow Lane Bar near St John's Hospital. To the north of the town was the hamlet of Whiston, a separate settlement whose precise location is uncertain. Indications are that it was on Mansfield Road, on the boundary between Nottingham and Basford, but although identified in 1502–03, it had disappeared by the seventeenth century.[21]

Immediately north of the town's defences were the common fields, and south of the town were the meadows.[22] The mechanism for the control of the fields at this time is unknown. Woodland, later known as the 'Coppice', lay to the north-east: this was probably a continuation of the 'King's wood' or 'thicket' outside the forest boundary. Nearby was the 'King's quarry' from which gifts of stone were made for buildings. Part if not all of the open fields were within the forest but not within *the regard*, the lands patrolled by the King's officers for offences. John, Count of Mortain had excepted the burgesses from the forest regard although 'Whiston Dale' (now known as the Forest) was excepted only in 1234. Certain forest restrictions still applied north of Nottingham ditch, for dogs had to be *hambled* (the ball of the foot cut or three toes of the forefoot removed) to prevent them from being used to hunt. Windmills had been erected by the early thirteenth century, and a few barns and buildings including 'Jecoryhous' and 'le Cornhous'.[23]

Local people held and worked land in the fields. Robert de Brunneby (bailiff 1329–30) found sheep had grazed his standing corn, and in 1315 pigs ate the corn 'on a strip where William Fox was growing corn'; Nicholas of Shelford (mayor 1330–31) bought twenty cartloads of hay for his land in 1322; and sheaves of barley and rye stacked for the autumn were stolen from the field in 1330. Outsiders were among those employed as agricultural labourers. Henry Wright of Colston Basset was engaged to plough and sow an acre of arable land with three bushels of oat seed for John Warde's profit in 1426; Robert Skelton was hired as a thresher for two weeks in 1432; and John Selers was paid to turn hay in 1441. William Halifax (mayor 1431–32, 1440–41) borrowed oxen to plough his land in 1435.[24]

The meadows were low-lying grassland valuable for pasturing animals; however, some land was also cultivated, as arable is mentioned in 1296 'in Nottingham field between the waters of the Trent and the Leen', and two areas of higher ground, East and West Ryehills, suggest grain production. From the early fourteenth century flooding became a problem because of climatic changes, and some land went out of cultivation.[25]

Religious houses

Outside the defences were the hospitals: in 1173–74 Henry II confirmed land which Robert de St Remi (otherwise unknown) had given to the palmers for a hospital, and Pope Lucius III in 1181–85 issued protection to the master and brethren of the 'alms house'.[26] The hospital of St John the Baptist (on the corner of the modern Glasshouse Street and Lower Parliament Street) existed before 1208 when the brethren undertook the custody and reparation of Nottingham bridge. It was refounded *c.*1220 by Robert (son of Ralph son of Fulk) of Nottingham, who provided a stable endowment. Its holdings included a windmill, arable land and meadow, rents from properties in Nottingham, and land in Stanton-on-the-Wolds and Kirkby-in-Ashfield. The advowson (the right to *present* [nominate] clergy) originally appears to have belonged to the burgesses but, because of a dispute (1273–74), the Archbishop of York presented, followed by the King and thereafter it remained with the archbishops. The hospital, which cared for both men and women, had a chapel and a cemetery, and its rule was administered by a warden with two chaplains.[27]

The evidence for the other hospitals is poor, and it is uncertain exactly where some were located. The hospital of the Holy Sepulchre is first documented in 1267, and the master and brethren were collecting alms in 1283. It had land and a cemetery outside the town ditch.[28] The fee of the 'sick men' of St Leonard was mentioned between 1207 and 1214 and the King permitted the lepers to collect firewood in Bestwood, the king's hay (enclosure) near Arnold.[29] The leper hospital of St Mary 'atte Westebarre' (Chapel Bar) was permitted to collect alms for its support in the 1330s. Many towns had leper hospitals at their gates which subsisted on casual alms and St Mary's was probably one of these. The evidence for another hospital, that of St Michael, is unsatisfactory. It was termed a 'hospital' in 1335 but a 'house' in 1416.[30]

Plate 7 **St Mary's Church**. An early print. There has been a church on the site of St Mary the Virgin in the Lace Market since Saxon times. The present church is largely the result of an ambitious rebuilding programme in the fifteenth century. One of the most impressive churches in the county, St Mary's was restored by Gilbert Scott and W. B. Moffatt in 1845–53, and in 1890 the Chapter House, by G. F. Bodley, was erected in the anticipation – not subsequently fulfilled – that it would become the cathedral of the new diocese of Southwell, created in 1884

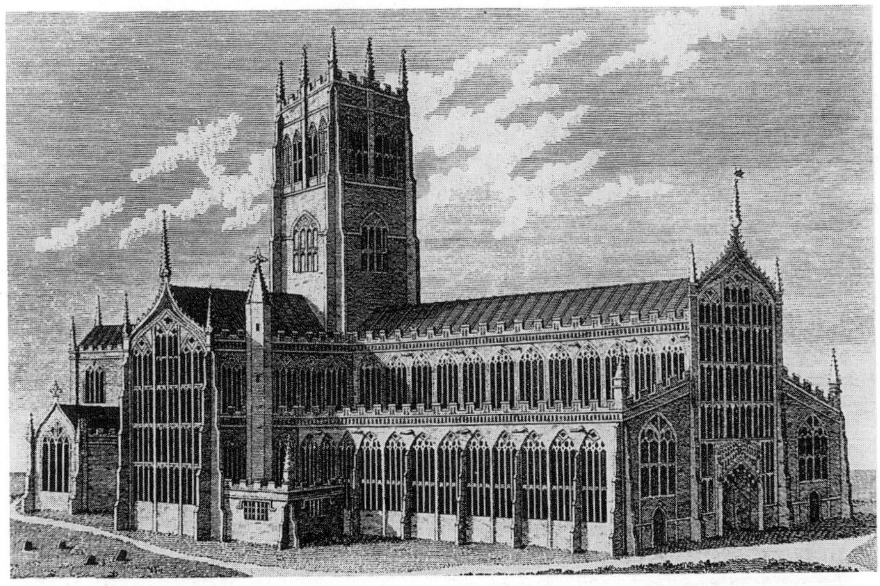

Within Nottingham there were three parish churches: St Mary's, St Peter's and St Nicholas's. All are located in elevated positions. St Mary's, the principal church, is a large cruciform building, with a central tower, of the fifteenth century; the fabric of St Peter's is thirteenth to fifteenth century. St Nicholas's, an early medieval church, probably cruciform, was destroyed in the Civil War and rebuilt in the late seventeenth century on the same site.[31] The advowsons of the three churches were held by the Cluniac Priory of Lenton, founded two miles to the west of Nottingham by William I Peveril in 1103–14.[32] As a result of the influence of the Peverils, Lenton Priory held a dominant position in the town, with a monopoly of rights in – and income from – the parish churches, the hospitals, the castle chapels, the bridge chapels, and other properties. A vicarage was created in St Mary's in 1234 but not in the other churches, and only St Mary's had land in the open fields. As a result, St Peter's and particularly St Nicholas's were poor, with incomes derived only from intra-mural tithes and offerings.

In comparative terms Nottingham had relatively few parish churches, which may reflect the influence of Lenton Priory, but there were other chapels. One was in the daily market in 1375. Another was St Michael's chapel, considered by antiquaries as the 'church' of Whiston; while a third was St James's chapel, between St James's Street and Moothall Gate. First mentioned between 1178 and 1180, it was the venue for the Peveril honorial court. It stood on a plot 210 feet long by 140 feet broad, with a lane for access and an attached plot 243 feet long by 17 feet broad. Mass had not been celebrated for some time in 1266, although a chaplain had received a 50*s* stipend from the King.[33]

The Carmelite Friars (White Friars) were established on a prime site between Moothall Gate and St James's Street near the Saturday Market by Reginald Grey before 1271, when the King granted them protection and gave them timber to repair their church. In 1316–19 the friars wanted to extend their site by acquiring the land on which the county hall stood, and the chapel of St James and its land. Lenton Priory was recompensed for the chapel and Leticia of Chesterfield, among others, granted them a plot in Moothall Gate. There was further expansion in 1356, and by 1495 the site was enclosed with gates and the prior had his own house.[34]

Within a few years of their arrival in England in 1224 the Friars Minor (Franciscans, Grey Friars) had reached Nottingham: in 1230 Henry III granted them timber to build a chapel. They were settled on common land since the King allowed the bailiffs 5*s* in the farm (an annual payment to the King) for the place where they were lodged. The site was in Broad Marsh on the edge of Nottingham. In 1256 the King granted them stone from his Nottingham quarry for their church and Margaret, Queen of Scotland, Henry III's daughter, petitioned timber from her father for their dormitory and chapter house in 1260. The stone church was completed 1303–10, and they also constructed a wharf (1236–37). The Friars Minor were particular about the quality of their water. They obtained a share of '*Brodewell* outside the town' and made a conduit to their house in 1282. Broadwell, probably the later 'Broad Oak Pool', was in Wood Field. The conduit was perhaps known as the 'Frerewatergonge' near the Leen. Additional water was brought by an underground conduit from a spring in 'Athilwelle', a lost hamlet in Lenton parish, through the castle park. This was, perhaps, the 'Cokwatergang' near Rotten Row (perhaps Walnut Tree Lane).[35] One of the earliest provincial ministers (head) of the Friars Minor in England was William of Nottingham (1240–54), noted for his encouragement of theological study. The Friars Minor included men of distinction, and they were involved in national unrest following the murder of Richard II in 1399: John Gounfrey, the warden, was arrested, and Roger Leicester imprisoned in the castle. Some friars were executed; the mayor and bailiffs were ordered to set the head of one of the Friars Minor on the walls or the pillory.[36]

Nottingham was one of seventeen towns in England where Jews could reside. The community lived primarily in and around Jew Lane on the southern edge of town within reach of the castle (for security), and near the synagogue, which was in Lister Gate, south of a substantial Jewish property on the corner of Castle Gate. It was probably established on land bought by David le Lumbard from William Bate, a prominent citizen.[37] The town must have offered business opportunities. Local Jews were primarily money-lenders, an activity which presupposes mutual trust between Christians and Jews, in contrast to neighbouring towns: Leicester expelled its Jews in 1231 and Derby prohibited them from residing in the town in 1261.[38] In 1199 David the Jew was fined for a forest offence. He was probably David le Lumbard, head of the Nottingham community, as he was termed 'bailiff of the Jews' and 'rabbi'. On his death in 1242 his three sons and a daughter continued his money-lending business.[39] The remainder of the community is not readily identifiable, although the evidence of *aids* (that is, grants or taxes) paid by the Jews to the crown shows that it was neither as large nor as wealthy as the communities of Lincoln and Stamford in the mid-thirteenth century. In 1290, at the time of the expulsion, twenty men were named, probably heads of households. Altogether they had assets of £450 14*s* 4*d* in money, £34 in corn and £36 in wool, but their houses realised only £13 6*s* 8*d*.

In Nottingham there is no evidence of friction even during the hostile climate prior to the expulsion of the Jews from England in 1290. An *arca*, an indicator of a community of some size and money-lending, was established before the mid-thirteenth century. This was a chest containing all documents involving Jewish business so that they could be inspected in case of fraud. Some records of its contents survive, and they show that only Nicholas of Warmsworth, the rector of St Nicholas's (1267–87), or possibly his father, also Nicholas, was in debt to the Jews.[40]

Government and administration

In the twelfth century the King appointed Nottingham's officials, and his officers retained many rights in the town down to the fifteenth century. He also held a substantial number of properties in the borough, some by virtue of the confiscated honor of Peveril.[41] Between 1155 and 1449 the burgesses obtained from the King a number of charters and letters patent applicable in both the French and English Boroughs. These confirmed existing rights and gave legal sanction to any new liberties. The 1155 charter records the customs (unspecified) and toll area as it was at the time and had been in the reign of Henry I (1100–35). The only industry mentioned is that of dyed cloth which no one was permitted to work within ten *leucae* (fifteen miles) of Nottingham (approximately a day's return journey).[42]

Between 1189 and 1194 John Count of Mortain was given Nottingham and Nottinghamshire by his brother King Richard, from whom the burgesses obtained additional liberties: a guild merchant and the ability to elect their own reeve, removable at pleasure, who was to pay the farm to John's demesne exchequer. When he became King, John confirmed these liberties in 1200.[43] Henry III's three charters added the right to elect coroners, powers concerning debt, and the important franchise of return of writs (1230, 1255, 1272). Edward I's charter of 1284 empowered the burgesses to elect their own mayor and one bailiff from each borough. The charters of Edward II (1314) and Henry IV (1399) gave further rights at law in civil actions determinable by the mayor and bailiffs, to keep the profits of justice, and the creation of justices of the peace. The charter of incorporation was granted by Henry VI in 1449.[44]

The administration of the medieval town is not known in any detail, although the story-book sheriff of Nottingham who clashed with the legendary Robin Hood was in fact the sheriff of the county. The town acquired a sheriff (in practice two, one for each of the boroughs) only in the fifteenth century. The office of reeve was mentioned in Henry II's charter, but little is known of the men who held the position. Orm the reeve was mentioned in documents in 1176–77, and Bartholomew the reeve witnessed the grant of an oven by Orm, son of the widow 'sometime reeve of Nottingham', to Rufford abbey. He was probably Orm 'the baker' who supervised work on Nottingham gaol (1180–81). The farm, an annual payment to the King to enjoy the liberties of the borough, is not accounted for in the Pipe Rolls as a separate item and it must have been collected by the county sheriff. Not until 1200, after King John's charter, is it recorded that the 'men of Nottingham' rendered their farm at the exchequer.[45] Henry III's charter (1255) referred to the 'bailiffs' (plural) and not 'reeve' (singular). Edward I's charter (1284) stated that one bailiff from each borough should be elected 'on account of the diversity of customs existing in the same boroughs'.[46] The French and English Boroughs were separate administrations, each with its own bailiff, and deeds were witnessed separately by the bailiff of the English or of the French Borough from *c.*1220. This 'separateness', however, should not be exaggerated. There were only two major differences between the boroughs: inheritance (primogeniture in the French Borough, ultimogeniture in the English Borough), and dower (a third of the husband's real estate in the French Borough, half in the English Borough). The principal duties of the bailiffs included the collection of the farm (£52), the regulation of the markets and, probably, summoning and presiding over the borough court. It is not clear how, if at all, their responsibilities changed when the office of mayor was created in 1284. They continued to be responsible for collecting the farm, which was increased to £60 in 1284, and until the fifteenth century only the bailiffs' names were noted for the record of the borough court sessions. The bailiffs had two sub-bailiffs by the mid-fourteenth century.[47] Cases of murder were the business of a coroner, a post dating from the charter of 1230. The duties of the coroner included enquiring as to treasure trove, rape, wrecks, deaths in prison, matters relating to outlaws, and deodands (any creature or article which may be instrumental in killing someone).

The grant of mayoralty in 1284 substantially altered the structure of town government. The mayor was 'to be set over the bailiffs and others of the same borough in everything pertaining to the government and advantage of the same town'. In witnessing charters the mayor's name preceded those of the bailiffs, but the mayor's role probably developed gradually. The mayoralty roll of John Samon in the 1370s records the mayor's great tourn and contraventions of the assizes of bread and ale. It also names those people not within the liberty of the borough. By 1395 the mayor heard and determined presentments for affrays and imposed the amercements. He also enrolled burgesses's names and recognisances under the statutes merchant. John Alestre's mayoralty roll of 1414–15 contains licences to traffic, sureties to keep the peace, and a list of affrays. By the fifteenth century the mayor had acquired a seal and his own group of officers: a clerk by 1410, and a bailiff who was responsible for attachments for affrays and, on information supplied, arresting those accused of market offences. The mayor had a limited expense account and may have had his own exchequer.[48]

No evidence has come to light of an inner core of advisers such as a council or aldermen, until 1446. The mayor's authority was considerable, although the burgesses who had been mayors or bailiffs formed an unofficial council. The role, if any, played by the guild merchant is unknown. A limited group of men seem to have exercised power: by the fifteenth century many burgesses had no voice in the selection or election of the chief officers. On 29 September 1412, the start of the civic year, a group of forty-nine burgesses who had previously held the office of mayor and bailiff met in St Mary's church to elect the new mayor and bailiffs. This exclusiveness was resented; indeed, a riot followed the meeting, and it is clear that the opposition had made careful plans and had its own candidates for office.[49]

The evidence for other civic officers is poor. The two chamberlains appeared in the late fourteenth century. Their duties were the collection and disbursement of the common monies which were expended on public works. The earliest account (1463–64) shows payments for hedging and fencing common lands; repairs to bridges or the Guild Hall; expenses for food and gifts of wine to influential persons; and uniforms for soldiers. In association with the mayor, they leased certain common lands. The Bridge Masters collected money and administered the legacies bequeathed for the maintenance of Hethbeth Bridge (Trent Bridge). Although the position of town clerk(s) can be seen evolving in the witness lists of thirteenth-century deeds, it is not until the late fourteenth century that this office is identifiable. John Clerk enrolled a deed on the borough court roll and attested another as 'scribe (*scriptore*) of Nottingham'. Other officials can be identified: the swinebote, who cleansed the streets in 1395; the common swineherd by 1352; and the pinder by 1467.[50]

By the late fourteenth century the enforcement of law and order was primarily handled by the mayor's tourn and the borough court, although market offences were presented to the mayor in his capacity as regulator of the market and 'lord of the manor'. The jury of the mayor's tourn was termed the 'Mickletorn Jury' (old English *micel*, great).[51] Policing functions were undertaken by Decennaries. The position existed by 1308, and by 1395 there were thirty-one Decennaries who supervised twenty streets, reporting to the Mickletorn Jury misdemeanours, nuisances, affrays and encroachments. These were presented by the jury to the mayor. Complaints reflected the trials and tribulations of urban life: rights of way had been impeded; butchers had sold corrupt meat; candles had been sold with short wicks; weavers and fullers charged too much; tanners prepared badly tanned leather; water-courses and ditches were filled with ordure and rubbish; stone was stolen from the town walls; a store-house was built on common land; a cellar door was left open. In the fifteenth century the Decennaries presented scolds (male and female). Its duties accomplished, the Mickletorn Jury was rewarded and given dinner.[52] The jury itself had no powers of arrest and imprisonment. The Decennaries, however, could arrest and imprison accused thieves *infangentheof* (caught red-handed) and, in association with the coroners, arraign them before the borough court.[53]

The borough court was probably descended from the Portmanmoot mentioned in the twelfth century, and in many ways it was quite dissimilar to the courts of other English Boroughs. In the fourteenth and fifteenth centuries 'the court of the lord king of his vill of Nottingham' did not concern itself with market offences, monitoring craft practices, regulation of the open-fields, and most things within the competence of the mayor's tourn. Its extant records, the borough court rolls (1303–1455) reveal that its concern was with crown pleas, real, personal and mixed, entered within its jurisdiction of debt, trespass, deceit and breach of covenant. In the early fourteenth century it heard pleas of defamation but this action declined in accordance with national trends. It did not hear criminal pleas which were reserved to the King. It was a court of record: that is, whatever was written in its record was authoritative. It functioned as a local version of the central courts at Westminster with which its procedures and processes were almost the same unless these were at variance with borough custom. The court heard and determined pleas initiated by royal writ. It did not distinguish between the French and English Boroughs unless the plaintiff or defendant invoked the difference in customs between the two where custom departed from the common law. The burgesses had obtained rights and liberties which enabled them to determine many of their own legal affairs and to exercise and preserve them was a function of the borough court. Consequently the court's rights were vigorously protected by the burgesses even against the King.

By the fifteenth century the court distinguished between pleas entered between burgesses, and between burgess and non-burgesses, who were termed forinsecers (outsiders). The burgesses were the privileged group and their pleas were always given priority over those of outsiders. The court's function was not the same as Nottingham's piepowder court which was a separate court, dealing summarily with offences committed at markets and fairs, and its records have been lost except for isolated examples copied onto the borough court roll.[54]

Other evidence for public life is thin. Civic processions are not recorded until the mid-fifteenth century, and no record survives of religious displays such as the feast of Corpus Christi or mystery plays. However, the quality of life was enhanced in various ways. The guild (fraternity) of St George collected money, malt, bread and cheese for its annual breakfast. This was held in the great hall of the Friars Minor and could be a lively affair: the friar's cutlery was damaged in 1479 and the hall itself in 1485. Its masses were animated by part-singing and organ accompaniment.[55] The townspeople played at dice, quoits, cards and football, and had the occasional horse-race. At one time there was probably a brothel: a vacant plot was known as 'Parodyse' situated significantly in Whore Lane in 1391. A bear may have been kept, as John Draper held the position of bearward in 1433. The borough court rolls mention musical instruments: lutes, harps and psalteries. Thrushes were kept, perhaps for their singing. Bonesetters set injured shins, and John Plumptre, 'fezician', owned analytical apparatus.[56]

The town came alive for its weekly Saturday market, which served the region for miles around, and for fairs. Nottingham Fair began on St Matthew's day, 21 September, and lasted for a week. Two miles to the west, Lenton Priory obtained from Henry II in 1164 the right to hold a fair during the week beginning on 11 November. This was increased in 1232 by four days. However, this clashed with a second Nottingham fair, lasting for two weeks, which was granted in the 1284 Charter and began on the eve of St Edmund's Day (19 November). Conflict between the Priory and the burgesses was inevitable, and the eventual solution turned out to be the transfer in 1378 of Nottingham's second fair to 22 February.[57]

Notes

1 PRO E 179/159/4; G. Vanderzee (ed.), *Nonarum Inquisitiones in curia scaccarii temp. regis Edwardi III* (1807), pp. 290–2; J. C. Russell, *British Medieval Population* (Albuquerque, 1948), p. 142.

2 C. Platt, *Medieval England: a Social History and Archaeology from the Conquest to 1600* (1988), p. 103.

3 PRO *Curia Regis Rolls* 16, no. 1750; *RBN*, I, pp. 48–53.

4 *CClR* 1242–47, 68.

5 T. Foulds, J. Hughes and M. Jones, 'Une Ville anglaise et ses rues à la fin du moyen-âge à travers ses archives méconnues: les *borough court rolls* de Nottingham (1303–1455)' (4[éme] Colloque international sur la sociabilité, Rouen, 1994).

6 A. Farley (ed.), *Great Domesday Book* I (1783), f. 280a.

7 C. S. B. Young, *Discovering Rescue Archaeology in Nottingham* (Nottingham, 1982); *RBN*, I, pp. 206–7; II, pp. 116–19, 372–3.

8 *RBN*, I, pp. 115–16, 158–9, 332–3, 340–1, 366; II, p. 416; NAO CA 1256 mm20, 22d; *Rufford Charters*, 19b.

9 NAO CA 1279 m11; NUMD Middleton deeds, MiD 1079.

10 Young, *Discovering Rescue Archaeology; CPR* 1399–1401, 459.

11 *RBN*, II, pp. 27–31, 390; A. Henstock, 'Late medieval building contracts for the Nottingham Area', *TTS*, 88 (1984), pp. 103–5.

12 *Thurgarton Cartulary*, 492; A. Saltman (ed.), *The Cartulary of Dale Abbey* (1967), p. 437; NAO CA 4469.

13 *Newstead II*, 160, 163; NUMD Middleton deeds, MiD 778.

14 NAO CA 1256 mm 10, 13.

15 PRO C 146/5291; *RBN*, I, pp. 116–17; *Thurgarton Cartulary*, 510 (1263–78).

16 *Newstead I*, fos. 82 (before 1168), 85v; NAO CA 1262 m13, 1304/I m15d (1408); 1255 mm 1, 1d (1315); 1297 m17d (1399); 1301 m8d (1404); 1303 m17d (1406).

17 NUMD Middleton Deeds, MiD 787 (1411); Young, *Discovering Rescue Archaeology; RBN*, II, pp. 40–1.

18 Barley and Straw, p. 2; *Rufford Charters*, 14 (1236–48), 1, 33; *Thurgarton Cartulary*, 495–8; *CClR* 1264–68, 300, 482; *CPR 1266–72*, 57; *RBN*, I, pp. 128–9, 274–6; II, pp. 60–1; III, p. 340.

19 M. W. Ponsford and A. Carter, 'Nottingham town wall: Park Row excavations 1967 and 1968', *TTS* 75 (1971), pp. 5–40; *RBN*, II, pp. 170–1, 356 (1435); *Thurgarton Cartulary*, 498 (1267–78); Saltman, *Dale Abbey*, 415, 416; NUMD Middleton deeds, MiD 769; NAO CA 1267 m1; 1269 m3; 1272 m8; 1274 m4d; 1324 m1d; DDP/CD 13.

20. M. W. Barley, 'Nottingham town wall', *TTS*, 69 (1965), p. 60; Deering, p. 4; L. Toulmin Smith (ed.), *The Itinerary of John Leland, 1534–43* (1907), I, p. 95; *RBN*, IV, p. 393; V, p. 188.

21 There was 'the highway from Cow Bar as far as the gallows of Whiston' infrequently known as 'Whistongate', and also the 'road from Whiston to Swine Bar': W. Stevenson and A. Stapleton, *Some Account of the Religious Institutions of Old Nottingham* (Nottingham, 1895), pp. 133–44, 155–6, 159–61; NAO CA 1251a m12; 1258a m20; 1282 m26d; 1311 m12d; NUMD Newcastle, NeD 4408–10 (1489–99); *RBN*, I, pp. 44–5; II, pp. 66–7; III, p. 478; *CPR* 1452–61, 615–17 (1460).

22 The fields are described in greater detail in ch. 8.

23 *CClR* 1256–59, f. 268: quarry of 'Gilpitwell' (? 'Gylpet dale' in Nottingham wood, *RBN*, II, p. 359). The well may be St Ann's Well: *RBN*, I, pp. 16–17, 120–3, 128–9, II, pp. 458–9; *CPR* 1232–47, f. 82; *CClR* 1251–3, f. 25; NAO CA 1262 m5d (1335), m20 (1336).

24 NAO CA 1256 mm4, 16d; 1258a m18; 1261 m8d; 1321/II m9; 1323 m3; 1332 m5; 1327 m9.

25 NAO CA 7530–1; *RBN*, I, pp. 16–17.

26 *RBN*, I, pp. 4–7.

27 T. D. Hardy (ed.), *Rotuli Litterarum Patentium in turri Londoniensi asservati* (1835), p. 87; *RBN*, I, pp. 12–47, 90–5; VCH *Nottinghamshire*, II, pp. 168–73; PRO Calendars of the Fine Rolls, 1413–22, f. 385.

28 *CPR* 1266–72, f. 46; 1281–92, f. 59; NAO CA 1251b m3d; 1256 m21.

29 PRO C 146/7788; T. D. Hardy (ed.), *Rotuli Litterarum Clausarum in turri Londoniensi asservati* (1833–34), I, p. 463; NAO CA 1282 m26d (1382); 1301 m11d (1404); *RBN*, I, pp. 16–17, 44–5, 222–3, 402; III, pp. 150–1; Newstead I, f. 85.

30 *CPR* 1330–34, fos. 10, 559; NAO CA 1256 m21; 1262 m5d; 1311 m12d; *RBN*, I, pp. 124–5; Vanderzee, *Nonarum Inquisitiones*, f. 290.

31 Barley and Straw, maps. Ex inf. Charles Young.

32 T. Foulds, 'The foundation of Lenton Priory and a reconstruction of its lost cartulary', *TTS*, 92 (1988), pp. 34–42.

33 *RBN*, I, pp. 188–9; III, pp. 150–1; *Thurgarton Cartulary*, 52n; J. Standish (ed.), 'Abstracts of the Inquisitiones Post Mortem and other Inquisitiones relating to Nottinghamshire 1279–1321' (*TSRS*, 4, 1914), pp. 274–5.

34 *CPR* 1266–72, f. 531; 1313–17, f. 382; 1317–21, f. 316; *CClR* 1268–72, f. 503; D. Crook, 'Moothallgate and the venue of the Nottinghamshire county court in the thirteenth century', *TTS*, 88 (1984), pp. 99–102; PRO C 146/4050; H. Gill, 'Notes on the Carmelite friary at Nottingham', *TTS*, 26 (1922), pp. 110–13.

35 *CClR* 1227–31, f. 305; 1254–56, f. 417; 1259–61, f. 326; 1234–37, fos. 309, 493; 1279–88, f. 163; *CPR* 1232–47, f. 118; 1272–81, f. 199; 1301–07, f. 131 (1303); 1307–13, f. 383 (1311); *RBN*, I, pp. 274–5, 278–9, 282–3, 371, 385, 387; NAO CA 1271 m7d; Standish, 'Abstracts', p. 85.

36 *CClR* 1399–1402, f. 528; 1402–05, f. 389; *CPR* 1401–05, f. 125.

37 B. L. Abrahams, 'The condition of the Jews of England at the time of their expulsion in 1290', *Transactions of the Jewish Historical Society*, 2 (1896), p. 100. The total reflects a respectable wealth for the community. Westminster Abbey Muniments, no. 6714 (before 1230).

38 *CPR* 1258–66, f. 153; C. Roth, *A History of the Jews in England* (3rd edn, Oxford, 1964), pp. 58, 69.

39 PR 1 John, 207; M. D. Davis (ed.), *Hebrew deeds of English Jews before 1290* (1888), nos. 95, 136; NUMD Middleton deeds, MiD 758/1; Saltman, *Cartulary of Dale Abbey*, pp. 440, 443.

40 Westminster Abbey Muniments, nos. 6690–1; *CPR* 1258–66, f. 186; 1266–72, f. 382.

41 *Rufford Charters*, no. 35; PRO Liber feodarum, *The Book of Fees commonly called* Testa de Nevill *reformed from the earliest manuscripts* (1920), I, p. 288 (1219).

42 *RBN*, I, pp. 2–5.

43 *RBN*, I, pp. 6–13 (a second charter is lost: pp. 120–3). The liberties granted by John Count of Mortain, had been lost when King Richard reassumed his brother's lands and honors in 1194.

44 *RBN*, I, pp. 22–5, 40–1, 52–3, 56–9, 76–81; II, pp. 2–11. For the 1449 charter see ch. 6.

45 PR Henry II, 11, 57; 2 John 8–9; *Rufford Charters*, 28 (c.1180). The Robin Hood traditions are clearly summarised in J. C. Holt, *Robin Hood* (revised edn, 1989).

46 *RBN*, I, pp. 40–1, 58–9.

47 S. N. Mastoris, 'The boundary between the English and French Boroughs of medieval Nottingham', *TTS*, 85 (1981), pp. 68–74; 'The reeves and bailiffs of the town of Nottingham before 1284', *TTS*, 87 (1983), pp. 36–9; 'Regulating the Nottingham markets: new evidence from a thirteenth century manuscript', *TTS*, 90 (1986), pp. 79–83; *Rufford Charters*, 8, 23, 24, 32, 34; *RBN*, I, pp. 146–7, 360–1.

48 *RBN*, I, pp. 178–9, 200–7, 268–309, 324–5, 411; II, pp. 98–9, 102–97, 368, 423.

49 PRO Calendars of inquisitions miscellaneous, 8, no. 469.

50 *RBN*, I, pp. 150–1, 184–5, 248–9, 268–9, 274–5, 410; II, pp. 220–3, 244–7, 368–80; III, pp. 425–6, 447–8.

51 *RBN*, I, pp. 268–9; II, pp. 38–9.

52 *RBN*, I, pp. 268–323; II, pp. 46–9, 377.

53 *RBN*, I, pp. 66–71, 158–61.

54 *Rufford Charters*, 28; T. Foulds, J. Hughes and M. Jones, 'The Nottingham borough court rolls: the reign of Henry VI (1422–55)', *TTS*, 87 (1993), pp. 74–87.

55 R. F. B. Hodgkinson (trans.), 'The account books of the gilds of St George and of St Mary in the church of St Peter Nottingham' (*TSRS*, 7 1939), pp. 22, 41, 49, 54.

56 NAO CA 1291 m11d; 1305 m23d; Foulds *et al.* 'Nottingham', p. 83; *RBN*, III, p. 284.

57 *RBN*, I, pp. 58–67, 192–5; VCH *Nottinghamshire*, II, p. 93.

5

TRADE AND MANUFACTURE

Trevor Foulds

Nottingham's overseas contacts and trade can only partially be traced in the records. A number of wealthy citizens had ships used to import and export goods to the town. The range was wide: a variety of spices and silk could be obtained in Nottingham, as well as timber, and ores and minerals used in dyeing cloth and leather. On his death in 1324 John Amyas, son of Nottingham's wealthiest citizen, had twelve pounds of Brazil (worth 2*s* a pound), the hard reddish wood of the East Indian Sappan tree used for dyeing, which he kept in a *fyr* chest, possibly spruce from Prussia. Exactly how he could have obtained it is not known, since the sources of supply, whether for use in the town or for trade elsewhere, are largely indiscernible. Direct import cannot be ruled out, but much was probably conducted through other merchants and middlemen at larger ports such as Hull or Boston. The evidence for the manufacture of goods within Nottingham is firmer, but the sources of supply of the raw materials and the distribution of finished products remains unclear.

The river and navigation

The River Trent played a crucial role in the economic life of Nottingham: the town was the last place upstream to which small boats could sail. The Trent flows into the Humber, and thus York, Hull and the North Sea were accessible. At Torksey the ancient Roman canal, the Foss Dyke, linked the Trent to the River Witham and provided the connection to Lincoln. From there, via the Witham, vessels could reach Boston, although by the middle of the fourteenth century the Foss Dyke was silting up, restricting access into Lincolnshire.[1]

The River Trent formed the administrative boundary between northern and southern England. It was unpredictable, difficult to control, and a formidable obstacle for road travellers from the south. The important York road and a number of lesser routes converged here because the Trent was fordable at Nottingham. It was an offence to impede the passage of ships (*navium*) on the river or encroach upon the York road and the Fosse Way. A bridge was built in 920 although nothing more is known of it until £6 13*s* 4*d* was spent on repairs in 1180–81. In the mid-twelfth century there were bridges downstream at Newark and Gainsborough, and a bridge upstream at Hemington was constructed at or soon after the Conquest, and repaired in the 1090s.[2] Otherwise, the river had to be crossed by fords or ferries.

The medieval bridge over the Trent was called 'Hethbeth Bridge', the etymology of which is obscure.[3] Two of its arches have been preserved close to the south of the modern Trent Bridge. Neither the town nor the wapentakes of the county were responsible for its maintenance; the building and repairing of bridges was an act of charity. In 1208 maintenance of Hethbeth Bridge was undertaken by St Joseph's Hospital, Nottingham; later it was handled by wardens who were licensed to collect alms (1251). The thirteenth-century bridge was of timber and stone, and due to the deterioration of the weather caused by the onset of the 'Little Ice Age', flooding became an increasing problem from the early fourteenth century.[4] The scouring action of flooding periodically caused the bridge partially to collapse or to be washed away, causing the town considerable problems. By the fourteenth century local people were beginning to take greater responsibility for maintenance, by acquiring income-yielding lands and properties. Together with pious gifts in alms or bequests in wills, these donations formed by 1416 the Bridge estate, with an exchequer to receive the income.[5] The process started as an act of charity by John le Palmer, a prominent citizen, and his wife Alice, who endowed the chapel of St Mary on the bridge in 1303 and undertook the bridge's reconstruction. After John's death his wife (d. 1334) continued lavishing money on it and obtained grants of pontage (the right to collect a toll on goods for the bridge's repair). The work was hampered by political bickering, poor accounting, and the occasional diversion of the proceeds of pontage by the King to other projects. In 1329 the repairs were said to be finished, but in 1335 the bridge was 'ruined and broken' and in 1463 a commission enquired if it would not be better to move it to a safer place.[6]

Hethbeth Bridge was a mile south of the town. A wooden causeway crossed the marshy grounds northwards to the Leen Bridge or Townsbridge (*Tounesbridgge*), which had twenty-three arches and was 664 feet long. It crossed the Leen and its subsidiary channels and must have been built shortly after the river was diverted in the twelfth century. Floods occasionally damaged the causeway, and the 'great bridge' over the Leen was a cause for concern in 1383, 1402, 1424 and 1458, as a result of floods and damage done by carts. The town was responsible for upkeep of the northern head of the bridge and the next two arches; the other six wapentakes of Nottinghamshire were responsible for the other twenty-one arches.[7] Horses and carts could be hired in Nottingham to carry merchandise from Hethbeth Bridge along the causeway into the town. Whether the River Leen, which joined the Trent near Hethbeth Bridge, was ever used to carry goods to and from the area of the Leen bridge is not known.

The burgesses regularly complained to the King about obstructions in the River Trent, but the response was often slow and accelerated only when royal interests were affected: as in 1324 when royal supplies could not get into the town.[8] Multiple river channels and a mill race were partly responsible for fluctuating water levels at Hethbeth Bridge, and the burgesses had to negotiate with local landowners in order to try to overcome them. During droughts, when there was not sufficient water at Hethbeth Bridge, burgess-owned vessels could manoeuvre and moor in the water at the Colwick landing-stage, two miles downstream. The merchandise was then transported to or from Nottingham on horseback. Near Hethbeth Bridge there must also have been facilities for loading and unloading vessels, and what may have been an oaken landing-stage was found during the construction of the New Trent Bridge (1871).[9] Vessels may also have been made in the area.[10]

Merchants and traders

Nottingham merchants owned or chartered ships, but little is known of where they ranged and what commodities they traded abroad. William Amyas (mayor 1316–17, 1324–25, 1328–29, 1333–34) owned ships, although as Nottingham's wealthiest person in 1341, and with established government connections, he may have been exceptional. Robert 'of the Sea' chartered one of Amyas's vessels for 20*s* to carry corn from the landing stage at Adbolton to Gainsborough, and another in 1316 from Robert of York to carry corn to York. Other Nottingham merchants with access to ships included John Remay, 'mariner', who rammed a boat from which three men were thrown overboard and drowned while he was sailing in the Humber near Gainsborough in 1366.[11] Other merchants ranged further afield. During the famine years of the early fourteenth century they went into France, possibly to Poitou, to buy corn and other foodstuffs.

Trading on the high seas could be dangerous. In the fourteenth century war with France and Scotland, and risk of piracy, made the English coast and North Sea hazardous. Nottingham merchants John le Colier and John of Tumby in 1317 laded a ship of Baldwin Skync at Boston with wool and other goods worth £1,000 to trade overseas. The ship was attacked between Dunwich and Orford by men of Sluys (Flanders). On behalf of the merchants the King contacted the Count of Flanders but the mayor of Antwerp proved dilatory in resolving the matter. Similarly, a co-operative venture between the burgesses of Nottingham and York came to grief in 1392. At 'Lescone' they put on board an Amsterdam ship forty-seven 'lasts' of herring, four barrels of eels and other merchandise worth £100. While passing the Scottish coast they were attacked and boarded by Scots 'arrayed for war', who impounded the ship and its cargo. In the same year another joint venture of the burgesses of Nottingham and York, consisting of a cargo of herring and other goods worth £400 which was also taken in Scotland, resulted in a Scottish merchant's goods being impounded at Great Yarmouth, and held on the sureties of John Samon, John Plumptre and Henry

Plumptre, all Nottingham merchants.[12] In 1380 Henry Plumptre, on two separate occasions, contracted Thomas Arnold to sail to Scotland and travel the country to search for a ship seized by the Scots. He even hired armour for Arnold. Conversely, war with Scotland was profitable for some well-placed Nottingham men, particularly for William Amyas. Nottingham merchants, by land and sea, supplied army provisions: John Fleming, Ralph Godard and Richard le Cupper in 1299, William of Beeston and Hugh Dammesone in 1323, and Richard of Hallam in 1333. Perhaps not surprisingly merchants were accused of supplying arms and corn to the enemy; and some transactions were dubious: the bishop of Norwich's crusade to Flanders in 1383 provided two Nottingham men with booty mostly in cloth, clothing and household effects which they looted from some unfortunate souls.[13]

Table 5.1 **Leaders of the medieval community, 1327 and 1341**

1327 (137 names)		*1341 (204 names)*	
50*s*	Walter of Lincoln (M, 2B)	£60	William Amyas (4M)
40*s*	William Amyas (4M)	£25	Roger de Botehale (2M)
20*s*	John le Colier (2M, B)	£16	John le Colier (2M, B)
15*s*	Laurence le Spicer (3M, B)	£15	Henry of Chesterfield (3M)
10*s*	Gervase of Bradmore	£15	Richard Samon (M, B)
10*s*	Richard of Chilwell (B)	£10	John of Tumby (2M, 2B)
10*s*	John Samon	£ 9	Hugh le Spicer (3M)
10*s*	John of Sneinton	£ 8	Thomas of Edwalton (M)
8*s*	William le Cupper (M, B)	£ 8	William of Rotherham
8*s*	Nicholas of Shelford (M)	£ 6	Richard of Chilwell's widow
6*s* 8*d*	John of Breedon (B)	£ 6	William of Edwalton
6*s* 8*d*	John Dun (B)		
6*s* 8*d*	Richard of Grimston		
6*s*	John of Tumby (2M, 2B)		

Source: RBN, I–III.
Notes: B = bailiff, M = mayor. Figures are the number of times the office was held (4M = mayor four times).

Peaceful contact with the Low Countries, particularly the duchy of Brabant (modern Belgium), was maintained into the fifteenth century. The trade was sufficiently robust for some Nottingham men to take up residence, while a small colony of Brabantines came to reside either permanently or for extended periods in the town. Robert de Ockley bought Brabant (*Braban*) cloth from John Skitson in 1408, and Michael Braban, who became a burgess, benefited from the sale of a woollen web-loom and a linen-loom with weaving implements in 1404. Foreign merchants found it profitable to trade in Nottingham: the exotically named Godekin de Reule, 'merchant of Germany', impleaded Robert son of Thomas Daft in the Nottingham borough court in 1324. Godekin, merchant of 'Estland' (Prussia), and his men had been granted safe conduct to trade in England the previous year. The court action did not proceed to judgment and we do not know what goods Godekin traded. Henry Plumptre had four cartloads of 'prusware' carted from Hethbeth Bridge in 1402.[14] The extensive forests of medieval Prussia produced timber from the spruce ('prus') fir tree and from its bark and leaves spruce beer was made, a popular drink of the period.

The men who owned or chartered ships and traded overseas were Nottingham's wealthiest men. They commanded resources far beyond the other citizens, they served as members of Parliament, and they were often justices of the peace. However, they were a small group, and disparity in the distribution of wealth was not unusual in English towns.[15] Only the wealthiest men became mayor, with the bailiffs drawn from lower economic strata. Few of the men who served as bailiff became mayor unless their fortunes improved, as in the case of John of Tumby – bailiff 1332–33, 1336–37; mayor 1343–44, 1345–46. In the early fourteenth century only four men whose incomes were assessed below £5 in 1341 became mayor: one was as low as 13*s* 4*d*, two at £1, and one at £1 10*s*.

Comparison of the taxation assessments with the charter evidence is instructive. For the period 1320–50, 160 men regularly witnessed charters, but many of these never became bailiff so that it can be assumed that there was a body of men with less economic power but some status. Comparison also reveals some notable absences. The prominent Fleming family of the mid- to late thirteenth century which supplied some reeves, bailiffs and mayors had gone by the 1320s, along with the Kitte (John Kitte, mayor 1308–09, 1309–10), and Bugge families. The Bugge family continued to hold property within the borough but preferred to be named 'Willoughby' or 'Bingham' from the Nottinghamshire vills in which they held land. The significance of the Palmer family collapsed with the deaths of John Palmer senior (*c*.1311) and John Palmer junior (mayor 1302–03, 1306–07; d. *c*.1320). Although Matilda, Agnes and Sabina, daughters of John and Alice Palmer, married prominent Nottingham men, William Amyas lost his son John in 1324,[16] but the children of Joan and Agnes, his daughters, were influential in the later fourteenth century.

Although the wealthy men of Nottingham were not comparable with the rich merchants of eastern England, their financial status was sufficient to encourage the crown to seek 'loans' to alleviate its financial difficulties. Obtaining repayment was often difficult. From the customs of Hull in 1338 John le Colier was owed £151 19*s* 1*d*, Roger de Botehale £746 2*s* 2*d*, William Amyas £1,075 8*s* 1*d* and Robert of Beighton £326 9*s* 2*d*. Two years later a further £400 was owed to William Amyas and John le Colier. John Crowshaw (mayor 1382–83, 1388–89) was owed 'great sums' from the Hull customs in 1389, and John Plumptre (mayor 1385–86, 1394–95, 1395–94, 1408–09), Henry Plumptre (mayor 1387–88), John Samon (mayor 1378–79, 1383–84, 1396–97) and John Tansley (mayor 1399–1400, 1410–11) lent £66 13*s* 4*d* for the Welsh war in 1404. Many of these men dealt in wool, but Henry Kitte and William Brian (both of whom were reeves) were vintners and the King's wine-keepers at the castle in 1240; William's father was Brian the Vintner; and Adam Kitte, probably Henry's son, was also a vintner.[17] Their status was such that they were responsible for the

King's treasure in 1241, and it is possible that their fortunes were founded on the supply and transport of wine and food to the castle, which acted as the distribution centre for King John's favourite residences in the region: Gascon wine was transported by land from Bristol in 1205 and from Boston two years later.[18]

Nottingham did not necessarily benefit from any surplus wealth these richer merchants may have generated. William Amyas repaired all the bridges between the Leen Bridge and Hethbeth Bridge in 1329, and John Plumptre founded the hospital of the Annunciation of the Virgin Mary (1390–1414) for poor widows (Plumptre Hospital). However, from the thirteenth century such men showed a preference for investing in land and founding chantries in order to demonstrate their piety. William Amyas held the manor of Watnall Chaworth and founded a chantry in St Mary's church in 1341. John le Colier held land in Sibthorpe, and in memory of his wife Agnes, daughter of John Passeys of Sutton Passeys, he founded a chantry in Sutton Passeys. Roger de Botehale founded a chantry in St Mary's church for his wives, Joan and Margaret in 1344. Thomas Thurland, who died in 1474, acquired the manors of Gamston, Houghton and West Drayton, which he used to re-found the Guild of Holy Trinity (1447–60) which had existed before 1395.[19]

Craftsmen

Nottingham had a wide range of craftsmen, although many worked part-time as the season demanded. Craft areas, as suggested by street-names, may be illusory: only one prominent craft or entrepreneur was needed to provide a street-name. One oven gave Baxter Gate its name, but it changed in the fourteenth century to Wheeler Gate when one or more wheelwrights were working there. 'Fullers' Street' became Lister Gate as dyers came to prominence in the thirteenth century. Goods traded or sold in Nottingham were not necessarily made in the town, and occupational surnames are unreliable indicators of craft activity. Little is known about craft associations. Possibly numbers were not sufficient to warrant the establishment of guilds, or perhaps their role was informally fulfilled by fraternities such as the Guild of Holy Trinity.[20]

The most prominent craftsmen were the weavers whose guild – the only one known in the town – was formed before 1155. The guild payment was the same as in Huntingdon (£2) but less than in Lincoln (£6) and York (£10). Only Alred the weaver appears in thirteenth-century charters, and it may be that in Nottingham, as in Lincoln, weavers were regarded as socially inferior. Weaving declined in the fourteenth century, and it was claimed in 1348 that since *c.*1302 some weavers had moved out of town, leaving fewer to make the guild payment. They may have gone into the countryside: in 1328 Richard Boby was accused of stealing cloths from country men. The early fifteenth-century evidence indicates a substantial recovery, in line with the economic buoyancy of the period, and the borough court rolls frequently mention weaving and weaving implements. There were complaints in 1395 that the weavers charged too much for their cloth.[21]

'Nottingham Cloth' was so called either because it was woven from local wool or because it was bought in the town. In national terms Nottingham cloth was designated 'northern cloth', and other types of northern cloth woven from 'northern wool' was dyed in the town. The standard northern cloth was 23–25 yards long and weighed 46lb: half pieces or dozens were 12–13 yards long and weighed 37lb. As in other towns, the wealthier men probably controlled the supply. John Plumptre supplied 'gode Notyngham shire woll' and 'northeren woll' in 1420. Although generally 'northern wool' was inferior to 'Nottinghamshire wool', which was itself not of the highest quality, both attracted Brabantine and Italian buyers.[22]

Raw cloth was fulled by fullers or walkers with fuller's earth, sometimes known as 'walker's earth', which absorbs grease. John Ingham, walker, was in debt for *walkerherth* in 1403, and the same year Thomas Dayne had a fulling-mill. A 'Walker Gate' had once existed near Goose Gate while 'Fullers' Street' is an older name for Lister Gate. Once fulled, the cloth was stretched to dry on tenters. Some were in crofts near the town wall at the postern in 1408 – one of them occupied forty feet of common ground, the length of a half-piece – and in Barker Gate in 1411.[23] Next, the nap of the cloth was raised by teazels and the loose fibres were sheared by shearmen, who were highly regarded, as the finish of the cloth depended on their skill.

Dyeing was another prominent craft. In 1434 Thomas Stretton dyed ten packs of Nottingham cloth and ten of northern cloth, blue, green, and murrey or tawny. Amongst the goods listed by John Amyas's executors in 1324 were a bale of alum, the mordant used to fix dyes in the cloth; a bale of archil, a lichen from which purple or violet dye is obtained; brazil, a red dye for leather; 3 bushels of woad, a blue dye; woad-vats; and madder, a red dye. The dyes were supplied by the spicers or apothecaries. Richard of Cotgrave, spicer, supplied sanders (red sandalwood), a red dye, and brazil in 1357; William of Spondon, apothecary, had saffron and verdigris, a green dye, stolen from his shop in 1325. Poytrees – contraptions for stretching or hanging dyed products on to dry – were owned by John Amyas, and were a nuisance as they encroached on roads.[24]

A fourteenth-century list states that Nottingham was known for its *boves*, which is often taken as firm evidence for a substantial tanning industry, but what *boves* (Latin, oxen, cattle) really meant in this context is uncertain.[25] The extent of full-time tanning is not known. Tanners are not numerically significant until the sixteenth century, which suggests that this was a post-medieval trade. Evidence for finished products is better in the fifteenth century.[26] 'Tanners's Street' was Barker Gate, a street-name interchangeable with Bellar Gate. By the late thirteenth century tanners were in Little (Narrow) Marsh near the Leen from which they would have drawn the water needed for washing and soaking. Complaints were made about tanners blocking the river at Little Marsh with stakes, poles and turves, and soaking skins. Sheepskins were stolen from the river in 1322 while being soaked. Cattle skins were soaked, treated with lime to remove the hair, washed and put in the tan vat, for which quantities of urine, alum and oak bark – hence barker – were required.[27] The longer the hide was soaked in this ooze the better the quality. Deer, sheep and horse skins were not tanned in this way, but tawed with alum and oil by tawyers, a separate trade, for which there is little evidence.

The Nottingham alabasterer's art had already attained some distinction by 1367, when Edward III commissioned an altarpiece or free-standing reredos for St George's Chapel, Windsor, from Peter the Mason. The altarpiece was large: it took ten carts with eight horses each seventeen days to carry the pieces by road from Nottingham at a cost of £200. Alabasterers are not found in the record again until 1479, but in 1491 they were working relatively mundane artefacts such as salt-cellars. The fame of locally worked alabaster reached the continent. In July 1414 Master Alexander de Berneval, architect–mason of Rouen cathedral, and two other men acting for the abbot of Fécamp (France) boarded the ship of Walter Neasham of Newcastle-upon-Tyne at Harfleur, and sailed to Newcastle. Three days later they reached

Plate 8 [*left*] **Bridlesmith Gate**. This was a main thoroughfare in the medieval town, although there may have been no more than one or two bridlesmiths living and working here. Timber-framed buildings of medieval and Tudor date facing down St Peter's Gate are shown on this Victorian painting by T.C. Moore. The single-bay building on the left is one of the few timber-framed buildings in Nottingham to survive to the present day. Its timbers have been dated to *c.*1443

Plate 9 [*right*] **The Tomb of Thomas Thurland (d.1473), St Mary's (1928)**. The manufacture of devotional objects in alabaster was well established in and around Nottingham. It underlined the religious conformity of the town prior to the Reformation, and although many of alabaster products were sold across England and Continental Europe, this is one of several in St Mary's

Nottingham. Walter introduced them to the merchant Thomas Prentis at Chellaston. Subsequently a deal was struck and the contract was drawn up in Nottingham, when it was agreed that the uncarved alabaster would be shipped from Hull.[28] To identify which surviving carvings originated in Nottingham is not easy, although the source (Chellaston in Derbyshire) is clear from the alabaster's particular geological composition.

Pottery kilns and wasters (discarded distortions of misfiring) have been found in various places, notably the site of the Victoria Centre, Glasshouse Street and Goose Gate, where two double-flue kilns were active *c.*1225–50. The apparent skill, consistency and efficiency of production point to a strong pottery tradition in Nottingham. Two distinct periods have been identified: first, splashed glazed ware in limited quantities from the eleventh century with a second phase in the mid-thirteenth century (Goose Gate); and second, the emergence of green glazed wares from the mid-thirteenth century, stabilising by the fourteenth century. Particularly fine pottery (jugs and kitchen wares) was produced in the early fourteenth century and is referred to as 'Nottingham reduced green glazed ware'. It has been found distributed throughout the East Midlands.[29]

We can trace one family of potters through five generations from the late thirteenth century: Henry le Potter, his two sons Richard and Matthew (d. *c.*1307), Matthew's son John (living 1322), and John's probable son Richard (1325), whose daughter Joan was living in 1376. By the early fourteenth century possibly as many as nine potters were at work in the town, although the only one who seems to have been wealthy was Margery, possibly the widow of Roger le Potter, who was assessed for taxation at £5, or Richard le Potter, assessed at £2 in 1341. Ralph, son of William le Potter, granted in 1301 to Matthew, son of Henry le Potter and Joan his wife a stall in the Saturday Market near one formerly occupied by Richard le Potter. For his part Richard le Potter acquired property in Fletcher Gate in 1327, while William le Potter had a tenement in Great Smith Gate. Robert and Roger le Potter had tofts on a 'Potters' Street', the location of which cannot now be identified. The fourteenth-century evidence suggests that the potters worked, if not lived, near the ditch on the east side of the town. John son of Matthew le Potter, William le Potter and Ralph his son had property on the ditch; Isabella wife of Robert le Potter was twice assaulted there in 1303 and 1311; and the same location is suggested in the case of Richard le Potter who lived in Barker Gate. It was here that his wife Alice was assaulted in 1313. Pottery production continued into the fifteenth century – William Farwell, potter, was bailiff 1390–91 and William Etwall engaged Richard Raven as a potter in 1440 – although by this time it may have been in decline.[30]

In the same part of the town as the potters were the tilers. Tiles, often made only for specific orders, were an important fourteenth-century craft and Nottingham floor-tiles are found throughout the East Midlands.[31] Tile making was established by the late thirteenth century. Around 1290 Robert Ruffus, tiler, had property within the ditch next to Richard son of Henry le Potter's, and in Barker Gate with a cellar, a kiln (not a tile-kiln), and access to the ditch. The later 'Tile Houses' are recorded in the ditch on the east in 1435 and 1440. Although little is known about floor-tiles, tilers are mentioned in the fifteenth century: 8,000 earthenware tiles worth £2 13*s* 4*d* were stolen in 1429. Hugh the Tiler of Lincoln made roof-tiles and guttering in 1330, John Sklater (Slater) put tiles on a house roof in 1397, and Thomas Slater was engaged in 'the slater's craft' to tile houses in 1410.[32]

Great Smith Gate, Bridlesmith Gate and Iron or Smithy Row hint at metalworking in the town. The wealthy John Samon had a forge in Great Smith Gate in 1414. Robert of Nottingham, merchant, supplied 'Nottingham iron' to make nails, bolts and chains for pontoon bridges built at King's Lynn in 1303.[33] Iron, steel, copper, lead, bronze, latten and pewter were worked into implements for everyday use, as were pots, pans, cauldrons, vats, table-ware, candlesticks, horse-shoes, bridles, stirrups, locks, armour, swords, knives and nails. Unexpectedly, five goldsmiths can be identified for the early fourteenth century. Henry the goldsmith sold and repaired silver bowls and spoons from his stall in the daily market in 1311 and had moulds for his work in 1328. There were fewer goldsmiths thereafter but they never entirely disappeared. Gold and silver may well have been worked into cloth by John Melburn, weaver, in 1436. Some metalworking was carried out on a part-time basis as anvils and other ironware could be hired.[34] Bell-founding, mentioned from the fifteenth century and probably controlled by a few specialists with workshops, cannot have been full-time: demand for bells would not have been constant and so the bell-founders supplied bell-metal and metal pots. Demand for armour cannot have been constant either. The evidence for two known armourers, Gilbert the armourer (killed 1339) and Richard of Langar in 1397, does not show them engaged in making or supplying armour. In the fourteenth century plate armour could be hired, but not necessarily from an armourer. John le Forbur carried swords by horse to Lincoln in 1316 which may have been made in Nottingham.[35]

Women

Women played a vital role in Nottingham's social and economic life throughout the medieval period. They had a defined area at the south-east of the Saturday Market and at the northern end of Bridlesmith Gate which was called the 'Woman Market'. Opportunities for women were limited by social convention and common law, but towns offered more scope and variety in work than the country. Nottingham women undertook a wide variety of jobs. Many worked as part of the economic unit centred on the family or supplemented its income: Cecilia Trevor helped her husband John to make silver decorations. Widows had to support themselves either by continuing their husband's business or in other ways. Margaret Potter was given money and metal to cast gudgeons for a mill, Joan Sheffield was a barker, Joan Burton an ironmonger, and Joan Rane worked as a labourer. Whether married or widowed, women traded in oak bark, cloth, skins, spices or bronze pots; they made saddles and cheese, baked bread and brewed ale; hired out cows, horses and geese; hired men for carpentry, agriculture and to collect their husbands' debts; borrowed and loaned money; undertook spinning, weaving, threading, embroidery and cutting cloth; mowed corn, weeded grain, drove animals to pasture, worked coalpits, nursed other people's children and sick women; and they were swineherds. Margaret Both, wife of John Both, wheelwright, in one year worked as a servant to one man and as a reaper to another.[36]

In May 1349 the Black Death approached Nottingham. The evidence shows a grant of pontage was cancelled due to 'pestilence threatening' its collection.[37] The Black Death was one of several disasters in the early fourteenth century. Nottingham, like many other towns, experienced considerable difficulties as population declined, but the record is almost silent. By the early fifteenth century the situation was improving: on the basis of social life, household effects, the colour and style of clothing, musical instruments, and rising meat consumption, we can deduce from evidence in the borough court rolls that the people of Nottingham in Henry VI's reign enjoyed a better quality of life than their counterparts in the early fourteenth century. These details perhaps reflect the buoyancy which carried Nottingham to its important charter of 1449, following which the swift decline of the borough court means that the life of the town cannot be recreated in the same detail. The late medieval town must be examined from a different perspective.[38]

Notes

1 *CPR* 1364–67, 138.

2 A. Farley (ed.), *Great Domesday Book* I (1783), f. 280a; *PR* 27 Henry II, 14; C. R. Salisbury, 'The excavation of Hemington Fields', *Current Archaeology*, 145 (1995), pp. 34–7. Dr Salisbury has provided dendrochronology dates for the bridge from 1065 to 1096.

3 J. E. B. Gover, A. Mawer and F. M. Stenton, *The Place-names of Nottinghamshire* (1940), pp. 22–3.

4 T. D. Hardy (ed.), *Rotuli Litterarum Patentium in turri Londoniensi asservati* (1835), p. 87; *CPR* 1216–25, 294 (1221); 1248–55, 120; *CClR* 1231–34, 391 (1234); 1234–37, 310 (1236); 1256–59, 258 (1258); 1268–72, 211 (1270).

5 The earliest extant Bridge-Masters' account is for 1457–58: *RBN*, II, pp. 108–9, 220–3, 364–8.

6 *CPR* 1301–07, 133; *CClR* 1327–30, 465; 1333–37, 390; 1360–64, 362; *CPR* 1361–64, 365.

7 *RBN*, I, pp. 152–3, 356–7, 364; II, pp. 222–41, 367; NAO CA 1307 m23d; *CPR* 1381–85, 327; 1401–05, 197; 1422–29, 193.

8 *RBN*, I, pp. 224–7, 412–21 (1392); *CPR* 1258–66, 480; 1324–27, 74–5; 1381–85, 189; 1321–24, 47.

9 *RBN*, I, pp. 88–91 (1316), 108–15 (1330), 226–9 (1383), 412–21 (1392); II, pp. 16–17 (1402); M. O. Tarbotton, *A Short History of the Old Trent Bridge with a Descriptive Account of the New Bridge, Nottingham* (Nottingham, 1871).

10 NAO CA 1262 m21d (1336) John le Shipwright; 1304/I m21d (1408) William le Shipwright. Neither reference is connected with ship-building: CA 1258b m8d; 1329/I m4d.

11 *RBN*, I, pp. 88–91; *CPR* 1364–67, 298.

12 *CClR* 1313–18, 319, 392, 500; 1389–92, 426; 1392–96, 33.

13 *RBN*, I, pp. 230–3; II, pp. 18–19; A. Cameron, 'William de Amyas and the community of Nottingham, 1308–50', *TTS*, 75 (1971), pp. 68–78; *CPR* 1292–1301, 481, 521; 1321–24, 288; 1330–34, 413; 1307–13, 256.

14 *RBN*, I, pp. 302–3, 320–1; II, pp. 16–17, 22–3, 52–3, 86–7; *Rufford Charters*, 17, 30; NAO CA 1258b m7; CPR 1321–24, 293. I am grateful to Dr J. B. Hughes for this latter reference.

15 C. Platt, *The English Medieval Town* (1976), pp. 107–11.

16 NAO CA 1259 m1. A commission of oyer and terminer for the death of John Amyas was not issued until 12 May 1344 (CPR 1343–45, 292). Two different people could, of course, have been involved.

17 *CClR* 1337–39, 425; 1339–41, 423; CPR 1338–40, 377, 406, 473; 1350–54, 143; CClR 1385–89, 571; CPR 1401–05, 417; CClR 1237–42, 184, 224; PR 2 John, 16; Rufford Charters, 3; CClR 1256–59, 420.

18 *CPR* 1232–47, 257; T. D. Hardy (ed.), *Rotuli Litterarum Clausarum in turri Londoniensi asservati* (1833–34), I, fos. 51, 89, 93b.

19 *CClR* 1327–30, 465; *RBN*, I, pp. 248–53, 264–5; II, pp. 96–9; *CPR* 1391–96, 116; *CClR* 1441–47, 29; *CPR* 1340–43, 343; *CClR* 1333–37, 478; *CPR* 1327–30, 100; 1340–43, 536; 1343–45, 317; 1446–52, 82; 1452–61, 615–17.

20 *RBN*, I, pp. 12–13, 196–7; V. W. Walker, 'Medieval Nottingham', *TTS*, 67 (1963), pp. 28–45.

21 *PR 2 Henry II*, 39; *Rufford Charters*, 27; *CClR* 1346–49, 448; NAO CA 1260 m25; *RBN*, I, pp. 272–3.

22 *RBN*, II, pp. 118–19, 146–7; W. Cunningham, *The Growth of English Industry and Commerce During the Early and Middle Ages* (5th edn, 1927), p. 630.

23 *RBN*, II, pp. 20–1, 60–1, 76–7; NAO CA 1259 m25; 1300 m16d.

24 *RBN*, I, pp. 40–1, 146–8, 166–7, 272–5; NAO CA 1259 m1d, m14d.

25 C. Bonnier, 'List of English towns in the fourteenth century', *English Historical Review*, 16 (1901), p. 502.

26 NAO CA 1255 m8d; T. Foulds, J. Hughes and M. Jones, 'The Nottingham Borough Court Rolls: the reign of Henry VI (1422–57)', *TTS*, 97 (1993), p. 81.

27 *RBN*, I, pp. 272–3, 369; NAO CA 1256 m22d; 1328/II m18d.

28 *RBN*, II, p. 302; III, p. 20. For Nottingham alabaster: F. W. Cheetham, *Medieval English Alabaster Carvings in the Castle Museum Nottingham* (Nottingham, 1973); W. Stevenson, 'Art sculpture in alabaster', *TTS*, 211 (1907), pp. 89–98.

29 Young, *Discovering Rescue Archaeology*. I am grateful to Victoria Nailer and Charles Young for making available their expertise concerning pottery.

30 *RBN*, I, pp. 42–3, 248–9, 370; II, pp. 172–3; NAO CA 1260 m8; 1256 m19.

31 E. S. Eames, *Medieval Tiles* (1968).

32 Saltman, *The Cartulary of Darley Abbey*, 410–15; Young, *Discovering Rescue Archaeology; RBN*, I, pp. 348–9; II, pp. 70–1, 272–3, 302–3, 316–17, 358–9, 391; NAO CA 1330 m4; 1323 m16d; 1261 m14d.

33 NAO CA 1308 m21d; D. M. Owen (ed.), *The Making of King's Lynn* (1984), p. 445.

34 NAO CA 1255 m4; 1260 mm17–18; 1324 m16; *RBN*, I, pp. 160–1; II, pp. 158–9, 270–1.

35 *RBN*, I, pp. 352–3; II, pp. 18–19, 144–7, 158–63, 166–7, 172–3; CPR 1338–40, 344; NAO CA 1260 m9; 1256 m20.

36 T. Foulds, 'Landeloupers and chullers: the evidence of the Nottingham borough court rolls 1303–1455' (unpublished paper 1995).

37 *CPR* 1348–50, 295.

38 Foulds *et al.*, 'Nottingham Borough Court Rolls', pp. 74–87; C. Dyer, *Standards of Living in the Later Middle Ages: Social Change in England c.*1200–1520 (Cambridge, 1989); T. Foulds, J. Hughes and M. Jones, 'Une Ville anglaise et ses rues à la fin du moyen-âge à travers ses archives méconnues: les *borough court rolls* de Nottingham (1303–1455)', 4ème Colloque international sur la sociabilité, Rouen, 1994.

6

THE LATE MEDIEVAL TOWN, 1449–1560

David Marcombe

The period 1449 to 1560 witnessed in Nottingham the breakdown of many customary patterns of behaviour, particularly in the political and religious spheres. Evidence of far-reaching social and economic development is more difficult to determine. The driving forces behind this change were the Charter of 1449, which revolutionised local government; the Wars of the Roses and the coming of the Tudor dynasty in 1485; and the Protestant Reformation of the mid-sixteenth century which ultimately swept away long-held traditions of Catholic belief and practice. These transitions were sometimes slow and painful and were certainly not all fully worked out by the time of Elizabeth's accession in 1558, by which time the face of the town was much altered.

Economy and society

It is impossible to comment constructively on the population of late medieval Nottingham, though it is possible to highlight periods when the town may have suffered greater than usual mortality due to plague. In April 1518 Richard Pace, Archdeacon of Dorset, wrote to Cardinal Wolsey making arrangements for Henry VIII's northern progress and pointing out that the King wished to avoid Nottingham since there was 'some death' in the town.[1] But the most reliable guide to probable mortality comes by way of an analysis of numbers of wills proved. Between 1460 and 1560 301 grants of probate survive, an average of three per year. Five phases stand out as remarkable: 1466–67 (nineteen probates), 1503–06 (twenty-one probates), 1515–16 (twenty-three probates), 1517–22 (twenty-nine probates) and 1557–58 (twenty-two probates).[2] This confirms Pace's comment that 1518 was a bad year and also draws attention to other periods, notably the extended difficulties which seem to have existed between 1515 and 1522. Obviously this kind of analysis is extremely rudimentary because it takes into account only will-makers, a small and comparatively affluent section of the community.

The same difficulties are encountered in attempting to assess the town's prosperity. Nottingham, which still drew its sustenance largely from textiles and a mixed-craft economy, was not a particularly wealthy community. According to the 1524 subsidy book the town's contribution stood at £50 6*s* 8*d*, significantly less than that of Leicester (£90 10*s* 0*d*) and Lincoln (£144 4*s* 0*d*), but more than that of Bath (£41 8*s* 6*d*).[3] From the King's point of view the loan 'lovingly advanced' by Nottingham and other communities in 1515 was infinitely more effective since it brought in more money (£147 13*s* 4*d* in Nottingham's case) and could be targeted at those with the ability to pay.[4] Several subsidy rolls survive, the best examples being *c*.1480–1500, 1504 and 1523/24.[5] The latter is unusually complete and provides a good picture of urban wealth and topography on the eve of the Reformation.

The 1524 subsidy was not a comprehensive tax, and it applied only to people with particular assets. Assessment was made on a variety of sources: land (though in practice this was rare); goods (excluding personal apparel and standing corn); and wages (a problematical area abandoned for taxation purposes in 1525).[6] In Nottingham there were 295 assessments in all, 1 per cent on land, 81 per cent on goods and 17 per cent on wages. The town had its prosperous inhabitants (John Williamson, assessed at £5, was the largest taxpayer), but 46 per cent of assessments were at the basic rate of 4*d* and a further 24 per cent were firmly pegged in the lower orders between 6*d* and 1*s*. In other words, 70 per cent of the inhabitants were taxed at 1*s* or less, indicating a community of moderate prosperity but with pockets of significant wealth.

The subsidy roll recorded taxable individuals according to the streets in which they lived. Areas such as Hen Cross, High and Low Pavements, Timberhill and Bridlesmith Gates were relatively prosperous; while Castle Gate, Friar Gate and Wheelwright Gate had a higher proportion of wage-earners and low-level goods assessments. Yet rich and poor lived cheek by jowl throughout the town and too rigid an attempt at social zoning would be misleading. Overall the findings from 1523/4 tend to confirm research on the topographical implications of the 1504 assessment – that there was a 'central core' of properties with few gardens; a 'second zone' comprising a mixture of tenements and gardens; and a 'periphery' with few tenements but a high proportion of closes, barns and gardens. Property values declined close to the periphery, the pattern dictated by 'proximity to markets or routes leading to them'. In the more marginal areas there was still room for expansion in early Tudor Nottingham, a point later amply confirmed by the maps drawn in 1609 and 1610.[7]

Was this space the result of late medieval urban decay, or had the town been set out with ample and perhaps over-optimistic bounds in the first place? The fifteenth century seems to have been a period of prosperity. Nottingham is not well-endowed with medieval buildings, but of those still surviving The Bell has timbers dated to the 1430s, The Salutation to the 1440s, and a house on Bridlesmith Gate to 1443. Thurland Hall, now demolished, was built in the 1450s, and contracts for secular buildings have survived for 1459, 1479 and 1513, and it was in the first half of the fifteenth century that St Mary's Church was built more or less as it survives today.[8] However, between 1480 and 1530 the accounts of various town officers and organisations comment fairly frequently on properties being in decay, and tenants negotiating reductions in their rent because of the letting difficulties faced by landlords. Clearly money was available, but it was being targeted at specific areas and projects, which no doubt bore a relationship to the identifiable zones. Certainly the fortunes of the town turned upwards after 1530 when population was once more increasing, and when references to 'decays' become less common in the surviving documents.[9]

Possibly the best guide to Nottingham's prosperity between 1460 and 1560 is provided by the annual admissions of burgesses which, amongst other things, indicate the willingness of individuals to commence trading.[10] In all 1,595 burgesses were admitted, an average of about sixteen a year or eighty per five-year period (figure 6.1). When admissions are analysed in these five-year units it emerges that before 1530 there were some above-average periods (1480–90 and 1505–10); but there were also periods of very low recruitment (1460–65, 1470–75, 1490–95, 1510–15 and 1520–25).

Plate 10 **Thurland Hall**. The quadrangle of Thurland Hall, recorded by a local architect, John Jephson, in 1825. Built by the wealthy wool merchant Alderman Thomas Thurland about 1458 and, after being rebuilt as the town house of the Earl of Clare, visited by James I and Charles I, it was demolished in 1831. Architecturally it displayed affinities to contemporary country houses such as Welbeck Abbey and Bolsover Castle, and combined rows of straight Jacobean gables with more fashionable shaped gables. The modern Thurland Street was cut through the site shortly after the house was demolished

Figure 6.1 **Admissions of Burgesses, 1460–1559**

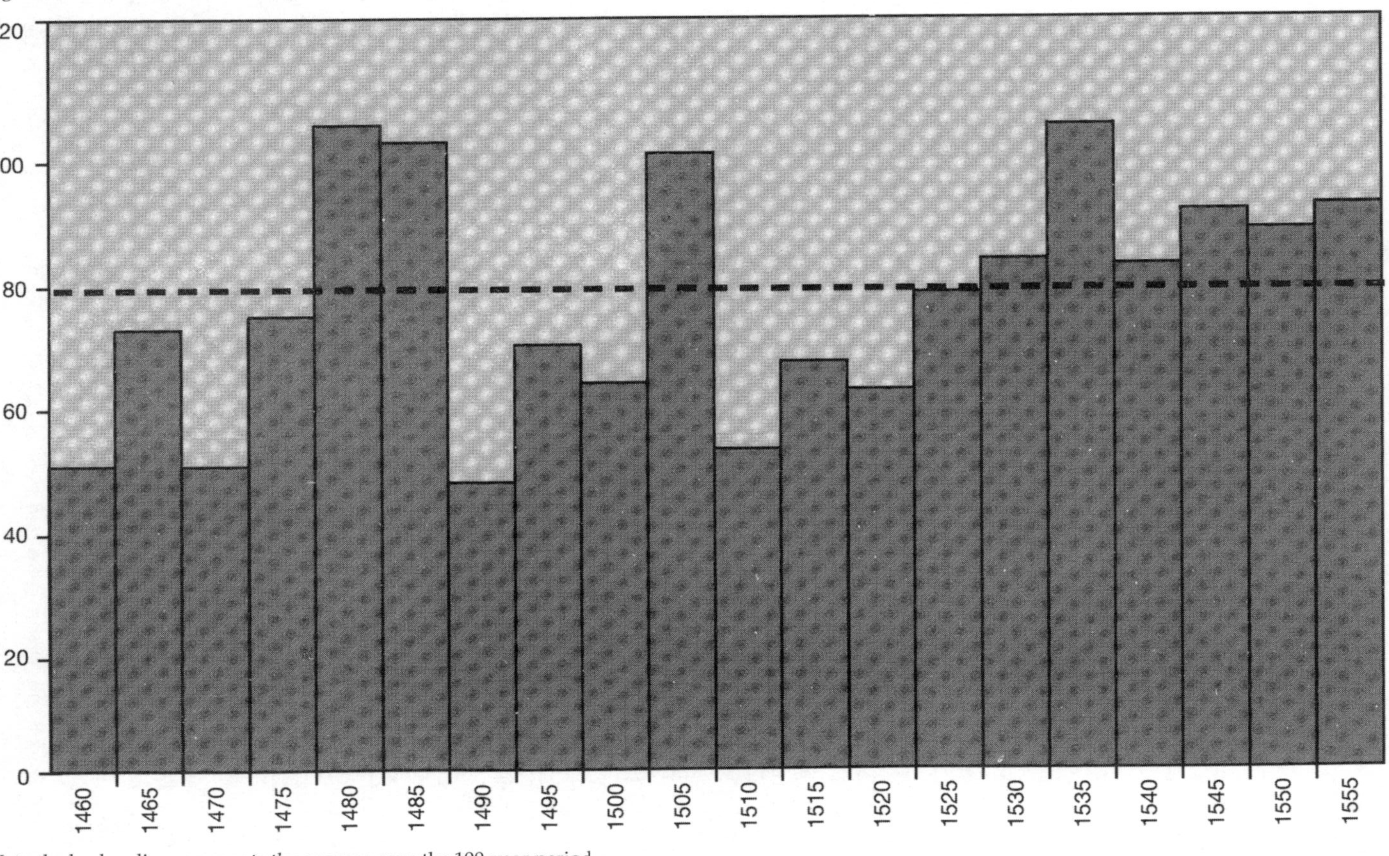

Note: the broken line represents the average over the 100-year period.

After 1530 the recruitment of burgesses was consistently above average, reflecting the recovery in the fortunes of the town.

The Wars of the Roses

The effects of the Wars of the Roses are not easily gauged, either politically or economically. Certainly the Yorkists always looked for support in Nottingham. Even before the crushing defeat of Henry VI at Towton there were those who wished the Lancastrians 'no good will' and took exception to the 'strong thieves' and mosstroopers who rode in the Earl of Northumberland's retinue and made their unwelcome presence felt in 1459. Once Edward IV was securely on the throne, he used Nottingham as a base first for his northern campaign of 1464, and later when he was forced to wrest control of the kingdom from the Earl of Warwick in 1471. The townspeople displayed conspicuous loyalty throughout, so much so that in 1462 Edward remitted £20 out of the fee farm of the borough for twenty years on account of their good services.[11] He erected new buildings at the Castle, including the state apartments and Richard's Tower. These were executed to the highest specifications and reflected the northern property interests of the Yorkists, especially those of the King's brother, Richard, Duke of Gloucester. Richard III, as King, received a Scottish embassy in the Great Hall of the Castle in 1484, yet it became his 'castle of care': here he received the news of the death of his only son, and from here he set out to his fateful encounter with Henry Tudor at Bosworth Field in August 1485.[12]

The way in which the town fathers watched the unfolding crisis speaks volumes for the very flexible loyalties of a corporation which had showered the Yorkist lords with gifts twenty years earlier. On 18 August 1485, four days before Bosworth, Thomas Hall was paid 6*s* 8*d* by the chamberlains for 'riding forth to espy for the town afore the field' and as soon as Henry's victory was assured a deputation was dispatched to procure a copy of his proclamation. In October Richard Nanfan, squire of the body, received 30*s* 'for a reward that should owe his good will to the town', and in March 1486 Henry VII himself visited Nottingham, being met a mile south of the Trent by the mayor and aldermen in their finery.[13] It was the beginning of a close and generally cordial relationship with the new Tudor dynasty. Henry VIII visited again in 1511 and placed an offering at the rood of the Carmelite friars. In 1525 his illegitimate son, Henry Fitzroy, was granted the ancient Earldom of Nottingham, along with other titles.[14]

Despite these marks of favour and a general harmony of interest between leading townsmen and the monarchy, all was not well. For some, the old Yorkist loyalties died hard. In 1495 John Lambton was alleged to have said that if the 'northern men' came south in support of Perkin Warbeck 'he might go with them'. More serious allegations were made against John Hewick, king's yeoman, in 1500, possibly the same John Howick, physician, who had been retained by Richard of Gloucester in 1483. Returning home after a spell in the royal service, curious friends and neighbours asked 'how he had done'. Hewick took some pride in the fact that he had spoken with the Queen, a daughter of Edward IV, 'and should have spoken more with her ... had not been for that strong whore, the King's mother ... with much other unfitting language'.[15] It is impossible to say to what extent opinions such as these were typical of grass-roots attitudes in the town, but such mutterings did not encourage the first two Tudors to maintain the Castle. This short-sighted policy was dramatically exposed in 1536 when the Lincolnshire Rising and the Pilgrimage of Grace erupted as a protest against Henry VIII's Reformation. The Castle, still vital in the context of a northern campaign, was hopelessly unprepared, with no artillery or garrison to speak of. With lingering fears of disloyalty in the town, especially concerning the monks of Lenton, it was left to the first Earl of Rutland to bring some order out of potential chaos. To his credit he not only successfully defended the Castle against possible attack by the rebels, but built it up once more as a base for the King's campaigns in Scotland in the 1540s. In all these conflicts the men of Nottingham dutifully played their parts. A detailed muster return of 1539 records, by street, the archers and billmen Nottingham could provide for the royal army; and in 1558 light horsemen were being kitted out for service on the borders, though it was argued they could not lawfully be diverted to fight in France.[16]

The 1449 Charter

The close harmony between Nottingham and the ruling dynasty was partly the result of a new charter the town received from Henry VI in 1449, granting it county borough status. In addition to a mayor the town was now to have an escheator, two sheriffs and seven aldermen, the latter elected by the burgesses. Once in office the aldermen served for life, had the status of JPs, and provided the pool from which the mayor was selected each Michaelmas Day.[17] This new 'inner ring' separated itself further from the main body of townspeople by distinctive dress and an increasingly ritualistic protocol. The Charter declared that they could wear scarlet fur-trimmed robes 'in the same manner and form as the mayor and aldermen of our city of London'. Subsequently a new guildhall was built at Weekday Cross, and the number of processions and civic services increased markedly. All of this was believed to be 'to the honour of God and conservation of good rule of the town' and even if the burgesses remained a force to be reckoned with when electing aldermen, the charter meant that they had lost a good deal of their customary influence in the vital mayor-making procedure. Between 1449 and 1560 local government became notably more oligarchical, and by that same token more easily influenced by the King, who periodically confirmed the borough privileges and whose authority the aldermen upheld as JPs.[18] Individuals such as Thomas Thurland, Thomas Mellers, John Williamson and John Rose were not only the wealthiest citizens, they were also the most politically active, deeply involved in almost every aspect of urban life. In 1534 David Cecil wrote gloomily to Cromwell about the situation in Nottingham 'where the King's laws are but smally regarded, except where they of the town bear favour'.[19]

The main difficulty faced by these new town fathers was to maintain their credibility with the King – which they did by lavish distribution of gifts and careful monitoring of political change – while opposing those forces which threatened to undermine the stability of the town (as they saw it) and their own vested interests. There were two particular threats, one external, the other internal, though at times they were closely linked. Towns, especially those which returned MPs, had always been vulnerable to the influence of ambitious magnates who were looking for ways to enhance their influence. In the troubled years of the fifteenth century this became entangled with so-called 'bastard feudalism' and was manifest by attempts on the part of the aristocracy and gentry to persuade townsmen to take their liveries, a move strongly opposed by corporations, since it implied the loss of control over their own citizens. In about 1463 it was decreed that a Nottingham burgess accepting a livery was to be disenfranchised, imprisoned and fined, a series of penalties which left no one in doubt as to the gravity of such offences.[20] Even so a trickle of burgesses always turned out to be bold or desperate enough to engage in acts of defiance, particularly during the uncertain circumstances of the civil wars.

In June 1471 Nottingham was shaken by a series of severe riots during which at least two men were killed, several people seriously injured and the mayor and sheriffs fired upon with arrows by individuals shouting 'Where are the traitors that will resist us? Let them come now and we will kill them.'[21] The instigators were possibly demobilised Yorkist soldiers, who wore the livery of Henry, Lord Grey of Codnor, an erstwhile Lancastrian who by 1471 had become a committed supporter of Edward IV. Between October 1470 and April 1471 Edward had suffered temporary deposition at the hands of Henry VI and the mayor, Robert English, had apparently given at least tentative support to the Lancastrian restoration, despite the broadly Yorkist sympathies of the town. By June 1471, when the riots broke out, Edward was once more firmly in control and loyal Yorkists were seeking revenge on those who had displayed ambivalence during the recent troubles – hence the rioters calling the mayor and sheriffs 'traitors'.

The aftermath gives further credence to this interpretation of events. The mayor, anxious to maintain his authority, complained to the King and worked through Lord Hastings, an implacable opponent of the Greys, to try to see justice done. In October 1471 both parties were heard before Edward himself in Star Chamber and were ordered to live in peace and harmony with one another. The King refused the mayor's request to send the rioters to prison, and ordered that the matter be dealt with by the town JPs. The case dragged on until April 1472 when the major protagonist, Thomas White, appeared with a royal pardon prohibiting the mayor and justices from molesting him further. Neither had Lord Grey's wings been clipped, because although the order of Star Chamber required him to make no more retainers in Nottingham, another four burgesses were prosecuted in 1495 for promising 'to serve him and to take his part against all persons'.[22] In the end the rioters, who had shown utter contempt for the authority of the mayor, escaped punishment and the corporation, faced with Crown inertia, had no redress.

Plate 11 **Sir Thomas Lovell, 1518**. Artist unknown. A man of considerable national and local influence Lovell, among other achievements, helped to defuse the urban crisis of 1512–13 and was involved with the foundation of the High School

Individuals other than Lord Grey attempted to retain citizens of Nottingham, but the issue died out in the early sixteenth century partly owing to stricter enforcement of Parliamentary legislation and partly because the town came under the influence of various individuals on whose merits the Crown and town fathers were in firm agreement. The first was Sir Thomas Lovell who, as Chancellor of the Exchequer, Constable of Nottingham Castle and Steward of Lenton Priory, spanned a range of key national and local offices. Next were his kinsmen Thomas and Henry Manners, successively first and second Earls of Rutland. The first Earl, a personal friend of Henry VIII and ennobled by him in 1525, was a capable military leader who dominated the town until his death in 1543. The second Earl successfully negotiated the troubled decade of the 1550s, deftly transferring his support from Lady Jane Grey to Queen Mary, and was Elizabeth's Lord President of the Council of the North when he died in 1563. Both were Constables of Nottingham Castle. The Earls of Rutland, in particular, were permitted considerable influence over the choice of MPs and they reciprocated by using their power at court to Nottingham's advantage.[23] Such mutual support, so evidently lacking in the case of Lord Grey, was vital in terms of the political aspirations of the town governors.

A second problem was less easily resolved because it concerned the perceived loss of power as a result of the new Charter by the main body of burgesses and the broader-based 'commonality'. Although the mayor and aldermen were vested with considerable executive authority, the burgesses and commons were still vital to the smooth running of the town, and by means of agencies such as the Mickletorn Jury and Common Halls, were capable of waging effective guerilla warfare against unpopular civic leaders. Their frustrations were expressed at fairly regular intervals, the years 1512–13, 1527 and 1553 being particularly notable. The targets were invariably leading aldermen such as Williamson, Rose and Mellers. They might be accused of making leases which were detrimental to the town, appointing corrupt or incompetent officers, or dealing in secret, even to the extent of unlawfully creating new aldermen.[24] In one bizarre instance in 1504 they were accused of rowdy and riotous behaviour, of dragging around the streets a barrel filled with stones at midnight, and causing terror to their slumbering neighbours. The accounts for the bridges and school were not 'made openly' and there was no information concerning expenses given to burgesses who attended Parliament 'for our money was therein as well as yours was and therefore it [is] convenient that we know'. Moreover, certain aldermen were using their positions of authority to evade the payment of subsidies to the King, putting their own interests before those of the town. But the most persistent complaint was that mayors and aldermen, whose livelihoods were tied up with the food and drink trades, were not enforcing legislation to regulate prices 'by reason whereof the town hath been greatly disordered'.[25]

These disorders came closest to anarchy in 1512–13 when Common Halls claimed the right to depose and elect aldermen and other officers, a privilege which was quite at odds with the Charter but which reflected contemporary upheavals. The 'inner ring' was united in its opposition to these democratic aspirations. Thomas Babington, the recorder, wrote ominously to the mayor, 'if ye shall suffer the commons to rule and follow their appetite and desire, farewell all good order'. Sir Thomas Lovell took an even tougher stance, asking for the conspirators' names so that they might be given some 'condign punishment' which would 'not be to their contentment'.[26] Such reactions seem to have defused the situation and though the attacks on the oligarchs continued, no fresh attempt was made by the commons to make and break mayors before 1560. The main weakness of the charter was that it did not define the role of the burgesses and commons in the corporation or make the ruling cabal accountable to the broad mass of citizens. These loopholes were subsequently mercilessly exploited, to the discomfort of Nottingham's elite. Moreover, the divisions could be seized upon by mischief-makers, as Lord Grey had done in the fifteenth century and the Prior of Lenton was to attempt in the sixteenth.

Town life

The routine preoccupations of town government – the pursuit of territorial disagreements, the regulation of trade and the maintenance of the bridges over the Trent and Leen – continued virtually unaltered. What was new, perhaps, and reflected the desire for 'good rule', was an increased effort directed against patterns of perceived anti-social behaviour which it was believed might undermine the moral basis or economic well-being of the community. In 1463 the corporation approved a comprehensive set of orders directed against prostitutes, brothels and disorderly alehouses, identified as those receiving 'suspicious persons' or open after nine o'clock at night. This did little good: disordered houses continued to be exposed at an alarming rate (eighteen in 1484 alone) and citizens were presented for engaging in a wide range of unlawful games including dice, bowls, cards, penny-prick and slide-groat.[27] One fear was that too much pleasure would wean people away from the discipline of work and as early as 1482 two men were presented because 'they do wander about unemployed ... and will not work although they be able in body to labour'.[28] After 1530 there was much concern about vagrants and 'valiant beggars', and the issue divided the community. Some people encouraged the vagrants because of cheap labour or the quick and illicit profits which could be made by lodging them: Alice Fyllypsun was in trouble for slandering the town in 1530 and again in 1534 for lodging vagrants and thieves 'and that she roasts them capons and hens at night the which be stolen from true men's houses'.[29] In 1540–41 a scheme was started to provide badges for the deserving poor to separate them from such deviants, but there was constant concern that mayors, justices and constables were not doing enough to identify the rogues 'for the town is not able to relieve them'.[30]

Institutional religion, the origin of many of the moral imperatives directed against whores and vagrants, was well represented in the town. Indeed, it provided another vital prop to the corporation's authority. The three parish churches attracted some outstanding incumbents, many with distinguished academic careers or who as canon lawyers were involved in the diocesan administration. John Hurt, vicar of St Mary's (1462–77), and William Gull, rector of St Peter's (1445–84), were both Cambridge Doctors of Divinity and had colluded in the foundation of God's House, later Christ's College, of which Hurt was Master between 1454 and 1462. Gull had preceded his time at Nottingham by twenty-five years as Master of Clare Hall and Hurt's will, drawn up in 1476, itemised a valuable library which was disbursed around a number of Cambridge colleges.[31] Much routine pastoral work was carried out by anonymous curates and cantarists, the latter linked to the plethora of chantry foundations dating from the fourteenth century onwards. Yet the presence of high-profile clerics gave the town status in the context of late medieval religious life and added credibility to the authority of the 'inner ring' members who rubbed shoulders with the clergy on civic occasions.

The three parish churches were objects of communal pride, and the impressive rebuilding of St Mary's had turned it into a church of considerable stature.[32] On the eve of the Reformation building work was taking place in all three churches and at the Carmelite friary.[33] Legacies were by no means unusual to support this work, both in terms of structural improvement and decorative embellishment, and occasionally an element of competition can be detected in the relationship between 'rival' parishes. Upset by what he saw as an undue emphasis on the beautification of St Peter's, John Rose willed in 1528 that his executors 'shall cause to make the best cross now belonging or being in the foresaid church of Our Blessed Lady St Mary to be of more value that [*sic*] the best cross in St Peter church in Nottingham in the sum of ten ounces of silver'.[34] Church giving of this sort was not wholly altruistic since it was often linked directly or indirectly to requests for *obits* or prayers for the soul, a means whereby the benefactor hoped to shorten his or her passage through the uncertain realms of purgatory. The wills of Thomas Thurland (1470) and John Williamson (1529) provide good examples of leading citizens whose charitable concerns were closely connected, effectively, with the purchase of salvation.[35]

For poorer people, in addition to the framework created by the parish churches, religious enthusiasm is best seen in the guilds and confraternities of which Nottingham had several, although not a high-status Corpus Christi guild to match those of York and Retford.[36] From a remarkable documentary survival, the account books of the guilds of St George and St Mary in St Peter's Church, it is possible to piece together the important social and economic function of such groups in the hundred years before the Reformation.[37] Membership was open to men and women for an entrance fee and an annual subscription. The guild member was entitled to wear a special livery and to participate in a regular round of functions such as the Corpus Christi Day procession and the theatrical festivities, complete with a fierce canvas dragon, which marked St George's Day. These high days and holidays generally concluded with feasting and revelry, the members drinking in turn from a communal mazer bowl. In 1490 the guild received 2*s* 1*d* 'for the garbage and for the dregs of beer left from the aforesaid feast', evidently an occasion of some merriment. But the guild also had a more serious side. On a member's death the funeral was marked by conspicuous ceremonies involving vigils and the burning of torches, and the soul of the deceased person was prayed for by a chantry priest supported out of communal funds. The guild also carried out good works, such as the support of pilgrims and the poor, and it accounted for income drawn from a wide range of sources – comparable in scale to that handled by some of the town officers. This was organised and administered by an alderman and two wardens elected from the members. Such involvement gave those in the middle ranks of society – increasingly alienated by the 1449 charter – a sense of civic responsibility and experience in the mechanics of corporate management. Even more importantly, it provided a broad mass of people with a sense of focus and social cohesion based on the generally accepted values of late medieval Catholicism. In 1500 the wardens had to pay 4s to a glazier 'for mending divers holes in divers windows … broken by insolent boys', but this was a comment on the unchanging exuberance of youth rather than an attack on the fundamental principles which the Nottingham guilds upheld.[38]

The atmosphere in the town before 1530 was steeped in ideologies which stemmed from the received notions of the Catholic faith, and there is no evidence that these had been seriously undermined by apathy or by the teachings of the Lollard heresy. Indeed, the town had a reputation for the production of alabaster religious imagery sold in England and abroad.[39] Devotional objects were commonplace. Margaret Allestre owned a gold ring with engraved images and a piece bearing the names of the Three Kings of Cologne, a sure safeguard against the falling sickness.[40] Hethbeth Bridge was still partly supported by alms given to licensed collectors as an act of piety; and when the town and Henry Pierrepont finally patched up their territorial squabbles in 1467, oath-taking in St Mary's Church was regarded as a prominent feature of the settlement procedure. The bonds between Nottingham's citizens and the Catholic faith were long and deep. It was with evident pride that William Turner, mercer, left his son five yards of cloth in 1521 made by his mother's own hand 'to make him a gown and a hood at such time as he shall be priest, and, by the grace of God, sing his first Mass'.[41]

Plate 12 **Agnes Mellers**. Widow of a bellfounder, her deep sense of personal piety and belief in the efficacy of education was marked by the foundation of Nottingham High School on Stoney Street, in 1512

These themes of conservative religious practice, charitable giving and a preoccupation with the afterlife are best drawn together in the person of Agnes Mellers, the widow of Richard Mellers, a bellfounder and 'inner ring' member. On her husband's death in 1507 Agnes became a 'vowess', a gesture of lay piety which pledged her to remain unmarried and devote her life to pious causes. It was a promise she took seriously. In 1512, with the support of Sir Thomas Lovell, she procured a licence from Henry VIII to re-establish a grammar school at Nottingham. A grammar school had been established before 1382 when William of Adbolton, *scolemaystre* or 'master of the grammar school', held property in St Mary's Gate, or Bellar Gate. By 1430 Thomas Ridley, clerk and master of the school, owed rent for the *scolehous*, which may have closed shortly afterwards.[42] In line with the accepted educational priorities of the day the refounded school had a curriculum based rigidly on the classics, spiced with a generous measure of Roman Catholic theology and prayers for the souls of the founders. But Widow Mellers managed to persuade a wide range of local people to support the scheme, and a list of 'divers well disposed persons' who had given lands and money for the support of the school included sponsors contributing sums ranging from 4*d* to 10*s*. With the corporation, in effect, nominated as the governing body, it was a remarkable instance of broad-based support for new-style education merged with old-style soul praying. Some townsmen followed the educational lead enthusiastically, although there were to be growing doubts about the soul praying. When John Williamson made his will in 1529 he ordered that his son should be sent to 'some good school' until he was fifteen; to Oxford or Cambridge until he was twenty; and then to the Inns of Court until he was twenty-four – the archetypal Tudor gentleman.[43] Agnes Mellers, intellectually steeped in the old order, had done as much as anyone to broaden the social and educational horizons of her neighbours. If there is a single figure who, Janus-like, links Medieval and modern Nottingham, then it is surely her.

Despite these notable instances of piety and conformity, it would be wrong to assume that all was well in the relationship between Church and people in the town. The hospitals were a particular area of concern. Although the corporation continued to nominate masters of St Leonard's until 1534 there is no evidence that the appointment was anything more than sinecure; and at St John's similar apathy had set in, the master and chaplains being said to have abandoned the place in about 1529 and the support of the poor having lapsed. At Plumptre's Hospital the story was the same – 'although the foundation hereof was to be an hospital for the relief of the poor, yet a priest hath the whole revenue thereof and the poor thereby nothing relieved'.[44] These difficulties were partly a result of the late medieval obsession with soul praying, in that endowments were being directed to this purpose rather than the relief of the poor. Indeed, itinerant hucksters regularly tried to persuade local people to join fraternities as far afield as London, Warwick and Ripon, all in fervent competition for the concessions offered to their members' souls after death. While the rival pardoners squabbled over their collecting areas and membership lists, George Bredon was quietly embezzling 11*s* 6*d* collected for the parish light of St Mary's, which became evident only after his death in 1512.[45] Such dishonesty was not the exclusive preserve of the laity. At some time before 1536 the priest in charge of the chapel on Hethbeth Bridge had sold all of the altar plate and ornaments, forcing his successors to go cap-in-hand to Sir John Byron to borrow the equipment for the services.[46]

Possibly the most serious concerns were bound up with the regular clergy. In 1500 and 1522 wardens of the Greyfriars were accused of procuring women for sexual favours. In 1532 Richard Sherwood, Prior of the Carmelites, killed one of his brethren, William Bacon, with a blow meted out in a drunken disagreement. He received a royal pardon, but the circumstances of the case could hardly have inspired confidence in those who looked to such as Sherwood for an example. Indeed, it is surprising, given the accusations levelled against the friars, that they were the recipients of so many legacies, in sharp contrast to the monks of Lenton who received virtually none.[47] Lenton's unpopularity was tied up with economic privilege, particularly the fact that during Lenton Fair normal trading in Nottingham was suspended for eight days.[48] By 1516 there was said to have been considerable 'strife and debate' over the issue and on 8 June this escalated dramatically and unexpectedly. Henry Steper, a Nottingham mercer who had taken the livery of the Prior of Lenton, attempted to assassinate the Mayor, Thomas Mellers, while he was dining at the home of John Williamson. Steper's precise motives are now impossible to determine, but the incident seems to have concentrated the minds of the warring factions on reaching a settlement and on 8 August an arbitration, worked out by Sir Thomas Lovell, was agreed upon.[49] It kept the peace in the short term, but whether it allayed the deep-seated hostility to some of Lenton's aspirations is another question altogether.

The Reformation

The Henrician Reformation of the 1530s was primarily the result of practical considerations connected with Henry VIII's desire to annul his marriage to Catherine of Aragon and marry Anne Boleyn. Even so, it unleashed anti-Catholic rhetoric, and local people did not have to look far to discover their own examples of neglect and corruption, and the abuse of privilege by the clergy. Lenton was particularly vulnerable. The priory first endured unwelcome scrutiny in September 1534 when it was visited by the mysterious confidence trickster or government informer, James Billingford, who made a number of cryptic allegations to Thomas Cromwell, principally that 'the King has no such mortal enemies as the abbots and priors'. In December 1535 Cromwell acceded to Sir Anthony Babington's request and intervened to have Nicholas Heath appointed as prior. Heath was a religious conservative who promised Richard Cromwell, the Secretary's nephew, £100 for the favour, but failed to provide the full amount since he claimed that the house 'is not of so clear state as I thought my predecessor had left it'. Consequently, Cromwell had at least two reasons to be gravely suspicious of Lenton and when one of its monks, Hamlet

Pentrich, apostatised in 1536 and again in 1537, his stories of dubious goings-on were readily heard. Pentrich, who was believed to have been encouraged by some local people 'who love not this poor house', alleged that treasonable conversations had taken place in 1536, the year of the Pilgrimage of Grace. In one a monk called Ralph Swenson had said of the King following the rebellion 'he that will not keep no promise with God himself but pulls down his churches he will not keep promise with them [i.e. the rebels]; but if they had gone forth onward up and stricken off his head then had they done well'.[50] Worse still, the Prior was reported to have said of Henry following his marriage to Jane Seymour, 'The devil is in him for he is past grace: he will never amend in this world. I warrant him [to] have as shameful a death as ever King had in England. A vengeance on him!'.[51]

Damning though these statements seemed, there is some evidence that Cromwell was uncertain what to do – Pentrich was hardly the ideal witness – but since he was eager to pressurise larger monasteries into submitting to voluntary surrenders, the charges were held on file.[52] In February 1538 Prior Heath, along with seven of his monks and a secular priest, were tried at Nottingham and charged with treason. All the defendants were found guilty, although only three, including Heath and Swenson, were sentenced to death. The judges were fêted with two gallons of wine after the trial and one Ross was paid 2*d* for cleaning Cow Lane, the site of the executions.[53] Since the priory was dissolved by attainder, the remaining monks were expelled without pensions and the site and lands were seized by the Crown, a salutary warning to others.[54] Why did Lenton perish in this singular and highly dramatic fashion? Certainly, there had been loose talk amongst the monks, but this was probably no worse than had gone on undetected or unpunished elsewhere. The notion of a conspiracy initiated from Nottingham, attractive thought it might be, is unproven. The most likely explanation of events is tied up with the Pilgrimage of Grace and with Nottingham's importance as a front-line base during and after the rebellion. The rebels had high hopes of achieving support in Nottingham – Lenton may even have been a focus of their ambitions – yet from the King's point of view it was essential that the loyalty of the town was guaranteed and any possible centres of resistance rooted out.[55] Heath and Swenson suffered on the anvil of political expediency rather than as true martyrs to the faith.

Following the brutal suppression of Lenton, the last stages of the dissolution passed off relatively peacefully. Early in 1539 Dr Thomas London requested a commission to take the surrenders of the friars in Nottingham and elsewhere 'for they would fain be gone and the longer they do tarry, the more waste they do make'. London got his wish. On 5 February the Franciscan and Carmelite friaries signed voluntary surrenders and their fifteen inmates were turned out into pensioned retirement.[56] In 1547 it was the turn of the chantries, guilds and confraternities and also hospitals, since the soul-praying provision incorporated at their establishment was now deemed unlawful. The Chantry Certificates provide a sometimes poignant picture of these institutions during their last days. Their properties were small and their priests were classified universally as 'unlearned', but the chantry commissioners conceded the assistance the cantarists had given to the overworked local clergy.[57] With these endowments stripped away, the parish clergy were never again to enjoy this valuable assistance in the day-to-day management of parochial affairs.

Plate 13 **St Anthony's Chapel, Lenton**. Formerly serving a hospital annexed to Lenton Priory, this building became a parish church after the Reformation and is the most substantial surviving fragment of the once-great monastery. Other fragments were used in the foundations of Wollaton Hall

Who were the beneficiaries of the secularisation of so much church property in Nottingham? Lenton, with possessions valued at almost £330, represented the lion's share, but these went almost exclusively to individuals unconnected with the town. Major long-term beneficiaries of Nottingham properties were the courtier, Sir Michael Stanhope, William Statham and William Fitzwilliam. Thomas Heneage obtained the more modest property of the Franciscans, and James Strelley that of the Carmelites, converting the old friary into a residence. The bulk of the chantry property – mostly houses, shops and gardens in Nottingham itself – went to John Howe of London and John Broxholme of Louth Park, Lincolnshire, as part of a job lot costing over £1,500. There is little direct evidence of citizens of the town benefiting, unless it was by purchasing from Howe and Broxholme; indeed, when the corporation petitioned the King for the small windfall of the advowson of Barton-in-Fabis, part of Lenton's property, a commission of inquiry was appointed and in 1542 it was ruled that it should be enjoyed by the Archbishop of York.[58] The only exception was a grant made in 1551 to the corporation of the hospital of St John and the chantry of St Mary in St Mary's Church. These properties, valued at £14 15*s* 6*d*, were given to the town with the specific intention of maintaining the bridges over the Trent, a far-sighted if not over-generous move, since the Protestant Reformation had undermined the tendency to pious almsgiving which had helped sustain these important structures for centuries. But even this could not be enjoyed without a struggle. Thomas Webster, the last Master of St John's, alleged that the corporation had misrepresented the Hospital's state of decay and he complained to Chancery in 1553 and to the High Commission in 1561, alleging that it should never have been dissolved. He was ultimately unsuccessful. The only medieval religious institution to survive the storm was Plumptre's Hospital, taken into the King's hands in 1549 and allowed to live on though with its charitable provision shorn of its 'popish' prayers for the dead.[59]

Evidence for the extent of Protestant commitment in the Reformation changes which beset Nottingham prior to 1560 is ambiguous. In July 1523 Richard Taverner, vicar of St Mary's and official of the Archdeacon of Nottingham, was berated in church by Robert Taylor, a shoemaker, who spoke 'malicious and contemptuous words' against him. In 1530 Taverner was again in the firing line, this time for taking excessive and extortionate fees for grants of probate and for over-assessing poor people and servants for tithe, a complaint which was also levelled against 'Sir Christopher', parish priest of St Peter's.[60] If this was an instance of the anti-clericalism Henry was anxious to whip up in the early stage of the Reformation, it did not develop into a sustained attack on the local clergy who, in general, held firm during the bewildering religious changes which characterised the reigns of Edward VI and Mary. The most remarkable incumbent to serve during this period was John Plough, who succeeded his uncle and namesake as rector of St Peter's in 1539. Plough was a man of real Protestant zeal who fled to Basle on Mary's accession and was the author of several polemical tracts, principally *An Apology for the Protestants*. However, like some of his Catholic predecessors, his local influence may be questioned. During his time at Nottingham his attentions were diverted by his studies at Oxford and by a living he held in plurality in Hertfordshire; and just as he was making a major impact in reformist circles, he resigned St Peter's in 1550.[61]

There were those, no doubt, who were sorry to see him go, but Nottingham, like the nation at large, was sharply divided in its religious loyalties. Francis Colman, the town clerk, and Nicholas Powtrell, recorder, shared Plough's Protestantism; but Humphrey Quarnby, bellfounder and one of the town's MPs in 1553 and 1554, was a religious conservative who did nothing in Parliament to oppose Mary's restoration of Catholicism, despite the fact that he had already profited from the Reformation by purchasing a bell from the dissolved Franciscan friary and obtaining a grant of some tithes belonging to Beauchief Abbey.[62] Apparent contradictions such as these were a feature of the age, brought about partly by genuine confusion and partly by the inevitable conflict of interest between individual conscience and expectations of loyalty to the Crown, which were deeply engrained. When Elizabeth Gellesthrop made her will in 1543 she left money for a light in St Mary's Church, but only 'if the laws of the realm will it permit and suffer'; and in 1545 Richard Willoughby, an alderman, created a preamble to his will which sums up the doubts which beset his mind over the important question of salvation. He left his soul to God: 'the maker and redeemer of the same, most humbly beseeching him that through the merits of his bitter death and passion that I may be one of his elect and chosen in heaven, and for succore and help thereunto I beseech Our Blessed Lady and all holy saints to pray for me'.[63] It was a formula which would have satisfied both Cranmer and Gardiner, a circumspect pronouncement of personal faith in a deeply divided age.

If Nottingham was a conforming community rather than one which ran forcefully with the tide in either a Protestant or Catholic direction, this character was in part moulded by the first and second Earls of Rutland who were both notable religious conformists, upholding the interests of the Tudor dynasty over and above the vagaries of doctrinal change. The dominant MPs during these years were Sir John Markham and his sons, Thomas and William. Sir John, a staunch supporter of Henry VIII and a well-known soldier, became noted for his Protestantism, Cranmer once describing him as one who 'hath unfeignedly favoured the truth of God's word'. Yet, like their Manners, patrons, the Markhams mended their fences under Mary only to re-emerge with renewed vigour after 1558.[64] Beneath the veneer of conformity the real loyalties of the Earls of Rutland and their followers may have slanted towards Protestantism and the new settlement of religion finalised by Elizabeth in 1559. This might serve as an epitaph for Nottingham, which was well aware of the benefits of obedience, but also of the high price that might be paid for disloyalty.

Notes

1 *Letters and Papers Foreign and Domestic of the Reign of Henry VIII* (hereafter *LP*), 2 (1515–18), pp. 1258, 1263.

2 Based on *Wills in the York Registry*, Yorkshire Archaeological Association Record Series, 6, 11, 14. I am grateful to Terry Bourne for help with this analysis.

3 *LP* 4 (1524–34), p. 421.

4 E. L. Guilford, 'Extracts from the records of the Borough of Nottingham', *TTS*, 26 (1922), pp. 23–4.

5 E. L. Guilford, 'Extracts from the records of the Borough of Nottingham', *TTS*, 29 (1925), pp. 68–80; S. N. Mastoris, 'A tax assessment of 1504 and the topography of early Tudor Nottingham', *TTS*, 89 (1985), pp. 41–56; *RBN*, III pp. 163–81.

6 J. Cornwall (ed.), *The County Community under Henry VIII* (Rutland Record Series, 1, 1980), pp. 5, 12–13.

7 Mastoris, 'Tax assessment', pp. 37–9. The 1609 and 1610 maps are analysed in ch. 7.

8 R. R. Laxton *et al*, 'Nottinghamshire houses dated by dendrochronology', *TTS*, 99 (1995), pp. 47–52; A. Henstock, 'Late medieval building contracts for the Nottingham Area', *TTS*, 88 (1984), pp. 103–5.

9 *RBN*, III, pp. 69, 95; E. L.Guilford, 'Extracts from the records of the Borough of Nottingham', *TTS*, 27 (1923), pp. 53, 65; R. F. B.Hodgkinson and L. V. D. Owen (eds.), *The Account Books of the Gilds of St George and St Mary in the Church of St Peter, Nottingham* (*TSRS*, 7, 1939), p. 84.

10 *RBN*, II, pp. 430–2; III, pp. 458–66; IV, pp. 416–17.
11 *RBN*, II, pp. 257, 368–9.
12 Drage, *Castle*, pp. 54–9.
13 *RBN*, III, pp. 238, 245, 262, 263–4.
14 *LP*, 1 (1509–14), pp. 454, 464; 2 (1515–18), p. 1452; 4 (1524–30), 638–9.
15 *RBN*, III, pp. 300–1, 401.
16 Drage, *Castle*, pp. 66–7; *LP*, 11 (1536), p. 465; 20, (1545), pp. 253–4, 351, 369, 387; 14 (1539), p. 286; *RBN*, IV, pp. 121–3.
17 *Royal Charters Granted to the Burgesses of Nottingham, AD 1155–1712* (Nottingham, 1890), pp. 51–69.
18 *RBN*, II, pp. 299, 448–9; *Royal Charters*, pp. 79–83.
19 J. Raine (ed.), *Testamenta Eboracensia*, III (Surtees Society, 45, 1865), pp. 184–6; V (Surtees Society, 79, 1884), pp. 265–6, 278–80; J. W. Clay (ed.), *Testamenta Eboracensia*, VI (Surtees Society, 106, 1902), p. 50; *LP*, 7 (1534), p. 186.
20 *RBN*, II, p. 425.
21 *RBN*, II, p. 283.
22 Guilford, 'Extracts', *TTS*, 26, pp. 19–21; *RBN*, II, pp. 384–7; III, p. 37.
23 *DNB*, 12, pp. 175–6, 935–6, 941–2; Guilford, 'Extracts', *TTS*, 26, pp. 24–5.
24 *RBN*, II, p. 420; III, pp. 359–60; IV, pp. 106, 108, 111.
25 *RBN*, III, pp. 95–7, 359–60; IV, pp. 108, 110.
26 *RBN*, III, p. 341, 343.
27 *RBN*, II, pp. 325–7, 347–9, 425; III, pp. 79, 327–8, 337; IV, pp. 52, 102–3, 112.
28 *RBN*, II, p. 325.
29 *RBN*, III, p. 373.
30 *RBN*, III, pp. 374, 390, 399–499; IV, 112–13.
31 Raine (ed.), *Testamenta*, III, pp. 222; K. S. S Train (ed.), *Lists of the Clergy of Central Nottinghamshire* (*TSRS*, 15, part II 1954), pp. 29–30, 37–8, 43–4.
32 Pevsner and Williamson, pp. 219–24.
33 *RBN*, III, pp. 21, 33–5, 43; J. Raine (ed.), *Testamenta*, IV, (Surtees Society, 53, 1868), p. 34; V, pp. 136–7.
34 Raine (ed.), *Testamenta*, V, pp. 265–6.
35 Raine (ed.), *Testamenta*, III, pp. 184–6; V, pp. 278–80.
36 D. Marcombe, *English Small Town Life: Retford, 1520–1642* (Oxford, 1993), pp. 216–18.
37 Hodgkinson and Owen, *Account Books*, pp. 1–14.
38 *Ibid.*, pp. 23, 53, 68.
39 *RBN*, III, pp. 23, 29, 181–3.
40 Raine (ed.), *Testamenta*, IV, p. 64.
41 *RBN*, II, pp. 265–7, 380–4; III, p. 23; Raine (ed.), *Testamenta*, V, pp. 136–7.
42 NAO CA 1290 n1d; *RBN*, I, pp. 246–7, 262–3; II, pp. 122–3, 138–9.
43 *LP*, 1 (1509–14), p. 685; A. W. Thomas, *A History of Nottingham High School, 1513–1953* (Nottingham, 1957), pp. 13–26, 77, 86, 88–9, 286–90; Traine (ed.), *Testamenta*, V, pp. 41–2, 278–80.
44 *RBN*, III, pp. 151–5, 442; A. H. Thompson (ed.), 'The Chantry Certificate Rolls for the County of Nottingham', *TTS*, 18 (1914), pp. 94–8, 107–8, 111.
45 *RBN*, III, pp. 119–21, 149, 151, 157, 191.
46 'Chantry Certificate Rolls', pp. 101–2.
47 *RBN*, III, pp, 75, 147, 153–4, 355; *LP*, 5 (1531–32), p. 485; Traine (ed.), *Testamenta*, III, p. 184; V, p. 266. Thomas Thurland was one of very few Nottingham citizens who left money to Lenton.
48 *RBN*, III, pp. 135–7; J. T. Godfrey, *The History of the Parish and Priory of Lenton* (1884), pp. 141–2; P. Grieg, 'The layout of Lenton fairground, 1516', *TTS*, 96 (1992), pp. 130–4.
49 *RBN*, III, pp. 9, 345–52, 423.
50 *LP*, 7 (1534), pp. 238, 247, 606, 636; 8 (1535), pp. 27, 30; 9 (1535), p. 367; 10 (1536), p. 261 (also printed in *LP*, 5, p. 440, but with the incorrect date), 514; 12 (1537), pp. 398, 414, 601.
51 G .R. Elton, *Policy and Police* (Cambridge, 1972), p. 359.

52 *Ibid.*, pp. 359–60; F. A. Gasquet, *Henry VIII and the English Monasteries* (1893), 2, pp. 189–91; D. Knowles, *The Religious Orders in England* (Cambridge, 1961), 3, pp. 372–3.

53 *RBN*, III, pp. 376–7; *LP*, 13 (1538), pp. 225, 294; Godfrey, *Lenton*, p. 191.

54 *LP*, 13 (1538), p. 502; 14 (1539), p. 402.

55 The rebels had requested a Parliament at York or Nottingham, indicating that they expected some sympathy in those towns: *LP*, 11 (1536), p. 507.

56 *LP*, 14 (1539), pp. 4, 92; A. Stapleton, *The Churches and Monasteries of Old and New Nottingham* (Nottingham, 1903), pp. 154, 169.

57 'Chantry Certificate Rolls', pp. 94–114.

58 J. Caley (ed.), *Valor Ecclesiasticus* (1825), 5, pp. 147–9; *LP*, 14 (1539), pp. 76, 160, 161; 15 (1540), pp. 294, 326, 344; 16 (1540–41), p. 643. See also F. A. Barnes, 'Lenton Priory after the Dissolution; its buildings and fairgrounds', *TTS*, 91 (1987), pp. 80–93; Godfrey, *Lenton*, pp. 214–20; Stapleton, *Churches and Monasteries*, pp. 155, 170; *CPR* 1548–49, 2, p. 235.

59 *CPR* 1550–53, 4, p. 128; Stapleton, *Churches and Monasteries*, pp. 110–12, 200.

60 *RBN*, III, pp. 159–61, 364.

61 *Lists of the Clergy*, p. 44; C.H. Garrett, *The Marian Exiles* (Cambridge, 1938), p. 252; *DNB*, 15, p. 1312; J. W. Clay (ed.), *North Country Wills* (Surtees Society, 116, 1908), pp. 157–8.

62 S. T. Bindoff, *The House of Commons, 1509–1558* (1982), I, pp. 677–8; III, pp. 144–5, 166; *LP*, 16 (1540–1), p. 724; Stapleton, *Churches and Monasteries*, p. 155.

63 *RBN*, III, p. 395; Clay (ed.), *Testamenta*, VI, p. 220.

64 Bindoff, *Commons*, II, pp. 568–71.

Part II

EARLY MODERN NOTTINGHAM

7

THE CHANGING FABRIC OF THE TOWN, 1550–1750

Adrian Henstock

Visitors during the reign of Elizabeth I approached Nottingham along a road from the multi-arched Trent Bridge across the flood plain occupied by the town's common meadowlands.[1] This route was the main approach from Leicester, London and the south. The town, on its low cliff a mile north of the River Trent, was dominated by the Castle, now a decaying medieval structure perched on its dramatic rock. Adjoining the Castle was the deer park, still stocked with fallow deer until at least the mid-seventeenth century. To the north of the town, beyond the line of its ruined town walls, were the two common arable fields separated by the road to Mansfield and York as far as the ridge which formed the boundary of the town's lands. Beyond were stretches of unenclosed rough grazing interspersed between the village fields of Basford and Arnold, vestigial fragments of the once extensive wastes of Sherwood Forest, which was still a royal possession. Some three miles from the town lay the large royal hunting park of Bestwood Park, containing a hunting lodge and a sizeable herd of deer (324 in 1594); by the end of the century its stocks of timber were being exhausted and enclosed land was being given over to raising crops or rearing cattle and horses.[2] To the north-east part of the Forest towards Mapperley rose to nearly 400 feet above sea level. Here two large coppiced woods within the borough boundary were called Nottingham Coppices, and were still 'well stored with oakes and underwood' as late as 1641. Fallow deer also grazed in the area, and frequently invaded the town's cornfields in summer and gardens in winter.

The main road to Derby and the north-west left the town through Chapel Bar, climbed over the ridge and then skirted the edge of the private deer park of the Willoughby family at Wollaton. This park was to be graced from the 1580s with one of the most magnificent 'prodigy houses' of Elizabethan England; its unique central prospect tower, prominently sited on the top of a hill, could be seen for miles around.[3] Nearby – at Wollaton and Strelley, and around Bramcote – were coal mines which brought both riches and ruin to the Willoughbys and their fellow speculators the Strelleys, Zouches and Beaumonts during the latter part of Elizabeth's reign.[4] To the east another road led towards the minster town of Southwell, with a branch to Newark and Lincoln. By the late seventeenth century the course of the latter route ran alongside the north bank of the Trent from Burton Joyce for some eight miles before crossing it by the ferries at Hoveringham and Bleasby.[5]

Although the forest land to the north of the town was suited mainly to stock rearing and some poor arable farming, the Trent floodplain, together with the broad Vale of Belvoir some ten miles away to the south-east, afforded a good surplus of corn. Much of this – whether wheat for bread or barley for malting – found its way to Nottingham's markets. The abundance of this area's produce was remarked on in 1641; and Richard Franck, a visitor in 1654, even claimed that the town was the 'inland mart and storehouse of Great Britain' for both corn and malt.[6]

The Elizabethan and early Stuart town

The earliest topographical description of Nottingham was by John Leland, who wrote in the 1540s that 'Nottingham is booth a large town and welle buildid for tymber and plaster, and standith stately on a clyminge hille'. He was especially appreciative of the market-place; its size, its clean paving and its buildings he considered combined to make it 'the most fairest without exception of al Inglande'. The antiquary William Camden visited in 1598 and later described Nottingham as 'a towne seated most pleasant and delicate upon a high hill, for buildings stately and number of faire streets surpassing and surmounting many other cities, and for a spacious and most faire Market Place doth compare with the best'.[7] Richard Corbett in *c.*1620 remarked on the fine 'churches and houses, buildings stone and wood'; John Taylor in 1632 commented on the 'faire buildings, many large streetes and a spacious Market Place'. Distinctive features of the town noted by nearly every visitor from Leland onwards were the caves. Some of these, particularly in the narrow climbing street aptly called Hollow Stone, were used as dwellings; as this was the main approach into the town for travellers from London and the south the excavations made an instant impression. Corbett penned several poetical lines about this area 'where gardens cover houses' and repeated the strong local rumour that the 'powder-traitors', i.e. Guy Fawkes and his fellow conspirators, had practised their undermining skills in the rock of Nottingham.[8] Both Corbett and John Evelyn in 1654 also commented on the number of crosses in the town. Four of these were depicted on John Speed's town plan of 1610 which, together with a plan drawn on a 1609 Crown Survey map of the southern part of Sherwood Forest, provide the earliest cartographic representations of Nottingham.[9]

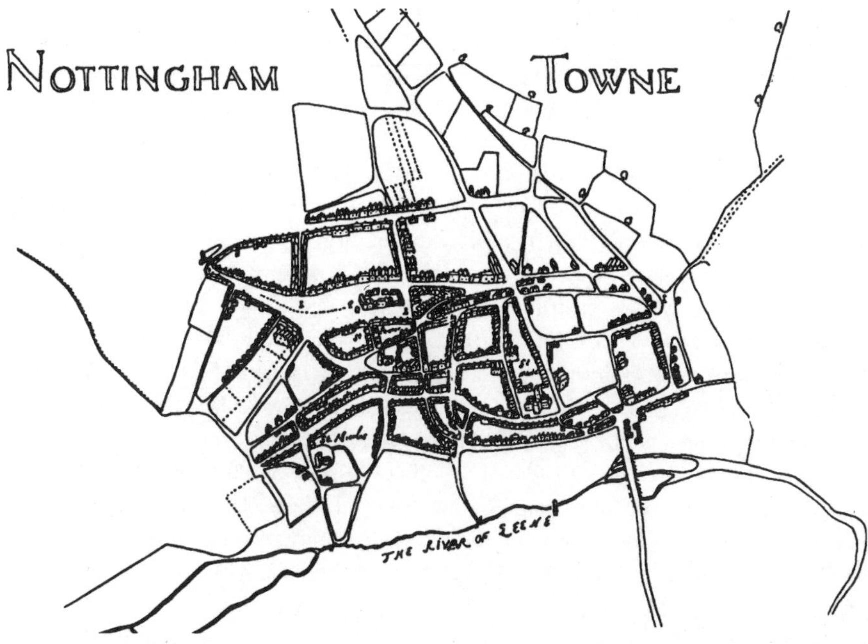

Plate 14 **Nottingham, 1609**. The earliest detailed map of the town, prepared for the Crown Survey of Sherwood Forest. It differs in some significant details from John Speed's better-known map of 1610, but both depict the town from a 'bird's-eye' perspective and buildings are shown in a stylised form. Development beyond the medieval limits of the town is shown along Backside, running west–east along the north side of the town, and forming a wide bypass route around the north and east of the town for use by coal wagons *en route* to the riverside wharfs at Trent Bridge

Continual robbing of the town walls for building stone resulted in their virtual disappearance; in 1625 a citizen was prosecuted for demolishing part of the wall near Chapel Bar and appropriating it to his own use. However the ancient town gateways of Chapel Bar (demolished 1743) and Cow Lane Bar (demolished 1649), as well as the small postern gate at the top of Vault Lane (later Drury Hill), still survived. Backside (now Parliament Street) had been formed to the east and west of Cow Lane Bar by the amalgamation of two narrow lanes on either side of the former wall. A small island site to the west of the Bar 'on the Backside upon the towne wall, nowe builded on' was sold into private hands in 1625. It survived until 1884.[10] Backside was part of a route around the north and east sides of the town used by heavy commercial traffic; by 1576 another section of this route was known as Coalpit Lane.[11] There was no comparable development on the Meadows south of the River Leen on the Trent floodplain. This is hardly surprisingly since, as Leland remarked, 'when any land waters cum doune, much of the vale and medowis ther be over flowen'.[12]

Within the town limits development was uneven. The two main focal points were the spacious Saturday market-place and the smaller Weekday Market. Near the latter on High Pavement were the major administrative buildings – the Guildhall or Town Hall and the Shire or County Hall – as well as the town's largest church, St Mary's. The two areas were linked by the main north–south street, Bridlesmith Gate. To the east of Stoney Street together with the whole north-east sector of the old English Borough was an area virtually devoid of building, probable evidence of late medieval shrinkage. There was also an empty area at the west end of Friar Lane and St James's Lane.

By 1609–10 both market-places had been partially infilled with permanent buildings which had gradually replaced temporary stalls. Near the Weekday Cross a row of permanent butchers' shambles divided the area into two alleys (later known as Blowbladder Street). The east end of the Saturday Market was taken over by a mass of permanent shambles and other stalls, some of them two-storeyed and divided by a series of alleys. The open market-place contained a Hen Cross, Butter Cross and a Malt Cross as well as the town's stocks and pillory; the whole space was divided into two by a low market wall (probably intended to separate the livestock from the other commodities). The Saturday market-place was the commercial centre of the town, and there was competition for properties on the favourable north side – Long Row; numerous outbuildings, workshops, stables and cottages had been built in the narrow yards which ran back up the slope from Long Row towards Backside.

The town plans show several larger properties of medieval origin such as the Plumptre Hospital in Fisher Gate and St John's Hospital on Backside, the latter converted into a House of Correction. The former White Friary is shown between Friar Lane and St James's Lane; following the Dissolution this had eventually passed to the Manners family and in 1574 John Manners of Haddon Hall had constructed a small mansion out of the old buildings.[13] It was the Manners' ownership which preserved the land to the west of the Friary from development until the nineteenth century. The other Friary site – the Grey Friars south of Broad Marsh – was also occupied by a rebuilt mansion, in this case with a large walled garden stretching down to the River Leen.

Although it is not prominently featured on the plans the largest private house in the town was Thurland Hall, a fifteenth-century merchant's residence in Gridlesmith Gate (now Pelham Street). By late Elizabethan times this was used as an occasional town house by Sir Francis Willoughby of Wollaton; here in 1587 he entertained the Earl of Rutland, the Archbishop of York and sundry gentry before showing off his newly-completed country seat at Wollaton. Thurland Hall came into the hands of the Stanhopes and from them was inherited in *c.*1613 by John Holles, 1st Earl of Clare. As the only house in Nottingham large enough to accommodate a royal retinue, it was used to entertain King James I on most if not all his six royal visits between 1612 and 1624, and also Charles I in 1634 and 1642. The frequency of these visits may have prompted Clare to rebuild the house, probably in the 1630s. In 1633–34 part of it collapsed as a result of members of the royal party lighting a fire in the tennis court. By the 1670s the building was a large three-storey brick structure with stone facings built around a quadrangle.[14]

The presence of other smaller town mansions of the urban or country gentry can be inferred from a combination of cartographic and archival evidence. On Stoney Street near St Mary's Church was a house probably belonging to the Plumptre family, and there was another to the east of St Mary's Gate (opposite the end of Pilcher Gate) owned by the Stanhopes. In 1613 Sir Edward Stanhope's house with its 'furniture, wainscot and hangings' was let for over £13. Adjacent was a garden, apparently surrounded by a stone wall, a stable and four 'chambered' tenements with gardens, built by Stanhope some thirty years earlier. In 1632 Sir Thomas Hutchinson had a house on the south side of High Pavement west of the Shire Hall.[15]

Elsewhere in the town centre most of the houses were two- or three-storeyed timber-framed structures, many – like the Guildhall or the 'Severns' building on Middle Pavement – of medieval origin.[16] Some, like 'Severns', stood side-on to the street, but most stood end-on, presenting a single, double or occasionally a triple gable end to the street. The upper floor of both two- or three-storeyed buildings was usually a half-storey – an attic under the roof pitch. Typically each succeeding floor would be jettied out over the one below, as can still be seen in one surviving single-gable three-and-a-half-storey building in Bridlesmith Gate.

As in most towns, there was an increasing tendency for new buildings to encroach forward on to the common highway, either with steps, palings, pillars or even small shop-fronts. From the 1620s such encroachments were reported by the Mickletorn Jury, which regularly perambulated the town in the style of a manorial court jury. Most encroachments were accepted providing that a fine or rent was paid to the corporation. In 1621 a presentment was made for 'setting a bulke [shop] too far into the street', and in 1630 a resident was presented for 'making a shop before his house in Broad Marsh end'. In High Pavement three wealthy citizens – Mr Dyvall, Mrs Martyn and Serjeant Boun – were all presented in 1626–27 for setting palings in front of their houses. A distinctive form of encroachment, particularly around the market-place, was the practice of building projecting upper floors out over the street supported by wooden pillars, leaving a covered walkway at street level. This was especially common on Long Row, and in 1655 eight leading citizens, including the Mayor and one of the Aldermen, were presented for 'incrotchinge with his postes in the street one the Long Rowe'. Concern at the scale of such developments was such that in 1656 a committee was appointed to measure all such encroachments made in the town since the beginning of the Civil War.[17]

In 1627–28 Mrs Martyn was presented for 'a large windowe in St Peter's Gate'. This probably refers to the building illustrated in several Victorian paintings, decorated with panels of sculptured plaster 'pargeting'.[18] A similar but larger three-and-a-half-storey projecting gable supported on columns can still be seen (at the entrance to Flying Horse Walk on The Poultry) on Cuckstool Row. Although extensively reconstructed and with pseudo-Tudor decoration added in 1936, this retains the basic shape of a structure of *c.*1600.[19] A taller, even more ornate example of a jettied gable, decorated with pargeting, stood on Long Row (near the site of the modern Queen Street), and is depicted on Sandby's drawing of the market place of *c.*1740.

Virtually all the secular buildings of Elizabethan and Stuart Nottingham were timber-framed, because of the absence of good building stone within reasonable distance. Magnesian limestone from Linby and Mansfield was only occasionally used; when Wollaton Hall was built in the 1580s Jurassic limestone was brought by road from Ancaster forty miles away in Lincolnshire. Traditionally the town had enjoyed plentiful timber supplies, both from its own resources in the Coppices and also from nearby Sherwood Forest. Deering, writing in the 1740s, cited as evidence for the former widespread availability of oak the fact that at least two timber buildings – the White Friary (dated 1574) and a house in St Peter's Churchyard – had stairs made out of solid oak blocks rather than planks. By the early seventeenth century timber was becoming less plentiful, and the town had to look further afield for the larger structural timbers. In 1624 seven 'summertrees' and nine lesser trees were purchased by the corporation from Beauvale Woods ten miles away. The infilling of the timber frames was usually of a daub made of clay (sometimes supplemented by stone lumps), as on the warehouse at Trent Bridge in 1638, but there is evidence that many houses were rendered with a lime plaster coating. A few were ornamented with plaster pargeting: Leland remarked that the town was 'welle buildid for tymber and plaster', and before the royal visit in 1634 the corporation issued instructions that houses were to be newly painted or 'roughe cast', presumably with plaster.[20]

Plate 15 **Early Stuart housing**. A gabled two-storey porch with decorative carving in St Peter's Gate, from a painting by T.C. Moore in 1863. The porch may have been constructed *c.*1628. The panel of plaster 'pargeting' on the left is preserved in Nottingham Castle Museum

Plaster obtained from the gypsum deposits in the Cropwell and Gotham areas south of the town was commonly used on the upper floors of houses. Camden wrote of Nottinghamshire that

> therein groweth a stone softer than alabaster, but being burnt maketh a plaister harder than that of Paris; wherewith they flower their upper roomes, for betwixt the joysts they lay onely long bulrushes, and thereon spread this plaister, which being thoroughly dry becomes most solide and hard, so that it seemeth rather to be firme stone then mortar, and is trod upon without all danger.[21]

The usual roofing material was thatch. In 1558 the corporation paid for four loads of rye straw to thatch the town's mills and two houses in Rotten Row. Thatch was unfortunately prone to fire, and by 1620 the town had its own 'fyer hookes' for pulling burning thatch off a building or even for pulling down a framed house to prevent fire spreading. During a raid in the Civil War in 1644 retreating Royalists 'shot their pistolls into the thatched houses to have fired them' but apparently with little effect. Nottingham had been producing its own clay roofing tiles from medieval times and these were used on the higher-status buildings. A tilehouse existed at the east end of the town from at least the 1550s. The corporation paid for the tiling of Hygyn's bedehouse in 1580 and in the same year John Crytchley, a tiler, paid his burgess entry fee in 2,000 tiles.[22]

Window glass became gradually more common, especially following the opening of local glasshouses after 1615. As early as 1599 a farmhouse at nearby Sneinton had glazed windows, although such fittings were still regarded as a luxury; the will of Isabel Cooke, widow, in 1624 specified that the 'sealing and glass in the windows' of her house should be treated as heirlooms. In 1627 the corporation paid to have the windows of the Spice Chamber glazed.[23]

A typical example of the materials and processes used in the construction of a timber-framed building can be found in the corporation's account for rebuilding the victualling house at St Ann's Well in 1619 at a cost of £52. Timber was fetched from the nearby Coppices and sawn in two specially-made sawpits. Lime was carted from Bulwell to be burnt into plaster in a coal-fired kiln. 'Slate' (? tile) and sand was brought from the town, as well as bunches of reed, presumably for thatch. The building was glazed with 104 'foot' of glass, and 6*s* 8*d* was spent on bread and drink for the workmen 'att the rearinge the house', i.e. erecting the pre-fabricated timber frame.[24]

A combination of an increasing shortage of timber and the presence of clay suitable for tilemaking was instrumental in stimulating the growing use of brick as a structural building material. Brick had been used in the area at Holme Pierrepont Hall as early as *c.*1500 and at Wollaton Hall (for internal walls) in the 1580s, but does not seem to have been generally adopted until after *c.*1600. It was used for building Thrumpton Hall in *c.*1608 and Clifton Hall in *c.*1630, and Deering noted that the earliest dated brick building in Nottingham bore the date-stone 1615.[25] This may also date the earliest beginnings of a settled – as opposed to itinerant – community of brickmakers, since also in 1615 the county justices ordered a cottage to be built at Sneinton for John Griffin, 'an expert in the art of making bricks and tile', almost certainly with the intention of inducing him to settle.[26] The Nottingham tilemakers soon turned their hand to the new craft. Charles Morley, described as a brickmaker in 1637, had been prosecuted eight years earlier for digging a claypit in the common fields. The new Chapel Bar tollhouse erected in 1649 used 1,800 bricks in its construction. Thurland Hall was partially built of brick; in 1645 the 2nd Earl of Clare gave over a million bricks from the site towards the Parliamentarian defences of the Castle.[27]

How much damage to property resulted from the Civil War is not certain. The Castle was garrisoned for Parliament and several thousand troops were quartered in the town. However, apart from two brief incursions by Royalist forces in 1643 and 1644 the town escaped largely unscathed. During the raids the Parliamentarians fired from the Castle *into* the town and damaged some property; St Peter's vestry was destroyed during the war and St Nicholas's church tower was ordered to be demolished after it had been used as a gun platform to fire into the Castle in 1643. 'Two or three houses' were also destroyed by arsonists.[28] Possibly some domestic property was also ordered to be demolished. It may be more than coincidence that a number of large new post-war houses were built at the west end of Castle Gate nearest the Castle, on the site of buildings shown on the 1609–10 town plans.

The 'urban renaissance'

From the Commonwealth period onwards, and especially after the Restoration of 1660, Nottingham began to exhibit characteristics of the 'urban renaissance' found in a number of English provincial towns over the ensuing century. Such towns became fashionable centres for the urban or 'pseudo' gentry who demanded and developed a range of private and public cultural and leisure facilities previously available only in London.[29] Many of the main elements of a renaissance in Nottingham were evident by the third quarter of the seventeenth century, especially the physical reconstruction of the town in a manner based on the principles of 'polite' as opposed to vernacular architecture.

The concept of a town-based gentry was not new. At least twenty-five members of the county gentry chose to live in Nottingham during the period 1590–1640, although many of these periods of residence were of a temporary nature; it was only after the Civil War that the town's status as a fashionable centre was confirmed. 'Many people of good quality, from several parts, make choice of habitation here where they find good accommodation', wrote Dr Robert Thoroton in *c.*1675. The Rev Thomas Cox remarked in 1720 that the town 'has perhaps more gentlemen's houses in it than any town of its bigness in Great Britain'.[30]

The new urban gentry were drawn from a wider social base than in the period before the Civil War. Some were the younger sons of county gentry, such as Francis Pierrepont, brother of the Earl of Kingston, or Rothwell Willoughby, brother of Lord

Middleton. Others were the heads of minor county gentry families who chose to live in a fashionable town house rather than on their country estates, among them Sir William Parsons, Lady Katherine Hutchinson, Francis Newdigate, William Hallowes, and Thomas Charlton, senior and junior. There were members of the old urban gentry such as the Plumptres, sole survivors of the wealthy medieval wool merchants, and *nouveau-riche* gentry such as John Gregory; he was the son of the Parliamentarian Alderman William Gregory who had, as Thoroton observed, 'by grazing raised a very considerable estate from the lowest beginning', which had enabled him to purchase the manor of Lenton in 1630.[31] Important newcomers included lawyers such as William Savile, Lawrence Athorpe, and James Farewell, the physician Dr Greaves, and office holders including John Bury, Receiver General of the Land Tax. They were complemented by wealthy tradesmen, prominent amongst whom were Laurence Collin, woolcomber; Thomas Smith, mercer turned banker; Samuel Fellows, hosier; and Francis Gawthern, white lead manufacturer. It was rare for such men to maintain a country seat as well as a town house; their Nottingham house was their main residence and their country estates, if any, were usually rented out. Several town houses were let for a season or for a number of years. Richard Pococke wrote in *c.*1751 that 'Nottingham begins to be much frequented by gentlemen, some who retire to it from their country homes, others who have left off trade, and many gentlemen of the neighbourhood have houses here for the winter.'[32]

These urban gentlemen began rebuilding their houses on a scale and in a style in keeping with their wealth and taste. Brick and tile were now firmly established as the standard building materials, stimulated not only by changing fashion but also by the danger of fire. Major conflagrations occurred in London (1666), Northampton (1675), and Warwick. Nottingham's citizens made a generous donation to Warwick in 1694. Two small fires in Nottingham in 1697 led the corporation to draw up regulations relating to the storage of gorse by the town's bakers; these were repeated in 1707 following a further 'dreadfull fire' in Friar Lane. By 1716 a fire 'engine' was stored in St Mary's Church, and another was in the new cross near St Peter's by 1733.[33] Increasing numbers of property owners began taking out fire insurance – between 1715 and 1730 257 policies were issued to Nottingham people by the Sun Fire Office.[34]

As early as 1669 James Brome observed when visiting the town that 'the houses [are] high and stately; they are, for the most part, built of brick'. Brick was the choice of material used for rebuilding the war-damaged St Nicholas's Church in 1671–82. The common pastureland on the Plains at Mapperley near the Thorney Woods became both the main source of the clay used in the brickmaking process and the site of the clamps and kilns, despite continuing prosecutions for encroaching on the common. They were considered an ideal location – close enough to the town to avoid expensive transport costs yet far enough away not to cause offensive pollution. Deering noted that the kilns produced both common and dressed bricks, as well as both flat tiles and the undulating pantiles characteristic of eastern England but rare in the counties west of Nottinghamshire.[35]

It was not only the use of the latest materials which characterised the new buildings; architectural fashion also played a major role. No longer was it acceptable to build in a rambling vernacular style; new town houses had to present a symmetrical frontage conforming to the latest Dutch or Italian fashion, ornamented with classical details to show the owner's taste and, if possible, incorporating the latest features such as sash windows. Deering described the Palladian front added to Plumptre House in the 1720s as having a 'grand stuccoed front and in the Italian taste'. Emphasis was placed on having a fashionable façade even if the rest of the building was not reconstructed; Thoroton in *c.*1675 remarked that local residents were vying with each other to be 'leaders of this dance of building new fronts in this town'.[36]

The fact that the rebuilding began before the Restoration implies a considerable degree of confidence. Apart from the need to reconstruct some war-damaged property, another reason was hinted at by Thoroton in his remark that 'since the late war, wherein this town happened to be on the conquering side, there are many houses new builded'. It is probably no coincidence that one of the largest and earliest of the new buildings – a detached mansion close to St Mary's Church – was erected in *c.*1650 by a victorious Parliamentarian colonel, Francis Pierrepont.[37] Only a few hundred metres away, on the north side of St Mary's Churchyard (now Kayes Walk), another prominent Parliamentarian was improving his ancestral home. Dr Huntingdon Plumptre was, according to Thoroton, 'accounted the best physician in Nottingham', and had been a leading – if somewhat half-hearted – member of the town's Parliamentarian Committee during the war. Having inherited the family property from his brother, he refronted it in more fashionable style, probably in the early 1650s. A plan and elevation drawn in the 1720s before the later alteration of the house shows it as a detached 'H'-shaped two-storey structure, facing south. The fronts of the two projecting wings appear Tudor in style, but the recessed central frontage was totally classical, an altogether more fashionable design.[38]

Building activity during the Commonwealth caused Richard Franck to claim in 1654 with some exaggeration that 'new fabricks are hourly lifted up into the ambient air'![39] A typical Nottingham house of the 1650s or 1660s was a two-, three- or four-storey brick structure with two or more gables, often on all elevations. Most had mullion and transom casement windows; Sandby's drawings of the market-place of 1742 show that at least half had these windows rather than the more fashionable vertically sliding sashes. A striking architectural feature of many houses in these years was the curved or shaped gable, one variation of which was the so-called 'Dutch' gable. Not a single example has survived to the present day in the ancient core of the town, even though they feature prominently on Hall's prospects of *c.*1675 and on Hawksmore's sketch of the castle area in 1680.[40] Such gables had appeared on Cambridge colleges in *c.*1630, and country houses in Nottinghamshire such as Owthorpe Hall were displaying them by the 1650s. The earliest example in Nottingham seems to have been built on the Plumptre Hospital in Fisher Gate, rebuilt in 1650. Sandby's 'prospects' show similar gables on St Mary's vicarage on Short Hill, erected in *c.*1651. Thurland Hall acquired some examples at an unknown date. Other dated but now demolished examples in the area included the White Horse in nearby Old Radford (date-stone 1661), and probably Laurence Collin's house in Castle Gate (1664).[41]

Four town houses (three of them now demolished) built in the 1660s and 1670s displayed the latest features of contemporary architecture. These were the former 'Oriental Café' in Wheeler Gate, the 'Howitt' house on Timber Hill, a house on Long Row (East), and the still surviving Newdigate House (built *c.*1675–80) in Castle Gate.[42] All four had alternating triangular and segmental pediments, an 'Artisan Mannerist' motif,[43] and all were in the forefront of architectural fashion. As early as 1669 James Brome could note that some of Nottingham's houses 'are rare pieces, as well for structure as design; and, in short, the whole front of their fabrick is beautified with sculptures, and glistening balconies, the inhabitants being very curious in the new modes and draughts of architecture'.[44]

Other new fashionable homes noted by Thoroton in *c.*1675 were those of Thomas Charlton, senior in Bridlesmith Gate, and of Samuel Staples and George Gregory, both in Swine Green (now Carlton Street). The latter had in 1674 'rebuilt most of the old mansion house, which is esteemed one of the best seats in the whole town'. Thoroton describes the house of Alderman William Toplady, a vintner, as one of the

Plate 16 **Late seventeenth-century town house**. The former Howitt House on Timber Hill (now South Parade) photographed before demolition. Note the alternating segmental and triangular pediments to the windows, the 'barley-sugar' columns flanking the central window, and the supporting pillars creating a covered walk at street level. The building to the left was the premises of Smiths' Bank, founded in the 1680s

first of the new fashionable buildings. It was probably on Long Row, and was no doubt financed out of his marriage in 1657 into the wealthy *nouveau-riche* family of Turner, coal masters from Swanwick in Derbyshire. The Hearth Tax assessments of 1674 reveal that the town had 13.5 per cent of its taxed houses with six or more fireplaces (compared with 12.7 per cent for Newark and 8.6 per cent for Mansfield). These included five properties with twelve hearths, two with thirteen, four with fourteen, two with fifteen, and one each with twenty-three (Pierrepont's house) and forty-seven (Thurland Hall).[45]

A major stimulus to Nottingham's standing both as a fashionable residential centre and as a leader of the latest architectural fashion was provided by the Duke of Newcastle's decision to rebuild the Castle. Thoroton wrote that in 'this present year, 1674, though he be above eighty years of age [he] hath a great number of men at work pulling down and clearing the foundations of the old tower that he may build, at least, part of a new castle there'. The Duke died two years later when the walls were only a yard high, but the building was completed in 1679 by his son at a total cost of £14,000. Newcastle appears to have been his own architect, assisted by the Lincolnshire mason Samuel Marsh. Although confusingly the building continued to be referred to as Nottingham Castle, it can best be described as a ducal palace owing its inspiration as much to Continental baroque as to English styles. Pevsner commented that it would be quite at home in northern Italy or Prague. Its main east front towards the town was rich with rustication, columns, pilasters, and windows with broken pediments.[46]

There may possibly have been a brief slowing in the pace of urban reconstruction in the decades around the turn of the century, although the three-storey terrace in Brewhouse Yard (now the Museum) was built in *c.*1700. Defoe in 1725 spoke of 'all the modern buildings erected lately … which are considerable, and of some just now going forward'. Architectural fashion had swung towards the more restrained and less ornamental 'Palladian' or 'early Georgian' style, with roofs now hidden out of sight behind low parapet walls. Deering noted that 'many of the inhabitants have taken to new fronting their houses after the newest manner, some with parapet walls'. Typical of the new style were three houses of the 1730s, two of which survive to the present day. The hosier Samuel Fellows' house in High Pavement (*c.*1737) has gone, but the houses of Francis Gawthern (1733) and Rothwell Willoughby (*c.*1738–43) still grace the upper end of Low Pavement. The former was built as a pair of identical houses; the latter, set back behind a flagged forecourt with entrance gates, was described by Deering as 'beautiful and well finished'. It has a handsome doorcase with pilasters under a segmental pediment.[47] The major residence reconstructed during this period was Plumptre House to the north of St Mary's Church. In the 1720s John Plumptre, MP, employed the prominent architect Colen Campbell to enlarge it into a Palladian mansion.[48] The culmination of this phase of Nottingham's architectural development was Bromley House, still standing on Angel Row. It was built for Sir George Smith, grandson of the banker Thomas Smith, in 1752, and has a plain façade with triangular pediments above the first-floor windows. The interior contains fine rococo plasterwork ceilings, ornate chimney pieces and other contemporary details.[49]

As with most of the Georgian town houses, Bromley House originally had a line of railings or 'palisades' in front of it. These were ornamental and gave protection to the ground floor windows. The town had numerous examples of fine ornamental wrought ironwork, including those at Willoughby House. The now-replaced railings at Newdigate House were probably made by the local ironsmith Francis Foulgham, who was active between about 1710 and his death in 1749.[50] Legally, these palisades were encroachments on the common highway, and the corporation attempted to exercise some planning controls over them. In 1737 a committee was appointed to view Samuel Fellows' house in High Pavement, 'which he is going to rebuild, in order to settle the limits of his foundation'. In 1743 Rothwell Willoughby was allowed to 'set his palisadoes before his house in the Low Pavement out into the street' to an agreed point on payment of 2*s* 6*d* per year.[51]

Similar considerations applied to the continuing encroachment by properties supported on pillars around the market-place, especially in Long Row. A process that had begun probably in the sixteenth century on an *ad hoc* basis, had by the late seventeenth century been elevated into a virtue as part of a conscious attempt to imitate an Italian *piazza* or London's Covent Garden by providing a colonnaded walkway. Richard Franck had written in 1654 that 'the ornament gaity and beauty [of Nottingham] is the Long Row', and in 1697 Celia Fiennes waxed eloquent about the large market-place, out of which ran two 'very large streetes much like Holborn but the buildings finer, and there is a pyaza all along one side ... with stone pillars for walking that runns the length of the streete'. The corporation tried to provide some direction and control over this development. In 1717 a committee of seven was appointed to 'sett out some ground on the Long Row for Mrs Willington to place columns on for the house she is going to build there'. On the opposite side of the market-place William Shepherd was allowed in 1714 'to range his house which he intends to build on Timber Hill equall with Mr Smiths house and Mrs Metcalfs and his pillars likewise'. In 1732 John Loveday wrote about the market-place that 'some of the houses have cloisters before 'em, upheld by pillars only, not arches'. By 1755 Patchen remarked that 'there is a small piazza on each side the market place continued from street to street, which makes it pleasant to walk here in all weathers and view the shops'. However it took some years before the vision of a continuous colonnaded walk was realised: Patchen observed that the market-place was 'surrounded with chiefly good buildings; tho' here and there is left an old low, ill-built house'. These occasional low timber-framed buildings, mainly alehouses, can plainly be seen on Sandby's view of the market-place of 1742.[52]

A feature closely associated with the development of fashionable houses was the pleasure garden, a status symbol which proclaimed both the leisure and taste of its owner. Little record has survived of gardens before the Civil War; most would have had a purely functional role to provide food, although it must be presumed that the Elizabethan and early Stuart gentry had small ornamental and herb gardens. Speed's plan of 1610 indicates features which appear to be ornamental beds, mounds and orchards to the north of both Long Row and Gridlesmith Gate and elsewhere in the town, but these may be purely conventional symbols. The post-war development of fashionable houses was, however, accompanied by a parallel development of new pleasure grounds for the well-off. Thoroton mentioned that after the Restoration Lady Katherine Hutchinson purchased the house next door to her own in High Pavement so that she could add its 'pleasant little garden' to her own 'for the garden's sake, wherein she takes great delight'.[53]

Late seventeenth-century garden design was largely French- or Dutch-inspired, with an emphasis on a formal geometrical layout, wide gravel walks, sunken terraces, fountains and statues. The grandest garden in Nottingham was at Pierrepont House.[54] A smaller garden which achieved national fame was the French-style *parterre* laid out in *c.*1705 adjacent to Newdigate House for the captured French Marshal Tallard,

Plate 17 **Pierrepont House and garden, *c.*1695**. Painted by an unknown Dutch artist. This brick mansion was erected by Colonel Francis Pierrepont *c.*1650, but 'L' shaped and – although impressive – lacking symmetry. The tall tower and balustraded flat roof evoked elements of Elizabethan building combined with more recent features. The garden formed a large formal rectangle, stretching eastwards down the slope in front of the house between St Mary's Gate and Bellar Gate. A series of sunken geometrical flower-beds were surrounded by a raised terrace walk around the perimeter, allowing a view into the garden. The walk was balustraded and ornamented with a variety of urns, some of them closely resembling stoneware 'flower-pots' manufactured locally in the 1690s. St Mary's church tower can be seen on the left

who lodged there whilst a prisoner of war in England. It was created by the royal gardeners London and Wise. Visitors were often disappointed by its size. 'The garden is but small but is kept very neat … it is well laid out into severall plotts', wrote Joseph Taylor in 1705; he added that the house and garden 'did not answer the great expectation we had from the generall discourse of their finery and grandeur'. Defoe in 1725 observed that Tallard had 'amused himself with making a small but beautiful *parterre*, after the *French* fashion, but it does not gain by *English* keeping'![55]

The Castle had grass courtyards but few gardens. Defoe noted that Newcastle had 'laid out a plan of the finest gardens that are to be seen in all that part of England; but they are not yet finish'd; they take up, as they tell us, threescore acres of ground in the design, and would, no doubt, be exquisitely fine, but it requires an immense sum to go on with it'. The 'immense sum' was obviously not forthcoming as nothing more is heard of them.[56]

In 1744 there were many small orchards around the town, including a large cherry orchard owned by the Sherwin family to either side of Coalpit Lane (now Cranbrook Street). Aligned with the front door of the enlarged Plumptre House, on the *opposite* side of Stoney Street, an avenue of trees led down the slope towards Bellar Gate, parallel to the Pierrepont House garden, leading the eye up to Sneinton church tower on the far hill. This concept of creating a 'vista' looking out to the distant countryside from the windows of a town house was a particular feature of Georgian Nottingham. In 1733 William Hallowes, a gentleman resident on the north side of High Pavement (now County House), purchased the former 'Castle' inn opposite his home and demolished it to open up a garden 'vista', a formal garden with a summer house, separated from the street by a low wall with iron palisades either side of a central gateway. It extended back to the edge of the cliff above Narrow Marsh and afforded an extensive view over the Meadows towards Wilford Hill from the first floor of Hallowes's house. Sandby's prospects show that the gardens on Short Hill, at the east end of High Pavement, also enjoyed a similar view. Some of these were terraced down the slope of the cliff. John Loveday in 1732 described the garden of the physician Dr Greaves as 'romantic enough all upon a rock, consisting of very small plots, one under another; the lowest is largest and looks down into one of the streets' (i.e. Narrow Marsh). Other areas of the town such as Castle Gate boasted the occasional vista; at Rothwell Willoughby's garden in Low Pavement the view was framed between two flanking summer houses on the edge of the cliff.[57]

The consumer revolution

Fashionable houses and gardens were, however, only two expressions of the increasingly affluent life-style of the urban gentry and the emerging 'middling sort' of lawyers, physicians, merchants, hosiers, maltsters and other well-off tradesmen. These people enjoyed a rise in their standard of living during the course of what has been termed a 'consumer revolution'. Aping the aristocracy and country gentry, they devoted much of their surplus income to the acquisition of non-essential and luxury consumer goods and status symbols. A detailed analysis of over a thousand probate inventories, listing the goods of deceased Nottingham townspeople between 1688 and 1750, shows both the number and quality of household furnishings; items such as silver, china, pictures, mirrors, clocks and books were increasingly commonplace in the homes of the better-off tradesmen as well as the urban gentry (figure 7.1). By 1747 even a plumber and glazier, Joseph Tuffing, could relax in his well-furnished parlour containing desk, bookcase, corner cupboard, three tables (one of them mahogany) and six chairs. The walls were decorated with a mirror, a 'weather glass', eleven pictures framed with glass and a 'prospect of Nottingham' (probably by Sandby). Guests could be entertained with the aid of a punch bowl, china salver, and a glass decanter and drinking glasses.[58]

Figure 7.1 **Selected household goods, 1688–1750**

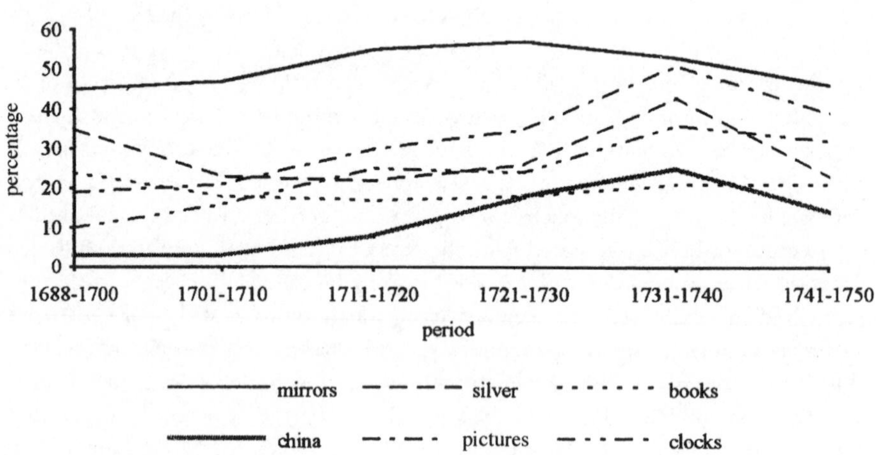

Source: NAO Probate Inventories.

This new-found affluence is also borne out by archaeological evidence. Excavation of a rubbish pit beneath Trinity House – a town house opposite St Mary's Church on High Pavement – has revealed the remains of a wide variety of expensive drinking vessels dating from between *c.*1650 and *c.*1730. During most of this period the house was occupied by the Hon. Lettice Stanhope, a widow, and then by James Farewell, a lawyer. The finds included imported Chinese porcelain, German stoneware, Venetian glass tableware of the late 1660s, Lambeth delftware, local Nottingham stoneware and green glass bottles, some sealed with initials and dates between 1660 and 1665. Drinking vessels were used not only for wine but also for tea, a growing fashion which spread rapidly down the social scale. In 1725 Defoe remarked that the Nottingham stoneware potteries were 'much increased since the increase in tea drinking', and Deering wrote rather sourly that even the lower classes had become addicted to their tea, coffee and chocolate: not only the 'gentry and wealthy traders drink it constantly but almost every seamer, sizer and winder [in the hosiery trade] will have her tea'.[59]

Tea was only one of a series of luxury commodities stocked by Nottingham shopkeepers. Thomas Baskerville in 1675 noticed 'shops full of all merchantable riches' and in 1755 Patchen remarked that the shops on Long Row were 'generally large and well furnished'.[60] In 1749 George Oldfield carried a wide range of goods in his grocer's shop, including tea, coffee, sugar, pepper, salt, ginger, seeds, allom, starch, indigo, soap, (lead) shot, paper, candles, brooms and thread. Upstairs in his 'flax chamber' he stored flax, tobacco, oils, ropes, sacks, spices and honey, and elsewhere he kept currants, snuff, brimstone, treacle and gunpowder. These were weighed out on the scales on the counter in his 'change shop'. Several shopkeepers now catered for the fashion market. Nicholas Sharpe, a haberdasher of hats who died in 1710, held stocks of hats for boys, youths and men as well as 'fine hats', all made in his garret out of hair, wool, hare and rabbit skins and gum. He also sold numerous bows, ribbons, twists and buttons. Gervase Wild, another haberdasher, in 1732 sold broadhats, 'carolines', straw hats and shopkeepers' hats. Beneath these hats wigs were also an important fashion accessory. Edward Brown, a tailor, in 1706 held stocks of wigs, perukes, hair, combs, razors both plain and 'silver lip't', wash balls, scissors and basins.[61]

Deering estimated that prior to about 1680 the town's shopkeepers would purchase mercery, drapery and grocery goods from London vendors visiting Lenton Fair, but after that date they began to travel regularly to London to buy direct. One wealthy mercer from Long Row, Gervase Rippon, had at his death in 1693 'in the shop, silkes, stuffes, linnen, gold and silver lace gowns, mens and womens garments with all kinds of mercers wares' valued at £400, in addition to outstanding shop debts owed to him totalling a further £950. Some tradesmen developed close links with their London suppliers; in 1724 Thomas Langford, a goldsmith, insured his property and stock both in Nottingham and at the Spotted Dog, Lombard Street, London. Local craftsmen diversified to serve the expanding luxury market; the inventory of William Smalley, a joiner who stored timber 'under the rock' in Hollow Stone in 1692, included several landscapes, picture frames and glass. By 1739 the town even boasted three toy shops.[62]

Another form of conspicuous consumption was in private transport, whether in ownership of a saddle horse or preferably a carriage. Samuel Hallowes left a coach and mares valued at £15 on his death in 1715. Deering recorded that there were in the town 'upwards of 400 saddle horses, above 130 coach chaise and team horses, eleven gentlemen's coaches and chariots, [and] a considerable number of chaises and chairs'.[63]

The townscape

This affluent and urbane life-style based on the example of London led to a demand for more comfortable and attractive public buildings for the conduct of fashionable social activities. Nottingham already possessed several buildings used for a variety of religious, administrative, educational or charitable purposes, including the three parish churches, the Guildhall, the Shire Hall, the Shambles with the Spice Chamber in the market-place, the Free School in Stoney Street, and a handful of 'bedehouses' or almshouses including the Plumptre Hospital in Fisher Gate. After the Restoration many were rebuilt or replaced.

The war-damaged St Nicholas's church was rebuilt between 1671 and 1683, although it has none of the sophistication of Wren's London churches of the same period. The Free School was extensively repaired in 1689 and largely rebuilt in 1708. The Guildhall in Weekday Cross was refronted in a more up-to-date style in 1744, although the medieval timbered hall where the corporation met was still retained. The street frontage was screened by a plain Georgian façade with a straight parapet, supported on a row of columns similar to those on Long Row. The old Shire Hall further up the street, despite a partial collapse in 1724, was not rebuilt until 1770. New public buildings were erected elsewhere in the town. After the long struggle for toleration was eventually achieved, nonconformist chapels were erected for the Independents in Castle Gate and the Unitarians in High Pavement, both in *c.*1690. The Quakers' permanent Meeting House on Spaniel Row was built in 1737. All three buildings have since been replaced.[64] A new charity school – the Bluecoat School – was founded in 1709 and moved into a pleasing new building (since demolished) on Weekday Cross in 1723. Collin's Almshouses were built in 1709 on a site between Friar Lane and Hounds Gate in a very urbane style.[65]

Between 1723 and 1726 the market-place was dramatically improved by the erection at its east end of the New Exchange, concealing a rambling conglomeration of butchers' shambles, stalls and the medieval Spice Chamber. The new building was an imposing structure with a straight parapet roof broken by a central semi-circular pediment enclosing a public clock. The whole was supported on a row of pillars echoing those around most of the market-place, obviously part of a conscious attempt at architectural unity. On the façade were three niches designed to hold statues. The Exchange was intended to house both borough and market administrative offices and a public meeting room, although it seems to have been rarely used for the latter purpose. The total cost was £2,400.[66]

The Exchange was designed and probably built by the Mayor for 1724–25, Alderman Marmaduke Pennell, described variously as a starchmaker, a feltmaker, and a bricklayer, but evidently also a builder and property developer. He was a prime mover in trying to develop the town's social amenities; he may have been instrumental in erecting the Theatre in St Mary's Gate and the Assembly Rooms in Low Pavement. He was also responsible, in partnership with 'Mr Smith' – probably Abel Smith the banker – for developing the Derbyshire spa of Matlock Bath, where

Nottingham gentry could stay for the sake of their health or recreation and mingle socially with similar families from expanding northern towns such as Manchester and Liverpool. Here business links could be forged, especially in the textile trades, and marriage horizons widened.[67]

Alongside the development of new public buildings went a demand for improvements to the town's infrastructure – the water supply and the muddy and congested medieval streets were especially in need of improvement. Perhaps the most important development was the attempt in the 1690s to provide piped water. Traditionally the town's water had been derived from numerous private and public wells sunk into the bedrock; Deering estimated that there were about 300 in use in *c.*1700. As population expanded these became inadequate, and by the late seventeenth century water was brought into the town from the River Leen, either by hand in pails or in water carts. Before 1700 many towns began to investigate mechanical means of extracting water and pumping it through wooden pipes laid under the main streets. In 1693 a private waterworks company was established, with the corporation holding six of the thirty-two shares. The company leased land adjoining the Leen at the foot of Finkhill Street, where a 'water engine' with a large water-wheel was erected: 'the main wheels of the hydraulic machine set in motion a number of crank levers, and itself moved, like the great waterwork wheels at London Bridge, by the power of water'. Many problems were encountered, and a whole succession of millwrights and engineers were employed to perfect the scheme. The main problem seems to have been the difficulty of pumping water up to the higher parts of the town, but Deering reported that the system had been 'brought to a competent perfection'. A reservoir was constructed on high ground near Butt Dyke to serve the west part of the upper town, and another at the south end of the Castle Park; this was ingeniously fed from the River Leen when in flood, and the water held back by floodgates. The overall result of the provision of piped water, Deering noted, had been a reduction from 300 to 200 in the number of active wells.[68]

Attention also began to be paid to the state of the streets. Although in 1641 the town was well paved with river boulders from the bed of the Trent, in 1717 the corporation appointed a committee to survey the streets and to ascertain the relative proportions to be paved at public or private expense. In 1718 they ordered the market-place to be paved, and in 1724 it was resolved to levy a highway rate for the first time on property owners in St Mary's parish to raise funds for repairing, cleaning, and paving the streets. Also in 1724 an order was passed by the corporation that all householders should remove dirt and sweep the streets outside their own properties. The area in front of St Peter's churchyard was paved; this was crossed by an open drain called the Rowell and was a notorious 'sink' in bad weather. From 1728 onwards the corporation entered into regular contracts with Charles Wheatcroft to pave different sections of the market-place with 'good large boulders'; members of the Wheatcroft family were regularly employed as the town's paviors until the 1770s at least.[69]

An increasing and more affluent population also meant an increase in traffic not only by private carriages but also by public transport. By Deering's day the town could boast five public 'Hackney glass coaches', a chariot and several chaises and chairs. There was also a 'Hackney sedan', the 'first ever used here, for hire', which was employed 'to carry persons who are taken sick from home, and ancient ladies to church and visiting, as also young ones in rainy weather'. Conflict between wheeled transport and pedestrians led to the erection of posts and rails at strategic points. To ease traffic flow it was decreed in 1728 that all free-standing signposts belonging to innkeepers and other tradesmen should be removed and replaced with hanging signs attached to the buildings.[70]

Road widening commenced on a limited scale in 1740. The impetus was probably the turnpiking of the main London Road from Trent Bridge to near Loughborough in 1737–38; this no doubt emphasised the narrowness of the steep and winding Hollow Stone. In 1740 the Duke of Kingston gave to the Corporation a house with rock cellars at Hollow Stone; this was demolished and the rock cut back to enlarge the road to a width that would allow two vehicles to pass. Earlier Lord Middleton had paid to level the deep hollow way at the Sandhills on the Derby Road outside Chapel Bar, no doubt to improve conditions for his coal wagons. In 1743 Chapel Bar itself was demolished to allow easier access by vehicles from Derby Road into the market-place. The narrow medieval postern gate at the top of Vault Lane had been similarly removed in the 1730s but there was no attempt at this period to widen any of the remaining medieval streets or to lay out formal new streets or squares as in some contemporary towns.[71]

Leisure interests

Little attempt was made to develop any formal walks or promenades for public use. The only recorded example was in connection with a spa or chalybeate spring which was developed on a site on the River Leen close to the waterworks. In 1707 Alderman Watkinson was recompensed for his costs in making a 'convenient walk to accommodate the water drinkers'. Trees were planted to create a walk and an arbour, and in 1709 the corporation agreed to construct a new bowling green on an adjacent site. This was presumably what Deering referred to later as the Town Green, which was open daily. He also mentioned other greens at St Ann's Well (open Mondays and Wednesdays), and at Basford (Tuesdays), both of which 'had good company' and where a good meal could be had. The best green, which he described as being 'as fine in any in England', was some two miles east of the town at Holme Pierrepont, open on Thursdays.[72] Bowling was one of the activities most closely associated with the gentry, who alone had the leisure and money to indulge themselves during the working week.

Another similar but more occasional leisure activity was that of horse-racing, which brought the town gentry into contact with their country counterparts.

Although some races may have taken place as early as Elizabethan times, the earliest reference to an organised meeting is 1689. Plate was purchased for a race to be held on Nottingham and Basford Lings (the common pasture to the north of the Sand Field, part of which still survives as the Forest) in 1699, in 1700 and again in 1704. The races attracted large crowds; Defoe wrote in 1725 that 'tis a most glorious show they have here when the running season begins, for here is such an assembly of gentlemen of quality that not Banstead Down or New Market Heath produces better company, better horses, or shows the horse and master's skill better'. Another gentry activity was hunting; Rothwell Willoughby of Low Pavement maintained a pack of hare hounds in the 1740s, and there was also a subscription pack in the town.[73]

Other less strenuous recreations were walks in the vicinity. Deering mentioned excursions along the Trent to Wilford and Clifton, to Beeston or to Colwick Spring. A traditional excursion was to St Ann's Well, near Nottingham Coppices, a venue popular probably for centuries. In 1641 it was said that 'this well is all summer long much frequented and there are but few fair days between March and October in which some company or other of the town … use to consort there … either to dine or supp or both …'. The situation had hardly changed a hundred years later, when Deering recorded that here was a 'cold bath' called Robin Hood's Well, an old wicker chair called Robin Hood's Chair, a rustic arbour, and a victualling house as well as the bowling green. Special entertainments were sometimes provided: 'here in the summer season you may be entertained with a concert of aerial musicians in Nottingham Coppices'. Shorter walks – for ladies – were around the Castle grounds, to the ancient maze near Sneinton called the Shepherd's Race, or to Trent Bridge where there were 'conveniences … to bathe unseen'.[74]

Most of these were traditional leisure activities. The greatest innovations which reflected the new-found fashionable consciousness of the townspeople were formal cultural and social activities such as theatrical performances, concerts, and regular dancing assemblies. Plays were being staged by the 1740s, although their development may have been retarded by the restrictions of the Licensing Act of 1737. Deering wrote that 'during the Race [meeting] a company of comedians always are in the town, who act at a theatre built for that purpose in St Mary Gate'. However a later writer described the building as 'an old barn' belonging to Mr Plumptre.[75] By 1726 the urban elite assembled in the purpose-built Assembly Rooms in Low Pavement while the 'tradesmen' emulated them with their own assemblies in a large room at Thurland Hall from at least 1721. At Low Pavement there was a 'handsome lofty and spacious room' nearly seventy feet long with a musicians' gallery, two withdrawing rooms and a refreshment room. By the 1740s there were regular monthly assemblies as well as special ones held in Race Week, Assize Week, or on similar occasions.[76] All these events attracted the country gentry into town, where they would stay with friends or take lodgings. They were the high points of the county's social calendar.

While the physical appearance of the Nottingham of 1650 was probably not dissimilar in many ways to that of 1550, the town of 1750 was very different. Brick buildings outnumbered timbered ones, and the architecture of the larger ones in their garden settings now conformed to the classical rules of the fashionable styles which had replaced the traditional vernacular. This physical change was stimulated by an increase in the number and wealth of the urban gentry and merchants, who were also instrumental in developing a social calendar of cultural and leisure activities as well as a number of public buildings to accommodate them.[77] This type of development was typical of the 'urban renaissance' experienced by many English provincial towns between 1660 and 1760. The physical and cultural changes in Nottingham merit the description of a renaissance, but with some reservations. First, being tightly encircled by a ring of inalienable common fields, Nottingham's development of public buildings and public spaces, in the form of planned promenades and squares, was limited in comparison with major cultural and leisure towns such as Bath, York, or Warwick.[78] Second, Nottingham's renaissance began before 1660 and lasted beyond 1760. New town houses were constructed in the Commonwealth period, and both private and public buildings were still being built after 1760. Stanford House, an 'Adam'-style town house, was built in 1775–82 in Castle Gate, and new public buildings included the enlarged Theatre (1760) and the rebuilt Shire Hall (1770). The town's social heyday, with its assemblies, plays and concerts, lasted into the next century. Finally, this fashionable renaissance was accompanied by, and in many respects supported by, sustained economic and industrial growth which fuelled a consumer revolution. Deering saw the rebuilding of the handsome town houses as 'manifest proof of the increase of riches among the inhabitants, owing chiefly to a beneficial manufactory', referring to the rapid growth of the hosiery industry, the economic basis of Nottingham's wealth.[79]

Notes

1 This opening description is based largely on the following: Anon., pp. 22–6; PRO MK 1142, Crown Survey and Map of Sherwood Forest, 1609; *RBN*, IV, V.

2 S. Gillott, 'Bestwood: a Sherwood Forest Park in the seventeenth century', *TTS*, 89 (1985), pp. 57–74.

3 M. Girouard, *Robert Smythson and the Elizabethan Country House* (Yale, 1983).

4 R. S. Smith, *Early Coal Mining Around Nottingham, 1500–1650* (Nottingham, 1989).

5 J. Ogilvy, 'Map of road from Nottingham to Grimsby', in *Britannia* (1675); Deering, p. 168.

6 Anon., p. 41; W. H. Stevenson, 'A description of Nottinghamshire in the seventeenth century', *TTS*, 11 (1907), pp. 117–30.

7 L. T. Smith (ed.), *Itinerary of John Leland, 1534–1543* (1906–10), pp. 94–7; W. Camden, *Britannia* (1610), pp. 547–51. The date of Camden's visit (1598) is inferred from the description in Anon., pp. 18–20.

8 R. Corbett, *Iter Boriale*, in J. A. W. Bennet and H. R. Trevor Roper, (eds.), *The Poems of Richard Corbett* (1955), pp. 35–7; J. Taylor, *Part of this Summer's Travels* (1632).

9 Corbett, *Iter*, pp. 35–7; J. Evelyn, *The Diary of John Evelyn* (1654); J. Speed, 'The Countie of Nottingham described…' in *Theatre of the Empire of Great Britaine* (1611); PRO MK 1142; I am grateful to Mr S. N. Mastoris for helpful comments about the two maps.

10 E. L. Guilford, 'Extracts from the records of the Borough of Nottingham', *TTS*, 29 (1925), p. 80;

Deering, pp. 3–5; *RBN*, IV, p. 393. The island site is depicted on town plans of 1610 (Speed) and 1744 (Badder and Peat) but not on those of 1609 (Crown Survey) or 1677 (Thoroton).

11 HMC, *Middleton*, p. 171; *RBN*, IV, p. 162.

12 Smith (ed.), *Itinerary of John Leland*, pp. 94–7.

13 H. Gill, 'Notes on the domestic architecture of Old Nottingham', *TTS*, 11 (1907), p. 108. The building bore the date-stone inscribed 'IM 1574'.

14 HMC, *Middleton*, p. 456; P. R. Seddon (ed.), *Letters of John Holles, 1587–1637* (*TSRS*, 31, 1975), p. xx; (*TSRS*, 36, 1986), pp. 455, 465; Bailey, *Annals*, II, pp. 578–620; A. C. Wood (ed.), *Memorials of the Holles Family, 1493–1656* (Camden Society, 3rd series, 55, 1937), p. 95; Thoroton's town plan (1677) illustrates the house named as 'Clare House': W. F. Webster (ed.), *Nottinghamshire Hearth Tax 1664, 1674* (*TSRS*, 37, 1988), p. 138.

15 NAO DD.FJ 11/1/8; F. A. Wadsworth, 'An assessment for St. Mary's Church, Nottingham, 1637', TTS, 33 (1929), pp. 16–22.

16 'Severns' building was dismantled and rebuilt on Castle Road in 1968: F. W. Charles, 'Severns: a fifteenth century timber framed building …', *TTS*, 74 (1970), pp. 45–61.

17 *RBN*, IV, p. 380; V, pp. 146, 111, 132, 286, 287; Guilford, 'Extracts from the records of the Borough of Nottingham', *TTS*, 28 (1924), p. 93.

18 *RBN*, V, p. 132.

19 A. Henstock, *Tracing the History of Your House* (Nottingham, 1988), pp. 83–7; S. P. Douglass, A. G. MacCormick, and S. N. Mastoris, 'The Old Flying Horse, Nottingham: a structural and documentary survey', *TTS*, 91 (1987), pp. 115–24.

20 *RBN*, V, pp. 123, 194, 166; IV, 388; Deering, pp. 86, 5–6; R. S. Smith, *Sir Francis Willoughby of Wollaton Hall* (Nottingham, 1988), p. 20.

21 Deering, p. 88; Camden, *Britannia*, pp. 547–51; *RBN*, IV, p. 335.

22 *RBN*, IV, pp. 120, 371, 376, 196, 197; J. Sutherland (ed.), *Memoirs of the Life of Colonel Hutchinson* (Oxford, 1973), p. 114.

23 *RBN*, IV, p. 250; NAO, PRNW, Isabel Cooke, pr. 7 October 1624; *RBN*, V, pp. 122–3, 152.

24 *RBN*, IV, p. 356.

25 Pevsner and Williamson, p. 49; Deering, p. 6.

26 H. H. Copnall (ed.), *Nottinghamshire County Records of the Seventeenth Century* (Nottingham, 1915), p. 125.

27 T. M. Blagg and F. A. Wadsworth, *Abstracts of Nottinghamshire Marriage Licences*, vol. 1 (1930), p. 158; Guilford, 'Extracts from the records of the Borough of Nottingham', *TTS*, 28 (1924), pp. 81, 84; Deering, pp. 139–40; *RBN*, V, p. 258; P. R. Seddon, 'Colonel Hutchinson and the disputes between the Nottinghamshire Parliamentarians, 1643–45: New evidence analysed', *TTS*, 98 (1994), pp. 71, 72, 79.

28 Sutherland, *Memoirs*, pp. 95, 100; Deering, pp. 34, 42. Speed (1610) shows a spire on St Nicholas's but the Crown Survey of 1609 does not and is probably a more accurate depiction: *ex. inf.* Mr S. N. Mastoris.

29 P. Borsay, *The English Urban Renaissance: Culture and Society in the Provincial Town, 1660–1770* (Oxford, 1989).

30 Anon., p. 55; Thoroton, p. 499; T. Cox, *Magna Britannia or Topographical, Ecclesiastical and Natural History of Nottinghamshire* (1720), p. 18.

31 Thoroton, p. 497; F. A. Barnes, *Priory Demesne to University Campus*, (Nottingham, 1993), p. 110.

32 J. J. Cartwright (ed.), *The Travels Through England of Dr. Richard Pococke* (Camden Society, New Series, 42, 1888), p. 168.

33 P. Clark, 'English country towns, 1500–1800', in P. Clark (ed.), *Country Towns in Pre-industrial England* (Leicester, 1981), p. 20; *RBN*, V, pp. 386, 394; VI, pp. 39–40, 63, 90, 140.

34 Guildhall Library, London, Sun Fire Office Registers.

35 J. Brome, *Travels over England, Scotland and Wales* (1669); Pevsner and Williamson, p. 224; *RBN*, V, pp. 323, 356; Deering, p. 88.

36 Deering, p. 6; Thoroton, p. 499.

37 Thoroton, pp. 492, 497. See plate 17, p.120.

38 Thoroton, p. 497; NAO, M 471.

39 Stevenson, 'A Description', p. 129.

40 Thoroton, facing p. 488; Royal Institute of British Architects, Drawings Collection, N. Hawksmore, sketch, 1680.

41 M. W. Barley, *The English Farmhouse and Cottage* (Gloucester, 1987), p. 190; Pevsner and Williamson, pp. 352–3; Thoroton, pp. 494–5; Deering, p. 33; Gill, 'Domestic architecture', pp. 105–8.

42 H. Gill, 'Nottingham in the eighteenth century, especially with reference to domestic architecture', *TTS*, 16 (1912), pp. 47–9; Henstock, *History of Your House*, pp. 20–1.

43 Pevsner and Williamson, p. 235. See plate 16

44 Brome, *Travels*.

45 Thoroton, p. 499; A. B. Clarke, 'Notes on the Mayors of Nottingham, 1660–1715', *TTS*, 41 (1938), p. 59; H. Lawrence, 'A Derbyshire visitation manuscript, 1687', *DAJ*, 32 (1910), p. 70; Webster, *Hearth Tax*, pp. xxvi–xxix, 137–42.

46 Thoroton, p. 490; Deering, p. 186; Pevsner and Williamson, pp. 226–7.

47 D. Defoe, *A Tour Through the Whole Island of Great Britain* (Everyman edn, 1928), II, p. 146; Deering, pp. 6, 231; Gill, 'Nottingham', p. 59; Fellows's house is individually identified on T. Sandby's *South Prospect of Nottingham* (1742), and is also illustrated in J. T. Godfrey and J. Ward, *The Homes and Haunts of Henry Kirk White* (Nottingham, 1908), p. 13; it is *not* the house illustrated in S. D. Chapman, 'The genesis of the British hosiery industry', *Textile History*, 3 (1972), 18; Gawthern, *Diary*, pp. 11–12; Willoughby's house is illustrated in Deering, facing p. 159; the timbers of Brewhouse Yard Museum have been dated to *c.*1700 by dendrochronology.

48 NAO M 471; H. Stutchbury, *The Architecture of Colin Campbell* (Manchester, 1967), pp. 63–4; the house is illustrated in Campbell's *Vitruvius Britannicus*, III (1725), plate 55 and in Deering, facing pp. 8, 19.

49 Pevsner and Williamson, p. 229; Gill, 'Nottingham', pp. 68–78; R .T. Coope and J. Y. Corbett (eds.), *Bromley House, 1752–1991* (Nottingham, 1991), pp. 49–75.

50 Pevsner and Williamson, p. 235; D. E. Holmes, 'A craftsman in iron: Francis Foulgham, Ironsmith, and the Newdigate family', *NH*, 24 (1980), pp. 7–8; James Foulgham of Nottingham executed a set of gates for Sir George Savile at Rufford Abbey in 1734; NAO DD.SR 215/13.

51 *RBN*, VI, pp. 155, 180.

52 Stevenson, 'A description', p. 129; C. Morris (ed.), *The Journies of Celia Fiennes* (1947), pp. 72–3; *RBN*, VI, pp. 64, 61; J. Loveday, *Diary of a Tour in 1732* (Edinburgh, 1890), p. 211; R. Patchen, *Four Topographical Letters* (1755); Sandby, *South Prospect*; a row of oak colonnades removed from a building in Long Row in 1896 and on display in Nottingham Castle Museum, is illustrated in Gill, 'Nottingham', p. 52.

53 Speed, *Theatre*; Thoroton, *Antiquities*, p. 493.

54 Yale Center for British Art: Paul Mellon Collection: painting of Pierrepont House and garden by unknown Dutch artist, *c.*1695; Nottingham Castle Museum, Prospect of Nottingham, by Jan Siberechts, *c.*1700; L. Knyff and J. Kip, Prospect of Nottingham from the East, *c.*1707: for a general discussion of the seventeenth- and eighteenth-century views of Nottingham see A. Henstock, 'A Prospect of Nottingham', *NH*, 21 (1978), p. 16.

55 G. London and H. Wise, *The Retired Gardener* (1706), appendix; J. Taylor, *A Journey to Edenborough in Scotland ...* (1705); Defoe, *Tour*, II, p. 144.

56 Defoe, *Tour*, II, p. 144.

57 Badder and Peat's Plan; A. Henstock, 'County House, High Pavement, Nottingham: a Georgian and Regency town house', *TTS*, 78 (1974), pp. 54–67; Gill, 'Nottingham', p. 59; Sandby's South Prospect; Loveday, *Diary of a Tour*.

58 J. V. Beckett and C. Smith, 'Urban renaissance and consumer revolution in Nottingham, 1688–1750' (unpublished MSS); NAO PRNW, Joseph Tuffing, admon. 28 September 1747.

59 R. C. Alvey, 'A cesspit excavation at 26–28 High Pavement, Nottingham', *TTS*, 77 (1973), pp. 53–72; Defoe, *Tour*, II, p. 145; Deering, p. 72.

60 *HMC*, *Portland*, II (1893), p. 308; Patchen, *Letters*.

61 NAO PRNW, George Oldfield, admon. 12 April 1749; Nicholas Sharpe, pr. 24 August 1710; Gervase Wild, pr. 13 June 1732; Edward Brown, pr. 26 June 1706.

62 Deering, pp. 91–5; NAO PRNW, Gervase Rippon, pr. 8 May 1693; William Smalley, pr. 5 May 1692; Guildhall Library, London, Sun Fire Insurance Registers, 1724.

63 NAO PRNW, Samuel Hallowes, pr. 22 June 1715; Deering, p. 96.

64 Deering, p. 9 and facing illustration; K. Brand, *The Shire Hall and Old County Gaol* (Nottingham, n.d.), p. 2; Barley and Straw, 7.

65 Deering, p. 158, and illustrations facing pp. 20, 159.

66 Deering, pp. 7–8 and illustration facing p. 8; *RBN*, VI, pp. 85, 99, 106.

67 Blagg and Wadsworth, *Marriage Licences*, p. 483; NAO DD.TS 16/19; Guildhall Library, London, Sun Fire Insurance Registers, 1720. A bathhouse (later known as the Old Bath) had been first built at Matlock in 1698 but Pennell and Smith purchased the lease, probably in the 1720s, and further developed the facilities, including cutting a new carriage access road through the limestone gorge to the village of Cromford: F. White & Co., *History ... and Directory of the County of Derby* (Sheffield, 1857), pp. 435; J. C. Cox, *Three Centuries of Derbyshire Annals*, II (1890), p. 231; NAO PRNV, Marmaduke Pennell, pr. 12 January 1732/3, Stephen Egginton, pr. 17 November 1744.

68 The engineers included Mr Wilkins of Leicester (1693), William Walker of 'Edtaine' (1693), John Rosse of Nottingham (1696), probably Peter Whalley of Nottingham (who set up Sheffield's waterworks in 1697), William Simmons of Woodstock, Oxon (1718), and Thomas Boulton of Nottingham (1732). Deering, p. 86; *RBN*, V, pp. 326, 380, 384, 391–3; NAO M7498; M19,858; Blackner, p. 25; F. Williamson, 'George Sorocold of Derby; a pioneer of water supply', *DAJ*, 57 (1936), pp. 43–73.

69 Anon., p. 46; *RBN*, VI, pp. 69–70, 93, 97, 101, 117, 120, 141, 167, 173, 176, 182, etc.

70 Deering, p. 76; *RBN*, VI, p. 117.

71 Deering, pp. 4, 167–8.

72 *RBN*, VI, pp. 33, 44, 48; Deering, p. 74; a bowling green to the north of the Sand Field is marked on the 1609 map.

73 *RBN*, V, pp. 364, 401, 403; VI, p. 20; Defoe, Tour, II, p. 143; Deering, pp. 76, 74.

74 Deering, pp. 72–3, 75; Anon., pp. 23–5; the probate inventories both of Richard Jackson of St Ann's Well and his widow Mary include 'Robin Hood's Chair', NAO PRNW R. Jackson, pr. 2 July 1713, M. Jackson, pr. 11 February 1713/14. I am grateful to Cathy Smith for bringing these to my attention.

75 Deering, p. 76; G. C. Robertson (ed.), *The Stretton Manuscripts* (Nottingham, 1910), p. 162.

76 Deering, pp. 75–6; *Nottingham Weekly Courant*, 30 June 1726, 3 August 1721.

77 In 1941 J. D. Chambers, his viewpoint shaped by early twentieth-century model housing developments, described this phase of Nottingham's history as its 'garden-city' period: 'Nottingham in the early nineteenth century', *TTS*, 45 (1941), p. 41.

78 Borsay, *Urban Renaissance, passim.*

79 Deering, p. 6.

8

DECLINE AND REGENERATION: SOCIAL AND ECONOMIC LIFE

Adrian Henstock, Sandra Dunster and Stephen Wallwork

In common with many English provincial towns, Nottingham suffered a relative decline in the late Tudor and early Stuart periods, followed after the Civil War by an era of increasing prosperity which became particularly marked after *c.*1700. The town's place in an approximate rank order of English towns rose steadily from forty-first position in *c.*1524 (based on recorded subsidy wealth), to twentieth in 1662 (taxable hearths). By 1750 it was well on its way to achieving the twelfth place (census population) recorded in 1801. It also gradually asserted its supremacy as the leading town in the East Midlands. In *c.*1524 it had lagged behind both Lincoln and Leicester but by 1662 had nearly caught up with the former and overtaken the latter; it exceeded both in population by 1801. Throughout it was always ranked above Derby, Newark, and other towns in the region.[1]

Population

One of the more significant indicators of the state of any town is population. From about 1575 it is possible to count the numbers of baptisms, burials and marriages for the three parish churches in the town, and to calculate that between the mid-sixteenth and the mid-eighteenth centuries the population of Nottingham grew from about 2,100 to 11,000 (table 8.1, figure 8.1).[2] Rapid growth during the second half of the sixteenth century was brought to a halt by an outbreak of plague in the mid-1590s, and although growth soon resumed it was more than twenty years before the population regained the late sixteenth-century levels. Growth continued at a slow but steady pace through the seventeenth century, punctuated by demographic crises; no decade escaped at least one year in which deaths exceeded births and growth was temporarily checked (figure 8.2). By the beginning of the eighteenth century population had reached about 6,000. There was then a dramatic change in the rate of growth, and by 1750 numbers had almost doubled to 11,000. Mortality crises, which continued to occur with relentless regularity, were largely the result of epidemic disease. Until the second half of the seventeenth century plague was the most devastating and persistent cause. In the 1590s about one in seven of the population died.[3] No other outbreak had such severe consequences, but the disease was a frequent and unwelcome presence in the town. Until the mid-seventeenth century not a decade passed without a 'visitation': 1588, 1593–94, 1604, 1611, 1617–8, 1625, 1635, 1639–42, 1647.

Figure 8.1 The population of Nottingham, 1575–1800

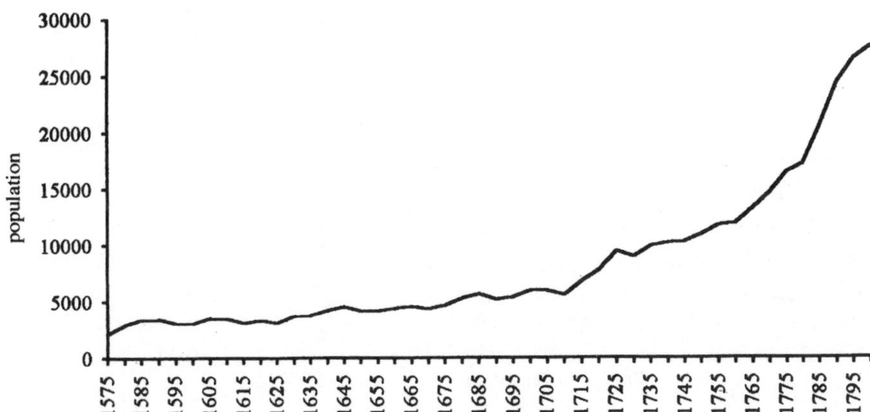

Sources: NAO PR 2019–23, 2138–42, 3630–4; NUMD Chambers MSS, notes on Nottingham parish registers, 1701–1800.

The response to plague remained virtually unchanged throughout the period. As news of its approach reached the town, steps were taken by the Corporation to try to prevent the 'sickness' arriving. Extra watches were set to prevent 'foreigners' from 'visited' locations coming within the town walls: in 1583 a poor man suspected of having the plague was bribed with 10*d* 'to avoyd the town' and in September 1646 the corporation 'voted and ordered generally that the Goose Fair shall be wholly cried down and proclamation sent to market towns to forbid the people to come to it by reason of the sickness in the country and to prevent danger to the town through God's mercy'.[4] Just as 'foreigners' were prevented from entering, local people were discouraged from leaving. In November 1601 access to Lenton Fair was restricted to livestock sales only, and a watch was set at various points between the town and Lenton to ensure that this prohibition on movement was upheld. Similar prohibitions were placed on local residents from visiting Derby in 1586 and Lincoln in 1631.[5]

Within the town a range of public health measures was adopted. Stray cats and dogs on Backside were slaughtered in 1647 and domestic animals such as pigs and dogs had to be kept inside. All alehouses on Backside were closed for two weeks in 1603. When, as was usually the case, precautions of this kind failed to prevent the spread of plague, attempts were made to isolate the afflicted from the rest of the community. When Thomas Locksmyth lay dying in 1593 'Robert Bullocke at a windowe did enquire and aske of him' what his last will and testament would be. Usually plague huts or cabins were set up outside the town boundaries. The high ridge of Mapperley Plains and the adjacent Gorsey Close and Trough Close were frequently used, as was Brewhouse Yard. There is no detail of the kind of care that was provided but, when the plague struck with severity, the financial costs could be high. The mayor's accounts for 1610 show that between 12 January and 6 April a total of £50 15*s* was paid out for the care of the 'visited' and the wages of the extra watchmen both on the approach roads to the town and on the 'Playnes'. These costs were not met by the corporation directly; local people were subject to the additional burden of a weekly levy during the height of any 'visitation'. In addition, charitable donations were made by individuals and by other communities spared by the disease. In 1592 the corporation recorded donations of money and food 'received for the relief of the poor and diseased infected' from members of the neighbouring gentry and clergy.[6]

As each successive attack of the plague receded, restrictive measures were relaxed. The watch was stood down, plague huts were destroyed and the land on which they were built was leased out for other uses. However, the corporation recognised the

Table 8.1 **The population of Nottingham, 1580–1750**

Date	*Population*	*Date*	*Population*
1580	2,920	1670	4,350
1590	3,440	1680	5,290
1600	3,080	1690	5,160
1610	3,480	1700	5,950
1620	3,310	1710	5,580
1630	3,750	1720	7,770
1640	4,250	1730	8,980
1650	4,190	1740	10,160
1660	4,342	1750	10,910

Sources: NAO PR 2019–23, 2138–42, 3630–4; NUMD Chambers MSS, notes on Nottingham parish registers 1701–1800.

Note: The population has been estimated from the number of baptisms, marriages and burials recorded in the registers of the three Nottingham parishes. The count was adjusted to compensate for gaps in the registers, and inflation factors were applied from 1686 for baptisms and from 1691 for marriages and burials to compensate for under-registration in the Anglican registers caused by the growth in nonconformity. After adjustments and inflation, baptisms were multiplied by 24 and the sum of baptisms, marriages and burials by 11.1. The figures given are the five-year averages of the mean of the two figures obtained from these calculations.

Figure 8.2 **Nottingham baptisms, marriages and burials, 1575–1750**

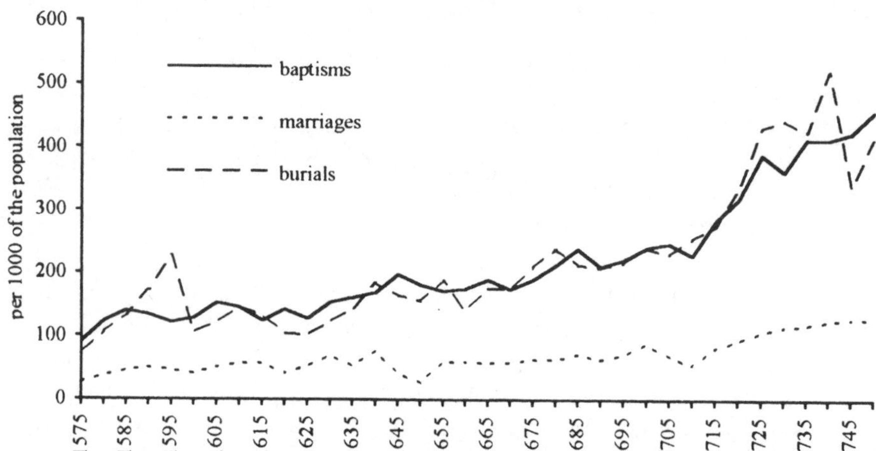

Note: The graph shows five-year averages of baptisms, marriages and burials as recorded in the parish registers. To compensate for under-registration resulting from the growth of nonconformity, inflation factors were applied to baptisms from 1686 and to marriages and burials from 1691.

Source: as fig 8.1

need for caution. In 1606 it let 'Gorsey Close ... at 50s rent with reservation for the town to use part of it to build on in any time of visitation'.[7] The ferocity and frequency of plague visitations waned towards the end of the seventeenth century, which was a common experience across the country.[8] Deering commented on what was probably the last serious outbreak in the town in 1667, when the plague

> made a cruel desolation in the higher part of Nottingham, for very few died in the lower, especially in a street called the Narrow Marsh, it was observed that the infection had no power, and that during the whole time the plague raged, not one who lived in that street died of it, which induced many of the richer sort of people to crowd thither and hire lodgings at any price; the preservation of the people was attributed to the effluvia of the tanners ouze ... besides which they caused a smoak to be made by burning moist tanners knobs.[9]

The plague was rapidly succeeded by smallpox. Although smallpox had claimed many lives in the sixteenth and seventeenth centuries, it reached epidemic proportions only in the eighteenth century. 'As healthful as Nottingham is', wrote Deering in 1739,

> there mostly happens once in five years some distemperature in the air, which either brings along with it some epidemical fever, (tho' seldom very mortal) or renders the smallpox more dangerous than at other times, of this last, the year 1736, was a fatal instance, for from the latter end of May to the beginning of September, this distemper swept away a great number of souls, (but mostly children) and in the single month

> of May, there were buried in St Mary's church and churchyard only, 104; in short, the burials exceeded that year the births by above 380.[10]

Every decade in the first half of the eighteenth century saw at least one year of exceptionally high mortality resulting from smallpox. Where plague was a universal threat smallpox struck particularly severely among the young; those who survived childhood had usually gained immunity from the disease by exposure to it early in life. The ravages of smallpox seem to have been met with a stoic acceptance; there is no evidence of the kind of basic preventative measures prompted by the threat of plague.[11]

Disease was not the only threat to population growth. Food shortages resulting from poor weather conditions and bad harvests were a recurring feature of English life in this period and Nottingham was no exception. Although death from starvation was comparatively rare, resistance to disease was lowered by poor nutrition. When, as in the 1580s and 1590s, the 1630s, 1720s and 1740s, food supply was interrupted, many died from plague or smallpox, and the number of marriages and births temporarily fell. In these circumstances the town's population was not able to replace its losses by natural increase. Between 1575 and 1750 there were many years in which fewer baptisms than burials were recorded in the parish registers (figure 8.2). Even in the years 1710 to 1750 when population doubled, burials (15,720) outnumbered baptisms (15,050). To explain this anomaly we need to study the pattern of migration.

Table 8.2 **In-migrants to Nottingham, 1570–1739**

Date	*Average number of in-migrants p.a.*	*Estimated total number of in-migrants*
1570–1593	46	1,050
1594–1644	5	242
1645–1711	26	1,742
1712–1739	194	5,420

Sources: As table 8.1.

Note: These figures have been extracted from parish-register data to provide an indication of the general trends in in-migration during each of the periods.

The migrant was a familiar figure in the early modern town. Nottingham offered the promise of opportunity, or at least an escape from rural poverty, to many men and women from small towns and villages throughout the East Midlands. The drift to the town varied at different periods (table 8.2). Although many arrived seeking to share in the economic prosperity of the late sixteenth century, the frequent outbreaks of plague from the 1590s until the 1650s made the town seem more threatening than welcoming and, combined with a long stagnation in trade, had the effect of discouraging migration. By the late seventeenth century Nottingham was more attractive to the potential migrant as new employment opportunities arose. Combined with the retreat of the plague this helped to attract a growing stream of migrants: as the frame-work-knitting industry expanded in the early decades of the eighteenth century the stream became a flood.

Table 8.3 **Origins of Nottingham apprentices, 1567–1753**

Place	*1567–1579*		*1692–1753*	
	No.	*%*	*No.*	*%*
Nottingham	30	40	542	45
Nottinghamshire	16	22	317	26
Derbyshire	4	5	137	11
Leicestershire	3	4	89	7
Lincolnshire	2	3	35	3
Yorkshire	4	5	25	2
Others	2[a]	3	43[b]	4
Not known	13	18	24	2
Total	74	100	1,212	100

Sources: NAO CA 3363, CA 1553.

Notes: [a] Staffordshire and Cumberland.
[b] Bedfordshire, Cheshire, Cornwall, Essex, Kent, Lancashire, London, Middlesex, Northamptonshire, Hampshire, Somerset, Staffordshire, Surrey, Wales (*sic*), Westmorland.

Some indication of the catchment area for one group of migrants can be gained from the surviving register of indentures of the young men apprenticed to Nottingham burgesses (table 8.3).[12] In both the late sixteenth and the early eighteenth centuries, most of the young men apprenticed to a master in Nottingham came from within the town or from elsewhere in Nottinghamshire; indeed, the proportion of 'local' recruits rose from 62 per cent to 71 per cent. About two-thirds were from Nottingham and the remainder from the county.[13] Most of those from the latter came from the more densely populated and easily accessible southern half of Nottinghamshire, particularly from the neighbouring village communities of Lenton, Radford, Sneinton, Wilford, Beeston, and Clifton. Market towns, particularly Newark, Southwell, Bingham and Mansfield, exported a steady flow of new apprentices. From beyond the county border apprentices often travelled many miles. In 1577 Robert Saunder, the fourteen-year-old son of a butcher from Barwick-in-Elmet near Leeds in Yorkshire was apprenticed to a Nottingham cutler, and the following year a tailor's son from Keswick in Cumberland was apprenticed as a baker. Serving an apprenticeship to a burgess conferred burgess rights, and some two-thirds of the burgess population was constantly being renewed by incomers. Some of these rose to high office; Richard Hurt, mayor on three occasions between 1595 and 1609, was a rich mercer who also owned several mills in and around the town. He came from Haldworth in Yorkshire. A notable feature of eighteenth-century apprenticeships was the number of young men entering the expanding hosiery industry. William Chapman, a weaver's son from Billingborough in Lincolnshire, was apprenticed as a framework knitter in 1743, and Benjamin Bostock, a collier's son from Trowell, was bound to a framesmith in 1740.

Two main objections were lodged to newcomers settling in the town, and these are clearly stated in the mayor's request of 1647 that the constable should provide him with a note of 'all foreigners come into town within four years last, that a course may be taken to remove such as are poor and are likely to be chargeable, and such as hinder the burgesses by trading'.[14] Concerns about poverty and the threat to trade are a common theme in the borough records and the corporation worked with the parish authorities to limit the numbers of newcomers.

Migrants unable to support themselves were particularly unwelcome:

> All strangers, idle and vagrant persons shalbe diligently examined if they remain here above three days their state to be known, how they live and can maintain themselves; and that such as you find suspicious to drive them from the town or otherwise let them remain in prison.[15]

The corporation made strenuous efforts to prevent poor migrants from settling in the town. In 1606 it was ordered that the holes in Hollow Stone should be filled in to prevent them from becoming homes for beggars. In 1612 the corporation attempted to restrict the building of cottages and 'poor habitations' and to prevent non-established town-dwellers from living in existing housing. While some of the cheaper housing was to be found in the underdeveloped east end of town, much of the poorest was in Backside, both to the east and west of Cow Lane and outside Chapel Bar. Many of these houses were probably squatters' cottages built on the waste land just outside the limits of the old urban core. The maps of 1609–10 show some development in this area, which was also notorious for having large numbers of common alehouses; in 1619 it was claimed that 'every nooke of ye Backside suffered typlers'.

Other measures taken by the corporation included residence restrictions. Anyone who had been resident in the town for less than three years could be evicted by his landlord, or the landlord was obliged to stand surety for the sum of £20 to prevent the tenant from becoming a burden on the poor rate. This prohibition on providing a roof over the heads of migrants also extended to lodgers. Landlords were prosecuted under the 1619 orders for taking in lodgers or leasing their property to tenants. Those found guilty of harbouring 'strangers' were fined heavily if they did not carry out the ensuing eviction order. Alderman Leonard Nixe was a regular offender in the 1620s, housing people in his 'new tenements' in Broad Lane and elsewhere in the town. Whether his motives in continuing to provide housing for 'foreigners' were philanthropic or financial is not clear: however, he seems to have been prepared to pay a fine of £3 6*s* 8*d* for each offence.

The responsibility for identifying unwanted newcomers lay initially with the aldermen, each of whom oversaw one of the seven wards in the town. On several occasions they were reminded of their duty to search their wards 'weekly or once in a fortnight at the least to weed out idle persons that be come into this town of late'. This duty became all the more important when plague was expected. By the early seventeenth century, when fear of an uncontrollable flood of migrants seems to have been at its height, the aldermen were assisted in their search and eviction policy by constables and beadles. In December 1615 payments were made for 'keepinge out the cuntrie poore on Christmas even'.

The migration levels of the seventeenth century give an indication of the overall success of these measures (table 8.2). However the regularity with which offenders were prosecuted is an indication that these orders did not find favour with everyone. While the fervour of anti-'stranger' feelings declined as the fear of plague receded, new initiatives were taken to prevent the poor from settling in the town. In April 1732 it was ordered that the arrival of any lodger was to be reported to the churchwarden or overseer of the poor within twenty-four hours. This was a specific attempt under the settlement laws to lighten the load of the parishes burdened with 'chargeable poor and with vagabonds and sturdy beggars'.[16]

In the later sixteenth century there was little by way of official poor relief, although the corporation occasionally paid private individuals for taking in paupers. In 1579 John Woodman, an innholder, agreed to house, feed and employ one Humphrey Harrison in exchange for 4*d* per week. The payment for taking in a child was higher; Isabell Sellyoke received 25*s* for 'keeping a bastard child' for forty-five weeks in 1581. In 1601 the town responded promptly to the new poor law legislation and the former convent of the 'hospitallers of St John of Jerusalem' was converted into a workhouse and asylum for the poor. John Cooper was appointed as the first overseer and given a mandate to 'walk the town to take up rogues and such like and punish such as shall be committed to him'. He was also to provide care for such 'poor infants' as were lodged with him. The workhouse, although located in the parish of St Mary's, was also to be available for use by St Peter's for the maintenance of beggars.[17]

By 1615 all three parishes were making financial contributions towards the upkeep of St John's 'to be collected by taxation'. The priorities of this institution can perhaps be discerned from the distribution of expenditure on the improvements that were made that year: £6 13*s* 4*d* was spent on 'bedding and provisions' for the poor and £20 was set aside for the purchase of materials to put them to work. The preoccupation with work continued through the seventeenth century. In 1627 plans were made for twenty poor children to benefit from a new initiative to provide them with work. The plan was costly and required both the personal financial support of corporation members and the revival of a weekly assessment to be paid by the townspeople. However Martin Hill, the governor of St John's, does not seem to have been successful. By 1630 he was in debt to the corporation for £100 and it was decided that a new governor for the poor children and house of correction should be appointed 'with all convenient speed'. Later initiatives included flax spinning and candle wick making.[18]

By the 1720s the accommodation provided for the poor at St John's was no longer sufficient, and in 1725 each of the three parishes made plans for separate workhouse provision. This did not signal any softening in attitude towards those considered to be irresponsible in their poverty. In 1729 three women found guilty at Quarter Sessions of being 'lately delivered of bastard children now chargeable to the parish of St Mary' were sentenced to be whipped at the house of correction, tied into the ducking stool and paraded along Stoney Street, High Pavement, Bridlesmith Gate, and around the Malt Cross before returning to the workhouse to be ducked.[19]

The workhouse was designed to provide for the destitute, but those who struggled to maintain themselves and their families were also helped in times of food shortage. In the 1580s the charitable action of the Earl of Rutland in subsidising grain prices was acknowledged by the justices of the peace. In the winter of 1630–31 a small group of burgesses was given responsibility for buying and then distributing food to needy families. Twenty quarters of barley and five quarters of peas were to be purchased for weekly distribution 'at some reasonable prices, under the market'.[20] This subsidy was insufficient: in January 1631 a group of burgesses petitioned Quarter Sessions:

> We desire and entreat that there may be some redress and order taken for the poor, either to set them on to work to cloth making, or else that every man may be cessed according to his ability, so that they may be kept at home , and restrained from swarming in our streets, as they do, both old and young;

Four years later, again following bad harvests, each parish appointed men 'to collect … for the poor, against Christmas, to keep them from begging'.[21]

In addition to public responses to crises, many individuals made provision for the 'deserving poor' by establishing charitable trusts or leaving money in their will. This kind of provision was carefully targeted to assist the most vulnerable and deserving. Widows, the elderly and young children were frequently mentioned. In 1647 Mary Wilson left a bequest of 30s, the interest from which was to be used to purchase cloth for two 'poor and impotent' people to make gowns at Christmas. In 1650 William Gregory made provision for the weekly gift of bread to twelve 'old poor and impotent' townspeople. On a grander scale was Lady Grantham's gift of 1658: she gave £200 to the town, the interest to be used to provide apprenticeships and work for the poor. Alderman Staples gifted £5 in 1630 as an interest-free loan over a six-year period to each of eight young burgesses, to assist them in setting themselves up in trade.[22]

As well as receiving charitable gifts of food, clothing and work the elderly poor benefited from the provision of almshouses. Deering listed fourteen different 'bedehouses', almshouses and hospitals, together providing accommodation for over a hundred people. Most of this provision was reserved for poor widows or the elderly, although there were five houses in Pilcher Gate occupied by poor families. A few of the almshouses dated from the medieval period, including Plumptre Hospital, which was renovated in 1650. However, most of the provision noted by Deering was set up in the seventeenth and early eighteenth centuries as charitable bequests in the wills of substantial citizens. In 1617 William Gregory had provided eleven almshouses in Hounds Gate, known as the White Rents almshouses, for the rent-free use of 'poor, aged people'. These almshouses were still in use in the eighteenth century, and as each parish made separate provision for its poor, the accommodation in the White Rents almshouses was divided accordingly.[23]

Among the migrants it was not just the poor and unemployed who were seen as a problem. Throughout the period the burgesses complained about the threat posed to their trade and livelihood by allowing new artisans and craftsmen who were not burgesses to trade in the town. In 1577 the Mickletorn jury made the presentment that 'there be made no more foreign burgesses but that they pay £10 and no money abated, for there is too many already; by making of them the poor burgesses commons is eaten up to the great hindrance of all'. Complaints continued throughout the seventeenth century. Legal action was frequently taken against those who were trading in the town without having satisfied the entrance requirements for burgess status, i.e. being the eldest son of an existing burgess, serving an apprenticeship to a burgess, or paying an entrance fee. Those seeking to enter the trading community by paying a fee could be rejected on economic grounds. In 1629 Cornelius Launder was refused entry because 'there be already two pewterers in the town who have children and apprentices that are ready to set up trade themselves'.[24]

The desire to limit the number of new artisans establishing themselves in Nottingham was tempered by an understanding that the sale of burgess rights provided an opportunity for the corporation to generate much-needed income. In 1698 a by-law was passed reiterating the order 'to prosecute and suppress all foreigners from and for using any trade within the said town, and also all others who shall use any trade in the said town unto which they have not served as an apprentice within the said town'. After this the price of purchasing the right to trade was beyond the means of most migrants.[25]

The trades of enrolled burgesses provide some indication of the occupations legally practised in the town after 1675, but less clear is the relative importance of the respective trades or the employment structure over the whole period. Table 8.4 offers a numerical analysis of the occupations recorded in various different sources after 1600, classifying them into five broad categories of food and drink, leather, textiles and clothing, metal, building and miscellaneous trades. The figures allow some general conclusions to be drawn by comparing trends in the first half of the seventeenth century with the post-Restoration period (table 8.5). The basic food and drink trades declined slightly but continued to account for nearly a quarter of all occupations, as befitted a populous market and county town. The leather trades declined by well over half, while textile tradesmen, including both traditional drapers as well as the emerging hosiers, doubled in proportion, due to the expansion of the framework knitting industry. The metal trades remained fairly constant but the figures mask a decline in the traditional smiths' crafts, compensated for by a marked increase in textile machinery engineering. Building trades remained constant but the substantial increase in miscellaneous occupations is a result of a much greater variety of smaller service trades, reflecting the increasingly sophisticated life-style of the town's inhabitants. Those occupational groups which produced the wealthiest tradesmen are indicated in table 8.6.

Table 8.4 **Analysis of trades, 1600–1754**

	Marriage Licences, 1600–40		*Wills, 1600–40*		*Burgesses alive in 1625*		*Anon.: Trades List, 1641*		*Wills, 1660–1700*		*Burgesses enrolled, 1675–1754*		*Deering: Trades List, 1739*		*Burgess Poll Book, 1754*	
Trade	*No.*	*%*	*No.*	*%*	*No.*	*%*	*No.*	*%*	*No.*	*%*	*No.*	*%*	*No.*	*%*	*No.*	*%*
Food and drink	95	24	26	17	45	29	71	33	77	26	301	14	88	36	247	18
Leather	101	26	46	31	174	34	107	21	41	14	278	13	61	8	108	8
Textiles	44	11	17	11	59	12	79	15	51	17	367	17	145	18	582	43
Metal	34	9	12	8	44	9	31	6	30	10	224	10	65	8	95	7
Building	14	4	8	5	20	4	30	6	23	6	154	7	38	5	39	3
Miscellaneous	101	26	43	28	62	12	100	19	81	27	862	39	200	25	288	21
Total	389	100	152	100	504	100	518	100	303	100	2,186	100	797	100	1,359	100

Sources: (a) *Abstracts of Nottingham Marriage Licences*, 1 (1930); (b) and (e) Nottingham Archdeaconry Wills, indexes, NAO; (c) NAO CA 4649; (d) *TTS*, 2 (1898); (e) NAO indexes to burgess enrolments; (g) Deering, pp. 94–5.

Notes: The figures relate only to persons with a named economic occupation, excluding gentry, widows, spinsters and not stated. Textiles include clothing trades other than leather, e.g. shoemakers, which are included under leather trades. The 1739 Trades List (and probably the 1641 Trades List) includes only masters and not employees or outworkers.

Table 8.5 **Trades: pre- and post-Civil War trends, 1600–1754**

Trade	*1600–1640* %	*1660–1754* %
Food and drink	26	23
Leather	28	11
Textiles	12	24
Metal	5	5
Building	5	5
Miscellaneous	21	28
Total	100	100

Notes: The figures represent the mean average percentage of the data sets in table 8.4.

Table 8.6 **Wealth by trades, 1688–1750**

	Inventories over £100	
Trade	*No.*	%
Food and drink	51	35
Leather	8	5
Textiles	36	25
Metal	8	5
Building	7	5
Miscellaneous	36	25
Total	146	100

Source: NAO, PRNW; analysis by Cathy Smith.
Note: The figures represent the number of persons whose probate inventories exceeded £100 in value.

Trade

A few of Nottingham's tradesmen operated from purely retail shops, but most had workshops which doubled as manufacturing and retail premises. Some, however, also sold their wares from stalls or pitches at the weekly markets which were central to the town's economy. Basic foodstuffs such as meat, fish, poultry and dairy produce could be purchased from the daily market at Weekday Cross. In the great market-place the Saturday market was able to offer a wide range of commodities for sale, each with its allocated space. On the west side of the market-place were areas set aside for sales of livestock, with pens for cattle, horses, sheep and pigs, all of which were driven to market on the hoof. Along Long Row were pitches for corn, malt, oatmeal and salt, and nearby were tented stalls for milliners, bone-lace weavers, hardwaremen, chandlers, whittawyers (white leather workers), tanners, coopers, tripewives and herb and seedsmen. To the east were the permanent roofed structures called the Old and the New Shambles, between them housing sixty butchers' stalls, and a double row of shoemakers' booths. Concentrated also in this area were shops or standings for haberdashers, grocers and mercers, leather sellers, tanners and glovers, fishermen and fishmongers, ropemakers, and cloth merchants. The latter sold woollen and linen cloth, 'northern cloth', and Hampshire and Burton kerseys. Sawn timber was sold on Timber Hill on the south side of the market-place, poultry around the Hen Cross at the junction of High Street and Bridlesmith Gate, and fruit and dairy produce around the Butter Cross in front of the Shambles. By Deering's time the timber merchants and sheep pens had been banished to other areas, and the stalls of the market gardeners had 'mightily encreased', a trend which commenced about 1705. The Saturday market attracted traders from Nottinghamshire and the neighbouring counties, although changes took place from time to time in response to market forces. In 1641 grocers and mercers from Mansfield and Loughborough were selling on the market, but by Deering's day they had been ousted by the Nottingham tradesmen. Conversely, the local market gardeners were by the early eighteenth century facing competition from those at Newark.[26]

Two of the most important staple foodstuffs were corn for bread and malt for ale. Much of both the breadcorn and the malt barley came from south Nottinghamshire and the adjacent Vale of Belvoir, and Nottingham market was the point of exchange for these commodities to the whole region.[27] During times of famine, especially those of the 1580s, 1590s and 1630s, attempts were made by the corporation to control the market for the benefit of the townspeople. A particular problem was 'poaching' by corn merchants from Derby, who were anxious to buy up corn to supply the upland areas of the Peak District. In 1608 orders were passed forbidding corn to be sold secretly in private houses rather than on the open market (a practice known as 'forestalling'), restricting the maltsters from purchasing barley, and where possible preventing the Derby dealers from purchasing corn. In 1613 a local man was prosecuted for allowing Derby merchants to buy corn illicitly from a private house. A related problem to forestalling was that of 'regrating', i.e. buying a commodity then reselling it later for a higher price; one dealer in 1605 was even prosecuted for buying two oranges – presumably a rare luxury – and selling them for double the price! In 1631 there was a prosecution for buying up oatmeal before the market and then selling it later, and the same year the county justices wrote to the Privy Council bemoaning the shortage of corn in the county. In 1659 the corporation was forced to resort to buying up quantities of Danzig rye imported from the Baltic. During a food riot of 1701 Alderman Thomas Trigg made an impromptu distribution of corn without first seeking the permission of its owner, Mr Fotherby. Trigg was delivered from Fotherby's wrath only by the corporation's decision to pay for all the grain that had been given away.[28]

The regular weekly markets were supplemented by occasional fairs lasting several days. The oldest was St Matthew's Fair, popularly known since at least the 1540s as 'Goose Fair', although no record has survived of any particular specialisation in the sale of geese; indeed, in the seventeenth century it appears to have been predominantly a horse fair, and in the eighteenth a cheese fair. The records of the horse fair toll collectors for the Commonwealth period show that between thirty and a hundred horses changed hands annually, attracting dealers from across the East Midlands and occasionally further afield.[29]

Far more important in the sixteenth and seventeenth centuries was Lenton Fair, which lasted for eight days each November. Although a mile outside the borough boundary in front of the gates of the dissolved Cluniac priory, it had a direct effect on Nottingham's trade as the townspeople were bound by law to suspend their regular markets for the duration. Lenton Fair was of regional importance, attracting London merchants specialising in luxury goods, including mercers, drapers, goldsmiths and grocers. In 1549 the Manners family of Haddon Hall in north Derbyshire purchased their spices from a London grocer at Lenton Fair, as did the Willoughbys of Wollaton in 1572. In 1593 the Williamson family of Sawley in south Derbyshire purchased various wares from the fair. However the influx of Londoners also brought the danger of disease; in 1603 Nottingham tradesmen were forbidden to deal in London wares for fear of bringing plague into the town, and the following year the fair was cancelled for the same reason. Many of the London goods were brought by sea and river via the Humber and the Trent; in 1610 the Willoughbys' coal barges taking coal from Nottingham to Gainsborough 'refraighted with London goodes for Lenton faire' on the return journey. The London merchants continued to visit the fair until about 1680, but thereafter Nottingham shopkeepers started to travel regularly to the capital to purchase their mercery, drapery and grocery goods direct. As a result the fair declined and by the 1740s it was little more than a large market with local clientele.[30]

Markets and fairs also served the important social function of bringing together people from across the region and beyond, allowing them to conduct legal or financial business in the town, to extend their marriage horizons, or simply keeping in touch with relations. In 1623 the marriage arrangements between a young man from Hathern near Loughborough in Leicestershire and a young lady from Sandiacre just over the Derbyshire border were finalised between the groom and his fiancée's father at the Saturday market. In 1679 Leonard Wheatcroft, the parish clerk from Ashover near Matlock in north Derbyshire, arranged to meet two of his children, who were living in the Nottingham area, at Lenton Fair.[31]

The import of luxury goods for Lenton Fair was only a small part of the trade on the Trent. Since the Middle Ages the river had served as a vital artery connecting Nottingham and the East Midlands with the port of Hull on the Humber estuary and thence to London and the Continent. Along the river were a series of inland ports, generally of decreasing importance the further upstream they were situated: Gainsborough, Newark, Nottingham itself (Trent Bridge), Kings Mills near Castle Donington and Wilden Ferry near Shardlow in south Derbyshire. Each acted as staging points for the transhipment of imported goods into smaller boats or exported goods into larger ones, as well as being collection and distribution depots for the surrounding countryside. Goods were conveyed between Nottingham and Gainsborough 'by shallower vessels called flat bottomed boats or barges by reason of diverse fordable shallows betwixt Newark and Nottingham' in 1641. These vessels had a single square sail and could make reasonable progress downstream aided by the current and the prevailing south westerly wind, but upstream they frequently had to be towed from a haling path on the river bank. In 1609 coal bound for Gainsborough was transported in a series of 'barges, boats or keeles' bearing names such as the *Speedwell*, the *Elizabeth* and the *Great Trinity*. Both Siberecht's prospect of Nottingham in *c.*1700 and Buck's view of 1743 show laden boats at Trent Bridge, the vessel at the latter having a collapsible mast to enable it to pass under the bridge. Sandby's prospect of 1742 illustrates a sailing barge heading upstream being 'haled' by a group of four men from a rope attached to the masthead.[32]

The water-borne trade has left little record during the sixteenth century, although its importance was confirmed by events of 1592–93. Sir Thomas Stanhope had erected a series of fishweirs at Shelford, between Nottingham and Newark, which provoked civil disturbances as well as complaints from thirty-nine villages situated along the river about the interference to navigation. By 1641 wharves on both sides of Trent Bridge handled exports such as coal from Wollaton and lead from the Derbyshire Peak District or imports such as wine, fish, iron, flax, pitch and tar, many of which originated from Scandinavia. The small port acted as an entrepôt for the distribution of goods by road transport throughout the region; it also served dealers from 'diverse other market towns in the counties adjoining as Melton Mowbray, Leicester, Mount Sorrel, Loughborough, Ashby de la Zouch, Derby, Ashburn in the Peake, who from Nottingham fetch these commodities by land carriage'. However some goods were transported upstream from Nottingham. By the 1720s according to that great chronicler of inland trade, Daniel Defoe, the Trent was

> navigable here for vessels or barges of great burthen, by which all their heavy and bulky goods are brought from the Humber and even from Hull, such as iron, black tin, salt, hops, grocery, dyers wares, wine, oyl, tar, hemp, flax, etc. and the same vessels carry down lead, coal, wood, corn and also cheese in great quantities from Warwickshire and Staffordshire.

Deering repeated this same list, adding Norway oaks and deals (pine) to the imports, and pottery and Cheshire cheese to the exports. The pottery no doubt derived from Nottingham, Derbyshire and especially from Staffordshire.[33]

Despite the impressive catalogue of commodities, much of the trade took the form of through traffic passing up and down the river rather than emanating from Nottingham itself; Defoe observed that 'Nottingham, notwithstanding the navigation of the Trent, is not esteemed a town of very great trade, other than is usual to inland towns.'[34] The corporation attempted to exact passage tolls from all goods passing through Trent Bridge, while at the same time supporting its own merchants in their attempt to evade the payment of tolls elsewhere. Not surprisingly, tolls became a frequent cause of conflict and occasionally actually disrupted trade. In 1566 a dispute over the payment of the passage tolls on the river at Newark led to the seizure of parcels of fish, iron and other commodities being imported by Nottingham merchants. In 1634 the corporation invoked its ancient charter rights to demand that Alderman William Nix and six other fishmongers and ironmongers should be allowed free passage for their goods up the Trent. In 1659 a further dispute led to a lawsuit over the freedom from tolls of Mr Fillingham and Mr Hall and 'others of this town tradeing from Hull or Gainsborough'.[35]

As Nottingham formed the effective head of navigation for many commodities it made vigorous attempts to maintain its position. However, following a general increase in trade after the Restoration, persistent attempts were made by areas upstream to take control of the through traffic. From the 1690s until 1760 Wilden Ferry was leased by the Coke family to Leonard Fosbrooke and his descendants, who managed to operate a monopoly on all river trade between Wilden and Gainsborough. Nottingham's traditional rivalry with Derby was given new force by the attempts to make the River Derwent navigable from Derby to the Trent; no less than seven bills to this effect were introduced into Parliament from 1664 onwards until an Act was eventually passed in 1719. All the bills were opposed by Nottingham. The corporation's initial reaction in 1698 to a similar attempt to make the Trent navigable as far as Burton was to place chains across the arches of Trent Bridge and to prevent boats from Sawley and Wilne in Derbyshire from proceeding. This navigation was authorised by a further Act in 1699, although in practice it was barely implemented; an attempt in 1714 to make it more effective never reached the statute books.[36]

Of those commodities imported by water, some were of particular significance to Nottingham's economy, among them fish, iron and timber. Although the Trent was renowned for providing numerous varieties of freshwater fish, barrels of herring and other salt fish were imported from Hull, presumably mainly for winter consumption, by local fishmongers. They frequently combined their trade with that of ironmonger to import bar iron from Scandinavia, possibly because the two commodities were handled by the same Hull merchants. By 1641 there were sixteen fish and ironmongers in the town.[37] A growing shortage of local timber with the post-Civil War's building boom resulted in increasing quantities of Scandinavian timber being imported in the late seventeenth and early eighteenth centuries. The majority were 'deals', i.e. pine planks and boards for use as panelling, floorboards and stairs. Timber was originally displayed for sale on Timber Hill on the south side of the market-place, but by the 1740s it was stacked at the Trent Bridge wharf or in private timber yards.[38]

Nottingham's chief 'export' was probably coal, although this trade was in the hands of the local gentry rather than the town's merchants, and it brought great wealth to the Willoughby family before the 1580s. Mined in the pits of Wollaton, Strelley and Bramcote, coal was a notoriously bulky and expensive commodity to transport by road. It was brought by wagon to Trent Bridge and then distributed by boat to Newark and Gainsborough and villages along the river. In 1603 the now impoverished Sir Perceval Willoughby of Wollaton entered into partnership with a Leicestershire coalmaster, Huntingdon Beaumont, to lease the Strelley coal from the Byron family. One of Beaumont's first acts was to construct a wagonway from the pits to Wollaton Lane, with the ultimate intention of extending it through Lenton to the Trent; this is the first recorded use of rails in Britain. In 1604 Beaumont attempted to break into the London coal market, hoping to compete with the sea-borne coal from Newcastle; he sold the idea to Willoughby by suggesting that he had the opportunity to become 'the chiefe cities cheife collier'. The venture soon failed and the vessels were sold back to the promoters, who cut their losses and leased their coal sales along the Trent to Gainsborough to Robert Fosbrooke. His family was to be involved with the Trent navigation for the next 150 years. An insight into the comparative costs of road and river transport is provided by an estimate made by Fosbrooke in 1614. While it cost 3*s* to carry a rook of coal five miles from Strelley pits to Trent Bridge (two miles of which was presumably by rail), it cost only 1*s* 2*d* to convey it over twenty miles from Trent Bridge to Newark by water.[39]

Despite its comparatively high cost, road transport had to be used where there was no alternative. In the 1580s loads of stone were carried from Ancaster in Lincolnshire to build the new hall at Wollaton, returning with coal. Wagons bringing corn from neighbouring counties also frequently returned laden with coal. Various imported goods were collected from Trent Bridge and distributed by road through Leicestershire and Derbyshire. Some bulky commodities were transported by packhorse, especially across hilly areas such as the Peak District. Trains of packhorses brought salt across the Peak from the Cheshire 'wiches'; in 1630 six horse loads arrived for sale in the market on one day. The pack horses returned laden with Nottingham malt. Less weighty items could be sent in parcels by the increasing numbers of short- and long-distance carriers' wagons. There was a regular London carrier in Elizabethan times, and by the 1740s there were three wagons leaving weekly for London, as well as twice-weekly services to Derby, Leicester, Mansfield, Loughborough, Southwell and York, and weekly services to, among other places, Sheffield, Leeds, Manchester, Birmingham and Bristol.[40]

The carriers were based at local inns, which served an important business function as temporary warehouses for items of trade as well as their more obvious roles in providing hospitality and stabling for travellers and market visitors. Few records of their operation survive, but there were thirteen innkeepers in Nottingham by 1615, and fourteen by 1641. The inns were scattered throughout the town, but with concentrations in Long Row and around the market-place and, to a lesser extent, in High Pavement, the first major street encountered by travellers coming from the south. The most prominent inn was The Bullhead in Long Row, first recorded in 1577. John Taylor lodged at The Princes Arms on his visit in 1632. Others mentioned before the Civil War include The White Hart (1558) in Long Row, The Peacock (1615) in Smithy Row, The Lion (1563) in Chandlers' Lane (now Bottle Lane), The Nag's Head in Stoney Street, and The Swan (1549) and The Castle (1616), both in High

Pavement. William Higdon, one of the thirteen innkeepers listed in 1615, purchased The Flying Horse in Timber Hill in 1618 from Sir Charles Morryson. By 1624 he was living there with his wife, two daughters, a female servant and an ostler.[41] Inns were outnumbered by common alehouses. The marked proliferation of alehouses, many of them unlicensed, was a notable feature of Tudor and early Stuart towns. They offered cheap refreshment and lodgings to the poor. Economic necessity drove many men and women into keeping alehouses; a petition to the corporation complaining about the increasing number of alehouses in Nottingham in 1619 specifically noted that 'when all trades feaylle, [men] turne tiplers'. Some sixty unlicensed alehouses were counted in 1615.[42]

Following the Restoration the number of inns increased considerably. A War Office survey of available guest beds and stabling in 1686 found that Nottingham could provide 349 beds and stabling for 626 horses, over a third more than Newark or Mansfield. Between 1715 and 1730 some sixteen innkeepers and victuallers took out fire insurance policies with the Sun Fire Office, including the landlords of The Feathers in Wheeler Gate and The Eagle and Child in Chapel Bar.[43] One of the largest inns is described in the probate inventory of William Parkinson dated 1733. He was able to entertain his guests in three parlours, and a dining room furnished with four tables, twelve leather chairs, a clock, mirror, weather glass and pictures. He could offer five bedrooms, including the 'best chamber' and the 'yellow chamber', and his well-stocked cellar contained over forty hogsheads of ale valued at over £70. In 1739 Deering recorded forty-one innkeepers in Nottingham.[44]

Individual landlords brewed their own ale from local malt, and Nottingham ale enjoyed a wide reputation. Celia Fiennes, who in 1697 was 'very well entertained' at The Blackmoor's Head, wrote that 'Nottingham is famous for good ale so for cellars they are all dugg out of the rocks and so are very coole. Att the Crown Inn is a cellar of 60 stepps down all in the rock like arch worke over your head; in the cellar I dranke good ale.'[45]

Malting and agricultural interests

Quality ale could be made only from quality malt, the processing of which provided an increasingly lucrative local industry during the course of the seventeenth century. This involved steeping quantities of barley in vats, laying it out to germinate, and drying in a kiln before grinding it into a powder. There are surprisingly few references to the trade during Elizabeth's reign, although it may have been practised by tanners combining both occupations on a seasonal basis. Stray references testify to three malt mills during the early part of Elizabeth's reign – in Narrow Marsh, Goose Gate End and the Backside – and by 1603 there were apparently four, all belonging to the corporation. However, of the 516 burgesses living in 1625 only one was described as a maltster, and of all the tradesmen with a recorded occupation who left a will before 1640 none was described as such. Yet in 1641 there were sixty maltsters in the town, equalling the butchers as by far the largest occupational group. Ironically the initial stimulus for this boom may have been poverty, leading to an increase in 'tippling houses' in the decades either side of the turn of the century, both in the town and further afield. There is evidence of a rush of people anxious to get involved in this lucrative trade, and in both 1603 and 1620 the tenants of the town's malt mills complained to the corporation that other people had set up rival mills.[46]

Several new malthouses were built. Sometime before 1612 the Plumptre Hospital estate erected 'a great howse with many fayer malting romes' on Cuckstool Row. In 1626 property sold in Broad Marsh included a 'malt house, kiln and stable … under one roof', together with an adjacent 'bracken house'; the latter was a store for bracken which was burnt in the kiln to dry malt. However, a major reason for the success of Nottingham's malting industry was connected with the man-made caves and cellars cut into the sandstone bedrock. Not only were these used for keeping ale and beer cool in summer, but they were also used

> instead of barnes for harbouring of brakes [bracken] got in summer to drye malt withall in winter, and some that have floors that are large and level use them for making malt, having in them wells and cisterns for steeping of barley. In these they will make malt as kindly in the heat of summer as above ground in the best time of winter, by reason whereof there is great abundance made in this town.

Some of the caves were also used for retailing ale, as the Broad Marsh property also included a 'seller or tavern' and another 'vault or tavern'. Bracken was later replaced as a fuel by coke, and Deering attributed the quality of Nottingham ale to the fact that the malt was dried with coke or cinders which produced a sweeter malt than that dried with Yorkshire coal.[47]

After the Civil War malting became a recognised occupation in its own right. Among occupations recorded in local wills between 1660 and 1700 were seventeen maltsters. The trade was also a source of considerable wealth. Thoroton wrote in *c.*1675 that 'the good barlay which grows in the Vale of Belvoir and the parts adjacent are there [at Nottingham] converted into malt, yeilding thereby (as I suppose) more profit to the place than ever wool did heretofore'. An analysis of probate inventories between 1688 and 1750 shows there were more wealthy maltsters than practitioners of any other trade; fifteen had goods worth between £100 and £500 and four worth over £500, well in excess of mercers, framework-knitters and others. William Coppock, who died in 1689, owned goods worth £355, including 180 quarters of malt in store, his own malt mill, and the 'screen in the malt chamber'. Thomas Harding had stock worth £300 in 1723. Robert Linley, ironmonger and roper, was holding £140 worth of malt in 1696.[48]

Another reason for the success of the malting industry was that the product found a ready market outside Nottingham. In 1641 'there is great abundance made in this town, which they vend in Lancashire, Cheshire, Shropshire, Staffordshire and the Peak of Derbyshire, by badgers, carriers, or hucksters of those countries which fetch it … dayly'. This formed a useful two-way trade for the packhorse carriers 'especially they in Cheshire making a doubble return by bringing salt from the Wiches and carrying back malt into those parts'. Nearly a hundred years later Defoe noted that 'they make the best malt, and the most of it of any town in this part of England'.[49] Deering listed forty maltsters in the town in 1739, who between them paid over £1,000 in excise duty at each 'sitting'. Although the trade was 'not inconsiderable', he admitted that it was now facing considerable competition as 'the modern improvement of land has made some neighbouring towns sharers' in the trade.[50]

Nottingham's malting industry was supported by the prosperous arable farming of the countryside to the south and east, but the town was itself a farming community. Many of the town's commonest occupations such as butchery, baking, and tanning, with its associated leather trades, were closely allied to agriculture. Within the borough boundary some 1,500 acres were devoted to farming, including the two common arable fields – the Sand Field and the Clay Field – on the slopes to the north of the town, the common meadows on the flood plain of the Trent to the south, two common pastures – the Lings and Mapperley Hill – on the northern extremities of the borough, and common woodland at the Coppices. In addition there were several enclosed crofts and meadows of varying sizes. Basically the farming system conformed to that practised in common-field villages although by this period strict crop rotations and many other regulations had fallen into decay. In the arable fields many of the original strips were grouped into compact blocks enclosed with either permanent or temporary hedges. These were 'Lammas closes', i.e. often fenced for some three-quarters of the year, but thrown open for common grazing by the burgesses' animals, usually from Lammas Day in August to Martinmas in November. By Deering's day the fields were 'now almost all enclosed'. No other evidence exists for any communal agricultural activity, and it must be assumed that during the rest of the year each owner sowed corn or even pastured animals as he wished, totally independent of his neighbours. The Meadows were still divided into small narrow strips or 'doles' but were usually unfenced. After the hay crop had been gathered, normally around Midsummer Day, they were also thrown open to common grazing.[51]

It was not necessary to leave land fallow because the natural richness of the soil was supplemented by regular fertilisation with human manure. In 1641 the soil was described as 'so rich as that ground which this year beareth corn will the next year bear good meadow'. Deering noted that the meadows were frequently fertilised by floodwater from the Trent and the fields were 'so plentifully enriched by the great quantity of dung and ashes the town afford [from urban cesspits] that there is no need to look for marle or other kind of manure'.[52]

The farming land was owned in freehold by private owners, and subject to the common rights of the burgesses. By far the largest owner was the corporation with its Chamber, Bridge and Free School estates. The corporation also owned most of the enclosed crofts, many of which were divided into 'parts' and allotted to burgesses in order of seniority. These perquisites were a source of considerable income to the senior members of the corporation, and helped to maintain several of the better-off

Figure 8.3 **Nottingham and its common lands**

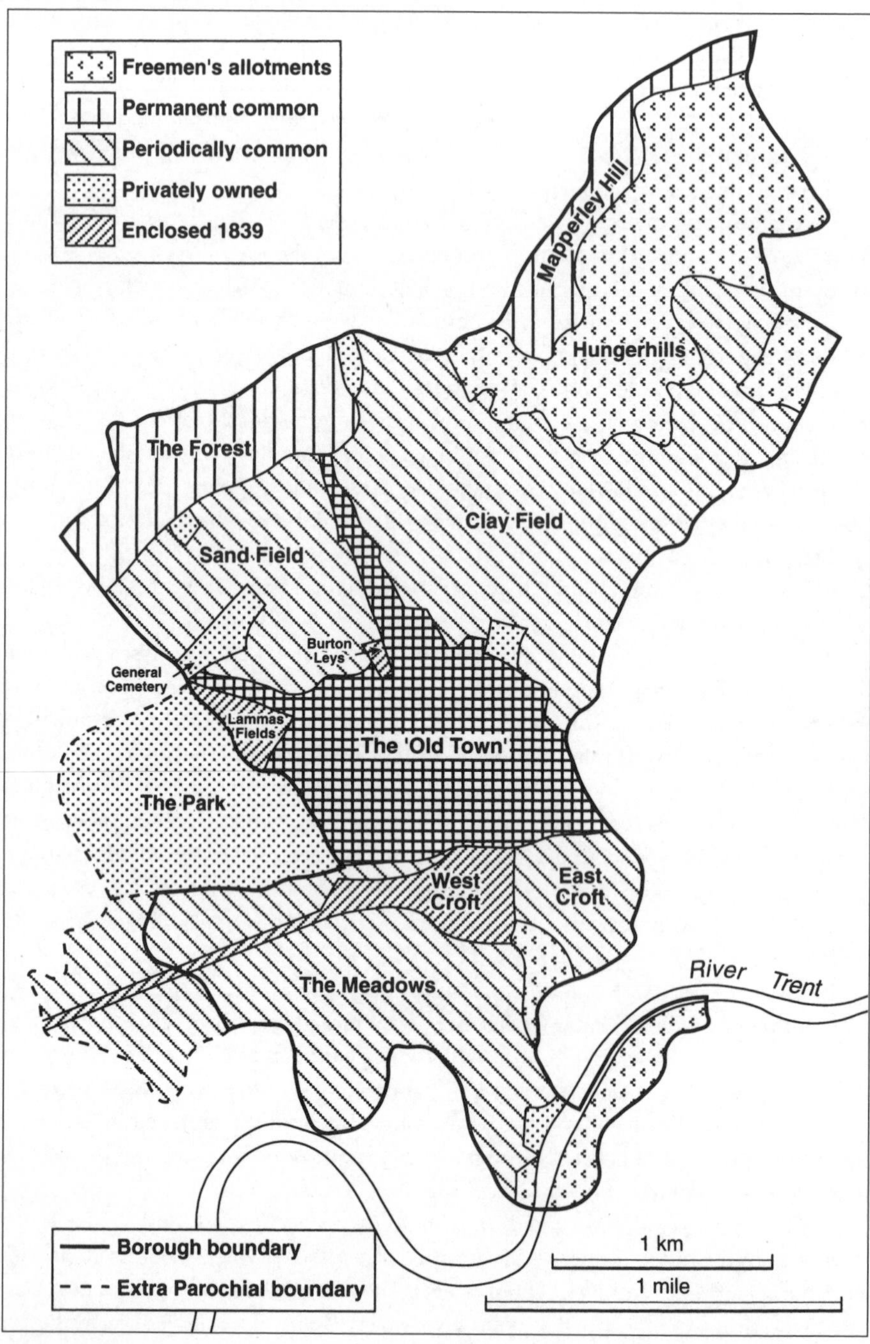

Note: Although this map replicates the situation on the eve of enclosure in 1845, so little had changed that it is almost exactly as depicted on the 1609 Crown Survey Map

butchers and graziers such as the Gregorys, who ran large numbers of animals on the town's lands. The corporation attempted to regulate the numbers of animals grazed. In 1578 the town's butchers submitted a set of rules to regulate their trade; these included the proposal that each butcher should graze no more than 'five score killing shepe' in the Meadows. In 1615 there were complaints that 'the multitude of shepe encreaseth her in this towne, and some men doo keepe 2 or 3 hundreth a peece in the feildes, which eate out poore mens commons' after Lammas day. As this inhibited the sowing of winter corn it was decreed that each burgess's allocation or 'stint' should be no more than sixty sheep. However, in 1630 the stint was ordered to be 'reduced' to six score, i.e. 120. The stint was further reduced to forty in 1698 and to thirty in 1727.[53]

Cattle were also grazed on the town's fields and pastures, and pigs and horses in the Coppices. In 1613 Hugh Varden, probably a typical burgess, owned a stint for eight cows to graze the fields after Lammas together with a 'burgess part' in the Dovecoate Close. An Easter book for St Peter's parish in 1624 lists sixty-four cattle owned by thirty-five householders; if projected in proportion to the estimated town population this suggests about 250 cattle. Many of these would have been dairy cows kept to supply domestic milk, and some would probably have been kept in cowsheds in the backyards of the owners' houses and stall-fed on hay, especially in winter. Others would be fattened for slaughter by the butchers and graziers. The stint for cattle was often exploited by senior members of the corporation for their own ends. It was claimed retrospectively in 1797 that:

> Soon after the Restoration two flourishing families in this town (viz. Mr Gregory's and Mr Sherwin's, graziers) used to go to Mansfield Fair to purchase large quantities of cattle. The fields at that time being unlimited, they turned to all they bought – the quantity being large the commonage was soon eat up – this passed for several years when the Mayor in consequence of divers complaints from ye burgesses called a general town meeting and by consent of that meeting, the number was limited to five head of cattle belonging to burgesses only.[54]

Manufacturing

The hides and skins from slaughtered animals were an important by-product of the butchery trade. They were sold to the tanners or members of a host of associated leather trades before being passed on to the numerous cordwainers (shoemakers), sadlers and glovers. Tanning had been a prominent trade in the town since medieval times, and was still concentrated in the low-lying area of Narrow Marsh beneath the sandstone cliff and adjacent to the River Leen. Some tanning vats had been formed out of the sandstone caves behind the cliff face. Here in 1654 the visitor Richard Francke noticed a colony of 'tanners, tawyers, fell-mongers, parchment and vellum-dressers, besides the glutiners, that dwell in houses contiguous with the rocks'.

These trades were notorious for producing offensive odours and waste, and it is hard to believe the claim in 1641 that 'I know no trades like to breed offence in that kind but tanners, fellmongers, and whittawyers, all which dwelling on a row on the bank of the River Leen, all the offals and refuse of these trades are by that river dayly swept away and cleansed.' Of those burgesses living in 1625 fifty were tanners or whittawyers and formed the fourth largest occupational group, and the trade provided the town with numerous mayors between the reigns of Elizabeth and Charles I, several of whom were from the Gregory and Sherwin families.[55] In the decades following the Restoration tanning went into rapid decline. According to Deering there had still been forty-seven tanners in 1667 but the numbers fell to twenty-one in 1707 and finally plummeted to three in his day. Nottingham's tanners had once been renowned for producing the best upper leathers for boots and shoes and also for harnesses and coach leather. Although dwindling timber stocks had been blamed for a scarcity of the bark used in the tanning process, Deering suggested that the decline was largely a result of the restrictive practices of the tanners.[56]

Tanning was not the only traditional trade to go into terminal decline during this period. In medieval times Nottingham had been well known for metal working of various types, hence street names such as Bridlesmith Gate. In 1641 it was still inhabited by some bridle smiths, but most of the smiths were 'now of a rougher stamp such as make plow irons, coulters, shares, stroake and nayles, harrow teeth and the like, of which trade there are at this day such store in this street and other parts of the town as serve to furnish not only the county of Nottingham but diverse other bordering shires as Leicester, Rutland and Lincoln'. Of those burgesses living in 1625 forty-four were metal workers, including twenty-two blacksmiths, three cutlers, three locksmiths and six spurriers.[57]

However, by 1739 Deering was able to list only three 'firesmiths', three cutlers and an ironfounder, a nailor and a pinmaker in the town in addition to four ironmongers, and he reported that 'this trade has moved its seat to Birmingham and Sheffield'. This was despite an increasing demand for specialist iron products, particularly in the expanding hosiery industry. Many smiths were now involved in building and maintaining stocking frames. By 1739 there were fourteen framesmiths and eight 'setters-up' of frames in the town. A quite different market had been created by the demand for ornamental iron railings and gates, some of them wrought by specialist smiths connected with the iron foundry near the glassworks at the east end of Barker Gate.[58]

A related traditional industry was that of bellfounding. Since the late medieval period Nottingham had been one of the few towns in the East Midlands to possess its own bellfoundry. In the early sixteenth century this had passed by marriage from the Mellors family to the Quarnbys. By Elizabethan times, however, the Oldfield family were supplying bells to churches all over Nottinghamshire and Lincolnshire and sometimes beyond. In 1586 Henry Oldfield married the daughter of the mayor of Congleton in Cheshire, where he settled and opened another foundry. In 1741 George Oldfield's foundry was situated in one of the yards behind Long Row, and it survived until the end of the eighteenth century.[59]

While such traditional trades were either declining or just holding their own, new ones sprang up, dictated by new fashions or consumer demand. Francis Gawthern moved into Nottingham in 1723 and leased the Grey Friars property near Broad Marsh from Thomas Smith the banker. Here he established what was reputed to be the first white lead works in the country, using lead presumably imported from the Peak District. The works specialised in the production of white lead for the manufacture of high-quality white paint which was used on many of the great country houses of the period.[60] Glassmaking also developed in this period. English glass manufacture was revolutionised following successful experiments of George Ravenscroft and others to produce clear lead or 'flint' glass in the 1670s and 1680s. A new glasshouse was established in Nottingham by 1675. A visitor in 1699 described how craftsmen 'make fine glass ware for drinking'. On a site near Glasshouse Street, it operated for nearly a hundred years under a succession of owners. In about 1700 a second glasshouse was erected by Robert Brentnall from Awsworth. He prospered, leaving at his death in 1713 an inventory of his possessions valued at £766 and including large stocks of bottles, drinking glasses, decanters and apothecaries' glasses. His glasshouse was at the east end of Barker Gate but seems to have closed in the 1750s.[61]

Plate 18 **Industrial buildings** ***c*****.1740**. This detail from Thomas Sandby's *East Prospect* of 1741 shows the smoking cones of two glasshouses (10) next to the iron-foundry chimney (11) at the east end of Barker Gate

The prosperity of the two glasshouses producing quality drinking vessels is further evidence of the consumer revolution, and the local industry also produced an offshoot in the form of a 'studio glassmaker' making trinkets or novelties. Celia Fiennes in 1697 was intrigued by watching him at work: 'There was a man that spunn glass and made severall things in glass, birds and beasts; I spunn some of the glass and saw him make a swan presently; with divers couloured glass he makes buttons which are very strong and will not breake.' This was almost certainly Nicholas Strelley, descendant of a prolific local gentry family who, according to Thoroton in *c.*1675, 'lives now in Nottingham upon some ingenious manufactures in glass which he spins and orders very commendably'. In 1712 Ralph Thoresby also watched him working and bought some glass 'curiosities'.[62]

Plate 19 **Trade Card, James Morley *c.*1700**. The card illustrates examples of Morley's wares, including 'carved' pots with a false outer body cut out into decorative shapes like fretwork, and a large garden urn similar to those in the gardens of Pierrepont House (plate 17) and Newdigate House, on Castle Gate

The medieval potteries had disappeared by the reign of Elizabeth, and the town was no doubt supplied with crude lead-glazed earthenwares produced in places such as Ticknall in south Derbyshire. However, the consumer revolution stimulated demand for better quality products such as delftware and stoneware. Following the first successful manufacture of German-style salt-glazed stoneware in the London area in the 1670s the technique spread to the provinces. By 1693 at least James Morley, a Nottingham brickmaker, was making a very fine orange-brown stoneware, using clay from Crich in Derbyshire, where his brother Thomas established an identical pottery in *c.*1698. James Morley's original works were situated at the east end of Barker Gate, but this site was abandoned in *c.*1715 and replaced by new premises in Beck Lane which remained in the hands of the Morley family for most of the century. Another pottery was opened by the Wyer family in *c.*1725 adjacent to the glass house in Glasshouse Street. The finest quality wares were made including ornamental mugs, jugs, tea and coffee cups, 'loving cups', 'flower pots' (garden urns) and the grotesque 'bear jugs', many of them illustrated on James Morley's trade card of *c.*1700. Some were commemorative pieces, incised with dates and the names of the recipients, such as the posset pot made for the mayor, Samuel Watkinson and his wife, in the year 1700, and decorated with the royal coat of arms. Nottingham stonewares were sold throughout the Midlands by road and sent down the Trent to London and even to America by water. They suffered increasing competition from finer Staffordshire wares and imported porcelain as the eighteenth century progressed.[63]

The adoption of new processes in the metal, glass and pottery trades was matched by developments in the textile industry, especially in hosiery. Stocking manufacture grew to become the town's staple industry, outstripping all rivals. Cloth had been manufactured locally since medieval times, but by the reign of Elizabeth it was of minor importance. In 1586 the county justices, speaking of the village of Wollaton, commented that it was 'far from any clothing townes, and near no market town but Nottingham'. However local wool was spun into yarn in many domestic households and then woven into cloth by local weavers. Linen was also woven from locally-grown flax. The list of burgesses living in 1625 included six weavers, and there were nineteen by 1641. The newly-woven cloth was subjected to a number of further processes, including fulling to shrink it, bleaching, or dyeing, the latter involving stretching it on tenters to dry outdoors. In 1574 the Willoughby family paid for cloth dyed by 'the Dutchman [i.e. probably a German] of Nottingham'; although his identity is unknown it is tempting to speculate that he may have been the mysterious Gutlake Dankes, a wealthy resident of Long Row in 1583, whose name suggests an origin in the Baltic states. At this time dyeing was presumably a rare craft in the town, although between 1585 and *c.*1590 Sir Francis Willoughby experimented with an ill-fated scheme to grow woad on his Wollaton estate. By 1630 there were enough dyers and clothworkers in the town to form themselves into a 'company'. Their ordinances were ratified by the corporation in that year. There was a fuller, a dyer and a clothworker amongst the burgesses in 1625, and three dyers, four clothworkers and eight bleachers (of linen) in 1641. Only three dyers left wills between 1660 and 1700; Deering's trade list of 1739 also enumerated three, together with one bleacher (of linen) and five linen weavers. No clothworkers appear in this list. In 1658 local drapers are recorded as purchasing cloth at Wakefield in Yorkshire.[64]

Wool was not only woven into cloth, it was also knitted into stockings and other garments by hand. This process was revolutionised by the invention of the stocking frame which enabled the operator to knit stockings faster than by traditional hand knitting. It had a complex mechanism operated by pedal and manual controls and was supposedly invented in 1589 by William Lee who, according to tradition, was a clergyman from Calverton, eight miles north east of Nottingham. Having unsuccessfully petitioned Queen Elizabeth for a patent he took his machine to France, where he died some time after 1614. His group of associates returned to London and began manufacturing stockings. They included his brother James, who subsequently returned to Nottinghamshire.[65]

Lee's pioneering products as well as those of his followers in London comprised fine silk hose catering for the luxury London market. The earliest local evidence suggests that silk stockings were being made in Nottingham from *c.*1640 onwards. There were two 'silk stocking weavers' (and two silk weavers) in the town in 1641. One of these must have been James Lord, whose will of the same year described him as a 'silk stocking worker'. The same description was applied to William Dally when he was enrolled as a burgess in 1650, presumably after serving the customary seven-year apprenticeship. These people would have been master framework knitters, often owning several frames, mostly rented out to journeymen working in their own homes. Thomas Selby's will in 1659 included bequests of silk stocking frames, two of them rented out. The development of knitting was accompanied by a parallel growth in machine building. By the late seventeenth century each stocking frame contained over 2,000 parts: one of Thomas Selby's frames in 1659 was described as being 'of my own making', but the town's long-established blacksmithing tradition provided specialist craftsmen capable of adapting to the new demands. Joseph Widowson is the first recorded 'silk stocking frame maker' in the town in 1661.[66]

After the Restoration of 1660 framework-knitters became more frequent, and the trade boomed in the 1690s. The apprenticeship registers kept by the Nottingham deputies of the London Company of Framework Knitters show that 104 apprentices were registered in 1695, 122 in 1696 and 54 in 1697; some 300 masters, including several women, are named. These figures relate to the whole region, not just to the town, but they provide evidence of the proliferation of the industry in the villages of west and south Nottinghamshire. Many knitters in the outlying villages were renting their frames from Nottingham masters, who also supplied the raw materials and purchased the finished products. As they controlled all aspects of manufacture from production to sale several of the master hosiers became very wealthy. An early example was John Hoe (*c.*1640–97), mayor in 1695. Between 1688 and 1750 framework knitters and hosiers formed the second largest occupational group of wealthy tradesmen, after maltsters.[67] The chief market for the finer silk hose was always London, and the large hosiers developed close links with the capital. Bales of hose were regularly consigned by carriers' wagon from the Nottingham hosiers' warehouses to London inns. In 1725 John Hoe (probably a grandson of the John Hoe mentioned above) had £500 worth of merchandise at the Golden Anchor in Leadenhall Street, London.[68]

Although Nottingham continued to specialise in silk stockings until well beyond the middle of the eighteenth century, some garments began to be made of worsted using local wool. In his will of 1714 Joseph Green, 'worsted weaver', left three worsted frames, together worth £10, all let out to different knitters in the town. In 1705 John

Hoe's widow Anne entered into a three-year partnership with another Nottingham framework knitter, Jonathan Labray, to 'buy make and sell worsted frame-wrought hose and yarn and frame-wrought thread and cotton hose' with a joint stock of £1,800. Labray's outworkers were spread around the Nottingham area; one of them, Henry Wright of Beeston, rented a worsted frame for seven years at £50 per annum in 1706. By his will of 1718 Labray left a large sum to the banker Thomas Smith to be put to charitable uses; six almshouses for 'decayed' framework knitters were duly erected near Chapel Bar in about 1726. Woolcombers supplied the worsted market and some of them, like Laurence Collin who successfully petitioned the corporation in 1654 to trade even though he was not a burgess, became very wealthy. Deering listed three woolcombers who 'all employ frames'.[69]

Plate 20 **The stocking frame**. A knitter at work, from Diderot's *Encyclopaedia* of 1763. The frame changed little in its essentials between its invention in *c.*1589 and its final extinction in the early twentieth century

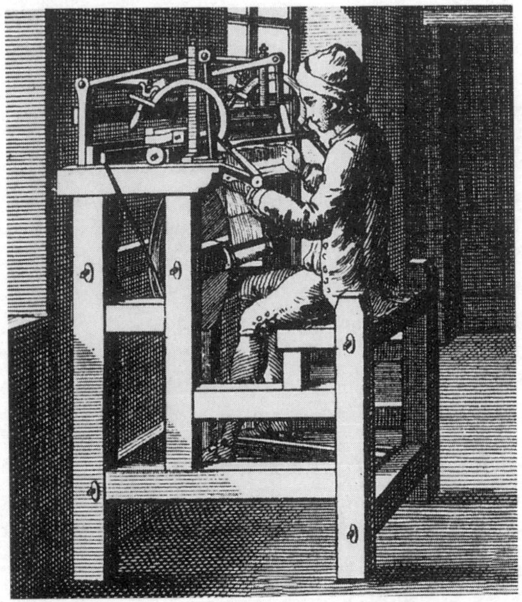

William Robinson (1664–1725), a hosier, was one of the richest men in Nottingham. He was also one of the provincial deputies for the London Company of Framework Knitters covering Nottinghamshire, Leicestershire and Derbyshire. At his death in 1725 he owned a seven-roomed house in Low Pavement, thirty-five stocking frames valued at £300, and 'sundry goods in ledger' worth £240. The total value of his personal goods amounted to £1,802, of which nearly half was owed to him in debts.[70] Robinson may have moved to Nottingham from London, as did another wealthy hosier Samuel Fellows (1687–1765). Fellows was able in 1737 to build himself an impressive three-storey town house in High Pavement, behind which was a yard crammed with a warehouse, a workshop for about twenty frames, and cottages for the knitters, many of them parish apprentices. He also owned another warehouse and workshop in Narrow Marsh, and no doubt had other frames rented out to domestic knitters. In 1730 his property was insured for £800 and his operation has been described as perhaps the 'most advanced hosiery manufacturing unit in the Midlands'. His name, like that of William Robinson, appears in the registers of High Pavement Unitarian chapel, and he served as mayor in 1755–56.[71]

In 1730 Fellows was one of the leaders of a group of Nottingham hosiers who successfully challenged the authority of the London-based Framework Knitters' Company (founded 1657) to govern the trade in the East Midlands. Within the next fifteen years it was claimed that at least 800 frames were moved from London to Nottingham, their owners attracted by lower wages, house rents and food prices. Deering wrote in the 1740s that 'within these thirty years last past, the merchants and hosiers in London, finding they could be fitted from the country with as good work at a cheaper rate than the London framework knitters could afford; the bulk of that trade has since shifted from thence'. Nottingham became one of the main centres of the hosiery industry, which soon dominated the town's economy and overshadowed all other trades. Deering wrote that:

> There are fifty manufacturers, employers of frames, or as they are commonly call'd putters out, who all trade directly to London, besides those who only deal with Leicester: Both together occupy above 3,000 frames, of which upwards of 1,200 are employ'd in Nottingham, and the rest in the villages about, who buy their provisions and other necessaries in this town: upon the just mention'd frames entirely depends, the masters, 3,000 workmen, and a considerable number of winders, sizers and seamers; woolcombers, frame-smiths, setters up, sinkermakers, stocking-needlemakers, not reckoning those trades who in part get their livelihood by this manufacture, as joyners, turners, &c in the whole upwards of 4,000.

Deering's estimates are borne out by the number of burgesses who were framework knitters and hosiers, and who are listed in the borough poll book of 1754. These totalled 470 out of 1,358 burgesses of known trades, i.e. 34 per cent.[72]

The increasing economic activity in Nottingham after the Restoration, and especially the development of the hosiery industry, produced a demand for capital investment, credit facilities and financial transfers between Nottingham and other towns, notably London. One of Nottingham's wealthy mercers, Thomas Smith (1631–99), began to fulfil this role by offering country banking services. The business expanded under his sons Thomas (1682–1727) and Abel (died 1757) in premises on Timber Hill, exploiting links with London through their brother Samuel who settled there. The Smiths' bank provided much of the financial backing for many of the town's expanding businesses. Banking facilities also helped solve one major problem of the immediate post-Restoration period which had hampered trade – a severe shortage of coin. This had led prominent tradesmen to issue their own tokens for use as currency.

Tokens survive bearing the names and often the occupations of some forty Nottingham tradesmen from this period, including drapers, shoemakers, sadlers, chandlers and apothecaries. Those which are dated range from 1664 to 1671, the latter issued by Thomas Toplady, a draper.[73]

Throughout the period under review, Nottingham's basic economic role remained unchanged: to serve as a market centre for the county and the region for the distribution and exchange of basic commodities, mainly foodstuffs and drink. The butchers, bakers, maltsters, publicans and similar tradesmen underpinned the town's economy, and in this respect Nottingham was no different from dozens of similar country towns. Again – like many other towns – the period between the 1580s and the 1630s witnessed a series of crippling visitations of the plague, poor harvests and severe winters, resulting in food shortages and major social problems.

During the course of the seventeenth century some traditional industries such as clothmaking, tanning and ironworking declined, while malting and hosiery manufacture boomed, leading to an increase in wealth, considerable migration into the town and, from about 1700, a rapid increase in population. From the Commonwealth period onwards the patronage of the expanding urban gentry classes created consumer demand for a wide range of luxury goods; these stimulated the growth of some new industries and increased trade by both river and road. However, it was the widespread development of hosiery, particularly after 1730, which gave the town a major manufacturing base. Population began to increase rapidly after 1710 and nearly doubled in the first half of the eighteenth century. A new phase in the town's history was about to commence.

Notes

1 W. G. Hoskins, *Local History in England* (2nd ed, 1972), pp. 239–41.
2 NAO PR, 2019–23, 2138–42, 3630–4.
3 There are no burial records for St Mary's from June 1591 to March 1600. The records of burials for St Nicholas are incomplete, no burials being recorded in November or December 1593 or for February and March of the following year. It seems likely that these latter omissions at least may be attributable to the upheavals in the town at the height of the plague.
4 *RBN*, IV, p. 200; V, p. 243.
5 *RBN*, IV, pp. 267, 213; V, p. 149.
6 *RBN*, V, p. 253; IV, p. 267; NAO PRNW, Thomas Locksmyth, pr. 20 July 1593; *RBN*, IV, pp. 281, 311, 299–300, 236.
7 *RBN*, IV p. 281.
8 E. A. Wrigley and R. S. Schofield, *The Population History of England 1541–1871* (1981), p. 668.
9 Deering, p. 82.
10 *Ibid.* The parish registers show this number of deaths occurred in July rather than May.
11 J. D. Chambers, 'Population change in a provincial town, Nottingham 1700–1800', in L. S. Pressnell (ed.), *Studies in the Industrial Revolution* (1960), pp. 113–16.
12 NAO CA 3363, CA 1553.
13 This level of recruitment from within a town was not unusual. See, for example, the evidence for

Bristol: C. Brooks, 'Apprenticeship, social mobility and the middling sort 1550–1800', in J. Barry and C. Brooks (ed.), *The Middling Sort of People: Culture, Society and Politics in England 1550–1800* (1994).

14 *RBN*, V, p. 253.

15 *RBN*, IV, pp. 191, 229, 347, 311–15.

16 *RBN*, pp. 361, 281,303, 311–15, 364, 381–2, 132; V, p.113.

17 *RBN*, IV, pp. 186–7, 199, 259; Date Book, p. 113.

18 *RBN*, IV, p. 332; V, pp. 131, 141, 174, 259, 309, 311.

19 *RBN*, VI, pp. 98,107, 124, 126.

20 *Calendars of State Papers Domestic* (hereafter *CSPD*), 190, 1586 June 11, No. 44; *RBN*, V, p. 147.

21 *RBN*, IV, pp. 148, 174.

22 Many of the more substantial of these charitable bequests are listed in Deering, pp. 132–53; *RBN*, V, pp. 254, 266, 296; IV, p. 149.

23 Deering, pp.132–53; *RBN*, V, p. 111.

24 *RBN*, IV, p. 170; V, p. 137.

25 *RBN*, V, p. 397.

26 Anon., pp. 35–8; Deering, pp. 7–9.

27 W. H. Stevenson, 'A description of Nottinghamshire in the seventeenth century', *TTS*, 11 (1907), pp. 117–30; J. Taylor, *A Journey to Edenbrough in Scotland ...* (1705); D. Defoe, *A Tour Through the Whole Island of Great Britain* (Everyman edn, 1928), II, p. 146.

28 *RBN*, IV, pp. 289, 310, 276; V, pp. 304, 174; E. L. Guilford, 'Extracts from the records of the Borough of Nottingham', *TTS*, 29 (1925), p. 85; *CSPD*, 185, p. 548, and 189, p. 18; *Date Book*, p. 179.

29 HMC, *Middleton* p. 392; NAO CA 1504–5.

30 P. Grieg, 'The layout of Lenton fairground, 1516', *TTS*, 96 (1992), pp. 130–4; HMC, *Middleton*, pp. 422, 170, 175; W. A. Carrington, 'Selections from the Steward's accounts preserved at Haddon Hall ...', *DAJ*, 16 (1894), p. 74; *RBN*, V, pp. 244–5; IV, p. 267; PRO SP 46/48; Deering, pp. 91–2.

31 A. Tarver, *Church Court Records* (Chichester, 1995), pp. 86–9; D. Riden, (ed.), *A Seventeenth Century Scarsdale Miscellany* (Derbyshire Record Society, 20, 1993), p. 92.

32 A. C. Wood, 'History of trade and transport on the River Trent', *TTS*, 54 (1950), pp. 1–54; Anon., p. 26; R. S. Smith, *Early Coal Mining Around Nottingham, 1500–1650* (Nottingham, 1989), pp. 71–3; Nottingham Castle Museum, Prospect of Nottingham, by Jan Siberechts, *c.*1700; S. and N. Buck, *South View of Nottingham* (1743); T. Sandby, *South Prospect of Nottingham* (1742).

33 S. Revill, 'A sixteenth century map of the River Trent near Shelford, *TTS*, 75 (1971), pp. 85–6; Anon., p. 26; G. H. Green, *Historical Accounts of the Ancient Kings Mills, Castle Donington, Leicestershire* (Castle Donington, 1960), p. 44, quoting Coke of Melbourne MSS; Defoe, *Tour*, II, p. 145; Deering, p. 91.

34 Defoe, *Tour*, p. 145.

35 *RBN*, IV, p. 398; V, pp. 15, 303.

36 C. C. Owen, 'The early history of the Upper Trent Navigation', *Transport History*, 1 (1968), *passim*; *RBN*, V, p. 398; VI, pp. 127, 143, 147–9.

37 Anon., pp. 29–30, 39–40; RBN, IV, pp. 398, 51–5; V, p. 15; F. A. Barnes, *Priory Demesne to University Campus* (Nottingham, 1993), p. 494; HMC, *Middleton*, p. 440.

38 Deering, pp. 8, 91.

39 Smith, *Early Coal Mining*, pp. 68–80.

40 R. S. Smith, *Sir Francis Willoughby of Wollaton Hall* (Nottingham, 1988), p. 20; Guilford, 'Extracts', p. 84; Anon., pp. 40–1; Deering, p. 97.

41 *RBN*, IV, pp. 336, 434; Anon., pp. 39–40; J. A. W. Bennet and H. R. Trevor Roper (eds.), *The Poems of Richard Corbett* (1955), pp. 35–7; J. Taylor, *Part of this Summer's Travels* (1632); NAO DD.VL 31/1; A. Henstock, 'Early Stuart Nottingham: new evidence from the St Peter's Easter Book of 1624', *TTS*, 97 (1993), p. 102.

42 *RBN*, IV, pp. 361, 336–7; Guilford, 'Extracts from the Records of the Borough of Nottingham', *TTS* 28 (1924), p. 90; P. Clark, 'English Country Towns, 1500–1800', in P. Clark (ed.), *Country Towns in Pre-Industrial England* (Leicester, 1981), p. 11.

43 PRO WO 30/48 (copy in NAO DD 1762); Guildhall Library, London, Sun Fire Insurance Registers (copy index in NAO).

44 NAO PRNW, William Parkinson, pr. 18 August 1733; Deering, pp. 94–5.

45 C. Morris (ed.), *The Journies of Celia Fiennes* (1947), pp. 72–3.

46 *RBN*, IV, pp. 95, 119, 162, 256–6, 368–9; NAO, CA 4649; Anon., pp. 39–40; Henstock, 'Early Stuart Nottingham', pp. 102–3; Guilford, 'Extracts from the Records of the Borough of Nottingham', *TTS*, 26 (1922), p. 30.

47 A. Henstock, *Tracing the History of Your House* (Nottingham, 1988), pp. 83–7; Henstock, 'Early Stuart Nottingham', p. 103; Anon., pp. 40–1; Deering, p. 87.

48 NAO, probate trade indexes; Thoroton, p. 492; analysis of probate inventories by Cathy Smith; NAO PRNW, William Coppock, pr. 16 August 1689, Thomas Harding, pr. 26 March 1723, Robert Linley, pr. 22 July 1696.

49 Anon., pp. 40–1; Defoe, *Tour*, II, p. 146.

50 Deering, p. 93.

51 R. M. Butler, 'The common lands of the Borough of Nottingham', *TTS*, 54 (1950), *passim*; Deering, p. 87.

52 Anon., p. 22; Deering, p. 87.

53 Deering, p. 96; *RBN*, IV, pp. 180, 340, 111–12; V, pp. 144, 399.

54 *RBN*, IV, p. 315; Henstock, 'Early Stuart Nottingham', p. 106; NAO CA 3974, quoted in G. Oldfield, 'The fields within the town: the story of Nottingham's Lammas Lands', *NH*, 19 (1977), pp. 4–5.

55 Stevenson, 'A description', pp. 117–30; Anon., pp. 46, 39–40; NAO CA 4649; A. B. Clarke, 'Notes on the Mayors of Nottingham, 1660–1715', TTS, 41 (1938), pp. 50–65.

56 Deering, p. 93.

57 Anon., pp. 34–5, 39–40; NAO CA 4649.

58 R. Johnson, 'Seventeenth century ironworks at Bulwell and Kirkby', *TTS*, 64 (1960), p. 44; P. Riden, 'The charcoal iron industry in the East Midlands, 1580–1780', *DAJ*, 111 (1991), pp. 64–73.

59 VCH *Nottinghamshire*, II, p. 369; NAO PRNW, George Oldfield, pr. 12 December 1741; Anon., pp. 39–40; Deering, pp. 94–5.

60 Gawthern, *Diary*, pp. 11–12.

61 R. S. Smith, 'Glassmaking at Wollaton in the early seventeenth century', *TTS*, 66 (1962), pp. 24–34; P. Hughes, 'Some civil engineering notes from 1699', *The Local Historian*, 26 (1996), p. 107. NAO PRNW, Robert Brentnall, pr. 16 October 1713; T. Sandby, *East Prospect of Nottingham* (1741).

62 Morris, *Journeys of Celia Fiennes*, p. 73; Thoroton, p. 231; J. Hunter (ed.), *Diary of Ralph Thoresby*, II (1830), p. 168.

63 HMC, *Middleton*, p. 440; the two 'potmakers' listed by the anonymous author in 1641 were almost certainly making metal pots; A. Oswald and R. G. Hughes, 'Nottingham and Derbyshire stoneware', *Trans. English Ceramic Circle*, 9, part 2 (1974), pp. 140–65; Bodleian Library, Oxford, Douce Portfolio 139, no. 283, trade card of J. Morley; Nottingham Castle Museum, Watkinson posset pot, illustrated in Oswald and Hughes, plate 90; I. Noël Hume, *Pottery and Porcelain in Colonial Williamsburg's Archaeological Collections* (Colonial Williamsburg Archaeological Series), no. 2, 1968, pp. 35–7.

64 R. S. Smith, 'A woad growing project at Wollaton in the 1580s', *TTS*, 65 (1961), pp. 27–46; *RBN*, IV, pp. 275, 205; V, pp. 147, 277, 297, 304; NAO CA 4649; Anon., pp. 35–40; HMC, *Middleton*, p. 450; NAO probate trade indexes; Deering, pp. 94–5.

65 Thoroton, p. 296; the account of the rise of the hosiery industry is largely based on S. D. Chapman, 'The genesis of the British hosiery industry, 1600–1750', *Textile History*, 3 (1972), pp. 7–50. See also J. Millington and S. Chapman, *Four Centuries of Machine Knitting* (Leicester, 1989), pp. 14–20.

66 Anon., pp. 39–40; NAO PRNW James Lord, pr. 20 May 1641, Thomas Selby, pr. 12 October 1661; NAO CA 3424, Q 267G; T. M. Blagg and F. A. Wadsworth, *Abstracts of Nottinghamshire Marriage Licences*, vol. I (1930), pp. 303, 210.

67 Chapman, 'Genesis', p. 26; Clarke, 'Mayors', p. 64; analysis of probate inventories by Cathy Smith.

68 Guildhall Library, London, Sun Fire Insurance Registers, Vol. 21; Chapman, 'Genesis', p. 26.

69 NAO M 8489 DD.AC 5/1/17, 5/1/14; Deering, pp. 153, 94–5; NAO PRNW, James Moore, pr. 31 May 1710; Lawrence Collin, pr. 30 January 1704/5; Collin's inventory totalled £1,052, but no less than £1,000 was owed in debts; *RBN*, V, p. 283.

70 R. Brocklesby, 'How they lived: William Robinson, sr., Nottingham hosier', *NH*, 11 (1973), pp. 5–7.

71 Chapman, 'Genesis', pp. 18–19; A. Henstock, 'County House, High Pavement, Nottingham: a Georgian and Regency town house', *TTS*, 78 (1974), pp. 54–67.

72 Chapman, 'Genesis', pp. 15–16; Deering, p. 101; S. Creswell, *An Alphabetical List of the Burgesses* (1754), *passim*; I am grateful to Mr S. N. Mastoris for details of his analysis of the poll book.

73 H. T. Easton, *The History of a Banking House* (1903), pp. 1–10; P. Preston Morley and H. Pegg, *A Revised Survey of the Seventeenth Century Tokens of Nottinghamshire* (1983), pp. 16–25.

9

TURBULENT CENTURIES: THE POLITICAL HISTORY OF NOTTINGHAM, 1550–1750

Martyn Bennett

In 1550 Nottingham was still experiencing the consequences of the dissolution of the monasteries. The changes invoked by Henry VIII's desire to secure the succession had long-lasting effects nationwide. While the period *c.*1550–1640 cannot really be regarded as a 'highroad to civil war', many of the structural difficulties in the mid-seventeenth-century state were germinated during the latter half of the sixteenth. This chapter covers the years from the struggle for church reformation, through the unification of the Scottish and English crowns in 1603, the Civil War of the 1640s, the final expulsion of the main branch of the house of Stuart in 1688, and the defeat of its last principal contender in 1745. In all these events Nottingham played a central role.

The corporation

The structure of the borough's administration changed little in the sixteenth century, but there were renewed attempts by the burgess body at large to challenge the power concentrated in the hands of the mayor and the aldermen who were in place for life as the corporation alone was responsible for filling vacancies. This was a common trend within boroughs to the end of the seventeenth century, as power was concentrated in the hands of a few as part of a defence against outside interference and internal disorder.[1] When the body of burgesses known as the Clothing was incorporated into the council in 1577, there appeared to be some possibility of increasing the burgesses' participation in local government. However, this made little practical difference, as the Clothing was composed of former chamberlains who had been selected by the corporation for that office in the first place.[2] Even so, there would seem to be some broadening of the trade composition of the corporation as reflected in the appointments to the two positions of sheriff. Between 1550 and 1575 representatives of only thirteen trades held the office. Roughly the same pattern held true for the remainder of the century, but between 1600 and 1625 twenty trades were represented.

The drift of power towards an almost self-perpetuating oligarchy was resented and challenged. Indeed, it is probable that such a broadening of the power base was brought about only because of the struggle to challenge the oligarchy. One of the principal leaders of the opposition was the glover Percival Millington, whose nephew was to be one of the town's MPs during the Civil War. In 1612 he was a sheriff.

The principal means of the sixteenth- and seventeenth-century protests at the power of the corporation was through the Mickletorn Jury. An attempt in 1577 to enlarge the Clothing into a lower house of forty-eight seems not to have been successful, but in 1579 the Jury protested at the composition of the corporation and demanded that it should be restructured. Of the present corporation it wanted to see only the coroners and the seven aldermen left in office, and the proposed lower house put into place and given responsibility for appointing to important posts such as the bridgemaster and school wardens. The corporation, not surprisingly as it had no desire to weaken its powers, ignored the suggestions. The argument resurfaced again in 1602, 1604 and 1605. Finally the burgesses appealed to the Privy Council. The matter was assigned to an assize judge who decreed a compromise, a council of twenty-four consisting of eighteen men from the Clothing and six 'commoners'. The six, later referred to as the Junior Council, acted as a means of allowing burgesses on to the corporation, even if they had not served either as chamberlains or sheriffs. The eighteen were later referred to as the Senior Council. The distinction between the commoners and the Clothing became blurred as commoners became chamberlains and then members of the Clothing. The aldermen voted with this corporation, but may have met separately.[3]

At the basis of these challenges to the established order was the crucial issue of the relationship between taxpaying and power. The rights of men to vote in borough and national elections were closely related to tax. However, a significant number of women paid tax in early seventeenth-century Nottingham but their political power was muted. Nationally women seem to have held between about 10 per cent and 30 per cent of property.[4] As men this would have entitled them to hold minor office and to vote, but gender barriers usually prevented this, although women in some Nottinghamshire communities did succeed to the offices of churchwarden and constable.[5] In Nottingham itself women did not achieve such positions and their ranking in the taxpaying community was towards the lower end of the scale. In St Mary's parish in 1582–83 nineteen of the 261 ratepayers were women, 7 per cent of the total, and they together paid just over 10 per cent of the total sum collected. In 1593 eighty-six people paid a levy towards Her Majesty's tax; ten (11.6 per cent) were women who paid 6.8 per cent of the total. However, in 1609 few women contributed to the subsidy levy of £11 11*s* 4*d*; only two (out of ninety people) were assessed, and between them they paid 7*s* 8*d*, only 3 per cent of the total sum. Five years later, when a benevolence was collected in the town, no women were assessed.[6] However, the influence of women behind the scenes could be significant. Lucy Hutchinson inferred that Alderman John James, while honest and loyal to Parliament during the Civil War, 'had no more than a burgher's discretion'. His wife, on the other hand, 'greatly assisted' him: she was 'a woman of great zeal and courage, and more understanding then woemen of her ranke usually have'. In Lucy Hutchinson's own biography of her husband, the Parliamentarian governor of Nottingham castle during the first Civil War, it is clear that she was involved in his decision to adopt the Parliamentarian cause and was the principal actor in his later conversion to Baptism.[7]

Nottingham castle continued its decline during the reign of Elizabeth, despite sporadic attempts at repair. The Queen's proposed visit in 1562 prompted major attention to some buildings, but others were declared to be beyond repair, including probably the Great Hall which was demolished by the end of the century. Repairs continued in the 1570s and the bills mounted to over £1,000 a year by the end of the decade. Possibly this was exceptional; since Elizabeth spent little on her other castles this may have been indicative of the strategic nature of the castle as well as the desire to keep it in a fit state as a potential but unrealised 'progress house' for the monarch's travels. James I used the castle in 1612 as the venue for meeting the local gentry, although he actually stayed in Thurland Hall. Costs of repair continued to mount, although they compared favourably with a further sixty royal castles regarded as unfit to be 'progress houses'. In 1622 the Manners family of Belvoir Castle in Leicestershire, long-time custodians, gained the hereditary holding in return for an annual rent. They began to strip the assets and pack barns at Belvoir with lead, bricks, iron, glass, timber and tiles. By the time the Civil War broke out the castle was in ruins.[8]

The road to civil war

When Duncan Gray commemorated the coronation of Queen Elizabeth II in *Nottingham: Settlement to City* he followed Wood in regarding the period from Henry VIII's reign to 1642 as a prelude to the Civil War, laying its roots firmly in the Reformation.[9] The vogue for seeing this period as a 'highroad to civil war' has faded a little from the historiography of the period, but the stresses brought about by fluctuations in the religious affiliations of the monarchs, coupled with some disastrous political decisions, created cracks under the surface of civility which were to rip apart the social fabric. The decision of Charles I to reduce the status of Parliament provoked deep discontent which by 1640 rendered him helpless to raise English support to suppress the rise of Scottish religious nationalism. These problems alone were insufficient to rend English society; indeed, by 1639 they had failed to undermine the King's political stability, but they ensured that the country was not sufficiently united behind him to withstand external shocks. In the late 1620s fiscal policy became a major political issue. Opposition grew once it became clear that Charles I was determined to extract taxation without recourse to regular Parliaments. When the commissioners for Charles's Forced Loan passed through Nottingham the streets were strewn with anti-taxation leaflets, and eleven local gentlemen refused to pay: Sir Thomas Hutchinson was imprisoned for his refusal. The corporation hoped, as did many others, that a Parliament would be called to which they could send MPs to 'ease the townes charges'. The county as a whole returned no more than £70 to the free gift or benevolence in 1626.[10]

Problems increased during the 1630s when a section of the county gentry was charged with fines of distraint of knighthood for failing to attend the coronation to be dubbed knight. In the middle of the decade, along with the rest of the inland counties, Nottinghamshire was for the first time assessed for Ship Money. The levy, for coastal defence, was usually imposed on seaboard counties only in times of danger, but under Charles this extraordinary tax was treated as an ordinary levy and collected nationwide. Nottinghamshire was assessed at £3,509, of which the county town had to find £200 a year. Opposition remained at a low level for the first two years of collection, but from 1637 increasing numbers of people appeared before quarter sessions for non-payment. By 1639 the High Sheriff of the county Lord Chaworth was being taunted by landowners who locked their gates in his face and challenged him to take distress if he dare. The following year Thomas Williamson, the new High Sheriff, could get nothing from the three boroughs in the county, and collection as a whole collapsed once the 'Short Parliament' met briefly in April 1640 and gave voice to national anger over the levy.[11]

In 1638, in the face of Charles I's attempt to impose what seemed to be a thoroughgoing model of the Anglican church on Scotland, the Scottish people united against him in defence of their kirk. Charles's continued intransigence drove the Scots into a steadily more radical stance and when he sought to impose his will through military might he was humiliated and defeated by the Scottish army. Nottingham had to contribute its trained band soldiers and provide them with money (in the form of 'Coat and Conduct' levies) and food for the King's wars against Scotland in 1639 and 1640. Troops heading north in 1640 passed through the town and expected to be quartered there. Three Nottingham residents, John Pye, Ann Clarke and Thomas Bagguiley, refused. Ann may have been opposed to the war itself, for when the three were presented at the October 1640 Quarter Sessions she was accused of 'giving ill speeches'. Thomas had abused the constable and John had refused money even to the soldiers. After the King's defeat the townspeople would have had to pay both the English forces and the victorious Covenanter Army lodged in the northern shires. In July 1641 they had to join with other areas to pay money to the receiver at York to cover the cost of disbanding the two armies.[12]

The second English Parliament of 1640 began to redress the balance between the executive and the legislative, taking advantage of Charles's financial and political bankruptcy. Political dysfunction in the country as a whole in 1640–42 was felt in Nottingham and one of the town's MP's, Gilbert Millington, played a small role at the centre. Millington and Sir Thomas Hutchinson, a county MP, were later to side with Parliament, but Gervase Clifton of Clifton, MP for Retford, was one of the King's supporters brave enough to make public his opposition to the execution of the Earl of Strafford in May 1641.[13] The other town MP, William Stanhope, and the other shire MP, Robert Sutton, were also Royalists. A year later a rebellion broke out in Ireland. Charles believed he had enough supporters in the four nations to turn upon his English enemies while keeping Scotland neutral, and while Ireland was in turmoil.

The King's gambit of 1642 was to end with his declaration of war on Parliament at Nottingham on 22 August. This followed in the wake of a sustained military and political campaign to secure loyalty across the Midlands, in which Nottingham played an early part. When Charles left London in February 1642 he made his way northwards and eventually settled at York. From there he spent the spring and early summer trying to gather military and political support around him. In the meantime, Parliament assumed responsibility for appointing the lord lieutenants in each county, and in Nottinghamshire it appointed the Earl of Clare, who had recently become Recorder of Nottingham in succession to Henry Pierrepont, Viscount Newark.[14] Charles, after initial offers of conciliation, decided to issue Commissions of Array, which effectively created bodies or committees similar to the Commissions of the Peace, to raise the county-trained bands. At the same time activists around the Midlands tried to seize control of the county ammunition stores. Lord Newark's attempt to seize the magazine in Nottingham was frustrated by the efforts of a crowd of townspeople and John Hutchinson, son of Sir Thomas, refused to let Lord Newark and the High Sheriff, John Digby, take the munitions out of the Guildhall. Hutchinson and members of the corporation argued that the arms and munitions were needed to defend the town. They would also have known that the King was aiming to use the weapons for his own army. While Hutchinson and the King's men debated the issue, the crowd threatened to 'break my lord's neck and the sheriff's out of the window'.[15] A compromise was reached which aimed to preserve local security and ensure that there would be in future two locks on the magazine, one held by the county in the person of the High Sheriff and one for the town held by the mayor, John James.

However the King made further attempts to gain possession of the arms and the town appealed for help; Mayor James and other townsmen and sympathetic gentry contacted Parliament. Westminster responded by ordering that any parts of the county magazine stored at Newark should be brought to Nottingham. John James, Millington and others were constituted as a committee to raise volunteer soldiers to defend the town.[16] The situation became increasingly fraught when the King began a tour of the Midlands, intent on drumming up support. On 11 July he was met at Newark by the trained bands, which had been assembled by the Lord Lieutenant, Lord Newark. On 21 July the King arrived at Nottingham to be greeted by the town council with the usual obsequies. Mayor James and deputy recorder James Chadwick kissed the King's hand, prompting Lucy Hutchinson to comment of the latter that 'never was a truer Judas since Iscarriott's time, than he, for he would kisse the man he had it in his heart to kill'.[17] Charles was following a studied policy of conciliation. He was in the process of offering positions of responsibility to those considered reluctant supporters and to seeming opponents, like Chadwick and Hutchinson, in the hope of drawing them on to his side. He was also aware that he could not count on popular support, and that Nottingham's administration may have been more impressed by the 800 soldiers accompanying him than by calls upon their loyalty.[18] The King's insecurity was confirmed after he left Nottingham as he failed to gain control of the Leicestershire magazine. By now neither conciliation nor Commissions of Array were enough, and he urged more drastic measures; on 19 August Digby broke into the Nottingham magazine and removed the store for the benefit of the King, who was passing through on his way to try to capture the magazine at Coventry. By this time Parliament had created an army in the south Midlands and Charles was attempting to gain control of the local county magazines, but Coventry defied him. Shots were fired at his party and he returned north.

The Civil War

On 22 August 1642 Charles I and his court repaired to a site immediately north of the castle (later known as Standard Hill) and, amid great ceremony, raised the royal standard 'in the evening of a very stormy and tempestuous day'. The omens were considered bad when the flag blew down, but the ceremony was repeated over the next few days and further forces gathered around the King. Historians have taken their cue from the Earl of Clarendon, when he looked back on the momentous day and proclaimed it very melancholy, as the Royalists looked at the small numbers of assembled troops, yet Charles was gathering troops rapidly. Many of those assembled in the Midlands, including horse regiments, were on active service in Warwickshire on 22 August and were only able to join him later.[19] Local forces were being raised in Nottinghamshire. From the Cliftons of Clifton came arms and ammunition; Sir William Staunton of Staunton raised a troop of horse; and Gervase Holles raised foot. The trained bands were gathered at such short notice that the village constable of Upton near Newark had to hire horses to get them to Nottingham quickly.[20] The King stayed until 12 September then moved on to Shrewsbury. Although he took most of the active supporters out of the region with him, it was still dangerous for some of his opponents to be seen in public, and John Hutchinson and others remained hidden for a while.

The Royalists and Parliamentarian armies clashed at Edgehill on 23 October 1642 and fought each other to a standstill. Both sides had to some extent created field armies in the belief (or hope) that one battle would end the struggle. That, clearly, had not happened, and it was necessary for them to begin building territorial control in the country at large. In November, Sir John Gell occupied Derby on behalf of Parliament and then assisted John Hutchinson and his political allies to take control of Nottingham.[21] This move did not go unchallenged. The King sent prominent supporters back into the region at the end of November to break the control established by the Parliamentary supporters. Nottingham was safe for some time because there were no significant Royalist forces in the area.

Plate 21 **The royal standard, as raised by King Charles I to rally his supporters to his side on 22 August 1642**. Detail from a Parliamentarian tract. The depiction of the town, with walls intact and at least five churches, suggests artistic licence!

The town rapidly became important to the Parliamentarian cause, although the power of the local Royalists kept this in check until July 1644.[22] Nottingham possessed strategic importance, allowing the Parliamentarians to block traffic on the River Trent and to deny the Royalists the use of Trent Bridge. Both sides had by the spring of 1643 constructed administrations within the counties of England and Wales under their respective control. These were managed by the revamped Royalist commissioners of array and (for Parliament) by county committees. Each body set taxation levels in the shires based on the demands received from the King at Oxford or from Westminster. Both sides then passed these assessments down to the local communities, and the constables either brought tax to collection points in the case of Parliament, or for the Royalists handed it to collectors who visited – accompanied by troops of horse – each week or two. Records of collection in Nottinghamshire show that the Royalists at Newark could expect in 1644 to collect money from most of the county, even from as near to Nottingham as Arnold and Clifton. However, the area of the county south-west of Nottingham and across the Trent could not be reached by Royalist collectors because of the town garrison. On only two occasions did the position alter.

Plate 22 **Lucy Hutchinson, wife of John Hutchinson, Parliamentarian governor of Nottingham Castle during the Civil War.** The memoir she wrote of her husband contains information about the politics of local Parliamentarianism and military events

On 18 September 1644 the Royalist regional general, Henry Hastings, and Sir John Henderson attacked Nottingham and occupied the fort that guarded the bridge. For about a month Royalist forces were able to cross into the south-west of the county and collect tax from hitherto untouched places such as Toton. The situation was repeated early in 1645 when an attack on the fort again placed it in Royalist hands, this time for about a week in January.[23]

Serious attempts to attack the town were made in 1643 and 1644. In May 1643 Parliamentarian forces gathered at Nottingham. These had come from the surrounding counties and included forces from Derbyshire and some from East Anglia led by Colonel Oliver Cromwell. The allied commanders were intending to launch an attack on Newark to interrupt the march of the Queen's army as it moved southwards towards the King.[24] In February 1643 Henrietta Maria landed at Bridlington with arms she had bought abroad. She assembled an army at York to escort the munitions to Oxford. In mid-June this army arrived unexpectedly at Newark, before the Nottingham forces were ready, and attacked the town. While there seemed to have been little chance of Nottingham falling to the Royalists, it marked the end of local Parliamentarian co-operation. Gell returned to Derbyshire where the Queen was soon to storm one of his garrisons, and Cromwell returned eastwards. Lord Grey was exposed as an ineffectual commander and replaced by Sir John Meldrum.[25] Hutchinson's garrison was left in relative peace but was reduced in size in July when Meldrum led the horse regiments to Lincolnshire for an attack on Gainsborough. When this resulted ultimately in their defeat,

> all the forces that went from Nottingham disperse into different services. Major Ireton quite left Colonell Thornhaúgh's regiment, and began an inseparable league with Colonell Cromwell, whose sonne in law he afterwards was. None of them could return to Nottingham by reason of Lord Newcastle's army, which lay between them and home.[26]

Military attempts on the town had ended for the time being, but the Royalist commander in the north, the Earl of Newcastle, tried to force Hutchinson to hand over the town. He began with a fairly conventional military threat in August 1643, which was rejected by Hutchinson who refused the yield to a 'papisticall armie led by an atheistical generall'.[27] He was even more uncivil to the new governor of Newark, Sir Richard Byron, his own cousin, as both men were regarded with suspicion by their own side because of their relationship. It was Byron who made the next representations to Hutchinson on behalf of the Earl. Hutchinson rejected this offer too. This was followed by an attack on the town which fell to the Royalists. The Trent Bridge fort was taken and occupied. The Royalists stayed in Nottingham for five days and used St Nicholas's church tower to fire into the castle. However, Hutchinson had fortified the castle, which held out with ease. The Royalists withdrew.

The town was attacked again on 16 January 1644 by Royalists from Newark and by forces under Sir Charles Lucas, who was gathering troops from the region to go northwards to assist against the Scots. Henry Hastings, now Lord Loughborough, was also present with forces south of the river, and Lucy Hutchinson reckoned that some 3,000 Royalists were involved in the attack. Again they failed to make any impression on the castle and after street fighting the Royalists withdrew, leaving

> for two miles … a great track of blood, which froze as it fell upon the snow, for it was such bitter weather that the foot had waded allmost to the middle in snow as they came, and were soon numbed with cold, when they came into the towne, they were faine to get rubbed to get life in them.[28]

This was the last attack on the town. Prince Rupert relieved a Parliamentary siege of Newark in March, only to be defeated at Marston Moor on 2 July, after which Royalist fortunes declined and the county committee at Nottingham was able to extend its administration and tax-gathering into the county.[29]

In April 1645 Royalists again occupied the fort in the Meadows, disrupting traffic over Trent Bridge. They hung on for some time – Lucy Hutchinson suggested nearly a month, although the Royalist press claimed only eleven days. While this should have eased access to the south-west of the county it is not clear if the Royalists were able to exploit the advantage to the full. When they left, after capturing a fort erected in an attempt to pen them in, they again broke down Trent Bridge to limit cross river traffic and hinder pursuit.[30] During the following months Nottingham seems to have been little disturbed during the major campaign which ended with the Royalist defeat at Naseby. With local Parliamentarians now on the offensive, Nottingham's garrison was soon involved in the third siege of Newark and its satellite garrisons at the end of 1645 and the beginning of 1646. This effectively ended any threat to Nottingham.[31]

The impact of the war

In a town which had seen strong attempts to gain broader control over the borough management during previous decades, it cannot be expected that the imposition of martial law on the townspeople of Nottingham was accepted easily, especially when it conflicted with borough interests. Concerns about Colonel Hutchinson's authority over the town were similar to fears about central government interference, and the corporation bridled uncomfortably. This was a problem felt in boroughs across the country which were occupied during the war.[32] Hutchinson's position as governor was secured in July 1643, but his role was questioned by some members of the county and borough militia committees.[33] His first challenge came when he removed cannon from the town into the castle in the summer of 1643. The townspeople, including several leading committeemen, protested that these belonged to the borough and their removal threatened the safety of the town. The protest developed into a mutiny and fifteen people were arrested. Disputes between the two parties continued to simmer for several months, and were not finally decided in Parliament until April 1645 when the scare caused by the Royalists' capture of the Trent fort forced the issue. Hutchinson had his powers confirmed and a small consultative committee was established to deal with him in military affairs. Despite Lucy Hutchinson's assertion that her husband was then left in peace, his opponents were placed on subsequent committees for the town and the shire for the rest of the war.[34]

When the first Civil War ended the town fortifications were demolished but the castle remained garrisoned, although Hutchinson, through illness, gave command to Thomas Poulton. For the first time in four years Nottingham became the sole centre of government in the county and the shire's constables began attending again to county affairs based in the town, such as the gaol, and to pay weekly taxes, known as the monthly pay, to officials in Nottingham rather than to Royalists or the Scots based around Newark. The new regiment at Nottingham, created in the summer of 1648, was also paid for at the expense of the local communities.[35] In 1648 the tide of the second Civil War ebbed and flowed around Nottingham. Gilbert Byron tried to capture the town, and in August fugitives from the defeated Scottish and Royalist army were defeated at Willoughby-on-the-Wolds, and brought as prisoners to the town.

The castle was repaired in 1648 and kept in good care until 1651, but even before the Battle of Worcester on 3 September, demolition had begun at the suggestion of both Poulton and Hutchinson. By 10 November that year the royal fortress which had dominated the skyline of the Norman town had been reduced to rubble.[36]

During Cromwell's Republican Commonwealth town government passed into the hands of the Parliamentarian victors.[37] James Chadwick and John Mason represented the town in the Protectorate Parliament of 1654, both having served as officers in the Nottingham forces during the war. In the Parliament elected in 1656 Chadwick remained in place, despite the fact that he was associated with the unpopular rule of the major-generals through his participation in Major-General Edward Whalley's county committee. This time Chadwick was joined by William Drury, an alderman since 1646. He served as mayor in 1647–48 and 1652–53. In the last Parliament held during Richard Cromwell's brief rule, Nottingham again proved loyal to the Protectorate, electing Alderman John Parker who had come on to the council via the office of chamberlain in 1645 and John Whalley, the former major general's son.

The new regime was not allowed to impose its supporters on the corporation without the traditional qualifications. When Laurence Collin, a woolcomber, petitioned the Lord Protector for a burgess place, the town made it clear that the usual procedures had to be followed. He was allowed to trade in the town as a freeman, but not to be a burgess. On the other hand Major General Whalley was admitted as a burgess, but the oaths were not imposed on him as his case was not to be held as an example for the future. The corporation retained a semblance of continuity with both the war and pre-war years with Alderman Parker coming into the council through normal channels and serving as mayor in 1653–54, but his wartime reputation lingered on, and in the turbulence of the Restoration he was replaced by Francis Toplady during his 1661–62 mayoralty. However, within two years he reappeared as an alderman.[38]

Some of the old figures were gone forever. Glbert Millington, the long-serving Parliamentarian, was exempted from the general air of forgiveness, arrested, tried and condemned to death. Although a signatory to the King's death warrant he had his sentence commuted to a prison sentence, and died in Jersey Castle in 1666. John Hutchinson, who returned briefly to public affairs when elected to Parliament in 1660, was soon expelled from the Commons on the receipt of the Declaration of Breda. He was able to retire to his Nottinghamshire country seat, but remained under suspicion, and in September 1663 he was arrested by the connivance of one deputy lieutenant, Francis Leake, against the wishes of the Lord Lieutenant, the Marquess of Newcastle, and the two deputy lieutenants. Attempts were made to link him with the Yorkshire Plot of that year, and he remained in prison, first at the Tower and then at Sandown Castle, Kent, until his death in October 1664. Other old faces returned, including Newcastle, raised to a dukedom in 1664, and the Earl of Dorchester, better known as Henry Pierrepont, Lord Newark, the former Royalist lord lieutenant, who became recorder in 1668.

Restoration Nottingham

After the Restoration in 1660 religious issues that had been part of the causes of the Civil Wars resurfaced. The restrictions on religious freedom which the Hutchinsons had deliberated in 1641 were again imposed on Protestants not in communion with the Anglican church. The sects or 'gathered churches', which had appeared during and towards the end of the first Civil War and matured in the years following the revolution, were declared illegal. More surprisingly the Presbyterian church, which had been established alongside them, was also persecuted. The liberal religious settlement which Charles II may well have envisaged upon his return was thwarted by the Cavalier Parliament, which sought nothing less than a reintroduction of High Church Anglicanism at the expense of all other forms of Protestant worship.

Under the Act of Uniformity of 1662 the ordination of ministers was enforced and the Book of Common Prayer was reissued. Ministers who did not conform were deprived of office. Thirty-eight, including the Revd John Barrett of Nottingham St Peter's, lost their Nottinghamshire livings. In 1665 the Five Mile Act forced the ejected to keep five miles away from their old parishes and away from any incorporated town. The ministers from Nottingham St Mary's moved to Mansfield.[39] Other sects, such as the Baptists and Quakers, long established in Nottingham, were prohibited from meeting by the Conventicle Act. The Baptists had been present in the town during the war, and Lucy Hutchinson was attracted to their beliefs. Most of the Independent groups had come into the town with the military forces, and the Baptists had been formed among the artillery. At the insistence of the Presbyterian ministers the original group had been suppressed, but Lucy Hutchinson read their confiscated papers.[40] The Quakers were established in the 1650s, but they too fell foul of the repression of the 1660s. Despite this onslaught the sect survived; in 1669 the Ecclesiastical Returns showed there was a small conventicle of 100 Quakers in the town, although there were far more in the county. About 400 Presbyterians were meeting at two conventicles in Nottingham, while Independents, Baptists or Anabaptists and Familists met in a further five conventicles. The Independents became the Congregational Church on Castle Gate after the Glorious Revolution of 1688. In 1669 there were only twenty to thirty Baptists in the town. The Familists, a communal sect with continental origins, had, like the Baptists, developed in the Parliamentary armies during the 1640s and had probably arrived in Nottingham during the days of the garrison. The town also had a few Catholics and a small Jewish congregation. For these groups Charles's failure to introduce long-lasting toleration was a blow. His Declaration of Indulgence of 1672, which established the practice of licensing premises for Protestant worship, lasted only one year, and repression followed hard on its collapse.[41]

It has been argued that 1669 represented the high spot of Protestant dissent in the county and that it became localised in particular communities in the wake of further repression. On the other hand, dissenters in general became overtly political in the town and nationally during the ensuing decade in a way which eventually ensured their religious freedom. The development at the end of the 1670s of political parties at Westminster opened up or perhaps consolidated divisions in Nottingham. It also tended to embrace the two principal religious groupings, the Anglicans and the dissenters, sweeping political and religious issues together in a manner as explosive as the pre-war years.

By the end of 1678, wars with the Dutch, battles over finance, plots threatening the King's life and that of the heir to the throne, and the Duke of York's conversion to Roman Catholicism, had served to polarise MPs and political society into two major groups. As with the cavaliers and roundheads of 1641 these groups gained names from the insults hurled at them by their opponents. The King's party which embraced the Anglicans became known as Tories. Their opponents, which included members of the dissenting sects, became the Whigs. Such divisions appeared in Nottingham and it is no surprise to find strong echoes of former political conflicts. The Tories included the second Duke of Newcastle, son of the Royalist general. The Whig faction included Charles Hutchinson, John's half-brother. When the Cavalier Parliament was dissolved in 1678 it was succeeded by three short Parliaments. In each of them the town returned one Tory, Robert Pierrepont and one Whig, Richard Slater of Nuthall.[42] On 10 December 1678 a riot broke out when the mayor, Ralph Edge, refused to accept the burgess's nominee for a vacant place on the Clothing. Edge claimed that William Drury was ineligible, not having served as a chamberlain or a sheriff. On his refusal to accept Drury, and the refusal of the burgesses to nominate another candidate, Edge had Robert Whortley sworn in. In the resulting fracas, the mayor and aldermen were pelted with cheese and bread. Whortley was a Tory who rose quickly, becoming an alderman in 1684 when Edge died, and mayor in 1685. He was displaced from the council when James II removed his Tory opponents. Drury had to await the Glorious Revolution for his seat. Gervase Rippon, whose elevation had caused the election, was one of the central figures in the conflicts of the next few years. Another was Christopher Hall, who with Rippon and Edge took the depositions of the witnesses in the wake of the riot.[43] The fierce debates in Parliament over the Exclusion Bill – the attempt to deny the Duke of York his right to succeed – were re-enacted in Nottingham.

The charters

As part of the polarisation at both national and local level the old debates about central interference in local affairs resurfaced in the battles over the reissuing of borough charters. Charles II sought to reinforce his power over boroughs to control the elections to Parliament in order to prevent the election of Whigs. In 1681 he began to meddle with the structure of town government, removing the odd Whig official where he had power to do so.[44] That year he interfered with the election of one Nottingham alderman, and a Tory mayor again refused to countenance a Whig candidate, discounting the successful election of a dissenting burgess to the position of alderman and placing the defeated candidate in his place. Mayor Gervase Wild alleged that John Sherwin was 'a busy and factious and turbulent man' who led the town's dissenters in all elections to oppose the interests of his majesty and magistracy of the town'. By May 1682 Sherwin had been indicted by the Grand Jury for the public defamation of the magistrates at the market cross. Wild felt unable to prove that Sherwin was an active dissenter, but others could. Obediah Kendal of Nottingham swore an affidavit to the effect that Sherwin had attended a conventicle on 8 May 1681 and had been at Presbyterian conventicles during his year as sheriff (1680–81).[45]

Charles II's desire to destroy the Whig party saw 119 incorporated boroughs receive new Tory charters.[46] Towns were 'requested' through a *Quo Warranto* to submit their charters for renewal. Nottingham's Tories, through the agency of and with encouragement from the Lord Lieutenant, the Duke of Newcastle, were naturally happy to do this and sought the necessary document of submission, known as an 'abhorrence'. In June 1681 Alderman Rippon went to London to collect the document and receive advice from Secretary Sir Leoline Jenkins, although in the end it was sent directly to the Duke of Newcastle.[47] The Whigs were alerted to this possibility and in 1682, fearing that the charter might be submitted to the King in an underhand way, placed four caveats with the Lord Chancellor, the substance of which would preclude serious changes. On 25 July 1682 the council had split 14:14 on the issue, which effectively meant that it rejected sending the abhorrence, but the mayor used his casting vote and had it sealed. Alderman Christopher Hall was sent to London to hand the charter to the Earl of Halifax who would lay it at the feet of the King. In fact, Hall was unable to carry it and the charter had to be sent to London by carrier. The abhorrence was then found to be inadequate, as it failed to detail the surrender of the town lands, and this meant that the King's re-grant of them was rendered nonsensical and illegal. To prevent the whole issue being fought out again, the mayor broke into the town chest to find the seal and attach it to a new abhorrence. The King finally re-granted incorporation on 21 September 1682, and rioting broke out almost immediately.[48]

The town's Whigs and their county allies, or dissenters, as the Tories labelled them, refused to attend the mayor to the Town Hall, and withdrew instead to St Mary's church. Two sets of ceremonies then took place and by the end of the day Nottingham had two governments: the Old Chartermen gathered around Mayor Greaves and Recorder Serjeant Bigland, and the new Chartermen around William Toplady. At one point the Old Chartermen went to the Guildhall to try to seize the insignia. They succeeded in getting hold of some of the books and one sheriff's mace. Greaves was then proclaimed at Weekday Cross. Toplady and his council went to his house nearby to complete their swearing-in, where they were visited by Charles Hutchinson demanding the mace. Toplady then went back to the Guildhall and had himself and his government proclaimed. At this second ceremony, John Sherwin appeared, leading a crowd which shouted down the new charter and bellowed in Greaves's favour.[49] The town was engulfed in disorder. Charles ordered the Duke of Newcastle to take up residence at his newly-built 'castle' to impose control. This was something the Duke appears to have resented, as Jenkins tried to assure him on 7 October that he could leave the town if he wanted to. The leading participants were apprehended and questioned. Newcastle, in his role as a county JP and as *custos rotulorum*, was at the heart of these proceedings in which twenty-nine leading Whigs were bound over to keep the peace. Some were more severely dealt with: Sir Thomas Parkyns was deprived of his place on the bench.[50] However, the problem was not solved, Greaves and Toplady were both summoned to the Privy Council, although it does not look as if they ever attended. Greaves and his supporters eventually gave way, and agreed to stop meeting as a mayor and council. The surrender of Greaves's 'ensigns of honour' took the impetus out of the 'rebellion' and the issue died down.[51]

The new charter was in many ways little different to the old one. The old fair was abolished and two new eight-day ones were instituted. The principal issue was the control exercised by the monarch in the selection of officers, removing all Whigs and placing Newcastle on the council as recorder in the place of Serjeant Bigland. The new recorder was clearly expected to keep a watchful eye on the activities of the corporation, and as such represented two evils in terms of borough independence: the interference of the county aristocracy and the interference of the crown. On the other hand, to the Tories Newcastle represented a continuation of the benefits of an aristocratic protector. Nottingham, because it had one of the earlier charters to be changed, suffered less interference in the short term than boroughs which had their charters renewed in 1684–85.[52] Yet this led to even more radical changes when, six years later, Nottingham's charter was one of the thirty-five to be surrendered and re-granted. James II also attempted fundamentally to curtail borough independence, to restore Whigs to corporations and to allow Roman Catholics to participate in local government. This was part of his attempt to win religious toleration for his own faith and because he believed that the Whigs – themselves oppressed by the Anglican establishment – would side with his demands. However, the dissenters and Whigs were less enamoured with this idea than the King, largely because they suspected him of advancing Catholicism, despite the Declaration of Indulgence which allowed toleration to dissenting Protestants. The King went ahead with preparations for a Parliament in 1688. He questioned county officials as to their support for abolishing the Test Acts and the penal laws aimed at Catholics, and he appointed a committee of lords to regulate boroughs. The effect was to alienate previously loyal Tories. The Duke of Newcastle seems to have been angered that the victorious Tories of 1682, William Toplady, Gervase Wild and several others, were replaced at the beginning of 1688. Two commissioners had effected their removal and ensured also that Mayor Rippon was replaced by, of all people, John Sherwin. In all sixteen men were removed in January and a further four in March.[53]

The surrender of the charter in May was to be followed by the grant of a new one designed to bring Nottingham's into line with the more stringent ones issued by Charles II. This action was the climax of outside interference in the seventeenth century.[54] The creation of Nottingham's new charter took up most of the summer of 1688 and involved long stays in London by members of the corporation. It was late September before the new charter arrived in Nottingham.[55] This abolished the two new fairs and re-established the old St Matthew's Fair. The eighteen members of the senior council were re-named the Capital Council and the King increased his control of the corporation by restricting the power of the burgesses in borough elections, thereby lessening their power to enter town government. He also reserved to himself the right to approve of the recorder and the town clerk, and the power to remove or to put in place aldermen.[56] The mayor, George Langford, a dissenter, recorded his objections partly because he felt that the Whigs and dissenters would be blamed for this curtailment of traditional democratic rights.[57] This was disingenuous, for he had specifically called for the exclusion of burgesses who had been displaced from the council, although he had supported the King's powers over the choice of recorder and clerk. Even though the Duke of Newcastle was a Tory who increasingly distanced himself from the monarch, he was reappointed recorder. The duke, the mayor and the eldest alderman formed the quorum of borough JPs.[58] It cannot have been easy for the duke to play this role, since his political allies had been driven from the corporation. He was instructed to question suitable men for Parliament on three points: their objection to repealing the Test Act and the penal laws; their willingness to vote for the men who repealed them; and their reaction to the Declaration of Indulgence. In September 1688 the King sent him a list of his candidates for the forthcoming elections in the county and its boroughs. All were Whigs.[59] The King's Parliament never sat. By the end of the same month the Prince of Orange, husband of the King's daughter Princess Mary by his first marriage, issued a declaration promising to intervene in the affairs of England: the 'Glorious Revolution' had begun.[60]

The 1688 Revolution

The Glorious Revolution or, as it was referred to in Nottingham, the 'Excellent Revolution', began with Prince William landing in the south-west on 5 November 1688, and with a series of risings against James in the North and Midlands. By the time William landed, James had reneged on some of his earlier actions. He had suspended his religious policy and restored the existing charters on 17 October, only about three weeks after Nottingham received its new one.[61] He had put new lord lieutenants in the counties, moving the Duke of Newcastle to Yorkshire in the process, and had restored justices who had failed to answer the three questions posed by the lieutenants earlier in the year. Newcastle had been accused of being too 'stunned or lethargic' to be of use to the King, but it is probable that his loyalty to the monarch had been severely strained during the period when his political enemies, the Whigs, were advanced to power under his very nose.[62] Prince William had moved to Exeter by 9 November, but the King was powerless to attack him. A landing in the north had been expected and the south-west was largely unguarded. In any case, prominent generals, including John Churchill, deserted James. Troops were sent from Scotland in an attempt to bolster the King's army, but they may have been less than enthusiastic for their cause: at Nottingham Lord Dunbarton's regiment rebelled and at least one soldier was injured, perhaps by William Cockle and Caleb Wilkinson, who were held partly responsible for paying the bill for the soldier's treatment.[63] On 14 November Nottingham was occupied by the Earl of Devonshire, the Whig conspirator from Derbyshire.

On 2 December the Revolution's focus switched briefly to Nottingham. The Bishop of London had smuggled James's younger daughter Princess Anne out of the capital in the company of Lady Churchill and brought her north via Northampton and Leicester to Nottingham. This was a turning-point in the loyalties of many uncommitted people. Anne was joined by members of the gentry on her journey northwards. The Earl of Chesterfield, who arrived at Nottingham once she was in residence, was prominent among those who cloaked their half-hearted rebelliousness under the cover of guarding the Princess.[64] The nobility and gentry issued a declaration in the town on 23 November setting out the reasons for their desertion of the monarch, and listing eight of the King's perceived illegal acts. One, the third, clearly had resonance for Nottingham: 'By destroying the charters of most corporations in the land' it was, they declared, 'tyrannical government' and they were not willing to deliver their 'posterity over to such condition of popery and slavery'. Inspired perhaps by their location, the charter issue recurred in the last section: 'the present restoring the charters, … [is] to still the people, like plumbs to children, by deceiving them for a while'.[65] Even though the Revolution had been set in train 'chiefly to ensure the dominance and to foster the influence of a propertied and privileged minority', the petition was often couched in terms which embraced the support of all social classes. It claimed that it was defending everyman's rights, declaring in Latin that the voice of the people was the voice of God ('*Vox populi vox dei*').[66] According to Deering, this may have had some grounding in the attitudes of people in Nottingham and its neighbourhood. He describes how on hearing that the King's forces were within four miles of the town, 'multitudes who had horses mounted and accoutred themselves with such arms as they had, whilst others in vast numbers on foot appeared, some with fire-locks, some with swords, some with other weapons, pitchforks were not excepted'.[67] This was a false alarm, but on the next day, crowds again gathered to cheer the leaders of the rebellion and declare their support for a free Parliament, although the presence of the Princess was not universally welcome because of the heavy expenses incurred. The town was already in debt and it was 'importuned by several lords to raise money towards defraying the charge of the souldiers kept for the guard of the Princess Ann of Denmark [she was married to Prince George of Denmark]'. Members of the corporation tried to raise the cash but failed and £100 was borrowed from Alderman Hawkins on 24 December and added to the sum outstanding.[68] By that time James II had fled the country, and on the same day members of the House of Lords then in London ordered the calling of a Convention which offered the crown jointly to Prince William and Princess Mary.

In the wake of the accession of William and Mary the charters of Charles II and James II were annulled and the charter of James I – essentially Henry VI's charter of 1449 – was restored. In a measure of independence, surely not unrelated to the town's reaction to years of interference, the repudiation of the new charters was largely undertaken by the borough itself; indeed, it was only in 1692 that the charter was officially redrafted.[69] Not everyone in Nottingham perceived the revolution as glorious. On 10 June 1689 a paper called *A Declaration of his most sacred Majestie, King James the 2nd, to all his Loyal subjects in the Kingdom of England* was circulating in the town. Copies were sent anonymously through the post. One copy was sent to Edward Bartliffe, who promptly handed it to the Town Clerk who alerted the corporation.[70] On the other hand the old Tory recorder the Duke of Newcastle died in 1691, and his office was handed to a Whig cousin the Earl of Devonshire. The town's aristocratic protector was now a supporter of the regime and of the old charter.

It was claimed in June 1690 that a plot had been discovered in the town whereby 'their Majesties' best and most loyall subjects' were to be disarmed by supporters of James II. An enquiry was set up and Charles Hutchinson, by now one of the town MPs, was asked to pass on the information to the Earl of Kingston. The Earl, the lord lieutenant, ordered houses to be searched for arms and, responding to slanders put about by Gervase Rippon, the Tory mayor displaced by James II, disarmed the mayor and others whom Rippon had accused of disloyalty. In the wake of these accusations the corporation took legal action against Rippon, and shortly afterwards against the town clerk who had been accused of betraying the secrecy of the corporation and neglect of duty. The outcome of neither case is clear, although the clerk disappears from the records shortly afterwards, while Rippon was soon serving as a trustee for rents in the town again.[71]

The Jacobite uprisings

The succession of the Hanoverian monarchs, and the Jacobite uprisings which followed, inspired outbursts of loyalty to the 'kings over the water' and purges of the disaffected in the corporation. On the accession of George I the mayor, Thomas Hawksley, knelt and pledged loyalty to the Stuarts at his house by Chapel Bar. He was promptly imprisoned and deprived of his office. In the wake of the 1715 uprising two others were displaced. On 7 June 1717 burgess Theodore Fosbrooke was disenfranchised for 'having been convict[ed] of being desaffected to his majesty King George'. Seven weeks later William Greaves was dismissed from his position of senior councillor and had his burgess rights removed for 'refusing to attend severall comon hall when he was only summoned and for being disaffected to his present majesty King George'. However, these individual stances seem to have posed little real threat.[72]

At the time of the 1745 uprising there was local support for the Young Pretender. The lord lieutenant, the Duke of Newcastle, disarmed the town's known Jacobites.[73]

Within a month of Prince Charles's landing in Scotland, the borough sent a declaration of loyalty to the King. On 26 September 1745 the town set aside £20 for gathering information about the rebellion and cleaning the town's weapons.[74] Other weapons were moved around the area. General Howard's regiment was at Mansfield by the end of August and two other regiments were at Loughborough; Nottingham was charged with the responsibility of ferrying materials back and forth to them. On 30 October a dinner was held in the town for the 'King's Friends' on the occasion of George II's birthday. However, something of a state of panic erupted as the Prince approached the Midlands. Chapel Bar had been removed only in 1743, the last physical presence of the town's walls, and suddenly the townspeople felt vulnerable.[75] A regiment of cavalry was raised at Nottingham by Evelyn Pierrepont, 2nd Duke of Kingston, with subscriptions from 350 people in the form of a loan, headed by Kingston himself and Thomas Pelham, Duke of Newcastle. The total raised was £8,526, which was more than adequate for funding the regiment, and enabled a profit to be made by the creditors.[76] By the time the Prince reached Derby on 4 December the regiment had already been involved in skirmishing with the Scottish Army at Congleton. It then went with the army into Staffordshire when the Prince arrived in Derby. In Nottingham, a degree of panic set in; the Scots were expected daily and their army was rumoured to be stationed between Nottingham and Loughborough, cutting communications with London. The road to Lincoln was packed with the carriages of the well-to-do fleeing the town.[77] In the event the Prince withdrew to Scotland. Kingston's regiment followed, and it went on to fight in the decisive battle at Culloden and to remain in Scotland until July 1746.[78]

The town had restructured its government again in 1727 to resist central interference, a measure reminiscent of the struggles at the beginning of the seventeenth century. The mayor and aldermen discontinued the practice of choosing six burgesses for a Junior Council, using as justification the old excuse that any election involving the broader community was bound to lead to disorder. The elections in January 1728 were accompanied by violence when the mayor declared that one of the candidates for the common council had not served as sheriff. Despite objections from the burgesses, there was no further Junior Council for fifty years, and the self-perpetuating corporation was unchallengeable.[79]

Nottingham's unparalleled role in the nation's affairs, particularly in 1642–49 and 1688–89, had given it a pre-eminence in the county with which neither Newark nor Retford could compete.[80] Like other towns Nottingham had seen both the benefits and drawbacks of aristocratic involvement in government during the two centuries covered in this chapter. The aristocracy, as evidenced by the new 'castle' in the 1670s, clearly saw a continuing role for themselves in the town. Yet Newcastle's interventions in the early 1680s demonstrated the dangers of an alliance between a powerful aristocrat and a reforming monarch. After the Revolution Newcastle was sidelined and the town demonstrated its independence in pre-empting the restoration of the new charter. It may only have been the combination of the 'right' political sympathies and his residence at Chatsworth in Derbyshire which allowed the town to develop without the active interference of Newcastle's successor as recorder, the Earl of Devonshire. Yet by 1750 the power of the aristocrats was almost broken,[81] while the closed oligarchy which ran the town was again coming under scrutiny.

Notes

1 P. Clark and P. Slack, *Crisis and Order in English Towns 1500–1700* (1972), pp. 21–2.

2 A. C. Wood, *The History of Nottinghamshire* (Nottingham, 1937), p. 154.

3 NAO CA3014; CA3015; *RBN*, IV, pp. xv–xvii, 171, 190–1, 262–3, 265, 274, 278.

4 For discussions of women, power and property see S. Ammussen, *An Ordered Society* (Cambridge, 1988) and A. L. Ericksson, *Women and Property in Early Modern England* (Cambridge, 1993). For similar discussions in a local context see S. Dunster, 'An independent life: Nottingham widows, 1590–1650', *TTS*, 95 (1991), pp. 29–37.

5 See M. Bennett (ed.), *A Nottinghamshire Village at War and Peace: the Accounts of the Constables of Upton 1640–1666* (*TSRS*, 39, 1995), pp. xvii–xix, 14–23 for an account of a Nottinghamshire woman constable.

6 *RBN*, IV, pp. 202–10, 293–5, 371–2.

7 L. Hutchinson, *Memoirs of the Life of Colonel Hutchinson* (1806), pp. 110, 78–9, 269–70.

8 Drage, *Castle*, pp. 66–8.

9 Gray, *Settlement*, p. 28. A. C. Wood, *Nottinghamshire in the Civil War* (Oxford, 1937), p. ix.

10 R. Cust, *The Forced Loan and English Politics* (Oxford, 1987), p. 171, Wood, *Nottinghamshire*, p. 167; Wood, *Civil War*, p. 10; *RBN*, V, p. 129; Orders to collect the taxation are to be found on pp. 125–8; *Calendar of State Papers Domestic* (hereafter *CSPD*) 1625–26, p. 434.

11 *CSPD*, 1639, pp. 150–1; *CSPD*, 1640, p. 244. These statistics come from an unpublished study, but a summary is included in M. Bennett, 'Nottingham Justices of the Peace and the Social Order', *NH*, 47 (1991), pp. 9–11.

12 *RBN*, V, p. 198, 202.

13 *CSPD*, 1641, p. 202.

14 The Militia Ordinance was dated 5 March; Clare became recorder on 2 February (*RBN*, V, p. 203)

15 Hutchinson, *Memoirs*, p. 86; All references to the Nottingham commission of 18 June relate to the transcript by William Dugdale, Northamptonshire Record Office, Finch Hatton MSS, 133.

16 For a discussion of this aspect of the war see M. Bennett, 'The King's Gambit: Charles I and Nottingham in the summer of 1642', *TTS*, 96 (1992), pp. 136–8.

17 Hutchinson, *Memoirs*, pp. 113.

18 Wood, *Civil War*, pp. 16–17; M. Bennett, 'Between Scylla and Charybdis: the establishment of rival administrations in the English Civil War', *The Local Historian* 22, 4 (1992), p. 199.

19 Clarendon, Earl of, *The History of the Rebellion* (Oxford, 1888, new imprint 1992), II, p. 290; Bennett, 'King's Gambit', pp. 139–40; J. L. Malcolm, *Caesars Due: Loyalty and King Charles* (1983), p. 43.

20 Wood, *Civil War*, p. 24; NAO PR1710, f. 12; Bennett, *Nottinghamshire Village*, pp. 8–9.

21 S. Glover, *The History, Directory and Gazeteer of the County of Derby* (Derby, 1829), appendix, 'A true relation of what service hath been done by Colonel Sir John Gell', p. 62. This is also now included in B. Stone, *Derbyshire in the Civil War* (Cromford, 1992).

22 Hutchinson, *Memoirs* is perhaps the fullest account of events in these years.

23 M. Bennett, 'The Royalist war effort in the North Midlands, 1642–6' (Loughborough University, Ph.D. thesis, 1986). Chapter Two carries an exposition of the system in Nottinghamshire. Historical Manuscripts Commission, Seventh Report, Various Manuscripts (1914), pp. 393–4; NAO DD39/5, Toton Rentals; see Lucy Hutchinson's account of the battle at the fort in *Memoirs*, pp. 157–64.

24 Bennett, 'Royalist war effort', pp. 190–2; Hutchinson, *Memoirs*, pp. 123–4.
25 L. Beats, 'The East Midlands Association 1642–44', *Midland History*, IV (1978), pp. 160–74.
26 Hutchinson, *Memoirs*, p. 138.
27 *Ibid.*, p. 141.
28 *Ibid.*, pp. 179–83.
29 Wood, *Civil War*, pp. 87–8.
30 *Ibid.*, pp. 90–1.
31 Bennett, 'Royalist war effort', pp. 239–43.
32 Clark and Slack, *Crisis and Order*, p. 23.
33 For a recent discussion of opposition to Hutchinson, see P. R. Seddon, 'Colonel Hutchinson and the disputes between Nottinghamshire Parliamentarians, 1643–45: New evidence analysed', *TTS*, 98 (1994), pp. 72–9.
34 P. Lloyd, 'Politics and personnel of politics in Nottingham 1642–1688' (University of Nottingham, M. Phil. thesis, 1983), pp. 109–16; Seddon, 'Colonel Hutchinson', pp. 72, 77–9.
35 Bennett, *Nottinghamshire Village*, pp. 37–45, 50–1.
36 Drage, *Castle*, pp. 73–4.
37 For a recent discussion of other towns see R. C. Richardson (ed.), *Town and Countryside in the English Revolution* (Manchester, 1992).
38 *RBN*, V, pp. 203, 204–5, 278, 301, 283, 288.
39 Wood, *Nottinghamshire*, p. 204.
40 Hutchinson, *Memoirs*, pp. 269–70.
41 S. B. Jennings, 'The 1669 Ecclesiastical Returns for Nottinghamshire: a reassessment of the strength of Protestant conconformity', *TTS*, 99 (1995), pp. 73–80.
42 Wood, *Nottinghamshire*, p. 208.
43 NAO DDE 8/5.
44 R. Hutton, *Charles II: King of England Scotland and Ireland* (Oxford, 1989), p. 423.
45 *CSPD*, 1682, pp. 192–3.
46 P. Clark and P. Slack, *English Towns in Transition* (Oxford, 1976), p. 139.
47 *CSPD*, 1682, pp. 247–8, 282.
48 *Ibid.*, p. 316; *RBN*, V, p. 321; Wood, *Nottinghamshire*, p. 210; NAO CA4209 is a draft of the charter.
49 *CSPD*, 1682, pp. 437–8.
50 S. Jennings, 'Bunny and Bradmore 1640–1690, change and continuity in an age of revolutions' (University of Nottingham, MA thesis, 1991), pp. 32–3.
51 *CSPD*, 1682, pp. 459–60, 477, 490.
52 Hutton, *Charles II*, p. 434.
53 *CSPD*, 1688–9, James II, 3, p. 138. *RBN*, V, pp. 336–9, 440–1; Deering, p. 255.
54 Clark and Slack, *English Towns* p. 139; *CSPD*, 1688–89, p. 244.
55 NAO CA4746, CA 4756.
56 NAO CA4212. This is a copy of the Patent Rolls entry: the original has been lost.
57 Deering, pp. 255–6.
58 NAO CA4752; *RBN*, V, pp. 345–7.
59 *RBN*, V, p. 273.
60 W. Speck, *Reluctant Revolutionaries* (Oxford, 1988) pp. 74, 220.
61 *RBN*, V, p. 354.
62 M. Ashley, *The Glorious Revolution* (1966), p. 219.
63 *RBN*, V, p. 354.
64 Speck, *Reluctant Revolutionaries*, p. 228.
65 There is a printed version of the Declaration in Deering, pp. 258–60.
66 A. McInnes, 'The Revolution and the people' in G. Holmes (ed.), *Britain After the Glorious Revolution 1689–1714* (1980), p. 81.
67 Deering, p. 260.
68 *RBN*, V, pp. 354–5; D. H. Hosford, *Nottingham, Nobles and the North* (Hamden, 1976).

69 NAO CA 4182; *RBN*, V, pp. 360, 376.
70 *Ibid.*, p. 357.
71 *Ibid.*, pp. 365–7, 370–1, 378.
72 Blackner, p. 379; *RBN*, VI, pp. 63n, 66–7; Wood, *Nottinghamshire*, p. 236.
73 F. J. McLynn, 'Nottingham and the Jacobite Rising of 1745', *TTS*, 83 (1979), p. 63.
74 *RBN*, VI, p. 195.
75 McLynn, 'Jacobite Rising', p. 63.
76 Blackner, p. 380; A. C. Wood, 'The Duke of Kingston's Regiment of Light Horse', *TTS*, 49 (1945), p. 75.
77 McLynn, 'Jacobite Rising', pp. 67–8; M. T. H. Hildyard, 'Some letters of Robert and Mary Thoroton and others', *TTS*, 57 (1953), pp. 25–8.
78 Wood, 'Kingston's Regiment', p. 80.
79 *RBN*, VI, pp. 113–15, 238–9, 247, 251–2.
80 Clark and Slack, *English Towns*, p. 104.
81 See ch. 13.

Part III

INDUSTRIAL NOTTINGHAM 1750–1914

10

AN INDUSTRIAL TOWN IN THE MAKING, 1750–1830

John Beckett

Nottingham in the later eighteenth century was a fashionable, elegant town: 'the situation is not exceeded by any in England', enthused Robert Sanders in 1772, 'and in the principal streets are many fine houses … . The streets are broad and open and well paved … . Many gentlemen of great fortune reside here, which is not to be wondered at, as the prospect from the streets over the fields, and the windings of the Trent are so delightful, that it even exceeds imagination.'[1] The following year another visitor was almost lost for words: 'this town, where nature and art has had an equal share in making it handsome, healthy and convenient, would puzzle a person well acquainted with most other in England to name its equal'.[2] Carl Moritz, a German travelling in England in 1782, found Nottingham to be 'of all the towns I have seen outside London the loveliest and neatest'. In his view everything had 'a modern look'. A decade later the Revd William MacRitchie called it 'a large and elegant town … . The streets, houses, and market-place here broad, cleanly, and elegant.'[3] MacRitchie highlighted the market-place, so long the unifying feature of the town, and a delight to all who passed through. One visitor noted that 'the market-place, though of an irregular figure, is reckoned the finest in the Kingdom … . The extensive colonnades add much to the ornament of the place especially as the fronts of the houses they support are tolerably well built.'[4] Moritz thought the market-place 'hardly less handsome than a London square'; the 1793 *Universal British Directory* described it as 'in spaciousness superior to most in the kingdom, and graced with many beautiful buildings'; and in 1830 William Cobbett called it 'a fine, most extensive and most beautiful market-place'.[5] John Blackner, perhaps a biased witness because he was a local man, nevertheless summed up the collective experience: 'when the traveller enters this town by way of Chapel-bar, he is highly charmed with a view of the finest market-place in England'.[6]

The elegant Georgian town which so charmed eighteenth-century visitors was destined to disappear by 1830. Nottingham, like so many English towns, stood in 1750 at a social crossroads: the next century and a half witnessed population and physical growth on an unprecedented scale, and with it came rapid changes in the urban environment. The pretty, uncrowded market and service centre was about to be transformed. By 1914 a Victorian town had been grafted on to a Georgian town – but the two were quite different. In 1750 Nottingham's better-off citizens lived in the town centre with their poorer neighbours around the periphery. This use of urban space was inverted in the Victorian town. The middle classes retreated to the suburbs and the better-off working classes found adequate accommodation to the north of the town centre. The central core of the town was turned over predominantly to business uses, with a residual area of poor-quality housing which seemed immune to improvement. Since 1914 the working classes have also left, and today the commercial heart of the modern city is largely non-residential.

These processes require explanation. In this chapter we follow the first stage of the reordering of the town, tracing the rapid growth of population and the various building booms down to about 1830. Chapter 11 tackles the second stage, with the

Plate 23 **The market place, *c*.1740**. Thomas Sandby's magnificent depiction shows: (foreground left) the malt cross from which proclamations were read; (background left) the colonnaded *piazza* along the frontages of the houses in Long Row dating from Georgian, Stuart and earlier periods and including examples (rear of malt cross) of late

coming of the railway and factory-based industry to the town, as well as the long-delayed attempts to exert some control over development through the Enclosure Act of 1845. Chapter 12 examines the expansion of the town in the final third of the nineteenth century, the growth of corporation control over development, and the attempts which were made to sort out the outstanding urban problems.

The urban landscape

In the years after 1750 many English towns began to experience population growth on a scale previously unknown. Rising real incomes drove forward demand for manufactured goods and services, and helped as a result to promote the expansion of urban employment. Towns became commercial and manufacturing centres and the resulting economic growth attracted labour from the surrounding countryside, which inevitably increased the density of population. In Nottingham population increase began around the turn of the eighteenth century in conjunction with the growth of framework knitting, but the pace quickened in the period down to 1831

seventeenth-century shaped gables; the narrow Sheep Lane (behind the malt cross) which was replaced by Market Street in the mid-nineteenth century; the four-storey, eleven-bay Exchange Building (erected 1724–25); and Timber Hill (now South Parade) on the right

(table 10.1). Taken at face value, these figures suggest that the pace of growth never approached the rate of increase which took place elsewhere in the early decades of the nineteenth century. In the 1820s growth was only 25 per cent in Nottingham, when Manchester, Birmingham and Sheffield all topped 40 per cent. In fact, this is illusory. Land restrictions produced a unique development pattern in Nottingham. The real extent of growth can be measured for the 1820s only by adding in the figures for the adjoining villages, which absorbed the overspill from the overcrowded town, and which were brought within its boundaries in 1877. The effect is shown in table 10.2. Nottingham's population grew by roughly 18 per cent in each of the first two decades of the century. When the surrounding villages are added the total increases to 23 per cent and 20 per cent respectively, and then to 43 per cent in the 1820s, roughly the ratio to be found in other great industrialising towns. This chapter is mainly concerned with the impact on the physical growth of Nottingham.

Table 10.1 **The population of Nottingham, 1750–1911**

Date	*Population*	*% increase*	*Date*	*Population*	*% increase*
1750	10,910		1841	52,164	3.9
1760	11,940	9.4	1851	57,407	10.1
1770	14,630	22.5	1861	74,693	30.1
1780	17,200	17.6	1871	86,621	16.0
1790	24,400	41.9	1881	186,575[a]	115.4[a]
1801	28,861	18.3	1891	213,877	14.6
1811	34,030	18.2	1901	239,743	12.1
1821	40,190	18.1	1911	259,901	8.4
1831	50,220	25.0			

Sources: Blackner, p. 77; J. D. Chambers, 'Population Change in a Provincial Town, Nottingham 1700–1800', in L. S. Pressnell (ed.), *Studies in the Industrial Revolution* (1960), pp. 97–125; VCH, *Nottinghamshire*, II (1910), pp. 307–17; NUMD Chambers MSS, notes on parish registers 1707–1800 (figure recalculated by Stephen Wallwork).

Note: [a] Increase largely due to the 1877 boundary extension (chapter 12).

In the years immediately after 1750 the orderly development of Nottingham which had been a feature of the post-Restoration town continued, but by the early nineteenth century a crisis was looming. Until the 1830s the relationship between Westminster and the rest of the country was a loose one, with responsibility being left in the locality wherever possible. Unfortunately the chartered corporations lacked the powers needed to govern growing industrial towns, but central government refused to invest them with greater authority. Alternative organisations were often regarded as preferable to the existing corporations when new powers were granted, and in many places the way forward was an Improvement Commission, established by Act of Parliament and empowered to clean up the urban environment. These commissions were not always a great success, partly because they frequently clashed with the existing corporation; but in a number of English towns they had a significant impact. Nottingham had no improvement commission, nor does one seem seriously to have been considered prior to the 1850s. With a relatively ineffective corporation, and no obvious alternative body – the Mickletorn Jury could still impose fines for 'certain classes of nuisances and encroachments' but it was effectively moribund[7] – the result was predictable: the physical development of Nottingham took place without any real planning, and with inadequate controls, particularly in relation to infrastructure.

Table 10.2 **The population of Nottingham and its industrial villages, 1801–81**

	1801	*1811*	*1821*	*1831*	*1841*	*1851*	*1861*	*1871*	*1881*
Nottingham	28,861	34,030	40,190	50,220	52,164	57,407	74,693	86,621	186,575
Radford	2,269	3,447	4,806	9,806	10,817	12,637	13,495	15,127	
Lenton	893	1,197	1,240	3,077	4,467	5,589	5,828	6,315	
Sneinton	558	953	1,212	3,605	7,079	8,440	11,048	12,237	
Basford	2,124	2,940	3,599	6,325	8,688	10,091	12,185	13,038	
Bulwell	1,585	1,944	2,105	2,611	3,157	3,786	3,660	4,276	
Total	36,290	44,511	53,152	75,644	86,372	97,950	120,909	137,614	186,575

Source: VCH *Nottinghamshire*, II (1910), pp. 307–17.

Since the upheavals of the 1720s the corporation had been unchallenged. The small size of the Clothing usually ensured that only sufficient candidates came forward for senior councillors as there were vacancies to fill. Contested elections were rare, although they were not unknown. In 1787 John Collishaw's election to the senior council was contested by Samuel Heywood, a member of the Clothing who wanted to see the common fields enclosed. The following year the mayor's nominee for a vacancy was defeated by Henry Green, a Tory. Other rogue elections occurred from time to time, but by 1833 four local families held three-quarters of the positions on the corporation. After a protracted legal case in the 1770s the junior councillors were reinstated in 1776, and the first election aroused considerable passions in the town. Abigail Gawthern, a middle-class Tory at the heart of genteel society in the late eighteenth-century town, recorded the events in her diary. Her father, Thomas Frost, was one of the six candidates. After breakfast at the White Lion the procession 'proceeded to the Town Hall with drums beating and beautiful blue flags trimmed with silver … . The next day they went to the Hall in grand procession to be sworn in.'[8] Despite the struggle for recognition, and despite the fact that the junior councillors tended to be Tories opposed to the Whig-dominated corporation, they lacked any real powers, and the Whig hold on power remained unbroken down to 1835.[9]

Since real power lay with the senior councillors, it is perhaps not surprising to find these positions occupied by the town's social and business elite. Between 1785 and 1835, of thirty-four men who held this position thirteen were hosiers, three were lace manufacturers, two were cotton manufacturers, and thirteen were from among the town's tradesmen and shopkeepers. They were overwhelmingly Whig in politics and nonconformist in religion. Subscribers to the High Pavement Presbyterian–Unitarian chapel held the mayoralty fifteen times out of thirty-eight occasions between 1797 and 1835. Twenty-four of the seventy-six appointments as sheriff were subscribers, and George Coldham and Henry Enfield – successively town clerks – were also subscribers.[10] Castle Gate Congregational Chapel and George Street Particular Baptists were also places where significant numbers of local politicians were to be found worshipping.[11]

What the corporation lacked were active powers of local government. Much of its work was concerned with registering burgesses, allocating burgess parts, administering the charity funds, and repairing its properties. It occasionally invested some funds in town improvements, but generally it was reluctant and frequently powerless to respond other than piecemeal to events. In 1764 orders were given to buy two fire engines, and when at a public meeting in 1783 complaints were voiced as to the state of the town's streets, the corporation announced that it was prepared to allocate £50 a year for cleaning and paving. Four years later the mayor was instructed to oversee paving repairs in the market-place 'where he shall think it necessary', and in 1804 the corporation funded the removal of the Malt Cross and Weekday Cross. In 1826 it paid for the sewering, levelling, and flagging of the market-place, and it subscribed £1,000 between 1826 and 1832 towards widening Chapel Bar.[12] But the corporation was most likely to spend money on improvements beneficial to itself, such as the £14,000 it laid out in 1814–15 reconstructing the Exchange.[13]

The position was further complicated by the question of money. In 1793 the corporation acquired powers to levy a rate. Daniel Parker Coke, when he stepped down as MP for the town in 1812, expressed his concern at the impact of these powers:

> I leave you I am sorry to say paying Taxes to a Corporate Body within your own bosom who have imposed a very heavy Town Rate upon you, to supply the waste of their own extravagance and to defray expenses which ought to have been paid out of those Estates which they hold in Trust for you, and which if well managed would have been fully adequate to the purposes.

Although the corporation responded by accusing Coke of a 'foul slander', his concerns were real enough.[14] No accounts were ever published, despite pressure from the burgesses and, although the town rate went ever upward, debts mounted. By 1833, despite its income from the Bridge and Chamber estates, from the rates, and from periodic sales of its property, the corporation had run up debts of £19,000. The Royal Commission investigating the activities of the corporation calculated that between 1812 and 1832 income from the Chamber estates totalled £67,422, and sales of property raised a further £47,474. However, from this total of £114,896, 'there will still remain a sum of above £93,996 of which nothing deserving of mention has been applied to the benefit of the town'. 'No funds', the town clerk admitted, had been 'specifically appropriated for the improvement of the town'.[15]

In these circumstances private enterprise was left to take the lead in the provision of utilities and the improvement of Nottingham's links with the wider world. Until the 1770s the waterworks remained a wholly private company. Water pipes were laid to various streets, but only about 150 households seem to have been connected and water was available only on set days of the week. In 1775 the corporation paid £12 to provide a piped water supply to the House of Correction, and four years later it started to make up for lost time by installing new pumps.[16] By 1782 thirty-nine streets in the town had customers attached to the water supply.[17] According to Blackner the real turning-point came in 1782 'when Thomas Hancock was chosen engineer … since which time, through his ingenuity their affairs have gone on in a prosperous way', and 'many parts of the town are supplied with water by pumps, erected by the corporation, within about the last thirty years'.[18]

Blackner's account put something of a gloss on affairs. Although the network was extensive, by no means all parts of the town had running water. Pipes had still to be paid for by the consumer, which put them out of the reach of many people, and significantly the marsh areas beneath the cliff face and the heavily infilled area between Long Row and Back Side (Parliament Street) were among those excluded. Tenants of Paul's Court wrote to the mayor in 1807 explaining the inconvenience they suffered 'for want of a regular supply of water'.[19] The quality of the water also left something to be desired: one of the pumps, at the bottom of Sheep Lane (now Market Street) had to be removed about 1804 because

> it was an eyesore in the day, and an object of danger in the night; and, as the ordure which accumulated year after year in the vaults on the Long-row had so far penetrated the rock as to ooze into the well, which rendered the water, at times, quite nauseous to the taste, and altogether unfit for culinary purposes.

Nor did it help that the River Leen was 'the common sewer of the town',[20] with disastrous consequences for the lower-lying areas when the river overflowed its banks.

It was not until the 1820s that a serious attempt was made to improve the quantity and quality of water supplied to the town. New waterworks were opened between Sherwood Street and Mansfield Road in 1826, and in 1831 the Trent Bridge waterworks were opened. These were the work of the 23-year-old Thomas Hawksley, the town's most passionate advocate of clean water over the next fifteen years. Hawksley's contribution was to bypass the polluted Leen to find purer water from the gravels of the alluvium. The water was pumped to a reservoir at the corner of Park Row and the Ropewalk. Next he drilled into the Bunter sandstone at the Park Row works to tap the pure water from below. Water was supplied by 1844 to 'about 4,000' houses, together with breweries, dye-houses and steam engines. Over the years which followed Nottingham came to enjoy 'the blessing of an almost unlimited supply of wholesome filtered water obtained from the River Trent, together with a supply obtained from copious springs in the neighbourhood'. By 1844 the town had three waterworks, and Hawksley was dreaming of streets cleaned by water-jets, water-closets and earthenware drains in each house – installed at a cost of less than £5 – and warm baths in public bathhouses.[21] Although Hawksley left Nottingham for London in 1852, and went on to become an international authority on water supply, lighting and sewers, he retained the post of engineer to the Trent Waterworks Company until it was taken over by the corporation in 1880.[22]

Street lighting was also less than ideal. Oil lamps were introduced only in 1762, much later than in comparable towns. Blackner complained that not enough lamps were put up even on the main streets, and the design was such that they provided little light. A woman walking along Greyfriar Gate in January 1778 fell into a place called 'The Sough', an open sewer. Unable to climb out, she was found dead next morning.[23] Progress came only with the formation in 1817 of a private company

Plate 24 **Thomas Hawksley (1807–93)**. After being articled to the Nottingham architect and surveyor, Edward Staveley, Hawksley went on to design the Trent Bridge waterworks in 1830, said to be the first scheme to provide a constant supply of pure water under pressure. He came to be widely acknowledged as the foremost waterworks engineer of his day, and was successively President of the Institution of Civil Engineers 1871–73, and the Mechanical Engineers 1875–77. He was elected an FRS in 1878

which, with the aid of legislation, erected gas lamps which were lit for the first time on 13 April 1819. The corporation subscribed for ten shares in the company.[24]

The state of the town's streets was another cause for concern. In the 1790s one contemporary was far from impressed:

> the streets are in general covered with sludge of the blackest kind, which sable hue is principally contracted from the dust of coal carts; and on a rainy day the heads of the passengers are saluted with streams of water from long projecting spouts issuing from the tops of the houses. The lighting and paving are articles which also require much improvement.[25]

Passing through in 1815 Elizabeth Fremantle considered 'the streets narrower than any I ever saw',[26] and as late as 1829 two vehicles could not pass on Milton Street or at the Chapel Bar end of Parliament Street. Pelham Street was only sixteen feet wide, Wheeler Gate was about one-third of its present width, and Sheep Lane was about the width of the modern pavement. As usual the corporation preferred to leave matters in private hands: it was grateful to the Duke of Newcastle when in 1811 he gave land to widen Cow Lane, subsequently renamed Clumber Street after his Nottinghamshire country seat; and to the trustees of Abel Collin's Hospital in 1829 when they funded the building of Carrington Street.[27]

Roads and the canal

Private enterprise also took the initiative when it came to turnpiking roads into the town, and cutting a canal. Movement into and out of Nottingham was helped by turnpiking schemes. The main road to London through Loughborough was 'very bad, not to say dangerous', according to Deering, prior to the 1738 Turnpike Act; but after improvements it was already 'as firm and good as any turnpike road in England'.[28] The logic of improving the road system was inescapable, and was largely connected with the transportation of coal. The mayor and several leading citizens of the town petitioned the Duke of Newcastle in March 1764, requesting his support for the Ilkeston turnpike:

> for the making of a turnpike from Nottingham to Belper in Derbyshire in order for the bringing of coals to Nottingham in the Winter Season .... By that means the exorbitant price of coals which from four pence or five pence a Hundred[weight] their former price are now risen to fourteen pence or sixteen pence a hundred[weight] (and from the badness of the road sometimes not to be got at any price) will then be reduced to a reasonable price which will be of prodigious advantage to the trade and poor of this town and the country adjacent.[29]

Concessionary rates were given for coal transport by several turnpike trusts. The road to Mansfield was turnpiked in 1787, and by 1832 it was in 'excellent condition'. Derby Road, to the west, was improved at the expense of Lord Middleton in the early eighteenth century, and in 1811 proper footpaths were laid and lighting introduced.[30]

The most problematic highway was the stretch of road to Trent Bridge. Leaving the town via Hollow Stone, it first crossed the Leen Bridge between Narrow Marsh and Fishergate. A new bridge 'of three good brick arches' was built in 1765 and at the same time Hollow Stone was straightened.[31] Once across the Leen, travellers had a somewhat perilous journey across planks and a causeway through the Meadows. The road had to cross two large pools. Wooden bridges were built across these in 1766, but replaced in 1792 by a ten-arch stone bridge erected by the corporation.[32] When the Trent overflowed its banks the roadway disappeared, and the whole low-lying area south of the town could be inundated. In Narrow Marsh in 1770 houses were flooded to a depth of several feet, and Samuel Marshall of Broad Marsh drowned on Christmas Eve 1790 while trying to rescue some sheep.[33]

The worst disaster of all was in February 1795. After seven weeks of frost, a rapid thaw brought severe flooding to the whole of the town below the Castle Rock and St Mary's Hill. Sheep and cattle were drowned, houses partly demolished, and 'the inhabitants of Narrow Marsh were made prisoners in their houses during two days and nights'. Food was taken to them by boat as they were 'obliged to be in their upper rooms'. Abigail Gawthern's lead works in Broad Marsh were flooded to a depth of three feet, and three pigs which drowned in a neighbouring sty turned out to be 'exceeding good meat' when they were divided among her work-force. The ten-arch stone bridge built across the pools was washed away.[34] The corporation responded by suggesting that the road should be turnpiked. This was not popular among those who were likely to become liable for tolls, and who questioned why some of the corporation's own funds were not made available for the repair work. In the end the corporation agreed to provide £500 towards repair costs and £100 towards the costs of obtaining the legislation. The bill received the Royal Assent on 19 May 1796, and within a couple of months workmen began to remove the ruins of the ten-arch bridge. The first stone of a new, seven-arch bridge was laid on 1 September 1796, and the result was a much improved Flood Road across the Meadows. Additional improvements over subsequent years included, in 1833, the provision of gas lighting.[35]

Finally the road across the Meadows reached Trent Bridge, which also had to be rebuilt following the 1795 floods. The bridge was 'narrow, irregular and inconvenient', but the corporation claimed in 1805 to be too hard-up to contemplate repairs. However, the following year, according to Blackner, it ordered 'the eastern parapet to be rebuilt, and the arches to be lengthened; which has rendered it tolerably commodious'. The northern end of the bridge was widened in 1810.[36]

How much traffic passed into and out of the town by road? In Deering's day three wagons left early on Tuesday mornings for London, returning on Friday evenings. By 1793 regular wagon services left Nottingham for London, Birmingham, Manchester, Leeds and York, as well as, more locally, Derby, Leicester, Mansfield and Lincoln. Orange's *Directory* of 1840 lists 150 destinations for carrier services from the town, with many places served more than once a week and by more than one carrier. In addition, according to Wylie, 'there were not fewer than four hundred saddle-horses kept by the middle and trading classes of the town, or about a horse to each twenty-

Plate 25 **View of Nottingham from the Flood Road, 1808**. Engraving by J. Dunn, *c.*1808, detail. A Royal Mail coach approaching the toll gate on London Road, near the junction with Meadow Lane. The Flood Road, as it was known, was administered by a turnpike trust under the legislation of 1795–96 following the winter floods of 1794–95. Note the canal on the right and in the middle distance the three Nottingham churches, St Nicholas's and St Peter's (centre), and St Mary's (right). The dominance of St Mary's on the skyline was lost with the building of the Lace Market warehouses from the 1850s

nine inhabitants'. A passenger service between London and Sheffield started in 1760, and called at The Blackamoor's Head. A regular London stage coach began in 1770, and by 1793 had been supplemented by daily coaches to Birmingham and Leeds.[37]

Individual coaches and carriers came and went, but William Stretton's private census carried out on 11 September 1819 uniquely captures the movement of people, horses, and conveyances on a single day. He and his fellow enumerators covered twelve entry points into the town over a twelve-hour period. They counted 14,474 people entering the town, 12,269 on foot, 957 on horseback, and 1,248 with carts, wagons, post-chaises, coaches (regular long-distance stage and mail coaches), gigs and canal boats. Nearly 500 of the people and 100 packhorses crossed the river on the Wilford Ferry, while twenty-three canal boats entered the wharves strung out between the Castle and London Road. This was a Saturday, market day, and therefore the traffic was heavy, but the picture it provides of a busy community should not be underplayed.[38]

Heavy and bulk goods were more likely to travel by water. The River Trent was improved for navigation purposes in the 1780s,[39] but the pressing need was for vessels to have access to the centre of the town. A canal link from the Trent to the Leen was the obvious answer, and by the end of the 1780s proposals were under discussion for such a link, proposals of which the corporation approved, but towards which it failed to offer financial help.[40] The scheme made no progress, but the threat of a glut of coal in Nottingham, as a result of expectations arising from the passing of the Cromford Canal Act in 1789, galvanised the local producers into seeking ways of protecting their livelihood. Legislation was passed in May 1792, and almost immediately work started on the construction of a canal link from the Trent into the town. The corporation subscribed for four shares. This stretch was opened in 1793 with decorated vessels drawn along the canal amidst enthusiastic rejoicing. The complete route to Langley Mill was opened only in 1796, partly as a result of delays during the 1795 floods. The Beeston cut was also opened in 1796, and traffic from the Trent was diverted along the canal from Meadow Lane to Beeston (figure 10.1).[41] The canal was soon flanked by wharves and warehouses handling coal, timber, corn, iron, stone, slate, plaster, tiles and night soil.[42] Stretton's map of *c.*1800 shows wharves all along the quayside from the Castle to London Road. Of the freight passing along the canal in 1800–01, 75 per cent was coal.[43] By 1834, according to Dearden, 'few commercial towns possess greater facilities for transporting merchandise or have more direct communication with the inland navigation of England than Nottingham'.[44] Traffic declined once the railway reached Nottingham, but the canal remained in commercial use until the 1920s. The original link through the West Croft was filled in when the railway line to Lincoln was opened in 1846.

Housing

Utility and communications improvements were not only privately sponsored, they fed on and stimulated the economic development in Nottingham, which was in turn responsible for population growth. And people needed houses. In 1829 the corporation banned the building of any further back-to-back houses on its own property. However, it seems to have gone no further and Moses Wood, the borough surveyor, commented in 1851 that 'it has long been a trite observation that "the Corporation property is known by its ruinous condition", and its truthfulness would not be much questioned by a rigid investigation in the present day'.[45] In fact, the great majority of housing in the town was erected by private developers, over whom the corporation had no powers of control. These were precisely the circumstances in which the speculative builder could flourish, and in Nottingham he could do so under conditions which were almost predisposed to produce high-density, poor-quality housing. The corporation might be excused for failing to introduce regulations, for which there were no national precedents, but it was the failure to enclose the open fields around the town – for which it could not escape some responsibility – that artificially constricted development.

In the 1750s the majority of houses in Nottingham had gardens, and on the eastern side of the town whole areas remained intact as orchards, market gardens or pasture. The most prominent working buildings on the skyline were probably the windmills around the town, together with the industrial premises near Barker Gate. A handful of cotton mills began to appear after 1769. The only really ominous signs of what was to come were several solid blocks of housing running north from the market-place to Back Side, and below the cliff edge in Narrow Marsh.[46] In 1755 'the first land ever known to be sold by the yard' changed hands, with clear implications for land values: the price was going up. The first identifiable building boom was from 1763–68, with another flurry of activity towards the end of the 1770s.[47] Early in the 1780s John Sherwin started to develop his two-acre cherry orchard on the east side of the town, with its adjoining paddocks of 3½ acres. He allowed the builders to erect either single houses or back-to-backs, and he provided some financial help for the craftsmen-builders, who purchased his land at about 5*s* per square yard. His cherry orchard became Cherry Street and Sherwin Street.[48]

Figure 10.1 **The waterways around Nottingham**

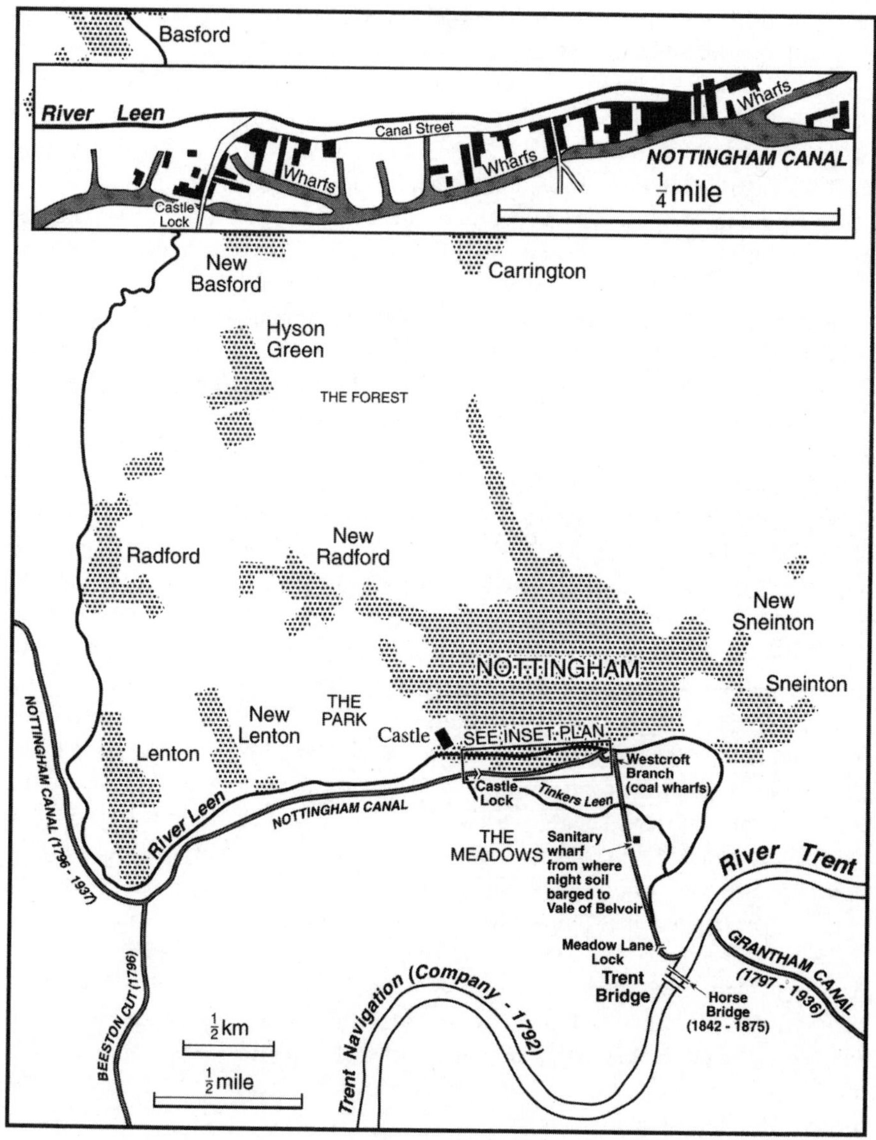

At this point there was no reason to anticipate anything other than orderly development along lines that were familiar elsewhere. The first stage was often the infilling of gardens, and plots behind houses. Usually the houses were small, and were often built back-to-back, reflecting the space constraints of what had often been burgage plots, and the price of the land. A second stage involved the colonisation of new land, but here developers frequently adopted the same building strategies. Consequently the typical back-to-back house built around a court spread from the inner core of the town, and was encouraged by rising prices, which in turn reflected a land shortage. Urban growth depended on the availability of land, and in almost every major English industrial town private owners were tempted by soaring prices to part with their holding. In Nottingham only three private landlords held any really substantial property around the town: the dukes of Newcastle on the west side, particularly the Castle Park Estate, and the Pierrepont and Musters families, to the east in the village of Sneinton. The major owner of undeveloped land within the existing town boundaries was the corporation, which was lord of the manor.

If Nottingham's pleasant inner core was to be sensibly developed it was vital for building land to become available, and the most straightforward means of achieving this aim was to enclose the open fields and meadows. In 1787 a plan was drawn up and presented to the corporation by an *ad hoc* committee of local people anxious to promote 'Improvements of the Town'. Their proposal was to finance these improvements from the profits arising as a result of enclosure, thereby effectively killing two birds with one stone. Enclosure, they argued, would make available land for the orderly expansion of the town, and the income generated from the sale of land to developers could be invested in infrastructure: roads, drains and the town's water supply. Ultimately, this was what happened, but not in the 1780s. Logic and emotions clashed head on, when it came to the sensitive issue of the open fields, and particularly the common rights: the commoners, Thomas Hawksley noted in evidence to a Select Committee many years later, 'are very tenacious of the right'.[49] The corporation decisively rejected the plans. Of the eighteen members present at the meeting on 15 May 1787, fourteen voted against and four abstained. Beyond this the record is silent: there is no mention in the Hall Book of any details of the plan, and neither the meeting nor the plan was reported in the *Nottingham Journal*. Yet the bitterness of the conflict was such that when Samuel Heywood, one of the promoters of enclosure, sought election as a senior councillor, he was decisively defeated by a majority of 600 in a poll of 1,051: 'the largest number of electors that ever exercised their privilege in one day, for the appointment of a senior councilman'.[50] Over the next half-century it proved impossible to bring enclosure back on to the political agenda. The effect was to keep out of the housing market land on to which the town might logically have been expected to expand. In turn this served to force up the price of development land within the existing town and – as a corollary – to force down the quality of new housing. For centuries the common fields had been effectively a green belt surrounding the town, but after 1780 they rapidly turned into a tourniquet.

It is no longer possible to reconstruct the complete pattern of housing development in the years after 1787, but enough is known to offer some idea of how Nottingham began to change as the premium on land soared. For householders with large gardens, the temptation to sell part or all of the land inevitably increased. As the lawyer Samuel Turner explained to Daniel Parker Coke in 1789:

> within these few years last past, entire land about this place being very scarce and difficult to obtain, and the great increase of inhabitants holding forth a prospect of advantage .... to builders and other adventurers of that description .... some of the closes immediately contiguous to the town have been bought at a very high price, and the purchasers .... have taken the opportunity of building several houses thereupon.[51]

House building peaked in the early 1790s as small orchards and closes on the east side of the town disappeared under brick construction. John Nixon, a builder, put up forty-eight houses in 1790, William Walters, a brickmaker, built twenty-two dwellings in 1791, and George Green, father of the Sneinton mathematician, erected a group of sixteen back-to-back houses known as Meynell Court. Not all the new houses were for the working classes. In 1793 the corporation made available some land between Back Lane and Derby Road, and better-quality artisan houses were erected along the frontage of Derby Road. At least 1,886 houses were added to the total stock between 1779 and 1801, although building details exist for no more than one-quarter of this total.[52]

A second area developed for housing in these years lay in a triangle north of Parliament Street and east of what is now Milton Street (effectively beneath the present Victoria Centre). Jalland's map of 1801, with its accompanying survey covering 1801 to 1812, shows quite clearly the house building going on between York and Glasshouse Streets, and the infilling on the eastern side of the town; but the most notable development was the decision of the Duke of Newcastle to sell Panier Close, a 16,000-square-yard plot on the north side of Parliament Street, for artisan housing. On Jalland's map Panier Close appears divided into three lots, one of which was a plaster yard. For sale purposes Newcastle divided the property into eleven lots consisting of forty-two plots. He placed no restrictions on the builders.[53] Lots sold for between 6*s* 9*d* and 13*s* a square yard. A mile from the centre of town land cost only 2*s* to 3*s* a square yard, but textile workers played into the developers' hands because they preferred to pay high rents, or even to double up in houses, rather than to live at a distance from the hosiers' warehouses.[54]

Most of the new houses erected in the town were built back-to-back in courts closed at both ends, with only a tunnel, twenty to thirty feet long, and eight feet high by three feet wide, providing access to houses in the centre (see figure 11.1). Three hundred such courts had been built by 1812, with little or no attention paid to planning.[55] Throsby complained about the lack of 'any design of forming regular streets'. His summing-up was apt; here was 'a resurrection of buildings generally without order, seated like clusters of mushrooms in a field cast up by chance'.[56] However, we must not assume that because the houses were crowded together they were, of necessity, poor quality. On the contrary, they may even have appeared to be relative palaces compared to some of the tumbledown thatched cottages illustrated by Deering, or the rock houses in which 'poor inhabitants on the east of the town' were living in 1768. When Robert Gregory bought a large orchard between Narrow Marsh and Sussex Street, and laid out Peach, Plum, Pear and Currant Streets, he provided each house with a small garden.[57] Blackner's description does not suggest that the new houses were, in themselves, inadequate:

> The houses of the working-class, at the present time, generally consist of a cellar, a room to dwell in called the house-place, a chamber [i.e. bedroom], a shop over it to work in, a room in the roof, called a cock-loft, and a small pantry; though in the manner of building there are many exceptions some for better and some for the worse; and they are generally composed of plaster floors for the upper rooms, lightly timbered with deal; brick walls some 4 and a half and some 9 inches thick; and cast-iron grates for fire-places, frequently with ovens and boilers of the same material.[58]

It was the absence of facilities which helped to determine the poor quality of the environment. 'Some of [the new erections] are extremely filthy passages', Throsby noted, and in more general terms he wrote of 'the gathered filth within doors' which was 'scattered daily, in the dirty passages without, in the front of the dwellings! – and many of these streets and lanes, if so they may be called, are without any sort of pavement, consequently without regulated water courses, and consequently pregnant with mischievous effects'.[59]

The middle-class retreat

Until 1815 Nottingham grew rapidly, but it was not yet an industrial slum: this came about largely as a result of events during the 1820s. The lack of leadership from the corporation might have made relatively little difference had the town not been changing. Private enterprise, with a little help from the corporation had, after all, brought urban renewal during the century after the Restoration. But this had occurred when a growing population had fitted easily within the existing boundaries, and such were the attractions of Nottingham that a core group of middling sorts lived in the town and influenced its development. In the second half of the eighteenth century in industrialising towns across the country the newly-emerging middle classes began to look to escape from increasingly dirty and overcrowded town centres, by beating an orderly retreat into suburban enclaves designed for their own benefit. Nottingham was no exception.

The signs of change were not hard to spot. Large houses were tenemented. In 1783 the Castle was still equipped as an aristocratic family house, but shortly afterwards it was partitioned up and let to wealthy tenants. It was used also as a boarding-school for young ladies, but the last genteel residents left in 1829, after which it was unoccupied except for caretakers and a lodge-keeper.[60] Similarly, Plumptre

House was tenemented in about 1785, and the family sold the adjoining land in 1796–97. The house was described as 'deserted for many years' until Alderman William Wilson took up residence in the 1820s. Thurland Hall was tenemented by 1790, when one of the apartments was occupied by the innkeeper of The Blackamoor's Head 'for the conveniency of large dining parties' – William Cobbett breakfasted with 200 gentlemen in this room in 1830, shortly before it was pulled down.[61]

The 1790s marked the beginnings of a definite movement away from the town centre. In its early stages 'suburbanisation' was little more than the coming-together of like-minded families at town edges. On the west side of Nottingham, Park Row was formed in 1797. Within the Park proper the first buildings date from 1792, but by the turn of the century the Dowager 3rd Duchess of Newcastle was considering more extensive developments for the estate. In the event it was 1807 before land on Standard Hill, divided into thirty-two plots crossed by four roads, was sold for about £7,000. The contrast with Panier Close was stark: the 4th Duke of Newcastle intended that the land should be used for quality houses renting at no less than £25 annually. No manufacturing was to be allowed. William Stretton built three of the first houses in this area between 1810 and 1814, at a cost of £4,000. They were occupied by wealthy manufacturers still able to live within walking distance of their businesses.[62]

Standard Hill was followed by other projects in the 1820s on the Ropewalk: what is now Park Valley (1828) and Park Terrace (*c.*1828–31). Derby Terrace, adjoining the Park's northern entrance, was probably started in 1829. It looked for a while as if Newcastle would go ahead with plans to develop the Park itself. This did not happen – partly because of the firing of the Castle in 1831 – but the splendid houses on Park Terrace, most still surviving today, were erected by the early 1830s. These were substantial properties with ground plans of over 120 square yards. White's *Directory* described them in 1832 as 'large and beautiful with hanging gardens in front descending by an abrupt but picturesque semi-circular sweep to the green pasture of the Park'.[63] It is the architectural structure of such houses, detached or semi-detached, which permitted the notion of 'separate spheres' to develop. The middle classes sought solitude and privacy of a kind which was quite different from the open promenading of the early eighteenth century, and which was reflected in the structures of some houses on the Ropewalk and in the Park where the back door faced the street and the front overlooked the gardens.

The problems of space in Nottingham encouraged some people to live beyond the town boundaries. In 1822 the *Nottingham Journal* advertised 'genteel furnished apartments' in the open country only five-minutes' walk from the market-place. Even larger houses were built further out, which were easily accessible to Nottingham only by horse carriage. At an auction in 1797 various middle-class families bought large plots of land on what is now the University of Nottingham campus to the west of Nottingham. Among the purchasers Wrights, the banking family, built Lenton Hall; Matthew Needham, 'surgeon and apothecary' of High Pavement, built Lenton House; Thomas Wright Watson, a hosier, built Lenton Firs; and the Lowes, another business family from High Pavement, built Highfield House. Elsewhere the Wright family built Mapperley House (later Hall) on land released under the Basford enclosure award in 1797, and promoted villa residences in the 1820s.[64]

The movement of the middle classes away from the town centre was a consequence of social change, and a clear response to the deteriorating environment. Nottingham lacked the smoke and grime contemporaries associated with northern industrial towns, and Nottingham's middle classes were escaping not from industry, but from the squalor which increasingly typified the town's inner core as, steadily and remorselessly, the garden town turned into an industrial slum with one of the most congested inner areas among the towns of Victorian Britain. It was still possible to enjoy southern vistas from Castle Gate and High Pavement as late as 1820 – indeed, Abigail Gawthern claimed that her husband paid £20 in 1789 to have the 'building which was erected for a new [St Peter's] workhouse to be taken down as where it then stood obstructed the view from the Meadows from the back part of our house'.[65] However, the surrounding areas made these streets less desirable than the vistas enjoyed from the Park edge, and by the early years of the nineteenth century visitors no longer went into raptures about Nottingham. One wrote mechanically in 1810 of how 'although the entrance on the western side is open and airy, yet the long line of streets filled with low manufacturing cottages does not impress the traveller with any high ideas of either the elegance or comfort of the town itself'. The following year Elizabeth Fremantle, travelling to Scotland from her home in southern England, was appalled by what she called 'a frightful old town … . oppressive, smoaky, noisy, riotous from the number of people employed in the manufactories, the inn detestable'. When she passed through again several months later the impression was no more favourable: 'at last to my great joy [we] drove away from this horrible town'.[66] Sir Richard Phillips, a journalist who spent two weeks studying the town in October 1828, left without regret a place which, he suggested, 'admitted of more social improvement' than any of the other towns he had visited.[67] William Cobbett's rather more upbeat remarks about Nottingham in 1830 – he found no evidence of 'that squalid misery which to me has been the great drawback in the merits of so many other places' – sits uneasily with these views, and suggests that his hosts carefully censored his viewing.[68]

The 1820s

What was happening is clear from contemporary maps. Stretton's map, dating from about 1800, shows the development of Nottingham in some detail, particularly the new streets on the eastern side. Yet it also reveals how much land even within the old core of the town remained to be developed, particularly perhaps in the area between Pelham Street and Parliament Street. Even as he was surveying, houses were going up. As a result, Smith and Wild's map of 1820 shows how the whole area east of Mansfield Road, and west of what was then the course of Glasshouse Street, had been substantially built over. In 1744 the area east of the line of Broad Street and Stoney Street was gardens and orchards; by 1820 it was largely covered with houses. To the south the Narrow Marsh area below the cliff face, where in 1744 there had been some substantial houses backed by long gardens running down to the River Leen, was by 1820 a network of yards, alleys and courts. Development had also taken place between the Leen and the canal.[69] The gardens were being surrendered for houses; in 1779 Nottingham had about 3,200 houses but by 1801 the total was 5,094, by 1811 it was 6,816, and by 1821 the number had reached 7,645.[70] A population of 40,415 was occupying physical space hardly expanded since 1750, and the elegant formal gardens had largely disappeared. Brick, often of poor quality, had replaced grass and trees.

By 1820 no one could any longer seriously regard Nottingham as a garden town, but it was events in the following decade which turned it into a slum. The particular impetus was the so-called twist net fever which followed the expiry of the patent on John Heathcoat's lace machine (see chapter 14). As news spread, skilled artisans poured into the town from the immediate neighbourhood and from further afield; smiths and mechanics, for example, travelled from Manchester, Birmingham and Sheffield. The result was chaos. In the course of the decade more than 3,000 new dwellings were built within Nottingham (an increase in the housing stock of 42 per cent), and the population rose by over 10,000 to reach 50,220 in 1831. Among the areas colonised in these years was the Broad Marsh. A lease on this area, granted in 1728, expired in 1827. The trustees of the Collin estate then built a new hospital at the northern end of the site, west of a new street, Carrington Street. The eastern side of this area was rapidly built up with small buildings, while the area to the west was soon covered with the familiar terraces of back-to-back houses.

Much of the land to the east of the Collin estate was owned by Lord Rancliffe, and this area was developed in the 1820s before Carrington Street was formed. New Bridge Street was laid out north from Canal Street and short terraces of back-to-back houses, perpendicular to the new street, extended west to the line of the Collin estate. Building to the east of New Bridge Street was mainly in the form of tightly-packed courts. Altogether 300 houses were built on Rancliffe's three-acre site. Even a superficial glance at Moses Wood's map of 1825, and at Staveley and Wood's map of 1831, which was drawn from surveys taken in 1827–29, shows the result: between 1820 and 1830 any available land was built over and hardly any open spaces had survived. As a witness told the 1833 commission of enquiry into the town's municipal corporation, apart from the market-place 'there is not one plot of 500 yards, unoccupied by buildings'.[71]

To make matters worse, this was speculative building of the most inappropriate kind, and the results soon became apparent. Absolem Barnett, overseer of the poor, recalled that 'thousands of houses were erected by greedy speculators, who studied, not the convenience and health of those obliged to take them, but how they might best secure 20 per cent on their outlay'. Garrets, stables, kitchens, cellars and the most unlikely places were converted into dwellings or workshops. Lean-to houses with one small room and a bedroom were run up in the corners of courts or yards. Many of the worst houses were located near to the River Leen, and others were built over open drains with perhaps only the floorboards to separate them from the contents of the drain. The boards often shrank and, in William Felkin's words, 'allowed noxious smells, and often other offensive matters, to arise. The health and morals of the residents are found to suffer greatly from so peculiar a state of their dwellings.' Nearly 200 dwellings were found under lace-dressing rooms, heated to 80°F for working purposes. As was all too obvious, 'the drainage was defective and ... many great nuisances existed some of which were of very long standing'.[72] In one part of the town 4,283 people shared 150 privies, 'one to every twenty-eight persons', and many of these thickly populated streets were 'unpaved, without sewers, and exhibited pools of filthy water and moist dungheaps'. By the 1840s life expectancy at birth in Byron ward was only 18.1 years.[73]

The impact was vividly described by Sir Richard Phillips:

> The court [in the Broad Marsh area] contained an abundance of small tenements, let to many stockingers like this, and there being many families, and even extra lodgers in all, it swarmed with population. Maggots in carrion flesh or mites in cheese, could not be huddled more closely together ... I entered, and found a dame busy washing her floor. I will not attempt to describe the furniture – it had been better – but all was worn out or broken. The woman was in rags, which scarcely covered her and everything bespoke hard work and inadequate pay.[74]

Phillips visited a recently built area and his comments related to the inhabitants and not to the property. Similarly William Booth, born in Sneinton in 1829, recalled that his mission to the poor had been inspired by 'the degradation and helpless misery of the poor stockingers of my native town wandering gaunt and hunger-stricken through the streets'.[75] These people almost inevitably ended up in the poorest quality housing. Father Robert William Willson described to a government enquiry into the state of the Irish poor how 'in one court containing about 16 rooms: 11 of them occupied by the Irish and 90 persons reside in the 11 rooms, I counted them myself last week. The rooms are very small and miserable dwellings.' In 1832 one group of 833 houses in the town contained 947 families with 4,283 people.[76] Nottingham, as a witness told an 1844 Select Committee, 'had been forced to receive at least three times the amount of population which could have been prudently and healthfully located within so narrow a limit ... in one part of the town more than 4,200 people were ascertained to dwell in a square of less than 220 yards on the same side'.[77]

Poverty

These conditions arose as a result of poverty which, in a town as dependent as Nottingham was on the textile trades, was an unpredictable but inevitable consequence of the trade cycle. It was also a problem which grew in proportion to the town. As with any large town, Nottingham had accrued its fair share of almshouses and other charities. Abel Collin's almshouses, twenty on Park Street and Houndsgate built in 1709, and twenty-four on Carrington Street built in 1831, were designed for people over seventy of 'irreproachable character' but 'in reduced circumstances'.[78] Some better-off families provided for themselves through friendly societies. Endowed and voluntary charities also offered poor relief, including the Vestry Society, established in 1713 in the vestry of St Mary's, with the aim of promoting piety and charity.[79] By 1839 the annual revenue from endowed charities exclusively devoted to the relief of poverty was £2,272, of which £1,392 was given direct to the poor and £880 to the support of fifteen almshouses.[80]

Most of the poor, however, had recourse to the parish officers. All three town parishes had workhouses,[81] but the most severe problems were in St Mary's, where the majority of the new working-class housing was erected. A Vestry Meeting in October 1790 considered a plan to spread the financial burden. The ratepayers were frustrated by the fact that most of the houses which had recently been erected rented for less than £10 a year, and were therefore not subject to the poor rate:

> The great number of small houses lately erected within the parish is a very serious and grievous burden upon the inhabitants in general … as such houses are principally occupied by very poor people, who are not only exempted by their landlords from payment of the parish rates, but their extreme poverty and numerous families are also the cause of a great increase of the poor within the said parish, and of the rates for the maintenance thereof, which several grievances require a speedy and effectual relief.

The remedy, or so it was thought, was a joint approach with the other two parishes to obtain legislation which would make the new houses liable to rating to the Poor Law, but this initiative made no further progress.[82] In retrospect the problem of poverty was still relatively mild. The annual cost of maintaining the poor of St Mary's was only £513 in 1768, and in difficult years the corporation occasionally contributed to relief. In 1783 the mayor called a public meeting to ask for help in relieving the poor, and the corporation subscribed £50. Public subscriptions to a relief fund brought in £1,200 in 1795, and in 1800 and 1801 soup kitchens were opened.[83]

Measures of this nature worked while the problem remained within bounds, but in 1809–10 the ongoing prosperity of the hosiery industry suffered a severe setback, which was succeeded by a long period of depression lasting to the middle of the century. By the end of the Napoleonic Wars the poor relief situation was becoming critical. It cost nearly £23,000 in 1812 and £17,202 in 1813. A particularly bad year was 1816, with between 7,000 and 8,000 people dependent on relief, and alarming estimates suggesting the annual cost would reach £40,000.[84] A committee set up to try to help with relief found that great numbers of the poor 'are in a most deplorable state of wretchedness, having from a want of employment been obliged to secure a scanty subsistence by pledging or selling every article of clothing and furniture that could possibly be spared, so as in many cases to leave them nearly destitute of clothes, furniture and bedding'. Visits had already been paid to 2,800 families, and the total was expected to rise to 3,500 families and 12,000–14,000 individuals. The committee decided to distribute tickets for the poor to redeem against meat, bread, flour, Scotch barley, potatoes or coal. In addition, the most distressed families were to be supplied with soup, if volunteers to make it could be found. There were 505 paupers in St Mary's workhouse, and nearly 14,000 existing on charity paid for from parish rates and voluntary subscriptions.[85]

The situation had hardly had time to improve when the textile workers were again badly affected by a trade slump in 1819. Destitute framework knitters paraded the streets. The Duke of Newcastle provided £500, and the Duke of Portland and Earl Manvers comparable amounts to set up a fund enabling the unemployed to emigrate to Cape Colony. Three hundred families eventually took advantage of the scheme.[86] In 1819 St Mary's parish appointed a Select Vestry, and in turn the Vestry appointed a paid assistant overseer, in place of the annual, unpaid 'volunteers' who had been responsible for the administration of poor relief. The man appointed was the 36-year-old former hosier, Absolem Barnett. For thirty years Barnett controlled poor relief in Nottingham. He was articulate and literate, a deacon at George Street Baptist Church, and a man of strong convictions as to how the Poor Law should be administered. It was these opinions, and the way he translated them into practice, which were to make him by 1840 one of the most detested men in the town.[87]

Barnett recognised that the cost of poor relief was running out of control, and he understood contemporary concerns about poor relief 'without strings'. In 1811 able-bodied applicants for relief had been set to sweep the streets, but from 1819 Barnett began to use work relief much more systematically. He also held the post of assistant to the surveyor of highways in St Mary's parish, and combining these joint responsibilities he put more than 500 able-bodied men to work laying drains and watercourses, repairing the banks of the Trent, and paving and metalling roads. Barnett considered this work to be for the good of the town, and funding was found from the public relief fund. The wages paid were below the average earned in comparable employment. In 1821 unemployed framework knitters were put to work re-laying pavements in the market-place. Again they were paid from a public subscription, in this case of £3,000. In almost all subsequent crises, while Barnett remained at the helm public relief committees were set up to raise money to help those out of work.[88]

The destitution of the framework knitters was in part a consequence of Barnett's policy. In normal conditions he offered relief only in the workhouse, which had been described as early as 1795 as 'dark, ill-ventilated and verminous' and, despite various improvements, was still in 1840 'very uncomfortable, and not so much like a workhouse as a prison'.[89] The poor preferred (as Barnett intended) to avoid applying for admission, with the consequence that despite the rapid growth of population in Nottingham prior to 1831 the cost of poor relief fell from £17,202 in 1813 to £10,666 in 1821, and to £10,827 in 1831. Expense per head of population, at 5*s* 5*d* in 1831, was lower than in 1803.[90] Barnett gained a national reputation for what was perceived to be his success in Nottingham, and his views were instrumental in shaping the 1834 New Poor Law. Yet this in no way reflected economic conditions within the town, and the conditions in which many of the framework knitters lived were such as to make Nottingham particularly susceptible to the ravages of cholera in 1832.

Asiatic cholera broke out for the first time in Sunderland in October 1831, and reached Nottingham in mid-1832: in the words of the *Nottingham Journal*, 'We regret that our duty compels us to announce that this fatal and alarming disease has appeared in Nottingham.'[91] Cholera had an effect out of all proportion to its statistical importance. It struck terrifyingly quickly – victims could be dead within hours of showing the first symptoms – and it affected rich and poor alike. Preparations commenced in November 1831 when an emergency Board of Health was formed, chaired by Archdeacon Wilkins of St Mary's. Sub-committees were created for each district of the town, with the brief 'to inspect the habitations of the poor with a view to their cleansing'. The first case in Nottingham was reported from the Narrow Marsh area on 6 July, and the first fatality on 11 July. Despite the efforts of the Board of Health – 'the town is now more cleanly than it was ever known to be' according to the *Review* on 22 July – altogether 930 cases were reported, of which 330 proved fatal.[92] The great majority of the fatalities were in the back-to-back houses on the east and southern sides of the town (figure 10.2). The outbreak lasted until October 1832, and services of thanksgiving (for the survivors) were held in St Mary's and St Peter's during November.[93] It was a time which stuck in the minds of those who experienced it; years later, when the town at last had a permanent Sanitary Committee, it was recalled that:

> This terrible scourge the Cholera fixed itself in 1832 in streets and courts filthy, ill ventilated and crowded with inhabitants too poor or dirty or dissipated to procure necessary food or use the most common means to secure health, and did not cease its ravages until it had destroyed the large number … out of that part of the population of our town.[94]

Cholera may not have been forgotten, but it had little impact on town life. The emergency Board of Health was dissolved, but some effort was put into paving and repairing streets in the lower part of the town, as well as improving sewage disposal, and a new cemetery was opened in 1836 – a grim reminder of one of the more pressing problems of 1832. But many people were complacent. They believed that the solution to Nottingham's problems was already in place. Hawksley's work in improving the water supply was considered to be of key importance, and it was believed that the availability of clean water was 'not sufficiently general' by 1832 to avert the spread of cholera.[95] To some extent this was true, but in reality such excuses were short-sighted.

By 1830 the middle classes were congregating on the western fringe, and the centre of Nottingham had been developed almost entirely with working-class houses. The shortage of land which had aggravated the housing crisis had also produced the development of outlying villages, as Nottingham could no longer absorb all those wanting to live in the town or the businesses wishing to locate within its boundaries. While Nottingham depended on domestic textile production, the land requirement for workshops and factories was relatively modest. By the 1820s, particularly in the lace industry, this was no longer the case, and the physical consequences were reflected in changes beyond the town boundaries.

Figure 10.2 **Irish settlement and cholera victims, 1830s**

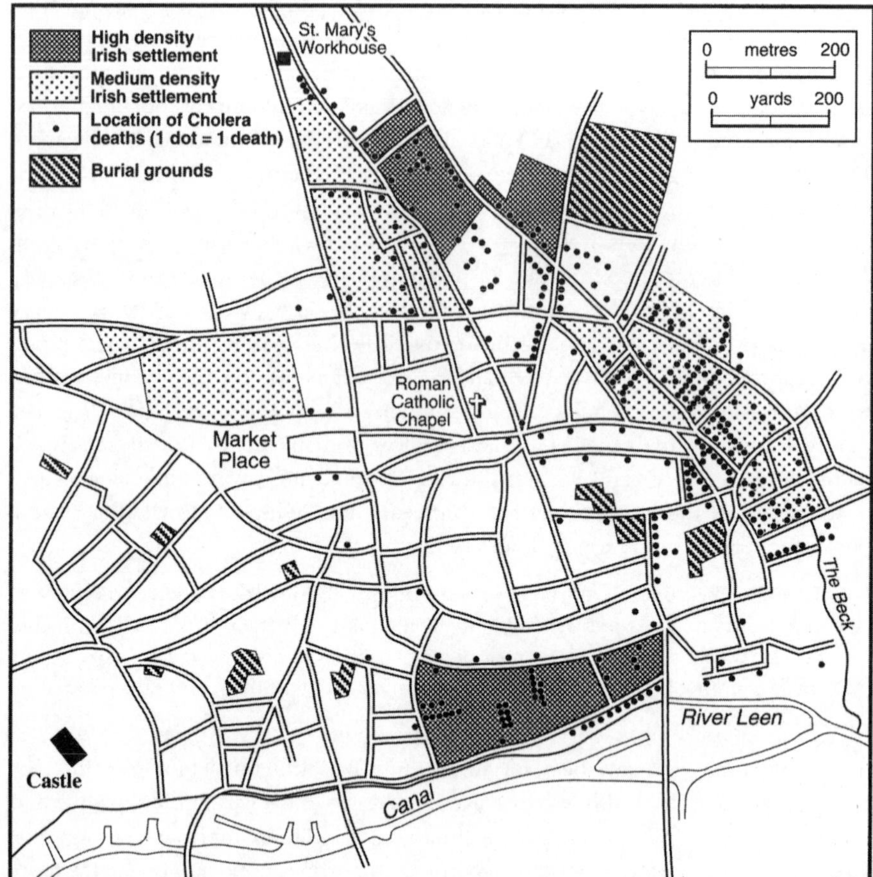

The industrial villages

In the 1790s local entrepreneurs looked to develop settlements north of the town along the River Leen. Throsby reported of Basford, enclosed in 1792–97, that 'this village appears like a new town, in consequence of its manufactory and improvements … . Its vicinity to Nottingham has much aided its population.'[96] Cotton mills and bleaching works had been established here and in Bulwell, but both villages were some distance from Nottingham. New opportunities arose when in 1796 the parishes of Radford and Lenton to the west, and Sneinton to the east of Nottingham, were enclosed. Until then Sneinton was a farming community apparently unaffected by its industrial neighbour, while Radford Folly was a pleasure garden.[97] The collective opportunities opened up by the various enclosure acts of the 1790s had considerable implications: by the 1820s the most dynamic physical expansion was in the villages just beyond Nottingham's town boundaries (figure 10.3).

Figure 10.3 **Nottingham and its surrounding villages, *c.*1845**

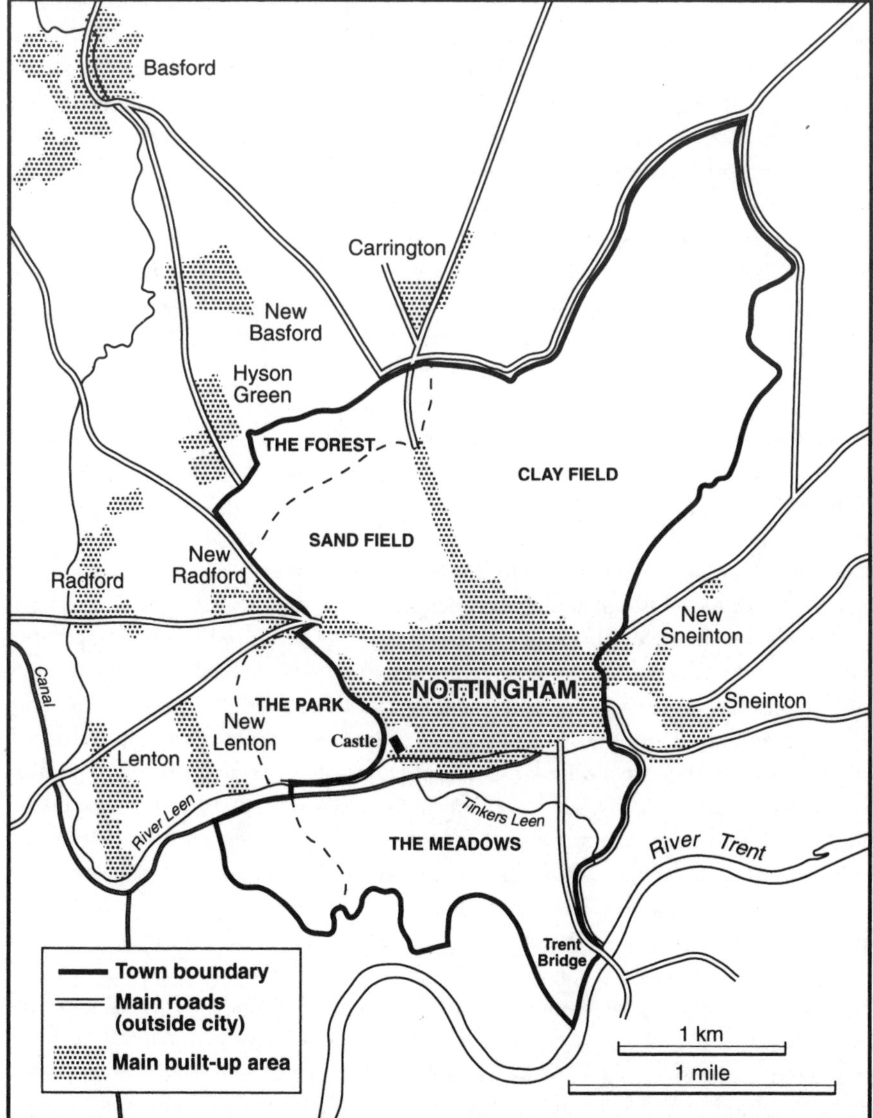

The impact on Sneinton is clear from events in the wake of the 1796 Enclosure Act. The chief landed interests in the village were those of the Musters family of Colwick Hall and the Pierreponts of Thoresby and Holme Pierrepont Hall. By the summer of 1795 agreement had been reached between them on an enclosure.[98] For the Pierrepont family the most immediate benefit was a rapid increase in the family's agricultural rental income from Sneinton, from £547 a year to £1,607, but it was the availability of land on the western edge of the parish – away from the village settlement – which made possible the building of New Sneinton.[99] The boundary between Sneinton and Nottingham lay along the River Beck which ran from St Ann's Well to join the River Leen. The Pierreponts were aware of the potential: their estate accounts record the building of a brick-kiln in 1798 and the wholesale cutting of timber in 1799, but the first house was erected in 1803 on land sold by John Musters to Benjamin Storey.[100] Building had begun on a substantial scale by 1809. Manvers' rental for 1810 from 'Sneinton-Nottingham' was £1,000. By 1820, building within Nottingham was pushing hard up against the River Beck, and five streets (Freemans, Independence, Snow, Richmond and Sun Hills) to the north-east of the Beck in Sneinton parish. A similar process began in the parish of Radford, the eastern extremity of which adjoins Nottingham at Canning Circus – the Admiral Sir John Borlase Warren still has a boundary marker. In the 1770s a traveller leaving Nottingham along Derby Road could pause at Sion Hill (now Canning Circus) to admire the 'very fine view of the Castle and Town', and then be most impressed in the opposite direction not by urban development, but by 'several coal pits belonging to Lord Middleton'.[101] The first houses at the eastern end of the parish were erected in 1796, but significant development really began as the lace industry expanded beyond 1809.

New Sneinton and New Radford were the first two suburbs to be opened up beyond the open fields, but neither experienced a great deal of change until the 1820s. The rapid development of the lace industry not only produced the building boom which so damaged the Nottingham environment – it also helped to spawn a series of recognisable suburbs as the better-paid lace workers sought a quality of housing they could not find, or build, in Nottingham.[102] Just as significantly, the introduction of factories into the lace industry made economic sense only in terms of green-field site development which was not available in the old town. Apart from Sneinton and Radford, Lenton and Basford also developed 'New' settlements, distant from the original agricultural-based villages, but proximate to the nearest border towards Nottingham. In Sneinton this simply meant that streets begun before 1820 were pushed across the Beck so that New Sneinton emerged as an eastern extension of Nottingham. New Basford was developed on land released by the Basford enclosure award. Here a new phase of house building began in 1820, and by 1822 3,000 people were living in the area between North Gate and Beech Avenue. White's *Directory* noted in 1832 that it was due to 'the lace and hosiery manufactures and its contiguity to Nottingham that the parish owed its wealth and consequence which has caused the population to triple in the previous years'.[103] Richard Birkin opened his first lace factory in the village in 1828.

Hyson Green and Carrington developed as green-field sites just across the town boundaries to the north. In Hyson Green house building began around 1822. In 1828 a reporter for the *Nottingham Review* found that 'there are now not less than 314 inhabited houses, most of them with private back yards, and gardens in front 35 yards long, which, for health and comfort, are inferior to none in or near Nottingham'. Nor was it static: 'there are also at this time building, or marked out to be built, upwards of 80 more houses'.[104] Carrington, just north of the Forest and west of Mansfield Road, was also an 1820s development. Ichabod Wright, who owned ten acres, including six he had purchased from the banker Robert Smith in 1798, planned a new settlement. In 1825 he began auctioning plots of land for development. His 'model village' was named after Smith, who took the title Lord Carrington when he was raised to the peerage in 1796. The first lace factory was built in 1831. Here, as in Hyson Green, many of the houses were built by societies of workmen.[105]

Of the new industrial suburbs generally, White's *Directory* of 1832 noted that 1,100 new houses had been built since 1821 to form 'handsome villages, occupied chiefly by bobbin-net makers, and forming a number of parallel and cross-streets ... and [with cottages] regularly built of brick and roofed with blue slate'. Even the back-to-back houses were offset by front gardens and 'the air is pure'. The result was a much higher quality of housing in these outlying areas than in the historic core of Nottingham.[106] Nor did the pace of growth slacken. While Nottingham was growing by fewer than 2,000 people in the 1830s, the surrounding villages increased by nearly 9,000. Between 1831 and 1851 929 new houses were built in Nottingham, and by contrast 1,654 in New Radford alone. Many of the incomers were moving from Nottingham. By 1851 29.4 per cent of heads of household in Radford were migrants from Nottingham, and possibly 15 per cent of Nottingham's population moved into the area in the first half of the nineteenth century. In addition, migrants into Radford were likely to have moved as part of a nuclear family, or to be seeking accommodation before starting their families. By contrast, it was single people, many of them lodgers, who were the most likely to be found moving into Nottingham in these years.[107]

In approximately eighty years the garden town became an industrial slum. The decision in 1787 to put the enclosure issue on hold was crucial because it produced three distinct trends: first, the centre of the old town was rapidly overcrowded with working-class housing; second, the middle classes retreated to new areas on the northern edge of the Park; and third, particularly in the 1820s, rapid development began in the suburbs. Nottingham stopped growing because it was saturated with buildings, and yet locked within narrow physical limits. It was a position which was intolerable for those who were trapped, particularly the framework knitters, but one which seemed to be incapable of resolution. Enclosure was off the local political agenda, the corporation lacked both the powers and the will to bring about change, and the more prosperous lace industry was finding a way of divorcing itself from its hosiery origins and moving out of the town. Furthermore, the response to the cholera outbreak of 1832 showed just how difficult it would be to change the direction in which Nottingham was heading: towards industrial stagnation, high levels of cyclical poverty to which there appeared to be no effective antidote, and unacceptably high death rates resulting from the unhealthy environment.

Notes

1 Robert Sanders, *Complete English Traveller* (1772), pp. 492–3.

2 BL Add MSS 32,232, Tour into Derbyshire, 1773, f. 28. The author is not known.

3 C. P. Moritz, *Journeys of a German in England in 1782* (1965), p. 176; Revd William MacRitchie, *Diary of a Tour through Great Britain in 1795* (1897), p. 70.

4 BL Add MSS 32,232, f.24.

5 Moritz, *Journeys*, p. 176; *The Universal British Directory of Trade, Commerce and Manufacture* (1793), p. 45; William Cobbett, *Rural Rides* (1982 edn), p. 156.

6 Blackner, p. 61.

7 *Royal Commission on the State of Large Towns and Populous Districts*, 1st Report: PP 572 (XVII) 1844, p. 132.

8 Gawthern, *Diary*, p. 31.

9 M. I. Thomis, 'The politics of Nottingham Enclosure', *TTS*, 71 (1967), pp. 90–6; Thomis, *Politics*, ch. 7.

10 NUMD HiA 1, Account Book 1797–1826, HiV 5, Pew Rents Book *c*.1833.

11 Thomis, *Politics*, pp. 134–5; Church, pp. 167–8.

12 *RBN*, VII, pp. 42, 205, 223; VIII, p. 38; Church, p. 178.

13 Blackner, pp. 410–11.

14 Gray, *500 Years*, p. 78.

15 William Stretton, *The Stretton Manuscripts* (Nottingham, 1910), p. 179; *Report of the Evidence given before the Commissioners appointed to enquire into Municipal Corporations* (Nottingham, 1833), pp. 36–7; *Royal Commission on the Municipal Corporations*, PP (XXV) 1835: Reports from Commissioners, appendix to 1st Report, part 3, p. 2006.

16 NAO M.7495, 7499; *RBN*, VII, pp. 143, 193, 196, 234, 251, 284.

17 NAO M.7496. The number of streets on which customers in arrears with rent are recorded is thirty-nine, so this total may be too low.

18 Blackner, pp. 25–6; T. B. Bailey, *In Memory of Thomas Hancock, civil engineer to Nottingham Water Works Company, 1782–1805* (Nottingham, 1898).

19 NAO M.7501; *RBN*, VIII, p. 60.

20 Blackner, pp. 23, 26.

21 *RBN*, IX, p. 72; *Royal Commission … Large Towns and Populous Districts*, pp. 133–7.

22 For Hawksley see R. Mellors, *Men of Nottingham and Nottinghamshire* (2nd edn, 1924), pp. 173–4.

23 Blackner, p. 75; P. J. Hammond, 'The collection and disposal of Nottingham's night-soil', *NH*, 34 (1985), p. 14; *Date Book*, p. 57.

24 Gray, *500 Years*, p. 66; D. E. Roberts, 'Controversies on Lighting in Nottingham', *Local Historian*, 11 (1975), pp. 327–30; *Stretton Manuscripts*, p. 184; White (1844), p. 179; *NJ*, 17 April 1819.

25 A. C. Wood (ed.), 'Nottinghamshire by G. M. Woodward', *TTS*, 61 (1957), p. 39.

26 A. Fremantle (ed.), *The Wynne Diaries* (1940), pp. 332, 343.

27 A. C. Wood, 'Nottinghamshire, 1835–1865', *TTS*, 59 (1955), p. 4; Church, p. 178.

28 Deering, p. 168.

29 BL Add MSS 32,956, f.218.

30 A. Cossons, *The Turnpike Roads of Nottinghamshire* (2nd edn, Nottingham, 1994); Deering, p. 168; Blackner, p. 27; White (1832), p. 54.

31 Blackner, p. 24.

32 Deering, pp. 164, 167; *RBN*, VII, pp. 59, 270–1; Orange, II, p. 919.

33 *Date Book*, pp. 84, 175.

34 Wylie, p. 274; *Date Book*, pp. 203–4; Gawthern, *Diary*, pp. 11, 62–3; Blackner, p. 15.

35 *RBN*, VII, pp. 311–24, 332, 334, 335; VIII, p. 429; Blackner, p. 18; Orange, II, pp. 919–20.

36 *RBN*, VIII, pp. 39–40; Blackner, p. 19; NAO M.23,868, f. 24.

37 *Universal British Directory*, pp. 47–8; Wylie, p. 278; Iliffe and Baguley, II, pp. 6, 14.

38 A. Henstock, 'A road traffic census of Nottingham in 1819', *TTS*, 90 (1986), pp. 94–100.

39 A. C. Wood, 'The history of trade and transport on the River Trent', *TTS*, 54 (1950), pp. 1–44.

40 *NJ*, 27 September 1788; *RBN* VII, pp. 230–1.
41 *RBN* VII, p. 264; *Date Book*, p. 187.
42 The decision to cut the canal parallel to the Leen looks odd at first sight, but was probably to allow wharf development on both banks. This would not have been possible on the north bank of the Leen due to residential development: F. I. Straw, 'An analysis of the town plan of Nottingham: a study in historical geography' (University of Nottingham, MA thesis, 1967), p. 120.
43 C. Hadfield, *Canals of the East Midlands* (Newton Abbot, 1966), p. 58.
44 W. Dearden, *Directory* (1834), p. 74.
45 L. F. Wilson, 'The state and the housing of the English working class with special reference to Nottingham, 1845–1914' (University of California, Berkeley, Ph.D thesis, 1970), p. 93; NAO M.23,868, p.2.
46 *NJ*, 1 January 1814; Deering, pp. 12–13.
47 NAO DD.TS/15/2/2; C. W. Chalklin, *The Provincial Towns of Georgian England, 1740–1820* (1974), pp. 237–8, 300.
48 Deering, p. 4; Chalklin, *Provincial Towns*, pp. 118, 165.
49 *Report from the Select Committee of Commons Inclosure 1844*: PP 583 (v) 1.
50 *RBN*, VII, p. 223; NAO CA 3546 f.17; *NJ*, 15, 22 July 1787; Wylie, p. 331.
51 *NJ*, 26 September 1789.
52 D. M. Cannell, *George Green: Mathematician and Physicist 1793–1841* (1993), p. 3; Straw, 'Town plan', p. 137; Chalklin, *Provincial Towns*, p. 232.
53 NAO DDTS 16/23; Straw, 'Town Plan', pp. 152–6.
54 Chalklin, *Provincial Towns*, pp. 121–2.
55 Blackner, pp. 72–4. This type of development, partially determined by the nature of landholdings, was rather different from the long rows of back-to-backs found, for example, in Leeds.
56 Quoted in F. C. Laird, *Topographical Description of Nottinghamshire* (1810), pp. 102, 224.
57 Deering, p.10; HMC *Verulam* (1906), p. 230; Straw, 'Town Plan', p. 138.
58 Blackner, p. 66.
59 Quoted in Laird, *Topographical Description*, pp. 102–3; Church, pp. 165–6.
60 NUMD NeI 1, An Inventory of the Furniture in Nottingham Castle, November 1783; Iliffe and Baguley, 8, p. 23; Wood (ed.), 'Nottinghamshire', p. 42; Blackner, p. 50.
61 *Strangers Guide to Nottingham* (1827), pp. 59, 80; *Stretton Manuscripts*, pp. 157, 168; Cobbett, *Rural Rides*, p. 156; Bailey, IV, p. 367; Absolem Barnett, *The Poor Laws and their Administration being an Enquiry into the Causes of English Pauperism and the Failure of Measures Intended for its Relief* (London, 1833), pp. 27–8; *NJ*, 19 May 1810, 17 August 1811.
62 Straw, 'Town Plan', pp. 138–9, 157–8; K. Brand, 'The Park Estate, Nottingham: the development of a nineteenth century fashionable suburb', *TTS*, 88 (1984), pp. 55–9.
63 Brand, 'Park Estate', pp. 60–1; White's *Directory* (1832), p. 132. It was from here that Thomas Chambers Hine (1813–99) tentatively set out on his architectural career in Nottingham.
64 *NJ*, 10 January, 3 August 1822; F. Barnes, *Priory Demesne to University Campus* (Nottingham, 1993).
65 Gawthern, *Diary*, p. 50. It seems more likely that he persuaded the parish to alter projected plans than to take down a whole building.
66 Laird, *Topographical Description*, pp. 77–8; *Wynne Diaries*, pp. 332, 343.
67 G. Syer, 'A visit to Nottingham in 1828', *NH*, 53 (1994), p. 15.
68 Cobbett, *Rural Rides*, p. 156.
69 NAO Ma 24/543; Chalklin, *Provincial Towns*, p. 115.
70 Blackner, p. 77. Nineteenth-century figures here, and in later chapters, are from the decennial census returns.
71 Straw, 'Town Plan', pp. 160–2; *Report … into Municipal Corporations*, p. 157. The Smith and Wild and Staveley and Wood maps have been regularly reproduced. Copies of the 1825 map by Wood are in NAO and NLSL.
72 W. Felkin, 'Statistics of the labouring classes and paupers of Nottingham', *Journal of the Royal Statistical Society*, II (1839), pp. 457–8.

73 *Report ... into Municipal Corporations*, p. 163; *RBN*, IX, p. 72; J. D. Chambers, *Modern Nottingham in the Making* (Nottingham, 1945), pp. 12–13; Felkin, 'Statistics', pp. 457–8; Wylie, p. 370; *NR*, 8 November 1833, 13 June 1845.

74 *NR*, 17 April 1829.

75 W. Booth, *In Darkest England and the Way Out* (London, Salvation Army, 1890), preface.

76 P. Murphy, 'Irish settlement in Nottingham in the early nineteenth century', *TTS*, 98 (1994), p. 83; S. D. Chapman, 'Working-class housing in Nottingham during the Industrial Revolution', *TTS*, 67 (1963), p. 82.

77 *Royal Commission ... Large Towns and Populous Districts*, p. 133.

78 E. L. Guilford, *A History of Abel Collin's Charity, Nottingham* (Nottingham, 1915), pp. 52–9, 71. The fullest accounts of charities and almshouses can be found in the early *Directories*, for example, White, 1832, pp. 161–71.

79 NAO DD.TS/15/2/2 Vestry Minutes, St Mary's.

80 R. Smith, 'The relief of urban poverty outside the Poor Law, 1800–1850: a study of Nottingham', *Midland History*, 2 (1974), pp. 215–24; Church, pp. 107–8.

81 Blackner, pp. 69–70; *Stretton Manuscripts*, p. 168; White, 1832, p. 166; NAO DD.TS 6/4/6 f.70.

82 NAO DD.TS/15/2/2 Vestry Minutes, St Mary's.

83 J. D. Chambers, *Nottinghamshire in the Eighteenth Century* (2nd edn, 1966), p. 242; *NJ*, 10, 17, 31 January 1801.

84 *NJ*, 29 September 1816.

85 *NR*, 20 December 1816; *Stretton Manuscripts*, p. 175.

86 *Third Report from the Select Committee on Emigration*, PP (550) 1827, paras. 4125–56; *Date Book*, p. 330.

87 S. D. Chapman, 'William Felkin, 1795–1874' (University of Nottingham, MA thesis, 1960), p. 183. Barnett set out his views in his book *The Poor Laws and their Administration*; for views of Barnett: W. Roworth, *Observations on the Administration of the New Poor Law in Nottingham* (Nottingham, 1840).

88 Barnett, *The Poor Laws and their Administration*, p. 12; Church, p. 114.

89 F. M. Eden, *State of the Poor* (1797), II, p. 573; Chambers, *Nottinghamshire*, pp. 237–42; Orange, II, p. 904.

90 *Report from Her Majesty's Commissioners for Enquiring into the Administration and Practical Operation of the Poor Laws* 1834 (PP XXVII (44), pp. 890–3, and appendix A pp. 111a–112a, appendix B, part v.

91 *NJ*, 14 July 1832.

92 *NR*, 18 November 1831, 27 July 1832.

93 *NJ*, 10 November 1832, NR 16 November 1832, both quoted in M. Walker, 'The Nottingham cholera epidemic of 1832', *TTS*, 95 (1991), p. 70.

94 *RBN*, IX, p. 71.

95 *NR*, 16 November 1832; *RBN*, IX, pp. 71–3; G. W. Lamplugh and B. Smith, *The Water Supply of Nottinghamshire from Underground Sources* (1914).

96 J. Throsby (ed.), *The Antiquities of Nottinghamshire*, II (1790), p. 230.

97 BL Egerton MSS, 3633–4, Court Rolls of the Manor of Sneinton, 1647–1796; Orange, II, p. 946.

98 NUMD M.3319/19, Daniel Coke to Charles Pierrepont, 17 August 1795.

99 NUMD Manvers papers, Sneinton rents. The family received 447 acres at enclosure.

100 NAO DD.TS 6/4/3/33.

101 BL Add MSS 32,232, f. 24; Blackner, p. 391; R. Mellors, *Old Nottingham Suburbs Then and Now* (Nottingham, 1914), pp. 32–3.

102 NAO DD.TS 6/4/3/2; Chapman, 'Working class housing', p. 77.

103 White, 1832, p. 585.

104 *NR*, 8 August 1828.

105 Liza Anne Tong, 'A local study of Carrington, Nottingham: industrial village to disappearing suburb, 1830–1930' (University of Nottingham, MA dissertation, 1995), p. 3; R. Mellors, *Radford and Hyson Green then and now* (Nottingham 1913), p. 12; NAO DD 3DN/46, M.13,477; NUMD Ma 2D 12/34–59; Mellors, *Old Nottingham Suburbs*, p. 70.

106 White, 1832, pp. 583–4; Mellors, *Old Nottingham Suburbs*, pp. 112–13; Chapman, 'Working class housing', pp. 79–80.

107 Church, pp. 164–5; R. Smith, 'The social structure of Nottingham and adjacent districts in the mid-nineteenth century' (University of Nottingham, Ph.D. thesis, 1968), p. 150; R. Smith, 'Population movements and the development of working class suburbs 1801–1851: the case of Nottingham', *Local Population Studies*, 47 (1991). In Radford the majority of the employed population was involved in manufacturing (48.2 per cent) with services and dealing poorly represented.

11

MUNICIPAL REFORM AND PARLIAMENTARY ENCLOSURE

John Beckett and Ken Brand

In the spring of 1844, James Ranald Martin, an assistant commissioner with the government enquiry into the state of large towns, described conditions in Nottingham as 'so very bad as hardly to be surpassed in misery by anything to be found within the entire range of our manufacturing cities'.[1] Seventy-two years after the gushing comments of Robert Sanders, with which we began chapter 10, the garden town had become an industrial slum. Help was, however, at hand. A year after Martin wrote his report the passing of the Nottingham Enclosure Act finally pointed the town in a new direction. From the 1850s new houses were built on land released for development; the warehousing typical of many great industrial towns of this period began to appear in the central area of the town; and an exclusive west-end estate offered a tranquil retreat for the middle classes. Yet the results of enclosure were mixed, partly because expectations ran too high. Cleaning up the environment created in the years prior to 1830 proved far more complex than supporters of enclosure anticipated. Our task in this chapter is to trace the gradual shift of emphasis from the *laissez-faire* attitude prevailing prior to 1830, towards regulation and control in the interests of orderly urban development, and to assess what had been achieved by the time the enclosure award was completed in the mid-1860s.

To understand this shift of emphasis, we need to appreciate the limitations of local government. National reforms affected Nottingham as they did other large towns, including the Poor Law Amendment Act in 1834, the Municipal Corporations Act in 1835, and the public health reforms of the 1850s. Despite these measures central government was still reluctant to lead the localities; the philosophy of devolving power remained firmly in place until the 1870s, and this approach was strongly supported by the prevailing Whig consensus in the town. When a government enquiry was threatened into environmental conditions in 1852 William Felkin, the mayor, complained that 'we despise the interference of any authority in local affairs and we will never admit into this borough any of the abuses which centralised authority would inflict upon us'.[2] The underlying assumption was that central government neither could nor should determine the structure and working of society. The best it could hope to do was to provide a firmly established and clearly understood framework within which society could largely run itself. Unfortunately, running themselves was what many of the new industrial towns were clearly failing to do, and even the municipal reforms of 1835 were of little significance. Two major developments marked the 1830s in Nottingham: the continuing move towards factory production in the lace industry, and the arrival of the railway. Both raised complex issues about the use of urban space, and serious questions about the continuing opposition to enclosure. The corporation lacked the legal powers to take any real initiatives, even supposing it had wished to do so, and ultimately it was shocked into action only by the local response to the findings of government enquiries in the early 1840s. This is the context in which the mid-Victorian decades need to be understood: it was not decisions taken at Westminster which changed attitudes in Nottingham, but a growing recognition within the town that something was seriously wrong. Municipal reform was driven from London, but enclosure bills sponsored in Nottingham created the conditions which led eventually to the transformation of the town.

Local government

The reform of the municipal corporations in 1835 grew directly out of parliamentary reform in 1832. This legislation (strongly supported in Nottingham) posed as many questions for the Whig government as it answered. One of the most pressing related to the future of the municipal corporations. This was not simply a matter of the powers, or more accurately lack of powers, exercised by the corporations; more critically, it was worries about the political complexion of corporations, and about urban law and order, which drove the Whig government to the conclusion that reform of the corporations was unavoidable. The politics were simple: most corporations were Tory-Anglican in composition, and the government feared they would use their local influence to return Tory MPs, thus undermining the position of the Whigs who had promoted Parliamentary reform. This was not the case in Nottingham, but its Whig-dominated corporation was an exception in the 1830s.

The problem of law and order was more complex: it arose from a fear on the part of the government that the new industrial towns had witnessed a decline in morality, law and order; that people had 'escaped' from the influence of religion; and that as a result towns were becoming ungovernable. Consequently, it was feared that without positive action to improve policing they would soon be out of control. The reform bill riots of 1831 in Bristol and Nottingham served to re-emphasise the reality of these fears. On the other hand, until the formation in 1829 of the Metropolitan Police, central government resisted calls for a permanent police presence. In Nottingham the justices appointed constables from each of the town's administrative areas, known as disnaries. There were thirty in 1740. In 1754 twenty-nine part-time constables were enrolled, with a range of duties including clearing small boys from graveyards during church services. Four watchmen were also employed, but were armed only with staves and a handbell. Efforts were occasionally made to apprehend offenders. In 1780 several constables were paid for attending 'at the Trent Bridge and River Leene to prevent people from Bathing on Sabbath days'.[3] By 1830 the number of constables in Nottingham had risen to 100. They were unpaid, although fees were given for performance, and they served part-time during the day only. The permanent police staff consisted of three constables. At night the town was the responsibility of the Watch, a ramshackle organisation roundly condemned by Blackner in 1815: 'The reader will judge for himself, whether this town is properly watched during the night, when he considers that about 35,000 inhabitants are scattered through upwards of 400 streets, lanes &c. and that nine or ten men, four of whom watch the market-place, are employed to walk *almost* twenty streets.'[4] It was an inefficient, not to say incompetent system, and the arrangements were hardly adequate when major outbreaks of civil disorder occurred. On those occasions it was necessary to swear in special constables or to call out troops.

How had this situation arisen? Until the early nineteenth century crime was not regarded as a serious problem in English towns, and criminal prosecutions were left to the discretion of the victim. Those apprehended were dealt with either by the magistrates, or for more serious offences by the Assize judges. In the lower court those found guilty were usually fined and sometimes subjected to physical ignominy such as the pillory – discontinued in 1808 – or public whipping, which came to an end after 1830. Those who went to trial were most likely, if found guilty, to be hanged or transported. Until 1827 executions took place on Gallows Hill, which was probably on the site of St Andrew's Church at the junction of Forest Road and Mansfield Road. In 1831 a new drop was erected near the prison wall, clearly visible from both Parliament Street and Broad Street. The Keeper of the House of Correction described dispassionately the fate of two young men in 1831:

> William Marshall aged 19 and William Reynolds aged 19 was executed on the New Drop Corner of the House of Correction Nottingham for Committing a rape on the Body of Mary Ann Lord, on the Night of Saturday the sixteenth of April 1831 in the fields near the Meadow Platts. The 2 young men were removed from the Gaol in the afternoon of the 23 of August at 3 o'clock in a Light covered cart. Executed at Eleven o'clock on the morning of 24th. Both confessing the crime laid to them on receiving the sacrament and which they had denied previously.[5]

Executions for offences prosecuted in the county took place on the steps of the Shire Hall on High Pavement. Gaols were mainly for debtors, or for criminals awaiting sentence, and were seldom maintained with any great energy. When John Howard visited Nottingham in 1773 he noted that the prison had been 'lately repaired and much improved'.[6] It was rebuilt in the 1820s. Alternatively offenders were sent to the House of Correction on the corner of Glasshouse Street and St John's Street, described by Howard in 1776 as 'two rooms, no fireplaces, a dark dungeon down nine steps'. By 1778 fourteen prisoners were occupied grinding beans in the prison mill, or weaving at the looms. It was rebuilt as the town prison, and a thirty-foot treadmill was introduced in 1825 which was used to pump water into the town.[7] It stood on the site of the Palais de Dance, now Ritzy and Zone.

Politics and law and order together dictated that the municipal corporations should be reformed. In June 1833 a Royal Commission was appointed to gather information about the existing corporations. Assistant commissioners were sent around the country to hold public enquiries. In Nottingham the enquiry opened at the Shire Hall on Friday 24 October and lasted for five days. Two commissioners, R. Whitcombe and A. E. Cockburn, visited the town, and a succession of witnesses appeared before them, more than willing, or so it seemed, to wash the town's dirty linen in public.[8] Not surprisingly, when the Royal Commission published its findings the corporation came in for a good deal of criticism. 'In the management of the Public Funds, the conduct of the corporation is open to severe animadversion', the commissioners commented, not through misappropriation of funds but because of 'the thriftless and unprofitable character of their general expenditure', which meant that the financial administration of the corporation was 'strikingly defective'. Expenditure on its own activities, running at 35 per cent of income, was 'disproportionate to the amount of the revenues'. The mayor's 300–guinea allowance to 'keep table and make friends' was irregular, and the annuities given to older members of the corporation and their widows was not 'a proper application' of funds, 'however benevolent the motives'. On the other hand the commissioners commented that the corporation ran its estates with some skill and public responsibility:

> No shadow of suspicion exists of any appropriation of the funds of the corporation to the purposes of individual members of the body: nor does there appear to have been any partiality or unfairness in the letting or selling of their lands and houses; and the general management of the property appears to have been judicious, the income having been for many years gradually increasing.

It was not the husbanding of resources which came in for criticism, but the 'thriftless and unprofitable character of their general expenditure'.[9]

It hardly mattered. The government had decided in advance that it wished to reform the municipal corporations. The 1835 Municipal Corporations Act replaced the old corporation with an elected body of forty-two councillors and fourteen aldermen. The town was divided for electoral purposes into seven wards, Byron, Castle, Exchange, Park, St Ann's, St Mary's and Sherwood. The corporation lost control of the Free School Estate and the Sir Thomas White charity, but not the Bridge estate.[10] The first election under the new act was on 26 December 1835 when six of the seven aldermen, but only three of the old councillors, were returned. Yet if some of the personnel changed, the political complexion did not. The Whigs won twenty-seven out of the forty-two seats, and promptly took this as a manifesto to elect thirteen (out of fourteen) Whig aldermen. The new corporation took office on 1 January 1836 with Thomas Wakefield, a hosier, cotton-spinner, colliery owner and newspaper proprietor, as mayor, and Henry Enfield continuing as town clerk. Wakefield had long experience of local government – he had been mayor in 1815 – but he set a significant precedent by refusing the 300 guineas normally allowed to the mayor for entertainment. This was an encouraging start, but the new corporation soon found it had few real powers. The motives of central government in passing the 1835 legislation owed less to concern about the quality of life in towns than to worries over the state of local democracy and financial accountability. The government succeeded in its desire to supplant the self-electing corporations with electorally and financially accountable democratic councils, but it offered the new corporations very little by way of effective powers.

The concern with law and order was reflected in the attention paid to policing, and one of the first tasks of the new Nottingham corporation was to set up a Watch Committee, with the intention of appointing policemen who would 'exert themselves to the best of their ability for the security of person and property, the preservation of public tranquility', and, of course, 'the prevention of crime'. In fact, three separate forces were established. The day police consisted of three constables, a force so small as to bring a protest from the market-place inhabitants who were 'continuously subject to annoyances and petty larcenies', and who complained that 'the numerous daring attempts upon the windows and doors of the Shop-keepers … by a gang of young thiefs … [show] the urgent necessity of immediate measures'.[11] At dusk the three constables were replaced by an evening watch of twelve constables who patrolled the streets until 10.30 p.m., when they were replaced by a fifty-strong night force. These arrangements soon proved inadequate. At a meeting of the Watch Committee on 27 October 1837, it was admitted that a mistake had been made in re-employing on the night shift many of the old, inefficient watchmen of pre-reform days. Thirteen men had been discharged for misconduct, and another twelve had left in anticipation of dismissal. Their replacements proved more vigorous but also aroused hostility, and a number of people were arrested for assaulting constables. In 1839 two more evening police and five day police were appointed, but the problems of managing such a disparate force were such that the various branches of the Watch were combined in 1841. Thereafter the size of the force grew with the expansion of the town, and gradually the police were able to relieve troops of the traditional burdens placed upon them in times of riot and disorder. As the force became more efficient and more respected locally, the number of assaults on policemen declined. A special 'Detective Police' was formed in 1854, following the example of the Metropolitan Police. There were 75 constables in 1864, 119 in 1874, and 188 in 1879.[12]

The gradual acceptance of the police also reflected a change in attitude towards criminals and in the criminal code. Public executions continued until 1868, but were rare in Nottingham after the 1830s. William Saville's execution outside the Shire Hall in August 1844 brought pandemonium in High Pavement, and in the stampede thirteen people died and more than fifty were injured. No further public executions took place until John Fenton's execution on 1 August 1860. Fenton was found guilty at the summer assizes in July of the murder of Charles Spencer, a cattle dealer of Walkeringham. The county justices, mindful of events in 1844, asked Richard Charles Sutton, a local architect, to devise methods of crowd control. Preparations for the execution began on 30 July when barricades were erected: 'eleven barricades across the High Pavement are erecting', recorded George Harwood, 'Garner's Hill and Commerce Square are stopped up with planks, and all the palisading, and many of the windows, are boarded up'. Preparations continued throughout 31 July. Samuel Collinson noted that 'numbers of people are looking on or sauntering about the place. I was out at midnight and there were some there then who had evidently taken up their place for the night.' The day of the execution dawned bright and sunny, and the crowds began to gather 'quite gay, laughter, jesting, swearing jeering all goes on the same as at a fair or races or any other occasion where crowds of Englishmen meet together'. The crowd was so considerable that Harwood could not get near 'or even within sight of the fatal drop'. Even so, he reported in his diary that

> Fenton, accompanied by the under-sheriff, the governor, the chaplain and the executioner, walked with unfaltering step out of the gaol to the scaffold, where he stood erect and firm during the few moments required for adjusting the rope etc., and then was launched into eternity. This was a little before eight o'clock and a sharp shrill cry or shriek from the excited multitude announced the completion of the tragedy.

Collinson described the 'sharp shrill cry', as a 'vague fear', but within a few moments:

> Again goes on the shouting, talking, laughing, jesting, here and there is perhaps a face that looks a little shadowed with seriousness – an hour passes, again the crowd seems strangely moved, and I hear one passing say 'they are cutting him down', and so the tragedy is ended.[13]

In the course of the nineteenth century greater emphasis was placed on improving prison facilities. County prisoners were kept in Shire Hall, where the gaol facilities were extended and improved on several occasions from the 1830s, until they were closed in 1878. Criminals convicted in the town were sent to the House of Correction. In 1857 the Visiting Justices informed the corporation that it needed to extend and perhaps rebuild the gaol. As a result a new gaol was planned for the site and work commenced in 1860. Further alterations took place at regular intervals through the following decade. By the mid-1880s it was insufficient to house the number of criminals being convicted, and work began on a new prison on Perry Road which opened in 1891.[14]

Despite its powers of policing, the new corporation was in many ways hamstrung. It inherited more than £20,000 in debts – twice its annual income, a sum which was not finally redeemed until 1853 – and it had no mandate to do anything about environmental conditions in the old town, or about enclosure. This was not a propitious beginning, given the state of the town. Staveley and Wood's map of 1831, updated by William Dearden after 1834, provides a graphic illustration of just how

Plate 26 **The Nottingham town gaol, corner of Glasshouse and St John's Streets**. In 1846 the old gaol under the Guildhall at Weekday Cross was closed when the gaol and the house of correction were combined in the building of the former St John's Hospital. After considering the erection of a new gaol for the town on a site in Burton Leys, the council went for a less ambitious solution by extending the building within the prison walls. Further additions were made in 1861 and 1867 before the prison was transferred to the Home Office on 1 April 1878, following the Prisons Act of 1877. The prisoners from the St John's prison were moved to the new prison at Bagthorpe when it opened in 1891. The old borough prison was left deserted pending the alterations to come with the arrival of the new railway line. In the end the whole prison was demolished and the site cleared after the council decided to form a new street from Lower Parliament Street to St Ann's Well Road in 1900. This is now King Edward Street

densely built Nottingham had become; indeed, few towns were more congested at this time. Hundreds of small dwellings characterised the south and east sides of the town. The majority of these houses had a ground plan with an area of only 20–23 square yards, and street densities in excess of 300 people per acre.[15] Congestion in the central and western town was less marked, but there was hardly anywhere left to build and the housing stock increased by just 5 per cent between 1831 and 1841. Nor was there any space for factories or institutional buildings, or for widening the narrow streets. William Felkin argued that high rents resulting from the land shortage were causing manufacturers to seek factory sites beyond the town boundaries, or to settle in Leicester, Loughborough, and Derby. In 1831 Samuel and Jonathan Burton, who had lace works on Mount Street, moved to Carrington in order to be able to build larger premises. In 1838 another factory was built in Sherwood, and in the lace industry most factories were built beyond the town boundaries in Radford, Lenton and Sneinton parishes. Between 1831 and 1836, according to Felkin, this trend was reflected in a fall in the number of lace machines in Nottingham by 600, while numbers in the surrounding areas increased commensurately.[16]

The railway

Clearly something needed to be done, but the corporation was in no position to give a lead and it needed an external agency to bring real pressure to bear. On 16 August 1832 a group of Erewash coal owners met in the Sun Inn, Eastwood, and from their discussions came a proposal to build a railway line from Pinxton to Leicester. The primary aim of the line was to protect their coal trade in Leicester, threatened by the opening a month earlier of the Leicester-Swannington line. One by-product would have been to put Nottingham, together with Derby and Leicester, on to the railway map with a link to the London-Birmingham line at Rugby. In August 1833 Felkin and William Hannay formed a local committee to support the Midland Counties Railway project. They believed the railway would speed up delivery times and lower transport costs, particularly for coal. The project was advertised in November 1833, but in the short term nothing was achieved.[17] Yet the railway posed a problem for Nottingham which had still to be addressed: if and when a line reached the town what route would it follow, and what space would be available for a station?

In 1836 the newly-formed Midland Counties Railway Company applied for legislation to open routes between Nottingham, Derby and Leicester. The reformed corporation had been in power for only a month when it was approached by the Company and asked to 'assent or dissent to the proposed Railway Bill in respect of parts of estates in either the Meadows etc., over which the line would pass'. This was an awkward moment. The newly-elected councillors were anxious to be seen to be doing the right thing, but they had to weigh up the obvious objections of the Nottingham Canal Company and the Trent Navigation Company, both of which opposed the measure, fearing that business on the canal and the river would be undermined; and those of the burgesses, still smarting from the failure of the canal company to compensate them for the land 'purchased, or rather seized by virtue of an Act of Parliament and appropriated to the use of the Nottingham Canal Company'.[18] The corporation sat firmly on the fence. 'Several members', reported the *Nottingham Journal* 'expressed their opinion that the time allowed to consider upon this momentous question was too short', and the council declined to offer assent or dissent 'at present'.[19] In the end the canal and navigation companies succeeded in forcing the abandonment of a scheme which would have brought the proposed line through the Meadows, across the canal, and right into the centre of Nottingham, where it would terminate at the junction of Lister and Castle Gates. The bill received the Royal Assent on 21 June 1836.

There were many in Nottingham who thought the corporation had been spineless in its attitude towards the railway. Thomas Bailey fired off a broadside with a letter to the *Nottingham Review* published on 21 October 1836:

> the apathy of the people of Nottingham on the subject of the railroads is astonishing. Whilst every part of the United Kingdom, nay almost every section of the civilised world, is entering with spirit upon the furtherance of these magnificent enterprises,

> encouraging their formation, and fostering their growth with the most enthusiastic ardour and patriotic solicitude, the population of this important town stand with folded arms and vacant minds, as uninterested spectators.

Bailey set the tone for a particularly stormy council meeting on 27 October 1836. One member spoke of 'the supineness and apathy' of the corporation:

> Nottingham from its geographical position might and ought to have been made a point through which the direct line of railway from south to north should pass … . That benefit has been lost to the town in consequence of the neglect and indifference with which the subject has been treated.[20]

Yet, as all those involved knew perfectly well, the problem was the route. The company had proposed that the line should cross the Meadows, but the corporation was neither willing nor able to resist the opposition of the canal and river companies and of its own burgesses. There was, however, a potential way around this problem. If the land was enclosed, the corporation could anticipate having the absolute right of sale. It could dispose of the land without appearing to favour the railway promoters at the expense of its own burgesses, let alone the canal and river companies. With this end in view the corporation set up two committees. Both reported in favour of promoting an enclosure of the common fields and meadows, with a proviso that the burgesses' rights should be protected. Before the end of 1837 the decision had been taken to promote a limited enclosure.[21]

Since 1787 the enclosure issue had rumbled along in the background to local politics as a divisive issue about which the corporation (both unreformed and reformed) seemed powerless to do anything. It was periodically debated in public – at some length, for example, before the assistant commissioners who took evidence on the state of the old corporation in 1833.[22] The corporation was obviously all too well aware of the continuing sensitivity of the question, and it decided in 1837 to approach the matter gently. The initial proposal was to promote separate bills to enclose the West Croft (to the south of the town, and the proposed site of the railway station) and the Lammas Fields, the eighteen acres between Park Row and Derby Road. This may have looked a small enough beginning, but the corporation quickly found itself squeezed between the obstructive burgesses on the one part, and a group of freeholders who wanted to go further and promote a general enclosure on the other. To retain the hard-won support of the burgesses the corporation had to oppose the general enclosure, while arguing that it might support such a measure if it safeguarded the rights of the burgesses and provided 'ample spaces for public walks and recreation'. A compromise was reached, and the two bills finally passed into law in 1839, by which time the corporation had laid out land in the West Croft allowing the railway company to begin building both the line and the station.[23]

The first train reached Nottingham on 30 May 1839, where it pulled into the Grecian-style, stone-built station. The company had also erected an engine house and a goods shed. The *Nottingham Journal* commented percipiently that 'new days are coming to Nottingham … a new impetus is now being given to the long declining affairs of our ancient town'. A public service between Nottingham and Derby began on 4 June with four trains each way each day, and two on Sundays. Fares were 4*s* first class, and 2*s* 6*d* second class.[24]

Ironically, in the longer term Nottingham enjoyed an unexpected benefit from the problems of these years. Railways had a major impact on Victorian towns, not least because of their demand for land for lines, stations, marshalling yards, carriage works and other facilities. Even a superficial glance at one of the large-scale Ordnance Survey maps for Nottingham reveals their physical presence, and physical relics survive around the town from lines which closed many years ago. Railways also affected townscapes in other ways. Areas adjacent to railway lines tended to become coal and timber yards, warehousing and factories and, almost invariably, to contain poor-quality housing which was either built as such or frozen in time by the arrival of the railway.[25] Almost none of these effects were felt in Nottingham until the Great Central line was cut in the 1890s because, apart from an initial desire on the part of the Midland Counties Railway to bring a line right into the centre of the old town, there was simply no need to drive the railway through built-up areas. Sufficient land was available in the West and East Crofts for the network to be developed within close proximity to the commercial quarters of the town – particularly from the 1850s the Lace Market area – without provoking any major upheavals.

The Midland Railway extended its services by providing a line from Lenton to Kirkby in 1848, and on to Mansfield in 1849. Further branches were opened in 1875 (Radford-Trowell), connecting Nottingham through the Erewash Valley to the northern manufacturing towns. The line ran around the town to the west and only created problems in Basford, where it effectively divided the parish from north to south. Industrial development occurred along the line but few houses were built close by. Similarly, lines to the east of Nottingham were developed in the 1850s by the Midland and the Great Northern Railway without impinging on existing built-up areas. Originally the intention was that both companies should use a single station, and the new Midland Station opened in 1848 as a replacement for the original station on land in the East Croft released under the 1845 enclosure. In the end, after considerable wrangling, the GNR gained the right to construct an independent line from Colwick into Nottingham, with its own station in the East Croft. The new (low-level) station, designed by T. C. Hine, opened in 1857. When, in the 1870s the Great Northern built a new line from Colwick to exploit coal resources north of Nottingham, it ran along the east side of the town well away from areas of housing.

The two enclosure acts which received the royal assent on 1 July 1839 were designed to do more than simply rubber-stamp the terms and conditions for allowing the railway to reach Nottingham. The West Croft enclosure act also included the Burton Leys area north of Parliament Street, initially occupied by a cattle and horse market, but since the later nineteenth century by the Guildhall and other buildings. The other act authorised the enclosure of the Lammas Fields, the eighteen acres between Derby Road and Park Terrace. This was designed as an area of quality housing. The legislation stipulated that there should be no industrial premises, and

Plate 27 **Milton Street, 1851**. Buildings on land released under the Burton Leys Enclosure Act of 1839. Holy Trinity, Trinity Square, on the left, by the Derby architect H.I. Stevens, was consecrated on 13 October 1841. It was a handsome Gothic edifice with a 177-foot spire, long prominent on the local skyline. It was demolished in 1958 and there is a multi-storey car-park on the site today. Centre is the Mechanics Institute, by the Nottingham architects Thomas Hawksley and Robert Jalland, which opened on 28 January 1845. Although burned down on 4 March 1867 it was rebuilt (enlarged) within two years. On the right is the General Baptist Church designed by William Booker at a cost of £2,900. It opened on 23 October 1850. Later unwanted, and offered for sale, it was purchased to allow expansion of the Mechanics

the houses were laid out on building plots of 100 square yards or more with large gardens. They were to have a value of £500, or £800 if they were on the Ropewalk. The fine houses on Regent Street with their Dutch gables were subsequently built to designs by T.C. Hine. Hine himself paid £218 for his plot (now 25 Regent Street) on 19 September 1845. His house, completed a year later, cost £1,053. William Parsons, a local solicitor and later mayor, moved into the area in 1851 when he described Wellington Circus as a cabbage patch. The Duke of Newcastle managed to ensure that the Act gave him land-use rights for his projected tunnel from the Park. Sensing that this enclosure reflected a local demand for quality housing, the duke also allowed development within the Park at the end of the 1830s.[26] Nottingham's middle class was now sufficiently buoyant to expand into leafy suburbs.

Neither Act of Parliament had any impact on Nottingham's environmental problems, but in December 1839 an 'Association for the Improvement of the Town of Nottingham' was formed under the chairmanship of Ichabod Wright, the banker. Its main function was to lobby the council to take action over what it considered to be the crisis threatening the local transport system because of the narrow lanes and alleys which, it was claimed, hampered the free flow of commerce. Sheep Lane, from the market-place to Parliament Street, was only ten feet wide, and other important thoroughfares such as Pelham Street and Bridlesmith Gate were less than five yards wide.[27] The Association passed a number of resolutions which were then presented to the corporation. William Felkin, elected to the corporation only the previous month, spoke strongly in favour of 'the necessity of improving the town … . If they did not attend to this, they would be distanced in the march of competition'. The Association also pressed for a General Improvement Act. Simultaneously notice was also given to the council of a private attempt to promote a general enclosure bill.[28]

The corporation responded to these pressures by establishing its own Improvement Committee, which put forward various proposals including the widening of Lister Gate. The projected cost soon aborted this scheme, but in 1842 it was agreed to extend Carrington Street by building a bridge over the canal. Originally the intention had been for the Midland Railway to bring its line across the Meadows to a terminal adjacent to London Road, but the terms of the legislation stated that the line should not run beyond the western side of Carrington Street. As a result, access to the town from the station was a problem because it was via an ill-lit path from Wilford Street, near the Navigation Bridge. Strangers arriving by train after dusk were 'in danger of getting very deep into mud or being liable to fall into the canal'. These dangers were rectified by the Carrington Street extension,[29] and when in 1843 Queen Victoria and Prince Albert paid a brief visit to the town the corporation sponsored a new road – appropriately named Queen's Road – across the West Croft enclosure.[30] By then the town was struggling with a deep and lasting depression in its textile trade, and some of the improvement impetus was lost, although the corporation did agree to cut Albert Street, at a cost of £8,000 raised from a special rate and a public subscription. It was completed in 1846.[31]

Poverty and environmental problems

The depression in the textile trades set in early in 1837, and brought Nottingham into national focus as a testing bench for the application of the New Poor Law in an industrial town. Under the terms of the 1834 Poor Law Amendment Act the three Nottingham parishes were formed into a single Union in 1836. Absolem Barnett was entrusted with putting the new legislation into practice, and the Poor Law Commissioners in London looked on anxiously to see whether the system would work. Within six months the town's textile trades went into a severe depression which posed problems for the board of guardians and for the Whig (and therefore pro-poor law reform) corporation. In particular, it was thought vital to enforce the 'workhouse test' whereby able-bodied males were refused relief except as inmates of the workhouse. With the passage of time it is now clear that such regulations were of little value in a town subject to the vagaries of the trade cycle and therefore to periods of short-term unemployment. But this was not how it looked in the spring of 1837. As the numbers applying for relief increased, and as the workhouse filled up, supporters of the new legislation looked for ways of keeping the unemployed in work. The logic was simple: there was not the space for all of them in the workhouse, and if they could not be kept in work, a central principle of the new legislation would have to be violated and outrelief paid to the able-bodied. Richard Morley, the mayor, organised a public subscription to raise money to put the unemployed to work. In under three months £5,000 was raised and at one time over 1,000 men were at work. Through the summer of 1837 occasional signs of an upturn in trade proved to be false dawns, and by late August the workhouse was full and the subscription fund exhausted.[32] The Poor Law Commissioners agreed to lift the ban on out-relief, but Barnett proposed instead a 'labour test' by which the able-bodied paupers would be put to work in return for poor relief. Barnett's opponents were not amused: they had argued for years that 'the cruelty of employing frame-work knitters upon such works ought to deter any overseer from resorting to it. The stockinger in general is delicate, badly clothed and badly fed; altogether unfitted for the hardships arising out of a situation so opposite to his usual mode of life'.[33] Able-bodied men with families were to be offered work digging and moving soil for the course of a road across Mapperley Common. Relief would be given partly in money, but not less than one-third would be in food substitutes, bread and potatoes, which would be delivered to their families twice a week.[34] More than 100 men were put to work through the autumn of 1837.

Throughout the winter of 1837–38 the workhouse was overcrowded, and the spring offered no respite. William Felkin estimated in March 1838 that 1,155 houses were vacant, including numerous retail premises 'of which seven were capitally situated in the market-place'. Families had been doubling up to make ends meet, and 'the pawnbrokers were unable to receive the amount of property offered in pledge, and it was thrown away by forced sales in the public streets'. His survey also revealed something of the 565 inmates of the workhouse in February 1838: 42 per cent were under sixteen, 35 per cent between sixteen and sixty, and 22 per cent over sixty. Of the 240 children 46 had both parents in the house, 65 had been deserted by their parents, 56 were orphans, and 73 had mothers who were unable to support them; 35 per cent were illegitimate. Among the reasons for being in the workhouse, 160 people were there through age and infirmity, 51 through some form of sickness including blindness, and 56 'mild insanity and total imbecility'. Outdoor relief was being paid in another 596 cases.[35]

After a brief respite in the summer of 1838, the textile trades were again in difficulty during the autumn of 1839. On 6 November 1839 Barnett reported that the unemployed were 'beginning this afternoon to parade the streets', and two weeks later 600 heads of families were out of work. A deputation of 1,500 people called on the mayor to provide work, and for a few days they collectively held out against an approach to the workhouse.[36] Early in December groups of unemployed men roamed the streets and presented a petition to the magistrates. In Barnett's words, they 'dispersed in many directions and are now begging in numbers in the principal streets of the town'. People were stopped in the streets, and shopkeepers 'beset by gangs of these persons bearing flags, from whom they almost demand money'.[37] The *Nottingham Journal* reported that 'large numbers of men assemble after dark in the evening and go to the bakers' shops in the town demanding bread, and have so much the air of intimidation about them as to succeed in most cases in obtaining it in large amounts'. Once again a subscription was opened to raise money for poor relief, and the mayor set up a committee to provide work for the unemployed and to distribute food and blankets to deserving cases. More than 500 able-bodied men with families were set to work on Mapperley Plains.[38] The arrangement was far from ideal. The men involved held a meeting at which they passed several resolutions: 'we, the unemployed operatives in Nottingham having been chiefly used to sedentary employments in warm workshops are totally unfitted to face the wintry blast on Mapperley hills, or to perform any useful labour thereon, without endangering our health, which is generally speaking rendered delicate by the nature of our usual avocations'. They requested more congenial work. Perhaps they were right, since Moses Wood, the borough surveyor, described the road built using unemployed textile workers as 'an interminable subject of complaint'. Meanwhile younger men, refused outdoor relief or work, wandered the town in gangs, forcing shopkeepers to give them food.[39]

The depression passed, but there were further problems in the late autumn of 1841. On 29 November a public subscription was set up to raise money for poor relief in the town, partly by feeding on bread and soup those not receiving parochial relief. Nearly 7,000 people, or 13 per cent of the town's population, benefited.[40] These years of difficulty for the textile trades – years sometimes known as the 'hungry forties' – shifted the focus of local attention away from environmental conditions towards poverty, and William Felkin was almost alone in his efforts to keep up the pressure for change. In February 1841 he prompted the corporation to set up a committee to enquire into 'the houses of the poor and the sewerage of streets'. No report has survived, but Felkin pressed on. In May 1842 he told a meeting of the corporation that the registrar general's figures showed that from 1800 until 1820 mortality in Nottingham decreased by 6 per cent, but between 1820 and 1840 it increased by 15.5 per cent.[41] Felkin described the 'fearful rate of mortality', and argued 'that the average of life was much less in Nottingham than the surrounding towns'. He was as yet, however, a lone voice: the *Review* later admitted that it had refused to believe that he could be correct.[42] In the meantime, problems were dealt with piecemeal, if at all. In July 1841 the poor law guardians agreed to refuse relief to anyone living in Cabbage Court since 'there was no possible means of drainage' and the area was rife with fever. Within a month the houses were flooded as a result of unseasonal rain: 'the water found its level and rose to several feet high inside their dwellings'. An editorial in the *Review* noted how 'filth, misery and wretchedness at all times more than abound'.[43] The guardians had a policy of refusing relief to people living in 'unwholesome situations', but it seems seldom to have been acted upon: Barnett claimed in 1845 that they were 'unable to accomplish their designs' because of 'the feeling in the town'.[44]

Figure 11.1 Back-to-back, court-style housing in Nottingham, 1844

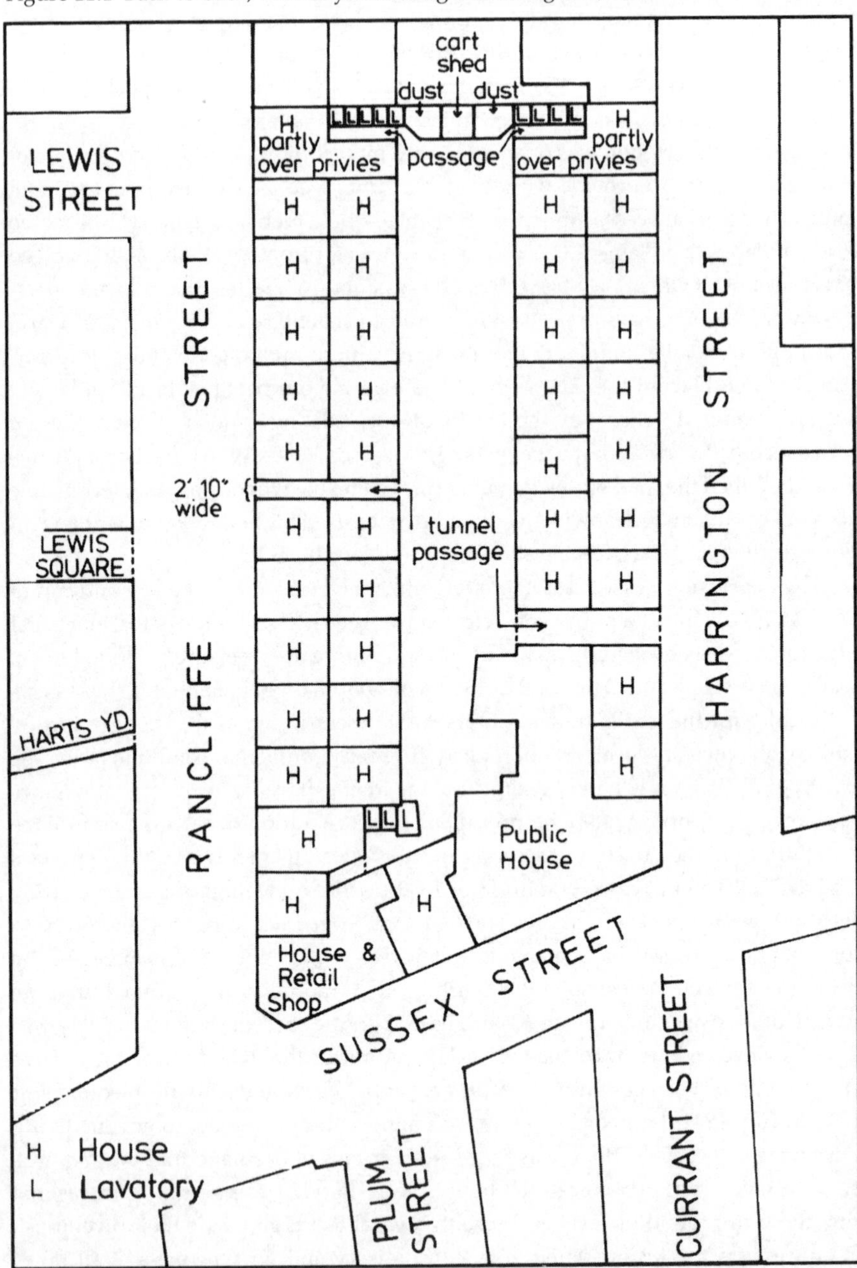

Note: The plan is redrawn from material presented by Thomas Hawksley to the Royal Commission of 1844. Hawksley's own caption ran 'Plan Shewing the Arrangement of "Back to Back" houses and the remoteness & exposure of the privies, also the deficiency of accommodation for the decent separation of the sexes.' He also noted that people living in houses which fronted the street had to pass through the tunnel and along the inside court in order to reach the privies.

As an issue of principle, environmental conditions were forced back on to the local political agenda in 1842, but – as with enclosure – as a consequence of pressures from outside rather than from within the town. Nationally, concern with poverty, public health, and the state of large towns had never been off the political agenda during the 1830s, but it came to a head with the publication in 1842 of Edwin Chadwick's *Report on the Sanitary Condition of the Labouring Population of Great Britain*. Chadwick, secretary to the Poor Law Commissioners, was deeply interested in the link between epidemic disease and environmental factors. His report drew on evidence gathered by approximately 1,000 Poor Law Medical Officers of Health. Nottingham corporation may have been relieved that the town was given nothing like the prominence of Manchester, Leeds and other new industrial towns, but Chadwick's report was a slighting indictment of urban local government and its unwillingness or inability to ensure even the most basic provisions for the new industrial working classes. It was designed to stimulate government action, and it succeeded, with dramatic results for Nottingham.[45]

In the shock-waves reverberating from Chadwick's report, a Royal Commission was established under the chairmanship of the Duke of Buccleuch to investigate the sanitary state of large towns and populous districts. Evidence was taken from experts up and down the country, and Nottingham's water engineer Thomas Hawksley appeared before the commission on 15 February 1844. Hawksley's evidence, backed up with statistics and diagrams, painted a grim picture of the industrial slum which was 1840s Nottingham. In dispassionate language suitable to the occasion he described for the Royal Commission the defective houses, the poor sanitary conditions, the 'absence of regulations ... with respect to new buildings', the 'accumulations of filth and moisture attended with the worst and most fatal consequences', the 'very defective and unsystematic' sewers, the absence of 'proper necessaries' in the smaller houses, and the streets where the poorer inhabitants lived which 'seldom or never receive the slightest attention'.[46] Two weeks later James Ranald Martin, one of the assistant commissioners, visited Nottingham and his report (dated 1 March) was equally lacking in sentiment. The streets where the working class lived were 'narrow, unpaved, uneven, ill-ventilated, noisome, and damp'. The houses of the poor were

> singularly defective ... damp and uncleanly ... . The courts are almost always approached through a low-arched tunnel of some 30 or 36 inches wide, about 8 feet high, and from 20 to 30 feet long ... . They are noisome, narrow, unprovided with adequate means for the removal of refuse, ill-ventilated, and wretched in the extreme, with a gutter, or surface-drain, running down the centre; they have no back yards, and the privies are common to the whole court; altogether they present scenes of a deplorable character, and of surpassing filth and discomfort. It is just the same with lane and alleys ... . In all these confined quarters too, the refuse is allowed to accumulate until, by its mass and its advanced petrefaction, it shall have acquired value as manure; and thus it is carted away by the 'muck majors' as the collectors of manure are called in Nottingham.[47]

Yet these descriptions of filthy conditions, however powerful, lacked the dramatic effect of Hawksley's statistics of life expectancy in the town. As the *Nottingham Review* noted in an editorial on 6 September:

> No one can read Mr Hawksley's report without being convinced that there is a vast, an appalling sacrifice of health and life every year in the town of Nottingham. This gentleman has proved beyond all doubt that the average duration of life among the males of the town is very little beyond *twenty years*!

Two years earlier, as the *Review* admitted, it had refused to believe Felkin: now, recognising that it had been wrong, the newspaper carried the full text of Hawksley's evidence in weekly instalments through the summer of 1844.[48]

Enclosure

What was to be done? For many years enclosure of the common fields and meadows had been seen by its supporters as the only obvious way of releasing land for building, and thereby offering some relief to the pressure on urban space. A long discussion along these lines took place during the 1833 hearings into the condition of the old corporation.[49] Hawksley and Martin made the same case in 1844, linking high land prices caused by land shortage to the erection of poor-quality housing. Martin placed the blame squarely on the failure to enclose, which was 'one of the greatest evils that can afflict a town':

> There is no other circumstance in the history of this great town that has so materially interfered with its moral and physical prosperity, with the proper regulation and construction of both streets and houses; indeed, with the just arrangement of everything above and below ground as these antiquated tenures. At a time when, through manufacturing prosperity, Nottingham would have expanded into the surrounding open spaces, this ancient right stood in the way, and forced the speculators in building, whom I there found to be the owners of the worst quarters, into ingeniously mischievous contrivances for heaping and clubbing buildings upon each other so as to amass the greatest number of dwellings upon the narrowest spaces.[50]

It was a claim picked up by the *Review*:

> If this be correct, what becomes of the long-repeated cry, that the open fields were necessary for the health and recreation of the inhabitants? Is it not evidence that these open fields and meadows, which can neither be improved nor built upon, nor brought into the proper service of the town, are the causes of disease and death to thousands? And this is brought about by cooping up the working classes in confined dwellings, and depriving all the families at home of the pure air of heaven, in order that a few and only a few, may gambol in the fields at meal-times … a remedy for some of these evils ought to be applied without delay.[51]

Fired with enthusiasm, the *Review* launched what was in effect a press campaign aimed at shaming the corporation and the burgesses into abandoning their entrenched opposition to enclosure. Throughout the autumn it ran leader columns on the subject. Meanwhile Hawksley was busy emphasising his point in evidence to a House of Commons Select Committee. The failure to enclose the Nottingham open fields, he argued, was 'materially' prejudicial to the health of the community: 'the public derive very little benefit from them, as to health, by recreation and exercise, while the town, certainly, at large is very greatly injured'. In the disputes which followed, even the most implacable opponents of a general enclosure recognised the need to release some land for building.[52]

The corporation was unmoved, but in mid-November 1844 an *ad hoc* group announced in the *Nottingham Journal* their intention to press for an enclosure act. Both the *Journal* and the *Review* welcomed the news – but there were others who did not.[53] Three days after the first announcement of this private initiative the burgesses met in the town hall. There was a heated discussion in which Hawksley was depicted as the villain of the piece. Nor was this surprising. 'Several influential members of the corporation', he had informed the Royal Commission, 'are extensive owners of the small houses inhabited by the working-classes in the worst conditioned districts, and have repeatedly avowed their hostility to the principle of enclosure.'[54] The burgesses believed they could count on the support of the corporation, and they concluded their meeting with a memorial to the effect that 'the freemen and the public at large would be forever deprived of the advantages which they and their families at present enjoy in some of the most healthy and delightful walks the loss of which nothing could ever repay'.[55] A struggle was inevitable, and the next six months witnessed something close to open warfare in the town.

The bill was ready by 3 February 1845. The following day the corporation appointed a committee to examine its clauses, and the burgesses held a public meeting on 17 February to condemn the bill and its intentions. The meeting ended in uproar after a motion was passed committing the burgesses to opposing the enclosure proceedings.[56] On 20 February the corporation met in extraordinary session to hear a report from the committee it had set up on 4 February. Thomas Wakefield, for more than twenty years an outspoken opponent of enclosure, launched a bitter attack on the bill. He particularly regretted 'the extinction of the right of the people to stroll over the Meadows … [and] the fields'. But the tide was turning. The corporation met again on 24 February and on 3 and 4 March to discuss the enclosure issue. Numerous objections were lodged, but in the end it decided to throw in its weight behind the private initiative. Wakefield, having made his last stand, moved the motion in support. A noisy public meeting conducted by the burgesses outside the council chamber failed to sway the corporation.[57] The bill now went to the Commons and passed through the normal parliamentary channels. At each stage in the process the burgesses presented counter-petitions. All were rejected.[58] Sixty years since enclosure had first been proposed, the legislation finally received the Royal Assent at the end of June 1845.

In the absence of any lead from central government, by the 1840s many industrial towns had taken their own action to try to improve the urban environment. The ways and means of proceeding varied. Some towns sought an Improvement Commission, while others adopted model clauses legislation and the permissive clauses in public general acts. Private acts often set the tone for later general legislation and individual towns pressed ahead of government action in the search for ways and means of improving the urban environment. The Nottingham enclosure act comes into this category. The people who framed the legislation regarded it as far more than a measure designed simply to deal with the enclosure of Nottingham's open fields and meadows. In the words of the preamble, it was to be an instrument of 'social, moral, commercial, and agricultural reform'. Many of the clauses were concerned with what could loosely be regarded as town improvement. The problem of narrow lanes was to be tackled by setting minimum width dimensions for new streets – 60 feet for main roads, 48 feet for medium roads, and 36 feet for inferior roads. Other clauses addressed the laying of sewers, and the construction of new houses. Significantly, further back-to-back house building was banned, minimum standards were laid down for houses built on the newly enclosed land, and builders of houses were to be 'at least 30 years of age, and properly educated, and skilled in the Art and Practice of Building'.[59] The problems identified by Hawksley were at last to be tackled.

Passing the Act may have divided the town, and implementing its terms was equally contentious, as a result both of unrealistic expectations and of political differences of opinion. The Whigs, almost permanently the party in power, were pro-enclosure, hence the coverage given by the *Nottingham Review* to Hawksley's evidence in 1844. They chose to regard enclosure as the cure-all for Nottingham's ills. In August 1846 the *Review* even carried an article extolling 'the progressive spirit everywhere manifested' in the town. It was referring primarily to the middle-class Wellington Circus area enclosed in 1839, but the impression conveyed was that everything was well.[60] The Whig argument was simple. Large quantities of land would be released for development and the price would fall. Consequently good quality working-class houses would be erected which would rent relatively cheaply, because land prices would no longer be the restraining forces which had created the slums. Market forces would then come into play: the working classes would move out of the slums into the new houses, the slums would become redundant and redevelopment would follow. By creating a 'New Nottingham' in the enclosed areas the social problems of the old town would automatically be resolved. The weak links in such a line of thinking are obvious, and Hawksley himself had specifically rejected the simplicity of this logic in his evidence to the Royal Commission: he argued that slum-owning members of the corporation who opposed enclosure did so 'under what I believe to be the very erroneous impression that their property would sustain permanent injury by the erection of better, more healthy, and more comfortable dwellings on the enclosed lands'.[61] Hawksley's position was closer to that of Nottingham's Tories, who supported the enclosure but canvassed for a separate improvement measure to complement enclosure.[62] The *Nottingham Journal* put the case succinctly in an editorial in February 1845; the writer expected to see:

> but little improvement from an inclosure in the condition of those whose welfare is made the prime motive for bringing more building land into the market ... we cannot see how ... the erection of cottages in the Sand and Clay Fields is to purify the Meadow Platts and Milestone Lane.[63]

Yet once the act passed the improvement question was shelved, because the Tory minority had little or no influence on policy. In the long run the Tory position proved to be correct, and so from the outset there was a fundamental flaw in the expectations of enclosure among the Whig majority.

The main point of the legislation was to make available development land to the north of the old town on the Sand (191 acres) and Clay Fields (408 acres), and to the south in the Meadows (241 acres). Prior to the legislation, and again as late as 1852, ideas were discussed with a view to zoning the town by restricting industrial development to the low-lying Meadows area, but such a scheme was never implemented.[64] The Act was also framed to ensure that the town had 'green lungs'. A government Select Committee reporting in 1833 highlighted the absence of open spaces in many industrial towns, and in 1839 Parliament adopted a standing order decreeing that all future enclosure bills should make provision for recreational space. Hawksley told the 1844 Royal Commission that Nottingham was oddly placed in respect of open spaces. There were no *public* parks, gardens or walks and local people had to travel to find recreation:

> At a distance of nearly a mile from the centre of the town there is a plot of land containing 124 acres, called the Nottingham Forest, an unstinted common, the soil of which is claimed by the corporation as lord of the manor. This is open during the whole year, and is partly applied as a cricket ground, an exercising ground for the military, and a race ground, and partly remains an unreclaimed waste.

At least it was better than Mapperley Plain, a fifty-seven acre open space, but two miles north of the town 'and therefore too remote for convenient recreation'.[65]

Hawksley was anxious to counter the corporation's claim that keeping the common fields open ensured plenty of recreation space for Nottingham people. As he rightly pointed out, for most of the year they were, technically, trespassing if they crossed the open fields, which were not strictly communal resources but the private property of the burgesses and freeholders. Hawksley's argument was heard: in 1845 the Forest and Mapperley were not regarded as sufficient to meet the terms of the 1839 standing order and, as a result, when the question of open spaces was discussed by the committee considering the Nottingham enclosure bill it was agreed that 'the quantity to be taken [for places of recreation] should be not less than a proportion after the rate of 5 per cent or 1/20th part of the total land to be enclosed, exclusive of the Forest and Mapperley Hill'. To fulfil this obligation the Forest was retained almost intact, the Arboretum was opened in 1852, four acres were set aside for Anglican and nonconformist cemeteries, and various walks were laid out: Elm Avenue, Corporation Oaks, Robin Hood Chase, and Queen's Drive.[66] As a result it was possible to stroll in a pleasant arc from the Castle, along Park Terrace to Canning Circus (Sion Hill), and then through the new cemetery and arboretum, along Elm Avenue and Robin Hood Chase to St Ann's (although by 1851 the Well was said to be dilapidated).[67] A green 'collar' had been created around the town. As a visiting journalist saw it:

> recreation walks – which are, in truth, almost a continuous avenue of trees – completely encircle the town, and afford a promenade of ten miles in extent ... the enclosure will exhibit almost an unique specimen of spirited and liberal provision for the public recreation and welfare.

However, the 'collar' diverted promenaders away from more distant attractions. Radford Folly, which was illuminated by night, and which was a popular retreat for dancing, fireworks and fêtes at regular intervals, suffered a decline in popularity. The lake was eventually filled in and the site became a railway siding.[68]

To fund their work the commissioners appointed to implement the legislation had to raise money. Land was sold in 1846 to the Nottingham Waterworks Company, which was itself created under the terms of legislation passed the previous year. Other land was set aside in the West and East Crofts to permit the Midland Railway to lay a new line passing south of the existing station, across Carrington Street, Queen's Road and the East Croft, and proceeding to Lincoln. The Nottingham and Lincoln Railway opened on 3 August 1846, although the land transaction was completed only in 1848, for £8,876. The Midland Railway decided that its original station was no longer adequate because trains to and from Lincoln had to back into and out of it. To solve the problem an entirely new station was built towards the eastern end of Station Street, and opened on 22 May 1848.[69] The enclosure commissioners also sold land from the western end of the Forest. The largest plot, of seven acres, was bought for a consortium headed by Revd James Orange, an Independent minister best known for his *History of Nottingham* published in 1840, and for his directory of the town which appeared the same year. He was a prominent supporter of allotments for working-class men in the 1840s, and he advocated cottages 'for the poorest and most industrious men with families'. The Orange consortium divided up their property into twenty-nine sub-plots, which they sold for quality housing development.[70]

It was not until 1851 that the commissioners were in a position to begin releasing land to the freeholders, the men and women who had successfully established claims to a share in the ownership of the open fields and meadows. By then, some of the high hopes which accompanied the passing of the enclosure act were beginning to fade. Disillusion was typified by William Felkin's complaints in 1852 about what he saw as the inadequate housing regulations. It took the commissioners twenty years to complete the enclosure award.[71] Moving from act to award always took time when an urban enclosure was involved, but this was excessive by any standards.

The delay partly arose from a misjudgement as to the likely impact of enclosure. The commissioners' brief was to lay out a handful of necessary roads north and south of the old town, and to make provision for further roads which would be constructed when housing demand dictated. A combination of an upturn in the business cycle, and the natural optimism which accompanied the town's escape from its old boundaries, quickly left these plans in disarray. Between 1841 and 1851 only 318 houses were built in Nottingham, but between 1851 and 1861 the housing stock increased by more than 5,000 units and the population grew by 17,000. The great majority of the new houses were erected on the enclosed land and the housing stock in St Mary's parish increased by 55 per cent through the decade. The building industry, in particular, enjoyed a boom.[72] In the meantime the commissioners found themselves without the resources to build all the necessary roads. They had raised from land sales sufficient capital to fund only the initial road programme. Since the corporation refused to accept any responsibility for roads on the newly enclosed areas, an impasse arose which was finally sorted out only in 1867.

The misjudgement about the likely effect of enclosure also had other implications. Since housing demand was greater than anticipated the price of land rose, and the stipulations in the legislation meant that developers could not compensate for rising prices (as they had done in the 1820s) by lowering the quality of the buildings they erected. The new houses simply could not be let cheaply enough to attract migrants from the slums: only 4 per cent were let for 3*s* a week or less.[73] When Wil-

Plate 28 **Sandfield Housing, Addison Villas, Addison Street**. After enclosure the old Sand Field provided the most advantageous sites for quality housing. The area rose northwards, away from the town centre towards the Forest, and although at times development was chaotic and building control far from adequate, many fine streets with suitably impressive housing were set out. Addison Street was one of the earliest, with twelve houses already occupied by 1854. Addison Villas, 2–24 Addison Street, were built *c.*1865

liam Eyre, frustrated by this situation, suggested in 1852 the formation of a company to purchase land and build houses which would rent at no more than 3*s* a week, he struck a chord. A committee was formed, 5,000 square yards of newly enclosed land adjoining St Ann's Well Road was purchased from the enclosure commissioners, and a prize was offered for the best design of artisan dwellings for the area. More than ninety houses were built, but the scheme had to be adjudged a failure because rents could not be kept below 3*s*.[74] In 1856 the *Nottingham Journal* lamented 'the want upon our inclosed lands of suitable dwellings for the working classes at such moderate rents as to come within their means'.[75] As the Tories had predicted, the new housing did not lead to the abandonment of the slums. They were quickly occupied by migrants seeking work in Nottingham, among them lace workers and skilled artisans, clerks, agents and travellers employed in the textile trades. On Ortzen Street, one of the areas developed following the land sales of 1849, 44.5 per cent of occupiers who were in work in 1861 had jobs in the lace trade, and only 6.2 per cent of household heads were in the hosiery industry. By contrast, cotton workers from the Mansfield area, and the Leen and Derwent valleys, all areas where the industry was in decline by the 1840s, together with agricultural workers from Lincolnshire and Northamptonshire and textile workers from the Coventry area, flocked to the town, often to the poorest housing.[76] The result was an imbalance in the housing market with a mismatch between the conditions of supply and demand, which meant that much of the old and insanitary stock was still in great demand, particularly from an ageing population, from the poorest members of the work-force, and from single people, many of them living in lodging houses.

Improvement

To complicate the enclosure issue further, the 1845 legislation had effectively created two towns: the new town, growing up on the fields with by-law housing and regulation roads, under the control of three (part-time) enclosure commissioners; and the old town, unregulated and unimproved, and still the responsibility of the corporation. The corporation was well aware of its responsibility for the old town, and in 1846 it established a Sanitary Committee, partly with the intention of enforcing the Nuisances Removal Act in the town. 'Nuisances' in this context included undrained and unpaved streets, open manure pits, pigsties, slaughterhouses, and other offensive intrusions. Between 1849 and 1852 the Sanitary Committee was responsible for removing sixty-three houses or groups of houses which had been built over privies, the reconstruction of seventy-three sets of privies, and the building of another thirty-seven sets. Many of the enclosed courts were paved and drained, public lavatories were built, and unhealthy buildings were cleaned and whitewashed. As a result, the committee claimed the credit when Nottingham was virtually untouched by the 1848–49 nationwide cholera epidemic. The constant and plentiful supply of fresh water in the town and the well-drained streets and courts were held to be responsible.[77] On the other hand the committee lacked positive powers: its mandate was to clear up the existing mess, not to take measures designed to prevent it from recurring. However, satisfied that the committee was making adequate progress, the corporation decided it had no need to adopt the 1848 Public Health Act, the first piece of national legislation to pay serious attention to urban environmental conditions. It did, however, adopt the 1851 Common Lodging Houses Act, and passed the regulation of boarding houses to the Sanitary Committee. Despite the upbeat tone of the committee's work, progress was slow. In 1852 the town was threatened with a Board of Health enquiry because the death rate had reached 26 per 1,000. The town clerk objected that these figures had been inflated by wandering paupers and Irish immigrants, and the corporation produced a long report on action taken in the town since 1846.[78]

Although the enquiry was headed off, the threat served to reinvigorate demands for an improvement measure for the old town on the grounds that the Sanitary Committee was not making sufficiently rapid progress. In its report of 1854 the committee listed its achievements, but they make depressing reading. Nineteen cases had been successfully dealt with in which leakages from privies or cesspools had gone into adjacent houses. In eighteen cases 'the construction of privies has been amended', while in a further eleven cases 'swine kept in confined situations and which had been complained of as being a nuisance have been removed'. In addition, twenty-six sets of 'offensive privies (many of them situated under rooms) have been converted into water-closets'. Finally:

> Crosland-court, leading from Red Lion street to Leen-side, has been materially improved by taking down part of a dwelling-house at one end, so as to make the communication nearly the full width of the court, instead of a covered entrance as before. Similar alterations are imperative in order to secure health in many other courts in this town.

This was doing little more than scratch the surface, as was clear when a year later the Sanitary Committee reported an outbreak of cholera in Foundry Yard off Red Lion Street in the Narrow Marsh. Property was demolished 'to allow air to circulate' – still at this date the common response to cholera which was assumed, incorrectly, to be spread by poor-quality air.[79] Hard though it undoubtedly tried, the Sanitary Committee was not winning the battle. Its 1859 report noted how the method of removing night soil was 'of the most defective character; the carts employed are not properly constructed for the purpose, and are often in so bad a state as to allow the liquid contents to flow into the public streets. The ashpits are seldom thoroughly emptied, and considerable quantities of offensive matters accumulate in them for a longer period.'[80] No one could any longer really doubt that the Whigs had been mistaken when in 1845 they had believed that the enclosure legislation was all Nottingham needed to cure its ills. The Tories, still convinced that an improvement measure was needed, brought forward plans for an Improvement Bill in 1854 and 1857. Both schemes were defeated in the council chamber.

In 1858 the government passed public health legislation, which the corporation agreed on 28 February 1859 to adopt. The 1858 Public Health Act offered the corporation extensive powers of self-government. Three new committees were established: for highways, for town improvements, and for markets and fairs, with the corporation becoming a Board of Health. A borough engineer had to be appointed, and the position went to Marriott Ogle Tarbotton (1834–87), whose first task was to prepare a report on the sanitary condition of Nottingham. What he found made uncomfortable reading for the enclosure commissioners and the corporation alike. In the Meadows, still the responsibility of the commissioners, Tarbotton found that numerous houses had been built which were 'not raised above the ordinary level of the ground and are consequently on the level at which the sewers must be laid, and are liable to be flooded and rendered permanently damp'. In the old town, Tarbotton could hardly conceal his astonishment when he found that the corporation possessed no accurate plans of its sewage disposal facilities. He set about preparing plans as a matter of urgency.[81] Neither corporation nor enclosure commissioners emerged with much credit from these initial investigations.

Tarbotton had no intention of wasting time. He took urgent practical action, including culverting the River Leen to make it flow into the canal, and he set about the task of widening and improving some of the more notorious streets in the town. Property was compulsorily acquired and then demolished in Sheep Lane, which was widened to become Market Street. At the same time Victoria Street was cut to relieve the strain on Bottle Lane.[82] Critically, Tarbotton needed to bring together the corporation and the enclosure commissioners to reach an agreement on responsibility for the new town which would permit the enclosure award to be completed. As borough engineer he could represent the corporation, but he also needed support from the commissioners, and this came when he was appointed in 1861 – in practice if not in theory – to the position of referee. The position itself involved checking new buildings in the town, but the symbolic importance was in enabling him to bring the corporation and the commissioners together. In June 1865 the commissioners finally completed the enclosure award. Long before then the effective legality of allotments made since 1851 had been accepted, and the award made few ripples in the town. Tarbotton still had work to do: in 1866 he brought together the corporation and the enclosure commissioners to begin talks on a compromise over issues outstanding between them since the 1850s, particularly the road network between old and new towns. In September 1866 agreement was reached to apply for an Improvement Act which would transfer powers still being exercised by the commissioners to the corporation's Highways Committee which would, in turn, take responsibility for completing the new roads and sewers, and for clearing a debt of £6,500 incurred by the commissioners.[83] The legislation passed in the spring of 1867, and for the first time the problems of old and new Nottingham could be considered as a whole rather than as two competing sets of interests under the control of two different bodies.[84]

The impact of enclosure

Altogether it was twenty-two years from the passing of the Enclosure Act until the commissioners finally laid down their office. Although the division of responsibility between old and new Nottingham over that period had created difficulties in regard to the relationship between old town and new, it had done little to slow down the pace of change in the town. With land being released for development long before the enclosure award was completed it was not only houses which were built. The Sanitary Committee reported in January 1857 that apart from 2,101 new houses erected since 1851, seventy-four factories and forty-one warehouses had been built. Nor was this surprising, since the availability of land coincided with mechanisation in the hosiery industry, and a move towards centralising warehousing in the lace industry. Wylie produced a long list of the factories and warehouses erected in the course of 1852, concluding with the comment that 'many other similar establishments are in contemplation'. Such was the prosperity that there was a 'scarcity of hands in almost every branch of business'. And when Samuel Collinson took a walk to Trent Bridge in July 1859 he looked over his shoulder to see 'the smoke from all the factory chimneys [rise] straight up to a considerable height and then gently inclined towards the town. Old Nottingham was thoroughly enveloped in a black pall of smoke.'[85]

Responses to the work of the enclosure commissioners varied. Alderman Robert Mellors was one of the more forthright critics:

> We complained of the narrow streets set out, of the winding streets, involving houses being built with zig-zag fronts, and of there not being reserved sufficient land to pay for paving the streets, and so rates had to be made on allottees. A grand opportunity was lost, as the Town might have been made a model one, with squares, boulevards, and open spaces.[86]

Without doubt there were reasons to criticise the enclosure proceedings, over the length of time taken to move from act to award, over the unfinished state of many of the streets, particularly in the meadows area, and over the lack of movement out of the slums. Yet other contemporaries saw the end result rather differently. 'The old town was clearly indebted to the new town for its vitality', one of the councillors was reported as saying during the debates of September 1866, 'but for the enclosure where would Nottingham be at the present time … it would have cut a very sorry figure throughout the country'.[87] This upbeat tone was echoed in the words of Wylie and Potter Briscoe, writing in 1893:

> the commissioners … proceeded to set out public and private roads to the extent of more than eighteen miles in length, Factories, warehouses, and residences sprang up all around, as if by the wave of a magician's wand. Land and building societies were formed, by means of which persons of limited means have been able to purchase small allotments at a moderate price and to build upon them on the most favourable terms. The transformation wrought upon the town as to its extent and aspect

surpasses anything which has been witnessed elsewhere in Britain within the same brief space of time.[88]

By the time the enclosure commissioners laid down their office other areas of Nottingham were also changing, notably the area around St Mary's church, known today as the Lace Market. In this area large mansions with gardens survived into the 1830s, and a few elegant residences with street frontages are shown on Dearden's 1844 map. In 1799 only one of Nottingham's six lace manufacturers lived in the area, but the outward movement of the middle classes in the early nineteenth century brought change. By 1832 there were 186 lace manufacturers in Nottingham, of whom sixty-six had addresses on St Mary's Gate, High Pavement, and Stoney Street. In the early 1840s the *Nottingham Journal* reported that the town had two groups of lace warehouses, the older being centred on Houndsgate and the newer on St Mary's Gate. The movement from the older to the newer area was rapid; within a few years the same newspaper was of the opinion that 'Mary Gate is the seat of the Lace Market'.[89] The concept of a 'Lace Market' area, roughly within the bounds of the old Saxon town, was further strengthened when in February 1853 Richard Birkin bought Plumptre House and grounds for £8,410. Birkin had come to New Basford during the twist net fever of the 1820s, and he now engaged T.C. Hine to exploit the site. Over the next two years Hine cut a new street, Broadway, through the grounds linking Stoney Street with St Mary's Gate. In this new street he erected a suite of warehouses for the Birkin family. Hine was also the architect of the fine new premises for Adams & Page, later Thomas Adams & Co., close by on Stoney Street, which opened in July 1855. These buildings, which contained many innovative facilities for the work-force, began a new generation of warehouses for the town. Commensurately the number of people living in the area began to decline. In 1841 many of the buildings were still residences, with 223 people living in the thirty-eight houses on High Pavement. By 1881 there were few people living on High Pavement or the adjoining streets, and by 1914 there were 158 buildings in the area, occupied by 346 firms, mostly in the lace trade.[90]

Another area of the town which was also changing was the Park. The fourth Duke of Newcastle made three unsuccessful attempts to develop the 'people's park' as a means of 'supplying his exhausted treasury', in 1822, 1827–31 (a phase abruptly terminated when the Castle was burnt in the Reform Bill riots), and *c.*1837–39 when he divided up the land into building plots.[91] He died in 1850 and it was left to his son, the fifth duke, to plan and execute a development plan. As in the Lace Market, the scheme was masterminded by T. C. Hine, who was appointed surveyor of the estates on 14 January 1854. Hine produced a geometrical layout based on two linked, tree-lined circuses, named Newcastle and Lincoln after the family's aristocratic titles. The first houses were under construction by 1856, after extensive roadworks were undertaken. From the outset it was intended as an exclusive housing estate for a wealthy middle-class elite. Textile manufacturers constituted the majority of householders, followed by professional men including lawyers, clergymen, architects and bank managers (but few doctors because the house leases forbade them from practising), and wholesalers and retailers. Between one-quarter and one-third of householders had unearned incomes, and the genteel prosperity of the area was reflected in the number of servants. Residents were tied to a strict code of behaviour and activities. By 1887 Hine's plan was virtually complete with around 600 houses on the site. A bowling green and tennis courts were part of the plan, but no other facilities – including a church planned in the initial stages – were included. The Park estate became a garden suburb *par excellence* for the upper middle classes, the Nottingham address of achievement. It was one of several such 'west end' developments attempted by landlords in growing Victorian towns, and its small size and configuration, together with its ideal situation to the west of the town centre, helped to make it the most successful enterprise of its kind.[92]

Between the cholera outbreak of 1832 and the passing in 1867 of Nottingham's first Improvement Act, the physical form and shape of the town changed dramatically. For this the 1845 Enclosure Act, and the ensuing reorganisation of the town, were largely responsible, but it was by no means a straightforward picture of change for the better. The 1830s and 1840s were difficult decades with high levels of unemployment, poverty, and little attention being paid (at least until towards the end of the 1840s) to the town's environmental problems. Economic difficulties, in particular, did not necessarily go permanently away. In April 1848 1,600 people were packed into the workhouse, furniture was being pawned, and children were absent from school because they had no clothes to wear. The vicar of St Mary's proposed setting up a permanent soup kitchen. Distress was said to be 'prevalent to a frightful extent among persons heretofore in a higher class, who are ashamed to apply for relief and are almost, if not altogether, in a state of starvation'.[93] Such years were fewer and farther between, although in 1857 8,000 unemployed people demonstrated in the town, applicants to the workhouse were set to work labouring on the Forest, and soup kitchens were opened in the winter. There were bad winters in 1860–61 and 1862–63, when soup kitchens were opened, and an Emigration Society was formed. Two thousand framework knitters applied to the workhouse in the closing months of 1864.[94]

Yet these problems took place against a background in which a new town was created. Although it turned out to be less perfect than some of its designers had intended the long-term impact was enormous, particularly after the tribulations of the 1830s and 1840s. Nor was change simply physical: attitudes were also changing. In Victorian towns the 1830s and 1840s were the decades of the shopkeepers. The mayor of Nottingham in 1833 was a retail tobacconist, and four of the six aldermen had retail businesses in the town.[95] By the 1850s and 1860s manufacturers were taking a more active and confident role in urban political and cultural activity, and this change was as clear in Nottingham as elsewhere. By the early 1850s four of the fourteen aldermen were hosiers, while seven were lace manufacturers. In the course of the 1850s and 1860s two of Nottingham's most prominent public figures were lace manufacturers, Richard Birkin (mayor in 1850, 1855, 1862 and 1863) and William Felkin (mayor 1851 and 1852). Birkin led the Improvement Committee, and Felkin chaired the Sanitary Committee, and both were examples of the kind of men who began to seek election to councils up and down the country in the post-1835 period. Another of the 1850s mayors was Lewis Heymann (1857), the town's first foreign mayor, and one of several wealthy Jewish merchants and manufacturers who worshipped with the Unitarians. The corporation's Finance Committee, established in 1860, included some of the town's leading lace and hosiery manufacturers.[96] Dissenting and business interests brought to civic government a fusion of business sense and religious ethics which provided some of the practical driving force behind civic progress.

Working out what civic progress amounted to took time, but much of the credit for moving the corporation in a forward direction lay both with its employees, men like Hawksley and Tarbotton, and the architect T. C. Hine. Moses Wood, the borough surveyor, criticised the penny-pinching attitude adopted by the corporation in relation to the Exchange,[97] and Hine used the occasion of the opening of the Adams & Page warehouse in 1855 to attack the shabbiness of the town's municipal buildings,

Plate 29 **T.C. Hine's proposals for the market-place, 1857**. The Town Improvement Committee invited Hine to submit designs for an improvement for the market-place and a new town hall. In his design, shown here, in front of a new Exchange in the manner of a French château, he proposed 'the lowering of the central portion of the Market Place to a sufficient depth to allow an arcade for provision shows and extending underneath the surrounding roadways, a large fountain in the centre and balustrade parapets and steps after the manner of those around Trafalgar Square in London'

particularly the Exchange, which he considered a disgrace. This was apt timing: Birmingham had acquired a site for a new Council House in 1853, and Leeds was currently building its great new town hall. Hine was invited to submit plans in 1857, and he proposed a new Exchange in the style of a French château and a redesigned market-place with a sunken quadrangle lined by a series of arched covered stalls. It was a magnificent scheme, but Hine was ahead of his time.[98] The politicians lacked the confidence to redesign Nottingham in such a grand way, and the scheme was shelved. New Nottingham had not yet developed the civic pride of its northern industrial neighbours.

Notes

1 *Royal Commission into the State of Large Towns and Populous Districts*, 2nd Report, part II appendix, PP 610 (XVII), p. 250.
2 *RBN*, IX, p. 89, 15 March 1852; *NR*, 24 June 1853.
3 *RBN*, VII, p. 175.
4 Blackner, p. 280; Bailey, *Annals*, IV, p. 287.
5 NAO DD 808/1 Diary of John Rainbow, governor of the House of Correction, 1813–36.
6 Iliffe and Baguley, 19, p. 55.
7 William Stretton, *The Stretton Manuscripts* (1910), p. 168; Blackner, p. 59; NAO DD 808/1; *Nottingham Mercury*, 23 August 1826; *A Report of the Evidence given before the Commissioners appointed to enquire into Municipal Corporations* (Nottingham, 1833), pp. 37–41.
8 The Tories, anxious to let the people of Nottingham know what the Whig Corporation had been up to, sent a reporter to take down the proceedings verbatim. These were published as *Report … into Municipal Corporations*. The report provides a detailed study of the structure and operation of the old corporation.
9 *Royal Commission on the Municipal Corporations*, PP (XXV) 1835: Reports from Commissioners, appendix to 1st Report, part 3, pp. 2006–7; *Report … into Municipal Corporations*, p. 6.
10 Gray, *500 Years*, p. 81; Church, p. 176.
11 Gray, *500 Years*, p. 83.
12 Iliffe and Baguley, 19, pp. 5–16; Church, p. 177.
13 NAO M.383 Diary of Samuel Collinson; M. 23,788, Journal of George Hodgkinson Harwood. There was a further public execution in 1864 when Sutton's barricades were re-erected. The last execution in the town, inside the Shire Hall, was in 1877.
14 *RBN*, IX, p. 50; Iliffe and Baguley, 19, p. 65–68.
15 Church, pp. 180–1; *RBN*, IX, p. 106; F. I. Straw, 'An analysis of the town plan of Nottingham: a study in historical geography' (University of Nottingham, MA thesis, 1967), pp. 146–7, 162–8.
16 W. Felkin, *History of the Machine-Wrought Hosiery and Lace Manufactures* (1867), pp. 380, 341–2, 437, 463, 467; S. D. Chapman, 'William Felkin, 1795–1874' (University of Nottingham, MA thesis, 1960), p. 256; *NR*, 4 June 1858, 16 April 1844.
17 *NR*, 8 August 1833; *NJ*, 12 December 1833.
18 *Commons Journals*, XCI (1836), p. 106; *RBN*, VIII, p. 407.
19 *NJ*, 5 February 1836; RBN, IX, p. 2.
20 *NR*, 21, 28 October 1836; *Nottingham and Newark Mercury*, 29 October 1836, p. 348; *RBN*, IX, p. 4.
21 *RBN*, IX, pp. 4, 7.
22 *Report … Municipal Corporations* pp. 157–67.
23 *RBN*, IX, pp. 21–2; 2 & 3 Victoria, caps. 28, 32; H. S. Cropper, *The Freemen of Nottingham and their Estates* (Nottingham, 1880), pp. 57–60.
24 *NJ*, 31 May 1839; C. R. Clinker (ed.), *The Midland Counties Railway* (1989).

25 J. R. Kellett, *The Impact of Railways on Victorian Cities* (1969), chapters X-XII.

26 NUMD William Parsons' Diaries, 6 February 1851; K. Brand, 'The Park Estate, Nottingham: the development of a nineteenth century fashionable suburb', *TTS*, 88 (1984), pp. 65–8; Straw, 'Town Plan', p. 186.

27 S. Glover, *History and Directory of the Town and County of Nottingham* (Nottingham, 1844), p. 10; Church, p. 179; *NJ*, 13, 20 December 1839; *Nottingham Mercury*, 13 December 1839.

28 *RBN*, IX, pp. 24–5; Chapman, 'William Felkin', p. 243.

29 *RBN*, IX, p. 23.

30 *RBN*, IX, pp. 23, 25, 37; *NJ*, 27 December 1839; Orange, II, pp. 951–2.

31 *RBN*, IX, p. 37; Glover, *Directory*, p. 10.

32 *NR*, 12 May 1837; PRO MH12/9444, Absolem Barnett to the Poor Law Commissioners, 15 July 1837.

33 T. H. Smith, *Hints to the Churchwardens, Overseers and Rate Payers of St Mary's Parish, Nottingham* (Nottingham, 1834), p. 13.

34 *NR*, 8 September 1837.

35 W. Felkin, 'Statistics of the labouring classes and paupers in Nottingham', *Journal of the Statistical Society*, II (1839), pp. 457–9.

36 PRO MH12/9445, Barnett to the Poor Law Commissioners, 6 November 1839, Edward Senior to the same, 21 November 1839.

37 PRO MH12/9445, report by Edward Senior, 10 December 1839; *NR*, 13 October 1839.

38 *NJ*, 13 December 1839; PRO MH12/9445, Barnett to the Poor Law Commissioners, 3 December 1839; *NR*, 29 November 1839.

39 *NR*, 13 December 1839; NAO M.23,868, p. 18.

40 *NR*, 26 November, 3, 10 December 1841.

41 *BRN*, IX, p. 29; *Nottingham Mercury*, 6 May 1842.

42 *NR*, 6 September 1844; Chapman, 'William Felkin', pp. 251–2.

43 *NR*, 9, 16 July, 13 August 1841.

44 *NR*, 13 June 1845.

45 E. Chadwick, *Report on the Sanitary Condition of the Labouring Population of Great Britain* (1842), ed. M. W. Flinn (1965), p. 193. Chadwick quoted Absolem Barnett, whose original evidence was given at slightly greater length in the *Local Reports on the Sanitary Condition of the Labouring Population of England* (1842), p. 155, on which Chadwick drew heavily.

46 Hawksley's evidence is in the appendix to the *First Report of the Commissioners of Inquiry into the State of Large Towns and Populous Districts*: PP 572 (XVII), pp. 130–48.

47 *Royal Commission … State of Large Towns and Populous Districts*, pp. 249–57.

48 *NR*, 6 September 1844.

49 *Report … into Municipal Corporations*, pp. 157–67.

50 *Royal Commission … State of Large Towns and Populous Districts*, p. 254.

51 *NR*, 6 September 1844.

52 *NR*, 28 February 1845; *Report from the Select Committee on Commons' Inclosure* 1844, PP 583 (V) pp. 223–4.

53 *NJ*, 15, 22 November 1844; *NR*, 15, 22, 29 November 1844.

54 *Royal Commission … State of Large Towns and Populous Districts*, p. 145.

55 *NR*, 22 November 1844; NAO CA 3604, fos. 21–2.

56 NAO CA 3604 f. 60; *NR*, 21 February 1845.

57 *NR*, 21, 28 February, 7 March 1845; *RBN*, IX, p. 44 and note; NAO CA 3601, f.85. The burgesses also conducted a pamphlet war in the town: NUMD *A New Song, entitled No inclosure! Or, the Twelfth of August* (n.d.); Ann Taylor, *Original Poems* (London, 1905), cited in E. Bryson, *'Owd Yer Tight* (Nottingham, 1967), p. 18.

58 *RBN*, IX, p. 42; *Commons Journals*, 100 (1845), pp. 77, 122, 131, 183, 191, 195, 234, 261, 272, 319, 324, 386, 409, 553, 654; *Lords Journal*, 77 (1845), p. 273.

59 8 & 9 Victoria, cap. 7, session 1845: *An Act for Inclosing Lands in the Parish of St Mary, in the Town and County of the Town of Nottingham*. For an account of the implementation of the Act: J. V. Beck-

ett and K. Brand, 'Enclosure, improvement and the rise of "New Nottingham" 1845–67', *TTS*, 98 (1994), pp. 92–111.

60 *NR*, 28 August 1846.

61 *Royal Commission ... State of Large Towns and Populous Districts*, p. 145.

62 *NJ*, 15 November 1844.

63 *NJ*, 28 February 1845.

64 *NJ*, 28 February 1845, 22 July 1853; *Nottingham Mercury*, 14 May 1852.

65 Nottingham Enclosure Act (1845), clauses 53–4; H. Conway, *People's Parks: the Design and Development of Victorian Parks in Britain* (Cambridge, 1991), p. 40; *Royal Commission ... State of Large Towns and Populous Districts*, p. 133.

66 *RBN*, IX, pp. 42–3, 85, 93; *NR*, 22 May 1852; Enclosure Act, clause 53.

67 *RBN*, IX, pp. 85, 93; NAO M.23,868, f. 16.

68 *NR*, 22 May 1852; Iliffe and Baguley, *Edwardian Nottingham*, 3, pp. 31–2.

69 *RBN*, IX, pp. 45, 48, 50; NAO CA 7751; *Date Book*, p. 475.

70 Orange, II, p. 913; R. A. Church, 'James Orange and the allotment system in Nottingham', *TTS*, 64 (1960), pp. 74–80; R. Smith and D. Shaw, *The Changing Character of Inner Nottingham 1800–1983* (Nottingham, 1983), pp. 11–25.

71 *NR*, 14 May 1852; *NJ*, 23 November 1855, 18 September 1857; Beckett and Brand, 'Enclosure'.

72 R. M. Donbavand, 'The social geography of Victorian Nottingham, 1851–1871' (University of Nottingham, Ph.D. thesis, 1982), table 2.1; Church p. 229.

73 S. D. Chapman, 'Working-class housing in Nottingham during the Industrial Revolution', *TTS*, 67 (1963), p. 89, argues that 845 out of 2,100 houses built on the open fields 1851–56 rented for 3*s* 6*d* a week or less. L. F. Wilson, 'The State and the housing of the English working class with special reference to Nottingham, 1845–1914' (University of California, Berkeley, Ph.D. thesis, 1970), pp. 93–4 puts the figure for houses renting at 3*s* a week or less at 4 per cent.

74 *NJ*, 8 October 1852; Chapman, 'Working class housing', p. 91; Wylie, p. 373; *RBN*, IX, p. 89.

75 *NJ*, 5 December 1856; R. Smith, 'Towards the mature industrial city 1800–1880: the development of All Saints Parish, Nottingham', *Midland History*, XIV (1989), pp. 75–94.

76 S. M. Maude, 'Population, mobility and urban growth: a study of migration in the nineteenth century with particular reference to Nottingham' (University of Nottingham, M.Phil. thesis, 1974), pp. 38–9, 154–5, 161, 171, 173–5, 216, 270, 322–8, 332; Church, pp. 232–5.

77 *NJ*, 5 October 1849, 14 November 1851; *RBN*, IX, pp. 71–7.

78 N. A. Ferguson, 'Working class housing in Bristol and Nottingham 1868–1919' (University of Oregon, Ph.D. thesis, 1971), p. 51; *RBN*, IX, pp. 89–92.

79 *Report of the Sanitary Committee of the Town of Nottingham Presented to the Council November 1854* (Nottingham, 1854); *RBN*, IX, p. 106. Ironically, it was in 1854–55 that the significance of water for the spread of the disease was first conclusively shown. By the time cholera broke out again in 1871 the corporation was mainly concerned with ensuring that the water supply was regularly checked to make sure it was not contaminated; *RBN*, IX, p. 215.

80 P. J. Hammond, 'The collection and disposal of Nottingham's night-soil', *NH*, 34 (1985), pp. 14–15.

81 *RBN*, IX, pp. 75, 134, 141, 148–9; M. O. Tarbotton, 'Recent sanitary operations and town improvements', *Allen's Illustrated Hand-Book of Nottingham* (Nottingham, 1866), pp. 81–95.

82 *RBN*, IX, p. 161, 164, 166, 170, 173.

83 *RBN*, IX, pp. 177–80; *NJ*, 28 September 1866; *NR*, 28 September 1866.

84 30 & 31 Victoria, sess. 1867; NAO CA 7732. A longer account of the tortuous negotiations which were finally completed in 1867 can be found in Beckett and Brand, 'Enclosure'.

85 *RBN*, IX, p. 118; Wylie, pp. 319–20; NAO M.382; Church, pp. 228–9.

86 R. Mellors, *In and About Nottinghamshire* (1890), p. 260.

87 *NJ*, 28 June 1866.

88 W. H. Wylie and J. Potter Briscoe, *A Popular History of Nottingham* (Nottingham, 1893), p. 117. The tendency among historians to adopt the downbeat Mellors line is discussed in Beckett and Brand, 'Enclosure'.

89 *NJ*, 14 July 1843, 18 June 1847; D. Lowe and J. Richards, *The City of Lace* (1982), *p. 27.*

90 *NR*, 13 July 1855; *S. A. Mason, Nottingham Lace, 1760s-1950s* (Ilkeston, 1994), pp. 132–5; G. Oldfield, 'The Nottingham Lace Market', *Textile History*, XV (1984), pp. 191–208; G. Oldfield, *The Lace Market, Nottingham* (Nottingham, Civic Society, n.d.).

91 *NR*, 14 June 1844.

92 K. C. Edwards, 'The Park Estate, Nottingham', in M. A. Simpson and T. H. Lloyd (eds.), *Middle-Class Housing in Britain* (Newton Abbot, 1977), pp. 54–75; L. Russenberger, 'The Villa Estate in nineteenth century England' (University of Chicago, Ph.D. thesis, 1988), ch. 4; Brand 'The Park Estate'; D. Cannadine, *Lords and Landlords: the Aristocracy and the Towns, 1770–1967* (Leicester, 1980), p. 406; Anne Bosworth, 'Aspects of middle class life: the Park Estate, Nottingham, 1841–1881', *Journal of Regional and Local Studies*, 5 (1985), pp. 28–42.

93 *NR*, 21 April 1848; Church, pp. 146–51.

94 *Outdoor Relief and the Labour Test* (1861); Church, pp. 154–5.

95 *Report … into Municipal Corporations*, p. 33.

96 Church, pp. 207–8. During the years 1860–69 the mayoralty was held by men described as lace manufacturers on five occasions.

97 NAO M.23,868 f. 12.

98 A. Briggs, *Victorian Cities* (Harmondsworth, 1968), pp. 158ff., 232; K. Brand, *Thomas Chambers Hine, 1813–99* (Nottingham, n.d.), pp. 12–13.

12

GREATER NOTTINGHAM AND THE CITY CHARTER

John Beckett and Geoffrey Oldfield

Between the Municipal Corporations Act of 1835 and the first Improvement Act of 1867, Nottingham had been groping uncertainly towards a more regulated urban environment and a civic consciousness. The environmental issues had been addressed in the enclosure act, in the formation of a Sanitary Committee, and in the practical work of Tarbotton. These were largely self-help measures, and the improvement legislation passed between 1867 and 1879 was not fundamentally different. Increasingly, greater uniformity of practice was imposed on local authorities through the establishment in 1871 of the Local Government Board – the most decisive in a series of steps from permissive legislation to central compulsion – while the 1872 Public Health Act created a coherent framework for Urban and Rural Sanitary Districts under the authority of the Board. Further public health legislation in 1872 and 1875 helped to develop a code of urban administration and recognised the need for a consistent system of local government to replace the *ad hoc* areas which had evolved over the previous forty years. This trend was extended in the local government acts of 1888 and 1894. Within the context of government prompting, individual towns struggled in the direction of a civic consciousness, characterised by increasing investment in sanitation, the taking-over of public utilities such as gas, water and the tramways, and the demolition of unhealthy property to improve public health and ease congestion on the streets. Nottingham corporation pursued each of these objectives, albeit with greater enthusiasm and financial support for some than for others. The results were positive. By 1871 the *Tourist's Picturesque Guide to Nottingham* welcomed travellers to the 'Queen of the Midland Counties'.[1] Civic improvements and industrial change propelled the town onwards, through borough extension in 1877 to a City Charter in 1897. This upbeat tone provides the background against which we can consider the physical growth of Nottingham in the last third of the nineteenth century, the reasons for growth, and the contradictions which remained.

Some idea of the appearance of Nottingham in the 1860s can be gathered from Edward Salmon's map of 1861, even if he occasionally shows buildings not as they actually were, but as architects had designed them. The 1850s had seen rapid change, with population increasing by 17,000, and a 43 per cent increase in the housing stock as nearly 8,000 dwellings were built on newly enclosed land. Salmon's map shows the result. Large areas of the Clay and Sand Fields were already well covered by houses, while to the south of the old town houses were going up in the West Croft, and in the Meadows area adjacent to Kirke White Street. During the 1860s the population rose by 12,000 and the housing stock by a further 10 per cent. More than 900 poor-quality houses in the old town were demolished between 1851 and 1871, although this still left a stock of 10,500.[2]

These gross figures tell us nothing about the division of social space in the town, but the divorce between the middle and working classes was reinforced by the way in which housing on the newly available land was in practice, if not in theory, separated roughly into middle- and working-class areas. The Sand Field, on rising ground to the north-west of the town, developed into a residential middle-class suburb. By 1901 7,944 people lived in 1,750 dwellings in the parish of All Saints. The corporation also encouraged schools and other institutions to move into this area, including the Boys' and Girls' High Schools.[3] By contrast, the heavier, damper soils of the Clay Field between Mansfield Road and St Ann's Well Road became an area of predominantly working-class housing. To the south the Meadows, periodically subject to flooding, soon gained a reputation for its inadequate housing. George Harwood, passing through the area in December 1860, noted that in one field 'entirely immersed' due to flooding there was a board announcing 'this eligible building land to be sold'.[4] Tarbotton attempted to counter the problem of flooding in the Meadows as part of his new Trent Bridge scheme in 1872, but he was not successful and a resolution of the problem was found only in the twentieth century. In the meantime, developers built houses which were inevitably subject to flooding and the Sanitary Committee complained in 1860 that more than 500 houses were 'quite destitute of drainage'.[5]

The Improvement Acts of 1867 and 1874

Problems of this nature made it imperative for Nottingham to be governed by one authority, and this was the background to the 1867 Improvement Act. As the preamble to the legislation made clear, it was regarded as a direct outcome of the unfinished enclosure proceedings. To this end it was designed to tackle the problem of roads left 'uncompleted … in an inconvenient state unfit for traffic', and to sort out the unsecured debts run up by the enclosure commissioners. In the wake of the legislation the commissioners were finally released from their burdensome office, and the sewer system was rapidly completed in the public streets within the enclosed area.[6] The corporation, in its role since 1859 as a Board of Health, could at last turn its attention to improving the now united old and new towns, and there was little room for complacency. An outbreak of cholera in 1871–72 offered a reminder, if any was needed, that the sanitary problems of the old town were far from being resolved, whatever the claims of the Sanitary Committee since 1848. Consideration was given to seeking wide powers of compulsory purchase, control of street lighting, and additional powers for improving housing and sanitation.[7] In the event, it was the 1872 Public Health Act which fundamentally altered the situation. This legislation made local authorities compulsorily responsible for providing an adequate supply of clean water, and stipulated that the Urban Sanitary Authority – which Nottingham corporation now became – was obliged to appoint a Medical Officer of Health and an Inspector of Nuisances – a post the corporation had declined to fill in 1859. In February 1873 Dr Edward Seaton was appointed as Nottingham's first full-time Medical Officer of Health.

Seaton immediately sat down with Tarbotton to frame a report on sanitation and health conditions in Nottingham. Seaton, doubtless encouraged by the like-minded Tarbotton, was in no doubt that many of Nottingham's continuing problems originated in the Enclosure Act. Those who had framed the legislation, he argued, in their anxiety to avoid a repetition of the narrow courts of the old town, had 'rushed into the other extreme', imposing limitations on housing which 'have proved serious obstacles to the natural growth of the town'. More significantly, the Act had not achieved all that had been hoped. While the town was generally 'well off' for sewers, 'a considerable number of streets still remain unsewered', and in 200 low-lying houses built below the flood plain in the Meadows the basements 'become actually filled with drainage' when the Trent overflowed its banks in winter. In the old town few houses had water-closets. Seaton condemned the privies and ashpits 'which, from structural defects, have become loathsome nuisances, prejudicial to the health not only of the men employed to empty them, but of the inhabitants of the neighbourhood'. Of the slum houses he had examined:

> nearly half had staircases so narrow, dark, and tortuous that it would be physically impossible to admit the upward or downward passage of air in any material quantity. Rooms, intolerably close and hot … [with] walls which were crumbling away, and everywhere infected by vermin … every hole that vermin had made … afforded a lurking-place for fevers and poisons.[8]

There was much more to it than this, but the overall tone reflected the problems which were known at least as early as the 1830s. Now, nearly thirty years after the Enclosure Act, the need for a comprehensive improvement measure – first advocated unsuccessfully by the Tory opposition in 1844 – had never been more pressing. In October 1873 the Improvement Committee recommended 'that it was imperative for the well being of the Town that Parliamentary powers should be obtained in aid of the ordinary legislation of the Country for the general improvement of the Borough', leaving the full council with little alternative but to order the preparation of an improvement bill. The vote was 35 to 3 in favour. Extensive consultation took place in the town as to the content of the proposed legislation: more than forty meetings of the council and its various committees were held to discuss the various clauses. The bill was then 'thoroughly made known to the inhabitants of the borough ... both in committee and in the press the clauses have undergone the most complete discussion'. The Nottingham Improvement Act became law on 7 August 1874.[9]

In print, the Act ran to seventy pages and covered a multitude of town affairs including burial grounds, markets and fairs, libraries, bathing places, corporation finance and building regulations. The corporation assumed the powers and duties of the Town Lighting Committee, and obtained powers to buy land for a new Guildhall. As one newspaper was later to recall: 'almost everything that was needed for improving the entire management of the borough was included in its provisions'.[10] Yet for most people the critical clauses concerned sanitary arrangements in the town. The powers of the corporation in regard to streets and sewers were now clearly set out. The official flood level of the Trent was to be raised to a level determined by the corporation, and no buildings were to be permitted below that level. The corporation obtained powers to enforce building regulations and to control the disposal of sewage and the collection of night soil, as well as powers to build artisans' dwellings.[11] Finally, the Act repealed the clauses relating to minimum house standards and sizes – a measure for which the Tories had argued as long ago as 1857, and which the Improvement Committee had called for in 1873 in the hope that cheaper-renting working-class homes would be built as a result.

As part of its efforts to improve the town, the corporation was also anxious to follow the examples set elsewhere, by acquiring the utilities. In towns up and down the country municipalisation of services was believed to be advantageous, and urban authorities took these over either to limit rate rises by reinvesting profits, or to subsidise the ratepayers by offering cheaper gas and water. Manchester and Leeds municipalised their gas in 1870: Nottingham corporation had been attempting to gain control of the Gas Company since the 1850s, and finally succeeded in 1874. Management was placed in Tarbotton's hands, and the municipal monopoly of selling gas in a rapidly expanding market gave the corporation an income which grew annually, and from which a major portion was placed in a reserve sinking fund.[12]

Ideally, the corporation wanted to control the water supply as well, partly because the Royal Commission on Sanitary Reform recommended in 1869 that water supplies should be removed from private into public hands. The Nottingham Waterworks Company had actively extended the water supply by building the Park works in 1850, the Bagthorpe works in 1857, and Bestwood Pumping Station in 1871. New reservoirs were built on St Ann's Hill in 1850, Mapperley Hill in 1857, Redhill in 1871 and Papplewick in 1880. The company refused voluntarily to part with its resources to the corporation, and the waterworks changed hands only as a result of a clause in the 1879 Improvement Act, which gave the corporation powers of compulsory purchase. These it chose to exercise on 25 March 1880. Almost immediately new works were started on Mapperley Plains and at Papplewick, where the pumping station, built in 1884, remains a local tourist attraction (although it ceased to supply

Nottingham with water in 1969). Sewage disposal was tackled with the opening of the Stoke Bardolph works in 1880, as part of a longer-term response to outbreaks of cholera in 1865 and typhoid in 1868. The 900-acre sewage farm, built with £150,000 borrowed from Public Works Loan Board, was impressive enough to attract foreign visitors. The profits derived from supplying water to the town, in excess of £10,000 per annum, were available to ease the rates and increase the reserves held by the corporation.[13]

Seaton and Tarbotton, working in tandem, were beginning by 1874 to come to terms with the town's most pressing problems. One of Tarbotton's greatest achievements was the new Trent Bridge. A replacement bridge had been under discussion for years, and plans were drawn up by Sir William Cubitt in 1853. The corporation shelved the scheme, probably because of the anticipated costs of £25,000–£35,000. In 1860 Tarbotton began pressing urgently for a new bridge to be built, and this was finally completed to his plans at a cost of £31,000, and opened in 1871, after which the old one was taken down.[14] The new Trent Bridge was doubled in width in 1926. Bridges at Wilford and Gunthorpe were opened in 1870 and 1875 respectively, greatly improving access to the town from the south.

The housing question

None of these changes had done much for the town's most pressing problem, the insanitary working-class housing, but here Seaton was aided by government intervention, particularly the public health legislation of 1875. The Artizans Dwelling Act was a recognition for the first time on the part of central government that due to the intense concentration of population in areas of British cities, living conditions were no longer tolerable. For the first time, the legislation offered local authorities the right to demolish property deemed to represent a health risk. They were also given powers to provide accommodation for the displaced in suitable dwellings within the same vicinity. This did not necessarily mean building; indeed, few urban authorities undertook rehousing programmes, partly because of ratepayer reluctance and partly because of debts run up acquiring utilities. When they did build little attempt was made to replace all the demolished stock, and often those displaced could not afford the rent for the new property. Usually it was sufficient for the local authority to be satisfied that there were enough houses available to be rented or to know that some other body or person was building new houses. Nottingham's City Engineer, Arthur Brown, noted of houses built on the Coppice Road by the Estates Committee *c.*1900 and let for rents of 6*s* 3*d* and 6*s* 9*d* weekly, that the Local Government Board had 'humorously decided' the properties were 'to re-house the poor who had to leave the back-to-back houses in the streets near the old gaol'. Such families could certainly not afford these rents.[15]

At the time, the 1875 Act appeared to offer Seaton the scope he needed for redeveloping the Nottingham slums. Under the terms of the Torrens Act of 1868, Seaton had regularly made recommendations to the Health Committee for the repair or demolition of property he considered unfit for habitation.[16] However, this legislation allowed only small-scale demolition, usually of individual houses rather than whole areas. Seaton's view was that such a piecemeal policy would never solve the town's problems. He calculated that 68 per cent of Nottingham's population lived in houses rated at £10 or less, 50 per cent in back-to-backs, and 25 per cent in houses which had been considered unfit for human habitation twenty years earlier.[17] The 1875 legislation offered the possibility of demolishing whole areas of insanitary housing, and within three months Seaton informed the corporation that he had identified an unhealthy area in the Broad Marsh affecting thirty-two properties in Darker's Lane and Darker's Court, 'the sanitary defects of the area not being capable of being effectually remedied otherwise than by an improvement scheme for the rearrangement and reconstruction of the houses within the said area'. The corporation agreed compulsorily to purchase the site, to demolish the older buildings, and to let or sell the land for commercial purposes. It also accepted the need to erect artisans' houses between Ortzen Street and Forest Road to accommodate those displaced.[18]

Having made his point with the Broad Marsh plan, Seaton initiated a second scheme on 12 October 1876 for an area in St Ann's Alley, near Glasshouse and Charlotte Streets. Once again the corporation agreed to purchase the property, to pull down the buildings and to sell the land at public auction or let it on long leases.[19] It was less easily persuaded of the need to build houses for those displaced. Alternative accommodation was already available on Waterloo Parade (adjoining the Forest), 'but hardly any of the working classes who were displaced are occupying the new houses'. Instead they went 'to other parts of the town', carrying with them 'their degraded habits' so that they soon helped to 'deteriorate the property in their new locality, crowding together in courts and alleys which are in a somewhat similar condition to those from which they were displaced'.[20] Despite such scepticism, an Industrial Dwellings Committee was established to consider building houses. The committee's original intention was to provide accommodation for council employees. A competition for the design was won by the local architects Bakewell & Bromley and, with a loan of £10,000, the building of Victoria Dwellings on Bath Street commenced in the second half of 1875. The name 'Victoria Dwellings' was agreed in November 1876, and in January 1877 it was decided that the apartments should be made available to any local working people, not just to council employees. Tenants willing to pay the rent were not easily found, particularly as the apartments turned out to be poorly constructed. In 1880 management was transferred to the Nottingham Town and Country Social Guild, founded in 1875. As far as the corporation was concerned this was an experiment that failed, and the position was not helped by a similarly unsuccessful scheme in Basford: Albert Buildings.[21] It took a quarter of a century for the corporation to recover from these experiences.

In 1878 Seaton looked back over his first five years in office with some satisfaction. 'By far the greater number of back-to-back houses are decently provided for in the matter of closet accommodation', he argued. In his 1879 report he went on to claim that a reduction in the number of typhoid fever cases was due to the fact that he followed up every case of enteric fever, and dealt with all reported nuisances under public health legislation.[22] Although it was taking time, Seaton was gradually unravelling the problems caused by unrestricted growth prior to 1830, and his success could be measured statistically, since the town's death rate fell from 26 per 1,000 in 1862, to 24.9 in 1871–75, and was steadily trending downwards. Yet there was no room for complacency. Lodgers and boarders represented nearly one-quarter of the population of Leenside at the end of the nineteenth century, and the vast majority of residents in this area were still operatives; it was a locality 'where drunkenness and depravity abounded, and where many children were running the streets in rags and dirt'.[23] In 1882 Seaton despaired of being able to do anything about the common lodging houses:

> Though we are obliged to permit their use, many of them, in Narrow Marsh especially, are of such faulty construction as to be unfit for the purpose. The erection of a few very inexpensively and plainly-built Common Lodging Houses, not too far away from where they are situate at present, would be of great benefit to the public health.[24]

The Borough Extension, 1877

By the time Seaton prepared his 1878 report, the terms of reference to which he was working had changed substantially, because in 1877 the Borough Extension Act brought the suburbs within the town boundaries to create Greater Nottingham. During the 1850s development on the former open fields quickly brought physical overlap between the town and its surrounding industrial suburbs. Already the 'villages' were rapidly growing into small towns: in 1851 Basford had a population of 10,093, Radford of 12,637, Sneinton of 8,440, and Lenton of 5,589 (table 10.2). As in Nottingham, the pace of growth had brought environmental problems. J. R. Martin, the assistant commissioner who reported on Nottingham in 1844, also visited Basford where he found 'numerous courts and alleys, closed at the end' in the newly built part of the village, and a sewer system 'of inferior arrangement and construction'.[25] Basford established a local board of health under the terms of the 1858 Public Health Act, but Radford was reluctant to take any such measures, and a Board was not formed until 1873. Under such circumstances death rates were high, and living conditions in some areas almost as bad as in Nottingham. However, the pace of growth slackened during the 1850s as developers turned their attention to the newly enclosed land; indeed, the value of building land in Sneinton reputedly fell from £1 to 1*s* a square yard.[26] Even so, by 1871 Radford, with a population of 15,127, was the second largest settlement in Nottinghamshire, larger even than Newark and Mansfield, and the five villages (including Bulwell: see table 10.1) had a combined population of 51,000. It was anomalous to have houses on either side of Alfreton Road in different parishes and under different administrative control, or to have streets running out of Nottingham into Sneinton divided for the purposes of local government. In 1861 Salmon suggested that Radford and Sneinton 'may be considered as suburbs of Nottingham'. With 51,000 people spread across 11,532 acres, compared to Nottingham where 87,390 people were confined within 1,933 acres, here was a conurbation simply waiting to be confirmed.

Locally it had long been recognised that, once the land surrounding Nottingham was opened up for development, the parishes of Radford, Lenton and Sneinton would soon be indistinguishable from the town. As one author commented in 1843, Hyson Green was 'separated from Nottingham by Lammas land, in which the burgesses of Nottingham have common right; should this privilege for any equivalent consideration ever be surrendered, and the intermediate land be made available for building, it is highly probable that Hyson Green would soon become united with Nottingham'.[27] As so often occurred in Victorian England, problems of water supply and sewage disposal proved to be the catalyst which brought town and suburbs together. The river Leen was a common sewer for Nottingham, Bulwell, Basford, Radford and Lenton. Joint action was needed to eradicate what was increasingly seen as an unacceptable hazard to health and prosperity. To try to achieve this, in 1872 the Nottingham and Leen District Sewerage Board was set up as a joint board with representatives of the town and the villages. The Board was not a success. It fell victim to petty territorial disputes, and by 1876 Nottingham corporation had decided that the most effective way to deal with the sewerage problems would be to promote a boundary extension. A single authority, or so it was argued, would not have to face the conflicts arising from the divided loyalties which were hampering the work of the Sewerage Board.

Negotiations designed to secure a boundary extension opened in April 1876 with the appointment of a committee 'to enquire into the necessity of the Town Council taking steps to extend the boundaries of the Borough'. After prolonged discussions the bill went to the House of Commons in December. Not surprisingly, the principal justification was the polluted state of the River Leen. The bill received the Royal Assent on 11 June 1877, and the new borough came into being on 1 November. The parishes of Radford, Lenton, Sneinton, Basford and Bulwell, and Wilford, north of the Trent, were added to Nottingham, and the area of the town grew to 10,935 acres (figure 12.1). The extended town had a population of 186,575 in 1881 and stood eighth in the rank order of English towns based on population size. It was now a major provincial town.[28]

The new corporation was to consist of sixteen (rather than fourteen) aldermen and forty-eight (rather than forty-two) councillors, elected from sixteen wards. The first elections for the new council were held on 1 November, and it met formally on 9 November when one of the town's lace manufacturers, Alderman W. G. Ward, was elected first mayor of the extended borough. Most of the existing boards and authorities within the newly incorporated areas were abolished. Police buildings and personnel were transferred from the county force to the town, new police stations were built, and others extended. The Boards of Guardians were also amalgamated. In 1836 the parishes of Radford, Lenton and Sneinton were formed into a separate union and built their own workhouse in Radford. With the borough extension this was converted into a 'Training Institute for Workhouse Children', and subsequently into an orphanage. It was demolished in the 1960s. Nottingham had opened a new workhouse in 1843. This was seldom full by the 1870s, and after some debate it was decided to retain it as fit accommodation for the enlarged Union.[29] In the event it did not survive for very long. With the building of the Great Central railway in the 1890s the workhouse was demolished. Various temporary premises were used until a new building was opened at Bagthorpe in 1903.[30] The major anomaly was the decision in 1877 to leave Basford and Bulwell out of the new Poor Law Union. An attempt to bring them into the Nottingham Union in 1894 was successfully resisted by the Basford Union.[31]

Post-1877 development

In conjunction with the borough extension Tarbotton produced a plan of greater Nottingham, which provides a snapshot of the town at this date. The old town was still densely developed, but the sharp distinction with the surrounding countryside, clear on all pre-1845 maps, was no longer apparent. To the north the Sand Field was being developed in the direction of Forest Road, while considerable building had taken place on the Clay Field to the east of Huntington Street and Mansfield Road as far as the junction with Forest Road. Beyond that a green belt stretched across the Forest and the Mapperley area, towards the outlying settlements of Hyson Green and New Basford to the north-west, and Carrington and Sherwood to the north-east. To the west New Radford was well developed, but there was still open land separating it from Old Radford. New Lenton lay beyond the still only partially built Park. South of the old town building was continuing in the Meadows, but little had changed to the east where – as in Radford – New Sneinton was still separated from the old village.

This was a picture destined to change very rapidly. In 1881 Nottingham had a population of 186,700 but this grew to 239,752 by 1901, an increase of more than one-quarter. The town speedily filled its new boundaries because the additional 53,000 people had to be accommodated. The green-field sites, so prominent on Tarbotton's map, soon began to disappear beneath bricks and mortar. By the time the Ordnance Survey produced its 1881 map several areas had undergone considerable development, including an area of New Basford between North Gate and what is now Valley Road, which was rapidly being filled in with terraced housing for working-class families. In the Hyson Green area, the Pearson-Gregory family's trustees sold thirty-four acres to developers in 1881 and a further sixty-five acres – the Forest Ville estate – in 1883. Both areas of land were rapidly developed, the latter as Forest Fields[32] – indeed, the pace of development was so fast that when the vicar of Hyson Green claimed in 1883 that the population had increased in two years from 6,049 to nearer 15,000, his calculations were treated in London with perhaps not surprising scepticism.[33] Other suburbs which grew rapidly in the closing decades of the century included Sherwood and Carrington.[34]

Figure 12.1 **Boundary extensions, 1877–1951**

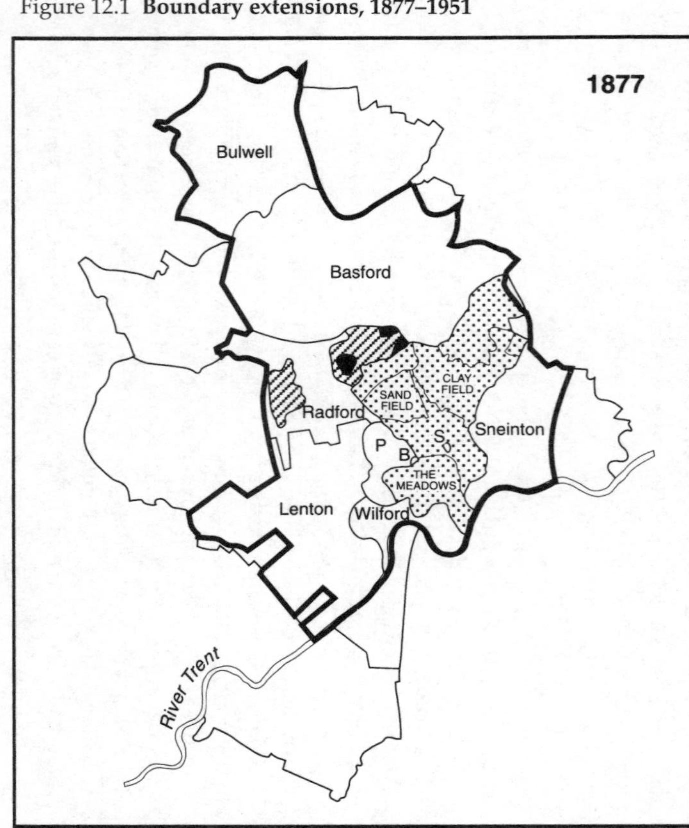

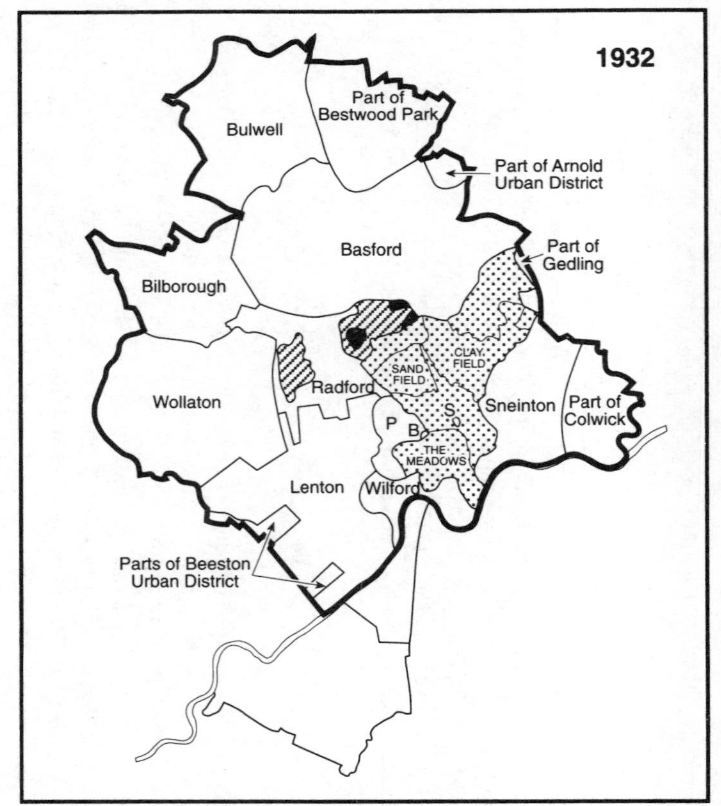

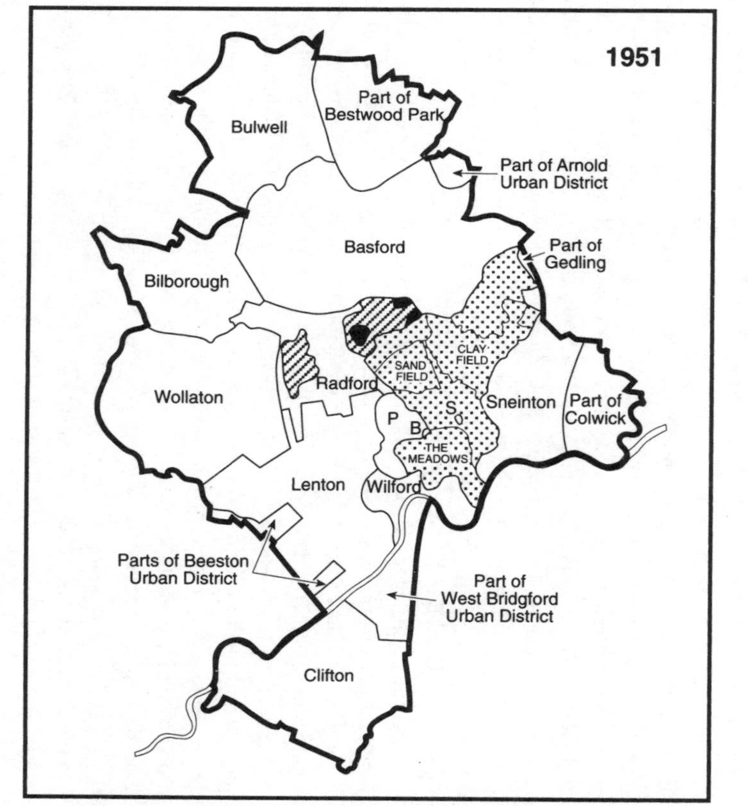
1951
Part of
Bestwood Park
Bulwell
Part of Arnold
Urban District
Basford
Bilborough
Part of
Gedling
CLAY
FIELD
SAND
FIELD
Radford
Wollaton
Sneinton
Part of
Colwick
P
B
S
THE
MEADOWS
Lenton
Wilford
Parts of Beeston
Urban District
Part of
West Bridgford
Urban District
Clifton

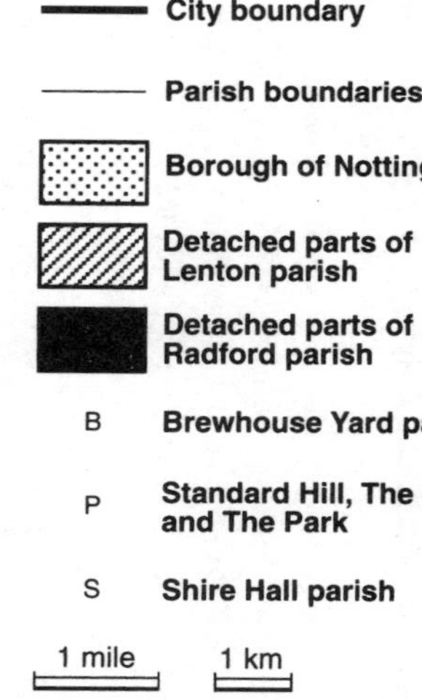
City boundary
Parish boundaries
Borough of Nottingham
Detached parts of
Lenton parish
Detached parts of
Radford parish
B Brewhouse Yard parish
P Standard Hill, The Castle
and The Park
S Shire Hall parish
1 mile
1 km

Nor was it just working-class areas which developed. In the middle decades of the century Sherwood Rise became a popular residential area for wealthy textile manufacturers with industrial interests in the satellite villages. In the 1850s work commenced on laying out a prestigious new area to be called Alexandra Park, although it took until the 1870s for a less grand scheme to be brought near to completion. Also in the 1870s Wrights, the banking family, sold off nearly six acres of their Mapperley Park estate for high-class residential development. Spacious detached and semi-detached houses were built for the industrial and professional middle classes in an area bounded by Mansfield Road, Redcliffe Road and Woodborough Road. This area was largely developed by 1901. Two years later the Wrights sold the rest of their estate, 129 acres running north from Ebers Road, to a syndicate of developers. They co-opted the architect W.B. Starr to set out a master plan for the new area and to design many of its houses. Mapperley Hall itself was sold to the corporation in 1906 and became a university hall of residence.[35] The desire for villa estates just beyond the town boundaries remained strong. Examples include Woodthorpe Grange, in Woodthorpe Park, built in 1874 by Henry Ashwell, a master bleacher; and half a dozen houses added to what is now the University of Nottingham campus in the late Victorian and Edwardian periods. These were occupied by Nottingham textile manufacturers, W. G. Player of the tobacco firm, and James Shipstone the brewer.[36]

For its part the corporation took the opportunity to plan additional roads designed to link together the various parts of the extended town. Gregory Boulevard, already inked in on Tarbotton's 1877 map, was planned as the first of a series of wide new roads: 'the town on this side will then be encircled by a magnificent road or boulevard, such as can be scarcely paralleled in this country'. It was well under way by 1880, when the Improvement Committee gave the go- ahead for a low-level road to connect Nottingham centre with Lenton, avoiding the steep gradients on Ilkeston and Derby Roads. This became Castle Boulevard which, together with Lenton Boulevard, was opened in September 1884. Radford Boulevard followed in 1887. Other major road constructions, designed at least partly to link Nottingham more conveniently with its outlying suburbs, included Vernon Road (1882), which was an extension of Radford Road, and Highbury Road.[37]

Such connections were also a reflection of growing employment opportunities in the industrial suburbs. Nottingham did not develop the pattern of social and industrial zoning and commuting characteristic particularly of London, but also of some other major towns. The one attempt to create such zones by limiting post-enclosure industrial development to the Meadows area failed. Consequently individual lace and hosiery factories were scattered around the town, intermixed with residential areas, and it was only towards the end of the nineteenth century that several substantial pockets of industry could be identified. Among these were the Radford Boulevard–Hartley Road–Norton Street area, both sides of Alfreton Road west of Canning Circus, and the manufacturing area which came into the town in 1877 between Gladstone Street and North Gate in New Basford. As these pockets developed the demand for public transport also increased.

Commuting, at least for the middle classes, became possible once the horse tramway was introduced. Horse buses were running regular services as early as the 1840s. In 1843 William Parsons took the omnibus to Sherwood to breakfast with his brother Sam, and by 1860 he was living in Daybrook and commuting into Nottingham.[38] By the 1870s regular services had been developed to Basford, Lenton, Carrington, Sneinton and West Bridgford, but the borough extension raised additional questions about the local transport network (see figure 12.2). In 1878 the Nottingham and District Tramways Company obtained permission to run horse-drawn trams from St Peter's Church to the Midland Station (at that time on Station Street) and the Great Northern Station on London Road. The following year the company opened a service to Carrington, terminating at stables next to St John's church, and in 1881 a service to Basford.

The number of new services proved inadequate to meet demand. The Directors of the Nottinghamshire and Midland Merchants and Traders Association petitioned the corporation in 1890, complaining that 'the tram service in Nottingham is not equal to the requirements of the town. That from the hilly nature of the town, travelling by means of horses is exceedingly slow and expensive.'[39] Such complaints seem not to have been heeded. Certainly tramway services remained in private hands until the corporation gained control of the Tramways Company in October 1897. Almost immediately plans for expansion and re-equipment were drawn up, and recommendations put forward for introducing electric overhead traction.[40] Commuting access to the town was in any case improved with the opening in 1889 of the suburban railway line, which served about 40,000 people in the Sherwood, Daybrook, Basford, Bulwell, and Old Radford areas. As with earlier railway construction, this caused little physical disruption to the town because it ran around the perimeter of the conurbation, largely on existing lines. However, passengers had to alight at the inconvenient Low Level Station until the Victoria Station opened in 1900.[41]

Once the borough extension was completed, the corporation sought to extend its powers in order to govern more effectively. In 1879 it promoted a further Improvement Act. Once again the utilities were a major consideration. The intention was to acquire powers to construct new gasworks and to purchase the waterworks. The Act, which was passed in August 1879, also gave the corporation powers to acquire Bulwell Forest, of which fifty acres was to be for a park and ninety acres for a cemetery, to construct new gasworks, and to acquire the water company.[42]

To these practical measures the corporation added schemes to improve the appearance of the town. Discussions were opened on the question of a new council building. The old Guildhall at Weekday Cross was neither large enough for all the corporation employees, nor was it adequate as a court of law. When Sydney Race went on a conducted tour in 1894 he noted that 'it was a musty old place.... The two courts are remarkably small and one wonders how business was ever carried on in them. The prisoner in the dock could almost reach across to the judge on his bench.'[43] In February 1875 Tarbotton outlined to the Public Buildings Committee three possibilities for new civic accommodation. T. C. Hine restated his proposals, first brought forward in 1857, for developing the market-place and the Exchange. 'We have here the grandest site in

Figure 12.2 **Tram routes, 1878–1902**

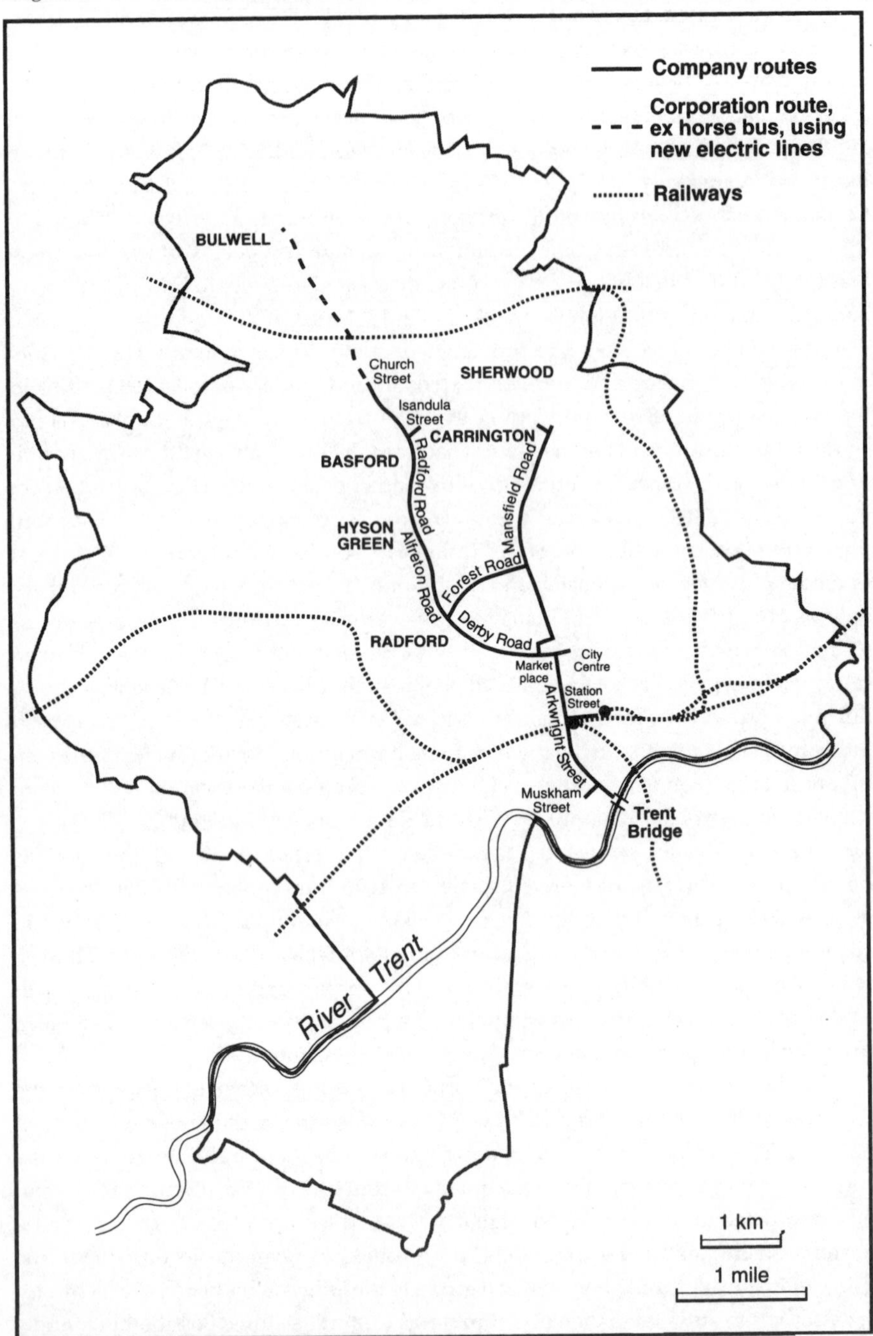

Note: The advantage enjoyed by the tram routes was in going straight through the heart of the built-up area where the railway lines, and particularly the suburban route, ran around the outskirts.

all England for a public building', he suggested; it should be developed to hold 'offices for the mayor, the assembly hall for the town council, the civic banqueting hall, and last, but not least, for the great hall in which the expression of public opinion would be heard'. Police courts and other facilities might go elsewhere.[44] The borough extension gave added impetus to the issue. The old Guildhall was not capable of accommodating the 64-member post-1877 corporation, which met initially in the Mechanics Institute until a room in the Exchange was converted into a council chamber. These arrangements were far from ideal, and in 1880 the corporation decided in principle that it needed a new building. A site was selected on the corner of Burton Street and South Sherwood Street, and land in the East Croft was acquired in order to relocate the cattle market. In 1882 the corporation advertised a competition with a prize of £600 to find a suitable design for the new building. From 117 entries a scheme by Verity & Hunt of London was selected at an estimated cost of £161,257. The corporation promptly got cold feet.[45] However, a revised and rather more modest plan was drawn up, with estimates running to only £60,100. As a result the present French Renaissance-style building was erected between 1885 and 1888. Although substantial – accommodation was found for the Police Courts, the Central Police Station, and the Fire Service – it lacked the grandeur and presence of Leeds, Birmingham, Manchester, and other town halls of this period. No attempt was made to alter the market-place: the outcome would certainly have been different if Hine's view had predominated.

Slum clearance

In any case, the corporation's attempts to foster a civic consciousness were inevitably tempered by the housing problem. Nottingham, like many similar towns, remained in the 1870s a walking town. Road building and transport improvements could not alter the fact that semi-skilled and unskilled employees working in the town centre needed also to live there, whatever the environmental drawbacks. As the Improvement Committee reported in 1873, employers needed their workmen close to the place of work:

> The manufactories of the Town require the services of workmen who must live within a certain radius of the factory or workshop, and the effect of strictly enforcing the sanitary laws with respect to overcrowding would be to cripple to a great extent the commercial interests of the town. Some thousands of workpeople are now driven into the outskirts of the Town and have to come to and fro long distances – in some cases two or three or even four or five miles to their work. In fact such is the demand in the Town for houses at the present time that the Magistrates are appealed to almost daily for help by persons who cannot find houses in which to dwell and as much as £1 is constantly given by a working man for the right of succession to a weekly tenancy.[46]

In these circumstances the corporation had to try to maintain a balance between competing interests. It needed to use the existing legislation to demolish the worst housing, and to insist on the improvement of other properties, without emptying the town centre of houses; and it needed to balance the competing demands for houses and for commercial premises at the heart of the town.

This is the context in which we should view Edward Seaton's most ambitious scheme. At a meeting on 29 March 1881 the General Purposes Committee of the town council resolved to accept a report from Seaton condemning as unhealthy an area of 12,000 square yards between Long Row, Market Street and Upper Parliament Street.[47] Over 100 houses, half a dozen common lodging-houses, public houses, hotels, warehouses, and shops were packed into the seven narrow alleys locally known as the Rookeries:

> Grocers, drapers, boot stores – every variety; eating houses and pie making establishments, some of which were not remarkable for their cleanliness; sweetmeat manufactories carried on in attics; fried fish emporiums, where a colouring material had to supply the lack of freshness and given an attractive look to please the eye; bacon curing establishments in dingy basements; rag and bone assorting rooms, a visit to which caused lively feelings afterwards; laundries, in which clothes and children, and steam and soap suds were strangely mixed up; bird fanciers and showmen.[48]

Seaton wanted to clear the area. Initially the Local Government Board, to which all such schemes had to be submitted, rejected the proposals because important details were omitted such as the number of houses to be built to rehouse those displaced, but by the autumn the scheme was ready to be implemented after the Estates Committee agreed to provide two acres from the Bridge Estate near the Hunger Hill Road and the Local Government Board agreed to allow building on the site to be undertaken by private entrepreneurs.[49]

The corporation saw, or thought it saw, a way of bringing about the required redevelopment without committing itself to any real expense. It proposed that the site should be used for a central railway station, on the basis that 'it has been felt that the present Railway Stations are not sufficiently central, and that their sites could not be regarded as final'. The three railway companies with interests in the town – the Midland, the Great Northern and the London and North Western Railway – were invited to tender jointly for the site. Unfortunately for the corporation, they refused to take the bait.[50] The corporation then offered a prize in a public competition for redevelopment. This also failed to attract takers.[51] As a result, demolition began on the site without any plan approved for redevelopment.

Although the demolition details were agreed in 1881 the scheme took time to bring to fruition, largely because of the complex negotiations over compensation to the property owners. The 1875 housing legislation had stipulated that they should receive full value. As a result, according to the town clerk, the corporation had been forced to deal with about 150 separate owners and had spent £160,000 acquiring the property and land. Overall, the corporation paid about £14 per square yard for the Parliament Street land (£160,000).[52] All this took time and it was not until April 1888 that redevelopment could begin. Eventually King Street (1891) and Queen Street

(1892) were cut at a cost of £13,000 and housing was replaced by commercial property including the new post office on Queen Street, Alfred Waterhouse's offices for the Prudential Insurance Company (1896), buildings by Watson Fothergill including Queen's Chambers (1897), and the new department store for Jessop & Son (1896). These were the plus-points, but from the point of view of the corporation the scheme was hardly a financial success. When it auctioned the Hunger Hill Road site in 1883 the land fetched only 4*d* or 5*d* a square yard on 99-year leases. The valuation had been about 10*s*. Overall the deficit on the scheme must have worked out at around £75,000, and although the benefits were largely uneconomic and unquantifiable most of the councillors saw this as a reason for future caution. Partly as a result, the 1875 legislation was not applied again in Nottingham.[53]

Even before demolition work in the Rookeries was completed, Seaton had left the town. He was increasingly concerned about the benefits of schemes such as this, writing in his 1882 annual report that 'there are within a mile walk of any of the slums hundreds of cheap and healthy houses being erected which would afford the accommodation required'. As the Poor Law Guardians had found in the 1840s, and Seaton's successors were to discover in subsequent years, persuading many of those who lived in the poorest areas to move to other homes was not always easy. However, his departure was less a question of principle than of money; the corporation refused to raise his salary and in 1884 he moved to a similar post in Chelsea. He left a substantial legacy. During his twelve years in post, Seaton had established an inspection staff, so that of 3,763 nuisances dealt with in 1882 only sixty-four were a result of complaints from the public and the rest had been discovered by his District Inspectors. The inspection staff survived him and by the 1890s Nottingham was among a number of boroughs which employed female sanitary inspectors as health visitors. Seaton could not solve every problem; the town still had an unusually high rate of infant mortality. Of 1,000 children born in 1882, 188 died before the age of one. He believed that many were 'improperly fed', and that their short lives were hastened to an end by 'the improper use of drugs which are given by the mothers to quiet the infants', a reference to the practice among women working in the textile trades of dosing their children with laudanum during the working day.[54]

The Rookeries scheme highlighted the problems faced by the corporation when it came to building houses, and the closing years of the nineteenth century were marked by inactivity and uncertainty. As elsewhere, heavy investment in the utilities brought a rising level of civic debt (£1.524 million in 1890, £2.093 million in 1900, and nearly £5.5 million in 1908). These figures naturally made the corporation cautious, and in any case the level of private house building developed rapidly after 1877. In fifteen months during 1881–82 as many as 3,235 houses were built in St Ann's, Byron, Castle and Exchange wards. Five separate house-building schemes started in Hyson Green around 1880, and the Forest Fields area was opened up for development from 1883. During the 1880s the town's total housing stock increased by 16 per cent, while the population rose only by 12 per cent. Dr Arthur Whitlegge, who succeeded Seaton, found few cases of overcrowding on which to comment in his first report as Medical

Officer of Health in 1885, and the town clerk claimed in 1888 that there were as many as 3,000 unoccupied working-class houses in the town.[55]

For those ready and willing to find reasonable accommodation, there were plenty of quality houses available in the town. Working-class families frequently occupied four- and especially five-roomed terraced houses, usually built straight from the pavement line, but with front and back entrances. By 1905 the five-roomed house was the predominant type of working-class dwelling in which 71.7 per cent of the town's population lived. Six-roomed houses were normally for white-collar workers and their families and other lower-middle class people such as foremen, insurance agents and clerks.[56] In these circumstances it is not entirely surprising that the corporation made little effort to implement the terms of the 1890 Housing of the Working Classes Act. With the 1891 census revealing a population density in the town of fewer than five persons per house, it was difficult to argue that there was any kind of crisis, even if 32 per cent of the population lived in houses of four rooms or fewer. Private housing development continued apace: the number of occupied houses increased from 46,613 to 52,537 in the course of the 1890s, and between 1900 and 1908 more than 1,200 building plans for new houses were approved by the corporation annually. In terms of slum clearance, the opportunity to redevelop a major slum area presented itself on the corporation's doorstep with the building of the Great Central Railway, the first line to have a marked physical impact on the town.

The Great Central was authorised by legislation passed in March 1893. One section was to run for ninety-two miles from Annesley to near Aylesbury where it would link with the Metropolitan Railway into London. *En route* it was planned to drive the railway right through the centre of Nottingham (and Leicester). Whereas in other Victorian towns railways had tended to determine the location of poor-quality housing, in both Nottingham and Leicester the corporations were faced with an opportunity of providing a site which would ensure the clearance of slum housing at no cost to the ratepayers. Since the Rookeries had already been cleared, and the Great Central wanted a north–south route, the final agreement was to build the station by clearing the housing north of Parliament Street and east of Mansfield Road. The line entered Nottingham from the north across the magnificent Bulwell viaduct (26 arches and 420 yards long), and then passed through the Sherwood Rise tunnel (665 yards), Carrington Station, and the Mansfield Road tunnel (1,189 yards) into a new station built on a site stretching from Woodborough Road to Parliament Street, and from Mansfield Road to Huntingdon Street. The railway company had compulsorily to purchase the land, and then to demolish 1,300 houses, twenty public houses, the Union Workhouse and a church. The land cost £473,000. The line left the station through the short Victoria Street Tunnel, to emerge into daylight at Weekday Cross, where the disused town hall had to be demolished and the High Pavement school moved to new premises. It then emerged on to a viaduct which crossed the Marsh area – necessitating the clearance of poor-quality housing in Peach, Pear, Currant and Plum Streets – before passing on to a massive low girder bridge crossing the Midland Station. There was a further viaduct across the Meadows before the line crossed the

Trent on a newly-erected bridge. Some of this structure remains today. The Great Northern, which was jointly responsible for the Victoria Station, constructed a new line from Colwick into the station, demolishing about ninety houses in the process. It built a further new station east of London Road which came to be known as the High Level Station. These developments had an enormous physical impact on the town, far more than any earlier lines had caused (figure 12.3). Furthermore the new station, of which only the clock tower remains, was sufficiently impressive to persuade the Midland Railway to abandon its facilities on Station Street and to commission the new building on Carrington Street, which opened in 1904 and is today the only operational railway station in the city centre.[57]

Plate 30 **Railways. An aerial view of Nottingham Midland Station, looking east, in 1927**. A.E. Lambert's buildings for the third Midland Station, opened in 1904, stand on Carrington Street bridge, almost facing the former Midland Railway Goods Office of 1873–74, and the Midland's 1896 Goods and Grain Warehouse at the foot of the photograph. The tracks in the station are spanned by the LNER (formerly Great Central) line from Nottingham Victoria to London Marylebone, and by three footbridges, one a right of way from Station Street to Queen's Road. To the left is the LNER line from Victoria Station to Grantham, while the gasholder at the top of the photograph stands between London Road High Level and Low Level Stations. The latter was the 1857 terminus of the Ambergate Railway, designed by T.C. Hine. A tram can be seen on Carrington Street outside the main entrance to the Midland Station

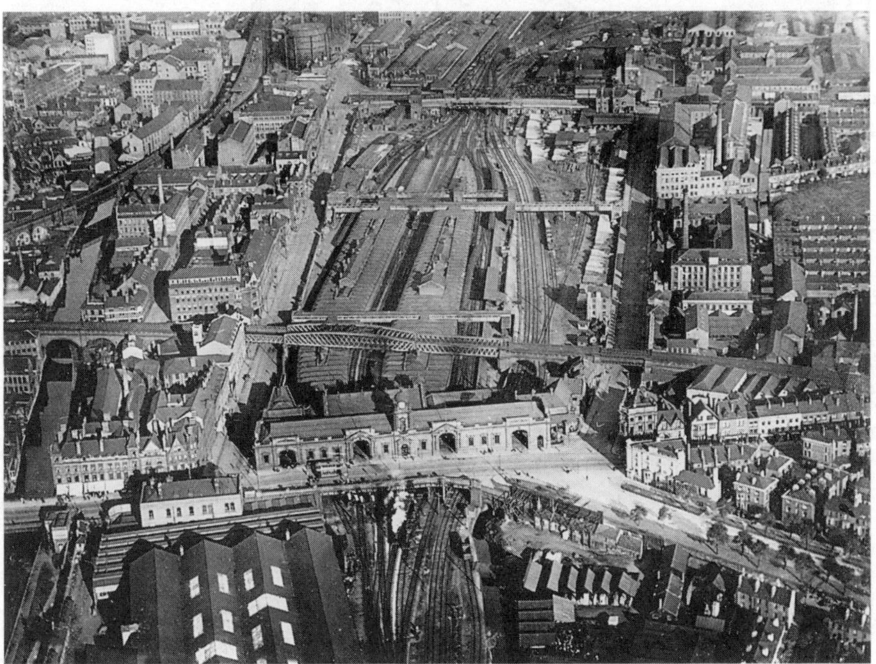

Figure 12.3 **Railways in Greater Nottingham**

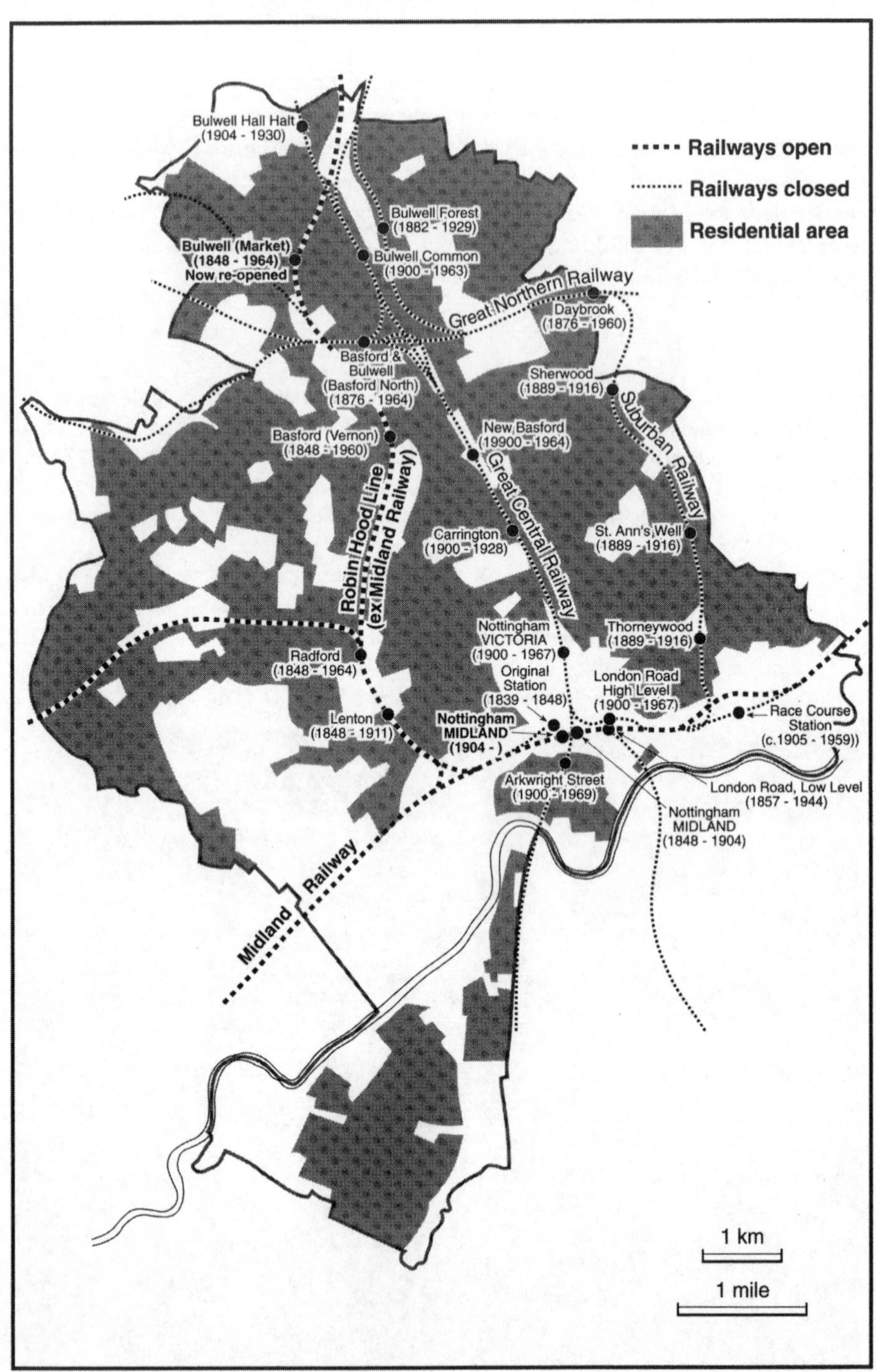

The Great Central brought disruption to the centre of Nottingham on a scale the town had not previously experienced, but it had less impact on the housing problem than many had hoped. One of the stipulations of the legislation was that the company should build houses for those displaced; in fact, it built only 300 homes, mainly in the Meadows and along new streets off the eastern side of Huntingdon Street, and these were too expensive for the uprooted families to rent. Pressure on the remaining back-to-back houses simply increased. Robert Mellors, who claimed that only one family from the area moved into a company house, noted the same reluctance Seaton had seen to moving: 'in little dark places the people expressed the wish to be let alone, for they wanted to live and die there'.[58]

As far as the corporation was concerned, no new housing initiatives were taken until shortly before 1914. Properties were regularly condemned and closed under the terms of existing legislation – sixty-eight in 1893 and fifty-seven in 1894, for example – and in 1897 a small redevelopment in Lower Parliament Street and St Ann's Street led to eighty-six new houses being built on Chandos Street, Cromer Road and Coppice Road at the upper end of St Ann's Well Road. However, these rented at rates which tenants in the slum areas could not afford.[59] A scheme for redeveloping the east side of the town was considered and rejected in 1898 and 1903, and the next moves came only after the Conservatives gained control of the corporation in 1908, and in the light of the 1909 Housing and Town Planning Act.[60] The Act coincided with the setting up of the town's first Housing Committee, which by 1915 had issued 1,145 closing orders and overseen the demolition of 499 properties. The committee also considered larger ventures, including an abortive scheme in 1911 to clear the Narrow Marsh area, but it made no attempt to build houses despite a rapid decline in the number of approved building plans between 1909 and 1913. Its one success was the Carter Gate and Manvers Street improvement scheme, which the Local Government Board approved on 31 August 1912 following a public enquiry. More than 1,900 people lived in the area, of whom only 498 were in work, and the aim was to clear the area to make way for the private development of new houses. Delay followed delay, and nothing had been achieved by the outbreak of the First World War, although the area was eventually cleared and replaced by a tram depot and offices for the corporation's transport undertaking.[61]

The slum areas were a major unresolved problem in Nottingham in 1914. The Medical Officer of Health claimed in the mid-1890s that 'most towns are adopting some system of water carriage', and urged the corporation to adopt a policy of putting water-closets in houses in Nottingham. Pail closets, adopted in 1868, were expensive to replace. As late as 1912 there were still 35,000 pail closets, processed at a cost of £18,000 annually, when a saving of £10,000 could have been achieved by converting them to water-closets.[62] The corporation offered a £2 10*s* subsidy to every householder voluntarily converting. Partly as a result the town still had problems removing its night soil, which was almost certainly still being physically transported from the town in the 1920s. Even in 1914 many of the back-to-back houses lacked piped water and adequate ventilation and sanitation facilities.[63] Not surprisingly, outbreaks of enteric (typhoid) fever continued well into the twentieth century.

The failure of the corporation to deal adequately with the town centre slum housing tarnished a great deal of work which was advancing to improve the urban environment. Considerable resources were invested in widening the remaining narrow streets and thoroughfares, among them Stoney Street, Pilcher Gate, Warser Gate, Upper Parliament Street, Greyfriar Gate and Wheeler Gate.[64] A new utility was added in the 1890s when electricity was introduced. By contrast with the gas, water and tramway initiatives, which began as private enterprises and were later taken over by the corporation, electricity was a municipal enterprise from the outset. Powers to establish an electricity authority had first been granted to local authorities in 1882, but there was little initial enthusiasm in Nottingham, and it was 1894 before electricity became available in the town. In 1895 the market-place was lit up by eight 4,000 candle-power lamps to mark the opening of the Nottingham Electric Lighting Station. The Theatre Royal and the John Player factories were first lit by electricity in 1898, but during its first five years in operation the company attracted only 863 subscribers.

Part of the trouble was that the corporation had begun cautiously, and the General Power Distributing Company, a private company, sensing a gap in the market, tried unsuccessfully to obtain powers to light parts of the town not covered by the corporation – and at lower rates. The corporation rose to the challenge, partly because to convert the tramway system to the overhead trolley the generating capacity had to be substantially increased. The original plant on Talbot Street was extended, and a new generating station built on St Ann's Well Road. On 1 January 1901 the first electric tram ran from the market-place to Sherwood: 'the cars were very extensively patronised'. As lines were laid and routes extended, electricity consumption (and profits for the company) grew.[65] Roads also had to be widened, including the Milton Street–Upper Parliament Street corner, Upper Parliament Street at its junction with Derby Road, and a new street from Lower Parliament Street to St Ann's Well Road passing across the site of the old gaol. Fires at warehouses on Stoney Street and near Carrington Street bridge enabled the corporation to set back the rebuilding lines and widen the streets. St Peter's Church, and possibly also Holy Trinity, had their churchyards cut back to permit road widening.

Horse-drawn vehicles, electric trams, and the occasional motor car competed for space on the streets of Edwardian Nottingham. Sydney Race saw a motor car for the first time in February 1897: 'it was low and looked just like an elevated trolley … . There were two men on it, and it came out of Circus Street and down Derby Road with a rattle.'[66] Cars took time to catch on; in 1903 only 125 vehicles (including motor bicycles) were registered for the whole county, despite the fact that there were various car-making plants locally, including the Humber works in Beeston (1898). From cars it was only one step to motor buses, and the first Nottingham service from the market-place to the Crown Hotel on Carlton Road began on 26 March 1906 – the first accident was two months later. The Barton Company began in 1908, running its first service from Long Eaton through Beeston to Goose Fair, and back again. It had a maximum speed of twelve miles per hour. By 1911 the corporation was seriously considering major road improvements to the town, including a route from Albert Street to Sneinton Hermitage, which would have had the additional benefit of clearing large areas of the Marshes.[67]

Plate 31 **An early car accident, 1904**. This accident, at the junction of Redcliffe and Mansfield Roads, occurred when Mr A.F. Houghton's 12 h.p. Sunbeam was in collision with an electric tram. A.R. Atkey, a pioneering motor dealer in the city (and later Lord Mayor), arranged to have the damaged car towed away. He referred to the incident as an argument which the tram won!

Living standards

The physical development of Nottingham in the forty years or so prior to the First World War was slowly matched by improvements in living standards and life expectancy. Textile workers were still subject to periodic unemployment as a result of the trade cycle. The bad winters of 1860–61 and 1862–63 saw soup kitchens being opened, and two thousand framework knitters applied to the workhouse in the closing months of 1864.[68] Nationally the provisions of the Poor Law were tightened in the 1870s, and in Nottingham a proposal was put forward for erecting an oakum-picking building at the workhouse. In October 1884 hundreds of textile workers gathered in the market-place and called on the corporation to provide them with work. Around 600 men were employed levelling land on Hunger Hills and the Coppice Estate. There were further problems in 1885 and again in the winter of 1886–87. In January 1887 the mayor opened a public relief fund, and £2,000 was contributed towards the cost of distributing soup and bread to the cold and hungry. Various church groups raised money to distribute blankets, soup and bread. The *Nottingham Daily Express* commented on the 'suffering' in the town 'from want of employment', although it suggested that in general the working classes

> of Nottingham are better fed and housed, their wages are higher, they work fewer hours, and they have opportunities for cultivating their minds and taking part in the settlement of public affairs of which their predecessors only dreamed in moments of optimistic vision. In fact a higher standard of comfort prevails among all classes of society.[69]

Charitable organisations attempted to help those for whom the level of poor relief was inadequate. The Nottingham Town and County Social Guild, modelled on the Charity Organisation Society founded in London in 1869, was set up in 1875 to co-ordinate the work of different charities in the town. The Guild was typical of the main current of Victorian philanthropy. The idea was to create what might be deemed a civic welfare system in which the moral conduct of the poor was assessed to ascertain their eligibility for charitable relief. The Guild secretary, Henrietta Carey, aspired to be Nottingham's Octavia Hill. For forty-five years she participated in events such as the annual competition for the cleanest houses and the prettiest flower-boxes, and much of her time was spent attending to the affairs of the Guild's convalescent home. In its first year the Guild investigated 655 cases, gave assistance in 472, but rejected the rest as undeserving. From the beginning one of its principal aims was the improvement of working-class housing on lines similar to those pioneered by Octavia Hill in the East End of London, but its activities represented a poor match for the overall poverty problem, and it was not particularly successful in its housing efforts on behalf of the working classes. On taking over Victoria Dwellings the Guild brought about some improvements, but without ever coming close to turning the dwellings into model housing for the poor and less well-off working classes. Straightforward relief to supplement the poor law was given by the Nottingham Society for Organising Charity, while from the 1880s a number of groups appeared in the town promoting socialist ideas.[70]

The ambivalent relationship between the Poor Law guardians and the corporation continued down to the First World War. Late in 1904, with unemployment running at record levels, the corporation put aside 'a considerable sum' for the Charity Organisation Society to distribute in the town. In four months, 834 people applied for relief, of whom 429 were helped and 405 were refused. Of the 405, 126 were said to be of bad character, 107 were found not to be destitute since others members of their family were in employment, 53 were referred to the guardians, and 35 were already in receipt of outdoor relief. The amount of actual relief distributed was £1,072. During the following winter, 1905–06, 270 pauper men were employed by the corporation 'levelling and laying out a playground and a street'. Their poverty was attributed not so much to depression in the textiles as to depression in the building trade. Until about three years before (*c.*1903) 'there was a large amount of building, there were public buildings, and amongst other things a new workhouse, and there was a certain amount of private speculative building'.[71]

Poverty remained a problem, but there is no equivalent for Nottingham of the social surveys carried out in London and York at the end of the nineteenth century. What little evidence there is suggests that for the majority of people living standards were improving, and since this must have been reflected in diet it would help to explain the falling death rates which reached 17.7 per thousand between 1896 and 1901.

The market stall had always been the most regular resort of the working classes, but increasingly the fixed shop was becoming popular.[72] This is of course evidence of supply rather than of consumption, but the one points in the direction of the other and is supported by the trends in death rates. The death rate fell to nineteen per thousand in 1889 and to twelve per thousand in 1912, although the rate among infants remained obstinately above the national average as late as 1911. By 1916 the main causes of death were no longer infectious diseases linked to poor sanitation, but tuberculosis, bronchitis, heart disease, pneumonia and cancer. The decline in death rates reflected rising living standards, a better balanced diet (which was itself a reflection of rising living standards), and a greater concern for the treatment of ill health.

For those who fell ill the standard of health care gradually improved. In 1780 the Duke of Newcastle gave an acre of land from the former northern bailey of the Castle which, together with a matching contribution from the corporation, became the site of the General Hospital. It was opened in 1782 with forty-four beds. This soon proved inadequate; ten more beds were added in 1784, and a new wing with ten beds in 1787. Accommodation remained stretched, despite numerous extensions to the hospital, including a third storey added to the main block in 1854–55 and an accident wing in 1879 (both by T. C. Hine). Edward Seaton was responsible for opening fever wards at the hospital. Finance was also a problem. The hospital relied on legacies and donations, and a constant round of fund-raising. Even so, in 1872 debts totalled £1,500, and the governors clamped down on the number of outpatients (reduced from 10,400 to 7,400) by enforcing the rule of no admission without a recommendation. To try to recover the situation, in 1874 a Hospital Sunday was organised in local churches, and a Hospital Saturday in local workplaces. The hospital bought a number of houses on the Ropewalk as additional accommodation, but to celebrate the Queen's Diamond Jubilee in 1897 a new wing (the five-storey, circular, Jubilee Wing by Alfred Waterhouse) was commissioned. Funded by private subscriptions, this opened in 1900 at a cost of £30,000, and provided sixty-six new beds. Other extensions at the same time included a new laundry, an enlarged power house, and a new mortuary and mortuary chapel.[73]

Plate 32 **General Hospital from St James's Terrace, 1830**. The hospital was erected in 1781–82 on a two-acre site, half given by the corporation and the rest by the 2nd Duke of Newcastle. Further additions were made in 1787 and 1812, and a long-promised Fever House was opened in 1828. The view in this painting by Caroline Mary Price was from the Hollows (St James's Terrace, Standard Hill), near the top of St James's Street. The front of John Simpson's original two-storey building, with its later wings, is clearly shown. Since the hospital closed, and the obtrusive 1960s Trent Wing has been demolished, the site has been restored, and the original hospital can be seen today, together with the Gothic chapel designed by T.C. Hine, and the Jubilee Wing opened in 1900. Since 1993 the main building has been the headquarters of Nottingham Health

To deal with mental health problems a general lunatic asylum was opened on a four-acre site in Sneinton in 1812. This was a joint venture between town and county, which relied additionally on voluntary subscriptions. The first six inmates were paupers transferred from the workhouse in St Mary's parish. By June 1815 it was full, and in subsequent years new buildings and extensions were added in an attempt to keep abreast of demand. The 1853 Lunacy Act handed over responsibility for the mentally ill to local authorities, which were required to satisfy the Lunatic Commission that asylums in their areas were adequate. As a result, from 1856 the Nottingham asylum was run jointly by the county and borough councils. Almost immediately a new building was erected. This was the Coppice Hospital (by T. C. Hine) which opened in 1859. At the same time a new wing was added to the existing asylum. In 1873 Nottingham corporation sold its share to the county, and two years later work began on building Mapperley Lunatic Asylum, which opened in 1880. Both Sneinton and Mapperley Hospitals had a preponderance of female patients. Under the Lunacy Act of 1890 the local authority was obliged to publish the report of the Committee of Visitors to the Borough Asylum at Mapperley, and the first appeared in 1893. A new wing was added to Mapperley Hospital in 1890. The Sneinton buildings continued in use by the county until the opening of Saxondale hospital in 1902.[74]

Other hospitals in the town included a fever house opened in 1828, a children's hospital opened in 1869, and the first women's hospital – in a house on Castle Gate which now houses Radio Trent – in 1875. The women's hospital treated 364 in-patients and 2,271 out-patients during its first year. One of the surgeons, Dr Elder, resigned in 1885 when he claimed to have been unable to perform a major operation because of the insanitary conditions. He and Dr Truman encouraged a Samaritan Hospital, which opened at Raleigh Street in 1887. The town thus had two hospitals for women, which were not amalgamated until a building on Peel Street was opened in 1930.[75] Despite these facilities, maternity services remained outside the hospital system until the twentieth century. The General Hospital specifically excluded 'laying in' women except in emergencies, and it was only from 1901 that the women's hospital accepted 'accouchement cases of married women', and even then they charged a minimum of five guineas a week. The Medical Officer of Health complained in 1908 about the shortage of midwives in the town, and called for the establishment of a Central Maternity Hospital.[76]

In 1885 the council bought a large area of land at Bagthorpe to build an isolation hospital and a sanatorium. It opened in 1891. All cases of diphtheria, enteric fever, smallpox, scarlet fever and tuberculosis were referred to the new hospital. By 1901 it had ninety-two patients. Tuberculosis peaked in 1909 when it accounted for 10 per cent of all deaths in Nottingham (234 males and 206 females).[77] Table 12.1 gives an indication of the size of the hospital population shortly before the First World War.

Table 12.1 **In-hospital patients in Nottingham, 1911**

Institution	*Males*	*Females*	*Total*
Children's Hospital	17	19	36
City Isolation Hospital	37	42	79
Lunatic Asylum (Mapperley)	396	463	859
Smallpox Hospital	–	1	1
Convalescent Home (General Hospital)	16	16	32
General Hospital	133	82	215
Women's Hospital	–	20	20
Coppice	39	48	87
Eye Infirmary	8	6	14
Samaritan Hospital for Women	–	13	13

Source: B. Arblaster, 'Health Services in Nottingham and the Provision for Women, 1860–1940' (University of Nottingham, MA dissertation, 1985), p. 23. The Union workhouses are omitted from this table.

By the end of the nineteenth century the older part of Nottingham was gradually being transformed into a service area, but the disfiguring effects of the late enclosure could never entirely be thrown off. The town had a seemingly haphazard juxtaposition of industrial and residential areas. It had developed industrial pockets rather than zones, with its factories scattered through the suburbs. An article in *The Builder* summed up the image problem at the turn of the century. 'Architecturally speaking', Nottingham was described as being

> one of the queerest cities in the provinces. Most of our cities have more or less well-defined areas, their central business quarter, their first-class dwelling quarter, their second-class dwelling quarter, their slum district, and their factory division. Nottingham is unique in having all these divisions hopelessly mixed up. It is a city without beginning or end. Public buildings, private dwellings, and factories are mixed up in endless confusion. Dirty warehouses and workshops face the Guildhall and loom up at the back of the University College. Furnace chimneys rise in the middle of the residential quarters and slums within a stone's throw of the market-place.[78]

T. C. Hine would doubtless not have been pleased to hear the Park housing described as having 'no architectural style or merit', but the general point of the article is indisputable: Nottingham has developed clearly defined zones, as opposed to pockets, only in the course of the twentieth century.[79] Yet by 1900 the form of the twentieth-century city was already taking shape. Within the central core the lace manufacturers had their warehouses and offices in the Lace Market area. The market-place was still the retailing heart of the town: 'what a wonderful institution is our Long Row', a commentator wrote in 1879, 'it is in fact the very pulse of the town and indicates the natures and habits of the inhabitants as does a barometer the state of the atmosphere'.[80] Numerous offices and commercial premises could also be found in the streets stretching from the market-place towards the Castle. In fact, Greater Nottingham was rather different from the compact pre-enclosure town: a sprawling conurbation had replaced the compact intimacy of those earlier days. Density per acre, having reached fifty-seven people in 1831, had fallen rapidly after enclosure and was just twenty-two in 1901. The canker was the back-to-back and unimproved housing, which was not just an eyesore but also limited the scope for commercial development. Significantly, in the late twentieth century the two main shopping centres sit astride what in the 1890s were slum housing areas.

Few people doubted that Nottingham had improved for the better. In 1887 the *Nottingham Daily Guardian* compared favourably the present time with Queen Victoria's accession half a century earlier. The streets were wider and houses were 'more healthy and convenient … . The provision of recreation grounds and public walks has greatly assisted in promoting the public health, and the town has become one of the most healthy, as well as one of the most attractive in the country.'[81] A decade later the town became a City, receiving its charter as part of the celebrations accompanying Queen Victoria's Diamond Jubilee. The corporation agreed to commemorate the honour by placing a memorial bronze in the Guildhall and by acquiring 'a proper badge ... for mayors to wear on special occasions'. This seemed rather low-key to the *Guardian*, which complained that 'the new honour has been received with a singular lack of enthusiasm. Even the deputy mayor seemed to have his doubts as to whether any benefits would follow from the change of title.'[82] Yet the *Guardian*, looking back over the nineteenth century in an article published on 1 January 1901, had no doubt that the new city had come a long way over the previous 100 years: it had been 'a century of progress and development, such as no previous era can in the faintest degree be compared with'. The century had seen in Nottingham 'a dazzling transformation'.[83] Perhaps in retrospect we might want to qualify such hyperbole – even the *Guardian* had complained in 1897 about the lack of an adequate city hall to go with the charter – but the late Victorian city of nearly one-quarter of a million people was a rather different place from the garden town of 15,000 people admired by Robert Sanders 130 years earlier.

Notes

1 Our research has failed to locate the origin of Nottingham's claim to be 'Queen of the Midlands', although this is certainly one of the earliest references.
2 R. Donbavand, 'The social geography of Victorian Nottingham' (University of Nottingham, Ph.D. thesis, 1982), table 2.1.
3 *NJ*, 1 October 1852; 1 April 1853; *RBN*, IX, pp. 94–5.
4 NAO M.23,788, 9 December 1860.
5 *RBN*, IX, p. 148.
6 *RBN*, IX, pp. 183, 200.
7 *RBN*, IX, pp. 222–3.
8 *RBN*, IX, pp. 221, 224; Edward Seaton, *A Report on the Sanitary Condition of the Borough of Nottingham* (Nottingham, 1873), especially pp. 4, 20, 31.
9 *RBN*, IX, pp. 232, 236, 238; 37 & 38 Victoria, The Nottingham Improvement Act, 1874.
10 *Nottingham Guardian*, 13 December 1909.
11 *RBN*, IX, pp. 240–1; *NJ*, 9 October 1874.
12 *RBN*, IX, p. 241: D. E. Roberts, *Nottingham Gas Undertaking 1818–1949* (Nottingham, 1977), pp. 5–22.
13 A. S. Wohl, *Endangered Lives: Public Health in Victorian Britain* (1983), p. 110; N. A. Ferguson, 'Working class housing in Bristol and Nottingham 1868–1919' (University of Oregon, Ph.D. thesis, 1971), p. 62. Profits from the gas and water undertakings were partly used to fund the University College.
14 *RBN*, IX, p. 97; Wylie, pp. 276–7; M. O. Tarbotton, *A Short History of the Old Trent Bridge with a Descriptive Account of the New Bridge, Nottingham* (Nottingham, 1871); Church, pp. 203–4.
15 Nottingham City Council, Estates Committee Report, 1901.
16 *NJ*, 21 September 1875; 14 October 1876.
17 Seaton, *Report*, pp. 4, 29.
18 *Nottingham Daily Express*, 24 September 1875; RBN, IX, p. 246; L. F. Wilson, 'The State and the housing of the English working class with special reference to Nottingham, 1845–1914' (University of California, Berkeley, Ph.D. thesis, 1970), pp. 162–4; Church, pp. 344–5; *Royal Sanitary Commission*, 1st Report and Minutes, PP C.4402–I (xxx), 1, p. 704.
19 *RBN*, IX, pp. 250, 252; Wilson, 'State', p. 163.
20 *Royal Commission on the Housing of the Working Classes*, PP C.4402–I, xxx, pp. 704–5.

21 The history of Victoria dwellings is outlined in S. Best, 'Minnitt's Folly', *Nottingham Civic Society Newsletter* 96–100 (1995–96).

22 *Medical Officer of Health's Annual Report* (1879).

23 E. P. Bailey, 'Leenside: the Churches and the making of a Nottingham slum' (University of Nottingham, MA thesis, 1993), pp. 27, 32, 35.

24 *Reports presented to the Council, 1882–3*, p. 824.

25 *Royal Commission into the State of Large Towns and Populous Districts*, 2nd Report, part II appendix, PP 610 (XVII), p. 257, 'The Suburb of Basford'.

26 Wylie, p. 363.

27 Revd J. Curtis, *A Topographical History of Nottinghamshire* (1843) p. 139.

28 *RBN*, IX, pp. 249, 252, 257. The Act was 40 Victoria, ch. xxxi; G. Oldfield, 'The Nottingham Borough Boundary Extension of 1877', *TTS*, 94 (1990), pp. 83–91.

29 Nottingham Union, *Observations of the Union Extension and New Workhouse Building Committee on the Building of a New Workhouse for the Nottingham Union* presented to the Board of Guardians at their Meeting held on the 29th October 1878.

30 K. Brand, 'Temporary accommodation', *Nottingham Civic Society Newsletter*, 93 (January 1994), pp. 17–21.

31 *EP*, 24 March 1894; *RBN*, IX, p. 382.

32 C. Weir, 'The growth of an inner-urban housing development: Forest Fields, Nottingham, 1883–1914', *TTS*, 89 (1985), pp. 126–31.

33 Church of England Record Centre, Bermondsey, 3459, Revd David Carver to the Ecclesiastical Commissioners, 28 February 1883. The figure of 15,000 is queried in the margin.

34 T. Fry, *The History of Sherwood: a Nottingham Suburb* (1989); L. A. Tong, 'A local study of Carrington, Nottingham: industrial village to disappearing suburb 1830–1930' (University of Nottingham, MA thesis, 1995), pp. 56–7, 67.

35 Tong, 'Carrington', pp. 44, 62–6; Ken Brand, *An Introduction to Mapperley Park* (2nd edn, Nottingham Civic Society, 1996).

36 Fry, *Sherwood*, pp. 54–5; F. Barnes, *Priory Demesne to University Campus* (Nottingham, 1993).

37 *Report of the Borough Extension Committee*, 9 July 1877, p. 5; Church, p. 349; Iliffe and Baguley, 2, p. 26.

38 NUMD William Parsons' Diaries, 19 September 1843.

39 *RBN*, IX, p. 344.

40 *RBN*, IX, p. 394; R. Marshall, *A History of Nottingham City Transport, 1897–1959* (Nottingham, 1960)

41 A 'Nottingham Suburban Light Railway' was floated in 1901 with routes to Carlton, Arnold, Hucknall and Ilkeston, but this was opposed by the Midland Railway and made no progress: Marshall, *History*.

42 *RBN*, IX, pp. 266–7; 42 & 43 Victoria, The Nottingham Improvement Act 1879; Church, pp. 193–204, 339.

43 NAO M.24,480/A8.

44 *NJ*, 5 May 1875.

45 *RBN*, IX, pp. 271, 304.

46 *RBN*, IX, p. 231.

47 *NJ*, 30, 31 March 1881; *Report of the Medical Officer of Health* (1882), p. 49; *RBN*, IX, p. 283.

48 R. Mellors, *In and About Nottinghamshire* (Nottingham, 1890), p. 474.

49 *RBN*, IX, p. 289.

50 *Reports to the Council* (1880–81), p. 717; RBN, IX, p. 289.

51 *Report of the Health Committee to the Council* (1881); *NJ*, 26 October 1880.

52 *Select Committee on Town Holdings* 1888, PP (313) XXII, pp. 557–8; *NJ*, 13 April 1882, 2 June 1885.

53 NAO CA/PE/III; *Royal Sanitary Commission, 1st Report and Minutes*, PP C.4402–I (XXX), 1, p. 704; *RBN*, IX, pp. 289, 303; Church, p. 344. To keep the matter in perspective, Nottingham was one of only twelve towns outside London which applied for permission to use the 1875 legislation: Wohl, *Endangered Lives*, p. 317.

54 *Report* (1882), p. 51; *RBN*, IX, p. 305; Wohl, *Endangered Lives*, pp. 41, 70.

55 Wilson, 'State', p. 148; *Report of the Medical Officer of Health* (1885), p. 53; *Select Committee on Town Holdings* (1888), pp. 557–8.

56 *Report of an Enquiry by the Board of Trade into Working Class Rents, Housing, and Retail Prices* (Cd 3864) (1908), pp. 352–3.

57 NAO TC2/255; *RBN*, IX, pp. 356, 357, 373, 375, 380, 385, 387, 390–1.

58 *Nottingham Daily Express*, 4 January 1898; Wilson, 'State', pp. 236–8; Mellors, *In and About Nottinghamshire*, p. 475.

59 NAO CA/PE/IV; Church, pp. 345–6, Wilson, 'State', pp. 200–31. The houses were of sufficient quality that they were retained during the St Ann's redevelopment of the 1970s.

60 *Nottingham Daily Guardian*, 3 November 1908.

61 Ferguson, 'Working class housing', p. 197; S. Best, 'Unfit for human habitation', *Sneinton Magazine*, 14 (1984), pp. 11–20; R. Smith, P. Whysall and C. Beuvrin, 'Local authority inertia in housing improvement 1890–1914', *Town Planning Review*, 57 (1986), pp. 404–24.

62 *Reports Presented to the Council* (1894–5), p. 11; Wohl, *Endangered Lives*, p. 100.

63 *Special Report of the Housing Committee to the Council* (1912). Night-soil disposal had long earned money for the corporation but it was a hazard for those involved. In 1867 several workers were reported to have been almost blinded for several days as a result of the condition of ashpits and privies, 'and in one instance it is yet doubtful if the sight will be recovered': *RBN*, IX, p. 189.

64 *RBN*, IX, p. 292.

65 *RBN*, IX, p. 395; EP, 1 January 1901; R. Iliffe and W. Baguley, *Edwardian Nottingham*, I (Nottingham, 1978), pp. 5–44.

66 NAO M.24,480, 3 February 1897.

67 Iliffe and Baguley, *Edwardian Nottingham*, I, pp. 60–93; NLSL 'Clearing the Marsh', from Anon. to Council ? 1911 (ref: L 38.8).

68 Church, pp. 154–5; *Outdoor Relief and the Labour Test* (1861).

69 *Nottingham Daily Express*, 18 June 1887; Church, pp. 250–2.

70 *Allen's Nottingham Red Book* (1900), p. 50, gives the objects of the Social Guild; Wilson, 'State', p. 158; *Queen*, 19 October 1895; H. E. Meller, (ed.), *Nottingham in the Eighteen Eighties* (Nottingham, 1971), pp. 21–8.

71 *Royal Commission on the Poor Law*, 1910 Cd 5066 XLVIII, pp. 445–623; evidence of John Kentish Wright, solicitor, chairman of the Nottingham Distress Committee, 1906–07.

72 NAO M.23,868, p. 2; Church, p. 346.

73 F. H. Jacob, *A History of the General Hospital near Nottingham* (Bristol, 1951), pp. 12–22, 113–20, 214–16; *Report of the Medical Officer of Health* (1878); B. Arblaster, 'Health services in Nottingham and the provision for women, 1860–1940' (University of Nottingham, MA dissertation, 1985), pp. 39, 44; A. Teeboon, 'The Nottingham and Nottinghamshire Hospital Saturday Fund, 1873–1948', *TTS*, 84 (1980), pp. 68–72.

74 Terry Fry, 'The General Lunatic Asylum, Nottingham, 1812–1902' (University of Nottingham Advanced Certificate in Local History dissertation, 1994); Arblaster, 'Health Services', pp. 32–6; NAO DD.TS 6/4/3/7; *RBN*, IX, pp. 111, 246, 286.

75 Arblaster, 'Health Services', pp. 25–9; minutes of meetings at the two hospitals are in NUMD UhW. The first annual report is UhW R1/1 (1876).

76 Arblaster, 'Health Services', pp. 68, 73; Jacob, *General Hospital*, pp. 113–217.

77 Arblaster, 'Health Services', pp. 30–1.

78 Quoted in Iliffe and Baguley, 20, p. 86.

79 Edwards, p. 378; Brazier, *New Geography*, p. 63.

80 *Midland Jackdaw*, 9 May 1879.

81 *Nottingham Daily Guardian*, 18 June 1887.

82 *RBN*, IX, p. 390; *Nottingham Daily Guardian*, 26 June, 20 July 1897.

83 *Nottingham Daily Guardian*, 1 January 1901.

13

RADICAL NOTTINGHAM

John Beckett

At the presentation of colours to the Loyal Nottingham Volunteer Infantry and Cavalry on 30 September 1799, the chaplain quoted in his consecration address the remark of a local gentleman that 'he had lived seventeen years in the town of Nottingham, and during that period there had been seventeen riots'.[1] Charles James Fox wrote of the 'uncontrollable spirit of riot' which pervaded elections in the town, and Sir Robert Peel in 1835 thought it 'a disorderly, radical city'.[2] That same year, according to the *Nottingham Journal*, local people travelling away from the town usually found themselves pitied 'when they find you are from Nottingham', and asked if it was currently quiet.[3] Nottingham, in the words of a modern historian, was 'the most riotous town in the kingdom'.[4] Turbulent Nottingham became a byword for troubles of one sort or another, although it was also a litmus test for Westminster governments anxious to take the temperature of political opinion outside the capital. As late as the 1880s elections, both local and national, were invariably marked by disorder and riot. In this chapter we shall ask whether it is possible to explain this remarkable track record. Was Nottingham simply full of individuals and groups ever anxious to pick a fight, or was there more to it than this? Did the disturbances reflect a natural tendency to riot, or should they be seen as the growing pains of a class society?

The towns and cities of Victorian England were the focal point of the economic and social changes which underpinned the social relationships of a class society. Contemporary observers were aware by the 1820s and 1830s that the experiences of particular towns depended on the specific nature of their economic structure. In addition, political debate was increasingly focused at the municipal level, and this was both part and parcel of the substance of local class action. Political activity, in other words, could be related to local economic structures. Thus we would expect to find that in towns with predominantly small units of production class tension was muted because the numerous opportunities which existed for social mobility blurred such distinctions. By contrast, cotton-rich Manchester was deeply divided. The large factories associated with textile production, together with the poverty of the displaced handloom weavers and the impact of world trade fluctuations, are held responsible for the emergence of antagonistic class divisions. Contrasts like these are perhaps too neat and tidy for comfort,[5] but they point towards a basic principle that class relationships can in part be explained by the interaction of general political and economic movements with the specific nature of local urban economic and social structures.

These ideas provide a starting-point for examining Nottingham's reputation. Like Birmingham and Sheffield it was a town of predominantly small businesses, at least until the 1830s and 1840s. At the time of municipal reform in 1835 the corporation was controlled by shopkeepers, but the development of large industrial organisations, as first the lace industry and later hosiery moved from domestic to workshop and factory production, was reflected by the mid-nineteenth century in the growing hold of industrialists on the mayoralty. It was the emergence of larger business concerns in industrial towns which is thought to have triggered social contradictions and class antagonisms, partly because for some employers this phase of development brought great wealth, while for many working people it brought economic obsolescence and impoverishment. This pattern holds good for Nottingham where a handful of entrepreneurs grew wealthy, as the framework knitters, with depression from about 1812 and increasing obsolescence after 1850, found themselves at the industrial margin.

Yet it would be unwise to try to locate emerging class antagonisms in Nottingham simply within the context of economic change. E. P. Thompson, Roger Wells and others have seen Nottingham as a classic exemplar of the view that political events and food scarcity in the 1790s alienated working people from the traditional society in which they lived: in Wells's words, 'considerable sectors of Nottinghamshire's working population were politicised'.[6] Others have argued that such views impose a perspective on events which is not borne out by the reality, since traditional social relationships remained strong.[7] Nottingham was certainly a *radical* town, epitomised perhaps by the election to Parliament in 1847 of Feargus O'Connor, the only Chartist MP. Yet, while each individual event – from food rioting in the 1750s and 1760s through Painite and electoral conflicts during the 1790s, the Luddite disturbances of 1811–16, the Parliamentary reform riots of 1831, and the Chartist disturbances from 1838–48 – is capable of being interpreted in class terms, the relationship between economic change and the emergence of a class society is imprecise. The electoral struggles of the 1850s and 1860s point towards a tradition of riotous behaviour rather than the birth pains and adolescence of a 'class' society.

Nor is the identification of changing social relationships aided by local politics in the town. Political debate through the war years (1793–1815) was fostered by regular town meetings called to debate everything from petitioning for peace to the establishment of a company to light the streets,[8] and the apparent Whig-dissenting hold on government was tempered by a significant Anglican–conservative minority. This was reflected in the election of junior councilmen, the monopoly of news enjoyed until 1808 by the Tory *Nottingham Journal*, and the continuing willingness of the electorate, at least until 1812, to return a Tory for one of the two parliamentary seats. Nor did the position change beyond 1815. In the 1820s several northern industrial towns witnessed the disintegration of an old Tory regime of merchant capitalists, professional men and clergy, and the emergence of a new generation of liberal reformers who were frequently nonconformists and usually industrial employers.[9] It was these Liberals who, benefiting from the repeal of the Test and Corporation Acts in 1828 and municipal reform in 1835, swept away Tory–Anglican majorities in numerous industrial towns, including Manchester, Birmingham, Leeds and Leicester, at the first local elections under the 1835 Act. No such change occurred in Nottingham, where dissent had never been a serious bar to holding public office and where the Whig hold on local government passed smoothly from the old to the new corporation.[10] Beyond 1835 the Tory minority occasionally found an issue on which to threaten the entrenched elite, particularly over the workhouse in the 1840s, but it was only in 1908 that the Conservatives finally gained an outright majority on the corporation.

The reality behind Nottingham's reputation can in fact be explained in terms partly of circumstances and partly of place. As a market centre the town attracted large numbers of visitors on Wednesdays and Saturdays. It was also on a Saturday that outworkers in the domestic hosiery industry came to the town to sell their wares and receive payment. As a result, the population was swollen by nearly 40 per cent.[11] Market stalls and shops stayed open late, awaiting custom from the framework knitters when they had been paid. The knitters would often cause disturbances when they learned during Saturday evening of changes in their working conditions. There were riots in 1783 when the employers lowered the prices they paid the knitters for their finished products; and in 1787 when a stocking frame was smashed in Narrow Marsh. In October 1790 troops were called from Peterborough 'in anticipation of a framework knitters' riot', but their presence did not prevent windows from being broken and thirty-seven arrests. As the Deputy Adjutant-General, Colonel De Lancey, commented in 1792, 'the people ... from the facility of getting money in the manufacturers and the dissipation which accompanies it, [are] very much disposed to Riot'.[12]

This disposition to riot was encouraged by the physical space in which to riot – the market-place – and to assemble, the Forest and Mapperley Hills.[13] The market-place, a large open area capable of holding many thousands of people, was the centre of electoral activities in the town; indeed, election riots only came to an end when, in the mid-1880s, Nottingham lost its position as the home of county elections and after the last burst of rioting in 1885, the town's three post-1884 constituencies began to count their votes locally. Until then almost every contest was accompanied by some form of violence, for which economic conditions alone do not provide an obvious explanation. Our difficulty is in trying to categorise Nottingham. Was the *Nottingham Journal* correct when it suggested in 1835 that the town was 'generally branded as the nursery of sedition and the stronghold of political and religious (or irreligious) agitation ... continuously the scene of some revolutionary tumult or other'?[14] Was there simply a tradition of riotous behaviour which was as much a part of election campaigns as candidates and polling booths? Or was it the case that radical politics and riotous behaviour were simply two sides of the same coin?

Food riots

Nottingham's reputation was established during the second half of the eighteenth century, initially because of food riots, but increasingly as a result of electoral and political struggles. In 1756–57 more than 140 separate food riots took place across thirty different counties as grain prices soared to record levels. On 25 August 1756 a group of colliers employed at Lord Middleton's pits in Cossall and Wollaton marched to Nottingham complaining of high food prices and irregular milling practices. Samuel Fellows, the mayor, recorded what happened next:

> about 9 o'clock this morning a great number of colliers, and other persons, entered this town armed with stakes, hatchets, pickaxes, shouting and making a great noise; upon which the proclamation against rioters was read, and these persons were seized and carried into the Guildhall, to wit, Thomas Johnson and William Johnson of Cossall, and William Waplington of Trowell.

Arresting the troublemakers was not necessarily the most prudent course of action:

> Before any examination could be taken the mob increased to a very large number demanding to have these men released. And beginning to grow desperate several of the foremost were admitted to a conference and promised to quit the town and go home quietly if the three men might be set at liberty.

The mayor decided that 'as no real mischief was then done, and finding that the men would be rescued; and that, probably, the Town Hall would be pulled down over our heads; we set the men at liberty'. If he thought his troubles were over – 'the mob was actually about to leave the town' – it soon became clear that worse was to follow. 'A number of women (of this town as 'tis supposed) gave them [the colliers] money to come back, and showed them to a windmill within our limits belonging to one Mr Foulds, having French [mill]stones.' This was sufficient provocation for the crowd. Foulds's millstones were broken and several other mills damaged. Although a number of rioters were arrested, prosecutions were dropped when witnesses refused to testify.[15]

In 1766, another year in which food riots took place across the country, Goose Fair was the occasion of a 'great cheese riot' when local suppliers demanded a price rise to 3*d* a pound. Stalls were attacked and ransacked, and cheeses distributed to the crowd. Being barrel-shaped they could easily be rolled, and soon they were being propelled down Wheeler Gate and Peck Lane. The mayor, trying desperately to intervene, stood in the middle of Peck Lane, only to be knocked over by an accelerating cheese. Troops were called out, shots fired, and one man was killed in the fracas.[16] Further food-related riots occurred in 1785, when an attempt was made to keep down the price of butter; in 1788, when a crowd complaining about high meat prices wrecked the butchers' Shambles; and on several occasions during the 1790s. In May 1792 a mob rioted 'on account of the high price of butcher's meat'. The butchers fled the Shambles, and the crowd helped themselves to the meat. A further group of shoppers, arriving in the evening, burned the empty stalls.[17] Worse was to follow in 1795. On 18 April a crowd assembled in the market-place 'with the avowed intention of sacking the Shambles'. The Riot Act was read, troops were called out to restore order, and the mayor used his authority to allow country butchers to set up stalls 'for the purpose of securing a better supply of meat, and a spirit of competition'. Over subsequent months the price of wheat soared, and by July hardly any was available in the town. On 20 April 'a large mob, consisting principally of women, went from one baker's shop to another, set their own prices on the stock therein, and putting down the money, took it away'. Although troops were again called out, it took twelve hours to restore order. The corporation sent agents to the ports in an attempt to acquire supplies, but without notable success.[18] Tension eased only when the new harvest brought an improvement in conditions.

The next crisis followed the disastrous harvest of 1799. Grain prices were already soaring by January 1800. A soup kitchen was opened in February, and in April Abigail Gawthern commented laconically on 'a riot in the market place on account of the high price of provisions'.[19] After that the town remained calm, and in August prices dipped in anticipation of a good harvest. When storms ruined much of the crop and the price began to rise again, the patience of local consumers finally snapped. On 31 August a crowd stoned the premises of bakers and millers in the town. The riot continued the following evening when barges on the River Trent laden with grain were attacked, and a warehouse stacked with flour near the canal was broken into. Troops were called out, but disturbances continued over the following days. According to a correspondent of *The Times* on 2 September there was a 'real panic' among 'all the opulent', and shops were closed. The trouble, he added, was that the riot was unlikely to subside while 'the women … the principal aggressors', remained on the streets.[20] When Mr Statham called on Mrs Gawthern he carried 'a brace of loaded pistols in his pockets'. The corporation printed broadsheets urging quiet: 'unless peace and good order be restored, it is impossible for any exertions to induce the farmers to send their corn to the town'. Also on 2 September the town clerk wrote to various farmers, millers and local landowners urging them to respond to the desperate plight in the town: 'we should be very happy to contribute to the relief of the town but at this moment we have not upon our premises a single loaf, not a strike of corn'.[21] Serious disorder broke out the following day. Fighting in the Meadows was followed by the ambush of a member of the Holme Pierrepont yeomanry cavalry, who was attacked and severely beaten as he guarded a cartload of grain being carried to the town. Two of those who took part in the riots wrote that

> your hearts would have ached to have seen the women Calling for Bread and declaring they would fight till they died before they would be used so any longer ... the conduct of the people ... who stood the fire from the yeomanry with such undaunted courage that astonished the gentlemen for they poured such showers of stones on them in all directions that they could load their pieces no more after they had fired them.[22]

The corporation sought ways of relieving the distress, and even tried the expedient of buying grain and selling it at a subsidised price. These measures had little impact. By 7 September there was hardly any grain in the town, and 'factors sent word that they would bring no more corn till the rioting was over'. On 11 September rioters 'broke the windows of the Leen Bridge Mill and went to Mr Jowitts at Colwick', and with supplies of wheat in short supply throughout September troop reinforcements were brought from Northampton on 16 September 'to keep the mob quiet'. It was not until 23 September that the magistrates believed they had established a 'tolerable quietness', but the town remained tense for several months. When a soup kitchen, opened on Christmas Day, ran out of supplies there was a further riot. Troops remained on the streets throughout the night, and reinforcements were brought in from Birmingham.[23]

After 1800 food riots were less frequent. The poor harvest of 1811 sent prices upwards and created the conditions for popular disturbances through the winter and spring of 1811–12. These culminated in a serious riot in September 1812, again led by women. As late as 1847, during Chartist disturbances, bakers were forced to reduce their prices, but the age of the food riot was more or less over by the end of the Napoleonic wars.[24]

The French Revolutionary and Napoleonic Wars

In any case riots in Nottingham had never been concerned solely with food supply. Elections, whether local or parliamentary, produced their fair share of trouble. As a county borough Nottingham returned two members to Parliament, but until the mid-eighteenth century had happily accepted candidates nominated by outside aristocratic interests. The Duke of Newcastle, owner of the Castle and Recorder of the town, was one such interest. His right to return an MP for Nottingham was first challenged in 1747 when the corporation proposed Lord Howe. John Plumptre, the sitting member, withdrew.[25] Thereafter the corporation began to flex its political muscle. Contests became both more frequent and, with a large (*c.*2,000) and volatile electorate, more lively. The political temperature finally reached boiling point when in 1790 the sitting members, the Whig Robert Smith of the local banking family, and the conservative independent Daniel Parker Coke, offered themselves for re-election. The campaign was marked by violence. On 17 June, the day before the polls opened, all the windows in Smith's bank (now the National Westminster Bank next to the Council House) were smashed, and when the re-election of the two MPs was announced late on 18 June windows were smashed in the Exchange and in adjoining corporation property:

'the ground was everywhere as an entire sheet of glass', wrote Thomas Bailey, who claimed never to have witnessed such a scene of destruction in the market-place.[26] Special constables, sworn in to try to restore order, 'drove the mob out of the and the mob went into the fields, and got hedge stakes and stones, and returned again into the Market Place, and drove the constables entirely away; they were obliged to run for the mob threw immense quantities of stones at them; many people much hurt'. A witness was later to recall 'life lost and your infirmary crowded with wounded – lives of [Smith's] adherents in imminent danger, their houses demolished as far as the mob could accomplish it, his own home attacked with such violence that scarcely a window or window frame remained'. When troops intervened to restore order one man, 'merely standing as a spectator' according to Mrs Gawthern, was shot dead.[27]

This was the kind of behaviour guaranteed to make the government at Westminster jittery, coming as it did so soon after the Revolution in France. Bailey argued that events across the channel had divided political opinion in Nottingham, although according to Blackner it was not until 1792 that Nottingham people split into 'two hostile parties, under the appellations of democrats and aristocrats'.[28] With its Whig corporation, a tradition of support for parliamentary reform, and a propensity to riot, Nottingham was a place an increasingly conservative government fearing 'seditious meetings and publications' needed to watch carefully. This became abundantly clear in May 1792 when the issue of a Royal Proclamation against seditious writings produced political conflict in the town. As elsewhere, a group of Tory gentlemen requested the mayor to call a public meeting to endorse the proclamation. On Tory-dominated corporations this was hardly a problem, but in Nottingham the Whig mayor, Samuel Oldknow, refused. Undaunted, the Tories held a meeting anyway, and a 'loyal address' was voted with more than 500 signatures.[29]

Plate 33 **C.J. Greenwood, Nottingham Park, *c.*1850, showing the Cavalry Barracks**. The barracks were largely erected in 1792–93 when the Duke of Newcastle let a four-acre site to the government for sixty years at an annual rent of £80. The picture also shows how limited development in the Park had been before T.C. Hine's work began in the mid-1850s, confined to the periphery, here fronting on to Derby Road

Nor perhaps is it surprising that the government, well aware of the town's reputation, and anxious to nip any potential trouble in the bud, nominated Nottingham for the dubious distinction of becoming the first sizeable English town to be awarded

Plate 34 **'The Contrast'**. A political broadsheet contrasting 'the pillars of the Constitution', with 'the tree of liberty'. A loyalist mob is shown outside the Exchange 'ducking' alleged supporters of the French Revolution in water from a public pump, *c*.1794

its own barracks for the permanent quartering of troops. The foundation stone was laid on 6 August 1792:

> The site is a most delightful one; and commands an extensive view to every point of the compass. These barracks [contain] well constructed apartments for the officers, a suttling house, stabling for three troops of horse, an hospital &c. the whole of which, embracing an extensive yard, is well walled round with brick.[30]

With additions between 1797 and 1799 the total cost must have been near to £20,000, and in 1798 a riding school was built for the gentlemen of the Nottingham Troop of the Yeomanry cavalry. While some Nottingham residents must have feared the presence of a permanent force of soldiers, at least the innkeepers found cause for rejoicing; so frequently had troops been called to the town to suppress riots that for years they had endured 'troopers almost continually quartered at their houses'. Billeting was a responsibility they were glad to shed.[31]

By the end of 1792 a popular democratic organisation had almost certainly been established in Nottingham, and Thomas Hardy, secretary of the London Corresponding Society, visited the town in November. The embryo Nottingham society grew through 1793, and had a mature organisation by February 1794. But with the outbreak of war on 1 February 1793 Nottingham – as happened in many other places – became a loyal and patriotic town. In March 1793 Tom Paine, the radical hero since the publication of his *Rights of Man*, was burned in effigy, and the Tory *Journal* – hardly able to believe the change of direction – recorded that 'universal joy beamed in every countenance'. The houses of radical sympathisers were attacked, and during boisterous celebrations of King George III's birthday a shoemaker accidentally shot his own father.[32] Some of the more enthusiastic of the loyalists began drilling, claiming that they were preparing to resist insurrection. In June 1794 'Republicans' in Nottingham were forcibly 'baptised' in the Leen and when, the following month, supporters of the Revolution were also rumoured to be drilling in nearby fields with the sanction of the mayor, a riot took place. Property was damaged belonging to people thought to be sympathetic to the principles of the French Revolution. On 2 July a mob marched from the market-place and 'set fire to the workshops' at Robert Denison's mill. Denison had opposed the war for economic reasons but, shocked by the attack, he closed the mill and re-opened it again only in 1801. It was burned to the ground in 1802, when arson was suspected. In the meantime, fear of invasion in 1794 led to the formation of the Nottinghamshire Yeomanry.[33]

This change of political allegiance proved relatively short-lived, and the town's radical undercurrent was never suppressed. Daniel Parker Coke introduced a petition from Nottingham into Parliament in 1793 proposing manhood suffrage, and in 1794 several burgesses unsuccessfully proposed that the radical leader of the opposition, Charles James Fox, should be invited to succeed the recently deceased Duke of Newcastle as Recorder of the town. Support for the war waned through the winter of 1794–95 with political discontent reviving against a background of sharply rising prices.[34] Opposition was mounted to the so-called Gagging Acts, the Treasonable

Practices Act and the Seditious Meetings Act. Petitions against both bills were sent to Westminster by the corporation, accompanied by an address to the King demanding an end to the French war. In taking this action the corporation was giving the kind of lead in Nottingham that democratic organisations were fighting for in London and elsewhere, but this did not mean it had displaced the radical movement in the town. So much became clear in the 1796 election campaign.

Coke and Smith, the sitting members, offered themselves for re-election in 1796, but many of the burgesses were dissatisfied with Smith, who was thought to be over-favourable towards the government. Dr Peter Crompton of Derby stood on a popular radical platform – Mrs Gawthern identified his supporters as Painites. The contest was marked by 'a great disturbance in the market place', and much window smashing. Gangs of partisans blocked the approaches to the polls and assaulted those whose views differed from their own. Fights broke out in the streets. In the end Smith and Coke were returned, but Crompton's 560 votes reflected the strong groundswell of radical opinion among the electorate: his supporters had shown their sympathy with events in France 'by carrying about a tree of liberty, which, on one occasion, they planted, or attempted to plant in the Market-place'.[35] The division of opinion in Nottingham was re-emphasised when, in November 1796, two senior councilmen had to be chosen for the corporation. The Tory Abigail Gawthern regarded Samuel Green and William Huthwaite, who were eventually successful, as 'the loyal candidates', and dismissed 'Mr Fellows and a Mr Wylde' as 'Painites'.[36]

Although the French Revolution clearly influenced thinking during the 1796 election, supporters were heavily outnumbered by those loyal to the government. Wartime victories could still prompt rejoicing in the town, but the volatile Nottingham crowd could never be entirely trusted. When in 1797 Robert Smith was elevated to a peerage as Lord Carrington, Admiral Sir John Borlase Warren of Stapleford was elected in his place. Large crowds had turned out when the war hero received the freedom of the town early in 1796, given to celebrate his capture of three French frigates while on active service, and his leadership of the expedition to Quiberon Bay in 1795. However, by the time of the 1797 by-election the national economy had slipped into recession, and the downturn was particularly severely felt in the Nottingham textile trades. The corporation petitioned the king, calling for the dismissal of the ministry and the immediate ending of the war. The Nottingham Corresponding Society convened a public meeting in the market-place, a meeting which could have been proscribed by the magistrates under existing legislation. Instead it was attended by the mayor and 'several aldermen', and a declaration was passed in favour of parliamentary reform. In these circumstances it is perhaps not surprising that during Borlase Warren's celebratory chairing following the declaration of the by-election result, 'a great mob of Painites broke the chair all to bits at the end of Greyhound Yard', and somewhat ignominiously the Admiral took refuge in the Tory headquarters, the White Lion Inn.[37]

After 1797 it is less easy to trace the activities of Nottingham radicals. The French invasion scare had a unifying effect on the town, although the corporation continued to oppose the war. 'A number of Painites dressed all in a blue uniform followed the High Sheriff who was in the same dress' when the Assizes opened on 22 March 1798,[38] and Nottingham was still considered a centre of radical activity in 1800 when Bow Street Runners were sent to ingratiate themselves among 'disaffected persons'. They reported that 200 or more people met in the Mason's Arms nightly where 'the conversation was always of the most seditious nature, and held without any reserve or restraint such as damning the King & ... praising the French ... declaring themselves highly in favour of a Revolution in England, and wishing for it immediately'. However, although the Home Office sent extra militia to Nottingham, it must be doubtful whether such open meetings could have continued, even in a town with radical sympathies, had they been suspected of serious intent.[39]

There were, without doubt, some supporters of events in France in the town, and they were again prominent during the 1802 election, held during a brief respite in the war. Coke and Borlase Warren stood, but the corporation was determined to play a part, partly because it believed Coke had been insufficiently vigorous in his opposition to the war. However, the corporation was unable to find a suitable candidate, and Coke and Borlase Warren were duly nominated. This should have been the end of the matter but the returning officer, instead of declaring them elected, called for votes on behalf of the two candidates. During the first hour of polling forty-four votes were cast, and then the corporation announced that it was putting forward Joseph Birch. Although Birch was unable to reach Nottingham until the fourth day of polling, this was sufficient to ensure a contest. Intimidation and riot reached new levels. Cobblestones were torn up and hurled at voters and candidates alike. Coke could not compete. On 8 July he was stoned by the crowd, after which he put a flyer around the town complaining of 'the various insults and threats which I have received in the [polling] booth for the last two days'. He had no option, he declared, but to withdraw from the contest. 'Everything is riot and confusion', recorded the *Journal*, and a petition of voters claiming they were prevented from polling for Coke due to the activities of the crowd gathered 537 signatures.[40]

Birch was duly returned, and was chaired into the town 'preceded by twenty-four damsels, dressed in white, ornamented with wreaths of flowers, and carrying leaves of laurel in their hands'. Somewhat surprisingly, 'the greatest good order prevailed'.[41] Coke petitioned Parliament, asking that the election be declared void, and the House of Commons committee which considered the petition reported that 'the freedom of the election was grossly violated, by disturbances and riots, accompanied with personal intimidation and violence'. On 16 March 1803 Birch's election was declared void, but no writ was moved until Parliament had passed the 'Daniel Parker Coke Act'. The legislation gave the county magistrates concurrent jurisdiction in the town to try to keep order and to ensure free elections. Not surprisingly, the corporation opposed the measure, which was denounced in the Commons by Charles James Fox as a straightforward election manoeuvre.[42]

While Parliament was busy with this legislation, Nottingham was in a state of electoral readiness. Through the winter of 1802–03, according to Bailey, the town witnessed 'one continued scene of drunkenness, disorder, tumult, canvassings, dancings, processions, and the like'.[43] Once the bill passed into law, a new election writ was moved. The corporation supported Birch, claiming that the Act was an invasion of 'the Charters which every Member of this Hall, and every Burgess has sworn to defend'. Birch arrived in the town on 23 March 1803 'with an immense mob up the Hollow Stone', and for the next two months the town was in a state of high tension. The election finally took place towards the end of May. Abigail Gawthern watched on 26 May when Coke's supporters met in the market-place 'with hundreds of people on horseback and foot', before moving off to the gates of Wollaton Park, where they met Coke *en route* from Derby and escorted him back to the town. The following day she noted acidly that 'Birch arrived and his Jacobin crew'. Coke defeated Birch by 195 votes in a poll of 2,523, and he was in the market-place again on 7 June to receive the congratulations of his supporters. He was chaired the following day: 'never was so handsome, so elegant a chair, nor such a concourse of people all with blue ribbons; the chair preserved whole owing to their throwing ribbons out of the Black's Head windows', as Mrs Gawthern recorded.[44] The contest was marked by incidents in which supporters of Birch allegedly had vitriol thrown on their clothes (a capital crime for the perpetrators), and Charles Sutton set up what would might now be called a support group for those victimised as a result of their voting behaviour.

The events of 1802–03 were only a temporary blow to the confidence of the corporation, and the county magistrates proved reluctant to intervene in town elections, despite the Daniel Parker Coke Act. However when, within a month of the 1803 election, the country was again at war with France, the corporation failed to raise a protest. Having in 1798 refused to make a donation to the war effort, the corporation now called a town meeting, and offered 400 guineas to the government together with its firm support for the conflict. Volunteers were called for, and about 750 men were formed into two battalions. By the end of 1804 almost the entire male population was being trained in the use of arms, partly because of the fear of invasion. Householders not among the volunteers were sworn in to act as special constables, and a large room in the Exchange became the local armoury. Whatever the allegations of disloyalty in the 1790s, there was little evidence of it during the Napoleonic Wars.[45]

The bigger problem was that of retaining interest in the war. Although the 'great news' of victory at Trafalgar was celebrated with 'three excellent vollies' by the infantry in the market-place, a Yeomanry dinner at the Flying Horse, and a 'general thanksgiving',[46] this was perhaps the last occasion on which the town turned out to celebrate. The 1806 and 1807 elections were quiet affairs. Borlase Warren stood down in 1806 when Coke was returned with John Smith, another member of the banking family. The corporation tried without much success to persuade its tenants and leaseholders to support Joseph Birch. Coke and Smith were returned again in 1807. With economic depression beginning to affect the hosiery trade, interest in the war declined. The volunteer yeomanry and infantry had effectively been dismantled by 1809.[47] In these years Nottingham voters returned to their older interest in Parliamentary reform, particularly with the founding in 1808 by Charles Sutton of the radical *Nottingham Review*.

Sutton launched the *Review* on the grounds that many people in the town did not have a newspaper congenial to their political sentiments. Initially the paper was pro-war, partly because of widespread indignation when France invaded Spain in 1808. Soon, however, Sutton began a campaign against the war and he championed the cause of Parliamentary reform. Simultaneously, the corporation gradually strengthened its electoral hand. In 1809 John Wheatley was chosen by 'a select meeting of the Corporation and Whig interest', although he was never in fact to run, but thereafter Whig candidates were assumed to have the backing of the corporation.

Coke, fearing he could not win in 1812 because he had become identified with those favouring the war, made over his interest to Richard Arkwright, son of the cotton magnate, but without much confidence. As Lord Liverpool told the Duke of Newcastle, 'the influence of government on a place like Nottingham cannot be considerable, but [Mr Arkwright] shall certainly have our best support in any way in which it can be properly given'.[48] It was not enough to return a Tory, particularly Arkwright, who opposed reform and peace at any price. As a result, and with the help of some judicious creations of honorary freemen, two Whigs were returned, Lord Rancliffe and John Smith. Rancliffe was summoned from Bunny Hall as the polls were opening, and he did not gain the approval of the corporation until the fourth day of the election. At the end of 1812 a petition calling for peace raised 5,000–6,000 signatures; by contrast, just 700 signed a counter-petition urging the continuation of the war. Only the publication for a short while from 1813 of the fiercely Tory *Nottingham Gazette* suggested the presence of a faction in the town willing openly to support the government, but the war was never again really popular in Nottingham. Although there was some rejoicing when Napoleon abdicated in 1814, there were no significant events in the wake of Waterloo and by then the *Gazette* had folded.[49]

Luddism

The closing years of the war brought industrial depression, and with it came Luddism. Frame-breaking as a form of protest had a long history in the hosiery industry, but the first outbreak of Luddite activity in March 1811 proved more serious. There was trouble during the autumn and winter of 1811–12, again in the spring of 1814, and a last outburst during 1816–17. Luddism started when some of the larger hosiery employers forced down wages to try to stimulate trade and open up new markets. Other employers looked for different, cheaper goods, which it was hoped would create new demands. To this end some hosiers began to produce 'cut-ups' rather than fully-fashioned garments, and lace manufacturers started to produce single-press lace. The Luddites particularly objected to the frames producing cut-ups, although action against the wide frames on which these were produced followed, rather than accompanied, action triggered by falling wages. Economic conditions underpinned Luddite actions. The framework knitters believed they had been badly treated by the hosiers during the depression of 1811–12. One of the town's MPs, John Smith, told the

House of Commons in February 1812 that he had never witnessed so much misery as on a recent visit to Nottingham. Trends in wages and food prices together ensured that the diet of framework knitters beyond 1811 was frequently little above starvation level. One of them claimed in 1812 that he fed his family on barley-bread, old milk, and potatoes. During a food riot in September 1812 one group of rioters was led by a woman nicknamed Lady Ludd. Yet, far from receiving any Parliamentary sympathy, in 1812 the framework knitters could only watch as frame-breaking was turned into a capital offence. An appeal to the Lords by the young Lord Byron of Newstead Abbey fell on deaf ears.

While Luddism originated in economic distress, the question which has taxed both contemporaries and historians concerns whether it turned into something more than a protest against prevailing conditions. The Tory *Nottingham Gazette* took the view that the disturbances were expressions of social conflict, whatever the industrial reasons that initially provoked them. Jacobinism, according to the *Gazette*, was the root and spring of frame-breaking in the town, and as such Luddism was a revolutionary protest.[50] Other contemporaries also believed that the Luddites might have seditious intentions, particularly in the later phases of the movement. George Coldham, the town clerk, was worried in 1815 that without a substantial increase in troop numbers within the town law and order could not be preserved. Coldham lived through the spring of 1815 in fear of physical attacks on himself and the magistrates. A further 'revolution' panic erupted in 1816, when Henry Enfield, who had succeeded Coldham as town clerk, reported to the Home Secretary suspicious meetings in public houses. On 9 December he even reported 'talk of revolution' among the Luddites. This seems to have been unnecessarily alarmist; in February 1817 the town magistrates rejected as unnecessary a proposal from the Home Office to transfer the Assizes to Newark.[51]

The problem for historians has been to decide just what the balance was between industrial and economic protest, and revolutionary intention. For E. P. Thompson, Luddism was a highly politicised movement, and his views have been developed by Roger Wells. By contrast, Malcolm Thomis has argued that in the years 1811–14 Luddism was essentially an industrial protest and any political overtones were to be found only in the last phase of the movement.[52] Others have suggested that the Luddite troubles came at a time of crisis common to both employer and employee, both of whom had doubts about the most appropriate means of solving the industry's structural problems.[53] The difficulty is that the Luddites did not use the revolutionary rhetoric and symbolism which would identify them as politically alienated, while from the point of view of industrial protest the movement died out before the structural problems were resolved.

Whatever the intentions of the Luddites, few of them joined the ill-fated uprising led by Jeremiah Brandreth in 1817. Through the spring of 1817 would-be insurgents were meeting regularly at the home of William Stevens, a needle-maker. Stevens was the leader of one of a number of secret committees planning an uprising on 9 June 1817. The delegate to this committee from Pentrich and South Wingfield, twelve miles away, was a framework knitter, Thomas Bacon. He organised a series of meetings at Pentrich, where he claimed that widespread preparations were under way. Jeremiah Brandreth was appointed by the Nottingham committee to lead the men of Pentrich to Nottingham on the night of 9 June. He told the Pentrich men that they would be provided with bread, beef and ale, as well as money, that by the time they reached Nottingham they would find it in the hands of its people, and that they would be joined by another 16,000 men from various venues. A provisional government would be set up in the town before the rebels marched on London. Brandreth marched from Pentrich as arranged, but once through Eastwood he and his men were caught and scattered by soldiers from the 15th Regiment of Light Dragoons. More than eighty were arrested, of whom fourteen were later transported and three, including Brandreth, executed. In Nottingham about 100 men assembled on the Forest but they dispersed peacefully. This was an ill-fated movement from the outset, but it was symptomatic of a wider belief that a revolutionary uprising might just begin in Nottingham, a reflection perhaps of the Home Office view of Nottingham formed as a result of events in the 1790s and again during the Luddite disturbances.[54]

From 1817 Nottingham corporation sought to cement its control of Parliamentary elections by creating new voters in the form of honorary freemen: 'many of these', the 1835 Royal Commission on Municipal Corporations noted, 'were wholly unconnected with both the town and the county. No previous communication had taken place between them and the corporation, but the freedom was voted to them on account of their known political opinions'.[55] In 1818 300 honorary freemen were sworn in prior to a contest which was 'attended with immense drunkenness and disorder, fights, intimidation, destruction of property, and party animosities'. Two Whigs were returned (Rancliffe and Joseph Birch) at this contest and again in 1820, although on both occasions with slim majorities.[56] To make sure slim majorities did not become minorities the policy was pursued more vigorously. Between 1819 and 1821 600 honorary freemen were created, and by 1826 it was alleged that the corporation had created around 1,200, many of them from Tory-dominated (and thus Whig-excluded) neighbouring Leicester. For their part, leading Tories took to purchasing and dividing freehold property in Nottingham in order to create additional voters. This was not of the same order: two Whigs were returned in 1826 when only ten of the 517 honorary freemen supported the defeated Tory. In 1830 two Whigs were returned, with the Tories failing to put up candidates. The corporation now controlled not only elections to its own number, but also the return of the town's MPs. It was a Whig monopoly against which the Tory–Anglican minority could make little headway.[57]

Parliamentary reform

Despite the Whig hold on politics, the continued existence of two power blocs was all too evident in the Reform crisis of 1830–32. Support for reform had been an issue in the town since the 1780s. In response to Peterloo, the Manchester reform meeting which ended in bloodshed, the corporation called a public meeting at which the magistrates were the chief speakers. In so doing it put itself back at the head of the reform cause in the town, a position it chose to exploit when the subject came back on to the national political agenda in 1830. In October that year the mayor organised a public meeting in support of reform. More than 8,000 signatures were gathered for a petition, and when Thomas Denman presented it to the House of Commons he claimed that it was signed by more than half the adult males of the town. A public meeting at the Exchange in March 1831 voted an address to the King and a petition to Parliament in favour of reform: 9,030 people signed the petition in only three and a half days.[58] It was followed in April by the uncontested return of the two sitting (Whig) MPs.

Through the summer months public meetings were generally orderly, but peaceful protest turned violent when, in October 1831, the second Reform Bill was thrown out by the House of Lords. News reached Nottingham late in the evening of the Saturday of Goose Fair, 8 October. The mayor immediately organised a public meeting for the Monday (10 October), but in the meantime revellers became rioters, with shops looted and disturbances continuing throughout the night. On Sunday 9 October, rumours that reformers in London were taking up arms fuelled rioting in the town. Windows were broken and personal violence threatened against those who had signed an anti-reform petition. The 15th Hussars were called out to restore order.[59] Crowds gathered early on the following morning for the public meeting timed to begin at 11 o'clock. By some estimates as many as 20,000 people gathered in the market-place. Order was maintained through the meeting, which was addressed by various prominent local leaders and which passed resolutions in support of the bill. Subsequently a group of rioters went to Colwick Hall, the home of John Musters, a prominent Tory magistrate. They broke in to the Hall, and 'attempted to set the house on fire by making a large fire of the Furniture in a lodging room; fortunately it was extinguished by the servants'.[60] Mrs Musters and her family took refuge with their solicitor in Nottingham. Returning to the town, the mob tried – and failed – to break open the House of Correction, before moving on to the Castle.

The fourth Duke of Newcastle, the owner of the Castle, was an implacable opponent of reform, and one of those who had been responsible for the rejection of the bill in the Lords. He had also presented the small Nottingham petition against reform. His reactionary views were well known, and during the election of April 1831 his London house was attacked by a mob with him inside, and the windows broken.[61] He remained unrepentant, and in Nottingham his Castle – although empty and largely neglected – was a symbol of his political views, so apparently out of line with thinking in the town. In pouring rain, a mob fired the Castle, and thousands gathered to watch the spectacle, which could be seen for miles around. Next morning the mob returned to the smouldering ruins to pull down what was left, and threats were issued against banks in the town, and against other property owned by Newcastle. The violence continued on 11 October. The rioters moved to Beeston, calling on Dr John Storer at Lenton Firs *en route.* After an acrimonious exchange they stole his carrots. At Beeston they burned down the silk mill belonging to a prominent Tory, William Lowe. Returning to Nottingham they called at Lenton House, the home of Matthew Needham. In his absence they ate all the food in the house and drank all his ale and wine 'at the same time laying their hands upon any portable article, which they carried off, together with about £40 worth of plate'. At neighbouring Lenton Hall 'John Wright gave them what money he had about him.'[62] Only the presence of the Yeomanry prevented an attack on Wollaton Hall. The rioters returned to the market-place, where shops were closed and the entrances barricaded. The mayor imposed a curfew, and order was eventually restored.

In the aftermath of these events, a good deal of energy was spent trying to distinguish between the rioters, many of them thought to be revellers from outside the town rather than local people, and the reformers. The local press tried to pass off the riots as the work of low and bad characters, who happened to be in the town for Goose Fair. In fact the rioters seem to have been politically well informed, and to have selected their targets with considerable care. Newcastle, lord-lieutenant of the county, and far from enamoured with the townspeople of Nottingham, happily raised the stakes by passing on to the Home Office gossip about money being collected for arms, and other signs of disaffection. The Nottingham Political Union, formed to promote a reform measure which would unite 'the middle and lower classes of the people of this town', had held its first public meeting in March 1831, but only now enjoyed an upsurge of support. Its membership reached 2,500 by January 1832, and it was rumoured to be buying muskets to hand around among its supporters. Such rumours proved to be groundless, and the town remained relatively calm, even during the trials in January 1832 of the handful of rioters who were arrested. No one was convicted for firing the Castle, but three men were hanged and four others transported for their role in the outrages at Colwick and Beeston.[63] And it was an event which lived on in the popular memory long after the participants had been forgotten. Writing in the 1880s James Hopkinson recalled the riots, which were 'so stamped on my memory that I cannot forget them', and reflecting on the nineteenth century the *Nottingham Daily Guardian* recalled that 'among the many local memorable events which have taken place during the century, the most striking is undoubtedly the destruction of the Nottingham Castle by fire'.[64]

When the reform bill finally passed into law in August 1832 the magistrates ordered the church bells to be rung and organised collections to pay for celebrations throughout the town. At a formal occasion on 6 August a procession supposedly numbering 15,000–20,000 assembled to welcome the two sitting MPs, and the 6,000–7,000 children involved each received a bun and a small mug of ale. The Keeper of the House of Correction noted that there was 'great rejoicing in Nottingham on account of the Passing of the Reform Bill, the morning was ushered in by the firing of cannon, ringing of bells, and the assembling of persons of all distinctions and of all ages'. But these were peaceful, garden-party-like celebrations rather than the rejoicings of a politicised working class which had finally won a concession. When William Cobbett lectured in Nottingham in February 1830 and was greeted by one member of his audience with the words 'Tom Paine for ever' others, according to the pro-Reform *Review*, 'instantly expressed their displeasure'.[65] Throughout the reform years the lead in Nottingham came from the corporation, and even the riots of October 1831 are difficult to interpret as class warfare in any meaningful way, although there was considerable local disquiet at the executions in January 1832. Petitions were raised in the town calling for the men to be reprieved, and the crowd at the execution was reported to be 'very far from being so numerous as on some former occasions; very few male inhabitants of the town were within sight of the scaffold, there were many women present'. In the afternoon shops closed in the town and 'the walking stationers generally abstained from calling aloud in the streets'.[66]

To contemporaries the 1832 Reform Act represented a watershed, the first significant change in the electoral system for four hundred years, and enough to make those opposed to the measure fearful for the future of the political system. It was not, of course, anything like as radical and serious as this, as distance from 1832 has revealed. In fact it took only weeks for many supporters of reform to become disillusioned, largely because so little seemed to have been achieved. In Nottingham, supporters and opponents of the 1832 legislation soon agreed that it had made little difference. The Nottingham Political Union remained in existence, and the pro-reform *Nottingham Review* continued to press for further measures. The newspaper believed that in Nottingham the electorate would remain much the same in size, with the 1,000–1,500 notorious honorary freemen being replaced by about the same number of new voters from the class of £10 householders, many of whom would in fact be the same people. No one disputed that the franchise would remain relatively broad-based, thus ensuring that electoral life in the town would remain vigorous. At the same time, since voters now had to be registered, party organisations were set up. The Nottingham Tories formed a Constitutional Club for this purpose.[67]

Chartism

In these circumstances the continued dominance of the Whigs in Nottingham politics comes as little surprise, particularly as the reform of the municipal corporations in 1835 served to confirm their position in local government. Disillusionment with 1832 festered outside the electoral system, and radicalism took on a new form in the shape of Chartism. Meetings to promote a Charter began in London during 1837, and mass meetings followed in major industrial towns during 1838. James Woodhouse told a meeting of 2,000 operatives in Nottingham in September 1838 that political reform was 'the means by which they could furnish their houses, clothe their backs, and educate their children'.[68] For the framework knitters, in particular, these were very real aims, and support for Chartism in Nottingham is hardly surprising. The first major meeting was held on the Forest on a wet and uncomfortable 5 November 1838. It was attended, according to the anti-Chartist *Journal*, by about 3,000 people and passed off peacefully. Many of these had come from outlying areas, and included a contingent from the Nottingham Female Association for obtaining the People's Charter, which was already holding weekly meetings in the town; indeed, women and children were prominent in Chartist demonstrations, reflecting their important role in the local textile trades. From the outset the *Journal*'s antipathy to Chartism was countered by strong support from the *Review*, which gave plenty of column inches to advertising and then reporting meetings, and also printed the Charter.[69]

The Chartist National Convention was called for February 1839, and there was a second public meeting in Nottingham on 25 March, this time in the market-place. Richard Oastler, the Tory-radical, was one of the speakers. In May the National Convention moved to Birmingham, plans were drawn up for a 'sacred month' – a general strike – and the first petition was presented to Parliament calling for a radical reform of the electoral system. With the movement bubbling, Chartists in large numbers attended a Whitsuntide Rally on the Forest on 22 May 1839. The magistrates feared trouble and swore in 400 special constables, but the meeting passed off peacefully. In July the first Chartist petition was presented to Parliament. Of the reputed 1.3 million signatures 17,000 came from Nottingham.[70] The House of Commons threw out the petition, provoking a wave of unrest across the country. Meetings were held regularly on Sundays at venues on the outskirts of Nottingham including the Forest, and during July the Chartists held regular evening gatherings in the market-place, attracting crowds of up to 3,000 people. These were in advance of the 'national holidays' called for 12 August, of which the outcome locally was something of a disappointment.[71]

The second phase of the Chartist movement can be dated to the formation in July 1840 of the National Charter Association, largely through the efforts of Feargus O'Connor. Just as O'Connor was stirring up the movement, Sir Ronald Ferguson, one of Nottingham's sitting MPs, died. At the by-election in April 1841 John Walter, editor of *The Times*, was returned on an informal Tory-Chartist, anti-Poor Law ticket, which was hailed as a Chartist triumph. Bribery and violence accompanied the contest.[72] Hardly had Walter taken his seat before a general election was held, and the town was embroiled in another blood-bath with voters abducted, windows smashed, and troops called in to break up gang fights. Two Whigs were finally elected although, following a parliamentary enquiry, a new election writ was issued in July 1842.

The return of the Tories to Westminster under Sir Robert Peel dampened the Chartists' spirits. For a while Nottingham was quiet: 'are they all asleep at Nottingham?', asked one enquirer.[73] Adverse economic conditions during the winter of 1841–42 fuelled the flames again and Feargus O'Connor received a tumultuous welcome when he came to speak in the town in February 1842. O'Connor, the inspiration of the movement by this time, had first spoken in Nottingham in 1836 when he had urged radicals to form a party for themselves, independent of either Whig or Tory. People arrived on foot from all over the county, and the renewed enthusiasm for the Charter lasted into the autumn, stirred by the rejection of the second petition in May 1842 and the by-election in August when one of the candidates, Joseph Sturge, stood on a platform which included five of the Charter points. O'Connor's presence in the town to support Sturge helped to raise the stakes, and Thomas Cooper, another national figure in the movement, came from Leicester to offer encouragement. The campaign reached a climax when the poll was declared on 4 August with Sturge losing by just eighty-four votes out of 3,686 cast. Two weeks later, on 18 August, a meeting of Chartists in the town proposed 'to promote a general strike, or cessation from labour, until the document known as the People's Charter become the law of the land'.[74] Over subsequent days there were disturbances around the town, and these culminated on Tuesday 23 August 1842 with what came to be termed the Battle of Mapperley Hills. About 5,000 Chartist supporters assembled on Mapperley Plains, the Riot Act was read, and despite the fact that the crowd was 'quietly sitting down on the grass preparing to eat their dinner', troops arrested about 400 men. Those detained were handcuffed, tied with ropes, and marched four abreast to the House of Correction. Such insensitive treatment provoked a riot and the guards were pelted with stones until 'the military were directed to clear the streets, which they did in a very few minutes by galloping about and brandishing their swords'. Most of those arrested were released within a couple of hours, although ultimately twenty-four were sentenced to terms of hard labour. The Battle of Mapperley Hills also represented the end in Nottingham of the second phase of Chartism, perhaps the period when its strength and influence as a working-class political movement reached a peak, although the 'Battle' was celebrated annually for some years as a reminder of the county magistrates' and military's transgression against popular rights.[75]

The Chartist movement was semi-dormant in the mid-1840s as attention focused instead on opposition to the Corn Laws which, since 1815, were believed to have artificially inflated the price of bread with particularly severe consequences for town-dwellers. Opposition was strongest in the industrial towns, and Nottingham was no exception. An Anti-Corn Law Association was formed towards the end of 1838, when Thomas Bailey tried without much success to rouse the corporation into active support.[76] It was not until January 1840 that a general meeting of the Anti-Corn Law Association was called and a recruitment campaign started. By the end of 1841 the Association was sufficiently buoyant to be able to plan what became in February 1842 the presentation of two petitions to Parliament. That same month 8,000 people attended an Anti-Corn Law meeting, but activity remained spasmodic in the town, even though nationally it was regarded as a strong centre of the movement. The Nottingham Association finally joined the national League in 1844, and in 1845 several leading Chartists publicly embraced the cause. When the *Journal* began to support Corn Law repeal in the early months of 1846, during a depression in the lace trade, the Tories responded by launching the *Nottinghamshire Guardian*, which claimed to be the only Tory and protectionist paper in the county. The corporation came out openly in favour of repeal by petitioning the House of Commons in February 1846.[77] The Corn Laws were abolished later that year, partly in response to the Irish famine.

The Chartist movement resurfaced in the summer of 1847 with a series of enthusiastic electoral campaigns, one of which saw O'Connor elected MP for Nottingham. O'Connor was invited to stand by Richard Sutton, editor of the *Review*, in a letter published in the *Northern Star* on 13 February. Nottingham, according to the *Review*, was showing that it was tired of 'do-nothing, kid-glove reformers'. A crowd reputedly numbering 10,000 gathered in the market-place to cheer the successful candidates, O'Connor and John Walter, and Chartists everywhere saw O'Connor's victory as a boost for the movement.[78] Chartism gathered renewed pace in the deteriorating economic conditions of the autumn, and following the Revolution in France in February 1848. O'Connor called a National Convention for 4 April 1848, with the intention of presenting a third petition on 10 April. In Nottingham a public meeting was called for 2 April 1848. There was talk of 10,000 Chartists assembling on the Forest, although this seems to have been a considerable exaggeration. The petition was presented in London on 10 April. The capital was fortified for the occasion, and for a parallel meeting in Nottingham the authorities went to considerable lengths to maintain order. The Irish Dragoons were quartered in the Park barracks, four troops of Yeomanry were held in readiness at Trent Bridge, Gamston, Wollaton and Gedling, and 1,500 special constables were on duty. Shops closed in the market-place before the meeting began at 1.00 p.m. Between 4,000 and 5,000 Chartists attended, but the meeting dispersed peacefully and, as nationally, Nottingham Chartism was never to be such a potent force again. Chartist candidates tried unsuccessfully to repeat O'Connor's electoral triumph through the 1850s, and Chartism continued to have an influence in local politics. James Sweet, the leader of the movement in the town, still considered himself to be a Chartist as late as 1872.[79]

The 1860s

O'Connor's brief interlude apart, Nottingham remained a Whig–Liberal stronghold in Parliamentary elections between the first two reform acts, but the party misjudged the local mood when in 1861 they put forward the Earl of Lincoln, son of the Duke of Newcastle, to stand at a by-election. To the surprise of some contemporaries, Sir Robert Clifton of Clifton Hall – 'of scampish notoriety' in Samuel Collinson's view – came forward 'on the extremely Liberal side', and with the support of the town's remaining Chartists.[80] He was returned with a substantial majority after a turbulent campaign. At the hustings William Parsons and his son Fred arrived early but suffered the indignity of having 'some fellows behind wishing to upset us or take our seats seized them and began to pull them from under us and break the form'. Fred, of whom under normal circumstances Parsons had no great opinion, 'settled the business by going into one of them and knocking him down which quieted the rest and we retained our seats'.[81] Samuel Collinson commented of the contest that:

> The town seemed to be given up to ruffianism, mobs of people were about every polling place insulting the voters for Lord Lincoln. Towards the afternoon all the shops in the Market Place, Pelham Street, Clumber Street, and Bridlesmith Gate were closed.

> Ruffians insulted all decent looking people, tearing their hats from the heads etc etc., pocket picking was carried on extensively, and the whole scene was a disgrace to the town and the times we live in.[82]

Clifton, despite his Liberal inclinations, was not chosen by the party at the 1865 general election when their candidates were Charles Paget (the other sitting MP) and Samuel Morley.

The 1865 campaign was marked by disorder, bribery and near-terrorism on the streets of Nottingham, with the so-called 'lambs' – in reality a group of bullies willing to sell their services as required – prominent on both sides. Conflict in the town reached a peak on 26 June when Morley and Paget were due to address a mass meeting in the market-place. Their supporters, brought in by rail from Mansfield and elsewhere, were attacked at the station by Clifton's 'lambs', who then proceeded to the town centre, burned the platform from which the speakers were to have addressed the crowd, and engaged in a spectacular display of window smashing.[83] In the riot fifty people were

Plate 35 **'The Fight for the Platform, 1865', by J. Holland Walker**. On 26 June 1865 supporters of Charles Paget and Samuel Morley arriving at the Midland Station from across the county were met by a crowd of stone-throwers. These supporters eventually fought their way into the market-place and on to the electoral platform from which, after surviving a shower of stones, they were driven off in a scene captured by the artist

injured. The mayor sent to Sheffield for troops, but it was after midnight before order was restored. Twenty-one men were prosecuted for their part in the disturbances, but discharged on promises of good behaviour. Troops were also present for the nomination on 11 July. Samuel Collinson, acting as a special constable for the occasion, noted when the nomination was taking place 'much stone throwing and now the mob seem to be in the ascendant. Ruffianism and terror seem to be the weapons with which Sir Robert Clifton means to fight this election.' Collinson had to be at the police station at 7.00 a.m. on polling day, and his job was to ensure that approaches to the Town Hall were kept clear. This was easier said than done: 'Paget and Morley's Committee Rooms in Milton Street and Burton Street completely wrecked and committees driven out … . Terror prevented numerous voters from coming up.' Clifton and Morley were returned, although from an electorate of 5,934 only 150 votes separated the candidates. Almost inevitably there was a petition, and both MPs were unseated. Morley, a strict Congregationalist, was particularly unnerved to find himself blamed for bribery and corruption of which he had been only dimly aware during the campaign. At the subsequent by election in May 1866, two Liberals were returned.[84]

Local elections

Whig–Liberal control of Parliamentary elections, albeit under conditions which many had expected to disappear after 1832, was matched at the local level beyond 1835. Party and sectarian identity played an important role in directing the actions of the urban middle classes as they sought to gain control of the institutions of town government. The unreformed corporations had shared power (not always willingly) with alternative agencies, including the poor law overseers and improvement commissioners. These had not necessarily been subject to political considerations. After 1835 the situation began to change. The new municipal corporations were ratepayer-elected councils which steadily gathered the agencies of local government under their control. Parliamentary and local council seats rapidly became the objects of party contest.[85] Nottingham was no exception, although breaking the Whig hold on local politics after 1835 was never going to be an easy task for the Tories. The composition of the corporation put them at an immediate disadvantage. With one-third of councillors retiring at each election, and with the aldermen being elected by the councillors, it was almost impossible to change the political complexion of the corporation in less than three years. In addition, the limited franchise until 1886, and the vested interest of the freemen in retaining the status quo, ensured that the Tories were always at a disadvantage. To try to strengthen their position in local politics the Tories sought to gain control of the agencies as a way of stirring political debate, and they were presented with an ideal opportunity within a couple of years of municipal reform – the question of a new workhouse.

With the creation of the Nottingham poor law union in 1836 the smaller workhouses of St Peter's and St Nicholas's parishes were closed and their inmates moved to the larger St Mary's workhouse, but in the trade depression of 1837–38 it became apparent that this was too small. While the Whigs, in a majority on both the corporation and the board of guardians, were perfectly willing to encourage the full implementation of the new legislation, particularly the relief of able-bodied men only in the workhouse, their hands were tied because the accommodation was inadequate. In November 1837 they brought forward proposals for erecting a new, larger workhouse.[86] When the likely costs became public knowledge early in 1839, the ratepayers swept the Whigs out of office and returned a Tory-dominated board of guardians, the party's first real political success in Nottingham. The Tories had promised to pay outdoor relief to the unemployed as a way of containing spending without incurring the anticipated capital costs of a new building. Unfortunately for the Tories, the depth of the recession meant that the relief payments reached unprecedented levels. The ratepayers lost faith and returned the Whigs to power in 1840. They promptly started building a new workhouse, plunging the town into political turmoil. At the municipal elections in November 1840, the Tories captured four seats from the Whigs specifically over the workhouse question. It was a vital issue at the parliamentary by-election in April 1841 when John Walter became the first Tory MP returned for the town since 1807. In April 1841 no fewer than eighty-seven candidates contested the twenty-four seats on the board of guardians. Seventeen Tories and seven radicals were returned. The new Board promptly stopped work on the nearly-completed workhouse.[87]

A further depression in the textile trades in the autumn of 1841 called the Tory bluff. With the old workhouse severely overcrowded the guardians were put under pressure to begin using completed sections of the new building. They attempted to ride out the crisis by offering ever greater sums of outdoor relief. The Poor Law Commission, whose rules were violated by this action, responded by sending a Harley Street doctor to condemn the existing workhouse. The commissioners ordered the opening of the new workhouse, and the Tory members stayed away from a meeting of the guardians at which it was agreed to implement this order.[88]

The crisis over the workhouse revitalised the Tories. Although they won twenty seats at the first post-1835 election, their numbers rapidly declined to only six in 1839–40, but increased again as the workhouse issue grew in importance. By 1844 they had twenty elected councillors sitting opposite twenty-two Whigs. Since only a small gain was needed to allow them to control the next election of aldermen (who were elected for six-year periods), the 1844 local government elections were unusually important. Bribery, intimidation and even abduction were all reported, with up to £20 paid for votes: 'so much for the purity of municipal reform', William Parsons noted in his diary. The infamous 'lambs' were called out to persuade voters, sometimes by browbeating, and by 'cooping' – confining them to public houses until the election was over.[89] The Whig–Liberals just survived, calling on the casting vote of their own mayor to nominate aldermen and retain control. It was a defining moment: municipal Toryism was never again the same force in Nottingham in the nineteenth century. Yet despite the Whig–Liberal hold on power through the middle decades of the century, contests were frequent. George Harwood noted in October 1860 that a contest was expected in every ward for the municipal elections. Harwood was a Tory, with little time for the

> Liberals, as they call themselves, [who] have long monopolized all power. A more illiberal selfish lot of fellows it is impossible to imagine … . as a rule the Nottingham whig is a narrow minded, grasping, conceited, animal; totally destitute of generous impulse and political principle; and who would rather infinitely give a poor man twenty shillings to buy his vote, than a single sixpence to relieve his distress.

After 'unblushing bribery' the Liberals came out in the ascendant. At the 1865 municipal elections Harwood complained that the bribery was 'something enormous … . Many thousands of pounds were spent in debauching the morality of the municipal electors.' A year later he complained that 'bribery of the most unblushing character has been employed by both parties. In this matter there is not one pin to choose between Whigs and Tories.'[90] The local elections held in November 1873 created such a disturbance that a public enquiry was held the following January. The Conservatives alleged that in St Ann's Ward the return of a Liberal had been possible only as a result of bribery, treating, and intimidation, and that between the election and the enquiry important witnesses had 'disappeared', allegedly with financial help. Food and drink, it was claimed, had been distributed in certain public houses at the – illegal – expense of the electoral agents, and voters had been intimidated 'by certain rough and disorderly persons' who had been plied with liquor. The case was upheld, only for the Liberals to be returned with larger majorities at the by-election.[91]

One persistent Conservative claim was that the dominance of the Liberals in local politics devalued the position of mayor. During the 1840s and 1850s Whig, dissenting, merchant hosiers were prominent on the council. Just occasionally the Tories enjoyed a success, as when Edwin Patchitt was mayor in 1858–59 and 1859–60. More often it was a small coterie of Liberal businessmen who held the position. When Thomas Cullen was chosen in 1860 Samuel Collinson complained: 'it seems a great shame that for a town like this the choice should be restricted to a few old fogies who must be every now and then re-elected'.[92] Richard Birkin was mayor in 1861, but the Liberals feared that unless he stood again the following year they would be forced to accept William Page. Birkin agreed to stand, to the annoyance of George Harwood, who suggested that 'the Whigs … have not another man available. One or two men are fit for the office, but are not willing. Several are willing, but are decidedly unfit.' Page, it transpired, had a drink problem. In Harwood's view he could not compete with the lace manufacturer and banker Thomas Adams, who,

> as a man of character, and a man of business, a man of position in the town, and a man of respectability, influence, and gentlemanly bearing, is vastly superior to any Whig in the whole Corporation, or any three Whigs put together. This really excellent, and in every way qualified man is passed by, is ignored, and why? Simply because he is a Conservative.[93]

The Tory William Parsons was elected mayor the following year, but in 1864 Page finally achieved his aim. Harwood was not amused:

> A more vulgar, impertinent fellow it would not be possible to place in the Chair. Parsons has fulfilled the duties of his office in a manner that has called forth the plaudits of everybody. For William Page to follow William Parsons is a tremendous descent from what is able, honourable and gentlemanly, to inability, meanness and vulgarity. If the Whigs could not find a better man, they should let the Tories try again.[94]

When the Whigs were not ensuring the election of one of their number to the mayoralty they were busy filling the magistracy. Parsons recorded that at a meeting of the corporation in February 1851 'Alderman Judd, a linen retail draper moved a recommendation to the Secretary of State for the appointment of six additional justices of the peace for the borough all whigs and dissenters of course; viz Felkin, Carver, Cullen, Cripps, J. Herbert and Birkin which was carried spite of our Tory opposition.' Unable to make any headway with the corporation, Parsons approached the more sympathetic board of guardians next day where he 'drew a letter or memorial to Sir George Grey, Home Secretary against the appointment of the six whig justices'. He persuaded several Tory members of the corporation to add their signatures, and sent off the letter.[95] Similarly contentious was the board of guardians, which remained a party issue for many years. In 1845 the *Journal* commented that 'as usual this contest, like all others which take place in Nottingham, has been made the subject of strong party exertions'. Harwood reported in 1860 'a strong contest between the Conservatives and the Whigs', and in 1865 he complained that the guardians had refused to accept an offer from Lady Clifton, wife of Sir Robert Clifton, 'to provide the poor people in the workhouse with a good dinner on New Year's Day'. In his view the reason was obvious: 'political feeling governs everything and everybody in Nottingham'.[96]

The last years of turbulence

Turbulence in municipal elections continued to be matched during parliamentary contests, even after the 1867 Reform Act widened the franchise and more than doubled the electorate. Following the Reform Act the Liberals established the Liberal Registration Association, largely to ensure all qualified voters were registered. It did them little good at the 1868 election when Sir Robert Clifton topped the poll. The Liberal vote was split and a Conservative captured the second seat. Clifton died the following year. As a mark of respect and as a reflection of his popularity, shops were shut on the day of his funeral (7 June), factory work virtually ceased, and an estimated 20,000–30,000 people made their way to Clifton. At the by-election he was replaced by a Liberal, but only after yet another contest characterised by disorder. At one point troops with fixed bayonets stood in front of the Exchange.[97] A further by-election in 1870 was followed by complaints of 'abundant use of the baton' by the police, who several times charged the crowd from the Exchange. Among those prosecuted for their part in the disturbances was Thomas Lees, a local carpenter who was both a qualified voter and a freeman. Despite the introduction in 1872 of the secret ballot, disturbances accompanied the 1874 election, contested by two radical Liberals, one moderate Liberal (Richard Birkin), and two Conservatives. One of the Conservatives was Saul Isaac, who had originally been associated in politics with Sir Robert Clifton, and who had become the first lessee of Clifton Colliery when it was sunk in 1869. One hundred Derbyshire police and fifty from Nottinghamshire supplemented, without noticeable effect, the local force during the contest. Miners from Clifton colliery pelted the police with herrings, potatoes, cabbage stalks and stones. With the Liberal vote split, two Conservatives were returned. The town was heavily defended for the 1880 election but there was little trouble. Only two Liberals stood and, with an electorate swelled following the borough extension in 1877, they easily topped the poll.[98]

Following the franchise reforms of 1883–85 Nottingham was divided into three single member constituencies, east, south and west, with 12,000–14,000 electors in each. At the 1885 election John Burns stood in Nottingham West as a labour candidate, representing the principles of the Social Democratic Federation recently founded by H.M. Hyndman. The decision to run Burns in Nottingham was a reflection of the town's radical reputation and its early flirtation with socialism. A local man, Thomas Smith, founded a branch of the First International in about 1870, and by 1872 the branch had an affiliated membership of around 400, including four women, and the more active members of the group met weekly at a coffee house on Houndsgate. It did not survive for long, but the Social Democratic Federation was well established in the town by 1884, when John Burns attended the annual conference of the Amalgamated Union of Engineers. As a result of speeches delivered in the market-place before and after the conference he was invited to stand in Nottingham West. He spoke frequently in the town as a result, and at the subsequent poll attracted 598 votes, which his supporters regarded as something of a triumph. At the close of voting in 1885 the ballot boxes began to arrive at the Exchange around 8.00 p.m. Despite the presence of extra police, some windows were smashed and stones thrown. The Riot Act was read, and the police ordered to charge the crowd. Batons were wielded without much care or concern and 150 people were injured. Of these, thirty-two, including one woman, sought help at the General Hospital. None of those treated was enfranchised.[99] These were the last serious election disturbances in Nottingham. The lesson was finally learned, and from 1886 the votes of each division were counted locally. Nottingham also lost its position as the home of county elections. Thereafter contests became relatively predictable and electorally quiet. 'At Nottingham', it was claimed in February 1887, 'the Socialist agitation is not in a very satisfactory condition.'[100] Even more surprising to old-time campaigners must have been the election results in the closing years of the nineteenth century, with two of the three constituencies returning Conservatives.

Radical, revolutionary, or just riotous? It would be neat and tidy to find in the activities mentioned in these pages a coherent thread, a growing class-consciousness running from the food riots of the 1750s to the socialism of the 1890s. Unfortunately consistency is the one feature missing. Nottingham in the 1790s was undoubtedly a radical town, but it is not easy to accept unreservedly the claim that 'the cohesive but violent crowds seemed to be shifting away from communal bargaining toward class conflict'.[101] Several historians have claimed that Jacobin activity was present in the 1796 election campaign, as well as in later events. Others have gone further to accept the claims of contemporaries who pointed to a revolutionary undercurrent during the war years, men like the notorious hard-line Tory John Bowles, who wrote of 'jacobinical tumults'.[102] Much depends on the credence to be attached to contemporary opinion, such as the spy-ring organiser who believed the people of Nottingham in 1799 to be

> extremely depraved in their Politics. In their Taverns and other Places of Public Resort little is held forth of a Political Nature but what has a seditious tendency, and so far is this Spirit from meeting with any Check from the Magistrates that it should be dangerous only to utter Sentiments of a contrary nature.[103]

Others claim that these sources are unreliable and exaggerate the reality. In their view, in Nottingham during the 1790s the accusation of Jacobin seems to have been levelled at more or less anyone who opposed the war, without necessarily suggesting more sinister overtones. Nottingham, so the alternative viewpoint runs, was little different from other towns across the country and, indeed, the loyalism of 1793–94, and the regular return of Tory candidates at elections, suggests that the town's radical leanings need to be kept in sharp perspective.[104] The most recent commentator has concluded that 'the evidence ... does not give the impression that a revolutionary atmosphere existed in the town'. In his view, political rivalry and socio-economic frustration fused together to stretch constitutionalism to, and in the opinion of some contemporaries, beyond acceptable limits.[105]

Nor has it been possible to reach a consensus over other phases of unrest. Luddism, while it may have done something to politicise the working classes, as was the case among northern textile workers, lacked an active underground sufficiently strong to raise support for *revolutionary* politics.[106] Trade unions, which boosted working-class radicalism, particularly in the years 1829–34, made little or no progress in Nottingham until craft societies were formed in the 1850s. This was largely a reflection of the nature of the textile trades. Parliamentary reform, while enjoying considerable support locally, was unusual in that the lead came from the corporation. Possibly the revulsion expressed at the three executions in 1832 points to some sort of local solidarity, and it certainly suggests the adoption of a moral viewpoint – that the punishment had not fitted the crime – but personal antipathy towards the Duke of Newcastle was just as significant, particularly when he won a claim for compensation for the burning of the Castle.

Nor was there much change beyond the Parliamentary and municipal reforms of the 1830s. Chartism was a political reaction to economic conditions. The framework knitters were always conspicuous, regarding the aims of the Chartists as likely to bring a remedy for depressed conditions. The first major Chartist meeting in Nottingham, in November 1838, was chaired by a prominent member of the early Framework Knitters' Union, and many of the leaders and more active members of the town's Chartist organisation were framework knitters. Opposition to the New Poor Law was another central theme in Chartist activities, and the upsurge of interest in Chartism in Nottingham in 1848 coincided with a trade depression.[107] As elsewhere, political radicalism was less obvious during the prosperous 1850s and 1860s, although electoral riots took place regularly. Possibly this helped to keep alive Nottingham's radical reputation, hence its targeting by the SDF and the early socialists. Yet by the end of the century election riots had come to an end and, with Conservatives being elected to Parliament and even to a majority on the corporation, socialism was able to make little progress. Once the rioting tradition had gone, Nottingham appeared to be no more radical than any other town of its size and composition. Despite the town's reputation there was relatively little socialist influence in elections, although the Nottingham branch of the Independent Labour Party was well established by 1893, and by 1894 it had built a formidable political machine, mainly for the purpose of fighting local elections. However, the willingness of the Nottingham electors to return Conservatives for two of the three Parliamentary seats at the end of the century suggests that, despite the strength of the Labour movement in the town, it represented only a small minority of the town's working class.[108] The radical, frequently disturbed and riotous town, had at last been tamed, and in 1908 even the corporation fell to the Conservatives.

Plate 36 **A suffragette.** The suffragettes played a low-key role in Nottingham, although following a meeting in the market-place on 28 July 1913 a near-riot ensued when 200 oarsmen from the Nottingham Boat Club stormed the meeting. The sequence of crazed shop windows was achieved by mischievously processing the negative

Notes

1 *Date Book*, p. 225.
2 Quoted in G. F. A. Best, *Temporal Pillars* (1964), p. 171.
3 *NJ*, 6 March 1835.
4 J. Bohstedt, *Riots and Community Politics in England and Wales 1790–1810* (1983), p. 206.
5 C. Behagg, *Politics and Production in the Early Nineteenth Century* (1990) has questioned the 'irresistible ... temptation' which has led English historians 'to relate the workers' sense of class to the size of the unit of production': p. 2.
6 E. P. Thompson, *The Making of the English Working Class* (1963); R. Wells, *Riot and Political Disaffection in Nottinghamshire in the Age of Revolutions, 1776–1803* (Nottingham, 1984), p. 37.
7 Thomis, *Politics*; M. C. Pottle, 'Loyalty and patriotism in Nottingham, 1792–1816' (University of Oxford, D.Phil thesis, 1988), especially pp. 280–3.
8 *NJ*, 15 April 1797; Blackner, pp. 403, 405; *RBN*, VIII, pp. 227–8; D. Fraser, 'The Nottingham Press, 1800–1850', *TTS*, 67 (1963), pp. 46–65.
9 One of the clearest examples is discussed in T. Koditschek, *Class Formation and Urban Industrial Society: Bradford, 1750–1850* (Cambridge, 1990).
10 F. M. W. Harrison, 'Nonconformity and the corporation of Nottingham', *Baptist Quarterly*, 21 (1965–66), pp. 364–7.
11 A. Henstock, 'A road traffic census of Nottingham in 1819', *TTS*, 90 (1986), p. 97.
12 *Date Book*, pp. 174, 177–8; Wells, *Riot*, p. 8.
13 The social significance of urban space in this context is emphasised by M. Harrison, *Crowds and History 1790–1835* (1988), pp. 57–101.
14 *NJ*, 6 March 1835.
15 BL Additional MSS 32,867 f.76; Egerton MSS 3437, fos. 374, 397; 3438, f. 41.
16 *Date Book*, pp. 69–70.
17 *NJ*, 12 May 1792; *Date Book*, pp. 181–2; Pottle, 'Loyalty and patriotism', p. 248.
18 *Date Book*, pp. 204–5, 207; Wells, *Riot*, pp. 13–17; Gawthern, *Diary*, p. 65; R. Wells, *Wretched Faces* (Gloucester, 1988), pp. 42–3; Pottle, 'Loyalty and patriotism', pp. 249–51.
19 Gawthern, *Diary*, p. 82; Pottle, 'Loyalty and patriotism', p. 256.
20 Gawthern, *Diary*, pp. 83, 85; Wells, *Riot*, pp. 26–8; NAO CA/3990 I/3, 1 September 1800.
21 NAO CA/3990 I/5, 2 September 1800.
22 Quoted in Wells, *Wretched Faces*, pp. 120–2.
23 Wells, *Wretched Faces*, pp. 47, 179, 238, 241, 312; Gawthern, *Diary*, pp. 83–4; Pottle, 'Loyalty and patriotism', pp. 257–61.
24 *Date Book*, pp. 286–7; Wells, *Wretched Faces*, p. 326.
25 BL Additional MSS, 32,711, fos. 358, 375, 395, 438, 448; J. H. Moses, 'Elections and electioneering in the constituencies of Nottinghamshire, 1702–1832' (University of Nottingham, Ph.D. thesis, 1965), I, pp. 135–44.
26 Bailey, *Annals*, IV (1853), pp. 136–7; R. Thorn (ed.), *The House of Commons 1790–1820* (5 vols., 1986), I, pp. 317–18; III, p. 475; V, pp. 199–200.
27 Thomis, *Politics*, p. 161; *Date Book*, p.173; Gawthern, *Diary*, p. 52; Bailey, *Annals*, IV, p. 137.
28 Bailey, *Annals*, IV, p. 136; Blackner, p. 386.
29 Wells, *Riot*, p. 9.
30 Blackner, p. 40.
31 K. Brand, 'The Park Estate, Nottingham: the development of a nineteenth century fashionable suburb', *TTS*, 88 (1984), p. 55; *Date Book*, p. 182; *RBN*, VII, p. 276. The Riding School survived until 1926.
32 *NJ*, 16 March 1793; *Date Book*, pp. 185–6; Gawthern, *Diary*, p. 58.
33 Gawthern, *Diary*, pp. 61, 98; *Date Book*, pp. 199–200; Thomis, *Politics*, pp. 173–7; Wells, *Riot*, pp. 11, 13; Pottle, 'Loyalty and patriotism', pp. 144–50. According to a later witness the 1794 'duckings' were organised by the Tory mayor: *Report of the Evidence Given before the Commissioners Appointed to Enquire into Municipal Corporations* (Nottingham, 1833), p. 107; S. Best, 'The destruction of

Denison's Mill', *Sneinton Magazine*, 23 (1986), pp. 13–21.

34 Thomis, *Politics*, p. 179.

35 Moses, 'Elections', I, pp. 186–8; Bailey, *Annals*, IV, pp. 167–8; Gawthern, *Diary*, p. 66; Wells, Riot, pp. 18–20.

36 Gawthern, *Diary*, p. 68.

37 Gawthern, *Diary*, pp. 66, 72; Thorn, *House of Commons*, I, pp. 317–18; V, pp. 492–3; Pottle, 'Loyalty and patriotism', p. 46; *Date Book*, pp. 186, 190, 210, 221. Borlase Warren is still commemorated in the name of a public house at Canning Circus.

38 Gawthern, *Diary*, p. 73; Wells, *Riot*, pp. 22–5.

39 R. Wells, *Insurrection: the British Experience, 1795–1803* (Gloucester, 1983), p. 45; Wells, Riot, p. 34.

40 *NJ*, 10 July 1802; Moses, 'Elections', I, p. 191; Pottle, 'Loyalty and patriotism', pp. 195–219.

41 *NJ*, 17 July 1802.

42 Moses, 'Elections', I, pp. 193–4.

43 Bailey, *Annals*, IV, p. 211.

44 Gawthern, *Diary*, pp. 99–100; Thomis, *Politics*, pp. 144–5, 162; Moses, 'Elections', p. 195.

45 Pottle, 'Loyalty and patriotism', pp. 52–6, 112.

46 Gawthern, *Diary*, pp. 119–20.

47 Moses, 'Elections', I, pp. 196–200; Pottle, 'Loyalty and patriotism', p. 164.

48 BL Additional MSS, 38,578, f.64.

49 Thomis, *Politics*, pp. 191–4; Pottle, 'Loyalty and patriotism', pp. 97–103; Fraser, 'Nottingham Press'.

50 Pottle, 'Loyalty and patriotism', p. 104. Jacobin was a loosely-used term for radicals who admired the French Revolution. Thomis, *Politics*, p. 178 suggests that it had 'no revolutionary connotation in the Nottingham context'.

51 Thomis, *Politics*, pp. 84, 196–7.

52 Thompson, *Making*, pp. 515ff., 604; Wells, Riot, pp. 37–8; Thomis, Politics, p. 95.

53 R. A. Church and S. D. Chapman, 'Gravenor Henson and the making of the English working class', in E. L. Jones and G. E. Mingay (eds.), *Land, Labour and Population in the Industrial Revolution* (1966), pp. 130–61; M. I. Thomis, 'Gravenor Henson: the man and the myth', *TTS*, 75 (1971), pp. 91–7; Thomis, *Politics*, pp. 77–99. Pottle, the most recent historian to look at Luddism in detail, suggests that the political uses made of Luddism by both the *Review* and the *Gazette* suggest that there may have been more to Luddism than simply industrial unrest: 'Loyalty and patriotism', pp. 104–11.

54 M. I. Thomis, 'The Nottingham Captain: a portrait of Jeremiah Brandreth, the Rebel', *NH*, 14 (1974), pp. 7–9; Thomis, *Politics*, pp. 207, 209; Thompson, *Making*, p. 733.

55 *Royal Commission on the Municipal Corporations*, PP (XXV) 1835: Reports from Commissioners, appendix to 1st Report, part 3, p. 2005.

56 Wylie, p. 317; Bailey, *Annals*, IV, pp. 287–8; Moses, 'Elections', I, pp. 204–5; II, p. 40.

57 Moses, 'Elections', I, pp. 216–18.

58 *NR*, 11, 18 March 1831.

59 *Report of the Evidence given before the Commissioners appointed to enquire into the Municipal Corporations* (Nottingham, 1833), pp. 94–107, 111–17, 186–7.

60 *NR*, 14 October 1831; NAO M.5586, fos. 61–3.

61 NUMD Ne 2F 4, f.19.

62 F. Barnes, *Priory Demesne to University Campus* (Nottingham, 1993), p. 233; Bailey, *Annals*, III, p. 378; NAO M.5586, fos. 61–3.

63 *NR*, 4 March 1831; Moses, 'Elections', pp. 220–2; M. I. Thomis, R. A. Preston and J. Wigley, 'Nottingham and the Reform Bill Riots of 1831: new perspectives', *TTS*, 77 (1973), pp. 82–103. Valentine Marshall, aged 17, one of those transported, became a successful florist in Tasmania. His great-great-grandson was an early visitor to the Galleries of Justice in Nottingham when they opened in 1995: *EP*, 26 October 1995.

64 J. B. Goodman (ed.), *Victorian Cabinet Maker: the memoirs of James Hopkinson, 1819–1894* (1968), p.

12; *Nottingham Daily Guardian*, 1 January 1901.

65 *NR*, 10 August 1832; Thomis, *Politics*, ch. 11; Bailey, *Annals*, IV, p. 388; NAO DD 808/1 Diary of John Rainbow, governor of House of Correction, 1813–36; *NR*, 5 February 1830.

66 *Date Book*, p. 406; *NR*, 3 February 1832.

67 *NR*, 4 March 1831, *NJ*, 1 September, 17 November 1832; A. C. Wood, 'Nottingham 1835–1865', *TTS*, 59 (1955), pp. 65–6.

68 *NR*, 7 September 1838.

69 The meetings were reported into the pro-Chartist *Review*, although in its coverage on 23 November 1838 it reported only speeches given by males while noting that the audience was 'composed of both sexes': *NR*, 23 November 1838. The Nottingham Chartist movement was co-ordinated by James Sweet from his shop in Goose Gate: *Dictionary of Labour Biography*, IV, pp. 171–3; *NR*, 9 November 1838.

70 J. Epstein, 'Some organisational and cultural aspects of the Chartist movement in Nottingham', in J. Epstein and D. Thompson (eds.), *The Chartist Experience: Studies in Working-Class Radicalism and Culture 1830–60* (1982), p. 229. Epstein is particularly strong on the cultural aspects, which have been only touched upon here.

71 Church, pp. 130–5; Wood, 'Nottingham', pp. 43–64; S. Foster, 'Nottingham Chartism and the Press, 1838–1848' (University of Nottingham, MA thesis, 1985), ch. 3.

72 NAO M.12,432, E. Alliott to A. Alliott, 27 April 1841; Epstein, 'Cultural aspects', p. 241. The events of 1841 are discussed in more detail below.

73 NAO M.19,795, T. Chapman to J. Worth, 3 October 1841.

74 Wood, 'Nottingham', p. 45; *Date Book*, p. 487.

75 *NR*, 26 August 1842; P. Wyncoll, *Nottingham Chartism* (Nottingham, 1966), p. 39; Epstein, 'Cultural aspects', pp. 247, 259.

76 *Full Report of the Speech delivered by Mr Bailey at a Meeting of the Nottingham Town Council February 19, 1838, on the subject of the Repeal of the Corn Laws* (1838). Bailey was unable to obtain agreement to his proposal of a petition to Parliament on the matter.

77 D. Fraser, 'Nottingham and the Corn Laws', *TTS*, 70 (1966), pp. 81–104; *NJ*, 9 January 1846; BL Additional MSS 40,584, fos. 176–7.

78 Wood, 'Nottingham', p. 77; *NR*, 13 August 1847; Wyncoll, *Nottingham Chartism*, pp. 43–4; Bailey, *Annals*, IV, p. 450. O'Connor is commemorated today by a statue in the Arboretum, erected – albeit somewhat contentiously – by subscription: NAO M.382, 14 February 1859. O'Connor made little impact in Parliament.

79 Wood, 'Nottingham', pp. 62–3; *Dict.Lab.Biog.*, IV, p.172.

80 NAO M.383, 5 December 1861.

81 NUMD William Parsons' Diary, 26 December 1861. Ironically Parsons had a cold and could not turn out to vote.

82 NAO M.383, 27 December 1861.

83 NAO M.383, 26 June 1865.

84 NAO M.383, 12 July 1865. The election is fully discussed in D. Cutting, 'The Nottingham parliamentary election of 1865' (University of Nottingham, M.Phil. thesis, 1972).

85 D. Fraser, *Urban Politics in Victorian England* (1976) is the fullest account of this process and sets events in Nottingham into a wider context.

86 PRO MH12/9444, 7 November 1837.

87 *NR*, 9, 16, 23 April 1841.

88 PRO MH12/9445, E. Senior to Poor Law Commissioners, 6 August 1841, A. Barnett to same, 4 December 1841; *NR*, 10, 17 December 1841, 18 March 1842.

89 NUMD William Parsons' Diary, 30 October 1844; A. C. Wood, 'Sir Robert Clifton, 1826–69', *TTS*, 57 (1953), p. 52.

90 NAO M.23,788, 30 October, 1 November 1860, 2 November 1865, 1 November 1866.

91 G. Oldfield, 'Municipal Elections in nineteenth century Nottingham', *NH*, 40 (1988), pp. 22–5.

92 NAO M.382, 9 November 1860.

93 NAO M.23,788, 10 November 1862.

94 NAO M.23,788, 9 November 1864.

95 NUMD William Parsons' Diary, 5 January, 4, 5, 6 February 1851.

96 *NJ*, 11 April 1845; NAO M.23,788 7 April 1860, 20 April 1863, 29 December 1865.

97 P. Wood, 'Political developments in Nottingham, 1868 to 1885' (University of Nottingham, MA thesis, 1989), pp. 11–32; Wood, 'Sir Robert Clifton', pp. 48–65.

98 A. C. Wood, 'Nottingham parliamentary elections 1869–1900', *TTS*, 60 (1956), pp. 50–65; P. Wood, 'Political developments', pp. 32–4, 40–7; *EP*, 9 October 1903. There were 16,154 electors in 1874 and 18,699 in 1880.

99 P. Wood, 'Political developments', pp 34–8; P. Wyncoll, 'The First International in Nottingham', *Marxism Today*, December 1968, pp. 372–80; Wood, 'Parliamentary elections', pp. 57–60. For the trade union attitudes towards Burns see P. Wyncoll, *The Nottingham Labour Movement 1880–1939* (1985), pp. 33–4, and for the SDF campaign pp. 77–80; Lord Snell, *Men, Movements and Myself* (1938), pp. 55–65.

100 Information contained in notes lent by Councillor John Peck.

101 Bohstedt, *Riots*, p. 206.

102 Thompson, *Making*, pp. 202–3; Thomis, *Politics*, p. 185.

103 Quoted in Wells, *Riot*, p. 3.

104 Thomis, *Politics*, pp. 169–73.

105 Pottle, 'Loyalty and patriotism', p. 219.

106 J. Dinwiddy, 'Luddism and politics in the northern counties', *Social History*, 4 (1979), pp. 33–63. Wells, *Riot*, pp. 37–8 disputes this.

107 Wyncoll, *Nottingham Chartism*, pp. 6, 49; Church, pp. 128, 146, 153. Epstein, 'Cultural aspects', pp. 230–1 claims there was significant if rather latent support from lace workers. C. P. Griffin, 'Chartism and opposition to the New Poor Law in Nottinghamshire', *Midland History*, 2 (1974), pp. 244–9.

108 Wyncoll, *Nottingham Labour Movement*, pp. 115, 117–20.

14

INDUSTRY AND TRADE 1750–1900

S. D. Chapman

Nottingham's gradual transformation from a country town with a range of manufacturing interests into an embryonic modern industrial city was traced in chapter 8. By about 1730 many traditional interests had gone into decline, and the growing dominance of the hosiery industry was changing the whole structure on which the town's economy was based. In the course of the eighteenth and nineteenth centuries hosiery production, and its offshoot lace making, came to dominate the economy not only of Nottingham, but of its surrounding region. Cotton spinning, bleaching, dyeing, and engineering were directly connected, and the overall influence of the textile trades cannot be underestimated. Although by the 1880s a range of new interests was beginning to broaden the basis of Nottingham's economy – particularly bicycle making, pharmaceuticals, tobacco, coal-mining and service industries – on the eve of the First World War Nottingham was still first and foremost a textile town. That dominance will be reflected in this chapter.

Hosiery, *c.*1740-1810

By 1750 the hosiery industry already had a mature organisation, with manufacturing operations organised by merchant-entrepreneurs based in Nottingham and Leicester and a few satellite towns (Derby, Mansfield, Hinckley and Loughborough) and merchanting in the Wood Street area of the City of London. The trade grew on these foundations in the second half of the eighteenth century. In Nottingham, the premier provincial centre, the number of merchant hosiers rose from something over fifty in 1740 to about a hundred in 1770–75, and then doubled again by the end of the century. Connections with the City of London also developed rapidly. Much of the enterprise and energy in the trade was dependent on accurate information from

London agents or partners on fashion movement – that is, on what could, or could not, be expected to sell. The coaching inns in and around Wood Street remained the centre of the trade, but by the early 1770s the more prosperous hosiers had their own warehouses built around these inn yards, while others were beginning to buy their own house or warehouse in the vicinity. The hosier whose trade was too small to justify holding stock in the City continued to sell through City agents (who occasionally advertised their services in the columns of provincial newspapers) or tramped around the wholesalers with samples strapped under their belt and cloak. Some features of marketing in the provinces, including sales at markets and fairs, and direct to hawkers, pedlars and shops, are summarised in figure 14.1.

The merchant hosiers were supplied by an army of framework knitters (or stockingers) working in garrets and workshops around the town and in scores of adjacent villages. When John Bilby's coach arrived in Nottingham in 1828 'our ears were saluted with the working of the stocking looms in all directions'.[1] The knitters collected yarns (linen, wool, cotton or silk) from the hosiers' warehouses every two weeks and returned the stockings or other knitted pieces (caps, gloves, waistcoat pieces, vests, etc.) for payment. Increasingly, knitters rented their frames (at 1*s* a week) as hosiers, and people of small capital, found them a good investment. In the villages the knitters were often organised by local middlemen known as 'bag hosiers'. Frames were usually worked by men, with women and children scaming, embroidering and ironing the finished goods; but some widows and grown-up daughters appear as framework knitters from the seventeenth century onwards.[2]

Figure 14.1 **Organisation of the Nottingham hosiery industry c. 1750–c. 1850**

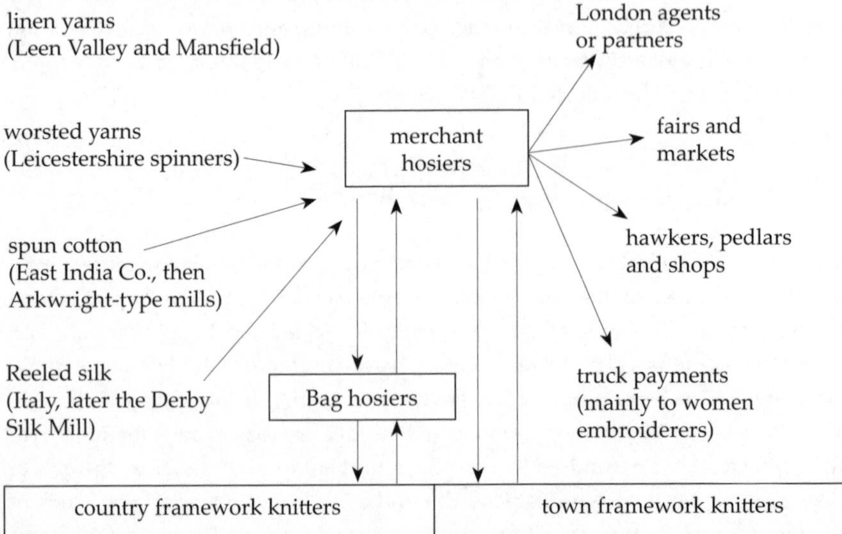

The second half of the eighteenth century was a period of great prosperity in Nottingham and Leicester as demand continued to grow, while the vestiges of the old London industry capitulated and the minor provincial centres (such as Tewkesbury and Godalming) were overwhelmed by the competition. The number of stocking frames in Nottingham increased from around 400 in 1727 to 2,600 in 1812.[3]

Nationally, an expanding 'consumer society' meant that fashion regularly dictated changes in colour and patterning – plain, striped, ribbed, mottled, embroidered, and numerous other types – and that a growing body of discriminating consumers appreciated quality and value for money. The most successful merchant hosiers and framework knitters were those who found ways of responding to these demands. When Sir Frederick Morton Eden visited Nottingham to collect evidence for his *State of the Poor* (1797) he noted that while knitters in the common branches earned no more than 10*s* weekly in full employment, the more skilled in the new fashion branches earned 20*s* to 40*s* a week. Evidence of rising consumption and rising expectations can be seen on every side. Friendly societies, the most popular and ubiquitous of all British working-class movements, and a genuine expression of confidence in present and future earnings, were notably prolific in Nottingham. The number of societies rose rapidly from sixteen in 1782 to fifty-one in 1795, some of them formed in the major firms.[4] The societies expressed their confidence in the trade by investing funds in stocking frames which, at 1*s* a week rental, paid a dividend equal to 10–15 per cent.[5] The French Wars (1793–1915) produced some erratic trading conditions, but down to 1807 the period was one of accelerated growth for hosiery, with wartime labour shortages pushing wages up.[6]

Technologically even in the first half of the eighteenth century increased scale of production presaged later developments. George Robertson (later called Robinson) came to Nottingham from Banff (Scotland) to introduce Dutch techniques of bleaching linen, linen stockings being among the most popular lines at this period as cotton was still very expensive. In 1738 Robinson built a mill at Bulwell, the first of a crowd of textile factories on the River Leen, in association with Cornelius Wyldbore of Nottingham, who was a specialist in dyeing scarlet. Meanwhile, William Elliott of Nottingham learned a new technique of dyeing black by using logwood with chrome, and built a large business on Beastmarket Hill. Elliott and Robinson built a second mill at Bulwell in 1761, and subsequently Nottingham's first silk-reeling mill, powered by a horse gin, was set to work in the yard behind Elliott's house.[7] Both in time and scale, these pioneer developments must take precedence over the better-known enterprises of James Hargreaves and Richard Arkwright in Nottingham in the late 1760s.

Improved bleaching and dyeing are the most obvious ways of enhancing the appearance of hosiery but, given the constraints of the vegetable dyes available in the eighteenth century, producing new knitted meshes had greater potential. Again, innovation began in the first half of the eighteenth century. About 1740 an unknown knitter discovered a simple technique of making silk stockings with the appearance of ribs called the tuck presser. Tuck fabrics had been in vogue for thirty or forty years, but because there was no patent and the tuck bar was simple enough for workmen to adopt, the technique was widely used and subject to numerous small improvements, introducing Nottingham framework knitters to the possibility of technical development of the stocking frame. The first important patented technique was for ribbed stockings and fabrics, the 'Derby rib' mechanism. Jedediah Strutt, the inventor, formed a partnership with Samuel Need, Nottingham's leading merchant hosier in the mid-eighteenth century. Need & Strutt made a substantial fortune, and their innovation had significant long-term consequences. First, a modification called Royal ribs (or British ribbed pieces) was a stout fabric that proved more suitable for outer garments, thereby extending the range of use of frame knitted fabrics. Second, Need & Strutt supplied much of Arkwright's capital when he brought his roller-spinning technique to Nottingham in 1768. Third, and most important for Nottingham, the ribbing attachment to the stocking frame was of exactly the same construction as the earliest successful lace-making system on the stocking frame.[8]

The innovator for the ribbing attachment was John Morris, the third generation of a well-known Nottingham family of merchant hosiers, who bought a patent taken out by two Mansfield framesmiths. Morris's eyelet-hole fabric or network was used to make gloves, aprons, handkerchiefs, hoods and caps, but the principal line was Spanish silk mitts for ladies' fashion wear. Information which emerged during a court action for patent infringement, *Morris* v. *Unwin*, in 1766, indicates the scale of the new venture. At the end of the patent period Morris owned forty-nine silk mitt frames, which were common stocking frames with the patent attachment, 'a set of working needles in the presser bar … which bar was hung on springs … and was caused to move sideways by means of which it moved the loop from between the needles and carried it to the next needle', an addition which could presumably have been made for a trivial cost. Production of six pairs a week for fifty weeks of the year would suggest an output of 15,000 pairs a year. In addition there were numerous pirates of the patent: sixteen Nottingham hosiers, three framesmiths, and seven framework knitters were sued for infringement. According to Henson, 'Morris was a generous man; no wages in the [hosiery] manufacture ever ran so high as those paid to the workmen employed on these machine mitts'. Felkin added that some workmen could make two pairs a day and thus earned wages of 25*s* (£1 25p) to 50*s* (£2 50p) weekly, unheard-of wages to Nottingham framework knitters accustomed to 10*s*–15*s* (50p–75p).

In 1787 Morris bought out another patent, this time for a technique called point net, but coming near to retirement he sold it to the Hayne brothers, three entrepreneurs who had moved from Ashbourne to Nottingham. After making some mechanical improvements, they produced a fast hexagonal net which, according to Blackner, possessed a 'lightness and beauty of texture' and 'regularity of mesh' which at the period 'had no parallel', and a rapid growth was inaugurated. The new fabric was made into sunshades, aprons, handkerchiefs, caps, mitts, gloves, purses, waistcoats, shawls, cauls, and other fashionable goods. When the technique of fastening the mesh was discovered,

> there were few more than twenty point net frames in existence, and some of them not more than 18 or 20 inches wide; whereas in 1810 there were at the least 1,500 frames employed in this manufacture, and many hundreds of them more than 30 inches wide; which taking the business in all its branches gave employment to from 10,000 to 15,000 persons, including women and children.

William Hayne 'had a most enterprising spirit, as well as judgement in manufacturing and mercantile affairs', and cornered the larger part of the new trade in both Britain and France. By 1812 the brothers owned machinery valued at £24,000, which at £25 a frame indicates 960 frames, or some two-thirds of those in the trade. Large quantities of point net were exported to Paris following the Peace of Amiens in 1802, but on the resumption of war in 1803 the French authorities seized some £25,000 worth. Even when allowance is made for the fact that the Hayne brothers became legendary figures in their own lifetime, their record must place them in the vanguard of industrial pioneers of the period. They disappeared in the collapse of the silk lace trade following the conclusion of the French Wars, along with most of the other pioneer generation of lace merchants in Nottingham, but not before the machine lace industry was well established.[9]

Cotton and worsted spinning

The growing prosperity of the hosiery industry, and the enterprise of the merchant hosiers attracted two pioneers of mechanised cotton spinning to the town. Richard Arkwright arrived in 1768 in search of capital and formed a partnership with Need & Strutt. A house in Hockley, then on the north-eastern edge of the town, was acquired to accommodate his roller-spinning machines, and a horse-powered capstan. The installation was small, and was probably regarded by the partners from the outset as a pilot project for their more ambitious factory system of production. Arkwright left for Cromford in 1771 to develop his water-powered system, subsequently building a chain of mills in Derbyshire and Lancashire. Meanwhile James Hargreaves followed him to Nottingham in 1769, with the support of another merchant hosier partnership, Rawson, Heath & Watson. They built a factory to accommodate manually-operated spinning jennies. This was across the street from Arkwright's first factory in Hockley, and it was still in production in 1803 when it was advertised for sale in the *Nottingham Journal*.[10]

Cotton had hitherto been a very expensive yarn, acquired only at the irregular auctions of the East India Company in London, and Nottingham hosiers leapt at the opportunity of a continuous and cheaper supply. Eleven firms built their own spinning mills in the town, or on small streams round about. The sluggish Leen soon became overcrowded with mills so that most firms had to install steam engines, which in the 1770s and 1780s were still in the pioneer stage of development. The high cost of Boulton & Watt engines, and the meagre water power supplies, was a real constraint on the growth of this new industry. The biggest mill in Nottingham, that of Denison & Oates at Pennyfoot Street, cost £15,000 to build and equip. It had a 30 h.p. engine and employed 300 workers, but was burned out in riots in 1794.[11]

The greatest beneficiaries of the new system in the Nottingham region were most probably those who were already occupying textile mill sites before Arkwright arrived. Foremost among these were the Robinsons at Bulwell and Robert Hall at Basford. The Robinsons ultimately built six mills, at Bulwell, Linby, and at Papplewick, where some remnants of their activity can still be seen. When the fifth Lord Byron (uncle to the poet) cut off their water supply from his Newstead Abbey lakes, they erected the first Boulton & Watt engine to be applied directly to an Arkwright-type mill, in 1784. The Arkwright prototype mill was a simple basic factory unit, seventy by thirty feet, on three storeys, with a 10 h.p. water-wheel driving a thousand spindles. It was made the standard production unit by Arkwright's patent licensing system. Robert Hall was a bleacher who had a 'thread mill' at Basford as early as the 1750s, and built his first cotton-spinning plant twenty years or so later. In the 1790s this successful enterprise was also the first in the area to use chlorine for bleaching.[12] From cotton spinning it appeared an easy step to spinning worsted by power. Among the pioneers were Davison & Hawksley, Nottingham merchant hosiers who built a mill at Arnold in 1791, where they already employed hundreds of framework knitters. In 1800 the partners said they employed some 1,400 workers, perhaps 200–300 of them in the mill.[13]

Despite this bold enterprise, cotton and worsted spinning did not find a secure home in Nottingham and its locality. Lancashire regained the technical leadership with Crompton's mule and had the overall advantage conveyed by two centuries of experience with linen and cotton production, and of geography (abundant water power and access to Liverpool, soon to be the main port of entry for cotton). By the time of the first factory inquiry of 1833, Nottingham had only four small cotton mills in production. Leicester fared no better, soon losing its early interest in worsted spinning to Bradford. Enterprise was re-focused on Nottingham's emerging specialism, lace, which was beyond the encroachment of both Lancashire and the West Riding.[14]

Hosiery in decline, *c.*1810–1850

For a combination of reasons the prosperity which had been such a feature of the hosiery industry in the second half of the eighteenth century came to an end from about 1810. Most important was a critical change of fashion. Stockings, the universal dress for men and boys, were superseded by trousers, inspired by the Prussian army uniform. The Hayne brothers, the largest and most successful firm in Nottingham, ran into financial difficulties exporting to France following Napoleon's embargoes. For the first time, the industry was clearly over-equipped with stocking frames and in 1809 the lace manufacturers halved the rent from 1*s* to 6*d*. This initially placated the knitters, who acknowledged publicly that the employers were 'using their utmost exertions to retrieve the credit of the trade', but insecurity persisted. The confidence of investors evaporated, and the friendly societies saw the value of their investment halved overnight.[15]

Table 14.1 **Investment in stocking frames**

	1812 (Midland Counties only)			
	No.	*Cost each (£)*	*Total investment (£)*	*%*
Narrow frames (18–20 in.)	22,000+	15	330,000	79
Wide frames (28–34 in)	3,500+	25	87,500	21
Totals	25,000+		417,500	100

	England (1844 and 1865) and Saxony (1855)					
	1844		*1865*		*1855*	
	No.	*%*	*No.*	*%*	*No.*	*%*
Narrow frames	31,642	78.9	42,000	84.0	11,200	54.4
Wide frames	8,470	21.1	8,000	16.0	9,400	45.6
Totals	40,112	100	50,000	100	20,600	100

Sources: Blackner, pp. 238–45 for 1812 census of frames; P. M. Lewis, 'The Evolution of the Hand Stocking Frame 1750–1815' (University of Nottingham, M.Phil. thesis, 1985), p. 190 for calculations of the number of wide frames, 1812; W. Felkin, *An Account of the Machine Wrought Hosiery Trade* (1845), p.16. W. Felkin, *History of the Machine Wrought Hosiery and Lace Manufacturers* (1867), p. 517; Karin Zachmann, 'Die sachsische Stumpfwirkerei im Spannungsfeld von Tradition und Anpassung', *Neues Archiv fur sachsische Geschichte*, LXIV (1993), pp. 115–28.

The situation deteriorated further in 1810–11, scapegoats were sought, and militants called for decisive action. One of the targets of popular resentment was the wider stocking frames that, since 1776, had been built to cater for new fashions in hosiery. To put a vertical stripe in stockings it was easier to knit them lengthways on the frame rather than in the traditional vertical manner. When these stockings were no longer in demand, 21 per cent of the industry's investment suddenly appeared to be redundant (table 14.1). Employers responded by extending the established practice of 'cut-up work', i.e. knitting wide lengths of fabric and cutting them with scissors to shape particular garments. The Hayne brothers, among other lace manufacturers, had done this with point net for over twenty years, but it was fairly new for stockings, and it was bitterly resented by artisans who insisted that all hosiery must be 'fully fashioned', i.e. knitted to the shape of the leg.[16] The owners of the wide stocking frames were a large and anonymous group of investors whose motives were subject to much local scrutiny.[17] Nocturnal devastation of wide stocking frames grabbed the headlines and served as an outlet for framework knitters' resentment, but it did nothing to relieve the underlying causes of the trade depression.[18]

By 1816 the hosiery trade had slipped into a deep trough from which it began to re-emerge only at mid-century. The stream of new ideas dried up while promising new technology gathered dust; warp knitting was left to the Germans to develop, and circular knitting to the Americans. Despite falling yarn prices, investment in hosiery machinery was desultory. Antipathy to the wide frames was almost certainly the prime cause of stagnation, for those employed in the rival Saxony industry represented a much higher percentage (table 14.2). For a generation everyone in the trade seemed to be afraid of innovation.[19]

Bobbin-net lace and the Jacquard

The earliest machine forms of Nottingham lace were made on the stocking frame. The town's ingenious artisans produced increasingly intricate meshes, and towards the end of the Napoleonic War the process of evolution took off to form a whole new industry. The foremost mechanic of this development was John Heathcoat, who came to Nottingham in 1804 as a framesmith, having just completed his apprenticeship. For many years Nottingham framework knitters and framesmiths had striven to produce new meshes on the stocking frame in the hope of creating fashionable varieties that could bring them greater rewards. The merchant hosiers, the organisers of the domestic system, were keen to offer partnerships or licensing arrangements to inventors who could produce new fabrics which could be marketed as fashion varieties in London and through their provincial connections. Heathcoat conceived the idea of imitating mechanically the motions of a pillow-lace worker. In 1808 and 1809 he achieved his first, and greatest, success with the invention of the bobbin-net machine, which produced a fast hexagonal net by manual power. The originality of the machine was soon contested, since most of the components were used by rivals and other textile inventors but, as Don Varley has expressed it with a striking simile: 'If the claims of Mozart to be the composer of Jupiter symphony are to be rejected on the grounds that he employed notes and instruments which were already well known, albeit in different orders and combinations, then we must equally reject those of Heathcoat to the invention of the bobbin net machine.'[20]

Jealousy, and resentment of Heathcoat's success, produced numerous infringers in Nottingham: 156 were identified in 1816 and 200 in 1819. Two cases in the Court of Common Pleas, *Bovill* v. *Moore* (1816) and *Heathcoat* v. *Grace & Co.* (1817), established the patentee's rights, after which he arranged a system of licensing which brought in about £10,000 royalties a year for the remaining period of the patent. An unusual feature of the licensing, which contrasts with that of other successful patentees such as Arkwright and Boulton & Watt, was that it allowed the continuance of a considerable number of small producers. These were mostly Nottingham framework knitters, mechanics and tradesmen, who had shifted their modest resources into the profitable new business. Despite this generous policy, Heathcoat continued to be unpopular, which was no doubt a major factor in the Luddite destruction of machinery in his new Loughborough factory in 1816. It is not clear if the Luddites knew that he had already (December 1815) bought a large disused cotton mill in Tiverton (Devon) for conversion to power-driven lace net production. Despite the offer of £10,000 compensation by the Leicestershire magistrates, Heathcoat took the whole of his business and many of his skilled work-force to Tiverton, where he worked to establish a major lace net-making enterprise. In the 1820s he had a capital of £120,000 and a payroll, with outworkers, of as many as 3,000, larger than anything in Nottingham.[21]

Heathcoat's Tiverton enterprise was the model for several other lace net factories established in the West of England. Nottingham entrepreneurs, however, lacked the capital to challenge the innovator on his own ground. Instead, the hundreds of Nottingham mechanics who crowded into the new trade worked to outflank the colossus of the new industry by producing patterned meshes to supersede hand-embroidered machine nets. By countless small advances they eventually succeeded. Prominent mechanics were Levers in the 1820s, Croft and Birkin in the 1830s, and Hooton Deverill in the 1840s. The latter was outstanding because he succeeded in applying the Jacquard – which used punch cards to form the pattern – to the Levers lace machine, thereby opening up various possibilities for new and elaborate patterning. Only a handful of these men were able to unite mechanical and entrepreneurial skills as Heathcoat had done. However, by mid-century a generation of experimentation in Nottingham's attic workshops and small factories had created a power-driven lace machine which could pattern the net.[22]

The number of net manufacturers peaked at nearly 1,400 in 1831, after which many small producers were forced out as competition intensified. In 1862 there were only 250 lace makers.[23] A few able mechanics maintained a leading place in the industry; among the most prominent were Thomas Sewell, Richard Birkin (Biddle & Birkin), William Vickers (Vickers & Hine), William Herbert, and Francis Ball and his son Thomas.[24] This vigorous generation reached the pinnacle of its wealth and political and religious power around the middle of the nineteenth century.

The factory system in the lace industry

The factory system did not develop in the Nottingham lace industry until the early 1820s, half a century after Arkwright set up Nottingham's first cotton-spinning factory. Heathcoat drove his bobbin-net machine by water power after he moved to Tiverton in 1816, and the other West of England net manufacturers copied his system. The numerous small producers in Nottingham and the surrounding area lacked sufficient capital to erect their own premises and purchase steam engines, and the shortage of building land within the town boundaries prior to the 1850s restricted any ambitious programmes.

The earliest lace net factory in Nottingham was built by Kendall & Allen. They were financing William Morley, an 'eminent mechanic' who was building versions of Heathcoat's machines through the period of the patent. Their Leen Side mill was evidently small, with a 14 h.p. steam engine in 1825 superseded by 25 h.p. in 1834. Men of capital were able to develop more rapidly. Samuel Hall, the Basford cotton spinner and inventor of the patent method of 'gassing' lace (singeing off the loose hairs of thread) built a 'large' factory (120 x 30 feet) in Lenton in 1820. More impressive was the Radford factory of James Fisher, the most successful London lace merchant of the period. The most enterprising Nottingham artisans who moved into net production took time to catch up. Thomas Robert Sewell, an early associate of Kendall, built his own factory in Carrington in 1831, and in the mid-1830s Biddle & Birkin built at New Basford. However, even in the early 1840s, these concerns were smaller than those of Heathcoat, and of his early partners, Boden & Morley of Derby (table 14.2).[25]

Table 14.2 **Lace factories, 1840–42, by size of payroll.**

	No. on payroll
John Heathcoat & Co., Tiverton	800–850
Boden & Morley, Derby	500
James Fisher, New Radford	(500+)
T. R. Sewell, Carrington	420
Biddle & Birkin, New Basford	200
Thackerays, Radford	130
William Herbert, New Radford (two factories)	c.100
Thomas Robinson, New Basford	60–70

Sources: H. T. Fang, *Triumph of the Factory System* (Philadelphia, 1978), p. 203. *NJ*, 25 October 1842 (report of Chartist trial). Samuel & John Edmund Hall's factory at Lenton, built in 1822–24, was turned over to stall-holding; *NJ*, 1 January 1841. The figure for Fisher is the author's estimate.

As power-driven production became more effective and competition intensified, small producers were able to survive by the system known as 'standings', i.e. renting space and power in a purpose-built or modified factory. The system probably began with local auctioneers of machines, who advertised house-room for buyers of single machines.[26] The earliest mill to be let for this purpose was Green's Mill in Broad Marsh, which was built for steam-powered cotton spinning in 1791 but closed towards the end of the Napoleonic War. At first used as a school and for the early meetings of the Primitive Methodists, it was subsequently rented to small net producers, who could link their machines to the 20 h.p. engine. Another early factory of this type was Halls' in New Lenton, where space was rented out as Samuel & John Hall's business declined and then slid into bankruptcy in 1840.[27] It soon became common practice for lace manufacturers with capital to build larger premises than they themselves required, renting out a part of the property and engine power. An early exemplar of this enterprise was William Herbert. In 1844 he had two factories at Radford with twenty 'standings' for which he was charging an annual rental of £800.[28]

The proliferation of small producers in the lace industry makes it more or less impossible to identify any prototype or representative factory in the way one can in the cotton industry. It is possible to identify the size of capital invested by a few of the leaders, and to compare the figures with the better-known cotton industry, and with some small manufacturers. James Fisher, the dominant entrepreneur in the 1830s, insured his two steam-powered mills (28 h.p. together) and machine building workshops at New Radford for £15,415 in 1834. Stock was insured in a warehouse on Short Hill in Nottingham for a further £4,000. At a government inquiry in 1840 evidence was given to suggest that a lace factory and warehouse employing 200–250 workers would involve a capital of some £18,000, as follows:

Buildings, engine, transmission system	£	3,000
40 12-quarter (3 ft wide) lace machines	£	10,080
Extra sets of bobbins and carriages	£	2,000
	£	15,080
Working capital [stockholding]	£	2,920
	£	18,000

The 'capital to carry on the business' evidently refers to stockholding rather than merchanting, for which the capital requirements would have been several times larger.[29] A warp lace factory built by Thomas Ball (Mayor of Nottingham in 1865–66) in Ilkeston in 1851–52, cost rather less:

Buildings in Burr Lane	£	4,452
Machinery	£	4,822
Steam engine	£	450
Fixtures, etc.	£	175
Warehouse (Castle Gate, Nottingham) fixtures	£	630
	£	10,529[30]

These figures may be compared with the £4,500 recommended for building a cotton-spinning mill in 1836.[31]

The contrast between large and small manufacturers is evident down to the First World War. When Thomas Humber moved his cycle works from Beeston to Coventry in 1908, Sir Arthur Black MP bought the buildings for £10,000, installed twenty new plain net machines of his own, and rented the remaining space to stallholders, offering financial support, either directly or through guarantees, to Lloyds Bank. E. I. Lees began in 1909 in the Humber Road factory with four plain net machines, valued at £4,000, half of which he borrowed. He soon had thirteen machines and a capital of over £7,000. The next year A. H. Beard began with two Levers machines, valued at £900, with Black guaranteeing him for £750. By the end of 1914 Beard had moved to two standings in the Victoria Factory in Gamble Street, and had a capital of £4,000–5,000.[32] The lace industry contained scores of 'little men' of this kind until its sharp contraction in the 1920s.

Data for the first generation of Nottingham lace manufacturers and merchants nearly all relate to numbers of machines and owners, rather than to factories and workshops; indeed, lace did not begin to come within the orbit of the Factory acts until 1861, so official data is relatively late compared with that for some other branches of textiles. Table 14.3 represents the best available data for pinpointing when factory production overtook the cottages, attics and scattered workshops in and about Nottingham. The number of factories did not begin to grow significantly until the Nottingham enclosure commissioners began to release building land in the 1850s, and then again after the American Civil War (1865). By 1876, when the first full data is available, the number of factories was about to overtake the number of workshops, although factories were by now more than ten times larger. Even so, the *average* factory size was still small – the Arkwright prototype mill had employed 200–300 people a century earlier. The 1850s also saw an unprecedented investment in warehouses, in which the finishing process (primarily lace clipping and dressing) were conducted, largely (86 per cent) by women and girls. Despite the dramatic fall in the numbers of females employed in hand embroidering lace net following the application of the Jacquard principle to Levers machines, the proportion in the labour force (58.5 per cent in 1876) was still significantly higher than men and boys (41.5 per cent). The system summarised in table 14.3 lasted well into the present century, and as late as 1909 over 7,000 women were employed clipping and scalloping lace in their own homes.

Table 14.3 **Lace production in England, 1876**

	No.	*Payroll*	*Average size*	*Female %*
Lace factories	223	8,268	37.0	27.5
Lace workshops	298	929	3.1	76.6
Lace warehouses	405	8,679	21.4	86.2
Totals	926	17,876	19.3	58.5

Source: Calculated from *Factory and Workshops Act Commission Report*, Parl. Papers, 1876, XXIX, Appendix B (Statistical Tables). p. 132. There were six lace factories in the West of England and a growing number in the small towns satellite to Nottingham (Beeston, Ilkeston, Long Eaton, etc.).

The advent of the factory system in hosiery

Over the period 1810–50 the hosiery industry saw few if any significant innovations, and several leading merchant hosiers told a government inquiry in 1844 that they saw no prospect of any.[33] All the business enterprise and talented artisans deserted hosiery for lace, and new investment dried up. A small number of persevering, well-connected merchant hosiers increased their control by buying up stocking frames. In 1810 Nottingham's largest firm was probably Heard & Hurst, who employed over 1,000 frames locally. Nathan Hurst supervised the Nottingham operation while John Heard was in charge of the selling organisation in London; the prestige of the house was based on their royal appointment, making George IV's hosiery.[34] By 1844 several leading hosiery firms had many more frames: Hine & Mundella owned 3,000 I. & R. Morley 2,700, and Heard & Hurst 2,000.[35]

Plate 37 **Boots Company Offices, Station Street**. The original Hine & Mundella hosiery factory of 1851, designed by T. C. Hine for his brother's firm, and notable in having the first steam-powered stocking frames, stood on this site. It was burnt down in 1859, and its replacement, by Hine, opened in the early 1860s. The original firm was restructured as the Nottingham Manufacturing Company. Jesse Boot first moved into a few vacant rooms in the building in 1898. He gradually acquired the rest, and it became the headquarters of the Boots Company

When overseas competition (principally from Saxony) forced the industry to change, the key technical developments in mechanising production were made in Loughborough with the rival systems of William Cotton and Charles Paget. In Nottingham an early response came from Hine & Mundella, who built a five-storey steam-powered factory close to the Midland railway station on land released by the enclosure commissioners. It opened in 1851 but after a promising start profits slumped, and other major firms were reluctant to follow: only 31 out of 113 hosiers listed in an 1844 directory converted to factory production, and not all of them were successful.[36] Most of the early innovators were men who, like Mundella (the son of an Italian immigrant to Leicester), were relatively new to the industry. Other firms changed course only when a new generation took control, or foreign competition became acute. The majority of factory hosiery firms rented space and steam power in one of the tenanted factories built for lace manufacturers. Most were small firms run by men with technical rather than marketing or financial skills, and frequently they lasted only a short while.[37]

Only the major established East Midlands firms had the necessary resources of capital and commercial connections to accomplish the complete transformation of the industry. Rather belatedly, I. & R. Morley of Nottingham and Corahs of Leicester took the lead. Morleys began in 1799 when John Morley left Sneinton to open a small warehouse in Wood Street, London, while his brother Richard took charge of the production side in Nottingham. They were closely connected with some affluent members of Nottingham's corporate elite, notably their brother-in-law Alderman William Wilson, Francis and Thomas Wakefield, Arthur Wells, the solicitor, and Wrights the bankers. Consequently their credit was always good. A 'top of the market' policy brought them royal patronage and a premier position in Wood Street, where they built a prestige warehouse in 1849. By 1860 they had 3,700 framework knitters on their books, but they were one of the most conservative firms in the trade, still believing that factory products were inferior. The Nottingham manager inspected the knitters' work 'and if they were not absolutely perfect the workmen were in for a very bad time', one of them recalled in later years.[38]

Far-reaching changes began soon after Samuel Morley (son of Richard) took sole control of the business in 1860. The depots where Morleys met their bag hosiers became the sites of new factories: Manvers Street (Nottingham) in 1866, Daybrook and Heanor (1875), Handel Street (Nottingham) (1879), Loughborough (1884), Sutton in Ashfield (1887), and Leicester (1889). According to Morley's biographer the factories 'were the best in the North Midlands; special attention was given to cleanliness, light and ventilation; and, above all, the fullest and freest fraternity was established between capital and labour, between master and workmen, merchant and clerks'. Samuel Morley was meticulous in quality control, but the range of goods was now greatly extended.[39] In the course of continued expansion in the Midlands, Morleys absorbed some of the earlier pacemakers of the industry – I. I. & I. Wilson bought from Hine & Mundella in 1871 and the bankrupt Midland Hosiery Co. in 1887. At their centenary in 1899 Morleys towered above all other firms in the trade and probably handled 10 per cent of total output. They employed over 1,200 at their warehouses in Wood Street, London, and Fletcher Gate, Nottingham, over 3,000 in seven hosiery factories in the Midlands, 250 in a glove factory in London, and – perhaps surprisingly – 3,950 framework knitters, more than those on the payroll in 1860. Still owned and run by the family, the firm continued to be the largest producer until after the Second World War.[40]

While Morleys lead the field in hosiery and knitwear before 1920, their individual factories were not giants – in 1899 the largest was in Heanor with just over 1,000 employees. It included the firm's extensive dyeworks.[41] In Nottingham the biggest hosiery factory was probably that built by Rogers, Black & Co. in Dame Agnes Street, which employed over 1,000 young women on 'cut and sew', that is, making shirts, pants, combinations, vests, drawers and hose by sewing together shapes from fabrics knitted on rotary frames, cut out and machine-sewn. The principle was precisely the one against which the Luddites had rebelled, and which I. & R. Morley still abjured, confining themselves to the 'Cotton's patent' or traditional fully-fashioned garment production. 'Cut and sew' was cheaper and probably more profitable. Rogers' still

Plate 38 **I & R Morley, Winding and Manufacturing Machines, 1900**. Morley's factory in Handel Street was bought by the firm in 1879. In 1900 344 people were employed here, and some of the 245 women are shown here winding and operating the machines. Note the male overseer! Some of the frames at Handel Street were twenty-four feet in length and eight garments could be made at a time

produced superior quality work on hand frames but believed in 1886 that the breed of old framework knitters was 'fast dying out'.[42] The Rogers family, like the Morleys, were long-established merchant hosiers who had come to factory production after the pioneers, but in both cases the new generation seemed intent on making up for lost time, although adopting contrasting business strategies.

Textile engineering

From the earliest years of the hosiery industry, machine making was a distinct specialism. The fully-evolved stocking frame contained 2,000 parts. Some, like the needles and sinkers, demanded great precision, and these became ancillary specialist crafts. The greatest skill was in the manufacture of the barbed needles that were the essence of Lee's invention, for which strong but flexible steel was required. Angerstein, a Swedish industrial spy who visited Nottingham in 1750, believed that the tensility of the steel needles was at the very heart of Nottingham's industrial achievement.[43]

Plate 39 **Trade Card, John B. & S. Whitehall**. The card indicates the range of vital components, 'spares', manufactured locally by specialists to support the local textile trades. The firm was at 32 Greyhound Street, close to Parliament Street, in 1848, but had gone by 1876

The number of framesmiths fluctuated with the prosperity of the industry. Blackner records that 'the highest number ever known' was forty-seven in 1807, 'many of whom had large establishments of journeymen and apprentices'. In the depression at the close of the Napoleonic War numbers fell to twenty-nine, 'generally with small establishments', and then to twenty-five in 1818.[44] The boom in the bobbin-net lace trade in the early 1820s gave a huge boost to machine building, and the number of smiths increased to eighty. A range of new specialisms emerged, more particularly bobbin and carriage makers, and guide makers. Felkin, the self-appointed statistician of the lace and hosiery industries, tried to count the total numbers employed in 1825 and again in 1835, but his findings are difficult to reconcile with Dearden's *Nottingham Directory* (1834) (table 14.4). Some features of the emergent industry are noteworthy. Master smiths' (machine builders') establishments were still very small at this time, with only five men each on average. Dearden shows they were already developing rapidly in the new industrial suburbs, especially in Radford. Lace and hosiery machine-building had not yet separated, so Felkin should not have omitted new specialisms on the hosiery side, notably sinker makers, which have been added to his list on Dearden's authority. With the advent of the Jacquard, another specialism (card makers) emerged.

Table 14.4 **Textile machine-building specialisms in early nineteenth-century Nottingham**

	Section	*1825*	*1835*
Master smiths (machine builders)	L, H	80	30
Journeymen		400	150
Master bobbin and carriage makers	L	50	(37)[a]
Journeymen		250	140
Smiths privately employed	L, H	300	100
Guide, pusher, bolt, comb, point-hook and sled makers	L	150	30
Needle makers, turners, woodwork makers, casters, setters up, etc.	H, L	270	55
Sinker makers	H	14	17
Totals		1,514	559

(L = lace, H = hosiery)

Sources: *NJ*, 26 August 1836, p. 4 (Felkin's report). Glover's *Nottingham Directory for 1825*. W. Dearden's *Nottingham Directory* (1834) supplies defects in Felkin's data.

Note: [a] Felkin's figure (15) must be an error as Dearden names 37. The totals are higher than Felkin's as he concentrated on lace and so omitted sinker makers.

Further information is lacking until 1865, when the number of master machine builders was down to ten. The American Civil War (1861–65) severely affected Nottingham – one manufacturer wrote in his diary in 1864 that 'the lace trade is paralysed'.

In addition, as the hosiery industry mechanised, machine building became a distinct specialism, led by Hine & Mundella who initially made their own machines and then built for export to France (Troyes), Saxony (Chemnitz) and the USA (New England).[45] But the most important development was that some framesmiths or component manufacturers began to move ahead by building large and (rapidly) integrated factories, bringing together component manufacture and assembly in a single firm. The most able of these new leaders was John Jardine who, having served his apprenticeship to a Nottingham clockmaker, became a bobbin and carriage maker. His 'mechanical genius' was applied to making tools to produce standardised components, from which it was no doubt a logical step to assemble all the components in one place. Jardine's other achievement was his insistence on the highest standards. When he was seventy years old (in 1895) and had over 500 on his payroll, Jardine's *Monthly Register* maintained, somewhat improbably, 'every portion of lace machinery, from the heavy framework to the minutest accessory is made under his eye'; but the point was made that his factories permitted no second-rate work. Jardine's Levers lace machines were designed and constructed to last for ever, and some are still at work in the industry today.[46]

The merchant hosiers' conservatism inevitably affected the machine builders. A striking illustration of their disadvantage is offered by the experience of Manlove, Alliott & Co., a well-known engineering firm at Radford closely connected with I. & R. Morley through membership of Castle Gate Congregational Chapel. The firm introduced a patent circular knitting machine (i.e. one that makes a tube of fabric which is then cut to size) which they showed at the Great Exhibition in 1851, and which was described as the one original feature of the knitting machine section. Morleys refused to adopt it and the company was so discouraged that it abandoned hosiery-machine building in favour of more general engineering work, including plants for bleachers and dyers.[47] Some framesmiths persevered, and two or three were able to build substantial works almost comparable to Jardine's. Perhaps the most successful was Moses Mellor, who had a work-force of 130 in 1865, making circular machines in defiance of the deep-rooted prejudice. The other outstanding firm, George Blackburn & Sons (Atlas Engineering Works), was started by three mechanics from Platts of Oldham, who also concentrated on circular machines. The lifting of the ban on the export of machinery in 1845 helped these firms, as British hosiery manufacturers were resistant to new technology and factory production. Overall, however, hosiery machine building was not a major success in Nottingham.[48] There is no easy explanation, but the long period of depression in the hosiery industry and the related fear of innovation must be at the root of the problem.

Markets, merchants and designs for lace

In the eighteenth century the dealers or middlemen known as 'lacemen' collected the small packages of hand-made lace from the people who organised the trade in Honiton, Buckingham, and other craft centres, and sold them on to milliners, haberdashers, export merchants and others. Only about 10 per cent of the hand-made lace imported from Flanders was declared at HM Customs and numbers of London silkmen probably dealt in smuggled lace as well as in English-made goods.[49] Most were in business in a modest way, their insured stock seldom rising above £1,000 and often much less. Eruptions appeared in this old pattern of trade towards the end of the century when two Nottingham-based partnerships began to insure much larger stocks, reflecting both the greater productivity of machine-made lace and the level of sales. Robert & Thomas Frost's insured stock rose from £3,000 in 1791 to £12,000 in 1807, while the Hayne brothers' stock rose from £2,000 in 1797 to £15,000 in 1802.[50] However, middle-class women still preferred the traditional hand-made product, which in turn continued to provide the structures and fashions for machines to copy. As late as 1860, Richard Birkin maintained that 'the whole of our lace machinery [in Nottingham] was constructed to imitate lace made in France and the surrounding countries by hand … and unlike most other descriptions of producing machinery continues to imitate hand-made goods'.[51] Merchants often dealt in both hand- and machine-made lace, varying the proportions as supply, price and fashion required.

The old-established textile trade of the City of London changed rapidly after the French Wars. Cheap-selling warehouses were established to take advantage of the innumerable small hand-to-mouth producers in Lancashire, Yorkshire, and the East Midlands, by acquiring stocks at bargain prices and selling cheaply to country drapers and haberdashers. The leading firm of Todd & Morrison was the first to exploit the bargains to be had in Nottingham.[52] Others soon followed: in 1828 the *Circular to Bankers* remarked that 'we hear of warehousemen who deal in the more showy, ornamental or more petty articles of attire and not much in the substantial parts of clothing, who severally make returns in trade amounting to £1m to £2m per annum'. This was a reference to the two most energetic firms specialising in lace, James Fisher & Co. and Copestake, Moore & Co. Like most London warehousemen, James Fisher received his early training in retail drapery. He started on his own about 1800 and expanded rapidly from an early connection with John Heathcoat. After the expiration of the bobbin-net patent in 1823, he built a factory at Radford, followed by another at Beeston, and in the 1830s conspired to dominate the industry by taking out a sequence of patents in the name of his chief mechanic, William Crofts. Fisher's London business peaked in the mid-1840s when James Fisher junior declared that his firm bought brown net 'from almost every manufacturer in the [lace] trade, and to a larger extent than any other [merchant] house in Nottingham'.[53]

Copestake Moore & Co. was founded by Sampson Copestake, and built up by two of Fisher's most successful commercial travellers. Much of the enterprise and energy in the trade was dependent on accurate information from London agents or partners on fashion movements – that is, on what could, or could not be expected to sell. Following Fisher's example, the firm built a factory in Houndsgate in 1844. By the 1860s Copestake Crampton & Co. (the successor firm) was reckoned to be the largest of its specialism in the world, employing over 300 men in its London warehouse, far more than its closest rivals (Thomas Adams, Richard Birkin, and Heymann & Alexander) in Nottingham.[54] Initially most output came from small workshops served by a corps of 'brown net' agents, who took in unfinished ('brown') nets to sell on commission (usually 2.5 per cent) and advanced both cotton and cash to machine holders who needed credit.[55]

The advantages conferred by the technical achievements of Heathcoat, Levers and other Nottingham craftsmen might have been expected to create a large lace export business, but the town had little commercial experience in overseas markets. Heathcoat took the initiative by opening a factory in France (1818), but this simply advertised the new system to the main competitor. A string of Nottingham bobbin net makers, frustrated by Heathcoat's unjust (as they saw it) licensing system, established workshops in Calais, further curtailing export opportunities. Felkin calculated that exports fell from 75 per cent of output in 1832 to 50 per cent in 1836, a period of booming trade in the economy generally.[56] In fact, most of the export opportunities in the early years proved to be in central Europe, with the gap in mercantile experience being bridged by a handful of German merchants who migrated to Nottingham, often after some initial experience in the Manchester textile trade. The most successful was Lewis Heymann, while other lace merchants with Continental backgrounds included Simon, Meyer & Co. (now Simon May) from Hamburg, Marx Brothers from Leipzig, Kulp & Son from Frankfurt and Liepmann Kohn & Co., originally from Berlin. Some stayed for only a few years but others were prominent in Anglo–German trade for two or three generations. At the end of the century, Jacoby and Flersheim were factory owners as well as merchants, while others including Liepmann, Stiebel, Feilmann, and Seelig were well-known names in the trade. In the 1830s and 1840s the Hansa Towns took more Nottingham lace than the rest of Europe collectively.[57]

The other main target for lace exports was the Americas, especially the USA. A couple of Heathcoat's disgruntled workmen had left Loughborough for Ipswich, Massachusetts, in 1822, but the Ipswich Lace Company was short-lived.[58] The market was wide open to European exports. William Cripps, a Nottingham lace merchant who began his career in the USA, wrote in 1830 that 'scarcely a packet ship left Liverpool without goods for our New York houses'. Frearson & Vickers were shipping large quantities of lace to New York in the mid-1830s, and also to Melbourne and Lima (Peru). James Fisher had New York agents in the 1840s and George Moore visited agents in cities including New York, Philadelphia, Baltimore, Montreal and Boston in 1844, and studied the 'dry goods' trade. The later part of the American Civil War interrupted progress and several firms went bankrupt, but when peace was restored a small number of firms, including Thomas Adams, Richard Birkin and Frank Wilkinson, the lace curtain manufacturer, built up a large American export trade. Other lace makers sold direct to American agents visiting the Lace Market. Towards the end of the nineteenth century, as Germany industrialised, the export trade increasingly depended on the American market.[59]

Lace merchants were more than simply middlemen, agents or financiers to the trade: they were the real entrepreneurs, selecting designs from samples submitted by the manufacturers and holding stocks of 'brown net' until the bleachers, dyers and finishers could take them and the market was ready. In this context, French complaints that Nottingham lace manufacturers lacked design sense or training is somewhat misplaced because they produced what the merchants commissioned (i.e. what the market could afford), and the popular demand was for something 'cheap and cheerful' rather than of original artistic merit. At the height of the Victorian lace boom in 1886 the head of Thomas Adams & Co. maintained that Nottingham was noted for a 'low class cheap effective article', which was what the major consumer markets required.[60]

This did not indicate any lack of original artistic merit. Some manufacturers relied on French designs copied from goods on sale in London or bought from itinerant artists, but this dependence ceased by mid-century. The government inspector appointed to examine the work of the School of Art reported in 1850 that 'the fabrics of the town are competing with those of France and Belgium in … beauty of design'. Lascelles's *Directory* of 1848 listed twenty-five designers and draughtsmen, and by 1865 there were said to be thirty-four, including several free-lancers. Good designs were produced when machine technology permitted (after the introduction of the Jacquard) and consumers demanded it: thus William Vickers (1797–1882) made a fortune and founded a dynasty by specialising, between about 1840 and 1870, in large shawls and mantles of the richest materials and most elaborate designs. He successfully imitated the hand-made production of Chantilly and Bayeux. William Vickers II received a thorough technical education and studied at South Kensington College of Art.[61] In fact, the manufacturer's ideal was to produce an elaborate and expensive-looking design which would capture the market long-term and so keep unit costs low. In this sense the most successful design on record was probably Birkins' rose pattern called Valenciennes, designed in 1883, of which sixteen million yards had been produced by 1906.[62]

The Nottingham lace industry faced stiff competition in export markets. While Britain maintained the principle of free trade, industrialising competitors protected their industries with high tariff barriers, as a result of which between the 1860s and 1880s the industry's growth was arrested and some branches slumped. Plain net, still dominated to a remarkable degree by the West of England producers, was easiest for a newly-industrialising country to take up. The Germans made warp net their specialism and strength while the Swiss concentrated on Schiffla embroidery and Raschel machines.[63] Nottingham, however, continued to be the world centre in Levers lace.[64]

Lace curtains

Lace manufactured on machines developed by Heathcoat and his rivals was always known as Levers lace because John Levers was the most genuine claimant to having produced an effective machine. Levers and plain net machines were ubiquitous until mid-century when a new branch offered fresh chances of fortune. Curtain machines were properly speaking refinements of the Levers machine, but they were much larger and more complicated and expensive to build, so that manufacturers were forced to specialise.

Like almost all other developments in the Nottingham textile industry, the lace curtain branch originally sprang from the enterprise of a handful of mechanics. In the late 1840s and 1850s Livesey, Elsey and Sisling developed a viable machine, and several firms were launched.[65] The initiative was soon taken up by entrepreneurs with good marketing and financial connections, better able to exploit the commercial potential. Lewis Heymann's firm (Heymann & Alexander) commissioned a young Nottingham artist, S.W. Oscroft, to design a panel incorporating the rose, thistle and shamrock as emblems of England, Scotland and Ireland. James Sylvestor, who had a plant of 'superior curtain machines' at New Lenton, was commissioned to turn the designs into fabrics. The magnificent curtains he produced were sent to the 1851 Great Exhibition at the Crystal Palace, where they won a gold medal, and were so admired by Queen Victoria and Prince Albert that a large order was placed for curtains of the same pattern to adorn the principal windows of Buckingham Palace. This royal patronage set a fashion and Sylvestor was kept fully employed by Heymann & Alexander. The firm won another prize at the 1862 Exhibition with an Oscroft design and the Art Journal *Illustrated Catalogue* declared that its productions 'now surpass those of France', which had always boasted of its superiority in design. Heymann's brother Albert followed him to Nottingham, where he became a director of the old-established bank Fellows, Hart & Co. (now part of Lloyds Bank), a connection which may have originated at High Pavement Chapel where both the Heymanns and the Fellows were leading members.[66] The 1862 Crystal Palace Exhibition also featured lace curtains by Thomas Adams & Co., Copestake, Moore & Co. and S. Wills & Co., all of Nottingham. Adams tried to upstage Heymann & Alexander's 1851 triumph by producing a highly-ornate imperial panoply featuring the royal arms in a setting of exotic vegetation, but Buckingham Palace was not induced to replace its curtains. Birkins belatedly moved into the profitable new branch of the industry in 1869.[67] The lace curtain branch continued to flourish: Wright's 1910 *Directory* listed forty-one lace curtain manufacturers plus fourteen others with standings. By this time there were a few in the suburbs, but probably no more than four.[68]

The lace market

Throughout the nineteenth century there were two national markets for lace. The Wood Street and St Paul's area of the City continued to be a major emporium, and most of the larger Nottingham firms including Fisher, Copestake Moore & Co., Thomas Adams, and Birkins, were well represented. Increasingly, however, a number of manufacturers began to keep sales offices in the area around St Mary's Church which came to be known as the Lace Market. All the major buildings, including the prestige warehouses of the larger firms, were erected after easy communication with London was opened up, namely the Penny Post and the Midland Railway. Consequently this second national market was not simply a matter of long tradition or inertia, and its existence needs to be explained.[69]

From the beginning of the machine-made lace industry a strong *esprit de corps* emerged among the hundreds of small producers who resisted the encroachments of the more substantial capitalists who sought to control the trade. In the 1820s the villain of the piece was Heathcoat and in the 1830s Fisher, but the small firms always feared what they called the 'slaughter houses', the London firms operating the system pioneered by Todd & Morrison of squeezing the last penny out of those least able to resist. One response was the commission agency set up in 1832 by William Felkin and William Vickers (Felkin & Vickers), with the intention that in trade depressions they would make 'adequate advances to the Machine Owners on goods deposited with them, and thus obviate the necessity of forced sales at depreciated prices'. In 1833 Felkin claimed he had sold 'more brown net than anyone in Nottingham',[70] but fears were not easily allayed, at least until in the 1850s Thomas Adams created a centre to challenge the metropolitan lace merchants.[71]

Also significant was the continuing importance of hand-made lace in the nineteenth century. Although machine-made lace could undercut bobbin lace, the more affluent and fashion-conscious class of consumers preferred the traditional product, which enjoyed a revival in the mid-Victorian years. Hand-made lace exhibited at the Crystal Palace Exhibition of 1862 attracted as much attention as the Nottingham imitations. Haywards of Oxford Street, one of the exhibitors of Honiton-made work, were said to employ some 2,000 women and children, and the *Art Journal* insisted that Devonshire lace 'sustains its supremacy' and still employs 'tens of thousands of young women'.[72] In 1914, when King George V and Queen Mary visited Birkins' factory and the firm was drawing as much prestige from the occasion as possible, the purchase of Malherbe's patent was trumpeted. The Frenchman's invention 'enabled an exact reproduction of hand-made lace by machinery to be put on the market for the first time in the history of the lace business, the threads being manipulated by machine in exactly the same manner as the hand workers'. This was the path on which Heathcoat had embarked more than a century earlier and was only now, it seemed, fully accomplished.[73]

The growing ascendancy of Nottingham was part of the long drawn-out process in which machine lace gradually usurped the proud position of the hand-made product, and the provincial centre accumulated experience in design and marketing. Felkin estimated that in 1836 about half of Nottingham's output was sent to London to market. Birkin maintained in 1862 that 'the entire production continues to be finished and sold in Nottingham' but in this remark there was more provincial pride than realism, for the leading houses (including Birkins) maintained their London outlets to the end of the century. The important distinction was made by Birkin's brother-in-law, Thomas Ball, at the time of the Anglo-French trade treaty (1860). He acknowledged that London was 'the seat of the English home trade', implying that the lace export trade was largely conducted by German, American and other buyers visiting Nottingham and (later in the century) setting up their partners or agents in the Lace Market. The Great Exhibition of 1851 gave a major impetus to this process, persuading foreign buyers to take the train to Nottingham to visit the warehouses of Heymann, Birkin, and other medal winners.[74]

Work in the lace and hosiery industries

The early lace net and Levers machines were expensive, complicated, slow and cumbersome to work, so that skilled workmen were able to command high wages. Felkin, building on the legends of the golden age of the Heathcoat innovations, maintained that the best workmen could earn as much as £5 to £10 a week in the 1820s, fantastic wages when agricultural labourers could expect no more than 8*s*–10*s* and framework knitters in the common branches 12*s*–15*s*. However other writers record more modest sums, and it seems that while Heathcoat paid his workmen 30*s*–60*s* (£1 50p to £3) a week, according to their strength and skill, most skilled men earned 15*s* to 20*s* (75p to £1) in the period 1812 to 1820 and higher rates in the 'twist net fever' of 1822–25. After that wages fell, especially in the slump of the mid-1830s, when French competition began to be felt.[75]

The heavy and exacting nature of work in the early lace machines, combined with the high cost of the investment and seemingly insatiable demand for the product, was responsible for the introduction of unusual work patterns. It quickly became standard practice for machine operatives to work two shifts a day of four or five hours each, and this continued even when power-driven machines were introduced. These arduous conditions were tolerated in the 1820s, while wages were exceptionally high, but as they declined and the opportunity to become an independent machine owner evaporated, the men began to form strong craft unions and to voice bitter complaints. *The Petition of the Masters and Workmen of the Town of Nottingham and its Vicinity engaged in the Manufacture of Bobbin Net and Warp Lace*, addressed to the House of Commons in 1845, complained of 'the horrifying, degrading and slowish system of night labour, as practised in all Lace Factories, Shops and other places, where the manufacture is carried on, whether by hand labour or by steam power'. It was 'usual for two men to work each machine and the time is so divided that each man works twelve hours and in addition to this he has other labour to perform, such as looking over [i.e. checking] bobbins, entering beams etc which employ him about two hours per day, making the whole about fourteen hours.'[76]

By 1850 bobbin-net machines were commonly driven by steam power, and it was usual to work the machinery eighteen or twenty hours a day, with the twist-hands working two shifts daily on one or other of two patterns:

Worker	*1st factory*	*Shift system (hours)*	*Worker*	*2nd factory*	*Shift system (hours)*
A	6.00 a.m.–9.00 a.m.	3	C	4.00 a.m.–9.00 a.m.	5
B	9.00 a.m.–1.00 p.m.	4	D	9.00 a.m.–1.00 p.m.	4
A	1.00 p.m.–6.00 p.m.	5	C	1.00 p.m.–6.00 p.m.	5
B	6.00 p.m.–12.00 p.m.	6	D	6.00 p.m.–12.00 p.m.	6

A & B and C & D changed at the end of the week

The intensity of the work was explained by the *Nottingham Review*:

> So long as the machinery works steadily and without hitch, and there is no breakage in the array of threads, the workman may be a mere spectator, but he must be a vigilant one. His eye must be continually fixed upon the hundred threads, wires, hooks and wheels which throb and quiver before him. The breaking of a single filament of course involving the necessity of stopping the machine, and carefully and delicately repairing the damage.[77]

However, in the national context, Nottingham lace workers fared pretty well. A government factory inspector wrote in 1862 that Nottingham men were never overworked, for they were seldom at their machines more than ten hours a day. The women and children were not employed continuously or systematically, but they had to be 'on hand' for long hours, keeping the men supplied with materials. In the cotton industry, the restriction of hours of women and juveniles by the Factory Acts had the effects of reducing men's hours, but this did not happen in lace.[78]

Thousands of women and girls in Nottingham and its villages were employed embroidering machine nets by hand and repairing runs in the net. The Nottingham lace runners were organised by mistresses, who were subcontractors of the lace manufacturers; they often charged their female employees more than the conventional penny in the shilling commission and then paid them in 'truck' (or kind), usually in bread.[79] If there was ever an exploited 'underclass' it was these badly paid domestic needlewomen. At the peak, about 1830, 150,000 were employed, but this dwindled to 25,000 in 1865 as pattern-making machinery was developed.

While it was perhaps inevitable that there would be winners and losers in the far-reaching changes of the Industrial Revolution, it was unusual for them to live in close proximity in the same town, but this was the situation in Nottingham with lace-makers and framework knitters. In the third quarter of the century, hosiery workers in the factories benefited from greater productivity and earned better wages, while the framework knitters, though less well paid, enjoyed an Indian summer as consumer spending rose in the mid-Victorian years. But from the 1880s greater competition at home and in export markets renewed pressure on incomes, brought the factory workers into industrial strife, and squeezed out the framework knitters. The introduction of the overlocking machine (1887) raised cut-up work almost to the standard of fully-fashioned, thereby greatly increasing women's employment at the expense of men. In

1892 there was said to be 5,000 framework knitters left in employment in the midland counties; if this was true around 80 per cent of them were on the payroll of I. & R. Morley. Morleys also gave pensions to many of their long-serving knitters.[80]

Nottingham had a strong and articulate labour movement from the middle of the eighteenth century. In 1778 the framework knitters were so well organised that they were able, with the support of Abel Smith, one of the town's MPs, to promote a Bill in Parliament to protect their trade. The Bill failed, but the knitters continued to be vociferous group in all matters pertaining to their welfare. They were particularly active in 1805–12, when they organised a national hosiery union and pressed two high court actions to enforce the regulations of the Company of Frameworknitters (of London) protecting them against abuse of the apprenticeship system, and against hosiers' combinations. This period produced some outstanding trade union leaders, notably John Blackner (1769–1812) and Gravenor Henson (1785–1852). E. P. Thompson has described Henson as one of three outstanding figures in the history of working class movements between 1780 and 1832.[81] The failure of these pioneer trade union initiatives produced a reaction in which Luddism was born.

At the close of the French Wars (1815) young and enterprising knitters were attracted by the unprecedented opportunities offered by the new lace net industry, while the less skilled framework knitters became an underclass. When trade unionism took a new hold towards the middle of the century, it was on the basis of so-called 'new-model' unionism, the well-paid 'aristocracy of labour' forming themselves into tightly-controlled self-help organisations, tacitly acknowledging the power of the employers and the government's *laissez-faire* policy. In 1850–51 craft unions were formed in each of the three major sections of the lace trade, Plain Net, Levers, and Curtain, and various framework knitters' societies followed shortly. The wide frame society was involved in a particularly long and bitter strike of eleven weeks in 1860, when employers threatened a general lock-out. The three largest employers, led by A. J. Mundella, persuaded representatives of the workmen to join them in a board of arbitration. This organisation not only kept the industrial peace for a dozen years; it actually encouraged the formation and growth of new trade unions and branches by offering their leaders seats on the Board. The Board became a model for conciliation arrangements in other industries, including lace and coal. Arbitration boards promoted the idea that trade unions could be a positive help to business enterprise, and that discussion of basic issues of hours, wage rates and working conditions was mutually beneficial.[82]

Peter Wyncoll asked in the Introduction to *The Nottingham Labour Movement 1880–1939* why in 1873 Nottingham was a 'Banner town, always at or near the front of the Reform movements', while by 1918 it was considered by many (particularly on the left wing) to be the 'Despair of Labour Politicians'. Down to the First World War the answer was partially to be found in the continuing domination of the 'labour aristocracy unions', with only limited interest in the numerous semi-skilled and unskilled workers in the lace, hosiery and machine-building industries. The Lace Makers' Society had around 3,000 members in an industry employing (*c.*1900) over

20,000, and members were most interested in maintaining their elite status. In the hosiery industry from 1871 there was conflict between the Rotary (full-fashioned) Union, the Circular (cut-ups) Society, and the hand Framework Knitters' Union, with the badly-paid rural knitters and female workers scarcely unionised at all. The traditional craft unions were reinforced by the strength of chapel, co-operative and friendly societies, which shared similar ideals.[83]

Coal

The main developments in the coal and iron industry were in the Erewash Valley between Ilkeston and Alfreton, and further north in the Chesterfield area. Only a small part of the enterprise and capital came from Nottingham. Ichabod Wright II, son of the founder of the town's second bank, was a partner in the Butterley Company at Alfreton in the 1790s, and William Stretton – the best known Nottingham builder of his day – was a partner in the much smaller Cossall Iron Company near Ilkeston.[84] By the early nineteenth century the demands of the Nottingham market encouraged entrepreneurs to look for workable seams closer to the town. Francis and Thomas Wakefield inherited a thriving family business in hosiery, cotton spinning and brass and iron founding. Thomas Wakefield, whose partners included Thomas North, took leases of small collieries ('gin pits') at Babbington, Strelley, Awsworth, Greasley, Newthorpe and Stanton by Dale in the 1830s. They built eighteen miles of private railways to help promote their enterprise, and in 1841 Wakefield, North & Company sank the first deep-level mine in the area at Cinderhill, reaching the coal seam at 222 yards. A 30 h.p. engine was installed to raise the coal, and they employed the latest in mining technology. The total investment was more than £75,000. The seams suffered from faulting, and the company struggled to survive. Wakefield became bankrupt in 1847, and the concern was kept going by Wrights the bankers. It became profitable only after North's death in 1868.[85]

Between 1869 and 1874 the number of collieries in and around Nottingham increased from seven to eighteen as demand grew from the new factories. Collieries close to the town included Clifton on the north bank of the Trent, sunk 1868–69 after coal was 'proved' in 1867. The works were completed in June 1871 and demand peaked in 1871–75.[86] Smaller concerns were owned by the Wollaton Colliery Company, established in 1874 with a capital of £105,000 and shortly thereafter the owners also of Radford and Clifton Collieries. Gedling Colliery, for a long time the only mining enterprise east of Nottingham, was sunk in 1902.

Banking and retail trade

The commercial and financial importance of Nottingham in the later seventeenth and early eighteenth centuries can be seen in the establishment in the town of

Plate 40 **Clifton Colliery**. Borings for coal, on a site just south of the River Trent, began on 1 May 1867, and a workable seam was found on 7 August. On 14 October 1867 exploratory work began on the north side of the river, and by March 1868 four seams had been located. Sir Robert Clifton did not live to enjoy the mineral wealth of his estate, and the commercial development was taken over by Saul Isaac, seen here addressing those who attended the festivities following the opening of the mine. He represented Nottingham in Parliament between 1874 and 1880

the earliest provincial bank and of the first provincial insurance agency. Thomas Smith's prosperous business as a mercer brought him close connections with the City of London which led, in 1671, to his appointment as a revenue farmer (collector of taxes). Holding large balances for long periods, he developed a second line of business as a banker. Thomas Smith II continued the banking enterprise and acquired (as his monument in St Mary's Church records) 'a handsome fortune'. In the next generation, Abel Smith opened the London Bank of Smith & Payne (1758). Surviving records show that support was given to the rising hosiery industry, and to cotton spinning in the age of Arkwright. The Sun Fire Office's first agent, Thomas Partridge, opened an office in Nottingham in 1721, providing further invaluable support to local business. Other banks followed at intervals: Ichabod Wright & Co. (Baltic merchants in the iron trade) in 1759, Hart, Fellows & Co. from silk and hosiery in 1808, and Moore, Maltby, Evans & Middlemore from lace about 1812. None have left any substantial records although they are likely to have provided some of the financial support needed by the town's growing textile and retail trades.[87]

The proliferation of small country banks in England was blamed for the severity of the 1825 financial crisis, and legislation was passed to allow the formation of joint-stock banks which, it was assumed, would be able to assemble more capital and therefore be able to survive major losses. The Nottingham & Notts. Joint Stock Bank was formed in 1834 by nine local entrepreneurs. They had heard reports of bank dividends of 6–10 per cent in Lancashire and Yorkshire, and hoped to raise £½ million. In fact, it was mid-century before £200,000 was reached, a capital that had been attained by Smiths in the first decade of the century. The new bank was unlucky: its customers included two of the town's former mayors: Thomas Wakefield, the colliery owner who became bankrupt in 1847, and William Cripps, the lace merchant who lost his fortune in 1858. Nevertheless, a second limited liability bank was opened in 1865, the Nottingham Joint-Stock Bank. It was headed by the lace manufacturer Thomas Adams and the entrepreneurial lawyer Jesse Hind. Its best known customer was Jesse Boot, but he moved his firm's account to the National Provincial Bank in 1905 when the local bank could not support the huge expansion of his retail empire. Neither of the Nottingham joint-stock banks caught up with the town's major private bank: on the eve of the bank amalgamation movement at the turn of the century, Smiths' subscribed capital totalled £2.6m. while Nottingham & Notts. had only £300,000 and Nottingham Joint-Stock Bank £200,000.[88]

Nottingham's historic market-place continued to be the principal focus of retail trade and the growing number of shopkeepers took a rising proportion of the retail turnover in the town. It is practically impossible to take a full measure of their numbers as there were so many ephemeral concerns which went unrecorded in the directories. The figures in table 14.5 give some impression of orders of magnitude. All major trades contained numerous small firms prior to the First World War.

Table 14.5 **Major retail categories, 1834 and 1885**

Category	*1834*	*1885*
Innkeepers and beer sellers	266	576
Butchers	142	393
Milliners and dressmakers	149	482
Tailors	174	277
Mercers and drapers	45	159
Bakers	97	225
Clothes dealers	11	61
Boot and shoemakers		526

Sources: W. Dearden's *Nottingham Directory* (1834); C. N. Wright's *Directory of Nottingham* (1885).

In the eighteenth century the mercers were the elite of the retail trade. Prior to mechanisation fabrics were expensive and most people, apart from the wealthy, made their own clothes. This trade passed gradually to tailors for men's and dressmakers for women's clothes but despite a few pioneers there was little ready-made before the mid-nineteenth century except for special needs such as servants' liveries and mourning outfits. The needs of the poor were supported by a corps of second-hand clothes dealers.[89] In the later decades of the century a handful of successful drapers became prominent, including Fazackerley, Griffin & Spalding – who by 1890 employed 200 assistants, half of them milliners – and Jessop & Son, on Long Row.

The publicans and beer sellers were much the largest group of retailers.[90] A handful still brewed their own beer, although by 1885 the majority were supplied by one or more of the twenty-nine brewers, nine of them in the town and others at Newark, Burton, Kimberley and elsewhere. Simply by counting names in trade directories it can be ascertained that the number of food retail outlets increased substantially during the nineteenth century, and by the 1870s dairy products and fish appeared more regularly in the town. Milk came in by rail and from numerous dairies close to the town, many of which survived as late as the 1890s; indeed, the Medical Officer of Health complained in 1894 that there was still 'much work to be done in the way of bringing dairies and cowsheds, and the trade carried on in them, into reasonable conformity with the regulations'.[91] The number of fishmongers increased rapidly, particularly after mid-century, and towards 1900 came the ubiquitous fish and chip shop. There were twenty-two fried fish sellers in 1883 but over 130 by 1905/6. By the end of the nineteenth century there were more than 300 greengrocers/fruiterers and potato merchants. In 1874 there were only eight fruiterers recorded in the market place, but by 1880 there were forty new fruit and vegetable stalls. Reports from the Market and Fairs Committee point in the same direction; in 1868 it was considered appropriate to approve the appointment of an inspector of fish, meat and vegetables.[92]

Readers of the local newspapers will be struck by the growing numbers of advertisements for bargains and cut-price goods in all sorts of trades. Thus in 1885 William Cotton's dress, cap and millinery warehouse in Weekday Cross offered pairs of lace curtains from 1*s* 9*d* to 21*s*, '20 per cent lower than any other house in the trade' while James Bell, bookseller in Carlton Street offered 3*d* in the shilling (25 per cent) on 10,000 books 'consisting of works in every branch of literature'. The most successful of these cheap promotions proved to be that of Jesse Boot in Goose Gate, who in 1885 was advertising 'patent medicines, perfumery, toilet soaps and household requisites sold at a reduction of 30 to 50 per cent'.[93]

With the exception of Boots, Nottingham's greatest originality in retailing is probably expressed in the co-operative movement, which began with the projected union flour mills of 1778 and 1808 and the friendly societies.[94] It reached a new high point in the lace-trade boom of the early 1820s, when prosperous artisans moved to the new suburbs of Hyson Green, where several of the rows of superior housing were built by workmen's co-operatives, followed by a grocery store in 1830. Club Row at Carrington and Union Street Lenton are thought to have had similar origins. The present 'Co-op' traces its direct descent to a temperance group of workmen meeting in Lenton in 1863, but the inspiration was much older.[95] Like so much else in nineteenth-century Nottingham, it grew out of the prosperity of the town's staple industries.

The country town of the early modern period had become a textile giant by the nineteenth century. Hosiery, and more particularly lace, came to dominate the town's economy and, apart from a network of banking and retail outlets, most people were employed within these industries. In 1910 a witness to the *Royal Commission on the Poor Law* noted that the town had a number of other trades, including leather work, coal mining, engineering, and furniture and cloth making.[96] This was, of course, an incomplete list, because from the 1880s the basis of the town's economy began to expand, particularly into bicycle making, pharmaceuticals and tobacco. In 1914 these concerns had yet to challenge textiles as the city's staple interest, but their growing importance was undeniable, as will become clear in chapter 20.

Notes

1 Norfolk Record Office, MC 27/2, 501 x 4, f.53.

2 S. D. Chapman, 'Enterprise and innovation in the British hosiery industry 1750–1850', *Textile History*, V (1974), pp. 14–37.

3 G. Henson, *History of the Framework Knitters* (1831), p. 106; Blackner, pp. 238–45.

4 F. M. Eden, *State of the Poor* (1797) II, p. 574; *NJ*, 16 November 1782; NAO CA 3993.

5 *NR*, 4 August 1809; *NJ*, 5 August 1809. Lace frames were invested in by many small capitalists 'who speculate in the same and let them out to hire as a means of obtaining more than legal interest for their money' – Thos. Hayne, 12 February 1812, quoted in M. I. Thomis (ed.), *Luddism in Nottinghamshire* (TSRS, 26, 1972), p. 38.

6 Chapman, 'Enterprise and innovation', pp. 28–9.

7 S. D. Chapman, 'The Robinson Mills: proto-industrial precedents', *Industrial Archaeology Review*, XV (1992), pp. 58–61.

8 P. M. Lewis, 'The evolution of the hand stocking frame 1750–1815' (University of Nottingham, M.Phil. thesis, 1985), pp. 51, 56, 65, 72; Blackner, pp. 245–9.

9 Chapman, 'Enterprise and innovation', pp. 23–4.

10 C. Aspin and S. D. Chapman, *James Hargreaves and the Spinning Jenny* (Helmshore, 1964), p. 36; R. S. Fitton and A. P. Wadsworth, *The Strutts and the Arkwrights* (Manchester, 1958), chs. II–IV.

11 S. D. Chapman, *The Early Factory Masters* (Newton Abbot, 1967), chs. 5–6.

12 N. Greaterix, 'The Robinson Enterprises at Papplewick, Nottinghamshire', *Industrial Archaeology Review*, IX (1986–87), pp. 37–46, 119–39; F. M. Wilkins-Jones, 'The Firs, Old Basford: relic of an 18th century textile complex', *NH*, 18 (1976), pp. 5–8.

13 Chapman, *Early Factory Masters*, pp. 110–13.

14 *Factory Inquiry Commission Report*, PP, 1833, XX, p. 383.

15 Chapman, 'Enterprise and innovation', p. 24; *NJ*, 5 August 1809.

16 Lewis, 'Hand stocking frame', especially pp. 91, 157. 'Cut-ups' were already a subject of complaint in 1798: *NJ*, 26 January 1798.

17 *NJ*, 30 September 1809: the lace manufacturers blame the anonymous investors; cf. PRO HO 42/131, Thomas Hayne letter.

18 R. A. Church and S. D. Chapman, 'Gravenor Henson and the making of the English working class', in E. L. Jones and G. E. Mingay (eds.), *Land, Labour and Population in the Industrial Revolution* (1967), pp. 130–61. See pp. 296–7 above for Luddism.

19 Chapman, 'Enterprise and innovation', pp. 24–5.

20 D. E. Varley, 'John Heathcoat (1783–1861) founder of the machine-made lace industry', *Textile History*, I (1968), pp. 2–45.

21 W. Felkin, *History of the Machine Wrought Hosiery and Lace Manufactures* (1867), chs. 14, 17; Devon R. O., Heathcoat MSS; *NR*, 20 May 1825 for number of employees.

22 D. E. Varley, *A History of the Midland Counties Lace Manufacturers Association* (Long Eaton, 1959), ch. 2. This remains the best survey of the machine lace industry, although see also D. Lowe and J. Richards, *The City of Lace* (1982), and S. A. Mason, *Nottingham Lace, 1760s–1950s* (Ilkeston, 1994).

23 Felkin, *Hosiery and Lace*, pp. 245, 248, 333, 336, 340–2; K. Honeyman, *Origins of Enterprise: Business Leadership in the Industrial Revolution* (Manchester, 1982), ch. 8.

24 Felkin, *Hosiery and Lace*, pp. 151–2, 315–9, 368–71; [Anon.] *Centenary: Vickers & Hine Ltd 1818–1918* (Nottingham,1918); Records of Baltex Ltd, Ilkeston (for F. Ball).

25 *Factory Inquiry Commission Report*, Parl. Papers, 1833, XX, p. 383; Felkin, *Hosiery and Lace*, pp. 301–22, 368–71.

26 *NR*, 10 December 1819, 21 May 1824.

27 *NJ*, 12 August 1797, 29 August 1801. Blackner, p. 128. *NR*, 13 September 1833; William Stretton, *The Stretton Manuscripts* (1910), pp. 53, 167, 175, 181.

28 Felkin, *Hosiery and Lace*, pp. 151–3; *NJ*, 1 January 1841.

29 Guildhall Library, Sun Fire Office registers MSS 11,937, 212/1177731, 213/1198474 (1836). 18409: data cited in H. T. Fang, *The Triumph of the Factory System in England* (Philadelphia, 1978), p. 204.

30 Records of Baltex Ltd, Ilkeston.

31 J. Montgomery, *Theory and Practice of Cotton Spinning* (Glasgow, 1836), pp. 248–55.

32 Lloyds Bank MSS, Alfreton Road Branch (Nottingham), private memo books, B25a/6–8.

33 C. Erickson, *British Industrialists: Steel and Hosiery 1850–1950* (Cambridge, 1959), pp. 174–8.

34 NUMD Felkin MSS, 'The story of William Felkin III, written by Himself' [1872].

35 S. D. Chapman, 'Hosiery Industry 1780–1914', in D. T. Jenkins and N. B. Harte (eds.), *Cambridge History of Western Textiles* (Cambridge, forthcoming), ch. 22, table 3.

36 T. S. Nutting, 'History of the British knitting machine building industry' (University of Nottingham, M.Phil. thesis, 1994), pp. 18–57.

37 Erickson, *British Industrialists*, pp. 171–3, 179–80, 185–6;. W. H. Armytage, *A. J. Mundella 1825–97* (1951), p. 21.

38 Erickson, *British Industrialists*, pp. 175–6; NUMD I. & R. Morley MSS; *Reynolds' Miscellany*, XVI (14 June 1856), pp. 1–2; *Threads* [I. & R. Morley house magazine] (April 1928), p. 2.

39 E. Hodder, *Life of Samuel Morley* (1889), p. 26; *Threads* (March 1925), pp. 9–10.

40 Hine & Mundella (Nottingham Manufacturing Co.) annual reports; F. M. Thomas, *I. & R. Morley. A Record of a Hundred Years* (1900), p. 100.

41 Thomas, *I. & R. Morley*, pp. 38–44.

42 *Hosier & Glover's Gazette*, 1 October 1886.

43 S. D. Chapman, 'The genesis of the British hosiery industry', *Textile History*, III (1972), pp. 7–50. By 1798 framesmiths, needle makers, sinker makers and 'setters-up' were recognised by the framework knitters' trade union as distinct trades: *NJ*, 27 January 1798; information on Angerstein from Peter Berg.

44 Blackner, p. 245; Sutton's, *Nottingham Directory* (1818).

45 Felkin, *Hosiery and Lace*, pp. 397–9, 516; NAO M 23,788, Diary of George Harwood, 3 November 1864; inscription on exhibition model at Ruddington Framework Knitters' Museum.

46 *Jardine's Monthly Register* (NLSL), 1892–95.

47 *The Illustrated Exhibitor* (1851), pp. 431–2; White (1854, 1862); NUMD Manlove Alliott & Co. MSS.

48 Nutting, 'Machine building', especially chs. 25–28.

49 PRO BT 1/311/3158, 25 May 1835.

50 Guildhall Library MS 11,936. Sun Fire Office policy registers 377/582971 (1791), 438/800307 (1807), 409/668031 (1797), 424/735606. Haynes also had £4,000 stock in Nottingham.

51 *NJ*, 14 February 1840; *Report on Lace Manufacture*, PP, 1861, XXII, evidence of R. Birkin, pp. 108–9.

52 Guildhall Library, Sun Fire Office registers 481/966014 (1820), 503/1028068 (1825); the sum insured rose from £12,000 to £17,350. For background see S. D. Chapman, *Merchant Enterprise in Britain* (Cambridge, 1992), pp. 176–7.

53 *Circulars to Bankers*, 17 October 1828; Felkin, *Hosiery and Lace*, chapter 22; *Children's Employment Commission*, PP, 1842, p. f13.

54 The traveller in the north of England, George Moore, another product of a retail drapery apprenticeship, is celebrated in one of Samuel Smiles' panegyrics on self-help enterprise. *George Moore, Merchant and Philanthropist* (1878); Chapman, *Merchant Enterprise*, pp. 176–7; *Nottingham Illustrated. Its Art, Trade & Commerce* (1891) pp. 43–5.

55 Felkin, *Hosiery and Lace*, pp. 340, 399. For examples of net agents see advertisements in *NJ*, 25 June 1833, 11 June 1847.

56 *Select Committee on Artisans and Machinery*, PP, 1824, V, pp. 269–82; PRO BT 1/287/514, 24 July 1832; Felkin, *Hosiery and Lace*, p. 343.

57 Bank of England, Leicester Agent's letter book, 1848–55; Allen's *Nottingham Red Book* (1903). *NJ*, 1 April 1842 for export data.

58 Jesse Fewkes, *Fine Thread, Lace and Hosiery in Ipswich* [USA] (Salem, 1904), pp. 13–21; *NR*, 23 July 1830.

59 NUMD Fisher MSS; Smiles, *George Moore*, pp. 103–8; J. D. Chambers, 'Memoir of a Nottingham lace merchant, William Cripps 1798–1884', *Bulletin of the Business History Society* (June 1950), pp. 3–47; Varley, *Lace Association*, pp. 66, 68, 76; *Jardine's Monthly Register* (NLSL), p. 49. *Centenary: Vickers & Hine Ltd 1818–1918*; NAO Adams MSS M 10751/3.

60 Varley, *Lace Association*, pp. 53–5; Felkin, *Hosiery and Lace*, p. 421, quoting S. Ferguson, who took the French view, in 1851. Felkin himself commended the manufacturers for their 'elegant taste' and 'judicious designs'; *NJ*, 19 August 1836.

61 H. Williams, 'The lives and works of Nottingham Artists, 1750–1914' (University of Nottingham, Ph.D. thesis, 1981), pp. 101, 174.

62 Lascelles' *Directory* (1848); Felkin, *Hosiery and Lace*, p. 399; *NJ*, 24 December 1847; *Centenary: Vickers & Hine Ltd 1818–1918*.

63 Varley, *Lace Association*, p. 88; E. Doughty, 'Lace machines', *Jardines Monthly Register* (NLSL), p. 173; Records of Guy Birkin Ltd, Nottingham.

64 *Report on the Lace Manufacture*, PP, 1861, XXII, pp. 32, 68, 130; Church, p. 304; A. Reisfeld, 'Historical outline of the warp knitting art', *Knitting International* (May–August 1984), especially p. 47.

65 Felkin, *Hosiery and Lace*, pp. 381–2.

66 G. Oldfield, *The Heymann Family of West Bridgford* (typescript, Nottingham, 1983). *Jardine's Lace Register* (October 1894). *Art Journal Illustrated Catalogue of the International Exhibition 1862*, pp. 79, 80.

67 *Art Journal Catalogue*, p. 62. Records of Guy Birkin Ltd.

68 *British Warehouseman, Supplement*, August 1897.

69 G. Oldfield, 'The Nottingham Lace Market', *Textile History*, XV (1984), pp. 191–208.

70 S. D. Chapman, 'William Felkin (1795–1874)' (University of Nottingham, MA thesis, 1960).

71 *NJ*, 5 February 1841, 26 December 1845. *Select Committee on Export of Machinery*, PP, 1841, evidence of W. Felkin.

72 *Art Journal Catalogue*, pp. 113, 132.

73 Records of Guy Birkin Ltd, *Visit of King George V and Queen Mary 24 June 1914* (brochure).

74 Felkin, *Hosiery and Lace*, pp. 343, 397; *NJ*, 3 March 1860; *NJ*, 5 September 1851.

75 Felkin, *Hosiery and Lace*, p. 369; *Date Book*, pp. 389–91 is more restrained on wage data.

76 BL, Peel Papers, Add. MSS 40,581, f.423.

77 *NR*, 25 January 1850.

78 *Factory Inspectors' Reports*, 1863, VIII, p. 437f.

79 *NJ*, 4 December 1840, 6 January 1843; Felkin, *Hosiery and Lace*, pp. 340, 399. The payment of women by truck was already well established in 1812 – PRO HO 42/131, Thos. Hayne report.

80 F. A. Wells, *British Hosiery Industry* (1935), ch. XI; S. C. Wallwork, 'A review of the statistics of the growth of the British hosiery industry 1844–1984', *Textile History*, XXII (1991), pp. 83–104.

81 A. Aspinall (ed.), *The Early English Trade Unions* (1949); Wells, *British Hosiery Industry*, ch. 6; Church and Chapman, 'Gravenor Henson'; E. P. Thompson, *The Making of the English Working Class* (1968 edn), pp. 541–2; J. C. Warren, 'John Blackner', *TTS*, 30 (1926), pp. 161–5.

82 N. Cuthbert, *The Lace Makers' Society* (Nottingham, 1960), chs. 4–5; R. Gurnham, *A History of the Trade Union Movement in the Hosiery and Knitwear Industry* (Leicester, 1976), p. 27; Church, pp. 270–1.

83 P. Wyncoll, *The Nottingham Labour Movement 1880–1939* (1985), p. 19 and ch. 3; Church, p. 275.

84 R. Mellors, *Men of Nottingham and Nottinghamshire* (1924), pp. 82–3; *NJ*, 6 May 1797, 13 July 1799 (Cossall Co.); Lascelles, *Directory* (1848).

85 A. R. Griffin, 'Thomas North: mining entrepreneur extraordinary', *TTS*, 76 (1972), pp. 53–73.

86 Church, pp. 230–6; A. R. Griffin, *Mining in the East Midlands 1550–1947* (1971), pp. 97, 104–5.

87 J. A. S. L. Leighton-Boyce, *Smiths the Bankers 1658–1958* (1958); P. G. M. Dickson, *The Sun Insurance Office 1710–1960* (Oxford, 1960), p. 67; *High Pavement Chapel Biographical Catalogue of Portraits* (Nottingham, 1932), p. 26; Blackner, p. 248.

88 National Westminster Bank Archives: Nottingham & Notts. Joint-Stock Bank records (especially Manager's Letter Book 1844–1861, and Minute Books), and Smiths' Bank records (especially private ledgers 1810–1820). Midland Bank Archives: Nottingham Joint-Stock Bank records (especially Minute Books).

89 *NR*, 24 September 1813 – the advertisement for Mackenzie's Warehouse selling 'cheap ready-made new and second-hand clothes' is probably the first of a growing number. *Nottingham Illustrated* (1891), pp. 75–6.

90 Wright's *Directory* (1885).

91 Dr Philip Boobbyer (Medical Officer of Health), *Annual Report* (1894), p. 63.

92 D. Amos, 'Food and health in nineteenth century Nottingham' (University of Nottingham, MA dissertation, 1994).

93 This selection is drawn from advertisements in Wright's *Directory* (1885).

94 *NJ*, 16 November 1782, 22 October and 19 November 1808; F. W. Leeman, *Co-operation in Nottingham* (1963).

95 S. D. Chapman (ed.), *The History of Working Class Housing* (Newton Abbot, 1971), pp. 146–7. *NR*, 19 February 1830, 19 November and 10 December 1830.

96 *Royal Commission on the Poor Law*, PP Cd 5056 (1910), evidence of John Kentish Wright, pp. 445–52.

15

CHURCH, CHAPEL AND SCHOOL

John Beckett and Brian H. Tolley

It was once broadly agreed that the growth of the industrial city and the decline of religion were two sides of the same coin. Secularisation and the break-up of traditional communities produced what many believed to be a retreat from religious observance, which was reflected in the findings of the 1851 religious census. Such a view is too simplistic. Nottingham in 1750 had three Anglican churches and a handful of nonconformist meeting houses. None offered an educational facility. Private, fee-paying schools were frequented mainly by the children of the middling sorts, and only the Bluecoat school offered education to the children of poor parents. A century later religion and education were bound up together and booming. The number and size of nonconformist groups had grown rapidly; the Anglican establishment had responded with new buildings and missions; indeed, churches and chapels were built at a rate which seems scarcely credible in the late twentieth century. But increasingly churches and chapels were not simply places of worship. From the late eighteenth century they were running Sunday Schools, and by the early years of the nineteenth century they were promoting day schools. Ministers of all denominations saw themselves as agents of civilisation in a society which badly needed, among other socially responsible developments, elementary education. The churches favoured more schools as long as they themselves controlled them, and as long as some variety of Christianity was taught within them. By the end of the nineteenth century the position had changed again. Although the churches now promoted a whole raft of social functions, the link with education had slowly been loosened in the wake of the 1870 Education Act. From the 1880s, religious observance was in decline, and the education system was gradually becoming an arm of the state.

In this chapter we look first at the response of the churches to urbanisation down to the mid-nineteenth century, and the growing role they played in education. Second, we examine the response of the churches to the 1851 religious and education censuses, and the growing secularisation of church activities in the decades to 1914. Third, we look at the growth of elementary education in the wake of Forster's Education Act of 1870. Fourth and finally we look at secondary, technical and higher education as it developed in the years after 1860.

Church, chapel and school, 1750–1850

The 1851 census of religious observance was the only attempt ever made at an official level to collect statistics of church attendance. To some commentators the figures came as a profound shock: 'the labouring myriads', wrote Horace Mann who oversaw the census and collated the statistical returns, 'are never or but seldom seen in our religious congregations'. Urbanisation, it seemed, was strangling church attendance. Yet viewed in the longer perspective, the situation looks rather different. The decades immediately prior to 1851 witnessed an astonishing growth in church and chapel provision across the country. The number and size of the dissenting sects grew rapidly, and from the 1830s and 1840s the Anglican church responded with a policy of church and mission building.[1] As figures 15.1 and 15.2 reveal, buildings had been erected in abundance: more problematic is the question of who was inside them on a Sunday.

Church and chapel alike thrived on competition. Both Anglicans and nonconformists responded to social and political change with considerable vigour, particularly in the wake of the evangelical revival which began among the Wesleyan Methodists in Nottingham in 1798 and spread rapidly to other groups. The General Baptists illustrate something of the rising tide. Formed in 1770, they purchased in 1783 the Tabernacle, a chapel on Boot Lane opened in 1764 by the Methodists. By 1783 they had outgrown it, and it soon turned out to be too small for the General Baptists, who by 1799 had built a new chapel of their own on Plumptre Place, off Stoney Street. Attendances exceeded 1,000. In 1817 a schism saw one branch go temporarily to Hockley Chapel (opened by the Methodists in 1783 but vacated for larger premises the previous year), while work commenced on a new chapel on Broad Street, with accommodation for 580. The Plumptre Place chapel was enlarged in 1834 to accommodate 1,400 hearers.[2] As in so many industrial towns, Methodism also flourished. John Wesley was a regular visitor. He preached at the Tabernacle for the first time in 1766, and opened Hockley Chapel which he considered 'one of the most elegant in England'.[3]

By contrast with the nonconformists and the Methodists, the Church of England was slow to respond. Mrs Gilbert was baptised and married in St Nicholas's, but she recalled of the 1840s that 'the Church of England's conception of duty was but meagre; the three parish churches being content with the two Sunday services year in year out. I never heard of a week–night service, a tea-meeting, a social gathering in connection with any one of them.' The Church of England, by comparison with the nonconformists, was 'lethargic in the spiritual oversight of her flock'.[4] This was perhaps unusual, since nationwide by 1800 Anglican Evangelicalism was

Figure 15.1 **Anglican and nonconformist places of worship, 1750 and 1851**

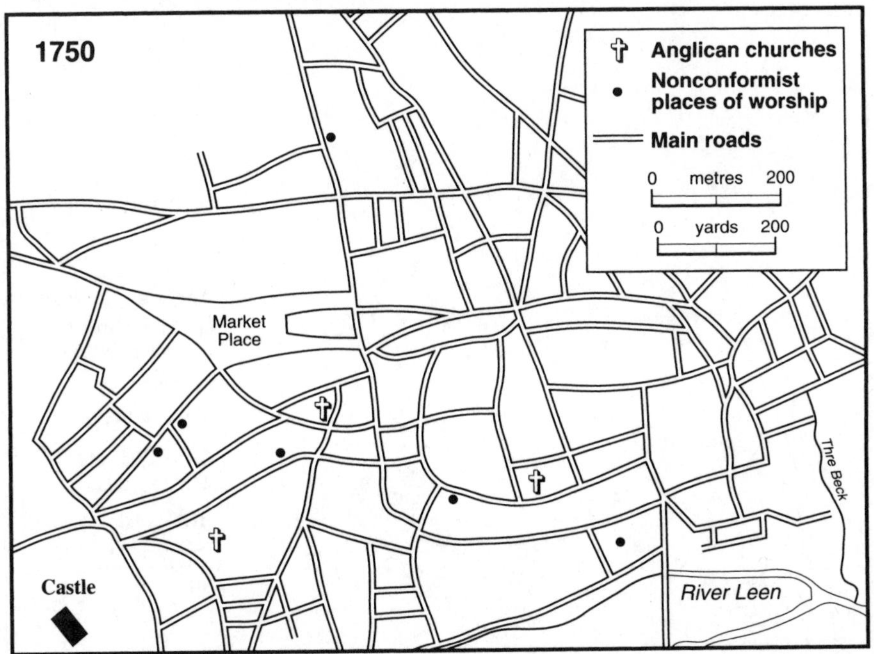

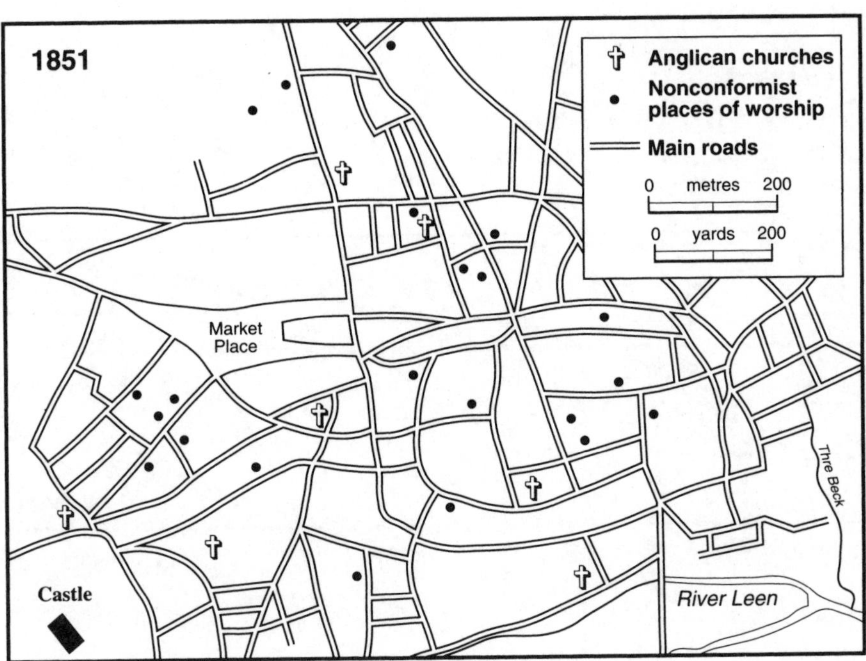

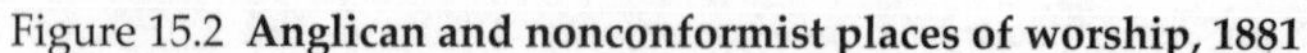

Figure 15.2 **Anglican and nonconformist places of worship, 1881**

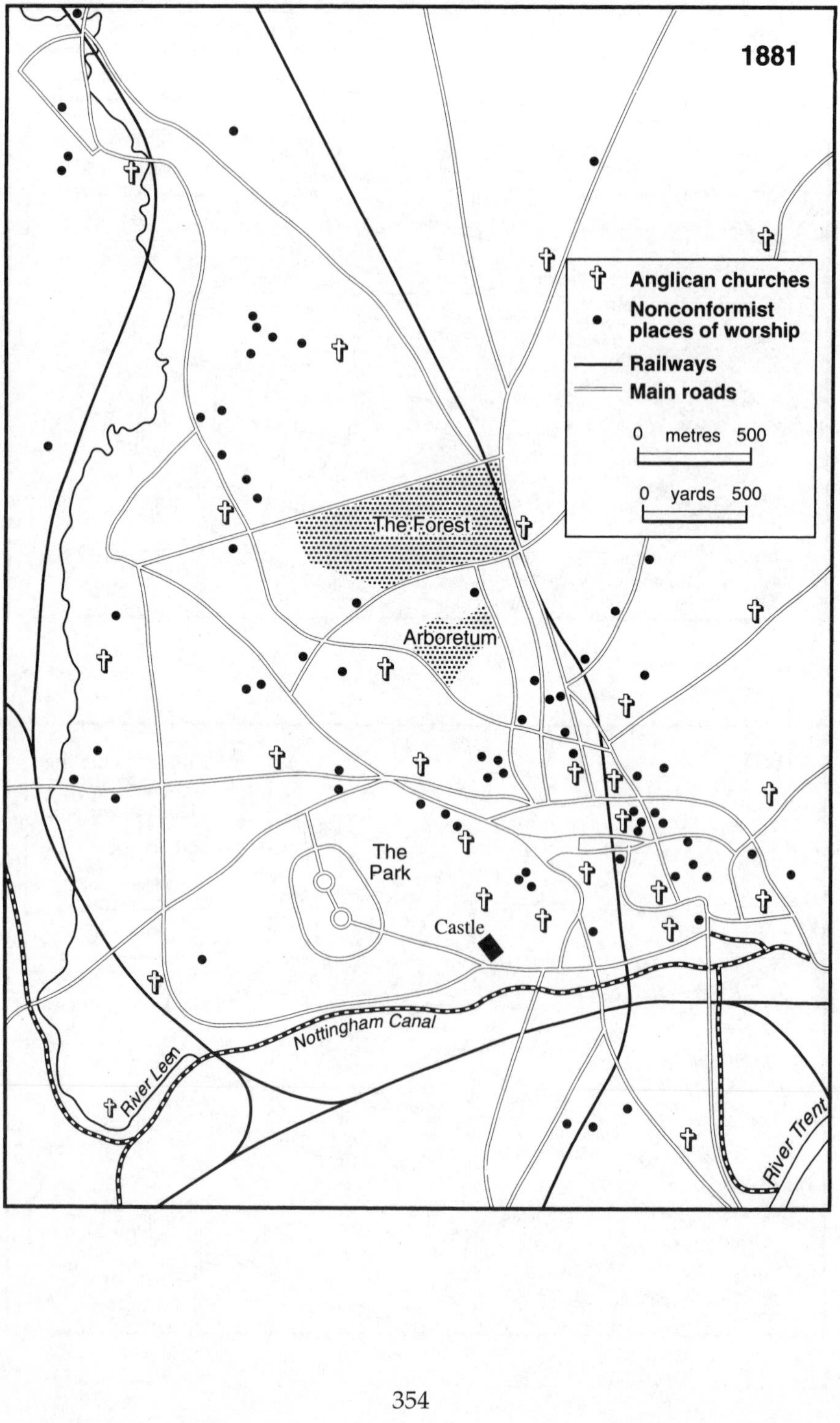

flourishing among the middle classes, with both clerical and lay support. St James's Church on Standard Hill, consecrated in 1809, reflected this trend in Nottingham. This was an evangelical Anglican church in an area on the west side of the town where the middle classes were beginning to make their homes. It was privately promoted by Act of Parliament in the teeth of opposition from the incumbents of St Mary's, St Peter's and St Nicholas's, who feared a loss of income. The church was built with subscriptions of nearly £13,000, but flourished only as long as the middle classes continued to live in this area.[5] It also struggled after another evangelical Anglican church, Holy Trinity, was built on land released under the 1839 enclosure of Burton Leys. Financed by middle-class subscriptions, by 1851 it could boast the largest congregation in Nottingham.[6]

The number of churches and chapels grew, partly because of divisions and splits within Methodism and among the Baptists. Other groups meeting in the town included Independents, Quakers and, from the passing in 1778 of the Catholic Relief Act, Roman Catholics. The first Catholic chapel was opened in about 1790 and numbers increased steadily to about 150 in 1824, when Father Robert Willson arrived in the town. He masterminded a new chapel on George Street which was opened in 1828 with full Catholic pomp and circumstance. Father Thomas Rimmer, a Catholic priest who ministered to the poor in the Narrow Marsh area, commented in 1840 that 'the Catholic body amounts to 1,000 English and Irish. I speak of those who attend chapel.'[7] This of course was the estimate of a biased witness, and the first real opportunity we have to assess the level of religious observance in the town is the evidence of Richard Hopper's 1833 survey (table 15.1).

Table 15.1 **Richard Hopper's survey of religion in Nottingham, 1833**

Denomination	*No.*	*Congregation*	*Communicants/members*
Church of England	5	5,800	330
Methodists	5	5,480	2,080
Baptists	4	2,300	1,362
Independents	5	2,800	645
Quakers	1	150	107
Roman Catholics	1	600	240
Unitarians	1	450	70
Others[a]	3	220	20
Total	25	17,800	4,854[b]

Source: *NJ*, 13 December 1833.

Notes: [a] Huntingtonians, New Jerusalem and Sandimanian. Only the Huntingtonians returned membership figures.

[b] Hopper's own figure was 4,864, which is wrong.

Hopper's figures have to be understood for what they were. He gathered the information in the course of preparing a paper he read to the Literary Society at Bromley House, but the figures were incidental to his main theme which was 'the propriety and practicability of National Education'. They do not record church attendance as such; rather, they show the number of places available (17,800), representing accommodation for about 35 per cent of the town at any one time, and membership. The latter is complex. For the Anglicans it depended primarily on Easter communicants, but in 1780 800 people took Easter Holy Communion in the three Anglican churches, and Hopper does not explain the origin of his figure of 330. Attenders undoubtedly exceeded communicants (see table 15.2) and among the nonconformists they greatly outnumbered members. The pastor of Castle Gate Congregational Church noted in 1817 that fewer than 200 of a congregation of between 900 and 1,000 were members. James Hopkinson described the process when he became a member of Stoney Street Baptist Church in 1837 as 'quite a trial', which may account for some of the discrepancy.[8] Consequently Hopper's survey offers an indication of scale without the details of attendance we associate with the 1851 census. And the most notable point about scale is that, in a town known for its nonconformity, the Anglican church provided less than one-third of the seats available for public worship.

By 1833 the Anglicans nationally, but more significantly locally, were in disarray. The controversy over St James's had served to delay further church building, which came back on to the agenda only when the government provided grants – in 1818 and 1824. As a result of these initiatives more than 600 new churches were built in rapidly growing towns. Nottingham first benefited with the building in 1822 of St Paul's church on George Street, which was consecrated as a chapel of ease of St Mary's (thereby ensuring no loss of fees to the vicar of St Mary's). It was the first attempt to provide for the new working class areas, and when the Church Pastoral Aid Society made a grant of £100 towards the incumbent's income in 1840 the parishioners were described as 'very poor, ignorant and immoral'.[9] No further progress had been made by 1833 when a combination of the repeal of the Test and Corporations Act in 1828, Roman Catholic Emancipation in 1829, and the opposition of Anglican bishops to Parliamentary reform in 1832 had raised significant questions about the future, questions brought sharply into focus when church rates were abolished in Ireland in 1833.

Between 1833 and 1868, when church rates were abolished in England, the rates issue represented a running sore in places where dissent was strong. In Nottingham it surfaced in the context of St Mary's. Archdeacon George Wilkins, who became the incumbent in 1817, found himself with a badly dilapidated building, and to procure money for repairs Wilkins tried in 1838 to raise a church rate. This was the traditional and legal means of funding repairs to the parish church, but dissenters outnumbered Anglicans by six to one. Nonconformists had, after all, raised considerable sums to fund their chapels, and they saw little reason to pay for the upkeep of a church with which they were not in communion. Thwarted but undaunted, Wilkins launched an appeal for £2,000 for restoration work. The repairs were carried out – badly. In 1842

Plate 41 **St Paul's Church, Broad Street (pastel by Tom Hammond), 1922**. Built in 1822, this was the first attempt by the Anglicans to build a church designed to serve a working-class area. It was demolished in 1925. Hammond uniquely captured late nineteenth- and early twentieth-century Nottingham in his numerous sketches, some of scenes and places which no longer exist and for which there is no known photographic evidence

the church had to be closed because the tower was deemed to be unsafe. Services continued in the Shire Hall and a schoolroom, and despite various renovations and attempts to reopen the church – one of which ended with a riot in April 1843 when the congregation thought the tower was about to fall in – it was not permanently restored until 1848, after the tower had been underpinned. At the same time a new west front was built, to designs by W. B. Moffatt. In the meantime, Wilkins again failed to raise a rate in 1843, and this was one reason for his decision the following year to resign the benefice.[10]

Whether deliberately or not, Wilkins had helped to provoke bitter controversy in Nottingham between Anglicans and nonconformists. The town first hosted a public meeting to consider disestablishment of the Church of England in 1834, when Wilkins argued that 'the sectarians have sounded the tocsin of religious strife'. In 1837 he widened the debate to claim that the Anglican church was being crucified between two thieves, the Roman Catholic and dissenting congregations.[11] Once Wilkins had gone the situation eased. His successor, Revd Joshua Brooks, concentrated on the pastoral care of his parish and, with the church still out of repair, he 'proposed carrying on eight services in the parish weekly and that at least four of the school rooms would be licensed in which there would be a church service or cottage lectures, many of which would be continued after the church was reopened'.[12]

In 1843 Sir Robert Peel, the Tory Prime Minister, steered legislation through Parliament permitting the division of over-populated parishes in industrial towns. Peel refused to follow this up with state funding for new buildings, although he allowed the Church Building Commissioners to borrow a further £600,000 to help fund new Anglican churches. This was not sufficient to bring about a rush of church building in working-class areas. What was also required was the nineteenth-century equivalent of sponsorship: the middle classes had to be tapped for money, and their consciences had to be pricked to persuade them to fund new churches in working-class areas. The only public money on offer was in the form of loans from Queen Anne's Bounty, in anticipation of revenue generated by the parishes once they were established. These arrangements were fundamentally unsound because the bulk of the finance had to be generated voluntarily which, in working-class areas, was almost impossible. New churches with their new parishes carved out of existing parishes were not allowed any claim on the endowments historically attached to the original parish church: in other words, new churches designed for poor and underprivileged areas were expected to be more financially self-reliant than the existing and sometimes affluent parish churches in middle-class areas.

Despite these problems the opportunities had never been so good. Wilkins had refused to contemplate the division of St Mary's parish, primarily because he feared giving the evangelicals a platform in the centre of the town. He was happy to promote new churches (such as St Paul's) as chapels of ease within the parish because he would have influence over their churchmanship and incumbency. Brooks had no such scruples, and the first church planned under the new rules was St John the Baptist, designed to serve the working-class areas on the south side of St Mary's parish, an area 'inhabited chiefly by people of the humbler rank of life', according to the prospectus. The building committee estimated its costs at £7,050, but even with grants from various church-building societies – including the Nottinghamshire Church Extension Society, founded in 1841 with a branch in Nottingham – it proved difficult to raise sufficient capital. However, the church was built in 1843–44 to plans by Sir George Gilbert Scott.[13] Ironically, although planned as a working-class church – the seats were 'free' – it came to be frequented by middle-class people from the Park attracted to its churchmanship. In 1892 Sydney Race described it as 'quite filled with fashionable people which is a good sign as the surroundings of the Church are very poor … the ceremonial was dignified and English and quite different from the Romish way of St Albans'.[14]

By the 1840s the local Roman Catholic community was thriving. This was partly due to an influx of Catholics from Ireland after the famine, so that by the late 1840s and 1850s the majority of Roman Catholics in British towns were Irish. The size of the Catholic community was sufficient to warrant the building of a larger church, and Father Willson was the moving force, as he had been in 1828. A plot on Derby Road, made available in the wake of the 1839 Enclosure Act, was acquired in 1841 and a new church built to designs by A. W. N. Pugin. It was not well received by every part of the town. *The Tablet* reported a wave of anti-Catholic demonstrations, and a Nottingham Protestant Association was founded to hear lectures on 'the doctrines and superstitions of the Romish church'. When the foundation stone of the new church was laid in 1842 – at 8.00 a.m. in an attempt to avoid demonstrations – the Association launched a stinging attack on Catholicism, aided and abetted by both the *Journal* and the *Review*. Archdeacon Wilkins dismissed Catholic worship in 1842 as 'awful mockeries, all founded upon the rudiments of a gross superstition'. The attacks were maintained throughout the building period, with anti-Catholic speeches at the Protestant Reformation Society being reported in full in the press. The new church, which cost £20,000, was opened in 1844, but it did little to stem the opposition: a meeting of the Protestant Operative Association held in the Assembly Rooms in March 1845 ended in a riot.[15] In the wake of the re-establishment in 1847 of the Roman Catholic hierarchy, Joseph Hendren was appointed first bishop of the diocese of Nottingham, and enthroned in 1851 when St Barnabas became a Cathedral. The diocese was believed to include 10,000 Irish immigrants, 7,500 'Old Catholic Stock', and 2,500 new converts.[16]

The activity of the various denominations had not been channelled only into building. From the beginnings of the Sunday School movement in the 1780s the churches had become increasingly concerned about education, and for many Nottingham children prior to 1870 their major learning experience took place at a Sunday School. Many of the early Sunday Schools were on a non-denominational basis, organised by evangelicals and middle-class philanthropists, and the first Nottingham Sunday School met in the Exchange. By 1787 it catered for about 450 children. Nearly 2,000 children were attending a variety of Sunday Schools in the town in 1802, and the Nottingham Sunday School Union was formed in 1810. Volunteer teachers, drawn from a wide variety of social backgrounds, sought to instil more than the rudiments of religious knowledge into their pupils, and in such institutions many Nottingham children received their only instruction in how to read. A few also learnt writing and arithmetic, although the content of the curriculum was a regular source of conflict.[17] Nationwide, by the early 1830s over one million children and adolescents were attending Sunday School, and in Nottingham possibly 60 per cent of all children were registered with one. Even in the 1860s Sunday Schools were still attracting large attendances: in 1865 a total of 6,388 pupils were attached to Anglican Sunday Schools in Nottingham, Radford and Lenton, and estimates for 1868 suggest than nearly 8,000 children attended Sunday Schools of all denominations in the town.[18]

The interest of the churches in education was formalised with the move into day-school education associated with the Church of England National Society founded in 1811, and the nonconformist British and Foreign School Society of 1814. The first school established on the nonconformist principles espoused by Joseph Lancaster was set up in 1810 to provide instruction in reading, writing and arithmetic. It subsequently occupied an old cotton mill in the Broad Marsh before moving to a permanent site on Derby Road in 1815. A Girls' British School was founded in Houndsgate in 1820 and then, after a gap of some eleven years, the nonconformists opened two new schools for boys and girls, one in Barker Gate in 1831 and the other in Canal Street in 1835. The latter moved to new premises in 1851. The momentum of the nonconformist educational crusade had already begun to wane, and by 1836 Nottingham nonconformists were openly talking about the intervention of the state to provide schools for working-class children. Their own efforts to supply elementary education could not compete with those of the Anglicans, who were rapidly recovering the ground lost to dissent.[19]

The first Church of England elementary school for boys opened in High Cross Street in 1811 and a Girls' School of Industry was opened in Rutland Street. Like the nonconformists, the Anglicans initially found it difficult to sustain the financing of school projects after initial enthusiasm had dwindled. Subscriptions and donations fell away and the number of children being educated correspondingly declined. Although the Church had shown interest in developing two of the four infants' schools set up in the town during the 1820s, the real thrust of the Anglicans to establish their dominance in the provision of elementary education came only after 1833, when the government made building grants for schools available for the first time. A total of £20,000 was to be distributed to schools by the National Society and the British Society, but as the money went only to existing schools – and then only as a supplement to a local subscription – it made no difference to areas with little or no educational provision. Even so, it was a help, particularly as churchmen were convinced that the demand for education was so vigorous that they would be best advised guiding and channelling it since, or so it was widely believed, any education worth the name would have a moral and therefore a religious core.[20]

In tandem with these initial grants Richard Hopper produced his survey of education in Nottingham published in 1833. In St Mary's parish he counted fifty-four day schools 'exclusive of Infants Schools', which were educating 1,960 boys and 860 girls. His calculations suggested that only 43 per cent of the children in the parish were at day schools, and that the rest, if they were receiving any instruction at all, must have been attending Sunday Schools. He calculated that 1,678 were attending Anglican Sunday Schools, 4,312 were attending nonconformist Sunday Schools, 200 went to High Pavement Unitarian School and 200 to the Catholic School. With 336 in the two adult schools the total was 6,726 from a total population of 50,000. Hopper's paper does not seem to have stimulated immediate action, although a Girls' National School was opened in Barker Gate in 1835, and another infants' school was set up at St Paul's Church in George Street in 1840 to serve the depressed area north of the present Lace Market. A boys' department was added to the Girls' National School in 1845.[21]

Changing attitudes had less to do with Hopper's survey, and more to do with a shift of emphasis nationally. During the 1840s ministers of all religious denominations saw the working class as ignorant and easily led astray by agitators, particularly in the wake of the Chartist disturbances. Consequently, ministers saw themselves as agents of civilisation in a society which was in danger of falling apart at the seams. To the belief in the need to be charitable towards the poor was added the desire to stabilise society, and to do so through education of a rudimentary sort which emphasised obedience and an acceptance of the status quo. Church and chapel alike favoured more schools of an elementary kind, as long as some variety of Christianity was taught in them. This emphasis on education took a particular form in Nottingham, where the small units of production which characterised the town's staple trades militated against the introduction of Owenite schemes for promoting social harmony through the education of a large work-force employed in one factory. Thus, even more reliance was placed upon the role of the church and the chapel in providing moral and religious education for working-class children, initially through the Sunday Schools and then, when these seemed inadequate, the voluntary day schools of Nottingham.[22] For the working classes the ability to read gave access to new ideas, to an intellectual world from which they had hitherto been excluded. J. W. Hudson, writing in 1851, described the 'active thirst for knowledge in this town' which 'led to a vivid perception of political rights and wrongs, to political unions and Chartism' and 'threw off the veil that darkened the vision of human intellect'.[23] The attraction of the Artisans' Library was further evidence of interest in education (chapter 16). Church and chapel school building was designed to cater for the need. The Anglicans opened the Trinity and St John's schools in 1847, and St Mark's in 1850. Two ragged schools were also opened: the Town Mission (Ragged) School founded in 1847, which moved by the 1850s to Glasshouse Street; and a later one opened in 1859 in Sneinton, where it still stands.[24]

The Roman Catholic community in Nottingham sought to cater for the needs of its own children by building schools. The first school, for girls, opened in Stoney Street in 1828 and six years later a boys' school in Bell Yard, off Long Row, was established.

The Roman Catholic Chapel in George Street was turned into an industrial and ragged school run by nuns when St Barnabas's was opened in 1844, and new school buildings were erected in Kent Street. Efforts were then concentrated upon opening Catholic schools to serve the areas around George Street, Derby Road and Narrow Marsh, where there were large numbers of children from Catholic families.[25]

Private enterprise also played a significant role in education. The Bluecoat School, like the Boys' High School, moved in the wake of the 1845 enclosure act out of the increasingly crowded lace-market area to larger premises on the rising ground north of the town centre. The new Bluecoat building, designed by T. C. Hine, opened in 1853, and was in effect a small Anglican elementary school at this date. It had accommodation for twenty girls and sixty boys.[26] The Boys' High School moved from Stoney Street to its present site in 1868 and flourished. The Girls' High School was founded in 1875 by the Girls' Public Day School Trust. Although it was supported by leading educational figures in the town, it was a fee-paying establishment which (unlike the Boys' High School) would not entertain the idea of scholarships to allow working-class children to attend. Most middle-class girls were educated in the private academies in Nottingham.

For the majority of the poor the common day or dame schools that were to be found in nineteenth-century Nottingham offered some sort of educational facility. Sometimes this amounted to little more than a child-minding facility that enabled women to carry on working to augment the meagre family income. These establishments were often short-lived and left few records of where they were located and what they taught. Individual schools can be identified only by the occasional advertisement inserted into a contemporary local newspaper or trade directory. The 1851 Education Census suggests that Nottingham and its neighbouring poor law districts had around 100 such day schools.[27] Most seem to have been quite small, occupying one or two rooms over a shop, an old warehouse, or a converted chapel. Since no licence was required, it was easy to become the proprietor of such a school, charging a small tuition fee, which was usually insufficient to allow anyone to rely upon teaching as their only means of earning a living.[28] The standard of work done in the common day schools varied enormously but, believing that an education which was purchased was better than that provided free in the schools run by the denominational bodies, many working-class parents preferred to send their sons and daughters to these establishments. Whatever their failings, the private schools offered an important additional facility through which a substantial number of children in the town received their basic education.

Little attempt was made to relate educational provision in the town to the demands of the major industries, except for the founding of the School of Art in 1842. The lace trade, in particular, acclaimed the value of art instruction as a means to improve design and to raise public awareness of good taste. In the early days of machine lace making many of the designs used were French, but to encourage local Nottingham talent William Felkin campaigned for the setting-up of a government school of design in the town. His inspiration was the £10,000 made available by

Plate 42 **Ragged School, Glasshouse Street, 1852.** In 1842 the Children's Employment Commission recommended an extension of the ragged-school system to try to accommodate the children of the lower working class for whom the ordinary elementary schools were out of reach. The first Ragged School in Nottingham was founded in 1847 by the banker J. Smith Wright, as a Sunday School. It occupied a first-floor front room in a tenement in Sherwood Lane, Charlotte Street. In 1852 it moved into a new building in Glasshouse Street, which included a teacher's residence, and quickly became a day school with an emphasis on welfare. Anonymous donors initially provided funds for some 200 meals two days a week

Parliament in 1841 to assist in the formation of schools of design in provincial centres like Nottingham. The campaign was successful and the Nottingham Government School of Design opened in a building on Beck Lane (now Heathcote Street) in 1843. Coincidentally with the opening of the school, Deverill's application of the Jacquard system to the Levers frames had brought the artistry and variety of handmade lace within the scope of the machine industry. Designing for the lace trade, which was a relatively well-paid job, became the ambition of many young people whose first attempts at drawing had been encouraged in the elementary schools by peripatetic teachers from the School of Design.[29] These encouraging beginnings were not maintained. Partly for financial reasons, by the 1850s emphasis was being placed on still life and figure drawing rather than industrial design and draughtsmanship. The School was little more than a drawing school and the number of artisans employed in the lace and hosiery trades who attended classes represented a decreasing proportion of the total, although some firms stayed loyal. Heymann & Alexander, Jacoby & Co., Thomas Adams, Barnett, Maltby & Co., William Vickers, and Bradbury, Cullen & Co., all attributed their success at the International Exhibition of 1862 to their designers, ex-students of the School.[30]

Continuing support from these larger firms encouraged the corporation to offer a new site for the School on enclosed land between Peel Street and the Arboretum. Plans were drawn up with the approval of the Department of Science and Art, and the new building opened in 1865.[31] The appointment of J. R. Rawle as Principal in 1866 began a new phase in the fortunes of the School. Responding to criticism that it had been rather better at educating middle-class than artisan children, he set about establishing a new relationship with the lace manufacturers, demonstrating that the teaching of the School was relevant to their needs, and even persuading the leading houses to send their young designers and draughtsmen regularly to classes for the first few years of their employment.[32] Rawle had less success with the smaller lace manufacturers. For many years the School was in financial difficulties. It was rescued when the corporation took it over in 1888.[33]

Church and chapel, 1851–1914

The 1851 religious census provides an indication of the strength of church and chapel in mid-century. Despite the reservations expressed about some of the findings, the figures provide a vital source for our understanding of religious observance in these years. Nationally, it was accepted that about 39 per cent of the population attended a church service on census Sunday, of whom about half went to an Anglican church. In Nottingham there were 34,157 'attendances' (table 15.2). When these figures are converted into actual people (in order to exclude double or triple attenders) we calculate that 23,964 people attended church on that day, 41.7 per cent of Nottingham's population of 57,407. Of these, 14.8 per cent attended an Anglican church, and 27.6 per cent worshipped at nonconformist and Roman Catholic services.[34] Half the churches and chapels in Nottingham had more than three-quarters of their pews occupied for at least one service on 30 March 1851.

What are we to make of these figures? At one level they were a cause for encouragement to church leaders in the town. At 42 per cent Nottingham had a relatively high attendance rate compared to other large industrial towns. Yet to churchmen in Nottingham and in most industrial towns the figures came as a shock. The assumption, fuelled by the much higher figures for rural than for urban church attendance, was that the new working classes had been alienated from the church. Horace Mann took the view that 'especially in cities and large towns is it observable how absolutely insignificant a portion of the congregation is composed of artisans'.[35] No one, it seemed, could further doubt the fact that in the new manufacturing towns of industrial England large numbers of working people permanently absented themselves from the churches, or at least from the Anglican churches. Consequently, in the wake of the 1851 census the spiritual destitution of the working classes became the key issue for Anglicans and nonconformists alike.

Table 15.2 **Attendance at church and chapel in Nottingham, 30 March 1851**

Denomination	*Morning*	*Afternoon*	*Evening*	*Adjusted totals*	
				(i)	*(ii)*
Church of England	6,117	508	4,584	7,899	7,814
Methodist	4,452	45	5,588	6,337	7,087
Congregational	2,014	277	1,345	2,601	2,555
Baptist	2,359	84	2,691	3,298	3,505
Roman Catholic	1,420	312	604	1,777	1,725
Others	1,039	224	494	1,316	1,278
Total	17,401	1,450	15,306	23,228	23,964

Source: M. R. Watts, *Religion in Victorian Nottinghamshire: the religious census of 1851* (Nottingham, 1988), II, pp. 176–94.

Notes: The adjusted total (i) is derived from the formula used by Horace Mann, the registrar-general, who counted all morning attenders, half the afternoon attenders, and one-third of evening attenders. Total (ii) is the formula used by Watts, adding together the best-attended service to one-third of the others. It is the one preferred here.

The initial response was to build more churches. Anglicanism was traditionally parish-based, and to retain this (essentially rural) concept in towns large parishes had to be divided, and new churches built and endowed. This policy was given substance by the New Parishes Act of 1856. Under the terms of this legislation St Mary's was subdivided seven times between 1856 and 1871.[36] Six of the new churches served a parish in working-class areas of the town, while All Saints was promoted by the silk manufacturer William Windley in the middle-class area opened up on the Sand Field. Significantly, of all the Anglican churches built between 1809 and the 1860s, only St Saviours in the Meadows and All Saints have survived, partly because at the time they were erected on green-field sites enclosed after 1845.

The division of St Mary's parish into smaller pastoral units provided not simply a new church in each area, but also an elementary school. Schools were opened in the parishes of St Matthew's, St Luke's, St Ann's, and St Saviour's, each serving a large working-class district of the town. New schools were also opened in St Peter's parish in 1855 and St Nicholas's in 1859. By 1865 6,237 children were on the books of Anglican schools as day scholars, and the tremendous enthusiasm of the Established Church in these decades made it unquestionably the chief provider of elementary education in Nottingham by 1870. In 1835 it had five schools and 665 pupils; by 1870 these numbers had increased to twenty-two and 5,354. By contrast, nonconformist schools increased from six to eight, and pupil numbers from 1,082 to 1,197 over the same period. By 1870 three-quarters of the school places identified by the School Board's statistical committee were in Church of England schools. Some gaps remained, particularly in the Leenside and Broad Marsh areas where provision was most neglected, and the greatest deficiency of places was found in 1871.[37]

Parish subdivision continued beyond 1871, but increasingly by this date for reasons of churchmanship. By 1866 the three town parishes were all under the control of evangelicals, but Nottingham was already being influenced by the Tractarian movement, launched in 1833. The Oxford movement, as it became known, pressed for the adoption of more ritualism, and high-church clergymen schooled in these new ways of thinking soon found their way to the Nottingham area. The vicar of Sneinton in the 1850s and 1860s was determined to break the evangelical monopoly, and he promoted the division of the parish into four, orchestrating in the process the building of St Alban's, St Matthias's, and St Christopher's. As early as 1851 St Alban was the local centre of Anglo-Catholicism. However, the high churchmen did not have things all their own way. St Andrew's on Mansfield Road was carved out of St Ann's and St Mark's parishes in 1871 as a new evangelical Anglican church. Other new churches in these years included St Thomas's on Park Row, which was an amalgam from the parishes of St Matthew, St Nicholas and St Peter in 1873–74. St Philip's, Pennyfoot Street, was created out of St Luke's parish in 1879–80. St George's on Kirke White Street was split from St Saviours in 1887–92. Where it was not possible to provide churches, chapels and meeting rooms were erected. These included St Jude's, Woodborough Road in 1879, Emmanuel on Woodborough Road in 1880, and St Catherine's on St Ann's Well Road in 1884.[38] Nine of the churches within the borough of Nottingham had associated mission rooms by 1881.

Not to be outdone, the nonconformists were also on the move. George Harwood noted the flurry of building that was going on, writing in his diary in 1863 that:

> Nottingham has, during the last few years, increased very fast both in houses and inhabitants, and the religious bodies seem to be trying to outstrip each other in providing for the additional population. The Church of England has added several new Churches, and is adding more. The Unitarians are building a Chapel in Pease Hill Road. Mr Little has recently opened the Methodist Independent Church in Great Freeman Street. The New Methodists have purchased a piece of ground on Woodborough Road for the purpose of building a chapel thereon. A piece of ground has been secured for the same object in Great Alfred Street by the United Free Church. The Wesleyans of the North Circuit have built a small chapel in Hartwell Street, and we of the South Circuit are about to erect a good chapel in the Meadows.[39]

He could have added to this list the Particular Baptist Church alongside the Derby Road entrance to the Park Tunnel, completed in 1850. Altogether, the Methodists built more than twenty chapels and missions between 1851 and 1881; as a result, at the latter date, the extended borough of Nottingham had forty-five Methodist chapels with sittings for 17,363 and a total attendance of 14,364. A new Roman Catholic church was opened on Woodborough Road in 1879 and another on London Road in 1883, neither of them provoking the hostility which was aroused in the 1840s.[40]

All this effort might have been expected to produce rapid results, but the Church of England objected to any re-run of the 1851 religious census, so that measuring the impact was not statistically possible. However, after discussions at the 1881 Church Congress, local newspapers across the country began to conduct their own surveys of religious worship, and to compare the findings with those of 1851. The *Nottingham Journal* published just such a survey on 4 December 1881 (table 15.3). On a simple statistical measure, church attendance had improved since 1851, from less than 24,000 attenders to nearly 47,000, so that church and chapel building had at least been matched by an increase in numbers coming through the doors. Unfortunately the position was not as straightforward as these totals might imply. With the borough extension of 1877 the population of Nottingham now stood at 186,575, so that the proportion of people attending a church service had fallen from 42 per cent in 1851 to only 25 per cent in 1881, although the latter figure is almost certainly too low since Sunday School attenders were not counted in 1881.[41] What was clear to anyone who examined the figures in detail was that thirty years of church building, far from solving the problems of attendance, had witnessed a decline in numbers. The distribution of churches beyond 1851 can be seen from figure 15.2.

Table 15.3 **Church attendance in Nottingham, December 1881**

Denomination	*Morning*	*Afternoon*	*Evening*	*Adjusted total*
Church of England	8,874	2,836	12,171	16,074
Methodist	4,940	573	8,447	10,285
Congregational	2,787	–	2,690	3,683
Baptist	3,394	410	5,170	6,438
Roman Catholic	1,857	385	1,072	2,343
Others (incl. Jews)	2,435	2,237	6,580	8,137
Totals	22,822	6,441	36,130	46,960

Source: *NJ*, 7 December 1881.

Note: The adjusted total is calculated according to the same formula used for (ii) in table 16.2, numbers from the best attended service added to one-third from each of the others. The survey may have omitted some of the mission churches, especially those of the Church of England: A. Rogers, 'Religion in Nottingham in the Nineteenth Century', in J. F. Phillips (ed.), *Town and Village in the Nineteenth Century* (Nottingham 1972), p. 49.

The informal census of 1881 coincided with a recognition on the part of many Anglicans that they were losing the battle for the working man's soul. Increasingly, the Church of England was becoming concerned with its peculiar responsibility as the 'Church of the Nation', its responsibility to bring the new working classes to worship. The problem was how to achieve these ends. In the middle decades of the nineteenth century education had seemed to be the key but, as we shall see, by the 1880s this was increasingly being delivered by the State rather than the Church. In addition, working-class families were less willing to accept the restrictions on their behaviour so beloved of the middle classes. Even Parliament accepted that the restrictions on Sunday needed to be eased, and in 1896 it voted to allow museums and art galleries to be open. So serious were the perceived problems that the Anglicans and nonconformists found common ground. The best example was the Pleasant Sunday Afternoon movement, which was religious in tone but non-sectarian in organisation, offering recreational and educational activities to working men, including brass bands and choirs, and sporting and cultural activities.[42]

In these changing circumstances the Anglicans adopted two interrelated policies designed to win back the working classes. First, as in the 1850s, they set about building new churches, but in addition mission buildings were erected and energetic young clergymen were appointed as missioners within existing parishes. The impetus was provided in 1882 by the Bishop of Lincoln, when he formed a Spiritual Aid and Church Extension Society for Nottingham, with the aims of founding mission centres in the 'unwieldy Mother parishes and chapelries of Nottingham', and of making the missions self-supporting. To this end sites were obtained and grants given towards new permanent churches or for temporary iron churches, and towards the support of mission clergy. Above all, the Society intended to try to provide for the spiritual welfare of the newly developing areas of the town which the 1881 figures showed to be inadequately served. Within three years of its establishment, the Society was responsible for helping to finance the restoration of Lenton Priory Church, the completion of the nave at Emmanuel Church, and another ten or eleven projects within the town. An early ledger mentions nineteen churches which benefited from the fund. By 1889 the society claimed to have helped three new parishes, to have purchased four iron churches, and to have enabled five new churches to be completed. They supported 'a large number of mission curates'. One-sixth of the town was receiving additional spiritual help, and £20,000 had passed through the fund in seven years.[43]

Mission rooms were popular in expanding areas of the town. By 1881 nine of Nottingham's eighteen churches, and five of the twelve churches in the suburbs, had associated mission rooms. To provide staff for these organisations the Church of England established in 1882 the Church Army, partly in imitation of William Booth's Salvation Army, founded twelve years earlier as a breakaway Methodist connection. Mission clergymen were also appointed, under the auspices of a parish, but with separate pay and status. The mission room or church often took the form of an iron church or tin tabernacle, a temporary place of worship made from iron and wood on a brick foundation which could easily be removed once the permanent church had been erected, or, as was often the case, converted for use as a church hall. The Spiritual Aid Society was responsible for at least four iron churches in Nottingham during the 1880s: in Hyson Green (1883), at St Catherine's (1884), St Bartholomew's

(1886) and All Souls (1887). Normally the Society met the erection costs and paid the annual rental for the building.[44]

The second policy adopted by the Anglican establishment to win the working classes back to the church involved an expansion of its social activities. By the end of the nineteenth century many churches had boys' brigades, men's fellowships and women's guilds, each with a secular content to their activities and epitomised by the expansion of church football and cricket clubs. The church was beginning to accept that it could not stand above and outside society, but that it had to compete with the secular world for the leisure time and financial resources of working people. Mission and leisure together are best illustrated from St Catherine's on St Ann's Well Road. In 1883 Revd Selwyn Charles Freer came to the district as a mission clergyman. He had no church, and so he began to take services in a cemetery chapel. An iron church was built with accommodation for 350 people, and dedicated by the Bishop of Lincoln on 22 January 1884. It soon proved too small and had to be enlarged. Bishop Ridding, the first Bishop of Southwell, opened the extension in November 1885. Freer promoted wholesome recreation. He organised social and recreational activities to attract working-class people to the church, and raised a subscription for an institute, which opened in November 1884. This quickly became the centre of parish social activities. In fact, much urban mission work in later nineteenth-century Nottingham had an emphasis on matters of a socio-religious nature, including the Temperance Movement and various other forms of church-orientated social work, including the Salvation Army.[45]

The activities of the Anglicans were partially matched among the nonconformists. By 1891 the four main branches of Methodism had eighty chapels and 7,752 members. By 1911 the twenty-four Baptist churches in the district had 3,500 members. Like the Anglicans, nonconformists often used iron mission churches. A 'tin chapel' was opened in Lenton in 1887 by the united Methodist Free Church, at a cost of £1,850.[46]

Elementary education, 1870–1902

Just as church and chapel alike were losing the battle for the souls of the working class by the end of the nineteenth century, so they had largely lost a battle which, in the middle decades of the century, they had seemed close to winning: the control of education. In 1861 the Newcastle Commission rejected the idea of state provision in favour of continuing the voluntary initiative, but with greater financial support on a payments by results basis. Within a few years the government had finally bowed to the inevitable: from the passing of Forster's Education Act in 1870 state provision was introduced as a way of filling gaps in the voluntary system – the Board School was born.

When the first Nottingham School Board was elected in November 1870, it was an important milestone in the provision of popular education in the town. Those who framed the legislation of 1870, which created the school board system, had in mind the need to meet a deficiency in the supply of elementary schools which was in evidence in many parts of the country, despite the tremendous efforts that had been made by the churches, chapels and other voluntary associations. The Nottingham School Board began with a specific responsibility to do this job for the borough of Nottingham, but in the course of the next thirty years, like many other school boards serving large conurbations, by force of circumstances it came to take on a more extensive role. In 1900 the Board was functioning like a modern education authority whose purview included secondary, technical and adult education, as well as the running of those elementary schools which were its legitimate field of concern. In the process of this transformation, the Board found itself in competition with the municipal authority which, armed with the new financial and administrative powers conferred upon it by the Technical Instruction Act of 1889, aspired to become responsible for all education in the borough. The rivalry which ensued attracted widespread publicity and gave the town a prominent place in events leading to the Education Act of 1902.

The first school board was elected with the mission of making good the deficiency in the supply of elementary education in the town. The thirteen elected members (rising to fifteen after the borough extension in 1877) included several clergymen – twenty-eight out of the ninety-seven members elected to serve on the Board between 1870 and 1902 were clergymen – as well as members of Nottingham's business and professional elite. The first woman was elected in 1883. Fortunately, the Board was not plagued by the religious schism found elsewhere, which might have obstructed its work. The absence of strife owed much to the presence of men like Canon Francis Morse of St Mary's, and Revd J. B. Paton of the Congregational Church. Both men were imbued with the ability to help resolve sectarian differences, and both were determined to see the Board accomplish its mission.[47] With such staunch support, the School Board was able to fulfil its task relatively quickly. It then became a victim of its own success when a whole new vista of popular education began to emerge in the closing years of the century.

The initial work of the School Board was to determine the deficiency of places, and the statistical committee set up by the Board found that there was a shortage of only 1,190 school places to meet an estimated need for 13,112 children between the ages of three and thirteen years.[48] The voluntary bodies had clearly done their work well in providing school places in the town, and the new Board built only two new schools, Bath Street and Huntingdon Street, before the borough extension in 1877. The position then changed dramatically. Three schools passed into the care of the Board, in Basford, Radford and Sneinton, but the estimated shortfall of places rose to some 4,600. As a result, over the following fifteen years the Board was engaged in a continuous building programme, partly to fill the gaps and partly as a consequence of population growth in the expanded borough. The Forster Street School, which had been planned by the now disbanded Radford School Board, was the first new school to be completed by the Nottingham Board after 1877, but this was just the beginning.

By 1882 new schools had been completed in Coventry Road, Quarry Road, Queen's Walk, Alfreton Road and St Ann's Well Road, and extensions were being added to the Bath Street and Huntingdon Street Schools. Four more schools were opened by the Board in 1885 and eight more were being built by 1889. Some temporary premises were also used to accommodate children during these years, and the Board also took over the running of several more voluntary schools, most of which needed extending and refurbishing.[49]

By the mid-1880s, the School Board had overtaken the denominational bodies as the chief provider of elementary education in the town. The efforts of the Church of England and the Roman Catholic Church to provide their own schools reached a peak in 1884 when between them they were able to offer 19,700 places. Thereafter the number of voluntary schools being closed or transferred to the School Board exceeded the number of new schools the two denominational bodies were able to build. By 1900 the Board was educating 28,957 pupils and the Church of England and Roman Catholics 15,781. Arguably the Board also provided a better quality of education, with lower staff–pupil ratios and fully trained staff. It set the academic pace in the 1880s, leaving the church schools to try to emulate the Board schools.[50]

The School Board persisted with its building plans in order to try to keep pace with the continued growth of population, but even after the great efforts of the early 1880s there was a deficiency in 1886 of more than 3,139 places. When a recession in trade hit Nottingham about 1890 and slowed down the influx of new workers entering the town, the Board was at last able to move closer to satisfying the demand for school accommodation. Although it continued to enlarge its existing schools, the only new ordinary elementary school it built after 1890 was on Sycamore Road. After this date it concentrated upon improving the quality of existing school buildings and the related facilities. By the end of the decade the Board was able to find places for 28,546 children in its thirty-six schools. It had also built thirty-nine special centres which provided accommodation for some of the other educational activities in which it was engaged, including woodwork, experimental science, cookery and laundry work, swimming and gymnastics.[51]

Building schools was relatively easy using a precept upon the rates which the School Board was empowered to do. Enforcing regular attendance was a more difficult nut to crack, and one which had bedevilled the attempts of the denominational bodies before 1870 to improve the education of children in the town. Employers demanded cheap child labour and parents were willing to supply this demand because it was a means of supplementing family income. Shops, markets, warehouses, and a variety of service industries had all made use of child labour. In both the lace and hosiery trades, large numbers of children had been employed 'as soon as they could tie a knot or thread a needle'.[52] However, lace had almost always been a factory-based industry and the provisions of the Factory Acts regulating the employment of children had been extended to the lace trade after 1861. The employment of children under the age of thirteen had then been forbidden. In contrast, hosiery was less mechanised than lace. Children worked alongside their parents in the home or

Plate 43 **Carrington Schools, Nottingham School Board (1884), junction of Hucknall Road and Claremont Road**. Many of the new Board Schools had a large tower to hold water and to help ventilate the building. The tower also accommodated a bell, which was needed to summon the children to school. Solidly built, the schools took their place alongside the churches, chapels, factories and warehouses of Nottingham. Their windows were positioned to exclude the sights and sounds of traffic from the street outside, and high ceilings also absorbed the noise of sixty or sometimes seventy pupils in each class. Children sat at iron-framed, immovable desks, and they were regularly admonished by teachers who liberally dispensed punishment for the smallest transgressions of the strict code of behaviour they were expected to follow. This school was designed by T.C. Hine & Son

small workshop, winding bobbins, repairing needles and even beginning to knit on the frames themselves from about the age of twelve. Consequently, the introduction of legislation which restricted the employment of children and stipulated attendance at school for prescribed periods met with a mixed response.[53]

The 1870 Education Act allowed the School Board to impose compulsory attendance at school when there was a reasonable chance of being able to offer accommodation to all children in the town. By-laws securing the attendance of children between the ages of five and thirteen for a minimum of twenty-five hours each week were introduced by the Board in November 1871. Any pupil who had reached Standard V of the Elementary Education Code might be granted full exemption from attendance.[54] Visitors were appointed to cover the various districts of Nottingham in order to enforce the by-laws and parents and employers were fined for non-compliance with the attendance regulations. The most severe cases of regular non-attendance were sent to the Day Industrial School, opened in George Street in 1886.[55] On a more positive note, the School Board provided incentives in the form of certificates and medals which were awarded to pupils for exemplary attendance. As a result, attendances improved, and by 1891 when elementary education became free, a daily attendance rate approaching 80 per cent of those expected to be in the Board's schools was being achieved. The Board then raised its exemption from compulsory education from Standard V to Standard VI. Regular attendance led to an improvement in the quality of the work and encouraged the Board to widen the curriculum. The Elementary Education Code controlled what could be taught in order to receive government grants and the Board emphasised the need for proficiency in the basic subjects of reading, writing, arithmetic and religious knowledge. Gradually other subjects were added, including science and drawing, practical woodwork and metalwork for boys above Standard V, and lessons in practical cookery and laundry work for girls who had attained Standard IV.[56] The Board encouraged its teachers to introduce class and specific subjects in the senior departments of the schools. The most popular class subjects were geography, English literature and physiography. Many of the specific subjects were science subjects such as algebra, mechanics, magnetism and animal physiology. The number of passes in specific subjects increased from 420 in 1873 to 2,822 in 1887 and to 7,821 in 1895.[57]

Perhaps not surprisingly, the Board was soon under pressure from pupils and parents to go beyond the delivery of the very basic schooling that had been its first target, and to introduce secondary education. There were considerable numbers of boys and girls in the elementary schools who had passed Standard VI, who were still under the age limit laid down by the Code, and whose parents were anxious to keep them at school. The solution was to bring these pupils together into a higher grade of elementary school. The Elementary Education Code of 1882 recognised for grant purposes a Standard VII, attainable by the very best pupils. If the Organised Science School regulations of the Department of Science and Art were applied the Board could grasp the opportunity of extending the education of these same children to the age of sixteen.[58]

Secondary, technical and higher education, 1860–1914

The first higher grade school established by the Nottingham School Board was People's College, which had opened in 1847. George Gill, its founder, was a prominent Nottingham Unitarian well known for his liberal political views, and the aim was to give working-class children – girls were admitted in 1850 – a non-denominational education equivalent to that obtained in a good writing school or private academy. The College was managed by representatives of the subscribers and parents, and the curriculum included English, French, German and commercial subjects as well as reading, writing and arithmetic. Since a small fee was charged for tuition, it had become increasingly like a secondary school, but with an impressive range of adult evening classes.[59] The decision to hand over the College to the School Board in 1879 was taken by the management in the full knowledge that when the planned University College opened its doors, much of the more advanced evening and adult education available in Nottingham would be concentrated in this institution. Aware that the Board was interested in developing more demanding day-school courses for senior pupils, the management of People's College saw every advantage in transferring their responsibilities. The Board immediately enlarged and remodelled the premises.

As a higher grade school, People's College was open to pupils from both the School Board's elementary schools and from those managed by the denominational bodies. All pupils had to have reached Standard IV and to have passed an entrance examination before they were admitted. The curriculum included the old Elementary Code subjects plus specific subjects such as music, history, geography, French, German and English grammar. A Standard VII was introduced for the most senior pupils who were prepared for examinations such as the Oxford and Cambridge Locals. In 1886 there were 104 boys and sixty-five girls in Standard VII. By 1888 a commercial department had been added to the College. It had also, by then, been chosen to be the School Board's centre for the training of pupil–teachers, a system first introduced in 1846 and which by the 1880s was the normal route followed by those who wished to become qualified teachers.

Two further higher grade schools were opened in 1889, on Queen's Walk and Huntingdon Street, and in 1891 High Pavement School became the fourth higher grade institution run by the Board. High Pavement had been founded in 1788 by the Unitarian congregation as a day charity school, primarily for the children of their own poorer members. It passed into the hands of the Board when the Unitarians were no longer able to support it financially. Guided by its headteacher, William Hugh, High Pavement School had established a reputation for its teaching of science to boys in its upper classes. In 1878 it had become an Organised Science School under the regulations of the Department of Science and Art, the governing body of national education. The school fabric was badly out of repair, and with closure becoming a distinct possibility it was transferred to the School Board in December 1891. New buildings were erected on Stanley Road, Forest Fields, into which the school moved in 1895. Thereafter High Pavement Higher Grade School took its place in the system of advanced elementary education which the Board had by now effectively created.[60]

All four higher grade schools were well equipped with laboratories, lecture and demonstration rooms, and workshops built to provide the facilities needed to teach the courses which earned grants from the Department of Science and Art. Eventually the decision was taken to establish Organised Science Schools in the senior departments of People's College and Queen's Walk School so that, with High Pavement Organised Science School, the Nottingham School Board had three such institutions under its control, offering a four-year course of study for pupils who were able to stay on in full-time education to the age of fifteen or sixteen. Facilities at the Queen's Walk School soon proved to be inadequate and the Board opened a new higher grade school named to commemorate A. J. Mundella's connection with the town. Mundella, formerly a businessman and local politician in Nottingham, was the government minister responsible for establishing higher grade schools. The design of the laboratories and science teaching areas in the new school incorporated all that was then perceived to be the best available for the most advanced teaching; indeed, the Board attracted widespread acclaim for its gymnasia and swimming-pools at High Pavement and Mundella, the science laboratories at the higher grade schools, and the full development of the Pupil Teachers' Centre.[61]

A growing number of pupils from the higher grade schools moved on to higher education, sometimes after spending a brief period at the Nottingham Boys' High School. In 1896 about 38 per cent of pupils at the school had previously attended public elementary schools in the town. Some became students at the new University College, and by 1900 there was a steady flow of former Nottingham pupils from the higher grade schools going on to universities such as Cambridge, London and Manchester.[62] For those who did not go on to college and university, the higher grade schools provided an education that equipped them for careers and professional occupations which would have been denied to them if the old elementary system had not been challenged in this way by one of the country's most enterprising school boards.

This enterprise also included the development of an extensive programme of evening adult education, which embraced commercial and technical classes as well as those in collaboration with the Revd J. B. Paton's Recreative Evening Schools Association, founded in 1882 to protect (or so it was hoped) young people who had recently left the elementary schools from the social and moral evils of the town. This was to be achieved by continuing their education.[63] The Board's enterprise also included the provision of special facilities for teaching handicapped children in its ordinary elementary schools, and the introduction of an extensive scheme of welfare and pastoral care. Children from the poorest backgrounds were given the opportunity to participate in school sports, and to enjoy trips by train into Derbyshire or to the seaside. This was a clear departure from the mandate given to the Board when it had first been elected in 1870. Its enterprise also included the creation of a body of teachers trained and equipped to work at all levels, whether in the kindergartens or

Plate 44 **Anthony John Mundella (1823–97) born in Leicester where he started a hosiery warehouse**. He moved to Nottingham to a partnership in what was to become B. H. Hine & Mundella & Co. Hosiers. Mundella was also a town councillor and Sheriff of Nottingham before being elected MP for Sheffield. He was twice President of the Board of Trade, Vice-President of the Council for Education, where he introduced the Mundella Code in 1882, and Vice-President of the Privy Council. Many felt his finest achievement was the formation of the Nottingham Board of Conciliation in 1866, to resolve labour problems in the hosiery trade. The Nottingham plan was the first in the country to be successful

nursery schools established by the Board or in the higher grade institutions. A good salary structure and conditions of service meant that the School Board had no difficulty in recruiting well-qualified men and women teachers, including graduates, to work in its schools. A school meals service was also provided.[64]

The University College was formally opened by Prince Leopold of Albany, the youngest son of Queen Victoria, on 30 June 1881. Its foundation was the summation of a campaign by a small group of men drawn from the professional and commercial life of the town, to establish an institution in Nottingham which would be of university standing. They included churchmen such as Paton and Canon Morse, both of whom had served on the School Board, solicitors Richard Enfield and G. B. Rothera, the medical practitioner W. H. Ransom, the lace curtain manufacturer Lewis Heymann and the silk importer and influential town councillor Edward Goldschmidt. These were the people who, in 1873, appealed to James Stuart and the Cambridge University Syndicate to establish a centre for University Extension in Nottingham. The appeal resulted in the first lectures being given in the town in the Mechanics Institute in the autumn of that year. Shortly afterwards the idea of a local college began to take shape. When the Heymann family – initially anonymously – offered £10,000 to endow extension lectureships, Enfield attempted to persuade the corporation to provide a suitable building. The council, which had been considering the erection of a public library and museum, agreed to incorporate these facilities into a building which would have lecture rooms and laboratories suitable for extension teaching. The site of the new building was on Horse Fair Close. It was built of Ancaster stone in a High Gothic style to the designs of Lockwood and Mawson.

By the time the new building opened in 1881 the scheme for a University Extension centre had been transformed into a more ambitious project, a University College. Nottingham at last had an institution to match the civic colleges established in centres such as Newcastle (1871), Leeds (1874), Bristol (1876), Sheffield (1879), Birmingham (1880), and Liverpool (1881). In each case, civic pride had undoubtedly contributed to the foundation, and to its credit Nottingham's town council agreed to shoulder the financial responsibility for the new College. The £10,000 endowment was invested to pay the expenses of visiting lecturers from Cambridge, but the council found the £50,000 required to pay for the buildings, and provided about £6,500 a year running costs.[65] Additional income from fees, a grant from the Department of Science and Art, and charges for popular lectures were enough to maintain the steady growth of the College during the 1880s.

Within the new institution extension teaching – the original inspiration – formed only a minor part of the instruction, and technical and scientific education related to the economic development of Nottingham and its region was emphasised as the most important function of the College. The shift of emphasis was possible only because the College was able to gain support from the principal industrialists in Nottingham. In the past, leading figures in the town's textile industries had considered commercial rather than technical education to be most relevant to their concerns.[66] In the 1860s, Mundella, while President of the Nottingham Chamber of Commerce, had tried to gain their support for technical education, but there was little response and it had been left to the supporters of the Mechanics Institute, using the system of courses and examinations prescribed by the Department of Science and Art, to organise various classes in scientific subjects which were felt to be appropriate for young artisans in Nottingham. This was the only organised system of scientific education which could be adapted for the purpose, and the transfer in 1881 of the Science and Art classes to the University College provided a starting-point for developing links with local industry. Paton, who had been co-opted to the University Committee, pressed for further initiatives to be taken, but his efforts fell on stony ground, and although classes in hosiery and lace making began in 1884 any hope of establishing a lace and hosiery school equivalent to the textile department being established at the Yorkshire College of Science, the future University of Leeds, was frustrated. In 1890 the corporation used powers and financial resources placed at its disposal by legislation of 1889 and 1890 to promote jointly with the University College technical schools on unused land at the rear of the building. In addition, in March 1888, the council took over responsibility for the School of Art.[67]

These different responsibilities were partly facilitated by the Residue Grant or 'Whiskey Money' arising from legislation of 1890 which, among other decisions, created a general purpose fund to be distributed to county and county boroughs to be used – if they so wished – for the promotion of technical education. Like many other authorities, Nottingham corporation chose to use the money to support educational development, and the windfall provided the means to support both the University College and the School of Art. Between 1891 and 1901 the two institutions received an average of 68 per cent and 20 per cent respectively of the Residue Grant available to Nottingham. Generously supported by the corporation, and in receipt of the new Treasury Grants to the universities which also began in 1889, the University College was able to begin a more secure period of development. In 1890 it was one of the first five university institutions to establish a day training department for elementary school teachers, and in 1893 engineering was added to the original four professorships which had covered language and literature, physics, maths and mechanics, chemistry, metallurgy and natural science. Other new subjects were slowly added to the academic curriculum and the first students began to prepare for the London External Degree. Meanwhile, university extension courses quickly diminished in importance, and had virtually disappeared by 1896. Most of the young men and women attending classes came from the elementary schools in the town, entering the College at the age of fourteen, so that the institution was perceived as performing the role of a secondary or finishing school for many of them. The technical school set up in 1890 survived, moving into purpose-built accommodation in 1893. Classes in lace and hosiery continued, although never developing in the way anticipated by the founders of the College. A variety of low-level technical courses was offered, and artisan students from Nottingham and surrounding districts came in the evenings and on Saturday mornings to learn trades related to a wide range of occupations such as electrician, gas fitter, plumber, carpenter and joiner.[68]

The corporation's commitment to the College was an act of great munificence, well understood by Professor Symes, the first principal from 1890 to 1911.[69] However, difficulties arose because the corporation became highly protective of the College, which it increasingly chose to consider as its own creation. It was equally sensitive about the School of Art, which it had rescued from closure. There was hostility to any moves which it feared would threaten its control of both institutions, and it stood opposed to any organisation which seemed to represent a threat to its position. Under these circumstances, a collision with the School Board was almost inevitable. Relations between the Board and the corporation had long been strained. The corporation never really came to terms with the fact that the Board could legitimately finance its building programme by means of the precept upon the rates.[70] The Board's higher grade schools and evening commercial and technical classes now seemed to pose a threat to some of the work being done at the College, since there was only a limited pool from which students could be recruited. Suspecting that it was the government's intention to create new local education authorities upon which the school boards would be represented, and fearing that this would mean that the Nottingham Board would then have access to the residue grant, the corporation proposed a private bill in 1901 to abolish the Board and to take over its powers in respect of elementary education.[71] In the event, the Nottingham Education Bill was withdrawn because Sir John Gorst, Vice-President of the new Board of Education, fearful of setting a precedent, was able to assure Sir Samuel Johnson, Nottingham's town clerk, that the government would itself introduce legislation to make the county and county borough councils the new Local Education Authorities with control over both elementary and secondary education. Nothing would be allowed to interfere with the corporation's powers to determine how it would spend the residue grant. The proposed legislation became, in due course, the Education Act of 1902.

In the mid-nineteenth century many informed contemporary commentators accepted the view expressed most cogently by Friedrich Engels in 1844. 'All the writers of the bourgeoisie', he wrote, 'are unanimous on this point, that the workers are not religious, and do not attend church.'[72] In the new manufacturing towns of industrial England the Church seemed to have no relevance but, as we have shown in this chapter, such gloom and doom was misplaced. Religion, in many senses, was more relevant to urban society in 1850 than it had been a century earlier, partly because Anglicans and nonconformists alike had run to keep pace with the population explosion by building new churches and chapels, but partly because of the contribution that they had made to educating the urban working classes. The running continued after 1850 with new churches and schools being built, and with the churches increasingly reaching out to the social needs of their parishioners. However, the education legislation of 1870 altered the rules. It did not so much decide the future as write off the past. The best efforts of Anglicans, nonconformists and Roman Catholics alike had failed to bridge the gap between educational requirements and places available. The School Boards, whatever the rivalry between Anglican and nonconformist – and

Nottingham was mercifully spared some of the clashes which occurred elsewhere – pointed towards the secular state. The schoolteacher rather than the priest would in the future be the guiding hand. And just as the role of the churches in education came into question, their problems were compounded by competition from a range of new leisure opportunities which they embraced without successfully monopolising. But the decline should not be exaggerated: at the end of the nineteenth century the churches were still providing many of the school places in Nottingham, and church attendance was rising on the eve of the First World War.

The development of Nottingham in the 150 years after 1750 was greatly influenced by church, chapel and school alike. Physically, the range of new buildings, many of which survive, albeit altered, affected the appearance of the town. Socially, the churches became the centre of a range of activities in addition to their primary role in Christian worship. Educationally, the needs of the new working classes were addressed first by the Anglicans and nonconformists, and then increasingly by the State. Nottingham also enjoyed the remarkable example of a corporation ready to fund a University College. Finally, the changing structure of the late nineteenth-century town was reflected in church and school provision. The informal religious census of 1881 revealed that Nottingham was relatively well provided with church and chapel accommodation, but that the suburbs incorporated in 1877 had been neglected. They also had a greater shortfall in elementary school places than the town. Beyond 1877 the emphasis moved away from the town to the suburbs, with a redistribution of resources to match population movement. When St Stephen's, Bunkers Hill, was demolished in 1895 as part of the Victoria Station redevelopment, its assets were transferred to a new church in the expanding part of Hyson Green; when High Pavement school needed new and more appropriate accommodation it was moved to the newly developing Forest Fields area. These are just two examples of a trend which has gathered pace in the twentieth century: today the only Anglican churches in central Nottingham are the three which were already in place in 1750, and many of the nonconformist chapels have either been demolished or converted to other uses. And today, except at People's College, hardly a scholar is educated within the built-up area of the pre-1845 town.[73]

Notes

1 *Census of Great Britain, 1851: Religious Worship, England and Wales, Report and Tables* (1853), p. clviii.

2 M. R. Watts, *The Dissenters, Volume II: the Expansion of Evangelical Nonconformity 1791–1859* (Oxford, 1995), pp. 49–50; J. C. Weller, *Say to the Wind: a Study of the Revival of Religion in Nottingham 1780–1850* (Nottingham, 1957); J. Severn, 'Church building in Nottingham 1660–1851' (University of Nottingham, MA thesis, 1991). The fullest account of the Baptist movement in Nottingham, prior to 1815, is J. T. Godfrey and J. Ward, *A History of Friar Lane Baptist Church* (Nottingham, 1903), and for the Baptist movement in both town and county F. M. W. Harrison, 'The life and thought of the Baptists of Nottinghamshire' (University of Nottingham, M.Phil. thesis, 1972).

3 N. Curnock (ed.), *The Journal of the Rev. John Wesley* (1909 edn), V, p. 160; VII, p. 341; R. C. Swift, *Lively People: Methodism in Nottingham 1740–1979* (Nottingham, 1979), pp. 1–10, 19–28. The façade of Hockley Chapel can still be seen today.

4 A. Gilbert, *Recollections of Old Nottingham* (2nd edn, Nottingham, 1904), pp. 24–5.

5 Wylie, pp. 103–5; Gawthern, *Diary*, p. 144; A. Bosworth, 'Nineteenth century churches in Nottingham', *NH*, 46 (1991), pp. 7–12. St James's was demolished in 1936.

6 Wylie, pp. 106–8. Holy Trinity was demolished in 1958. It was on the site of the modern Trinity Square car-park.

7 NAO DD 808/1; P. Murphy, 'Irish settlement in Nottingham in the early nineteenth century', *TTS*, 98 (1994), p. 86.

8 Watts, *Dissenters*, p. 674n.; J. B. Goodman (ed.), *Victorian Cabinet Maker* (1968), pp. 40–1.

9 Wylie, pp. 105–6; *NJ*, 25 October 1822; Birmingham University Library, CPAS MSS, Register of Grants 1836–53, 5 March 1840. St Paul's was demolished in 1925.

10 Watts, *Dissenters*, p. 223; A. C. Wood, 'Nottingham, 1835–1865', *TTS*, 59 (1955), pp. 24–5; Wylie, pp. 88–97; Pevsner and Williamson, pp. 219, 221.

11 Wood, 'Nottingham', p. 25; Watts, *Dissenters*, pp. 457–8.

12 Birmingham University Library, CPAS MSS, List of Grants 1836–53, 4 January 1844.

13 Lincolnshire Archives Office, Cor B/5/8/5/2–13.

14 NAO M.24,480/A4; Wylie, p. 96; Severn, 'Church building', pp. 93–6; Weller, *Say to the Wind*, pp. 47–58; E. P. Bailey, 'Leenside, the Churches and the making of a Nottingham slum' (University of Nottingham, MA dissertation, 1993), pp. 49–53. The church was badly damaged during a bombing raid in 1941 and demolished in 1951.

15 Wood, 'Nottingham', pp. 23–4; Diary of W. B. Carter, 6 March 1845 (privately loaned).

16 Murphy, 'Irish settlement', pp. 82–91; A. Bosworth, '"Grandeur and Trumpery": the creation of the Roman Catholic diocese of Nottingham, 1850', *NH*, 47 (1991), pp. 2–6; M. Cummins, *Nottingham Cathedral* (3rd edn, Nottingham, 1994), pp. 17–35. Father Willson left to become Bishop of Tasmania about six months before the new church opened. He died on a visit to Nottingham in 1866 and was buried in the Cathedral.

17 S. D. Chapman, 'The evangelical revival and education in Nottingham', *TTS*, 66 (1962), pp. 35–66; *NJ*, 27 January 1787, 9 October 1802; Watts, *Dissenters*. pp. 292–301; D. Wardle, *Education and Society in Nineteenth-Century Nottingham* (Cambridge, 1971), pp. 38–45.

18 Lincolnshire Archives Office, DBE/8/4/47; D. H. Williams, 'The contribution of the Church of England to education in Nottingham during the nineteenth century' (University of Nottingham, MA thesis, 1991), pp. 17–34; *Red Book of Nottingham* (1868), pp. 59–60.

19 *NJ*, 28 July 1810; Wylie, p. 342; Chapman, 'Evangelical revival', p. 64. A further experiment in 'moral and religious' education was the workhouse school set up by Absolem Barnett in 1832: A. Barnett, *The Poor Laws and their Administration* (1833), p. 63.

20 Wardle, *Education*, pp. 45–50.

21 *NJ*, 13 December 1833; Wardle, *Education*, pp. 50–5.

22 *Children's Employment Commission, 1842*, PP 1843 [XIV] F3–5. When R. D. Grainger, the Childrens' Employment Commissioner, spoke to hosiers about the benefits of education, there was general agreement that 'exactly in proportion as mechanics are better educated so they become more valuable to their employers because educated mechanics are more respectful in their behaviour to their superiors'.

23 J. W. Hudson, *A History of Adult Education* (1851), p. 146.

24 Wardle, *Education*, p. 49; Lascelles and Hagar, *Directory* (1848), p. 127; Wylie, p. 347; *Date Book*, p. 508; *EP*, 23 November 1995. For working-class libraries see ch. 16.

25 Wardle, *Education*, p. 49; Murphy, 'Irish settlement', p. 87.

26 F. W. Taylor, *The History of Nottingham Bluecoat School, 1706–1956* (Nottingham, 1956), p. 28.

27 *Census of Great Britain, 1851: Religious Worship, England and Wales, Report and Tables* (1854), pp. xxxiii, 164. The poet, Henry Kirke White, corresponded with his mother, a dame school mistress, about her school *c.*1800: C. V. Vernon, 'The poems and letters of Henry Kirke White' (University of Nottingham, Ph.D. thesis, 1980).

28 NAO *Nottingham School Board*, report of the Statistical Committee, 15 May 1871. Nine of the original ten private schools examined by the Board and thought to have been efficient were subsequently removed from estimates of capacity.

29 B. H. Tolley, 'Technical education in the East Midlands. A study in educational administration and history' (University of Nottingham, Ph.D thesis, 1979), pp. 6–7, 174; *Date Book*, p. 459; Committee of Council *Annual Report* (1851), pp. 295–6; Carol A. Jones, *A History of Nottingham School of Design* (Nottingham, 1993).

30 R. Lyon, *1843–1968. The Nottingham College of Art and Design* (Nottingham, 1968); *Reports of the Science and Art Department*, vol. 1 (1854), pp. 150–9, 362; vol. 5 (1858), p. 36; vol. 10 (1863), appendix, L, pp. 169–70; Minute Book of the Nottingham Chamber of Commerce (1860–63), 5 July 1860.

31 *RBN*, IX, pp. 118, 151, 153.

32 *Samuelson Commission*, PP 1883 [XXI] Second Report, vol. III, appendices, pp. 769–770, evidence of J. R. Rawle; *NR*, 10 January 1868.

33 *Samuelson Commission*, appendices, p. 666, no. 37, evidence of R. H. Steegman of Steegman & Co.; *Report of the Science and Art Department*, vol. 20 (1873), pp. 19–20; School of Art Subscription List (1869); Tolley, 'Technical Education', p. 184; *Nottingham Guardian Journal*, 26 January 1870; *Nottingham Daily Express*, 26 January 1871.

34 A. Rogers, 'The 1851 religious census returns for the city of Nottingham', *TTS*, 76 (1972), pp. 74–87 with the figures recalculated according to the formula in the notes to table 15.2. The Nottingham returns are also reproduced in M. R. Watts, *Religion in Victorian Nottinghamshire: the religious census of 1851* (Nottingham, 1988), I, pp. xxix–xxx, II, pp. 176–94, although the estimates for attendance differ from those given in Watts, *Dissenters*, pp. 704–5. However, as Watts points out (p. 673), the figures can only be regarded as rough guides.

35 *Religious Worship*, p. clviii.

36 St Mark's, Windsor Street, 1855–56, 850 seats (demolished 1958); St Matthew's, Upper Talbot Street, 1856, 700 seats (reduced to 450 seats in 1881 after the galleries were closed, and demolished 1956); St Stephen's, Bunker's Hill, 1859, 700 seats (demolished 1896); St Luke's, Carlton Road, 1863, 550 seats (demolished 1920s); St Ann, St Ann's Well Road, 1863–65, 1,000 seats (demolished 1971); St Saviour's, Arkwright Street, 1863–65, 750 seats, All Saint's Raleigh Street, 1864–65, 848 seats.

37 Wardle, *Education*, pp. 49–53; Lincolnshire AO, DBE/8/4/47; Chapman, 'Evangelical revival', pp. 63, 66. For a discussion of the size and structure of some of these schools, as well as their educational achievements, see Williams, 'Church of England', pp. 38–55.

38 A. Rogers, 'Religion in Nottingham in the nineteenth century', in J. F. Phillips (ed.), *Town and Village in the Nineteenth Century* (Nottingham, 1972), pp. 48–59.

39 NAO M.23,788, 5 December 1863.

40 Swift, *Lively People*, pp. 149–58; Bosworth, 'Nineteenth century churches', p. 12.

41 A possible if somewhat crude way of compensating for the missing Sunday School scholars is to omit from the calculations all those under fifteen. In 1881, 36.5 per cent of the population was under fifteen, so if we reduce the figure of 186,575 by the same proportion and then repeat the calculation the attendance becomes 46,960 out of 118,475, or 39.6 per cent. A fall from 42 per cent to 31.6 per cent is rather less dramatic than to 25 per cent, but given the crudity of the calculations the general point made here holds good.

42 K. S. Inglis, *Churches and the Working Classes in Victorian England* (1963), p. 23; H. Meller (ed.), *Nottingham in the Eighteen Eighties* (Nottingham, 1971), pp. 34–5.

43 *Allen's Nottingham Red Book* (1895), p. 113; *White* (1885), p. 243; NAO DR/3/2/2/1. The churches aided were Emmanuel, St Mary's Cemetery Church, St Bartholomew's, St George's, Kirke White Street, Lenton Priory, St Margaret's Mission Hall (Meadows), Alfreton Road Church, Cobden Park Church (All Souls), St Alban's, St Augustine's New Basford, St Christopher's Sneinton, St John's Bulwell, St John's Carrington, St Clement's, St Aidan's, St Luke's, St Matthias's, St John the Baptist, and New Radford. Altogether, the Anglicans built, or rebuilt, no fewer than twenty-three churches in the years 1855–1905: N. Truman, *Nottingham and its Churches, 1449–1949* (Gloucester,

1949), p. 12; S. Best, 'Mission accomplished: the early years of St Christopher's Church', *Sneinton Magazine*, 49 (1993–94), pp. 9–26.

44 J. V. Beckett, 'The Church of England and the working class in nineteenth-century Nottingham: the building of St Stephen's, Hyson Green', *TTS*, 92 (1988), pp. 59–73; NAO M.396, p. 263, list of iron churches built by Nottingham Spiritual Aid and Church Extension Society; DR.1.1.12.14, Southwell Diocesan Magazine 1899, p. 189.

45 NAO M.392–6; [J. M. F. Lester], *Dear St Catherine's* (1929), pp. 26–36; Meller, *1880s*, ch. 3.

46 Swift, *Lively People*, pp. 152, 156; F. M. W. Harrison, *The Nottinghamshire Baptists* (1978), pp. 64–5; *Lenton Listener*, (Nov./Dec. 1983).

47 *RBN*, IX, p. 209; NAO *Nottingham School Board*, Regulations for Management, 1878; *Nottingham School Board*, Final Report (1903), p. 36. Scripture teaching was examined each year alternately by local clergy and nonconformist ministers: D. Wardle, 'The work of the Nottingham School Board' (University of Nottingham, M.Ed. thesis, 1961), p. 62; E. M. Becket, 'The development of education in Nottingham in the nineteenth and early twentieth centuries' (University of Nottingham, MA thesis, 1922), pp. 98–104.

48 Using the census returns, the statistical committee established that there were 17,988 children between the ages of three and thirteen in the town. About 15 per cent of this number were believed to be children of middle-class parents who would not wish to use the School Board's schools. It was also estimated that about 15 per cent of the remainder, including half-timers, would, for a variety of reasons, not attend the new schools. All existing private elementary schools in Nottingham charging less than 9*d* per week were considered to be potential sources of accommodation. Of the 105 elementary schools examined by the Board, 72 were thought to be 'efficient' with 12 others likely to become 'efficient'. NAO *Nottingham School Board*, Minutes of the Statistical Committee, 15 May 1871; Wardle, *Education and Society*, p. 86.

49 NAO *Nottingham School Board*, Abstract of Reports of Committee on Borough Extension, November 1877; *Nottingham School Board*, Final Report (1903), p. 30; S. Best, 'Sneinton School Board's brief life', *Sneinton Magazine*, 50, (1994), pp. 25–34; 51 (1994), pp. 15–26.

50 Wardle, 'Nottingham School Board', p. 106; Williams, 'Church of England', pp. 65–78.

51 NAO *Nottingham School Board*, Triennial Report, 1883–86, p. 9; Final Report (1903), pp. 30–1.

52 *Second Report of the Childrens' Employment Commission*, Appendix, PP 1843 [XIV] F, pp. 1–2 *passim*.

53 *Children's Employment Commission* (1863), Children Employed in Trades and Manufactures not regulated by Law. PP 1863 [XVIII], pp. 187 *passim*. Although the Act seems to have been effective there were still some difficulties concerning children who worked in domestic premises which could not be described as a 'factory'.

54 *Committee of Council Annual Report* (1877). Report of HMI Capell-Sewell. p. 533. A child of ten might be allowed to attend half-time if he or she was 'beneficially employed' and had passed Standard II of the Elementary Education Code. This was a concession to Nottingham employers but in the confused situation brought about by the overlap of factory legislation and by-laws, the latter grew increasingly reluctant to take on children for half-time work.

55 NAO *Nottingham School Board*, Final Report (1903), pp. 10, 18. Two 'visitors' were appointed in 1872. In 1903 there were twelve district visitors, a superintendent and a deputy superintendent; Wardle, *Education and Society*, pp. 110–12. Before 1886, the most difficult cases were sent to industrial schools in Bradford and York as well as to training ships in Southampton and Bangor.

56 Wardle, *Education and Society*, p. 90; NAO *Nottingham School Board*, Report on Science Teaching, 6 October 1885. The Board employed the services of a science assistant who took his equipment round to the various schools on a specially constructed handcart.

57 Tolley, 'Technical education', pp. 85–9; Wardle, *Education and Society*, p. 92.

58 *Report of the Science and Art Department*, 19 (1872), pp. 25–7.

59 NAO SB 47/1/1/7; Church, pp. 150, 314; Wylie, p. 347; *NR*, 6 August 1847, 7 December 1855, 3 October 1856.

60 B. Carpenter, *Some Account of the Original Introduction of Presbyterianism in Nottingham* (Nottingham, 1865), pp. 165–7; J. P. Russell-Gebbett, 'High Pavement: Britain's first organised science

school', *History of Education Society Bulletin*, 43 (1989), pp. 17–29; J. P. Russell-Gebbett, 'High Pavement School Science 1885–1905: struggle and survival Part I, *History of Education Society Bulletin*, 52 (1993), pp. 22–34, and Part II, 53 (1994), pp. 23–34.

61 NAO *Nottingham School Board*, Final Report (1903), pp. 30–1; W. H. G. Armytage, *A. J. Mundella 1825–97* (1951), pp. 203–36.

62 *Higher Grade Schools and Public Secondary Schools* [Statistics] 22 June 1898, PP 1898 [LXX], p. 521; NAO *Nottingham School Board*, Triennial Report, 1898–1901.

63 *Royal Commission appointed to Enquire into the Working of the Elementary Education Acts. [The Cross Commission]*, PP 1887 [XXX], Third Report, Minutes of Evidence, questions, 53,024–53,034.

64 NAO *Nottingham School Board*, Final Report (1903), p. 41; Wardle, 'Nottingham School Board', pp. 191–3.

65 B. H. Tolley, 'Nottingham University, 1881–1911: the formative years', in *One Hundred Years of Nottingham Life: the Centenary Lectures Delivered at the University of Nottingham* (1981), pp. 6, 12.

66 J. L. Paton, *John Brown Paton: a Biography* (1913), p. 181; C. Erickson, *British Industrialists, Steel and Hosiery 1850–1950* (Cambridge, 1959), pp. 110–18.

67 Tolley, 'Technical education', pp. 143–6, 153–6, 163–71, 174; *RBN*, IX, p. 345; *Application by the Committee of the School of Art to the Corporation of Nottingham for Financial Assistance*, 23 February 1888.

68 Wardle, *Education and Society*, p. 157; A. C. Wood. *A History of University College, Nottingham. 1881–1948* (Oxford, 1953), p. 71; Tolley, 'Technical education', pp. 229–31.

69 *Royal Commission on Secondary Education* [Bryce Commission], vol. IV, p. 373, questions 15,947–8.

70 *RBN*, IX, pp. 226–7.

71 Tolley, 'Technical education', pp. 200–2, 238–40; B. H. Tolley, 'University College, Nottingham, and the Nottingham Education Bill of 1901', *Journal of the History of Education*, 10, 4 (1981), pp. 263–72.

72 F. Engels, *The Condition of the Working Class in England* (1844; 1969 edn), p. 155.

73 To People's College should perhaps be added Clarendon College, which has recently taken over premises within the old town.

16

LEISURE, RECREATION AND ENTERTAINMENT

John Beckett

The physical and social transformation of English industrial towns had a significant impact on life-styles, perhaps no more so than in the use of leisure time. It was not simply that towns were inappropriate venues for some of the traditional recreations associated with rural England. The processes of change were more complex and subtle than the straightforward substitution of one culture for another. Older forms of entertainment often survived, albeit in an altered form, among them the annual Goose Fair. On the other hand the greater stratification of urban society was reflected in the social calendar. In rural England the gentry had patronised the sports and entertainments of the rest of society; in urban England the middle classes developed their own exclusive entertainments in which great stress was laid on the rationality of the activity and the importance of avoiding moral corruption. The enabler in this process was the club, or voluntary association, which grew in importance from *c.*1780, initially among adult middle-class males. These men often sought an intellectual and cultural environment separate from family and work, and they frequently created private spaces such as coffee clubs and libraries for this purpose. In turn, the search for privacy produced a growing polarisation of polite and popular culture, and the middle classes became concerned to apply their values to working-class interests. In particular, they sought to wean the industrial operatives away from their customary pursuits – particularly animal sports – and from the public house, although here the position was complicated by the role of pubs in providing accommodation for working-class clubs and societies. By the 1850s 'rational recreation' as both preached and practised by the middle classes, coupled with greater leisure time for the working classes, were bringing about a new social environment.

Nottingham experienced these various trends as clearly as most other industrialising towns, although naturally with local variants. A distinctive 'polite' culture emerged in the eighteenth century, although the strong nonconformist tradition among the middle classes ensured that it was more intellectual and less convivial than in some other places. As elsewhere, the town endured considerable teething problems in the development of working-class recreations in the period to about 1850, although the late enclosure of the open fields at least meant that it avoided the space constraints on sporting and other activities which affected many industrial towns. Finally, Nottingham enjoyed or endured a rapid transformation of leisure interests from the 1830s and 1840s, which brought a realigning of middle- and working-class interests in the second half of the nineteenth century.

Polite society and middle-class leisure

Nottingham in 1750 was a genteel town with a distinctive urban culture. The expansion of the middling sorts in the second half of the eighteenth century coincided with the increasing commercialisation of leisure pursuits and a boom in consumer spending on household goods. Luxuries began to appear in middle-rank households, just as their occupants began to retreat from the socially mixed use of space which had characterised earlier periods towards a more exclusive culture. It was still fashionable to promenade and to be seen. Colwick-Spring and the walk along the River Trent to Clifton Grove were favoured routes, together with Wilford – reached by ferry – Lenton, and Radford Folly, the latter 'a delightful place of public resort' laid out in 1780 by William Elliot. The fittest of all could take the entire ten-mile footpath encircling the town, refreshing themselves at the tea gardens designed for middle-class promenaders.[1] Promenading took place in the open air, but the new middle classes sought to associate together and to put social distance between themselves and the rest of society by creating their own places of recreation, either for entertainment – Assembly Rooms, theatres and concert rooms – or for educational and other purposes through subscription libraries and voluntary associations.

Purpose-built provincial theatres appeared in many towns in the middle decades of the century. In Nottingham, James Whitley opened the 758-seat St Mary's Gate Theatre in 1760. It was an immediate success, particularly among the Tory–Anglicans. The *Nottingham Journal* reported in 1774 a visit by 'the best travelling company at this time in England', and in 1778 the building was substantially improved. Abigail Gawthern was a regular patron.[2] Theatres, like churches, often doubled as venues for concerts, and the rise of organised music festivals nationally dates from about 1760. Subscription concerts in Nottingham began at least as early as 1759, and members of the audience in 1769 included 'the Duke of Portland, Lord George Cavendish, Sir Gervase Clifton, Sir William Boothby, and the principal ladies and gentlemen of the town and neighbourhood who were highly pleased with the performances and expressed great satisfaction on seeing so brilliant an audience'. Subscription concerts were held at the more socially active times of the year, often in the Assembly Rooms. John Pearson, a singer and music teacher in Nottingham between 1783 and 1796, gave concerts at the Assembly Rooms. Occasional music festivals in the town, as in

1763 and 1772, were supplemented on a regular basis from 1782 by an annual musical festival in support of the General Hospital. Other benefit concerts were given for charitable reasons. Mrs Gawthern attended a concert in 1781 which was arranged to raise money for Mrs Melville, 'left a widow in distress'. Concerts were also held at St Mary's Church. A large organ was installed in 1742, and replaced at the end of the 1770s by a Snetzler organ costing £800. Samuel Wise, organist 1756–1802, promoted concerts with children from the Bluecoat School – only a few yards away at Weekday Cross – among the choristers.[3]

Theatres and concerts are still familiar, but perhaps most typical of the urban leisure activities of the middling ranks by the later eighteenth century were the socially exclusive assemblies. The Assembly Room was altered in 1790, and refurbished in 1806–07 when, according to Blackner, 'this seat of gaity and refined amusement was fitted up in a superb style'. In Deering's day assemblies were held monthly on the first Tuesday, but there were others associated with particular events. Some were annual: the Assize Assembly was held in the spring, and several assemblies took place during race week – they were advertised in 1768 for Tuesday, Wednesday and Thursday. In 1782 an annual assembly was introduced for the support of the General Hospital. Assemblies were also held to celebrate royal birthdays and elections, although the prevailing Tory consensus at Low Pavement ensured a somewhat exclusive gathering. At election balls held in the Assembly Rooms in 1803 and 1806 everyone who attended wore something blue. Finally, assemblies were occasionally convened to celebrate particular events, such as the centenary of the Glorious Revolution in 1788, and Nelson's victory at the Battle of the Nile in 1798.[4]

What were Assemblies for? Primarily they were for participants to be seen socialising in public. The young went to show off their fashionable clothes and their dancing skills, as well as to look for marriage partners: 'the Assemblies of Nottingham', wrote an observer in 1812, 'are, as in all other places, the resort of the young and gay, who go to see and be seen; and also of those, who, having played their matrimonial cards well in early life, are now content to sit down to a game of sober whist or quadrille'.[5] Woodward commented that the old maids of Nottingham appeared old-fashioned except at an Assembly or card party 'when a consultation at the milliners in the Long Row usually produces a long train, and a few modish decorations by way of head-dress'. Tea, coffee and light refreshments were served, and it was late into the night before Assemblies broke up: Mrs Gawthern frequently returned home at three o'clock in the morning, and after one Assembly in 1804 she listened to the birds singing before retiring to bed.[6]

Assemblies were an important and fixed part of the annual calendar, but Nottingham's social élite did not rely upon them exclusively for entertainment. Mrs Gawthern regularly attended balls and concerts around the town. She went to the grand ball at the Castle in 1776 given by officers of the Nottinghamshire Regiment of Militia. This was a one-off: 'there had not been a ball of 50 years before', she noted – nor would there be any repeats. Other occasions were also sociable. On her daughter's twenty-third birthday in 1807 Mrs Gawthern was too ill to have guests to dinner, but entertained twenty people to tea and sandwiches, 'cards, music and dancing', until 2.00 a.m.[7]

Mrs Gawthern frequently entertained in her own home, but private celebrations were also allowed in the Assembly Rooms where, in 1782, the mayor gave a ball attended by many of the county families. By the late 1820s the Assembly Rooms were 'not now so much used as formerly, the large room at the Exchange having in some measure superseded it'.[8] Lord Middleton hired the large room in January 1824 for a ball and supper to which he invited 400 guests. Similar events included a ball to celebrate the installation of the Duke of Newcastle in December 1860 as Provincial Grand Master of the Order of Freemasons. The room was also used for concerts and exhibitions. George Harwood took his wife and son to the Exchange in 1860 'to see "Eastward Ho!" and "Home Again", two celebrated paintings by Henry O'Neil Esq.'.[9]

Middle-class leisure was not only about entertainment: it also had an educational and improving angle expressed through subscription libraries and intellectual debating societies. Subscription libraries date from the mid-eighteenth century. In 1744 Dr Standfast left over 1,000 volumes to the Nottingham Bluecoat school to establish a public library for 'clergy, lawyers, physicians, and other persons of a liberal and learned education', and this provided the basic stock for various organisations. There was a book society in the town by 1788–89 and half a dozen circulating libraries by 1815. The Nottingham Subscription Library was founded in 1816, and in 1821 bought for £2,750 Bromley House on Beastmarket Hill, which is still its headquarters, and where it quickly became a focus for the cultural and intellectual life of the town. Membership was exclusive, and limited to 300. The annual subscription of two guineas remained unchanged until 1919.[10] Formal voluntary associations began around 1780 but expanded rapidly in the 1820s. Typical were the Literary and Science Society founded in 1824, and the Literary and Debating Club, founded in 1837. A Secular Society was founded in 1852. Out of these emerged – later than in many provincial towns – a Literary and Philosophical Society. In 1866 Samuel Collinson, stockbroker, artist and poet, was one of 160 people who went on a Lit. & Phil. excursion to Buxton, and also that year he read a paper on heraldry.[11] Later in the century archaeological and antiquarian societies were formed. The Thoroton Society was founded in 1897 to take an interest in the county's history, archaeology and antiquities. It was based in Nottingham. The Cosmopolitan Debating Society was founded in 1898 to provide 'a free, impartial, non-sectarian, non-partisan forum of all views and opinions on all subjects', although it was politically to the left and Keir Hardie was an early speaker. Meetings attracted audiences of 400–500 people.[12]

The growth of intellectual and improving societies began alongside the more entertaining aspects of middle-rank culture, but long outlasted them. The distinctive character, particularly of eighteenth-century culture, was a stress on urbanity, manners, and the behaviour of a polite society. What placed these values under stress was a combination of the evangelical revival, the French revolution and the rise of radicalism. The exact way in which the mixture worked may escape us, but the results were clear. Activities such as theatregoing, novel reading and card playing were scrutinised to see whether or not they served any purpose of which God might approve, and at the same time the sociability of eighteenth-century society gave way to an emphasis on domesticity, from the frank enjoyment of leisure towards a more calculating performance of duty. This shift of emphasis coincided with the middle-class drift away from town centres into more exclusive areas, and towards private rather than public entertainment. As a result, provincial theatres almost everywhere suffered a decline, from which they began to recover only in the 1850s and 1860s. By the 1820s the St Mary's Gate Theatre was used for only about three months of the year, and was seldom filled more than two or three times a season, partly 'owing to the greater part of the middle classes being now dissenters, and averse to theatrical performance'. It usually housed touring companies doing the East Midlands circuit.[13] Samuel Collinson was a regular patron in the 1840s and 1850s, but he was not often impressed. In December 1854 a performance of the *British Legion* was 'middling', while a farce performed in August 1856 was 'not well performed by the London Company', and a melodrama in January 1862 moved him to write 'oh, such rubbish the performance was, melodrama of the most diabolical and bloodthirsty character'. Concerts – of which the evangelicals approved when they included sacred music – were also going out of favour.[14]

Similarly Assemblies were becoming less popular. At their height they attracted anything up to 300 people. Consequently Mrs Gawthern was disappointed when, following the Assizes in 1800, there was no Assembly: 'it has not been omitted (Miss Taylor who keeps the room says) of one hundred years'. So she held an Assembly herself and invited seventy guests. Attendance at the regular Assemblies was also falling. On 29 July 1803 there were only fifteen couples present, and only nine couples turned out on 9 August. Numbers kept up for race week, and for celebratory occasions: 176 people turned out for the Assembly on 18 January 1804 to celebrate the Queen's birthday. To make ends meet the rooms were increasingly used for private parties, and then in 1835 they were sold for £1,100, including fixtures and furnishings, to the committee of the News Society. One of the conditions was that the rooms should still be used four times a year for the Infirmary, Asylum, Assize and Race Balls, as well as for commemorative events such as the anniversary of the Glorious Revolution. In 1836 the old building was replaced by a splendid new suite of rooms built in Grecian style, which can still be seen today. They were primarily used for balls, concerts, public meeting and private societies. The latter included a literary society, a chess club, and a lodge of freemasons. Public exhibitions were regularly held in the rooms. Wylie commented that 'the character of the building has somewhat degenerated by its having become the scene of many gay gatherings of the humbler classes'.[15] It was a suitable epitaph on a building which, more than most, reflected a changing ethos in leisure pursuits among the middle classes.

Working-class recreations before 1850

The middle ranks, with time on their hands and money to spend, were perfectly capable of organising and developing leisure pursuits, both entertaining and enervating, in urban society. By contrast, the new working classes were much less well placed. The traditional sports and recreations of rural England transferred uneasily into urban life, partly because space was at a premium and partly because of a greater emphasis on work and personal discipline. In addition, middle-class voluntary societies, often with government support, sought to prosecute offenders against moral laws, while local authorities tried to regulate alehouses, to suppress fairs and wakes, and to prevent sporting events such as prizefighting. Largely as a result, traditional popular culture merged into new forms of entertainment suited to urban–industrial society.

One of the most serious problems associated with industrial towns was recreational space. A combination of late enclosure and the slow movement of the industrial work-force into workshops and factories, which meant that they continued to control their own work time, helped to ensure the survival in Nottingham of many popular recreations, particularly in the Meadows. Mary Howitt wrote of the

Plate 45 **Cricket in the Meadows**. Apart from the cricket match the picture shows, on the left, the new Midland Station, opened on 22 May 1848, on Station Street. It was a one-storey building in the Greek style, covering an area of 600 feet by 94 feet. The

'inimitable crocus beds' in the 'fine green meadows … their extraordinary beauty shining out clear and bright, in many places to the extent of twenty acres, one entire bed of lilac flowers'. Mrs Gilbert recalled of the 1830s how 'young and old alike' turned out 'during the fortnight the beauteous purple bloom lasted to revel among them'. James Hopkinson long recalled 'one of the loveliest sights in England … the Meadows about the middle of March … covered with purple and white crocuses'.[16] Others remembered the sporting activities in the Meadows. Traditionally, football matches were played here on Shrove Tuesday: in 1832 'a numerous party assembled in the Meadows to keep up old customs by a game at football. The players, to obviate any disadvantage from an external wetting imbibed considerable portion of inward moisture at the Royal Children, Castle Gate, where also they partook of a substantial supper paid by the losers.'[17] Much the same was true of cricket. Nottingham operatives reputedly rose at 5.00 a.m. to play the game in the Meadows, 'because there is no other town in the kingdom, perhaps, that offers so many advantages in having open spaces in the immediate vicinity of the town'.[18] Large crowds would also gather for foot racing. In 1773 15,000 people assembled on the Forest for a ten-mile contest between two of the most noted runners of the day. The runners performed their task – 'entirely naked, for they ran without any covering whatever' – in the creditable

station offices had a frontage of 180 feet with a stone portico in the centre. To the right of the picture, beyond the players, is the canal, while the smoking chimneys point to some of the factories of the new industrial town

time of 'fifty-six minutes and two seconds'. Open spaces also facilitated other sports: 'long-bowls' was played in the Duke of Newcastle's Park.[19]

Not all traditional sports required open space. As in the countryside, so in the town, blood sports were particularly popular. 'Every butcher', according to Wylie, 'was obliged to bait each bull before he slaughtered it'. The rear of the Leather Bottle Inn in Burton Leys was the place to go for bull-baiting, while 'cockpits were connected with the principal inns, and were regularly advertised in the local paper'. Competitions were held. One such match was arranged between London and Nottingham cocks in 1761, but called off when the London cocks were found to be doped. William Frost fitted up a cockpit at the White Lion Inn in 1768. Fights were advertised in the newspapers and continued until 1814. There were also cockpits behind the Lion Inn on Clumber Street, and the Peacock on St Peter's Gate. In March 1814 a contest was advertised at the Lion between Nottinghamshire and Derbyshire for five guineas a battle, with each county providing forty-one cocks.[20]

People would always turn out at the prospect of new ventures. In 1821 several hundred spectators in the Park witnessed an unemployed baker 'perform the arduous task of gathering 100 stones placed at the distance of a yard asunder, with his mouth, and deposited them in a basket'. Would-be entertainers had to run the wrath of the volatile Nottingham crowd if their act went wrong. Thousands gathered on the Forest to witness the first balloon ascent in 1785. Unfortunately Mr Cracknell, the aeronaut,

> had no proper apparatus for generating a sufficient quantity of hydrogen gas, and from twelve to seven o'clock kept the people on the tiptoe of expectation, and so severely tested their patience that they were at length for tossing him into the air. They took the matter into their own hands, and, regardless of the protestations of the unlucky experimenter, cut the cords, and liberated the balloon without an occupant.

They then broke up his equipment to make a bonfire. The balloon was later found at Horncastle. In the event it was 1813 before the first successful balloon flight from the town, when a Mr Sadler took off from the canal wharf. In 1826 a Mr Green took the precaution of completing the 'process of inflation' the day before his ascent, and he turned the occasion to profit by charging 10*s* 6*d* to anyone willing to be elevated above the market-place. He then flew to Edwalton, with a Mr Saywell as passenger. Saywell paid twenty-five guineas for the experience.[21]

What concerned the middle classes was that working-class activities were insufficiently enervating, and that popular pleasures led to a loosening of moral standards. Traditional pastimes came under sustained attack in the years after 1815. Fairs were denounced as being the resort of pickpockets, prostitutes, and others of a criminal disposition. Festivals such as Guy Fawkes' Night and Boxing Day were seen as socially subversive, and massed games of football as senseless disorder. Blood sports, such as bull running, cock-fighting, bear-baiting and ratting, were attacked for their cruelty and for the dishonesty attached to the gambling they attracted. Criticism was backed by legislation, which gradually outlawed animal sports, while the officers of the Royal Society for the Prevention of Cruelty to Animals (formed in the 1830s) made sure that it was enforced. Cock-fighting slowly disappeared in Nottingham, at least openly, although dog-fighting continued in the Meadows until enclosure. Boxing was widely followed, but often illegally. In the 1830s and 1840s William Thompson – 'Bendigo' – and Ben Caunt, a Hucknall miner, were the local heroes. They first fought in 1835, and this contest was followed by a string of other fights down to 1850. Bendigo excelled at all sports, but he also gained a reputation for being drunk and disorderly, and was sent to the House of Correction no fewer than twenty-eight times. Even so, crowds lined the route to his funeral at St Stephen's, Bunkers Hill in 1880. Bendigo's achievements were legendary in the era of bare-knuckle fighting, and he, like other local boxers, was largely backed by publicans, who had replaced the gentry as the patrons of this particular working-class recreation.[22]

The sports which survived were those which enjoyed patronage, or were considered to be socially acceptable. The most obvious example was horse-racing, the first sport in England to become highly organised across the country for the sake of both profit and entertainment. The popularity of racing increased as professional jockeys and thoroughbred horses came to dominate the major meetings, and as courses were shortened. The original Nottingham racecourse, although beginning on the Forest, was four miles in length and ran across much of Lenton and Radford parishes. It was reduced to two miles by Deering's day, although it still extended towards Basford. The annual race meeting traditionally took place on the Forest in July, moving to August by the early nineteenth century, and representing the high point of the town's social calendar. Deering had noted that competition from meetings elsewhere had taken some of the shine off the town's races by the 1740s.[23] If a new stimulus was needed it came from Sir Charles Sedley, MP for the town and a well-known sportsman. Sedley took a pride in ensuring that 'the races were kept up in a style far superior to anything that has been done in that way', and his 'efforts to make this ground rivalled by none ... [were] strongly visible in the fences and other improvements'. Whether it was Sedley's influence or not, by the 1770s landowners for miles around were converging on Nottingham for the annual races. In 1776 Mrs Gawthern noted that the Duke and Duchess of Portland and many other titled families attended the races. Here they encountered, and must literally on occasion have rubbed shoulders with the lower classes, who turned out in considerable numbers to sit on the slopes of the Forest, from where they had a good view of the races. The opportunities for gambling and drinking inevitably helped to raise the popularity of race meetings. Mrs Gawthern was not particularly amused when, in 1798, her postilion imbibed so freely that he was 'very near to overturning Mrs and Miss Wyldes'.[24]

The social mixing which characterised race meetings came under threat as the middle classes sought to control their own social space. Polite society demanded segregation, and by the 1760s grandstands and enclosures were being built at racecourses up and down the country. In 1776 at a meeting held in the White Lion Inn, a subscription was raised, and plans were then drawn by John Carr of York to replicate the grandstand in York. The building was to be 81 feet long with two storeys. On the ground floor there were to be tea and card rooms, and on the upper floor a large room which could be used for entertainment, but which was also designed to give an 'opportunity to see the race-course in every part'. Another 500 people could stand on the roof. Building began in February 1777, and the total cost was £2,460. Subscribers reflected the social élite which hoped to use the grandstand. The dukes of Newcastle, Norfolk and Portland subscribed 200 guineas each; Lord Middleton of Wollaton Hall, Sir George Savile of Rufford, Sir Charles Sedley, and John Musters of Colwick, 100 guineas each. Altogether there were seventy-four subscribers – the minimum subscription was twenty guineas – thirty-one of whom also contributed to the General Hospital in 1781. Apart from the local landowners, they reflected the commercial, business and professional interests of the town, the urban élite: at least six were manufacturers, and the list included four bankers, a merchant, two doctors, five clergymen, four lawyers, one clerk and two wealthy widows.[25] Admission to the grandstand was exclusive by price: in 1781 a single ticket for admission for one week was one guinea. Whether its early attraction was maintained is less clear. In the 1790s Mrs Gawthern wrote of the 'poor' and 'little company', partly a consequence of the quality of the horses being raced, and the fences were reputedly in 'a state of decay'.[26]

The corporation let the racecourse to a consortium in 1777, which controlled meetings until 1845. Following the enclosure of Radford and Lenton in 1798 it laid out a new course known as the Spectacle Course, 'being in the shape of a pair of spectacles, or nearly that of the figure 8'.[27] Attendances revived; in 1806, when Mrs Gawthern's postilion again drank too much, she noted that several local aristocrats and gentlemen were present. However, many patrons thought the view inadequate, and in 1813 the course was altered to an oval shape.[28] In 1829 the consortium moved the meeting from August to October. This was not particularly popular, especially in 1844 when the races clashed with Goose Fair. William Parsons was most put out:

> Called at the office and went thence to the races with [son] Fred which are this year very inconveniently and to the great dissatisfaction of the Townspeople held at the same time as the Fair. The people refused to subscribe and there was no Town Plate to run for in consequence. The races were however pretty numerously attended and there was some good running. Dined at my Father's about 3 and went into the Fair after and got home in good time.

He managed to fit in office, races and fair again the following day.[29] Despite opposition to the rescheduling of the meeting, the race ball was well patronised. In 1839 it was 'attended by a large assembly of the beauty and fashion of the neighbourhood, the dancing having been kept up with great spirit till a late hour'.[30] In 1845 the corporation exercised its right to cancel the consortium lease in the event of enclosure, and it immediately restored the races to August.[31] Samuel Collinson attended the first meeting under the new regulations on 5 August 1846:

> The weather glorious, the hillside covered with merrymakers enjoying themselves, some under cover of the booths, others with better taste preferred to sun themselves

> in the open air and breathe the invigorating breeze. On the low ground amongst the carriages from any indications that the deportment of the people offered a spectator might just as easily have judged that the crowd was collected to attend a political meeting as a mere holiday or recreation, so much quiet gravity, almost solemnity, pervades the middle and upper classes of this country. On the hill side among the humble classes, you would find more of what would remind you of what you have been accustomed to consider as Merry England. Good humoured groups sat on the green turf joking, laughing and passing round mugs of Nottingham ale, looked as happy as if they never had been and never would be 'shut up' from morn to dewy eve in close factories or closer attics barely able by long hours and hard work to earn enough to sustain existence.

In 1853 a Spring meeting was introduced, despite some opposition from the corporation.[32]

Nottingham's meetings illustrated many of the problems which middle-class reformers associated with horse-racing. They were largely a male activity associated with drinking and gambling, and they were the haunt of pickpockets and other social undesirables. This naturally offended the evangelicals, but racing was too well embedded in the annual calendar to be restricted. In 1847 the Ten Hour Act regulated working hours, and with the movement towards workshop and factory production in the Nottingham textile industries during the 1850s employers began to grant a half-day holiday for the races. This did not please the upstanding Wesleyan Methodist George Harwood, who wrote scathingly in his diary on 16 July 1861 that:

> Being the 'Nottingham Summer Meeting' of race-horses, gambler, blacklegs and scoundrels of every description, a half-day's holiday is vouchsafed to work-people in general. Not having any particular wish to mix up with the aforementioned respectable society, I embraced the opportunity of going … in a cart, on a journey of observation and pleasure to Stanton Iron Works.[33]

Collinson was equally uneasy, writing in 1856 of the 'villainous looking set' he encountered at the races, and the following year remarking on how 'men well known, occupying respectable positions, aye, married men, sitting in the drinking places at the stand, with an assemblage of whores, standing treat and hail fellow well met'.[34] On the other hand racing was regarded as an acceptable 'rational' recreation for the working classes because it could be regulated, particularly when, from the 1870s, enclosed racecourses were built which charged entry fees. By then racing was in decline. Off-course betting was made illegal in 1853 and over the following decades many courses closed, or were replaced by purpose-built enclosed courses. Open courses such as the Forest began to seem anachronistic, and the last meeting was held on 30 September 1890. Racing moved to a new course at Colwick, and the grandstand was demolished in 1912.[35]

Racing survived industrialisation despite the concerns, particularly of the evangelicals, and partly no doubt because in Nottingham it took place on land which was appropriated neither before nor after enclosure for development. Consequently it did not represent a threat to business interests in the town. The same could not be said of Goose Fair. Annual fairs came under attack after 1815 because of their association with disorderliness, drunkenness and immorality, but reformers had to take into account the charter rights which governed fairs, as well as their commercial functions. Fairs began to assume a distinctively urban form with business activities taking place alongside booths, peep shows and exhibits of natural and unnatural rarities and monstrosities. Pressure for suppression came mainly from evangelical and dissenting groups, aided by ratepayers and business interests who considered them to be an intolerable interruption of business. Traditionally Goose Fair began on St Matthew's Day, 21 September, but with the national calendar change in 1752 and the loss of ten days, it moved to early October. Traditionally also it was a produce and livestock market. However, attractions in 1805 included a lion, a Bengal tiger and tigress, four kangaroos from Botany Bay, panthers, beavers, a leopard and leopardess, wolves from the Alps and muscovy cats. 1805 also saw the first appearance of Wombwell's Menagerie, which was to return annually for more than a century. Mrs Gilbert recalled 'the glory of Wombwell's first magnificent collection. We owed much to Wombwell in our knowledge of the forms and habits of the savage beasts of the forest, of the curious ruminants from the East, of the gay-plumaged birds of the tropics, of the deadly reptiles.'[36] Here she summed up one of the problems for would-be reformers: the educational aspect of the fairground, of which rational recreationalists could only approve. It was the pure entertainments that the reformers attacked, and in 1813 the magistrates refused to allow 'those disgraceful and dangerous machines called merry go rounds' on to the site.

As a result, shows rather than rides were the main attraction for much of the nineteenth century, together with stalls which extended all the way to Chapel Bar. Madame Tussaud brought her famed collection of life-size wax figures to the town in both 1819 and 1829, displaying them in the Exchange. In 1819 she stayed for two months. By 1821 the local press was complaining about the number of shows and the space they were taking up, but no one seems seriously to have questioned the survival of the fair, despite the prominence of dissenters on the corporation and the success of fairground opponents elsewhere. William Howitt's view was that Goose Fair was too well entrenched: 'in the country, for many miles around, this fair is looked forward to by young and old, with views of business and recreation, for months: and what was done, and said, and seen at Goose Fair; who was met there, and what matches were made, serve for conversation for months afterwards'.[37] Howitt has left a vivid description of preparations for Goose Fair. 'Huge caravans incessantly arrive, with their wild beasts, theatricals, dwarfs, giants and other prodigies and wonders.' They were followed by 'covered wagons, containing the contents of sundry bazaars', and

> caravan after caravan, cart after cart, long troop of horses tied head and tail, and groups of those wild and peculiar-looking people, that are as necessary to a fair as flowers are to May; – all kinds of strollers, beggars, gipsies, singers, dancers, players on harps, Indian jugglers, Punch and Judy exhibitors and similar wandering artists and professors.

He witnessed the opening of the fair with the mayor and aldermen in their robes and with the 'mace borne and the trumpet blown before them, and the beadles with their staves behind'. Once it was declared open the market-place became 'one mass of moving people and unintermitted din' with animals, comedians, machines, panoramas, prodigies, musicians, and an array of other performances.[38] Mrs Gilbert recalled the fair as a family occasion in the 1830s and 1840s: 'everybody kept open house; the utmost bonhomie prevailed; the schools had a week's holiday'.[39]

Far from suffering any decline, the popularity of Goose Fair increased during the 1840s when visitors began to arrive by train. Mechanical roundabouts appeared by the 1870s, and by 1900 railways were bringing more than 50,000 people into Nottingham during the fair. The showmen tightened their grip on the fair, and its trading function gradually disappeared.[40] Sydney Race described it in 1892:

> All down these streets and Long Row and all around the market were ice cream sellers, cocoa nut galleries, shooting galleries, various games of chance, toy fruit and sweet stalls, phonographs, trial of strength machines, galvanise batteries and the like. These phonographs were new things attached to a little centre machine were a number of tubs each having a little bulb at the end to fit into the car.[41]

His comment on the phonograph is a reminder that many people had their first introduction to technical and mechanical inventions at the fair. In 1895 an empty shop on Long Row was temporarily converted to display Mr Eddison's Kinetoscope Machine, a sort of peep-show in which individuals could witness motion pictures. The cinematograph, which combined the kinetoscope with the magic lantern to project moving pictures on to a screen for a large audience, was demonstrated at Goose Fair in 1897, although it had been seen in July the previous year at the Grand Theatre in Hyson Green. In the last years of the 1890s Captain Payne's electric bioscope rivalled Collins Living Pictures in attracting an audience to watch moving pictures. In 1899 Payne's show advertised 'steadiness and no flickering'. Showmen adapted new technology to bring their amusements up to date. With the introduction of steam power the 1904 Goose Fair featured three and four abreast galloping horse roundabouts, steam yachts and gondolas. Rides were larger and more adventurous. The 'cake walk' was introduced in 1909.[42] To compete with cinemas showmen filmed the market day, which then became a great crowd-puller when shown at the Fair.

Not everyone appreciated the romance of the Fair. Samuel Collinson complained in October 1858 of 'the usual assemblage of vagabonds of all sorts coming into the town preparatory for the fair tomorrow'. This did not stop him from attending, although he stayed at home in 1860 and again in 1861 because of 'the row and noise'.[43] Asmodeus, who described in detail the 1860 Fair Collinson avoided, complained of the tricksters, impostors and thieves who were attracted to Nottingham for the festivities. Yet even a strict Methodist like George Harwood could not keep away: in 1861 his lace factory was closed for two days and he 'went with my wife, children and servant, through the Fair, and bought a few articles for amusement and use'.[44] Harwood's firm, like many others, granted their employees a holiday for Goose Fair, but by the 1870s the disruption to business was causing concern. In 1875 the Market Traders' Association lodged a protest against the roundabouts, and demanded a curtailment of the Fair. They won an unexpected victory when it was cut from eight to five days (to begin on a Tuesday rather than a Sunday). As one councillor put it, Goose Fair was 'a source of annoyance to many respectable inhabitants of the town, rather than a gratification'.[45] An enquiry was launched in 1878 'to collect and tabulate evidence as to the moral, social, sanitary and commercial effects of Goose Fair, upon the town'. In July 1879 the Nottingham Town and County Social Guild pointed out the disadvantages to trade, health, temperance and morals of Goose Fair, and unsuccessfully asked the corporation to cut it to one day. By contrast, the manager of a factory in Burton Street argued that the fair was 'a necessary relief from the cares and toils of business and the foul atmosphere of factory life'. The abolitionists gained a token victory in 1880 when it was reduced to three days, beginning on the first Thursday of October.[46]

Local newspapers continued to carry objections from disgruntled townspeople. Even the Roman Catholic bishop weighed in for the 1897 Fair, complaining about the organised 'rushes' of the crowd. Sydney Race knew about these:

> The crush is maintained by strings of young people … who go up and down [Beastmarket Hill] in two rows occasionally colliding and frequently getting up a rush which culminates in a sudden stop and consequent knot of heads and bodies. Three or four policemen stride up and down the hill and land any particularly energetic gentlemen out into outer darkness with a roughness which amuses every body but the party principally concerned.[47]

The bishop's view was simple:

> it does not appear to me to be a modest or decent thing that young women should voluntarily allow themselves to be crushed up and carried along in a dense crowd of all people, nor can I believe that it can be otherwise than very dangerous to their purity. I fear many a girl owes her first fall into sin, and subsequent ruin, to the crowded rushes in Goose Fair.[48]

In the longer term the fair had to change, but because of practical considerations rather than moral fears. The traditional Victorian layout of the market-place was altered in 1900 to accommodate the electric tram. Shows had to be banned from the pavement on Long Row. In their place came 'an appreciable addition' of roundabouts, although the swing boats were 'conspicuous by their absence'. The public perception of the fair was also changing. Rowdy conditions led many people either to avoid the event or, by the time of the First World War, to avoid the market place after 7.00 p.m. But there was never any shortage of alternative entertainment. The theatres and variety halls put on special programmes for Goose Fair to attract revellers already in the town.[49]

Industrialisation gave Goose Fair a new format but it survived, as did other traditional occasions. Among them, 5 November was perhaps the most important popular holiday in the annual calendar. Fireworks had been introduced by the middle of the nineteenth century. In 1863 George Harwood treated his son Tommy to some 'wheels and crackers. He also fired off his little cannon several times.'[50] Christmas survived, to be transformed by the Victorians. Mrs Gawthern usually spent the day with friends, dining and playing cards, and William Parsons' Christmas was much the same in 1838. However, in 1843 he 'decked my cottage with Holly and Ivy', and most years thereafter he entertained carol singers. Parsons dreamed of a white Christmas although, as today, the occasion was more likely to be damp, mild or foggy, and for many people snow was far from welcome. The hard winter of 1860 brought a white Christmas, but with gas meters and the water supply frozen, the frost, snow and biting wind on Christmas Day brought 'painful distress' among the homeless and poor: 'to many of whom Christmas has brought but little mirth or festive cheer', Parsons wrote in his diary.[51] The Methodist George Harwood refused to adapt to the Victorian Christmas: in the 1860s he regularly spent the morning of 25 December at the annual meeting of the United Friendly Society of Halifax Place Chapel.

Although some traditional working-class recreational activities disappeared during industrialisation, they were quickly replaced. Gardening, in one form or another, had long been popular. Numerous gardens were provided on the outskirts of the town by the corporation and by private landowners including the Duke of Newcastle and Earl Manvers. William Miles observed in 1843 that 'the poorer inhabitants of Nottingham ... seem, instead of frequenting the pot-house, to work early and late in the gardens'.[52] James Orange planned cottage garden cultivation 'to encourage industry, education, temperance and morality'; according to William Howitt in 1838 there were more than 5,000 allotments containing, as single gardens, 400 square yards each, with about 500 acres altogether given over to allotments; and the Chartist land companies helped to boost the movement in Nottingham. In 1853 there were more than 7,000 allotments, including the Hunger Hill rose-gardens which were 'known far and wide for the wonderful richness and variety of their bloom'.[53] Perhaps because so many of the allotments were outside the boundaries of the old town, they seem never to have been squeezed for space in the manner which occurred elsewhere.

With so much interest, it is no surprise to find that a number of gardening societies flourished in the town. The Notts. Horticultural and Botanical Society was formed and held its first show in 1761. In 1825 it became the Nottingham Floral and Horticultural Society, and by 1856 was holding its shows in the Arboretum. The St Ann's and Nottingham Amateur Floral and Horticultural Society, known as the St Ann's Floral Society, held its first show in 1858. By 1864 it was promoting the St Ann's and All England Rose Show, which was, for many years, the excuse for a festive procession involving stalls, hawkers, men on stilts, street performers, and even Swiss dancing bears, all of which gave the impression of a fair. The Society (and its roses!) flourished, and in 1896 and 1897 held its annual show in the

Plate 46 **Allotments**. The Hungerhill gardens provided many residents of the lower part of the town, particularly in the St Ann's area, with fresh air and the facilities of a small garden. Many of the allotment holders, including Mr and Mrs G. Bell, shown here, erected summerhouses where they could entertain, or just take tea! From the mid-Victorian period the area became famous for the quality of its roses. The improvised greenhouses of the working men who spent much of their limited free time here produced blooms which astonished enthusiasts: the rose expert Dean Hole of Caunton considered the finest rose he ever saw to have been grown on the Hungerhills – and displayed in an old bottle!

market-place, before moving to the Coppice recreation ground the following year. Perhaps because of Nottingham's reputation, the Royal Horticultural Society held its annual exhibition in the Park between 27 June and 1 July 1871. Between 15,000 and 20,000 visitors attended, and the St Ann's Society displayed its cut roses on 1 July.[54]

For some years the St Ann's rose show was held in a pub, the General Cathcart, and it is no surprise to find that the working classes, unable or unwilling to build separate premises, held their clubs in public houses. For middle-class reformers this posed a problem. Many were convinced that for the new working classes the public house was their prime source of entertainment, and that this was a cause for concern as to both their moral and physical welfare. In the 1760s Nottingham had 151 licensed premises, with no fewer than seventeen taverns or alehouses on the north side of Long Row between Clumber Street and Chapel Bar. By 1799 the town had 156 inns and public houses, and a drinking place for approximately every 185 men, women and children. The total increased to 182 in 1815 and to 382 by 1865.[55] Drink was, in fact, integral to working-class life. It was a painkiller, a morale-booster, a sleeping-draught, and a medicine. And some public houses undoubtedly had sinister reputations, particularly those associated with the hosiery industry. The occupations of publican and small-scale hosier seem often to have been combined. Isaac Johnson, landlord of the King's Head in Narrow Marsh, owned seven frames in 1844–45, hiring them to men who received board and lodging at the inn in part-payment for their services. Absolem Barnett condemned the practice of paying wages in pubs:

> Abject wretchedness is induced by the practice of a lower order of master settling the account of wages with their journeymen at a public house. The cost of liquor drunk during the week, and of food obtained, on the credit of the master, at the small shop, is deducted from a scanty pittance, and this is sometimes further reduced by the expense of a drunken debauch.[56]

Yet retail outlets for alcoholic refreshment were far more than simple drinking establishments. Hostelries ranged from coaching inns such as The Maypole in Long Row, The White Lion on Clumber Street and The Blackamoor's Head on High Street, to the numerous taverns and bars providing places for entertainment and business. Inns were the focal point of transport systems and places where news was disseminated. In 1832 thirty-five coaches ran daily from The Lion Hotel, The Black Boy, The Maypole, and The Milton's Head. Country carriers operated from inns: in 1846 275 carriers from Nottingham started from 47 separate hostelries. Public houses were meeting places for societies. The Glee Club met at The Poultry Hotel and the New Amateur Musical Society met at The Durham Ox. Practically all the pubs had concert rooms as well as makeshift stages to cater for plays, singing and lectures. Pubs were also the setting for money clubs and friendly societies. The Oddfellows met at The Three Salmons and The Eight Bells. Sporting, political and trade union organisations used pubs, including the Chartist demonstrators of the 1830s and 1840s. Trade unions met exclusively in public houses. Many public houses also had a skittle alley in the backyard, and sometimes a bowling green. Quoits and other games were the nineteenth-century equivalent of darts.[57]

Nor were pubs antithetical to education and learning. Just as the middle classes had an educational and improving angle to their leisure activities, so they tried to impart the same values to the working classes, primarily through mechanics' institutes and libraries. An Artisans' Library was founded in 1824, and the Nottingham Operatives' Library originated in the Rancliffe Arms on Sussex Street in 1835. Entrance was usually 6*d* and subscriptions 1*d* a week. By 1844 it had 1,600 volumes and, by 1853, 2,200, when there were 200 members. Other branches were set up in the King George on Horseback in King Street, and the Pheasant on Charlotte Street, both in 1836, the Queen Adelaide on Mansfield Road in 1841, the Cricket Players in Hyson Green in 1843, and the White Swan on Alfreton Road in 1844. The branches held in total more than 5,000 books in 1850, and 8,000 by 1893.[58]

In a very real sense public houses were the hub of working-class leisure and entertainment, but this was no consolation to the middle classes, who preferred to drink in the comfort of their own homes. Various attempts were made by local magistrates to restrict the hours and conditions of public houses. In November 1817 a search was carried out of all the town's public houses for illegal bagatelle boards or other forbidden gaming devices. At the same time instructions were issued to the effect that all public houses were to be closed by 11.00 p.m., and restrictions were placed on Sunday opening hours. The position changed again in 1830. For various reasons, some of them related to an increase in spirit drinking, the government passed the Beer Act which allowed any ratepayer to sell beer as long as they obtained a magistrate's licence at a cost of £2. Since the duties on beer were repealed at the same time, the legislation ushered in forty years of free trade in beer. The result was a proliferation of retail outlets. Nottingham had 180 drinking establishments by 1828, 225 in 1832, including forty-six beerhouses licensed under the new legislation, and 389 in 1864, of which 169 were beerhouses. After the boundary extension of 1877 there were 600 hostelries in the town.[59]

One of the major responses to the 1830 Beer Act was the development of the temperance movement, which sought to exert pressure on Parliament through the Central Association for Stopping the Sale of Intoxicating Liquor on Sundays. Nottingham had eight temperance inns in 1832, and thirteen by 1853. A Teetotal Society was formed in 1851, and a temperance operatives library was founded by a coffee-house proprietor in direct competition with the Rancliffe Arms Library. In 1853 the People's Hall was opened, partly as a counter-attraction to the public house, and incorporating a library, a reading room and a lecture hall. George Gill, the founder, hoped that 'intellectual pursuits and mental improvements might be substituted for the attractions of the tavern', and he aimed to attract friendly societies, money clubs, and other societies which he believed often met in pubs for want of alternative accommodation. Membership of People's Hall reached 450 in 1856, but declined to 300 in 1869. Nationally, the Sabbatarians achieved a victory for temperance when in 1854 Sunday opening hours were cut to 12.30–2.30 p.m. and 6.00–10.00 p.m.

Part of the problem for the Nottingham temperance movement was the attitude of the corporation. The Nottingham Licensed Victuallers' Protection Association was established in 1840 to safeguard the interests of the trade, and Thomas Wakefield, who had been the first mayor of the reformed corporation, presided over its annual dinner in 1843. The result of this relationship was clear in 1859, when a petition with 1,288 signatures was presented to the corporation opposing the licensing of public houses on the Forest. The petition referred to 'the vast amount of drunkenness in our midst, with its attendant consequences of poverty, crime, disease and premature death', but the corporation was unmoved, merely recording receipt of the petition in its minutes. In 1872 all drinking places were put under the oversight of licensing justices. For the first time since 1832 the number of permitted outlets was brought under control, and the local temperance movement enjoyed a revival. In 1878 the Nottingham Temperance Mission was formed as a local branch of the Church of England Temperance Society. Volunteer workers visited lodging houses, held gospel and temperance meetings including Band of Hope and Sunday School meetings, created drum and fife bands, and promoted mothers' meetings and sewing classes. Many of these activities took place in premises on Popham Street, Leenside, until they were demolished in the late 1880s to make way for the Great Northern Railway. In broad terms the temperance movement was never very effective. The most significant reduction in the number of public houses in Nottingham came not through the efforts of the temperance movement but because in 1896–98 twenty-six were demolished during redevelopment for the Great Central Railway.[60]

New leisure interests from the 1830s

The middle-class concern with rational recreation grew out of the movement to ensure that its own leisure activities were morally enervating. From the 1830s it increasingly turned into a programme designed to improve the leisure pursuits of the working classes, but it also started to alter as the activities favoured by the middle classes, particularly from mid-century in regard to sport, began to change. While rational recreation was never an organised movement, the various groups involved had a general distaste for public, annual and customary practices which upset the business life of the community, the work ethic, and middle-class notions of decorous behaviour. Regulated amusement was regarded as a safety valve for social disaffection, and the rational recreationalists looked to extend middle-class leisure interests to the working classes. As we have seen, artisan libraries with branches in pubs paralleled the subscription libraries of the middle classes, and mechanics' institutes, with their emphasis on education, paralleled literary and philosophical societies even if they rapidly became recreational rather than educational in emphasis.

The Nottingham Mechanics Institute was founded at a meeting in the Guildhall on 30 October 1837, with John Smith Wright as first president. It began life in a house in St James's Street, and twenty-eight lectures were given to Institute members in 1838. A Mechanics Exhibition was held in the Exchange in 1840 to raise money, and after the president donated land, spacious accommodation was erected on Mansfield Road. The lecture hall had seating for 1,000 people, and the building included a library, classrooms and a small museum. However, the Mechanics attracted the lower middle class rather than the working classes for whom it was intended. In 1850 236 out of the 579 members were described as clerks, warehousemen and shopmen. Most members were interested in recreational rather than educational pursuits, although lectures were well attended. Lecturers in the early years included Frank Waldo Emerson and Charles Dickens (who returned a number of times). Samuel Collinson heard Dickens read *Christmas Carol* in 1858, which he thought 'a great treat'. Jenny Lind, the Swedish nightingale, was among the singers who performed at the Mechanics: James Hopkinson likened her voice to 'a melodious flute and the vibrations thereof sent a thrill of rapture ... through the audience'.[61]

The Mechanics was an extension of rational recreation for the middle classes, but quite new as an improving concept in the mid-nineteenth century was the Arboretum. Derby, in 1840, was the first English town to acquire an arboretum, and the same principles were adopted in Nottingham with the intention of creating a botanical garden. The designer Samuel Curtis created a parkland with an artificial lake and an aviary. Existing trees were made to blend in with the site, and plants and flowers were labelled with information about their country of origin and details of size. The corporation's surveyor, H. Moses Wood, designed the refreshment rooms. The Arboretum opened on 11 May 1852 with a procession of civic dignitaries in what the *Illustrated London News* termed a 'festive atmosphere'.[62] The total cost was £6,554. Initially the grounds were open free on Sunday, Monday and Wednesday, and on other days to subscribers. Family subscription was £1 a year, and individual subscription 5*s* annually. Non-subscribers were to pay an entrance fee of 6*d*, or 3*d* for children, on fee-paying days. Considerable opposition was mounted to these charges, and they were abandoned after five years under pressure from ratepayers, and partly because they were of dubious legality. As with the Mechanics, it proved difficult to maintain the idea of the Arboretum as a place of educational improvement: Samuel Collinson noted with regret that 'the Arboretum seems to be merely a huge playground for young girls and boys'.[63]

Collinson summed up the problem faced by the middle classes in their efforts to guide working-class leisure interests, and it was a problem which multiplied as living standards rose and shorter working hours brought a recognisable leisure element into the lives of even the poorest of the town's workers. The emphasis moved towards positively aiding the working classes, and legislation which encouraged the setting-up of public facilities included the Museums Act of 1845, the Baths and Washhouses Act of 1846, and the Free Libraries Act of 1850. Under the 1850 Act libraries could be established provided the ratepayers showed their willingness in a ballot. It took three petitions from Nottingham schoolteachers and local ratepayers before a public library was opened in Thurland Street on 13 April 1868 on a temporary basis in the disused Artisans' Library. The argument in favour of the library was based on the premise that 'the more … the rudiments of knowledge are disseminated among labourers in the general field of employment, the more triumphs will be achieved. As we sow, so shall we reap.' A reference library was added two years later. The public library moved to purpose-built premises on South Sherwood Street in 1881, and by 1900 six branch libraries and a children's library had been established.[64]

The first free museum was set up in 1867 to house a natural history collection which the corporation inherited after a fire at the Mechanics Institute. Under the terms of the 1874 Improvement Act the corporation gained powers to lease the burnt-out shell of the Castle. Between 1876 and 1878 T. C. Hine turned the gutted Renaissance palace into the first provincial museum of fine art. It was opened on 3 July 1878 by the Prince of Wales and was, according to the town clerk 'a monument of municipal progress'. Initially an entrance fee was charged, but in 1890 two free days a week were introduced.[65]

The first public baths were opened on 16 December 1850 on New Bath Street, but William Parsons, a member of the Public Baths Committee in 1851, did not warm to them:

> Visited the public baths in the Evening. My attendance at these Baths has always been either as Visitor or Committee man, as the want of change of water more frequently in the large Bath (which is only changed once a week although above 1000 Bathers use it in that time) and the want of cleanliness in the small Baths have deterred me from being a Bather. The management at present is not efficient though much improved.[66]

Samuel Collinson went to the Turkish bath in 1861, part of the public baths complex, and 'very conveniently fitted up, heat of first room 120 degrees, second room 140 degrees, all is arranged very comfortably and the effect produced upon the body after the bath is very pleasant'.[67] Further public baths were opened towards the end of the century, notably Radford Baths, following the borough extension, in June 1880.

Libraries, museums and baths were examples of the move towards regulated leisure activities by the later nineteenth century, and they reflected also an increasing interest in communal leisure among the middle classes. Having drifted away from the town centre since the turn of the century, they began once again to take an interest in theatre and music. If there is a symbolic moment in the development of middle-class leisure interests in Victorian Nottingham it was the opening on 25 September 1865 of the Theatre Royal. Built in six months at a cost of £15,000 by two Nottingham (Anglican) industrialists, the Lambert brothers, and with seating for 2,200 patrons, it was designed in the manner of Nash's Haymarket Theatre by C. J. Phipps of London, and was intended to be 'a place of innocent recreation and of moral and intellectual culture'. Sir Robert Clifton, MP, was in the audience at the first performance. The opening programme was Sheridan's *School for Scandal*. As the curtain went up the manager, Mr Montgomery, told the audience that the theatre was to be a place of 'intellectual recreation', but the sensibilities of the town's dissenters led to objections, particularly to the renaming of Sheep Lane – which ran between the market-place and the new theatre – as Theatre Street. George Harwood noted that 'Baxter, minister of Sion Chapel, has proclaimed war from his pulpit. And our superintendent at the meeting of the Evangelical Alliance this week spoke very strongly on the subject.' The corporation bowed to these sensitivities and decreed that the newly-widened street would be called Market Street.[68]

The theatre became an active centre of local culture, with a programme including everything from farce to Shakespeare, and an annual post-Christmas pantomime. Sydney Race was at the pantomime in 1897 when Dick Whittington was performed:

> I fancy that the panto has not been doing so well this year. It was very incomplete, for one thing, on the opening night and the papers slated it while the people who went the first week or two spread a bad opinion of it. For my part I think it much better than last year's and came away quite pleased while we both had some hearty laughs, which was not so before.[69]

Race compared what he saw to events at the Grand in Hyson Green, also built to designs by C. J. Phipps. Funded by R. J. Morrison, a town councillor heavily involved in the post-1880 development of Hyson Green, the Grand opened its doors for the first time on 1 February 1886 when J. W. Turner's English Opera Company produced *Maritana*. The building was lit with gas. The Grand was famous for its water effects; on occasions the whole stage was converted into a lake, complete with boats and waterfalls. It flourished under the management of J.R. Mulholland from 1888 until the mid-1890s, with a range of entertainment including operas and plays. After Mulholland left the quality of the productions declined, and the Grand became chiefly the home of melodrama, which may have been more suited to the tastes of its predominantly working-class audience.[70]

The revival of theatre was matched by the revival of music. The Sacred Harmonic Society was founded in 1856 by a group of vocalists, and gave its first performance – *The Messiah* – in January 1857. The building of the Albert Hall, opened in 1876, provided the town with what was claimed to be 'the finest concert hall in the Midland counties', with seating for 2,550 people. The hall, designed by local architect Watson Fothergill and originally intended as a Temperance Hall (although the function changed before it was completed), opened with a performance of Handel's *Messiah*, in which an augmented Sacred Harmonic Society provided the chorus. It became the Albert Hall Methodist Mission in 1902. After a disastrous fire on 22 April 1906, the Hall was rebuilt to a design by A. E. Lambert with substantial financial support from Jesse Boot. As a result the enlarged hall, with its new Binns organ, reopened in March 1909. Boot's donation was conditional on popular organ recitals being given on Saturday afternoons, and concerts on Saturday evenings, with cheap seats to attract the working classes.[71]

Sport provides perhaps the clearest example of the movement towards regulating the leisure activities of the working classes in the second half of the nineteenth century. Until the mid-nineteenth century the middle classes had been wary of sporting activity, which they associated with the excesses of the aristocracy, and the unruliness of traditional rural pursuits, many of them associated with animals. However, the transformation of sport in the hands of the public schools during the 1850s had a profound affect throughout society. Sport now came to be seen as an instrument of physical health and social discipline. Football was traditionally played without rules or pitch, and frequently upset trade where games took place in town centres on calendar holidays. In the 1850s and 1860s it took on a new format, and the result can most clearly be seen in the emergence of the professional game, particularly the formation in the 1860s of Nottingham's two football clubs. A group of businessmen and cricketers, meeting in the Lion Hotel on Clumber Street in 1862, agreed to form the Notts. County Football Club. Football was still a middle-class sport, and Notts. County played their early games in the Park. From the 1880s until the Meadow Lane ground opened in 1910 they played their home matches on the Trent Bridge cricket ground. Nottingham Forest was formed in 1865 by a group of young people attached to St Andrew's Church on Mansfield

Road, and naturally they played their games on the Forest, hence the name. More than 4,000 spectators turned out for the first match against Notts. County, played on the Forest in 1866. Forest won 1–0. They moved from the Forest in 1879 and played at a number of grounds in Lenton and the Meadows, including Trent Bridge (1880–82), before settling at the City Ground in 1898. Crowd misbehaviour was not unknown. When Forest played Derby on Goose Fair Saturday 1886 at their ground on Bathley Street, just off Arkwright Street, a crowd of 17,000 went out of control, and the referee had to abandon the game. Forest beat Derby to win the FA Cup at the Crystal Palace in 1898: 'Sailor' Capes, who scored the first Forest goal, won a bicycle as a reward.[72]

Cricket became another popular working-class sport. The earliest game known to have been played in Nottingham was in 1771 with a match against Sheffield, but it is only from 1789 that reliable records exist relating to matches played locally. In August 1791 a match was played in the Meadows between the gentlemen of the Marylebone Club in London and the Nottingham team. Ten thousand spectators watched. The Marylebone Club won a two-innings match with something to spare, and then insisted on an additional game in which their eleven players took on twenty-two of Nottingham. It made no difference to the result: 'the style of play of their aristocratic competitors was new and irresistible'. Matches were played in the Meadows until a new ground was laid out on the Forest in 1815. A match was played there in 1817 between twenty-two of the Nottingham club, and eleven of England, for a purse of 500 guineas, which Nottingham won.[73] William Howitt has left a vivid description of the match between Nottinghamshire and Sussex on the Forest in September 1835. The match was announced in the *Nottingham Review* on 4 September. Admission to the grandstand was 2*s*, but the majority of spectators sat on the Forest slopes without paying. Stalls and booths, offering betting, food and games, were much in evidence, but both Howitt, and the newspapers, commented on the general good humour of the crowd. Here is Howitt:

> The booths and tents were occupied with a dense mass of people, all as silent as the ground beneath them; and all up the hill were groups, and on the race-stand an eager, forward-leaning throng. There were said to be twenty thousand people, all hushed as death, except when some exploit of the players produced a thunder of applause.[74]

Years later Mrs Gilbert also recalled the match:

> The slopes from the windmill-crowned crests down to the race-course resembled a military encampment; for the white tents for refreshment and various other purposes were dotted about in every direction ... . As the multitude squatted on the patches of sward watching the play and hailing with exultant shouts the achievements of the players, the white tents, the greenery, the wide expanse, and the clock-clack of the windmills appeared with fine effect to the senses and the imagination.[75]

Nottingham won by three wickets.

Cricket was a spectator sport but, like football, as it became professionalised and commercialised, it moved away from open areas where large crowds could watch free of charge into regulated grounds where spectators paid an admission fee. In Nottingham this was the Trent Bridge ground, laid out by William Clarke in 1838. Born in 1798 and trained as a bricklayer, Clarke became landlord of the Bell Inn in the market-place, and then married Mrs Chapman, landlady of the Trent Bridge Inn. The first county match was played at Trent Bridge in 1838, and Clarke charged 6*d*, to which the working classes – used to watching their cricket free – objected. Perhaps as a result, only ten major matches took place at Trent Bridge before Clarke left in 1846 to become a professional bowler on the staff at Lords.[76] Clarke may have departed, but cricket had now come of age in terms of respectability. For the rational recreationalists successful regulation was measured in terms of behaviour.[77] Moving the spectators into regulated grounds helped the process, and by 1866 Trent Bridge was said to be 'always in excellent condition', and available for letting to responsible parties, who were advised that 'the charge for using it may be ascertained at the adjoining public house'. However, judging from Samuel Collinson's occasional comments, the game lacked atmosphere. What had been a popular, and free, activity, if one associated with drink and gambling, was now regularised. When George Harwood went to Trent Bridge to see 'for the first time in my life a professional cricket match' in July 1866, he noted that 'the playing was in every respect most admirable'. As a closed ground it was also suitable for other events such as boxing.[78]

Plate 47 **Trent Bridge Cricket Ground**. Demonstration by lady cyclists, 1903. The famous cricket ground, laid out by William Clarke in the 1830s, has been used for many purposes in the past. Both Notts. County and Nottingham Forest played some of their games here prior to settling at their current permanent grounds

The county cricket championship began in 1873, and by the 1880s the Nottinghamshire team almost monopolised the championship despite a rift between committee and players which led to seven of the latter being temporarily sacked, an event which gave William Gunn (still commemorated in the firm of cricket equipment makers Gunn & Moore) an opportunity to break into the side. Gunn, born in St Ann's, was also a successful footballer for Notts. County. Among the more avid supporters was the architect Watson Fothergill, who arranged his London visits in the 1880s to coincide with the county's matches in the capital.[79]

Football and cricket, the latter in particular, were both spectator sports, but both had a participatory following often connected with a range of organisations designed to shape the values and behaviour of young men through youth clubs and semi-military organisations, the principle being that idle hands would otherwise find mischievous work. Some of the mission clergymen in late nineteenth-century Nottingham, among them the Revd Selwyn Freer at St Catherine's, encouraged wholesome recreation, sometimes known as muscular Christianity. Just as significant were the efforts of the middle classes to organise the leisure interests of working-class adolescents, particularly through the Boys' Brigade and the Scouting movements. The Boys' Brigade, founded in 1883, was introduced into Nottingham in 1888 by John A. Dixon JP. The North Nottingham Institute, comprising the four parishes of St Mark, St Luke, St Ann and St Andrew, formed a company in October 1888. Initially the activities were confined to bible classes and drill, but later band practices with drums and fifes were introduced. Antagonism among nonconformists towards the military methods of the brigades led in 1899 to the establishment of the Boys' Life Brigade by Revd J. B. Paton. The intention was to teach life-saving drill without military methods of the Boys' Brigade.[80]

Sports clubs proliferated in the late nineteenth century, with their own membership regulations and fees, and their own approach to competition. The River Trent remained a focus of water-sports activities with an Aquatic Club, regattas, several rowing clubs (1862–71) and, in 1887, a sailing club. Thomas Hawksley pointed out in 1844 that the town lacked any proper 'open bathing places'. People swam in the River Trent in warm weather, 'but neither very decently nor very safely'; indeed, more than fifty people had drowned in the river in recent years.[81] This did not apparently deter others, and in 1857 the corporation provided changing facilities at Trent Bridge. The Nottingham Swimming Club was formed in 1880. Cycling was popular, a reassuring local boost for a growing industry in which lace mechanics were switching their skills to manufacturing and assembling cycles. The Nottingham Cycling Club, the second oldest in Britain, was founded in 1876, and held races at Trent Bridge. During the 1880s Frank Bowden's rapidly expanding Raleigh Cycle Company became a national leader in style and innovation. In 1892 no fewer than 2,300 prizes were won worldwide on Raleigh bicycles, including the world championship. Cycling clubs abounded, with numerous competitions, especially on bank holidays. A cycle exhibition was held in the Albert Hall in 1897.[82]

The specialist clubs were not alone in promoting sporting activities. The Mechanics Institute was the focal point of many recreational pursuits, including a camera club in 1892, a cycling club, a rambling, archaeological and natural history club, a travellers' club and a reading circle. A small choir of male voices was formed in October 1892 and an Operatic Society in 1893. The latter performed *Madame Favart* in 1897, and the hall was crowded every night of the week. The YMCA opened in 1879 as one of two occupants of Morley House on the corner of Mansfield Road and Shakespeare Street. The other occupant, the Morley Club – taking its name from the MP Samuel Morley – was designed for the promotion of clubs for games, sports and gymnastics, with a heavy emphasis on temperance and the entertainment of working men and women.[83] The present building dates from the 1930s. The emphasis in all these cases was on organisation and the need to employ idle hands in order that they would not make mischief. Two final examples of regulated leisure were the excursion and the music hall.

Increasingly in the second half of the nineteenth century it was possible for people to spend their leisure hours away from Nottingham. The Mechanics Institute was planning railway excursions for its members as early as 1840, and from about 1850 firms began to treat their employees to an annual outing. In 1865 Hine and Mundella began taking employees on an annual outing to Thurgarton or Hoveringham, entertaining them with a brass band and sports, feeding them, and returning them home. Changes in working schedules ensured that by the 1860s individuals were able to plan their own excursions especially when, in 1861, many of the hosiery manufacturers introduced a half-day holiday on Saturdays. Other holidays were built into the factory year. In the lace industry during the 1860s Good Friday was a working day, but in George Harwood's factory the Monday and Tuesday following Easter were half-days. The introduction of the August Bank Holiday in 1870, together with the completion of the line to Skegness in 1873, enabled people to spend a day at the seaside. Ten thousand arrived in the town on August Bank Holiday 1874, and 20,000 in 1882. The majority came from the East Midlands, and numbers fell away during trade depressions in the textile industries. In 1883 shop assistants gained their half-day holiday, and a Thursday Half-Day Holiday Association was formed to help them to use it to advantage. By the 1890s the Midland Railway was offering deals designed to encourage local excursions, and cyclists took the opportunity of riding their newly-acquired bicycles between stations. More than one thousand people took a railway excursion to Radcliffe-on-Trent on Good Friday 1890 and another 2,674 on Easter Monday. On the same days, 571 and 2,170 travelled to Matlock, while on August Bank Holiday Monday, 2,251 people visited Chatsworth. For those not inclined to stray from the town on a public holiday there was always G. H. Ward's £17 10s Shrovetide 120 yards Handicap, run on the Castle Grounds with plenty of betting. Also popular were steamer trips on the river to Colwick Park.[84]

Music hall was one of the best known working-class leisure pursuits to emerge from public houses and the culture associated with them. The makeshift stages where travelling entertainers performed gradually moved from the occasional to the regular. 'Free and easies' marked the beginning of music hall, evenings when entertainment was free of charge, and members of the audience were invited to do a 'turn'. Generally they took place in hotels, inns or taverns. Among the pubs were The Old Rose Revived on Bellar Gate, The Albany on Birkin Avenue, The Bell on Parliament Street, and The Black Swan on Goose Gate. In time, the popularity of these events outgrew the taverns and other buildings were converted, among them the old St Mary's Gate Theatre, which closed prior to the opening of the Theatre Royal. It was converted into the Middleton Alhambra Palace of Varieties. Music Hall enjoyed a chequered existence. At the Alhambra, attempts to ensure that respectability was maintained led to the offer of:

> £1 reward ... to any giving information of any person using bad or obscene language or anyway annoying the audience or performer. Any stamping, whistling or shouting will be immediately expelled as the police are in attendance.[85]

In some cases new buildings were constructed as Music Halls, among them St George's Hall, the Malt Cross on St James's Street (1877), the Crown and Cushion on Fletcher Gate, and the Talbot, later the Palace of Varieties and briefly (1887–94) the Temperance Theatre of Varieties. St George's Hall opened in May 1854 with a Crimea benefit. It was here in 1868 that a very young Vesta Tilley made her debut. Samuel Collinson attended a free and easy at St George's in 1859: 'music not bad but the band deficient in strength'.[86] The appeal to the working classes is clear from the admission price, which was usually 2*d* for the main body of the hall and 6*d* for a box. The movement of music hall from the public house to separate accommodation enabled local authorities to introduce regulation. The small tavern concert room disappeared, often because the proprietor could not meet stringent fire regulations. The Palace of Varieties and the Alhambra Music Hall were among the premises deemed by the Watch Committee to be in need of improved safety regulations. The legal position was further tightened when in 1891 the Watch Committee adopted the Public Health Amendment Act of 1890 requiring annual licences for places of 'public dancing, singing, music or other entertainment'. The halls survived, and despite middle-class efforts to improve them, they retained a certain lack of respectability: Sydney Race recalled of the Hippodrome that 'it was not visited, except surreptitiously, by nice people'.[87]

Edwardian music hall really dates from the opening in 1898 of the Empire Theatre of Varieties offering 'variety entertainments of the highest excellence'. It enjoyed considerable popularity into the 1920s. Lily Langtry and George Formby senior were among the entertainers in 1902, and Charlie Chaplin was a regular visitor to the town. After Whitehall's factory on the edge of Theatre Square was burned down in 1905, the site was turned over to a new music hall, the Hippodrome, which opened in 1908.[88]

The divergence between the classes in their leisure pursuits during the nineteenth century was not absolute, and perhaps the clearest example of social mixing was to be seen in the one-off celebrations which brought thousands of people on to the streets and into the parks and open spaces. When the Crimean War ended in

Plate 48 **Fire at Whitehall's Factory**. Whitehall's Factory on Wollaton Street was a tenement factory with twenty-three lace and hosiery manufacturers. It was burnt down in 1905, and in 1908 the 2,500-seat Hippodrome Music Hall opened on the site. It was one of the premier variety houses until it switched to films on 7 July 1927. It became the Gaumont on 12 February 1948 and closed on 16 January 1971. Restyled, it is now a night-club. These changes reflect alterations in the use of space in Nottingham city centre. The Clarendon, right, is more popularly recalled as The County Hotel, Theatre Quadrant. It was demolished to allow for expansive refurbishment of the Theatre Royal in *c.*1977

1856 the town celebrated with a procession led by the mayor and corporation, which included the Sunday Schools and Friendly Societies. When the Duke of Newcastle inspected the Robin Hood Rifles on the Forest in 1861 the crowd was 'innumerable', according to George Harwood. Two months later a regional meeting of the Band of Hope was celebrated with a procession from the market place to the Arboretum. In 1862 the Oddfellows celebrated their Jubilee with a fête in the Arboretum preceded by a grand procession through the streets. Thousands turned out in 1865 for the Nottingham and Midland Counties Working Classes Art and Industry Exhibition, held in a temporary structure off South Sherwood Street, which was later used as a venue for meetings of the British Association during a visit to Nottingham in 1866. Thousands more attended the 1903 Industrial Exhibition in purpose-built premises at Trent Bridge, which were gutted by fire in 1904.[89]

Royal occasions were also popular. A 'general holiday' was called for Queen Victoria's coronation in 1838, with a civic procession from the Exchange to a service in St Mary's, festivities in the Park during the afternoon, and fireworks in the market-place in the evening. Scholars at Stoney Street Sunday School enjoyed a 'grand dinner' in the graveyard with 'a liberal supply of beef and plumb pudding' and sufficient ale for many of the children to become 'intoxicated'. Visits from Queen Adelaide, the Queen Dowager, in 1841, and Queen Victoria herself (albeit briefly en route from Chatsworth to Belvoir) in 1843 were occasions for celebration. On the latter occasion the corporation marched in procession to the Midland Station. 'Nothing could have been more loyal and enthusiastic than their reception', wrote William Parsons, 'nothing could exceed the demonstrations of loyalty and attachment which were everywhere manifested'.[90] On the Queen's birthday in 1860 30,000 people turned out to watch the Robin Hood Rifles go through manoeuvres in the Park. Shops and business premises in the town closed on 23 December 1861 for the funeral of Prince Albert, and in 1863 for the marriage of the Prince of Wales. Again there was a procession – from the market-place to the Forest – and the market-place was illuminated: 'And never have I seen such a grand and glorious display as was presented by the Exchange', wrote George Harwood, 'the whole front blazed with light. The effect was enchanting. Many individuals have also illuminated their places of business or residence, and Nottingham appears full of glory.'[91] When the Duke of York married Princess Mary in 1893 the shops, many warehouses and offices closed, flags were hung from buildings in the market-place and five different bands played in various parts of the town during the afternoon and evening.[92]

With this tradition of celebration it is not surprising to find the town in party mood for Queen Victoria's jubilees. Victoria celebrated her Golden Jubilee in 1887 and her Diamond Jubilee in 1897. Events in 1887 included a children's celebration on the Forest, and a demonstration in the market-place by the friendly societies. A decade later the children again celebrated on the Forest, but on this occasion Nottingham had the added opportunity for letting down its collective hair because it was as part of the celebrations from 20–24 June that it received its city charter. Celebrations included a civic service, and various parades and reviews of troops on the Forest. There was a mayor's banquet, a Jubilee Bonfire, and on 23 June a civic and representative procession on the Forest. Sydney Race described the illuminations:

> All up Mansfield Road and the route through the Forest that the procession of Wednesday was to take, along Alfreton Road and down Derby Road were Venetian masts and either across and from one to another were strings of little flags. In Chapel Bar, Angel Row, and Smithy Row, larger flags were hung across the streets from house to house producing a pretty effect. Most of the shops in the town hung out a flag. Griffin and Spalding had many out with shields and little banners decorating the whole of the front. One or two places were well illuminated at night. The Guardian office had Victoria the virtuous picked out in electric lights with other lights round a painted device. Boots had electric lamps, red white and blue in colouring and the groups of three round all their windows with a gold crown and two stars of red white and blue cloth, a light on the front. The effect was gaudy. The Exchange had long rows of lights in small glass lamps along its facade with the square windows picked out with the same and here a very good effect was produced.[93]

Many of the changes in leisure and entertainment during the course of the nineteenth century were pragmatic responses to perceived needs rather than anything more profound. The main concern of both local and national government was to control the use of space, while the middle classes sought to regulate working-class leisure pursuits for what they conceived would be the good of the whole community. The achievement of these varying aims differed. Sometimes regulation was little short of control, as with the attack on blood sports, but in other respects it was neither very far-reaching nor very successful. Public houses are an obvious example, but Goose Fair, far from going the way of the many urban fairs which were suppressed in the course of the nineteenth century, survived in a transformed but none the less recognisable form. Public parks, libraries and museums had the blessing of local councils because they were controlled through by-laws designed to enforce certain standards of behaviour. 'Perfect order', the Free Library Committee reported in 1880, 'has been observed in all the reading rooms.'[94] Other moves appear only in a negative light, such as the introduction in 1878 of fire regulations on music halls, which drove out of business some of the less salubrious outfits. Usually, however, regulation had a positive rather than a negative impact. The 1845 Enclosure Act was a serious attempt to promote civilised urban life, and in recreational terms this was reflected most clearly in the provision of open spaces. Nor were the aims forgotten after 1845. Following the borough extension in 1877 the Health Committee was asked by the corporation to investigate 'the propriety of leaving open spaces in crowded parts of the town as playgrounds for children'. Under the terms of the 1879 Improvement Act the corporation bought Bulwell Forest, fifty acres of which was designated parkland. In 1883 St George's Close, near Queen's Walk, was set aside for recreation, and the Gregory estate trustees allotted land just off Derby Road in Lenton as another public park in 1888. A further range of facilities was provided with the formation in 1901 of the Victoria Embankment.[95] Nottingham corporation may have lacked the courage to adopt T. C. Hine's civic regeneration plans in the 1850s, but it recognised the need to promote and encourage a civic culture which built on the open spaces laid out in 1845. The new city retained many of its older leisure activities, including its public houses and its Fair, but during the nineteenth century it had seamlessly added a range of new recreations suitable to its size and standing and, in its open spaces, it had recreated something of its eighteenth-century garden image.

Notes

1 Orange, II, p. 946; R. C. Sutton, 'Radford Grove or Folly', *TTS*, 17 (1913), pp. 56–8; White, 1832; 1853, p. 100; Wylie, pp. 360–3; *The Stranger's Guide through Nottingham* (2nd edn, 1827), pp. 81–97; A. Gilbert, *Recollections of Old Nottingham* (2nd edn, Nottingham, 1904), p. 54.

2 R. Evans, 'Theatre music in Nottingham, 1760–1800', *TTS*, 88 (1984), pp. 47–53; Gawthern, *Diary*, pp. 102, 103, 108, 109, 124.

3 *NJ*, 9 December 1769; R. Evans, 'Music in eighteenth-century Nottingham' (Loughborough University, MA thesis, 1983), pp. 27–72; Gawthern, *Diary*, pp. 38 50, 106, 109; R. Evans, 'Music in St Mary's Church, Nottingham', *NH*, 38 (1987), pp. 14–17.

4 Blackner, p. 68; Gawthern, *Diary*, pp. 40, 90, 100, 124, 126; Deering, p. 76; *NJ*, 25 June 1768, 7 March 1801.

5 Quoted in Gawthern, *Diary*, p. 20.

6 A. C. Wood, 'Nottinghamshire, by G. M. Woodward', *TTS*, 61 (1957), p. 46; Gawthern, *Diary*, pp. 82, 108.

7 Gawthern, *Diary*, pp. 32, 59, 68, 77, 81, 84, 112, 127; Evans, 'Music', pp. 5–6; Bailey, *Annals*, IV, p. 57.

8 Gawthern, *Diary*, p. 40; *Stranger's Guide*, p. 34.

9 NAO M.23,788, 8 December 1860, 1 October 1861; *NJ*, 13 September 1844.

10 R. T. Coope and J. Y. Corbett (eds.), *Bromley House, 1752–1991* (Nottingham, 1991), pp. 1–47.

11 NAO M.383, 26 June, 6 December 1866.

12 Ex inf. Aubrey Bush.

13 *Stranger's Guide*, p. 52; White (1844), p. 177; BL Additional MSS 41,073–4, T. H. Wilson Manly's theatrical notebooks of 1820–23, detail his tours and performances, including his regular visits to Nottingham.

14 NAO M.382–3, 18 December 1854, 7 August 1856, 29 January 1862; *NR*, 20 December 1816.

15 Gawthern, *Diary*, pp. 81, 82, 102, 105, 107, 126, 146; Wood, 'Woodward', p. 46; Orange, II, pp. 945–6; White (1844), pp. 176–7; *Stranger's Guide*, pp. 108–9; Wylie, p. 360.

16 Mary Howitt, *Autobiography* (1889), II, p. 201; Gilbert, *Recollections*, p. 28; J. B. Goodman, (ed.), *Victorian Cabinet Maker* (1968), p. 7.

17 *NR*, 9 March 1832.

18 Quoted in H. Conway, *People's Parks* (Cambridge, 1991), p. 24.

19 *Date Book*, p. 92; Wylie, pp. 358–9.

20 Wylie, p. 358; *NJ*, 4 April 1801; *NJ*, 22 January 1814; *Stretton Manuscripts*, p. 174.

21 *NJ*, January 1821; *Date Book*, pp. 153, 291, 377–8.

22 J. J. Rowley, 'Drink and the public house in Nottingham, 1830–60', *TTS*, 79 (1975), p. 80; Iliffe and Baguley, 2, pp. 98–111; G. Oldfield, 'Bendigo – A local hero?', *NH*, 44 (1990), pp. 6–11.

23 Deering, p. 76; Blackner, pp. 32–3.

24 *The Universal British Directory of Trade, Commerce and Manufacture* (1793), p. 45; J. Throsby (ed.), *The Antiquities of Nottinghamshire*, II (1790), p. 151; Gawthern, *Diary* pp. 32, 74, 79.

25 *RBN*, VII, pp. 156, 409–18; *NJ*, 28 September 1776; NAO DDE, 3/3, Subscribers to the Nottingham grandstand and the Assembly Room; *Date Book*, p. 108.

26 *NJ*, 4 August 1781; Gawthern, *Diary*, pp. 64, 67, 71; Throsby, II, p. 151; G. Davies, *A Touch of Colwick* (Chorley, 1994), p. 25.1

27 A. Wanderer, *Walks Round Nottingham* (1835), pp. 241–2.

28 Gawthern, *Diary*, p. 124; Blackner, p. 32.

29 NUMD William Parsons' Diaries, 2–4 October 1844.

30 *NJ*, 11 October 1839.

31 *RBN*, VII, p. 156; IX, pp. 41, 46, 48; White (1844), p. 177.

32 NAO M.382, 5 August 1846; *RBN*, IX, pp. 117, 132, 134. There had been a spring meeting in 1815 but it was not continued: Wanderer, *Walks*, p. 243.

33 NAO M.23,788, 16 July 1861.

34 NAO M.382 15 July 1856; 22 July 1857.

35 *RBN*, IX, pp. 348, 350; Davies, *Colwick*, pp. 60–83; S. Best, 'How the racecourse came to Colwick', *Sneinton Magazine*, 46 (1993), pp. 13–26.

36 *RBN*, VII, pp. 69, 261; VIII, p. 103; P. Wilkes, *The Great Nottingham Goose Fair* (Burton on Trent, 1989), p. 21; Gilbert, *Recollections*, p. 32.

37 Wilkes, *Goose Fair*, p. 22; W. Howitt, *The Rural Life of England* (2nd edn 1838), II, p. 251.

38 Howitt, *Rural Life*, II, pp. 251, 253.

39 Gilbert, *Recollections*, p. 33.

40 Wylie, pp. 325–7; Wilkes, *Goose Fair*, p. 26.

41 NAO M.24,480/A3.

42 Iliffe and Baguley, 3, pp. 40–1; 4, pp. 49–50; *Edwardian Nottingham*, 2, p. 65; Wilkes, *Goose Fair*, pp. 3, 4, 43.

43 NAO M.383, 1 October 1858, 4 October 1860, 2 October 1861.

44 English Asmodeus, *Revelations of Life in Nottingham* (Nottingham, 1860), pp. 181–8; NAO M.23,788, 2 October 1861.

45 *NJ*, 3 August 1875.

46 *RBN*, IX, p. 271; Wilkes, *Goose Fair*, p. 27

47 NAO M.24,480/A13.

48 *Nottingham Daily Guardian*, 14 October 1897.

49 *Ibid.*; Wilkes, *Goose Fair*, p. 2.

50 NAO M.23,788, 5 November 1863.

51 NUMD William Parsons' Diaries, entries for 25 December 1843, 1844, 1847, 1861, 1862.

52 *Report of the Select Committee on Labouring Poor (Allotments of land)*, PP C.402 (1843), 7, para. 1924.

53 R. A. Church, 'James Orange and the allotment system in Nottingham', *TTS*, 64 (1960), pp. 74ff.; Howitt, *Rural Life*, p. 310; Gilbert, *Recollections*, p. 55.

54 R. Mellors, *The Gardens, Parks and Walks of Nottingham and District* (Nottingham, 1926), p. 45; NAO M.382, 3 June 1856; *Nottingham Daily Guardian*, 9 July 1897.

55 *RBN*, VII, endpiece; White, 1832 and later directories.

56 Quoted in Rowley, 'Drink', p. 73.

57 J. Heath, 'Leisure provision in Victorian Nottingham', *NH*, 28 (1982), p. 9; M. Thomis, *Old Nottingham* (Newton Abbot, 1968), pp. 140–56; Rowley, 'Drink', pp. 77–80. Details of the numerous clubs in the town can be found in contemporary directories, and various editions of the *Nottingham Red Book*.

58 White (1844), p. 170; Rowley, 'Drink', p. 78; H. Meller (ed.), *Nottingham in the Eighteen Eighties* (Nottingham, 1971), p. 62.

59 Rowley, 'Drink', p. 72; *NR*, 6 September 1844; Iliffe and Baguley, 4, pp. 76–7.

60 Rowley, 'Drink', pp. 74, 81; *RBN*, IX, pp. 136–7, 285; E. P. Bailey, 'Leenside: the churches and the making of a Nottingham slum' (University of Nottingham, MA thesis, 1993), pp. 66, 91–2.

61 Gilbert, *Recollections*, p. 53; NAO M.383, 21 October 1858; Goodman, *Victorian Cabinet Maker*, p. 67; Wylie, pp. 343–5; *The Tourist's Picturesque Guide to Nottingham* (Nottingham, 1871), p. 33; D. Wardle, *Education and Society in Nineteenth Century Nottingham* (1971), pp. 139–40, 177–82; Iliffe and Baguley, 14, pp. 1–60; J. Granger, *History of the Nottingham Mechanics' Institution 1837–1887* (Nottingham, 1912); J. D. Atkinson, 'Working-class attitudes to education in Nottingham, 1836–1870' (University of Nottingham, Ph.D. thesis, 1976).

62 *Illustrated London News*, 15 May 1852.

63 Mellors, *Gardens*, pp. 48–9; NAO M.382, 16 June 1856, 28 May, 4 June 1857; Meller, *Eighteen Eighties*, p. 63.

64 *RBN*, IX, pp. 183–7, 310.

65 *Nottingham Guardian*, 13 December 1909; *RBN*, IX, pp. 229–30, 245–6. A full account of the opening is given in T. C. Hine, *Nottingham: its Castle: Supplement* (Nottingham, 1879); Iliffe and Baguley, 8, pp. 64–101; T. E. Pemberton, 'The art treasures at Nottingham Castle', *Windsor Magazine*, II (1895), pp. 435–43.

66 NUMD William Parsons' Diaries, 23 June 1851.

67 NAO M.383, 16 November 1861.

68 Iliffe and Baguley, 7, pp. 41, 46; NAO M.23,788, 13 October 1865; *RBN*, IX, p. 173.

69 NAO M.24,480/A14.

70 Iliffe and Baguley, 3, pp. 92–102; Meller, *Eighteen Eighties*, p. 63.

71 Iliffe and Baguley, 12, pp. 72–92; Iliffe and Baguley, *Edwardian Nottingham*. 2, pp. 38–43; C. Weir, *Jesse Boot of Nottingham* (Nottingham, 1994), pp. 51–2.

72 Iliffe and Baguley, 14, pp. 61–90; D. McVay, *Notts County Football Club* (Nottingham, 1988); P. Attaway, *Nottingham Forest: a Complete Record 1865–1991* (Derby, 1991).

73 J. F. Sutton, *Nottingham Cricket Matches from 1771 to 1853* (Nottingham, 1853), pp. v–ix, xii–xiii; P. Wynne Thomas, *Trent Bridge* (1987), pp. ix, 1, 3, 6.

74 Howitt, *Rural Life*, II, p. 275; *NR*, 4 September 1835; *NJ*, 4 September 1835; Sutton, *Cricket Matches*, p. 67.

75 Gilbert, *Recollections*, pp. 47–8.
76 Wynne Thomas, *Trent Bridge*, p. 13.
77 Howitt, *Rural Life*, II, pp. 276–7.
78 NAO M.23,788, 9 June 1860, 7 July 1866.
79 J. Lucas and B. Haynes, *The Trent Bridge Battery* (Glasgow, Collins, 1985), pp. 26–9; Iliffe and Baguley, 18, pp. 1–51.
80 [J. A. F. Lester], *Dear St Catherine's* (1929); Anon. *The Boys' Brigade 1st Nottingham (St Andrews) Company* (Nottingham, 1988); J. Springhall, *Youth, Empire and Society: British Youth Movements 1883–1940* (1977), pp. 44, 155.
81 *Royal Commission: State of Large Towns and Populous Districts*, 1st Report (1844), p. 133; Goodman, *Victorian Cabinet Maker*, pp. 7–8.
82 G. H. Bowden, *The Story of Raleigh* (1975), p. 18; Meller, *Eighteen Eighties*, p. 67; NAO M.24,480/A14.
83 NAO M.24,480/A14; *NJ*, 8 March 1879.
84 Church, pp. 209–10, 375–6; Meller, *Eighteen Eighties*, p. 63; *Nottingham Daily Guardian*, 5, 8 April, 6 August 1890; Iliffe and Baguley, 6, pp. 92, 99. The shop assistants' half-day holiday was granted reluctantly, particularly by Jessops: *Supplement to the Gazette of the John Lewis Partnership*, 26 June 1954, p. 5.
85 Heath, 'Leisure', p. 12; Asmodeus, *Revelations*, pp. 54–60, for a description of a 'free and easy'.
86 NAO M.24,480, 22 March 1859; Asmodeus, *Revelations*, pp. 100–4; Iliffe and Baguley, 12, pp. 17–31.
87 NAO M.24,480/B7; *RBN*, IX, p. 262.
88 Iliffe and Baguley, *Edwardian Nottingham*, 2.
89 NAO M.382, 13, 16 May 1856; M.383, 15 July 1862; M.5,588, 7 April 1856; M.23,788, 21 May, 1 July 1861, 15 July 1862; *Illustrated London News*, 7 October 1865; *EP*, 4 July 1904.
90 Gilbert, *Recollections*, pp. 50–1, 55–8; Goodman, *Victorian Cabinet Maker*, pp. 70–1; NUMD William Parsons' Diaries, 4 December 1843.
91 NAO M.23,788, 24 May 1860, 10, 13 March 1863; M.383, 23 December 1861.
92 NAO M.24,480/A5, 6 July 1893.
93 NAO 24,480/A15; P. Clay and J. H. Richards, *Official Record of the Celebration of the Diamond Jubilee of Her Majesty Queen Victoria, June 1897* (Nottingham, 1898), p. 50.
94 *RBN*, IX, p. 274.
95 *RBN*, IX, pp. 260, 295; Mellors, *Gardens*, pp. 69–71.

Part IV

TWENTIETH-CENTURY NOTTINGHAM

17

THE IDENTITY OF A TWENTIETH-CENTURY CITY

Colin Griffin

In 1932 W. G. Jackson, a Nottingham Schools Inspector who later became Director of Education, told a national conference on education that:

> The name of Nottingham has re-echoed down the centuries through the history of England. To-day it keeps its pride of place. 'Queen of the Midlands', some call it, and not without reason. For though it is now a great industrial centre, it has preserved beauty where that was possible, and added beauty when opportunity afforded.
> A Sylvan City.
> The City has a Council House to equal, if not surpass, any civic building in the land, or outside it for that matter. It has fine tree-lined boulevards; let it be added unto Nottingham that it has kept its trees! It has innumerable parks and open spaces; public walks, squares and gardens are to be found all over the City; there is no district, however poor, without its place of grass and trees. And the river, the smug and silver Trent, bordered by one of the finest embankments in the country and spanned by the widest bridge outside London, affords endless sport and leisure.[1]

This peroration echoed the words of a previous generation, written in 1908:

> For an industrial centre Nottingham is favoured in its situation ... In the matter of open spaces the town is well supplied. An insanitary area to the north of the Market Place has been recently cleared away, narrow thoroughfares widened, and boulevards made round the town, so as the streets are generally well paved and lighted, the impression given by much of the City is one of abundant air space.[2]

'Can it be true', says our visitor, 'that Nottingham has a population of over 240,000; the public buildings look so clean and fresh, unlike the dingy, smoke-stained edifices of the great manufacturing towns of the North?'[3]

'Queen of the Midlands', introduced into Nottingham phraseology about 1870, is today taken for granted. In the 1970s Emrys Bryson observed that 'Brushing aside

Plate 49 **'Queen of the Midlands'**. The feminine imagery, stressing at the same time Nottingham's hard-nosed industrial concerns, is carefully cultivated here on the front cover of the city's 1925 handbook

false claimants, like Leicester, a Nottinghamian refers to his city as the "Queen of the Midlands" without embarrassment.' Today it is still customary to preface popular histories with comedians making cracks like: 'Queen of the Midlands' I met him once in Clumber Street I think. Seriously, though, Nottingham is a great place, and I love going back home.'[4] These current attitudes of superiority are not altogether surprising, given that they have been assiduously cultivated by the local press, sections of the intelligentsia and, most notably, by the corporation itself, whose *Guidebooks* present Nottingham as the epitome of the progressive, modernising city:

> Nottingham has won renown through her industrial and commercial achievements, entitling her to a foremost place among the great cities of Britain and the Empire [1939] … the people have made their city a clean, healthy, happy and beautiful place in which to live and work … the textile trades have brought about a reputation for cleanliness in its manufactures which has helped to earn the description 'Queen of the Midlands'.[1947]
>
> … for a manufacturing city … the 'Queen of the Midlands' is no Cinderella. There are green parks and pleasant boulevards; there is a river as beautiful as it is commercially useful, and there are buildings of historic interest, yet in Nottingham thoughts and eyes are fixed on the future and not ever turned to that which is past. You will be certain to meet the claim that the city has the prettiest girls in the country, many of them engaged in making lace just as pretty and attractive as themselves.[1966][5]

This essentially soft, feminine image as an attractive place to live and work in contrast to the grim, harsh character of the industrial centres of middle and northern England could hardly have been sustained in the popular consciousness had it not reflected and served to symbolise certain characteristics of the city in the twentieth century.

Post-1918 national reconstruction provided a stimulus to modernisers among the civic leadership who in 1919 sought a large-scale extension of the city boundaries and embraced 'a comprehensive housing blueprint of slum clearance in the city centre, [and] the construction of well planned low density suburban council estates serviced by an efficient public transport system'.[6] The proposed extension was opposed by the neighbouring authorities, and an enquiry was mounted at the Guildhall in February 1920. Three months later Dr Christopher Addison, the Minister

Plate 50 **City of Nottingham Boundary Extension enquiry, Guildhall, 12–14 February 1920**. The enquiry was metaphorically presided over by Captain Albert Ball, VC, one of Nottingham's First-World-War heroes, whose portrait by Noel Denholm Davis had recently been completed. On the right is a rather optimistic map of a greatly expanded Nottingham. Had the boundary application been successful, the physical make-up of the twentieth-century city would have been rather different

of Health, announced that the extension had been refused. Rejection was a blow to civic self-esteem. In the years which followed the city fathers intermittently 'came to identify civic pride and identity with big, sometimes grandiose municipal gestures',[7] none more so perhaps than 'the great housing plans of 1923–33, an era of bold planning and gracious achievement'.[8]

New houses, however attractive, were distant from the centre, and a grand municipal gesture required something more at the heart of the city. Cecil Howitt, the architect responsible for much of the new council housing built in the 1920s and 1930s, planned a series of major projects, most notably the Council House and the redevelopment of the market-place. The projected cost of the new Council House was £½ million. Howitt's scheme included a new Exchange, movement of the open-air market to permanent quarters off Parliament Street, and the transfer of Goose Fair to the Forest. There was a public outcry at the projected cost, but where T. C. Hine had failed in the prevailing political conditions of the nineteenth century, Howitt now succeeded. A grand gesture was needed. In March 1926 the corporation placed a contract to build a new Exchange at a cost of £502,876 (although this was later reduced by £40,000). The foundation stone was laid in March 1927, and the splendid neo-Baroque Council House was opened by the Prince of Wales in May 1929.[9]

The corporation knew exactly what it was doing. The *Nottingham Journal*'s headline in May 1929 pronounced the scheme a major civic success:

> Queen of the Midlands Historic Day Nottingham's New Civic Centre Based on Milan's Famous Example Still a Modern Building in 100 Years Hence Beauty and Utility.

50,000 citizens from all classes of society were assured by the Lord Mayor on the royal inauguration that 'the site could be compared with no other in any provincial City in the country … and will mark a new civic era … a new standard of ideals to the citizens'.[10] Coincidentally, in 1928 the town's chief citizen was accorded the status of Lord Mayor.

At the same time the market-place was laid out as an ornamental public garden, with a processional way leading to the Council House, and with fountains as a focal point, 'a provincial Speakers' Corner for orators, religious revivalists, Salvation Army Bands'. And it worked: the old market-place, henceforth known as Old Market Square, or Slab Square, became a focal point to the town. Subsequently it has also acted as a stage for pop groups, a temporary beach for Punch and Judy shows, a location for protest rallies and – echoes here of the nineteenth century – a place of riotous assembly ('punch-ups'!) on Friday and Saturday evenings.[11]

In this heady atmosphere almost anything positive could be attributed to the good sense of the corporation. An airport was opened at Tollerton in 1928, which placed Nottingham 'in the forefront in the matter of aviation'. The council 'was one of the first of the city corporations to realise the great services which Redifusion can provide within a town'. The original cable radio mike was inaugurated in 1931 (television was added in 1952) and serviced 22,000 homes, fifty factories and numerous public buildings, including schools and hospitals. It played a valuable part in maintaining public morale in wartime.[12]

This upbeat tone was also reflected in some descriptions of the inter-war city. J. B. Priestley, visiting in 1933, knew of Nottingham's reputation for 'affluence' which made it seem 'gayer in its own robust Midland fashion than other provincial towns … a sort of industrial Venusberg', largely because of its numerous 'pretty, independent waged young women'. Yet to an extent Priestley was caught up with the mood of the times rather than the reality of economic conditions. Later commentators noted that the picture of industrial Nottingham between the wars was 'not one of unclouded prosperity'.[13] Even at the time it was argued that:

> Comparisons have been made from time to time with the industrial development of other large towns in the Midlands, such as Derby, Birmingham, Coventry and Wolverhampton, and there is no doubt that these places have achieved success in attracting men's industries where Nottingham has failed. If only engineering, motor, aircraft, transport or other heavy industry could be attracted to the City, employment would be found for those men who have been displaced in recent years and whose prospects at present in the district are poor. Hundreds of skilled men have been compelled to leave the city in order to obtain employment in their own trade.[14]

Unemployment was widespread. In the depths of depression in 1933 20,455 people were out of work, and the proportion of the insured population unemployed at the height of the 1930s recovery was 10.8 per cent compared to Coventry's 7.4 per cent and 9.9 per cent in Wolverhampton.[15] Even for those in work Nottingham was a low wage economy. Average weekly earnings for male and female workers in hosiery, for instance, were £2 9*s* 6*d* and £1 5*s* 6*d* respectively at a time when a weekly income of £2 13*s* 2*d* was required to provide the basic 'Human Needs' for a man, wife and three children and £5 18*s* to maintain 'a desirable standard of living' which had some allowance for 'luxuries' such as cigarettes or a cinema visit.[16] Short-time working played havoc with the standard of living of many workers, including coal-miners who could take home as little as £1 10*s* a week in the most depressed years.[17] It is hardly surprising that one-quarter of all Nottingham families had incomes of less than £1 10*s* a week in 1937 compared to 17 per cent, 15 per cent and 10 per cent in Wolverhampton, Leicester and Coventry respectively.[18] There was much poverty amidst plenty in inter-war Nottingham.

This contrast between the magnificent restructuring of the city centre and the ongoing poverty experienced by many working people was not unique; indeed, it can be drawn again for the post-war years. In these years of 'affluence', when unemployment was at its lowest, Nottingham became 'a place of old-time luxury' that could support 'the largest 10 pin bowling centre in Europe' in the early 1960s and more shops and expenditure per head than other Midland towns such as Leicester and Coventry.[19] Two major employers of both male and female labour, Boots and Players, were pioneers of the industrial welfare movement, based on the principle that superior working conditions maximised the productivity of the work-force by mitigating the strain of mechanised methods of production.[20]

The Festival of Britain celebrations provided further opportunity for self-congratulation for the 'housing campaign' which had won 'the admiration of the best judges not only in this country but throughout the world ... we have seen a splendid City begin to arise around us, a thing of beauty and design, a City for living in, not merely getting a living in'.[21] As 'a cultural renaissance' stirred in the post-war years the city found itself 'looking for a habitation and a name; an Acropolis of the Arts'.[22] The proposed civic centre remained an architect's dream, although civic pride eventually produced an outstanding new regional playhouse building in 1963, which was followed in the 1980s by the Royal Centre complex: the renovated Theatre Royal and a contemporary Royal Concert Hall with seating for 2,500 people.

Once again the contrast can be drawn with the city beyond the centre. A survey of St Ann's in the 1960s found that 'there are substantial numbers of people who earn weekly wages so low that they are constantly on the threshold of poverty' and employed 'in most of the industries of the Nottingham area ... some of which are household names. A pipemaker at Stanton ironworks; a soap processor at Boots; a coalminer employed by the National Coal Board ... a storekeeper at Raleigh cycles.'[23] Old age, chronic sickness, unemployment and single-parent families also helped plunge about a third of the inhabitants into poverty. St Ann's was typical of 'other twilight areas elsewhere in Nottingham',[24] such as the Meadows. These areas of deprivation had only just been redeveloped when the return of mass unemployment in the 1980s prevented the areas escaping from social deprivation and added new areas such as the outlying Broxtowe council estate.[25] 'For a long time', wrote *The Times* in 1989, it 'looked as if it might ride out the recession of the early 1980s ... . But somehow the City of nearly 300,000 people acquired a tarnished crown. For a while it became "Grotty Notty" and suffered from low esteem. Nottingham's manufacturing industries had the stuffing knocked out of them.' Even two of its newer companies, Players and Raleigh, suffered because of changing social habits: the decline of cigarette smoking and the abandonment of the cycle for the car.[26]

That all has not been well with the twentieth-century city, whatever the image makers may have suggested, can also be demonstrated from a single example: public health. At face value the statistical evidence is incontrovertible, the people of modern Nottingham are healthier and live longer than their grandparents and great grandparents at the beginning of the century. The late nineteenth-century fall in the death rate continued until the 1920s, stabilising thereafter at a relatively low level. First-World-War overcrowding in insanitary dwellings encouraged the spread of 'Spanish flu' which cost 1,350 lives and powerfully assisted the spread of diseases like infantile diarrhoea, which temporarily reversed the downward trend in infant mortality.[27] Since then a marked change in the cause of death is observable (table 17.1), with a remarkable decline in deaths from infectious diseases, including tuberculosis and traditional childhood diseases such as diphtheria, enteritis, measles and whooping cough. In 1947 Cyril Banks, the Medical Officer of Health, declared that 'the

Table 17.1 **Causes of death in Nottingham, *c*.1910–70**

Date	*Heart disease*	*TB*	*Cancer*	*Bronchitis*	*Pneumonia*	*Enteritis /diarrhoea*	*Diphtheria*	*Measles*	*Influenza*	*Whooping cough*	*Kidney disorder*
1911–15	484	422	279	368	268	180	29	95	23	57	110
1916–20	332	395	318	371	397	82	48	43	288[a]	41	82
1921–25	389	320	379	365	365	65	16	44	66	34	75
1926–30	571	305	387	344	365	74	53	16	84	29	83
1931–35	781	276	400	168	309	56	8	27	67	16	97
1936–38	956	256	444	142	310	50	12	17	55	15	94
1946–50[b]	1,010	203	535	230	203	29	2	4	21	7	62
1951–55	1,105	86	590	291	210	16	0	2	35	5	36
1956–60	1,166	37	605	276	190	14	0	1	34	0	28
1961–65	1,261	21	683	319	210	19	0	1	29	0.4	21
1966–70	1,233	16	756	297	247	16	0	0.4	33	0.4	16

Sources: As table 17.2.

Note: [a] 1,350 died in the influenza epidemic of 1918–19.
[b] Statistics not available for the Second World War.

greatest triumph has been over diphtheria, obtained by an immunisation campaign … launched in 1940 on a large scale and with a ready response on the part of parents'. Tuberculosis had been likewise tamed: 'whole families, father, mother and four or five siblings, all dying within the space of less than five years, is now unknown'.[28] Effective organisation meant that 'no stories of the spread of vermin or scabies or infectious disease in local homes' were heard following the reception of evacuees from London 'sent to escape the "flying bombs" of July and August 1944'.[29] Public health officers had less success with venereal disease which rose inexorably during both world wars 'because husbands and wives are wrenched apart … . Both make chance contacts which would not have occurred in normal times. Such contacts often prove exciting, unsettling and finally dangerous.'[30] Antibiotics enabled the 'dangers' to be combated after 1945. Finally, when poliomyelitis threatened to become a major killer of children it was effectively combated by vaccination between 1956 and 1958 though during the 1957 epidemic the public was advised 'even "as soon as possible" has a limit and that somebody will have to wait'.[31]

Of course there has had to be a down side to this picture of success. Chest diseases, like bronchitis and pneumonia, remained major killers in an area noted for its winter 'smogs' until the 1970s.[32] In Nottingham, as in the country at large, 'it seems as though the diseases which killed young and old alike in the nineteenth century have been replaced by diseases which attack and kill mainly the middle aged and the elderly'.[33] Hence the rise in deaths from heart disease and cancer shown in table 17.1.

Much of this success was achieved by a programme of public health reforms. Inter-war housing and sanitation improvements helped to improve the health of poorer inhabitants.[34] None the less, since it was impossible 'to bring about an entirely satisfactory reduction in the infant mortality rate so long as slum dwellings remained', it took the large-scale post-1945 clearance schemes, combined with vastly improved maternity and child welfare provision, to stabilise it at the lowest levels. The gradual elimination of private slaughter-houses amid domestic dwellings and their replacement with a public abattoir removed another 'menace to public health and decency'.[35] Post-1950 Trent flood protection schemes also ensured that there would be no repetition of the periodic flooding which could inundate as many as 7,000 houses and factories in the Meadows and elsewhere with polluted, sewage-laden water.[36]

Piecemeal improvements in hospital provision also helped 'to postpone death' though the city was endowed with two relatively impecunious hospitals, which were seriously underfunded after the creation of the National Health Service. The result was an unsatisfactory ratio of both beds and consultants to population size. The Queen's Medical Centre, opened in 1970, 'raised standards of medical practice across the board … so the people of Nottingham can now say we have the best'.[37]

Yet, against this generally upbeat picture of public health improvement in the 'Queen of the Midlands', has to be set the more uncomfortable fact that a clear link between low income and the level of ill-health and premature death is as apparent today as it was at the beginning of the century. Between 1907 and 1914 'the proportional number of deaths in houses above £26 per annum was only one-seventh of that of houses of a lower rental' because 'the general conditions of life among the poor, the relatively poor, and the industrially employed', such as insanitary and cramped housing conditions and lack of personal and domestic cleanliness, fostered the spread of the disease.[38] In 1915 the social-class dimension of diphtheria was equally clear: 'the distribution of the disease in all the poor neighbourhoods was again very general and relatively uniform, but the better class business and residential districts seldom affected'. Similarly, infantile diarrhoea 'is most prevalent and fatal in the densely populated and poor districts. The poorer parts of Sneinton, Leenside and Old Radford most acutely ... the better class districts, such as The Park, Mapperley Park, Upper Woodborough Road district and the area around the Arboretum were spared.'[39] During the smallpox epidemic of 1921–23, 'the disease displayed, as usual, a tendency to confine itself, and to spread in, certain districts of the City and certain social and industrial strata of the community', in other words those living in overcrowded housing conditions.[40] The average death rate in Nottingham in 1921–30 was 13.3 per 1,000 compared to neighbouring Carlton's 10.5 or West Bridgford's 10.6 because the 'highest death-rates and rates of infant mortality are always to be found amongst the very poor who inhabit the centres of our large Cities, and the lowest rates among the people with a higher standard of existence in the suburbs'. Table 17.2 offers statistical support for this claim.[41]

Table 17.2 **Average mortality in Nottingham and in some of its insanitary districts, 1930–33**

Area	*Death rate*	*Infant mortality rate*
Nottingham	14.1	79
Meadow Platts	19.3	174
Coal-Pit Lane	14.4	140
Sneinton Market area	20.0	132
East Street	31.7	183
Care Street	27.8	179
Sussex Street	16.0	126

Source: Evidence of the Boundary Extension Enquiry: *NJ*, 22 April 1933.

The high infant mortality rate compared to many other large cities was related to poor-quality housing, overcrowding and poverty, as Commonwealth immigrants found to their cost in the 1950s and 1960s, since 'the accommodation selected by these people cannot, in the nature of things, with a waiting list for homes of several thousands, be suitable in all regards'.[42] Respiratory infection had become the major killer of infants and this persisted beyond the rehousing programmes because the poor of 'the deprived areas' were unable to afford sufficient heating to keep cold and damp at bay.[43] A number of post-1960 housing schemes proved to be of doubtful utility in the drive for better health. Poor construction and maintenance problems meant that in

Hyson Green 'a substantial number of tenants found living in the flats an extremely unpleasant experience and the complex presents a serious risk to health'.[44]

In both the national and wider European contexts the city is now average with respect to morbidity and mortality rates for the major diseases. However, variations in rates of ill health and mortality between neighbourhoods are, in some cases, as profound as those between the most and least developed nations in the world. Geographical studies of low birth weight in babies, accidents, tuberculosis, limiting long-term illness, mental illnesses, deliberate self-harm, post neonatal deaths and deaths from stroke and coronary heart disease, have all confirmed the existence of substantial local variations in the health status of the city's residents.[45] A 1980s survey concluded that

> it can be stated with certainty that, with few exceptions, the geography of health in Nottingham is the same as the geography of socio-economic status. What is much more complex and controversial is how this state of affairs has come to be and what can or cannot be done about it. Medical opinion is coming around much more to the question of prevention, and the role of anti-poverty programmes in this process.[46]

In 1995 another comprehensive survey demonstrated both the association between poor health and social deprivation, and the huge differentials in health status between socially disadvantaged and more affluent residents.[47] Surveys of the health of Nottingham residents reveal marked improvements since the nineteenth century,[48] and yet at the end of the twentieth century there remains 'a dramatic and disturbing difference' between the health experience of different areas though, given the high quality of the housing stock, poverty and differences in personal behaviour are the most likely key explanations'.[49]

The contradictions between perception and reality, expressed in the public health debate, have not lessened over time. In August 1990 the corporation was able to glow with pride when the city came top of a *Moneywise* survey of the quality of life in sixty-three British towns and cities: 'Nottingham is a wonderful place with a pleasant environment, many attractions and a bustling, very friendly community.' It was:

> THE place to live .... Good local health care, low street crime, a low rate of vandalism, affordable housing and good hospitals make the Queen of the Midlands Britain's best City. Nottingham folk knew it all the time, of course. But it was still nice to have objective confirmation from outsiders who could never be accused of being biased.[50]

As recently as 1995 another survey made much the same point: 'the City Centre is being held up as a shining example for the rest of the country to follow ... dazzling night life, safe, well-lit car parks, park and ride centres ... high quality industrial and commercial development'. Such findings appeared to contradict media claims that Nottingham had an inner city 'plagued by poverty and deprivation, and rife with crime and racial tension'.[51] They also sat uneasily with the results of a survey carried out in January 1993 by Salford University and covering seventy-five English cities. The analysis was based on (among other factors) unemployment rates, one-parent families and birth weight. Nottingham was placed sixty-fourth and labelled 'a blackspot'. Defenders of the city's image as 'the place to live' observed that 'the survey cannot be described as anything to do with the quality of life; it is a survey of poverty' of which the city had, admittedly, its fair share.[52]

Nottingham's image as 'Queen of the Midlands' both asserts its perceived superiority as a place to work, live and visit over its provincial rivals such as Derby and Leicester, and conceals those elements of city life that might bring the image into question or challenge the limitations of urban renewal. The contradictions are redolent of the attitudes of the city's two most internationally acclaimed twentieth-century writers, D. H. Lawrence and Alan Sillitoe. For Lawrence, Nottingham was 'nothing more than an amorphous agglomeration. There is no Nottingham in the sense that there is a Sienna.'[53] Sillitoe's semi-autobiographical character, Arthur Seaton, a Raleigh lathe operator, is 'an anti-modern urban delinquent' who despises such post-1945 symbols of affluence as television, the motor car and the suburban council house.[54] He prefers the traditional working-class community of Radford with its opportunities for promiscuous social mixing, hard drinking and street-fighting, and he dreams about assassinating the city council and its officialdom for destroying his natural habitat.[55]

Lawrence and Sillitoe painted an unflattering picture of the city, an image quite different from the glamorous and vibrant one projected across the globe by world ice-skating champions Torvill and Dean, and by Brian Clough's European cup-winning Nottingham Forest. Yet these contradictions are symptomatic of images of the twentieth-century city, from the inter-war contrast of a major civic programme and house-building programme set against ongoing poverty, through the inequalities of opportunity in regard to health which continue to the present day. In subsequent chapters we shall see that contrasts have underscored much of Nottingham's history over the past century. Whether it has been sports facilities, grammar school places before 1974, or the problems of crime and drugs in the modern inner city, the soft image of the Queen of the Midlands so dear to the heart of the corporation has always had a hard and unforgiving edge. Yet, so long as there is perceived to be a need for a 'boosting' image, Nottingham will remain the 'Queen of the Midlands', despite predictions of its imminent demise.[56] At least in the late 1990s the contradictions are more openly recognised: recent official documents are notably more cautious than some earlier handbooks. Here, by way of conclusion, are the words of Nottingham City Profile as it has sought to present a balanced image:

> It is the commercial, retailing and administrative centre of the East Midlands with a busy and attractive city centre. Adjacent to the city centre is the Lace Market, both an important Conservation Area, with one of the country's finest collections of 18th and 19th century buidings, and an Industrial Improvement Area which is the home of the city's clothing, textiles and fashion industry .... The city, however, also has significant problems .... There are areas of extreme disadvantage, which have disproportionately high rates of unemployment, low income, poor health, and social problems.[57]

Notes

1 W. G. Jackson, *Nottingham – A Sketch of Its History and Industries* (Nottingham, 1933), p. 91.

2 Board of Trade, *Enquiry Into the Cost of Living of the Working Classes* PP Cd 3864 (1908).

3 Lemmon Lingwood, *The Illustrated Handbook to Nottingham* (Norwich, 1906), p. 39.

4 Emrys Bryson, *Portrait of Nottingham* (1974), p. 25; Foreword by Sue Pollard to Ian Manning, *Images of Nottingham* (Derby, 1994).

5 City of Nottingham, *Official Guide Books* (1939, 1945, 1966). Compare the construction of Manchester's image as Victorian 'shock city' in Asa Briggs, *Victorian Cities* (1968), ch. 3, and the 'invention' of traditions in Eric Hobsbawm and Terence Ranger (eds.), *The Invention of Tradition* (Cambridge, 1984), chs. 1 and 7. Angus Calder, *The Myth of the Blitz* (1991), ch. 1, is another example of image-making and mythologising.

6 Minutes of Enquiry on the Proposed Nottingham Boundary Extension, February 1920, NAO CMCAA/1920.

7 R. Silburn, *People in their Places, One Hundred Years of Nottingham Life* (Nottingham, 1981), p. 31; N. J. Hayes, 'Municipal subsidy and Tory minimalism: building the Nottingham Playhouse, 1942–1963', *Midland History*, 19 (1994), pp. 128–46 for post-war Tory resistance to what they called 'reckless and feckless' spending on major civic arts initiatives, particularly if they were supported by their Labour opponents. See also ch. 19 of this book.

8 J. D. Chambers, *Modern Nottingham in the Making* (Nottingham, 1945), p. 44.

9 E. Scoffham, *A Vision of the City: the Architecture of T. C. Howitt* (Nottinghamshire County Council, 1992), pp. 8–12.

10 *NJ*, 22, 23 May 1929.

11 Bryson, *Portrait*, p. 31.

12 *Guidebook* (1947), p. 191; *Guidebook* (1966), pp. 38–9.

13 J. B. Priestley, *English Journey* (1977 edn), p. 131; Edwards, p. 410.

14 F. Hampton (Employment Exchange Manager), 'A brief survey of Nottingham employment', July 1936, quoted in N. J. Hayes, 'Unemployment, employment and industry in Nottingham, 1930–39' (Open University, BA dissertation, 1986), p. 64.

15 N. Tiratsoo, *Reconstruction, Affluence and Labour Politics: Coventry 1945–60* (1990), p. 122; *Labour Gazette*, 1933 and 1939 when there were 14,000 unemployed.

16 G. D. H. and M. I. Cole, *The Condition of Britain* (1937), pp. 244–5, 262.

17 C. P. Griffin, '"Three days down the pit and three days play": underemployment in the East Midlands coalfields between the wars', *International Review of Social History*, 39 (1993), pp. 323, 330.

18 Tiratsoo, *Reconstruction*, p. 122.

19 *The Tribune*, 7 February 1964; Tiratsoo, *Reconstruction*, p. 150, quoting the Board of Trade's *Census of Distribution* 1 (1953).

20 Nottingham Society of Engineers, *Report on Reconstruction* (Nottingham, 1943), pp. 86–7.

21 J. D. Chambers, *The People of Nottingham, 1851–1951* (Nottingham, 1951), p. 8.

22 J. D. Chambers, *A Century of Nottingham History* (Nottingham, 1951), p. 24.

23 K. Coates and R. Silburn, *Poverty, Deprivation and Morale in a Nottingham Community: St. Ann's* (Nottingham, 1968), pp. 52–3, 59–62. Of the male wage earners in the sample, 24.5 per cent had an income of less than £10 a week and a further 17.5 per cent between £10 and £14 at a time when £15 a week was considered 'a living wage' by the Trades Union Congress. The actual numbers of unemployed were 1,447 in 1955 and 5,896 in 1967.

24 Coates and Silburn, *Poverty* (1968), p. 53. There were, of course, many far more salubrious residential areas, including the older council estates and the 'high status residential districts, such as Mapperley and Wollaton, largely owing to the physical and social attractions which they possessed': C. J. Thomas, 'The growth of Nottingham's residential area since 1919', *EMG* (1971), p. 35.

25 See ch. 18. 41,533 and 21,237 were out of work in 1987 and 1990 respectively, representing an unemployment rate of 19 per cent and 13 per cent: *Labour Gazette*, 1987, 1990; NLSL Nottingham Urban Programme, 1990–91, pp. 4–6.

26 *The Times*, 23 October 1989.

27 Medical Officer of Health (MoH), *Summary Report* (1916–28). The subject is examined in more detail in ch. 21.

28 MoH, *Annual Report* (1947).

29 MoH, *Annual Report* (1944).

30 MoH, *Annual Report* (1943).

31 MoH, *Annual Report* (1957).

32 MoH, *Annual Report* (1963).

33 D. C. Marsh, *The Changing Structure of England and Wales 1871–1961* (1967), p. 10.

34 MoH, *Annual Reports* (1929–34).

35 MoH, *Annual Reports* (1934, 1939, 1947). Other influences include rising average living standards, family limitation and individual medical care.

36 Edwards, pp. 147–51. There were major floods in 1901, 1910, 1932, 1946 and 1947.

37 MoH, *Annual Report* (1944); S. Ablett, 'The Medical School of the University of Nottingham: origins and development' (University of Nottingham, Ph.D. thesis, 1992), pp. 59, 67–8, 285. The General was an eighteenth-century hospital in origin and the City was developed out of the Bagthorpe workhouse complex.

38 MoH, *Annual Report* (1915).

39 MoH, *Annual Reports* (1914, 1915).

40 MoH, *Summary Report* (1916–28).

41 MoH, *Annual Report* (1931).

42 MoH, *Annual Reports* (1937, 1947, 1962). In 1962 infant mortality rates were 23.1 per 1,000 for the city and 35.6 for the West Indian immigrant community.

43 Nottingham Housing Action Group Report, *Sixty-Eight Child Deaths: a Case of Inaction* (Nottingham, 1978).

44 Hyson Green Tenants' Action Group, *Warning. Hyson Green Flats Can Damage Your Health* (Nottingham, 1984). For the evidence of a city planner, construction worker and numerous tenants, see J. E. Kingscott, 'Oral history in libraries with special reference to the Nottinghamshire Oral History Collection and the Hyson Green Project' (Loughborough University, MA thesis, 1988), pp. 115–25. Both complexes were demolished in the late 1980s.

45 Nottinghamshire County Council reports, *Disadvantage in Nottinghamshire: County Deprived Area Study* (1983), part 1, pp. 69–70; 'Social need in Nottinghamshire, 1994', pp. 80–3; R. Madeley, 'The geography of health in Greater Nottingham', *EMG*, 9 (1986), pp. 30–6; L. M. Davies, 'Aiming for health in the 1990s' (Nottingham Health District, Annual Report of the Director of Public Health, 1991), pp. 27–50; S. Wilson, *Aiming for Health in the Year 2000* (Nottingham Health District, 1995), pp. 19–21, 34–6; J. A. Giggs, 'Mental disorder and ecological structure in Nottingham', *Social Science and Medicine*, 23 (1986), pp. 945–61; S. Winn, 'Psychiatric disorders in Nottingham: a comparison of diagnostic and age groups', *EMG*, 9 (1986), pp. 21–9; M. W. Beaver, 'Aiming for health in the 1990s' (Nottingham Health District, Annual Report of the Director of Public Health, 1994), pp. 17–19.

46 Madeley, 'Geography of health', p. 35.

47 Wilson, *Aiming for Health in the Year 2000.*

48 *Ibid.*; C. A. Moser and W. Scott, *British Towns: a Statistical Study of Their Social and Economic Differences* (1961), pp. 136–7.

49 Madeley, 'Geography of health', pp. 30–5; Nottingham Health Authority, *Director of Health Annual Report* (1990), p. 10. Taking the Standard Mortality Rate for Nottingham as 100, that for Woodborough was 48 and Forest and Musters (inner-city areas) were 194 and 261 respectively (1984–88 average). Only 1.5 per cent of households were without exclusive use of a bath/shower and inside WC in 1991. There were still some dwellings in private rented accommodation in which 'living conditions were squalid and a threat to health'. Nottingham City Council Factsheet 1991: Director of Health Report 1990, p. 29.

50 *EP*, 31 August 1990; *The Times*, 22 August 1990. The survey took into account a cost of living index and rankings on litter, health care, crime, housing and education.

51 *EP*, 23 November 1995.

52 *EP*, 1 February 1993 under the headline 'Top … to near bottom.' How poverty could be divorced from the quality of life was not explained. Nottinghamshire County Council had been carrying out deprived area studies since the 1970s, notably those of 1975, 1983 and 1993: Brazier, *New Geography*, ch. 9.

53 D. H. Lawrence, *Nottingham and the Mining Country in Selected Essays* (1929), p. 121.

54 S. Daniels and S. Rycroft, 'Mapping the modern city: Alan Sillitoe's Nottingham novels', *Transactions of the Institute of British Geographers*, 18 (1993), p. 472.

55 A. Sillitoe, *Saturday Night and Sunday Morning* (1958), p. 38. Daniels and Rycroft, 'Mapping', p. 476, note that the 'Queen of the Midlands' officialdom reacted coolly to the international success of the novel.

56 G. Trease, *Nottingham: a Biography* (1970), p. 228.

57 NLSL *Nottingham Urban Programme* (1991), p. 4.

18

HOUSING, POPULATION AND TRANSPORT

John Giggs

If rapid population growth was one of the hallmarks of nineteenth-century Nottingham, suburbanisation has been its successor. From 1911 population growth was only modest (table 18.1), peaking at 311,899 in 1961. In both 1951 and 1961 Nottingham was the eighth largest city in England and Wales, but its position slipped to twenty-third in 1991. The net population increase between 1911 and 1991 was a mere 1.4 per cent. The city's experience has been characteristic of most large British towns since the Second World War.[1] Far more significant in many ways has been the sustained fall in household size, with a resulting explosion in the numbers of households needing accommodation. These trends can be attributed to changing social values, rising living standards, and improvements in housing, public health and health care. Collectively they have generated considerable alterations in the age structure of the population (table 18.2). A substantial decline, both absolute and relative, in the under-fifteen-year-old cohort has been overshadowed by a rapid increase in the size of the elderly population.

In twentieth-century Nottingham the rate of growth in household numbers has far outstripped that of population. The average household size in Nottingham declined from 4.33 in 1911 to 2.37 in 1991. The knock-on effect was an 82 per cent increase in the numbers of households and an 85 per cent rise in the number of occupied houses (table 18.1). This placed enormous pressure on the housing stock, and as a consequence the sheer physical size of the city's built-up area has grown to a hitherto unimaginable extent. In 1994 the residential area of Nottingham was almost four times larger than it had been in 1916. In just two decades (1919–39) the city's residential area doubled in size and, since 1945, it has grown by a further 82 per cent. Transport changes have facilitated this, triggering since the 1920s a profound loosening of the city's spatial structure and a progressive weakening of workplace–residential links.

Table 18.1 **Population, households and dwellings, 1911–91**

Date	*Population*	*Private households*	*Occupied dwellings*
1911	259,901	60,070	59,372
1921	262,624	61,876	63,167
1931	276,189	70,740	68,889
1951	306,008	93,491	87,114
1961	311,899	103,166	99,470
1971	300,630	102,980	102,575
1981	272,141	100,552	109,213
1991	263,522	109,356	109,818

Sources: Decennial Population Censuses.

Note: Due to wartime conditions a full census was not undertaken in 1941.

Table 18.2 **Age structure of the population, 1911, 1951 and 1991**

	England and Wales					
	%			% change		
Age	*1911*	*1951*	*1991*	*1911–51*	*1951–91*	*1911–91*
0–14	30.6	22.2	18.9	–2.3	–2.7	–14.7
15–59	61.4	61.9	59.8	22.5	10.2	35.0
60+	8.0	15.9	21.3	240.4	52.2	365.9
	100.0	100.0	100.0	21.3	14.0	38.3

	Nottingham					
	%			% change		
Age	*1911*	*1951*	*1991*	*1911–51*	*1951–91*	*1911–91*
0–14	29.2	23.2	19.8	–6.6	–26.8	–31.6
15–59	63.2	62.3	58.7	16.2	–18.8	–5.7
60+	7.6	14.5	21.5	224.5	27.7	286.7
	100.0	100.0	100.0	17.8	–13.8	1.4

Sources: Decennial Population Censuses.

1914–1939

The First World War marked the end of more than a century of unprecedented growth in Nottingham's population and physical fabric. It is not possible to portray in detail the city's social and spatial structure since the original census returns down to the level of the individual and the household are available only to 1891. However, broad variations in the social status of the city's residential areas in 1916 can be established using general rate books. C. J. Thomas has selected and mapped five categories of residential rateable values, and figure 18.1a presents a simplified version of his findings.[2] By 1916 Nottingham's central area was largely devoted to non-residential land uses. Middle-class professionals, businessmen and shopkeepers had moved to more salubrious areas, particularly the villas and large terraced houses clustered in compact enclaves around the Forest, in Sherwood, Mapperley Park, and the Park Estate. Here houses were valued at £35 and above, with the largest properties occupied by wealthy businessmen such as Sir Jesse Boot and Ernest Jardine, whose houses in the Park were valued at £200 and £335 respectively. Houses of middling value at £20–£34 were smaller and lay mainly on the boundaries between the higher and lower status residential areas. Within the city most houses were small terraced properties valued at under £20, many of them back-to-backs which the corporation had not yet been able to clear. Three large tracts of working-class houses dominated the built-up area: the St Ann's–Sneinton area east of the city centre, the Meadows area to the south, and the swathe on the western edge extending from New Basford in the north to New Lenton in the south. Smaller areas of working-class housing lay on the margins (for example, Carrington–Sherwood), and in the detached industrial suburbs of Bulwell, Old Basford and Old Lenton.

In Nottingham, as was the pattern nationally, house building came virtually to a standstill during the First World War, and the existing house stock continued to deteriorate. Between 1911 and 1921 the number of families sharing dwellings rose from 698 to 1,745. A Housing Committee report in 1919 designated seven areas in the city containing 8,804 houses and 12,416 people to be unhealthy. A further 3,012 single insanitary houses with 10,767 occupants were also declared unfit for habitation.[3] The seriousness of the situation became apparent in July 1919, when the corporation unsuccessfully applied for an extension of the city boundaries. The application was refused because the city council was found seriously wanting with respect to its statutory responsibilities. Sewage disposal arrangements were inadequate because not enough had been done to ensure that pail closets were replaced with water-closets. The Minister of Health suggested that no extension proposal could seriously be entertained until the corporation had made substantial improvements in sanitary and housing arrangements in the city.[4] The 1919 Housing and Town Planning Act had already provided the context for housing authorities to construct dwellings, and to let them at current working-class rents, with any shortfall being met largely by central government. Subsequent legislation in 1922 and 1924 subsidised both

Figure 18.1 **Residential areas, 1916–91**

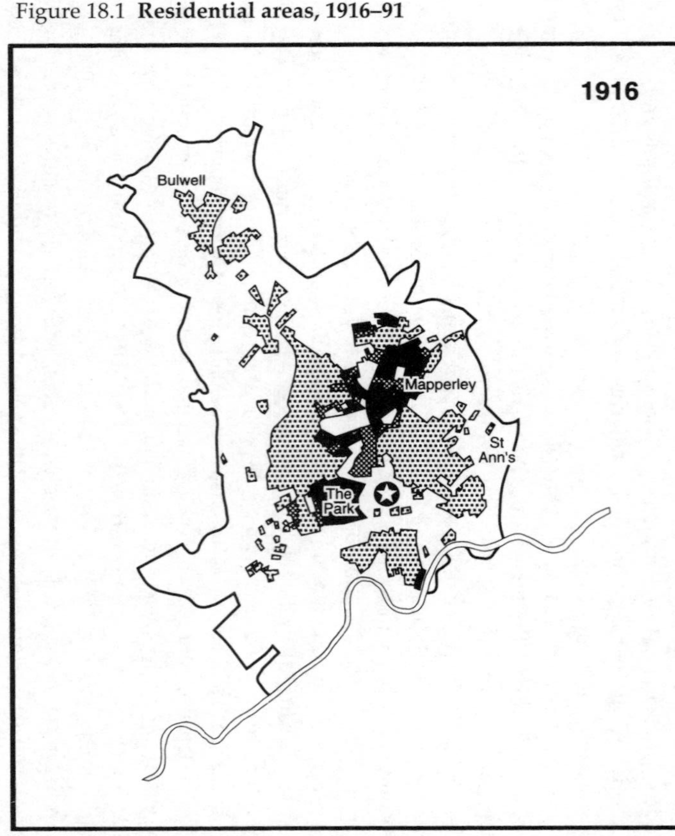

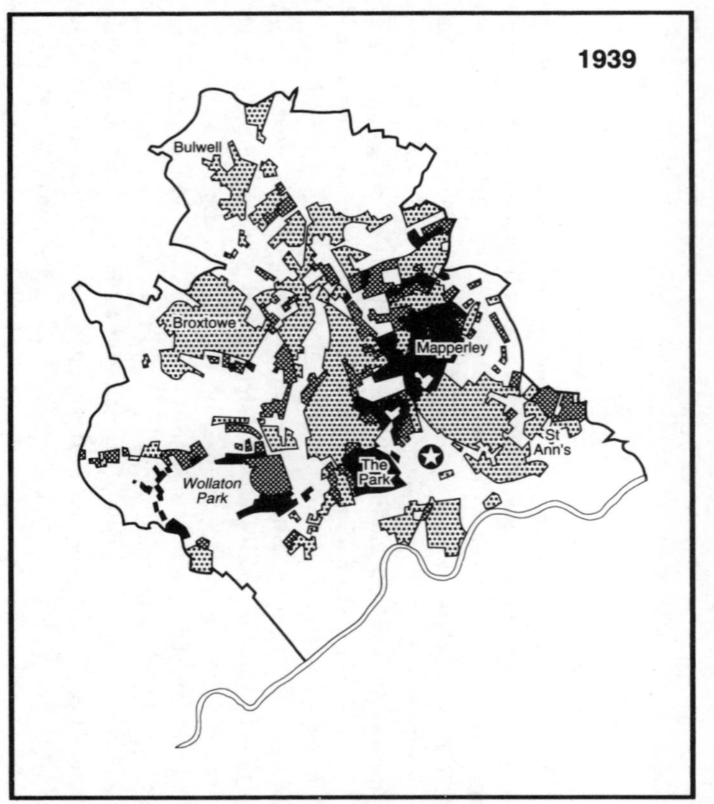

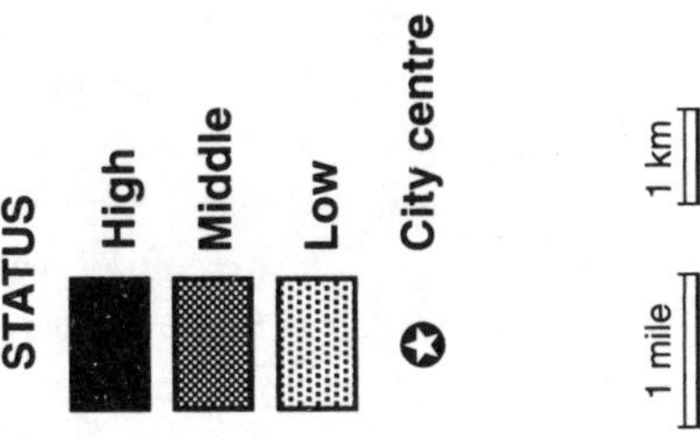
STATUS
High
Middle
Low
City centre
1 mile
1 km

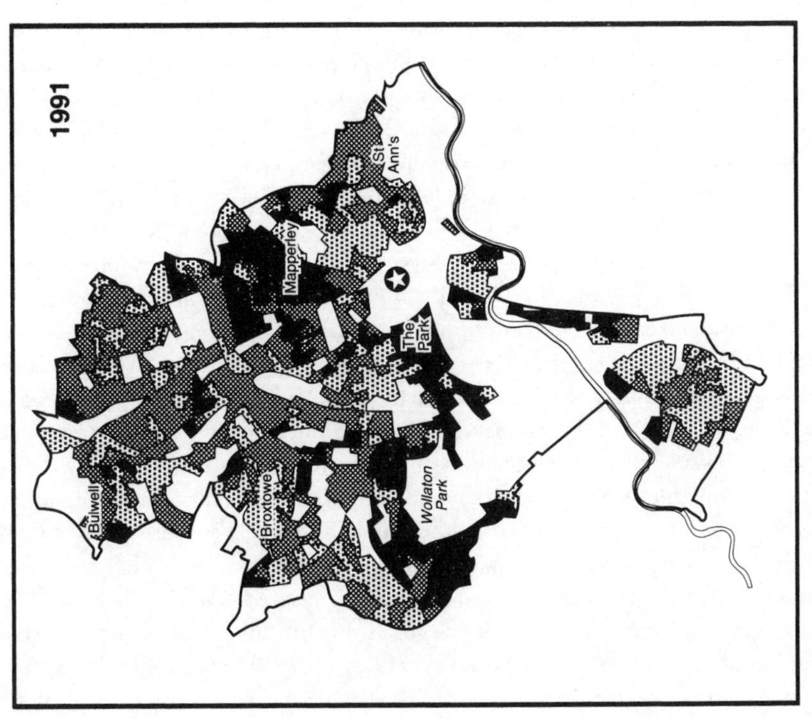
1991
Bulwell
Broxtowe
Wollaton Park
The Park
Mapperley
St Ann's

the private and public housing sectors. The corporation, stung by the rejection of its extension application, organised a massive modernisation programme for the domestic sewage disposal system. By 1926 nearly £2½ million had been spent converting around 30,000 pail closets, and by 1928 a new main drainage system had been approved. The following year extensive improvements costing £330,000 began at Stoke Bardolph.[5]

The corporation also embarked on a programme of house building. Of 26,603 houses constructed in the inter-war period 17,461 (65.5 per cent) were built by the local authority. Twenty municipal estates were built on green-field sites, ranging in size from 212 dwellings at Gordon Road to 2,838 at Aspley (figure 18.2). A further forty-one smaller schemes, involving up to 150 dwellings, were implemented chiefly on undeveloped tracts of land within the existing built-up area, although a number were built in older parts of the city on slum clearance sites. These included the Red Lion Street improvement scheme of 1923, under the terms of which the notorious Marsh district was redeveloped.[6] The architect Cecil Howitt, who designed house types which could be built relatively quickly and cheaply, deserved much of the credit.[7]

The new suburban municipal estates accounted for most of the expansion of Nottingham's built-up area during the 1920s and 1930s. The overcrowded and unhealthy living conditions in the inner-city slums contrasted starkly with the new estates, with their semi-detached houses incorporating three bedrooms, a living-room, kitchen, bathroom, toilet and garden. Housing densities in the 1920s peaked at twelve per acre (thirty per hectare), compared with up to 500 per acre (1,235 per hectare) in some of the slum areas. The dominant characteristic of the new estates was their spaciousness, a result of the standards specified in the Tudor Walters Report of 1918. To implement these standards the city's Estates Committee needed land. Between 1919 and 1928 it bought land on the open market, and in the years 1928–32 it made extensive use of compulsory purchase powers. By 1931 it was clear that the city boundary would have to be extended if the demand for housing was to be satisfied. In October that year the corporation proposed an extension designed almost to treble the physical area of the city by bringing in large parts of the adjoining urban and rural districts. Following a public enquiry in 1932 a limited extension was granted and the city area extended from 10,935 acres (4,425 hectares) to 16,166 acres (6,545 hectares) (figure 12.1). Almost all the territorial gains (92 per cent) were made in the Basford Rural District and, as a result, the council housing estates developed during the 1930s were mainly located west and north of the city.[8]

During the inter-war period the private sector played a secondary role in the construction of houses in Nottingham. Just over a third (34.5 per cent) of new houses were attributable to private enterprise. By comparison 80 per cent of all houses built in Britain between 1919 and 1939 were for owner occupation.[9] The disparity was largely due to the corporation having secured most of the suitable building land within the city limits. On occasion it sold off blocks of land to private builders, stipulating the type and quality of houses to be erected. Such sales were particularly

Plate 51 **Clearance and redevelopment, 1936**. These two pictures show the before-and-after effect of the redevelopment of what is now Brook Street. They were taken from approximately the same place (note in the background the trees of Victoria Park and the spire of the Victoria Schools complex on Bath Street). In this area 1,130 houses were demolished in 1936 and 4,095 people displaced in the process. In his annual report the Medical Officer of Health anticipated that people's subsequent residence in new housing would bring an improvement in health and 'habits of life'. To help attain these objectives the corporation provided a free removal and fumigation service to prevent the migration of bugs, and two female removal officers advised former slum dwellers on utilising their new facilities

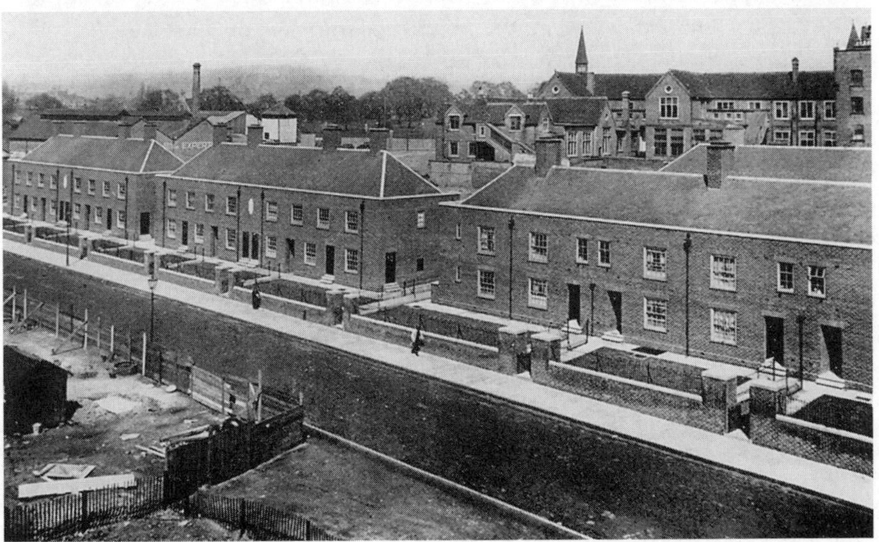

judicious around the fringes of Wollaton Park. In 1924 the corporation bought the Wollaton Park estate for £200,000 from Lord Middleton, and it then proceeded to recoup almost the entire cost by selling off parcels of land for development. Most owner-occupied housing developments in this period involved less than ten acres (four hectares), and given the limited financial resources of their builders, these estates were usually located where roads and mains services already existed.[10]

The scale and distribution of public and private residential developments in inter-war Nottingham were such that both the physical form of the city and its social geography were substantially altered. By 1939 there was a mosaic of social status areas, (figure 18.1b). Relatively little high-status development had taken place since 1916, except for the area around Wollaton Park and infill building on the Park Estate and at Mapperley Park. Suburbs in the middle-status range had commonly been built for owner-occupation. Small blocks of modest, three-bedroomed detached and semi-detached houses began to appear along the main roads radiating out from the city centre and along the new ring road (figure 18.2). Here they were intermingled with numerous low-status areas. Most of the new council estates fell into this category, being rated at £14–£18, although their facilities were far superior to those of similarly rated properties built before 1919.[11]

The corporation also paid attention to the city's road network. The 1919 Housing and Town Planning Act required local authorities with populations exceeding 20,000 to prepare town-planning schemes, initially by 1926. Schemes were prepared for Nottingham in 1926–27, and combined into a Draft Town Planning Scheme which was approved in 1932. Attention was paid chiefly to the road system, since the development of an outer ring road around the western and northern edge of the built-up area of the city had been advocated since 1919. The northern section (Valley Road) had already been built during 1920–22 as a corporation-sponsored scheme for the relief of local unemployment. The opening of Middleton and Western Boulevards in 1928, and Clifton Boulevard in 1932, completed the major dual carriageway route. Between December 1923 and 1926 Trent Bridge was doubled in width at a cost of £130,000, while the city was linked with the suburb of Beeston along Abbey Road and University Boulevard. In the inner city Parliament Street and Huntingdon Street were widened in 1932. These schemes eased congestion in the older built-up areas, and provided the framework for large-scale, low-density urban growth.[12]

The development of the road network was complemented by a sustained increase in cheap, frequent, and fast mass transport, enabling people to live on suburban housing estates while working and shopping in the city. The initial boost came with the introduction of electric trams in 1901. The fleet expanded from nine vehicles to 135 in 1914 and to 155 during 1915–19. By 1926, 200 vehicles were operating on 25.9 miles of routeways. From 1921 there was increasing competition from motor bus services and, from April 1927, trolleybuses. The Nottingham Corporation Act of 1930 facilitated the conversion of all tramway routes to trolleybus operation (figure 18.3). Electric trams were phased out rapidly and services finished in 1936. Already the corporation's fleet of 106 trolleybuses was the largest in the country, but

Figure 18.2 **Council house building, 1919–83**

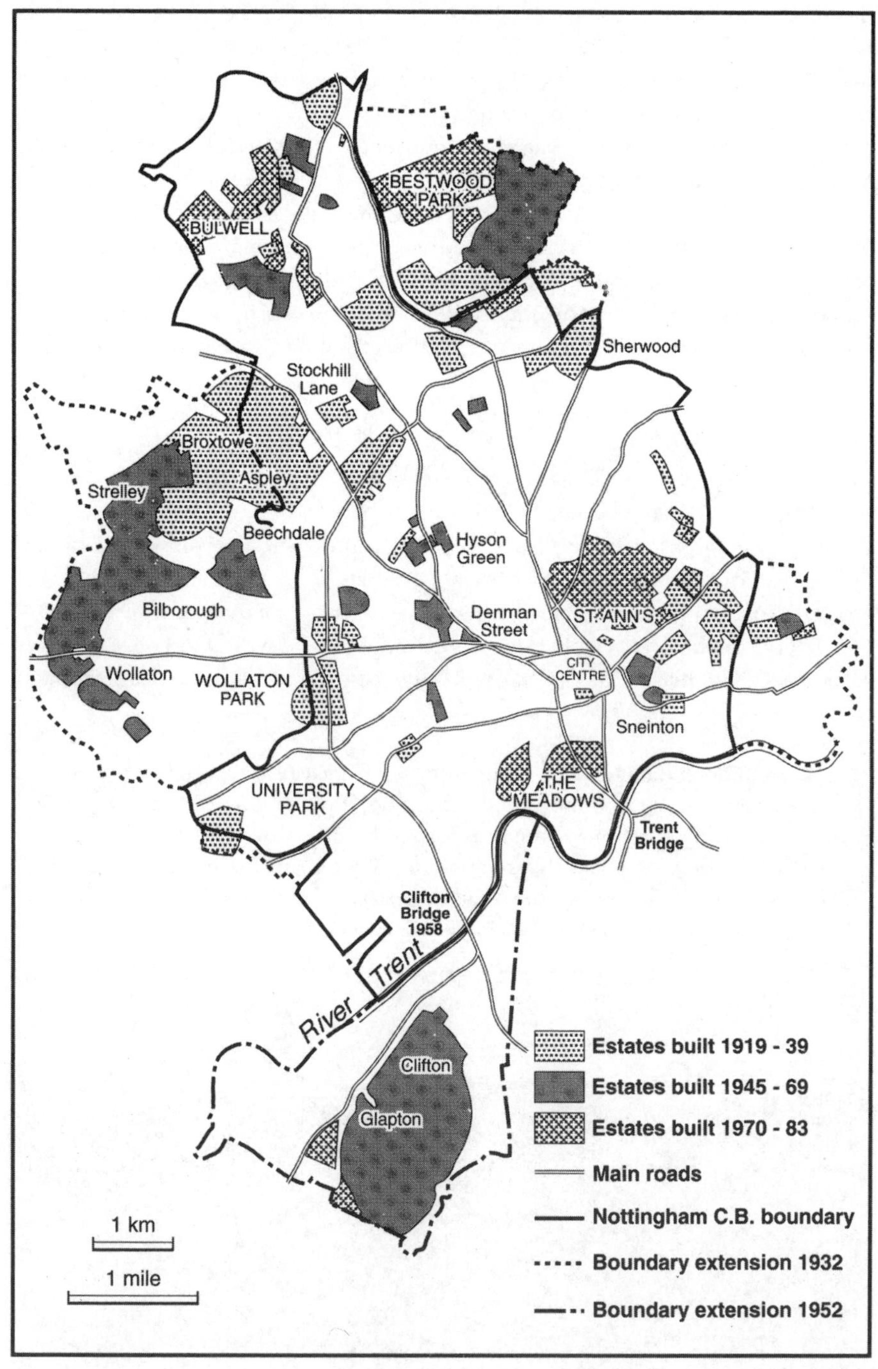

due to the introduction of the more economic diesel-driven bus, there were no further extensions to the route system. Between 1920 and 1939 the corporation's motor bus fleet increased from three to 217 vehicles.[13] The market-place became the hub of the network and, renamed the Old Market Square by 1928, it became the centre of an extensive road-based transportation system.

The railways, by contrast, made no contribution to the city's residential expansion during the inter-war years. Most of the railway network was created as part of wider regional and national passenger and freight systems, and the Suburban Line had already lost much of its passenger traffic to the tramcars by the time war economy measures resulted in the closure of its three stations from 1 July 1916. Through services were maintained until January 1931, but thereafter the line was used solely for goods traffic with only St Ann's Well station remaining open (figure 18.4).[14]

1939–1995

In two important respects the Second World War provided a re-run of the situation during the First World War. In 1939 there was still a large unmet need for dwellings, and the situation was exacerbated by the virtual cessation of construction during the war. Population and household numbers continued to grow, and in 1942 the Reconstruction Committee estimated that 6,325 houses would be needed immediately

Plate 52 **Middleton Boulevard, looking north, 20 August 1930**. Opened in 1928 on land recently purchased from Lord Middleton as part of the Wollaton Hall acquisition, this was part of the major dual-carriageway route around the town. The wide central reservation, where children once played, can still be seen today, but this is now a major traffic route, with vehicles regularly reduced to a crawling pace as they approach the Raleigh roundabout in the distance

after the war. By 1945 the Finance and General Purposes Committee had revised this figure upwards to 8,605 dwellings.[15]

During the decade after the war house building was firmly regulated by central government, with council house building favoured (via licences and subsidies) at the expense of the private sector. Initially, building was resumed in the Bilborough and Bulwell areas, but between 1951 and 1973 in Clifton, and in Bestwood Park between 1958 and 1968, the last major estates in the inter-war tradition were developed. Peripheral developments also continued, particularly at Top Valley (1973–6), but these were smaller in scale and often involved a mixture of public and owner-occupied property. Overall, between 1945 and 1981 32,551 new council houses were erected, and 49.8 per cent of city households lived in council-rented properties in 1981 (figure 18.5). By contrast, in the neighbouring suburbs of Broxtowe, Rushcliffe and Gedling the proportions were 20 per cent, 16 per cent and 18 per cent respectively.[16]

An important feature of the post-war period has been the sustained assault on the obsolescent nineteenth-century housing stock around the city centre. A lengthy survey (1947–52) identified 11,232 houses in poor or unfit condition. Government approval for tackling the city's slums came in 1955. In some instances the cleared sites were used to build deck-access and high-rise flats, although during the 1960s the corporation showed little enthusiasm for these novel forms of housing construction. This

Plate 53 **Huntington Street Bus Station, 1932**. Bus stations have lacked the glamour of railway stations. They were mostly open, with islands of raised paving forming platforms for loading and unloading, yet it was from Huntington Street (opened 1930) that many Nottingham residents set out for holidays and day trips – quite apart from daily journeys to work and home – in the days before mass car-ownership. The Bus Station closed in 1972 when it was superseded by the Victoria Centre Bus Station

Figure 18.3 **Nottingham City Transport trolleybus routes, 1950**

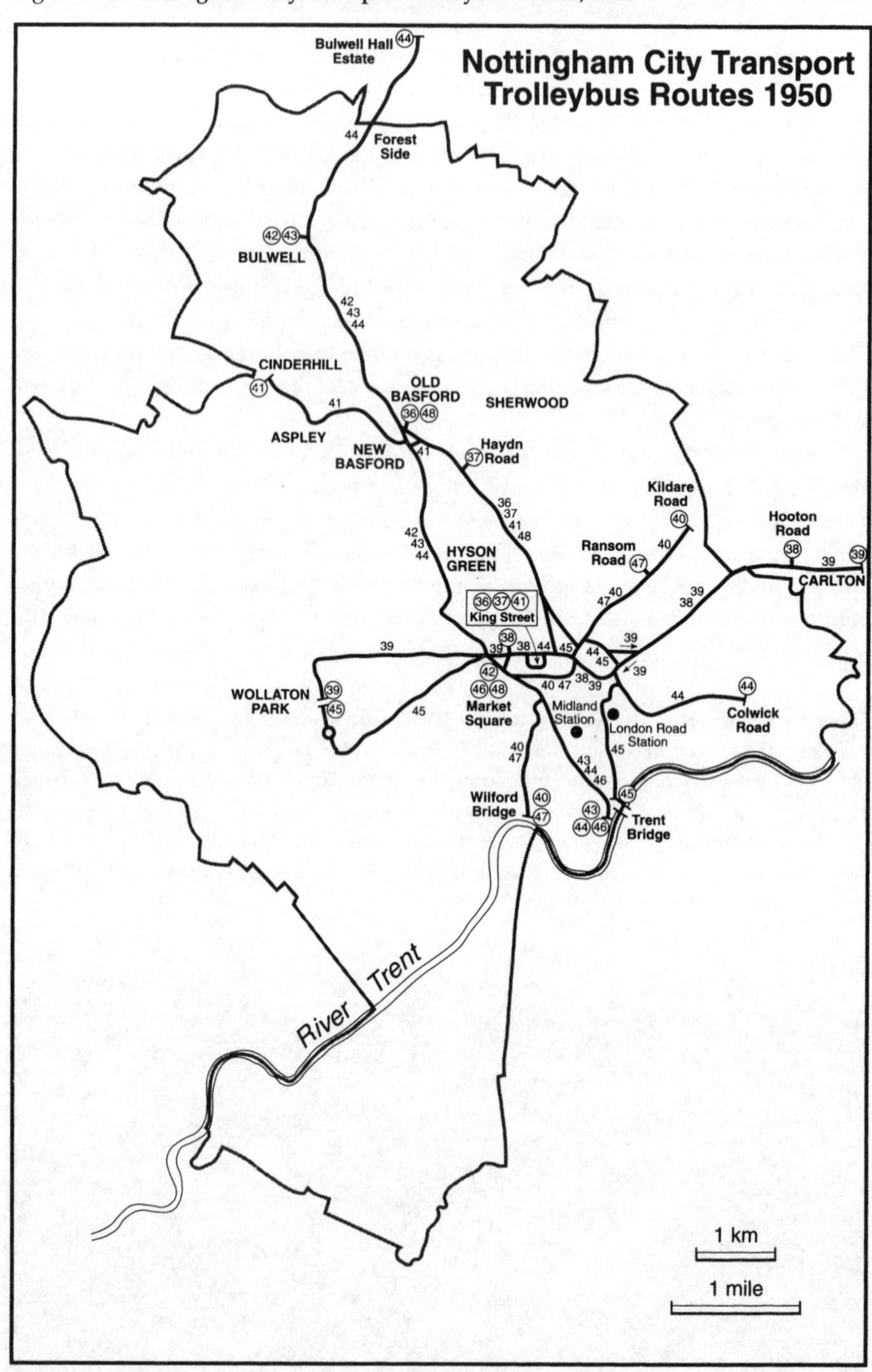

proved fortunate. Nationwide, serious structural faults developed within twenty years in many such dwellings, but in Nottingham only four sites have had to be cleared (Old Basford, Hyson Green, Denman Street and Balloon Woods).

During the 1960s and the 1970s comprehensive slum clearance and renewal schemes became fashionable. The St Ann's and Meadows projects were among the largest in Europe, involving the clearance of 25,000 post-enclosure slum houses. In St Ann's, the largest of these areas, 30,000 people lived in 10,000 houses, mostly built in the 1880s. Many were rotting, damp, difficult to heat, and lacking in basic amenities. The costs of such schemes could not be sustained, and housing policy, both locally and nationally, switched to the improvement of substandard dwellings with designated General Improvement Areas (GIAs) and Housing Action Areas (HAAs). In Nottingham over 7,000 grants had been given by 1982 for housing improvements in twenty-three GIAs and sixteen HAAs.[17]

The private sector and housing associations have also contributed to the city's housing stock in the post-war years. Indeed, since 1979 these agencies have become the main providers of new housing because central government has drastically curtailed financial support for public housing developments. However, because the corporation acquired most of the suitable building land, non-public housing schemes have mostly been small in scale and scattered within the existing built-up area (for example, infilling in Mapperley Park, the Park Estate and around Wollaton Park) and on green-field sites. Since 1980 new residential development has been limited to piecemeal infilling. The city's latest Local Plan identified just 198 acres (82.7 hectares) spread over thirty-two sites as being suitable for residential development by 2011.[18]

A further important change has resulted from the central government policy of encouraging sitting council tenants to buy their homes.[19] Between 1981 and 1991 the number of households living in council houses in Nottingham fell by 14,285 (28.6 per cent). Conversely the proportion of households living in owner-occupied properties rose over the decade from 37.5 per cent to 51.9 per cent. Households living in council housing fell from 49.8 per cent to 32.7 per cent over the same period. This policy has dramatically changed the city's housing-tenure map (figure 18.5). In both inner city and suburban council estates the proportions of households still renting in 1991 were much lower than a decade earlier. On some estates (notably Clifton) owner-occupiers now constitute more than half of the households.

Since 1919 the city council has endeavoured to provide decent housing. The corporation has done this directly, as landlord for its own tenants, and indirectly by using its statutory planning powers to enable other housing agencies to provide sufficient dwellings. As a result, in 1992 81 per cent of all dwellings in the city had been built since 1919. Yet the task facing the council is Sisyphean. Although only 1.9 per cent of the housing stock was classed as unfit in 1992, 47.3 per cent needed renovation. The financial constraints imposed by central government on local authority expenditure, combined with council house sales since 1980, have resulted in a growing failure to meet the demand for adequate local authority accommodation.

Figure 18.4 **Roads, railways and residential areas, 1916–95**

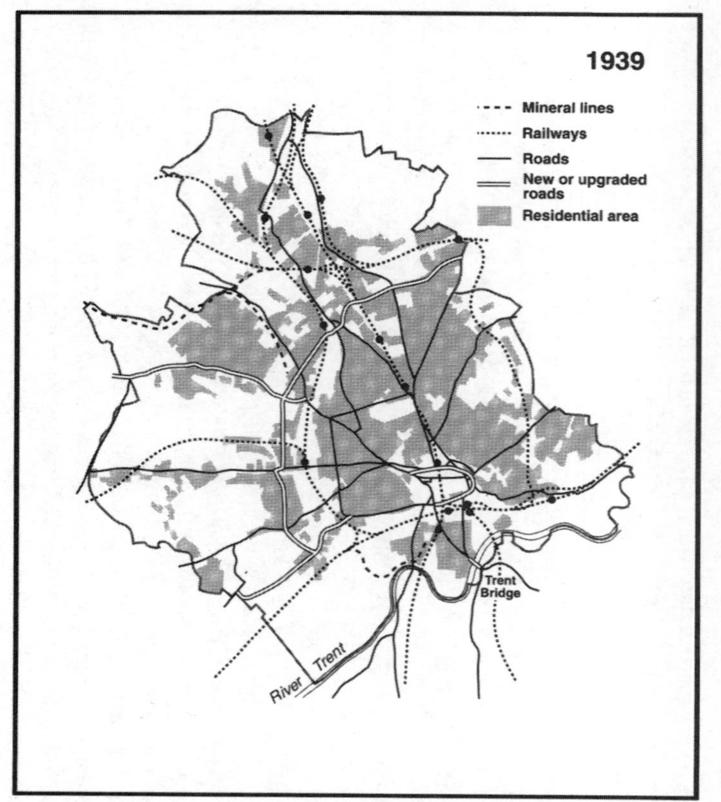

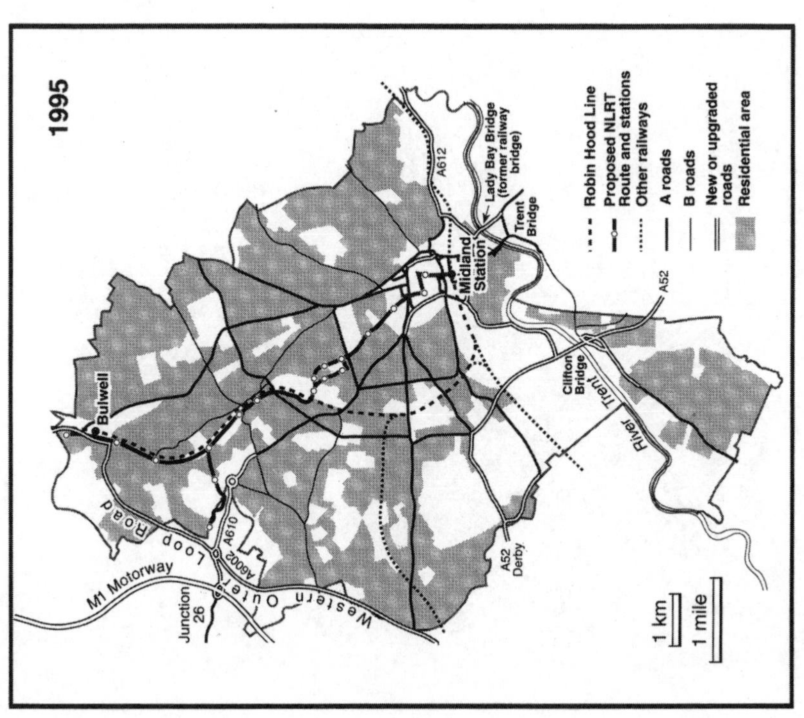
1995
Bulwell
Junction 26
M1 Motorway
A6002
A610
Western Outer Loop Road
A52 Derby
Clifton Bridge
River Trent
A52
Midland Station
Trent Bridge
Lady Bay Bridge (former railway bridge)
A612
Robin Hood Line
Proposed NLRT Route and stations
Other railways
A roads
B roads
New or upgraded roads
Residential area
1 km
1 mile

Figure 18.5 **The impact of council house sales, 1981–91**

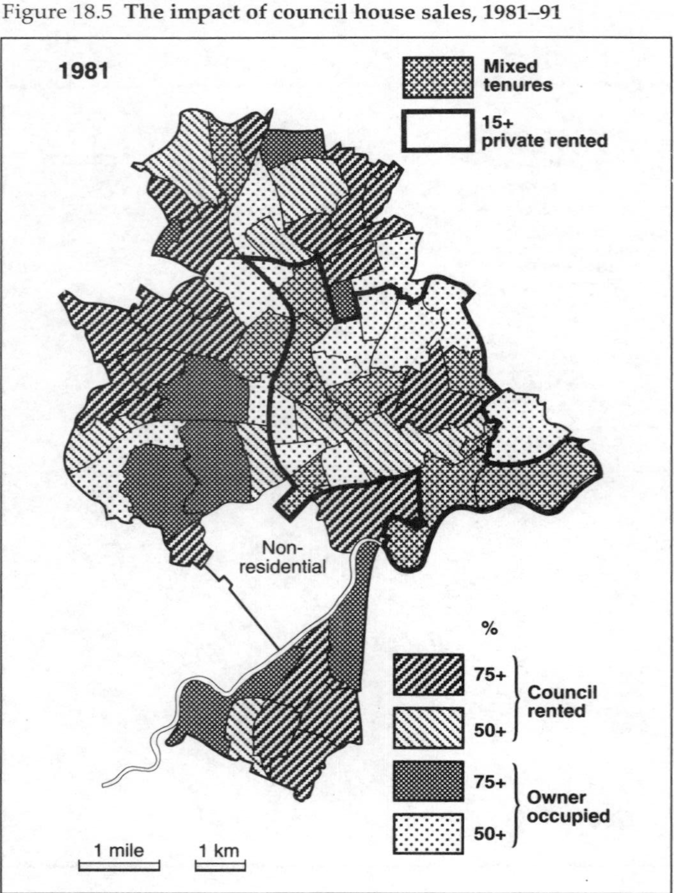

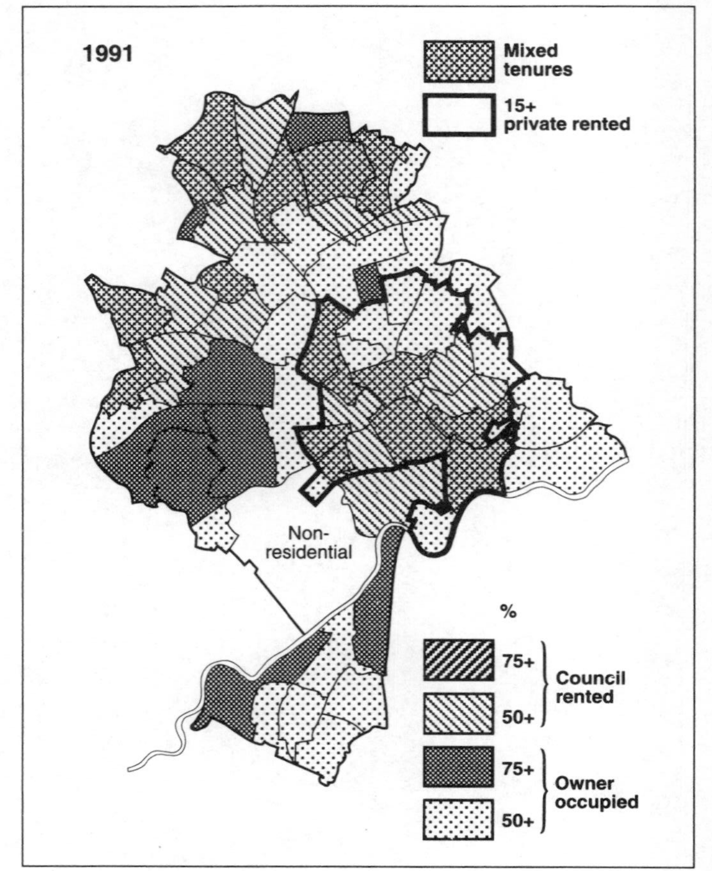

In Nottingham there were 10,378 households on the waiting list in April 1993, of which 6,869 were classed as being in priority need. Homelessness affects almost 1,000 households annually in the mid-1990s.[20]

The shortage of building land is a comparatively novel phenomenon. Far more serious and protracted has been demographic change. Until 1961 the city's population grew steadily, albeit at lower rates than in its neighbouring suburbs. Over the period 1961–91 suburban migration assumed major dimensions and the city's population fell by 18.4 per cent. In part this was a consequence of comprehensive renewal schemes in central residential areas such as the Meadows and St Ann's, where numbers were halved in the 1970s. However, the middle class has chosen voluntarily to leave the town and has been heavily over-represented proportionately in outmigration. In 1991 only 25.6 per cent of the economically active males and 22.7 per cent of the females in Nottingham were in social classes I and II, compared with much higher proportions in Gedling (35.4 and 29.4 per cent), Rushcliffe (51.2 and 37.4 per cent) and Broxtowe (37.1 and 31.1 per cent). The proportion of males in social classes I and II almost doubled in Nottingham between 1951 and 1991 (table 18.3), but the ratios of working males in the city – compared to England and Wales generally – fell from 75:100 to 72:100 for social classes I and II and rose from 114:100 to 136:100 for social classes IV and V.[21]

Table 18.3 **Social classes (males only), 1951 and 1991**

	1951		*1991*	
Classes	*Nottingham*	*England and Wales*	*Nottingham*	*England and Wales*
I	2.1	3.3	5.2	7.0
II	11.2	14.5	20.4	28.3
III	53.3	52.9	46.3	43.9
IV	18.9	16.2	20.6	15.4
V	14.5	13.1	7.5	5.4

Sources: Decennial Population Censuses.

Social polarisation, measured in terms of the spatial sorting of classes, was evident by 1916, and has been reinforced since by the growth of discrete council estates and owner-occupied suburbs. Despite the massive transfer of council houses to the owner-occupied sector during the 1980s, the city's high-status neighbourhoods constitute only a small part of the entire social mosaic. Nottingham is probably unique among British cities in the survival of two high-status areas (the Park and Mapperley Park) close to the city centre. Both are less grand than in their Victorian and Edwardian heydays, but they are still islands of affluence amidst a sea of low-status Victorian terraces and 1970s public housing. Their survival and enhancement have been ensured because the council designated them Conservation Areas (the

Park in 1969, Mapperley Park in 1974).[22] Elsewhere in the city the proportion of males in social classes IV and V exceeded the national average (20.8 per cent). Figure 18.1c shows that the majority of these low-status areas were in the suburban council estates. The former inner-city concentration of semi-skilled and unskilled workers has shrunk to a vestigial swathe fringing the eastern and southern margins of the city centre, and embracing St Ann's, Sneinton, and the Meadows. One other low-status area (New Basford/Hyson Green) survives north-west of the city centre.

Although socio-economic differentiation persists as the most important dimension of social cleavage in British cities, it is not the only one. Social life is also influenced by demographic attributes such as age and household structure, which usually display distinctive spatial patterns. In Nottingham the importance of the life-cycle phenomenon can be demonstrated by the use of two specific examples. In 1991 almost one in five of the City's population was aged under fifteen, compared with 18.9 per cent for England and Wales (table 18.2). Within the city's neighbourhoods numbers varied from 9.9 per cent in the Park Estate to 33.7 per cent in north Bilborough. Children were found in disproportionately high numbers within the peripheral suburban estates and in both old and redeveloped inner-city neighbourhoods. People aged over sixty now outnumber those aged under fifteen, both locally and nationally (table 18.2). In Nottingham the lowest value was recorded in Hempshill Vale (10.1 per cent) and the highest in Beechdale Ward (38.4 per cent). The greatest concentrations occurred in the city's western and southern suburban estates.

During the past twenty years important changes have occurred in household characteristics: 'the storybook family in Dick and Jane readers (with an aproned mother baking cakes for the two children as they await father's return from a day of breadwinning) has by no means disappeared, but it is fast being outnumbered by other kinds of families'.[23] In 1991 only 17.1 per cent of Nottingham households fitted Knox's graphic description (table 18.4). The proportions were much higher in the neighbouring suburbs of Broxtowe (23.9 per cent), Gedling (24.1 per cent) and Rushcliffe (25.8 per cent). Many couples choose to cohabit rather than to marry, while the number of people living alone in the city has risen from 21.4 per cent in 1971 to 30.3 per cent in 1991. However, the fastest-growing of all household types is the single-parent family, up from 1.9 per cent in 1971, to 8.1 per cent in 1991. The diversification of households has important consequences for socio-spatial segregation. In Nottingham the proportion of married couples with dependent children ranged from 8.1 per cent of all households in north St Ann's to 35.5 per cent in Rise Park. Although the greatest concentrations were found in suburban estates, only eight of the city's fifty-six planning zones had rates higher than the average for England and Wales (22.4 per cent). Cohabiting couples with dependent children, in contrast, are over-represented in Nottingham (table 18.4), exceeding the national average in two-thirds of its residential areas.

Table 18.4 **Household composition, 1991**

Household composition	*Nottingham*	*England and Wales*	*Ratio (1):(2)*
	(1) %	*(2)* %	*(3)* %
Households with no families	35.3	29.4	119
One person	30.3	26.1	116
Two or more persons	4.8	3.3	145
Households with one family	63.7	69.6	92
Married couple family	44.7	55.4	81
With no children	20.8	24.5	85
With dependent child(ren)	17.1	22.4	76
With non-dependent child(ren) only	6.8	8.5	80
Cohabiting couple family	7.2	5.5	131
With no children	4.1	3.5	117
With dependent child(ren)	2.9	1.8	159
With non-dependent child(ren) only	0.3	0.2	141
Lone parent family	11.8	8.8	134
With dependent child(ren)	8.1	5.2	156
With non-dependent child(ren) only	3.7	3.6	103
Households with two or more families	1.2	0.9	124

Source: Decennial Population Census 1991 (Part 2, Table 87).

Social problems

Studies of Nottingham's population have not been confined simply to delineating the major dimensions of social class and demography: social problems have also been identified and examined. In 1945 Chambers observed that 'the housing plans of the twenties triumphantly solved the problem of re-housing large sections of the population on a standard of amenity that was the equal of any in the world; but new problems, mainly of a psychological nature arising out of the transfer of large numbers of human beings, presented themselves'.[24] Since the 1960s a reduction in employment opportunities in manufacturing has only partly been compensated by gains in service employment. Unemployment levels have escalated quickly in all the large cities: in 1991 the rates among adults and youths (aged 16–19) in Nottingham were 14.7 per cent and 17.0 per cent respectively, compared with 8.6 per cent and 17.6 per cent for England and Wales. Within the city, levels of unemployment for both groups exceeded the national figures in most neighbourhoods. The highest rates were found in inner-city areas (peaking at 44.6 per cent for adults and 66.4 per cent for youths in Hyson Green), but there were also substantial outliers of high unemployment on the council estates. More than 47,000 households claimed benefits in 1995.[25] Many of the young people living in Nottingham's most deprived areas have few skills or qualifications. In 1991 51.4 per cent of 16–17-year-olds in the city had left full-time education compared with 45.0 per cent in England and Wales. The poorest areas of Nottingham had the highest rates of early school leavers, reaching 79.7 per cent on the Bulwell Hall Estate.

Lone parent families with dependent children have also been identified as an economically marginal group.[26] In 1991 these families constituted 8.1 per cent of all the city's households, compared with the national average of 5.2 per cent – a ratio of 156:100 (table 18.4). The majority (93.6 per cent) of these families are female-headed. Of all the city's families with dependent children, 28.7 per cent were headed by a lone parent and only a quarter of its neighbourhoods had proportions lower than the national average. The highest concentrations were found in inner-city locations, notably the Meadows, St Ann's, Radford and Hyson Green.

A key element of differentiation in British cities during the post-war years is ethnicity. During the inter-war years Nottingham's foreign-born population numbered only 4,290, of whom the Irish formed the largest individual group (table 18.5). The Second World War triggered a wave of immigration to Britain and large numbers of refugees, drawn mainly from eastern European countries (especially Poland), settled in Nottingham. A new phase began in the 1950s when thousands of New Commonwealth migrants settled in the city, attracted mainly by the prospect of both employment and accommodation. In recent years other groups have arrived in Nottingham as refugees from the Vietnam War.[27]

Table 18.5 **Growth of the immigrant population of Nottingham, 1931–91**

Provenance of immigrants	*1931*	*1951*	*1971*	*1991*
Irish Republic	1,107	2,337	3,990	2,686
Europe	761	5,198	5,770	3,498
New Commonwealth	335	810	10,567	11,982
India }		417	2,250	2,088
Pakistan }	243 }		}	3,390
Bangladesh }	}	85 }	1,790	165
Caribbean	23	98	5,421	3,975
Other sources	2,087	2,709	1,348	2,812
Total immigrants	4,290	11,239	21,675	20,978
Percentage of total population	1.6	3.7	2.7	8.0

Source: Decennial Population Censuses.

Table 18.6 **Ethnic groups, 1991**

	Nottingham		*England and Wales*	*Ratio*
	(1) No.	*(2) %*	*(3) %*	*(2):(3)*
White	235,184	89.2	94.1	95
Black				
Caribbean	8.516	3.2	1.0	321
African	618	0.2	0.4	55
Other	3,042	1.2	0.4	329
Indian	4,757	1.8	1.7	109
Pakistan	6,867	2.6	0.9	287
Bangladeshi	301	0.1	0.3	34
Chinese	914	0.4	0.3	121
Other groups				
Asian	699	0.3	0.4	71
Other	2,624	1.0	0.6	179
Total non-white	28,338	10.8	5.9	182
Total population	263,522	100.0	100.0	–

Source: Decennial Population Census (Part 1, Table 6).

The 1991 population census provided the first opportunity to establish precisely the sizes of individual population groups, categorised by both country of birth and ethnicity. Table 18.6 shows that Nottingham has a large ethnic community, with substantial over-representation (in relation to the figures for England and Wales as a whole) of Black Caribbean, Black Other and Pakistani groups and under-representation of Black African, Bangladeshi and Asian groups. Comparison with the data in table 18.5 reveals that the longer-established settlers are now outnumbered by their UK-born children: 65.2 per cent of Nottingham's Black community was born in this country. Among the more recently settled groups the UK-born populations tend to be progressively smaller (Pakistanis, 52.2 per cent; Indians, 49.6 per cent; Bangladeshis, 41.5 per cent; Chinese, 22.3 per cent).

Many of the city's immigrants had limited financial and vocational resources. Today, however, there is great diversity in the relative fortunes of the ethnic groups. The 1991 census showed that unemployment rates for most ethnic groups were higher than those for Whites, but not for the Indians and Chinese. The Indian, Pakistani and White groups had similar proportions of employees, managers or professional workers (19, 16 and 15 per cent respectively), whereas the Black ethnic group had only 5 per cent. In the housing market owner-occupation rates were highest among the Indian and Pakistani households (81.2 and 78 per cent respectively), compared with 51.5 per cent for white households and 44.7 per cent for black households.

The early New Commonwealth settlers moved into inner-city working-class residential areas including the Meadows, New Lenton, Radford, the Forest and St Ann's. Racial discrimination was commonplace, despite the efforts of the Nottingham Trades

Council which became concerned in 1953–54 about the operation of an unofficial 'colour bar' against Afro-Caribbean immigrants by some employers and publicans, and formed a Colour-bar Sub-committee. Offending publicans were reported to the Licensing Authorities, contacts were established with immigrant groups, employers were canvassed as to their attitudes and anti-racist publicity campaigns were mounted within the local trade union movement. Much of the campaign was focused on the employment policies of the city council, where the Transport Department was alleged to be operating a policy of discrimination. Although the Labour Group refused to meet the NTC to discuss the issue, the City Transport Committee agreed to act to remove any forms of discriminatory employment policy.[28]

Problems came to a head in 1958 when disturbances in the St Ann's Well Road area earned Nottingham the title of 'race-war city'.[29] On three consecutive Saturday nights in August and early September 1958 disturbances involving hundreds of people, many of them bystanders, occurred in St Ann's as a result of mutual resentment, although white youths were also prepared to fight each other and the police when black immigrants had prudently instigated a self-imposed curfew.[30] Further disturbances occurred in the 1980s. In Hyson Green in August 1980 individual black youths were attacked by gangs of white youths, and the perceived failure of the police to mount an effective response provoked a petrol-bomb attack on the police station by black youths.[31] Molotov cocktails were also in evidence during the so-called 'copycat riots' on the nights of 10–12 July 1981 when large multiracial groups, imitating events in Liverpool and London, engaged in widespread rioting and looting, particularly in the Hyson Green area. Nine houses, 155 shops and seven vehicles were damaged and police on duty in the Hyson Green flats complex 'came under heavy attack from petrol bombs'.[32] Further disturbances took place in 1986 when 'a number of forced entries into black people's homes, and a series of street searches, caused widespread anger'.[33]

Since the 1950s the immigrant ethnic groups and their British-born children have made many valuable contributions to the economic, social, cultural and political life of the City, not least the country's first black JP and Sheriff. Viv Anderson, then playing for Nottingham Forest, was the first black footballer to represent England at international level. Today, ethnic migrants and their families live in every part of the city, although spatial disparities persist.[34] In 1991 ethnic minorities (including the Irish-born) were still heavily concentrated in the inner city (peaking at 46.1 per cent of the residents of Lenton Sands) and least well-represented in most suburban neighbourhoods (2.1 per cent in Clifton Fairham). Among the individual ethnic groups the Indian population has experienced the most marked residential dispersal.

Some of Nottingham's social problems are attributable to groups which are legally as well as economically and socially marginal. They include illegal immigrants, down-and-outs, drug users, petty criminals and prostitutes.[35] Prostitution has been endemic in the twentieth century. The number of public drinking clubs increased from forty-one to seventy-nine between 1926 and 1936, largely providing a cover for illicit drinking and prostitution, which contributed to the city's reputation as a notorious centre of immorality during the Second World War and its aftermath.[36] In the 1980s, after one of the periodic 'clean-ups', a police officer admitted: 'I think by tradition every City has a red light district ... it's what we say, keeping the lid on the problem. You won't stamp it out.'[37]

Accurate information concerning the size, characteristics and residential and operational locations of marginal groups is, inevitably, difficult to obtain, although considerable attention has been devoted to the activities of criminals and illegal drug-users in the city. The official statistics suggest that Nottingham has long occupied a high position in the national league table for crime, and that the level of criminal activity has increased substantially since the 1970s in parallel with rising unemployment and social deprivation.[38] Violent crimes, 'economic' crimes (burglary, robbery, theft and handling stolen goods), vehicle crimes (especially theft and 'joyriding') and criminal damage have all shown substantial increases since the mid-1980s. The Chief Constable admitted in 1988 that

> By day Nottingham is a vibrant commercial centre attracting business people and shoppers from all over the region. By night the City is catering for a wide variety of tastes ... . The policing problems change little from year to year with shop thefts and autocrime featuring highly during the day and alcohol related public order offences and assaults by night.[39]

Nottingham's reputation for public disorder is reflected in the crime statistics (table 18.7), but on balance, in the view of the Chief Constable, 'firm, but friendly policing' generally contained the epidemic of street violence. Controlling 'football hooliganism' in the city centre has sometimes proved difficult, as in March 1984 when four hundred 'supporters' from Derby, Leicester and Nottingham 'met by arrangement to do battle'.[40]

Table 18.7 **Affrays, drunkenness and disorder, 1935–59 (annual average)**

Date	*Minor assaults*	*Drunkenness*	*Assaults on police*
1935–39	107	287	13
1940–44	124	140	10
1945–49	182	107	9
1950–54	218	288	13
1955–59	179	269	20

Source: Nottingham Chief Constable, *Annual Reports*.

An investigation of the spatial distribution of crimes committed in Nottingham during 1973 showed a strong concentration of both offence occurrences and offenders' homes in the city centre and contiguous low-status neighbourhoods. A second survey, using statistics for May–September 1982, also revealed high prosecution rates among adults living in inner residential areas and also on suburban council estates. Similar geographical patterns have been found for young offenders in both 1981 and 1992.[41]

Since the 1960s the United Kingdom has experienced an 'epidemic' of illegal (mainly recreational) drug-taking, with the numbers of notified new drug addicts rising annually. True prevalence is difficult to determine accurately because most drug users are unregistered, although users claim to have had little difficulty obtaining drugs. However, recent national and local community surveys suggest that drug use in Nottingham is close to the national average. Research has shown that the majority of Nottingham's opioid and cocaine users during 1985–86 lived in the inner city areas and in some of the newer, low-status suburban council estates. Most were young, single males, one-quarter of them living alone. They reported financial problems and they had engaged in criminal acts to finance their addiction. Of these males, 55 per cent claimed to have been the victims of crimes which had involved drugs, and 46 per cent had been victims of household crime.[42] A large proportion of citizens claimed to be 'worried' about becoming victims of crime and going out alone at night.[43]

It has come to be recognised since the 1960s that numerous social problems endemic to urban areas are interconnected rather than discrete phenomena.[44] Although the inner city had the largest concentration of deprived neighbourhoods over the period 1971–91, the problem has become progressively more severe and widespread in the suburban council estates. Collectively these problems reflect increasing socio-spatial segregation of the 'haves' and 'have nots' in large cities.[45]

Transport

The continued dispersal and polarisation of Nottingham's population since 1945 can be attributed mainly to the rapid growth in private transport. In 1966, 34 per cent of the city's households possessed at least one car; by 1991 the proportion had risen to 49.3 per cent, still substantially below the England and Wales average of 67.6 per cent. There is a considerable net daily inflow into the city, predominantly by people driving from the neighbouring suburbs where car-ownership levels are substantially higher than in the city (Rushcliffe, 78.9 per cent, Broxtowe, 73.1 per cent, Gedling, 73 per cent). These figures reflect the fact that Nottingham has retained its regional status as an employment centre, because economic activities have not dispersed significantly since 1945.[46]

Local bus services have changed substantially since 1945. The route network has remained largely radial, with routes being extending into the suburbs of Clifton, Bestwood and Rise Park. In 1961 the city council approved the gradual abandonment of the trolley bus system, but the end came more suddenly than anticipated, with the entire fleet being sold off by July 1966. More importantly, the Transport

Acts of 1980 and 1985 have 'undermined the virtual monopoly of bus companies within their designated territories'.[47] Consequently City of Nottingham Transport (now Nottingham City Transport Ltd, or NCT) no longer has protected status in the provision of services within the city and neighbouring suburbs. A 'mixed economy' exists as private companies compete with the municipal service. The combined effects of competition with rival bus companies and private motor cars has resulted in a decline in bus services along less profitable routes. People living in Nottingham's suburban estates have been most severely affected because overall levels of car ownership are low. Women are particularly disadvantaged by the cut-back in public transport.[48]

During the past forty years the use of buses in Nottingham has halved, whereas total road traffic has increased sixfold.[49] This pressure has prompted major improvements to the local and regional road networks (fig. 18.4). The bridging of the River Trent was improved by the opening of the new Clifton Bridge in 1958, and by its subsequent widening in the early 1970s. It was improved again in 1995. Related improvements to the A453 have enhanced links with Clifton and the city centre. The old railway bridge at Lady Bay (east of Trent Bridge) now carries road traffic. The A52 has been widened within the city and, together with a recently improved and extended section of the A610, provides Nottingham with more effective links to the M1 at junctions 25 and 26 respectively. To improve traffic circulation around the periphery of the city two orbital routes are being constructed. The western outer loop road, linking Bulwell with the A52, is nearing completion. In east Nottingham, the A612 has been completed from Lady Bay Bridge to Colwick, and should eventually form part of an eastern orbital loop.[50]

In the city centre town planners were faced with reconciling modern traffic needs to the medieval street plan. Maid Marian Way, built in the 1960s, cut diametrically across the fan of old Norman streets leading from the Market Square to the Castle. It was a controversial development, and plans were abandoned to construct an urban motorway around the town following a vigorous campaign by the Civic Society. This had been founded in the wake of the construction of Maid Marian Way.[51] Instead the council adopted a policy of widening selected roads and diverting traffic along a one-way system around the central shopping area. Measures were also taken to reduce road traffic flows into the city centre and to maintain the mobility of the 50 per cent of the city's economically active residents who go to work by car. One of these initiatives, the so-called Zone and Collar scheme, was particularly innovatory, but was quickly abandoned in the face of motorist opposition.[52] Underground, multi-storey and off-street car parks have been provided for some 8,000 cars. Many of these strategies were implemented in the early 1970s in conjunction with the pedestrianisation of the main shopping streets. Since the 1980s traffic control and flow has been improved by means of an underground computerised monitoring centre linked to strategically-placed television cameras. Traffic congestion in the city centre has also been reduced by the introduction of park-and-ride schemes on the Forest, the Victoria Embankment, and elsewhere.[53]

The Victoria and Broad Marsh Shopping Centres have increased retail floor-space and also provided new bus stations and car parks. Lying on the northern and southern margins of the historic core of the city on what, in the nineteenth century, were areas of poor-quality housing, the two centres serve as significant reminders of the demands of modern shopping and the motor car. The current development of out-of-town retail promises yet a further change of social habits.

Since 1945 investments in roads and motor transport have enhanced Nottingham's local and regional status. However, for the city's rail services the period has been one of virtually unrelieved decline (figure. 18.4). All the suburban services and most of those to neighbouring towns closed before the 1960s. By 1967 the line out of Victoria station to London (Marylebone) and Sheffield, and one from the Midland station to London (St Pancras) had also closed. The Victoria Station also closed, although the clock tower remains. Gains have been modest. In 1984 a two-hourly direct service to Birmingham was introduced.[54] On 17 May 1993 the Robin Hood Line was inaugurated by Regional Railways Central and Nottinghamshire County Council, thereby restoring passenger services between the Midland Station, Hucknall and Newstead. Bulwell Station was opened for hourly services in 1994. The Robin Hood Line is being co-ordinated and integrated with the planned Line One (figure. 18.4) of the Greater Nottingham Light Rapid Transit scheme. Parliamentary approval for this scheme was granted in 1994 and Line One opened in 2004.

Notes

1 B. Robson, *Those Inner Cities* (Oxford, 1988), pp. 17–25.

2 C. J. Thomas, 'Geographical aspects of the growth of the residential area of Greater Nottingham in the 20th Century' (University of Nottingham, Ph.D. thesis, 1968), pp. 62–80. Similar studies of other British cities have confirmed that the residential property rating value is a useful surrogate for the social class of the occupants: H. Carter and C .R. Lewis, *An Urban Geography of England and Wales in the Nineteenth Century* (1990), p. 63.

3 Thomas, 'Geographical aspects', pp. 79–80.

4 *Nottingham Journal and Express*, 29 May 1920.

5 G. Oldfield, 'The municipal boundary extensions of Nottingham, 1877–1952' (University of Nottingham, MA thesis, 1989).

6 Thomas, 'Geographical aspects', pp. 80–1.

7 E. Scoffham, *A Vision of the City: the Architecture of T. C. Howitt* (Nottinghamshire County Council, 1992), pp. 10–17.

8 Thomas, 'Geographical aspects', pp. 90–2, 121.

9 P. Lawless and F. Brown, *Urban Growth and Change in Britain* (1986), p. 73.

10 Thomas, 'Geographical aspects', pp. 100–18.

11 *Ibid.*, pp. 102–4.

12 *Ibid.*, pp. 94–7; J. D. Chambers, *Modern Nottingham in the Making* (Nottingham, 1945), p. 52.

13 F. P. Groves, *Nottingham City Transport* (Glossop, 1978), pp. 1, 19, 21, 39, 93.

14 J. R. Bonser, 'The Nottingham Suburban Railway', *The Lodestone* (October–November 1954), pp. 115–17.

15 Thomas, 'Geographical aspects', p. 123.

16 *Ibid.*, pp. 123–6; Brazier, *New Geography*, pp. 30–1.

17 Thomas, 'Geographical aspects', pp. 128–30, 145–7; Robson, *Those Inner Cities*, p. 18; Brazier,

New Geography, p. 37; R. Smith and P. Whysall, 'The origins and development of local authority housing in Nottingham 1890–1960', in S. Lowe and D. Hughes (eds.), *A New Century of Social Housing* (Leicester, 1991), p. 41; R. Silburn, *People in their Places, One Hundred Years of Nottingham Life* (Nottingham, 1981), pp. 31–3.

18 Brazier, *New Geography*, p. 36; Nottingham City Corporation, *Draft Nottingham Local Plan* (Nottingham, 1994), pp. 55–6.

19 Robson, Those Inner Cities, p. 123.

20 Nottingham City Corporation, *Draft Local Plan*, pp. 54–5; J. A. Giggs and D. K. Whynes, 'Homeless people in Nottingham', *EMG*, 11 (1988), pp. 57–67.

21 J. A. Giggs, 'Fringe expansion and suburbanisation around Nottingham: a metropolitan area approach', *EMG*, 5 (1970), pp. 9–18; Brazier, *New Geography*, pp. 67–78.

22 Nottinghamshire County Council, 'Social need in Nottinghamshire: County Disadvantaged Area Study, 1994', part 1 (West Bridgford, 1994); K. C. Edwards, 'The Park Estate, Nottingham', in M. A. Simpson and T. H. Lloyd (eds.), *Middle Class Housing in Britain* (Newton Abbot, 1977); K. Brand, 'The Park Estate, Nottingham: the development of a nineteenth century fashionable suburb', *TTS*, 88 (1984), pp. 54–75; K. Brand, *The Park Estate* (Nottingham, 1985).

23 P. Knox, *Urban Social Geography* (2nd edn, Harlow, 1995), p. 11.

24 Chambers, *Modern Nottingham*, p. 44.

25 *EP*, 5 October 1995. The earlier impact of these changes in St Ann's are discussed in K. Coates and R. Silburn, *St Ann's: Poverty, Deprivation and Morale in a Nottingham Community* (Nottingham, 1968).

26 H. P. M. Winchester and P. White, 'The location of marginalised groups in the inner city', *Environment and Planning D: Society and Space*, 6 (1988), pp. 37–54.

27 D. Lawrence, *Black Migrants, White Natives: a Study of Race Relations in Nottingham* (1974), pp. 12–45; L. Crewe, 'Skills, work and training: the employment experience of the Vietnamese community in Nottingham', *EMG*, 15 (1992), pp. 3–13.

28 NUMD Nottingham Trade Council, Annual Report 1955. I owe this point to Dr Richard Stevens.

29 M. S. Husain, 'The increase and distribution of New Commonwealth immigrants in Greater Nottingham', *EMG*, 6 (1975), pp. 105–29; Brazier, 'New geography', pp. 84–5; A. Lawrence, 'The social and spatial segregation of Asian immigrants in the Nottingham conurbation, 1971–86' (University of Nottingham, BA dissertation [Geography], 1988).

30 Lawrence, *Black Migrants, White Natives*, pp. 1–2; J. Wickenden, *Colour in Britain* (1958), pp. 30–4.

31 A. Simpson, *Stacking the Decks: a Study in Racial Inequality in Council Housing in Nottingham* (Nottingham, 1981), pp. 289–90.

32 Nottingham Chief Constable's Annual Report (hereafter CC), 1981.

33 J. T. Benyon and J. Solomos (eds.), *The Roots of Urban Unrest* (Oxford, 1987), p. 9; Lawrence, 'Segregation of Asian immigrants', pp. 85–96; Lawrence, *Black Migrants, White Natives*, p. 213. For the contribution of the Black community to the development of Nottingham see Len Garrison (ed,), *The Black Presence in Nottingham* (Nottingham, 1993).

34 H. Carter, *The Study of Urban Geography* (4th edn, 1995), p. 275; M. Chisholm, 'Britain as a plural society', in M. Chisholm and D. M. Smith (eds.), *Shared Space: Divided Space* (1990).

35 Winchester and White, 'Location of marginalised groups', p. 41.

36 CC, 1936; *Sunday Pictorial*, 25 May 1947, which also reported that the city centre was 'flooded with good-time girls', the Arboretum area was the 'pansies' beat' and professional prostitutes resorted to providing 'perversions' to maintain a clientele in the competitive environment.

37 J. E. Kingscott, 'Oral history in libraries with special reference to the Nottinghamshire Oral History Collection and the Hyson Green Project' (Loughborough University, M.A. thesis, 1988), p. 103.

38 Home Office, *Criminal Statistics in England and Wales* (1993); Central Statistical Office, *Social Trends 25* (1995), p. 154; D. T. Herbert and D. M. Smith (eds.), *Social Problems in the City: New Perspectives* (1989).

39 CC, 1988.

40 CC, 1984.

41 Nottinghamshire Police Authority, *Nottinghamshire Constabulary Annual Report* (1993); J. Bradbury, 'An investigation of the spatial distribution of crime in Greater Nottingham' (University of Nottingham, Ph.D. thesis, 1981); Nottinghamshire County Council, 'Disadvantage in Nottinghamshire, 1983', part 1, pp. 73–4, part 2, pp. 25–33; 'Social need in Nottinghamshire, 1994', pp. 86–7.

42 Central Statistical Office, *Social Trends 23* (1993), p. 104; Beaver, 'Aiming for health', pp. 26–8; J. A. Giggs *et al.*, 'Class A drug users: prevalence and characteristics in Nottingham', *British Journal of Addiction*, 84 (1989), pp. 1473–80; J. A. Giggs, 'Drug abuse and urban ecological structure: the Nottingham case', in R. W. Thomas (ed.), *Spatial Epidemiology* (1990), pp. 227–33.

43 M. Leitner *et al.*, *Drug Usage and Drug Prevention* (1993), pp. 16, 72, 81; Kingscott, 'Oral history', p. 99.

44 J. A. Giggs, 'Socially disorganised areas in Barry: a multivariate analysis', in H. Carter and W. K. D. Davies (eds.), *Urban Essays: Studies in the Geography of Wales* (1970); Robson, *Those Inner Cities*.

45 J. A. Giggs, 'Schizophrenia and ecological structure in Nottingham', in N. D. McGlashan and J. R. Blunden (eds.), *Geographical Aspects of Health* (1983); 'Disadvantage in Nottinghamshire, 1983' part 1; 'Social need in Nottinghamshire, 1994'.

46 Brazier, *New Geography*, chs 5, 6, 10.

47 *Ibid.*, p. 131; Groves, *Nottingham City Transport*, p. 64.

48 Groves, *Nottingham City Transport*, p. 93; S. Longford, 'Women's mobility deprivation: a case study of Strelley, Nottingham', *EMG*, 15 (1993), pp. 3–10; Nottingham City Transport Ltd, personal communication.

49 A. Jones, 'Developing a transportation strategy for Nottingham', joint report of the Director of Development and the Director of Environmental Services to the Nottingham City Transportation Committee, 21 July 1995.

50 K. C. Edwards, 'A new bridge over the River Trent', *EMG*, 9 (1958), p. 45; Nottinghamshire County Council, Construction and Design Department, personal communication.

51 M. Barley, *The Chiefest Grain* (Nottingham, 1993), p. 101.

52 Brazier, *New Geography*, ch. 10.

53 J. A. Giggs, 'Traffic reorganisation in the central core of Nottingham', *EMG*, 5 (1973), pp. 429–32; Brazier, *New Geography*, pp. 127–9.

54 V. Foster and B. Taylor, *Railways in and around Nottingham* (Huddersfield, 1991); Brazier, *New Geography*, pp. 119, 121, 132.

19

THE GOVERNMENT OF THE CITY, 1900–1974: THE CONSENSUS ETHOS IN LOCAL POLITICS

Nick Hayes

It has become commonplace to refer to the emergence and implementation of a national political consensus to reconstruct the country in the two decades after 1940, and to contrast this with the 'wasted years' after the First World War when promises to build 'a land fit for heroes to live in' fell victim to political partisanship and inertia.[1] The consensus came under increasing strain from about 1960 and was, in the face of increasing economic pressure, in terminal decline by the 1970s. This chapter will investigate the extent to which local politics in Nottingham conformed to this widely accepted interpretation of the national experience. To keep the subject within bounds, it will address in particular the issue of housing, a key focus of popular and public concern after both world wars.

Twentieth-century Nottingham inherited a clearly delineated local party-political system, albeit one in the process of transition. For fifty years a Liberal caucus of wealthy manufacturers had governed the town. Their leaders had endorsed a limited working-class candidacy to the party ranks and also certain trade union industrial demands, while the unions in turn approved both Independent Labour Party (ILP) and more commonly Liberal candidatures in local elections. 'Progressive co-operation', it has been suggested, 'was still a very real feature of local politics' in Nottingham.[2] From 1909 to 1911, the local Liberal/Labour MP and the Liberal *Nottingham Daily Express* openly supported ILP candidates and, with one exception, there were no Liberal/Labour electoral conflicts. Co-operation broke down in 1912 when both parties stood in wards where the other had sitting councillors. At the same time Liberals and Tories openly colluded, and Labour candidates were denounced collectively as a 'small, noisy band of ILP wire-pullers'. Sir Edward Fraser, the Liberal Group leader, claimed that the old parties were 'drawing together' and putting partisan feeling aside to face 'the rise of a new force which calls itself socialism'.[3]

In fact, Labour's local municipal pre-war advance was distinctly low-key: a high point in 1911 saw the party capture only four of the forty-eight elected seats, a figure halved in 1912 when in six contests it polled on average 26 per cent of the vote. By 1913, because of its 'strictly limited capital', Labour was unable to contest any wards.[4] But Labour default far from denoted Liberal success. In 1908, as in many provincial towns, the Conservatives had finally taken control of the council, and this domination was to last until 1945. The increasing popularity of protectionist policies amid local industrial decline, and general government unpopularity, helps to explain Liberal failure. Their electoral fortunes were not improved by concerted Labour campaigns highlighting the failure to redress the historically poor condition of large tracts of the city's working-class housing. The Conservatives talked of interventionism, although they turned out to be less willing to practise than to preach. Nevertheless, in establishing a Housing Committee that acknowledged, albeit cautiously, free market failure, local Conservatives provided a foundation for civic interventionism upon which the council could build after the war.[5]

In 1914 there were some 5,000 vacant houses in Nottingham, but 'the influx of munitions and other workers' meant that 'by the end of 1918 all ... houses in a reasonably habitable condition had been let'. More immediately, war saw the Treasury-directed termination of the Carter Gate clearance and planned rehousing programme. By 1915 the patchwork closure of property deemed 'repairable' had been abandoned and by 1918 all demolition work was indefinitely suspended because of the lack of alternative accommodation. Nottingham's post-war heritage of pre-war neglect, according to the city's Medical Officer of Health, was that some 7,000 of its 52,000 working-class dwellings, housing over 25,000 people, were judged to be inadequate.[6] In November 1918 the Housing Committee issued instructions that all unfit houses should be served with closing orders. This was seen as the prelude to an ambitious reconstruction programme combining house building with vigorous slum clearance. The scheme was quickly forestalled. Westminster insisted that 'the time was not ripe' to consider clearance as a practicable option; indeed, by 1921 so acute was the housing shortfall that dwellings which had been closed reopened. Since between 1919 and 1922 speculative builders constructed only 114 houses (of which fifty were state-subsidised), the political commitment to intervention was reinforced.[7]

Initially, 1,000 working-class houses were planned. This was a decision approved by a full two-thirds of council members, but it quickly ran into difficulties when an influential caucus – including the new Liberal leader (Huntsman) and a local Tory (Atkey) – called for the abandonment of all existing schemes and to limit provision to 500–600 tenement dwellings. This was a particularly surprising about-face by Huntsman who had previously declared that 'the real attraction for my entering public life was that I might take a share in carrying out social reform'. Now he spoke of the current misplaced 'passion of grant and subsidy', of high costs, the inappropriate focus on 'garden city' provision and of the usurping of council authority by the Housing Committee. At the longest council meeting then on record, the cuts were approved by 30–19 votes. The claim that this would 'deny brave heroes' homes provoked uproar and disorder in the chamber. The *Nottingham Journal and Express*, which was partly Liberal-financed, castigated Huntsman's stance as 'reactionary', and the decision needs to be judged against the generous nature of the central subsidy, which limited local liabilities to a token contribution.[8]

At this point Christopher Addison, the Minister for Health, formally intervened to endorse the 'enlightened view' of the Housing Committee. He rejected the tenements scheme and, by threatening to authorise construction in Nottingham himself – without benefit of subsidy – he effectively limited the city's options. By way of compromise the council – in one further about-face – partially endorsed the original proposals, which were subsequently revised upwards to meet some 90 per cent of the deficit of 3,700 working-class houses. As a result, 1,476 dwellings were completed before the public expenditure cuts of 1921. Most of the houses were let to the ex-servicemen for whom they were intended.[9]

The 1919 municipal elections, the first held since 1913, saw a significant increase in the number of wards fought by Labour and in its share of the vote, which rose to 55 per cent. Labour was successful in seven of the nine seats contested – six Tories and one Liberal were returned unopposed. Labour's improvement was bound up with structural and attitudinal changes associated with the war.[10] It was undoubtedly better placed, financially and organisationally, by 1918, although it took several more years to establish a city-wide structure. One key component here was Trades Council support for Labour municipal candidatures in 1919, which built heavily on wartime co-operative practice. Political unity, campaigning on emotive 'home front' issues centring on shortages and perceived inequalities, was forged within the broader labour movement and proved singularly beneficial to the party.[11] In 1919 Labour focused quite specifically on housing. As the local Liberal press noted,

> If a Progressive party is to be kept healthy, it must have regular constant and suitable exercise … . Possibly the successful onslaught which Labour has made on the old regime may be the best thing that could have happened … it was high time somebody imparted more vigour and life into the criticism of Corporation affairs. The attitude of the City Council towards housing has been a scandal.[12]

Inter-party relations at this juncture were unusually fluid. Although attention has been focused on the antagonism directed against Labour by the traditional parties – once again 'banding together to fight a common danger in the Socialists and their revolutionary doctrine'[13] – contemporary opinion was at times genuinely reflective, although both traditional parties readily indulged in playing the 'Bolshevik card': in this sense Labour's challenge appreciably altered local political discourse.[14] Anti-Labour rhetoric peaked at the 1920 municipal elections, but at the annual mayor-making ceremony, Huntsman made the following declaration supporting the nomination to civic office of Herbert Bowles, the Labour group leader:

> It is with the highest degree of satisfaction that not withstanding the peculiar views that the hot atmosphere of a recent election might have forced to growth that they should elect a representative of Labour to the position. They could not expect that Labour should permanently lie like Lazarus outside the house for crumbs which might fall, or might not.[15]

That year also saw the election of the first Labour aldermen, the party having argued that representation should be proportional to party strength. In fact, agreement was based not simply on party size but weighted to take account of individual length of service, to Labour's obvious disadvantage. As Bernard Wright, the Conservative leader, commented:

> To prevent unpleasant disputes ... it was felt desirable that some definite working arrangement should be arrived at ... [so] that, whatever occurred, there should remain upon the Council a certain number of aldermen of experience who would be in a position to criticise and protect against innovation or experiments which might be contrary to the city's interest.[16]

This first six-year inter-party agreement, which also stipulated alternating entitlement to the mayoralty and shrievalty, was signed in October 1920. Wright, under immediate pressure to renege on the agreement following heavy Labour defeats in the 1920 'Bolshevik' elections, steadfastly refused, arguing it would be both 'dishonourable' and 'unconstitutional'.[17]

By 1926, the initial two-clause agreement had grown to what was proposed should be seventeen, all of them designed to enhance inter-party co-operation and to lessen friction over patronage placement.[18] However, the all-important committee hierarchy was still dominated by the old parties, where tradition and arbitrary seniority reinforced Conservative control in the key committee initiating process. Yet as its strength grew, Labour increasingly controlled the junior posts in committee (table 19.1) and indeed chaired important areas of council business – Bowles chaired the Estates Committee from 1920. After 1932, the concordats formally acknowledged that committee offices should be allocated in proportion to party strength, with allowance being made for minor posts. Informal 'gentleman's agreements' (by word of mouth or exchange of letters) governing patronage distribution were not uncommon in other towns and cities, although in some places during the 1920s Labour was frequently and heavily discriminated against, provoking both bitterness and subsequent retaliation. What was unusual about Nottingham's concordats was their comprehensive and formal nature. In granting early recognition to Labour aspirations and limiting patronage disagreement (the most frequent cause of inter-party disputes elsewhere), the protocols came to symbolise an equitable co-operative ethos within a competitive party-political system, which was noticeably at odds with the city's pre-1914 patronage patterns.

Table 19.1 **Committee and patronage distribution in inter-war Nottingham**

	Chairs			*Vice-Chairs*			*Aldermen*			*Party strength*		
Date	*Con.*	*Lib.*	*Lab.*	*Con.*	*Lib.*	*Lab.*	*Con.*	*Lib.*	*Lab.*	*Con.*	*Lib.*	*Lab.*
1913	17	7	–	16	7	–	8	8	–	37	23	2
1920	22	5	1	12	12	2	8	6	2	34	21	9
1923	19	5	1	10	11	2	8	6	2	35	17	11
1926	18	5	2	7	9	6	7	5	4	30	15	18
1929	13	5	9	8	4	12	6	4	6	27	11	26
1932	17	3	7	11	3	12	8	2	6	34	8	22
1935	14	1	10	10	1	12	9	1	6	32	3	29
1938	14	–	10	11	–	12	8	–	8	34	1	29

Joint patronage was not always popular. Both Labour left and Tory right were at times highly critical of inter-party co-operation, claiming that it sullied political principle. In a similar vein, the open friendship of Wright and Bowles was held to work against their party-political responsibilities: Wright particularly, in cultivating 'a policy of collaboration ... caused umbrage to some of his more aggressive followers who thought he carried conciliation too far'. Yet as dominating figures, they 'formed a personal axis' which on occasion 'bulldozed' many an ambitious and contentious capital project (for example, the new Council House and boulevard ring road system) through the city council.[19]

This positive accommodation inside the council needs to be set against the almost continuous operation of a formal 'anti-socialist' pact in 1919–38, which was also common elsewhere. At times relations between the two parties were brittle and even hostile, but only rarely did Tory fight Liberal. More commonly each campaigned for the other. This contradiction can best be explained in terms of the separation of electioneering strategy from local Conservative *realpolitik*, bound up with the inverse yet parallel chronologies of rising Labour and declining Liberal power. Long-term, the pact worked to the detriment of the Liberals, placing the party perpetually in the Conservative's shadow in policy implementation, recruitment and identity; similarly its rigid rhetoric of financial orthodoxy and anti-Labourism juxtaposed uneasily with its progressive claims.[20] In predominantly working-class areas some Liberals lost to Labour, but middle-class wards became Conservative strongholds. Liberals, quite simply, lacked a solid base from which to campaign. Increasingly only in socially mixed wards were seats allocated between the coalition partners, and even here to the advantage of the Conservatives. The result was that by the 1930s Liberals had neither the organisation nor the will to contest local elections, and even in supposedly former nonconformist strongholds like the St Ann's ward, Conservatives (or later Labour) dominated, with the Tories seeing themselves – much to the annoyance of local Liberal activists – as the natural anti-socialist contestants.[21] Within this general picture of Liberal atrophy, there were resurgences. In general elections Nottinghamshire returned two Liberals in 1923 and one in 1929, all in constituencies where the Liberals regularly maintained a presence in both local and national elections.[22] In the 1924 and 1928 Nottingham local elections (when the alliance broke down) Liberals contested ten and nine seats respectively, but in only two wards did they receive more votes than their Conservative opponents, and only in Byron Ward – the last regularly contested non-working-class Liberal seat – was the party successful.

The causes of the 1928 rupture are instructive. Despite a growing acknowledgement, even by local builders, that free enterprise alone was incapable of meeting housing demand, the degree of corporation intervention remained contentious. Only Labour and the building unions promoted the use of direct labour for house construction. However, in seeking to avoid past delays, the Housing Committee adopted the unusual practice of contracting out its own sewer and road work. In several close votes in 1927 and 1928, a majority of Conservatives (with some Liberal support) sought to reverse this policy. Thwarted, they opted to oppose the only Liberal, who had voted against them and who was then also seeking re-election, accusing him of having 'socialist sympathies'. Liberals, however, maintained that the Tories were simply trying to 'pocket' one of their seats, and subsequently declared the pact 'broken ... absolutely and finally'. Yet they were so politically dependent that in subsequent years the anti-socialist alliance continued to operate, albeit in a rising atmosphere of resentment, as Conservatives increasingly claimed candidatureships in former Liberal wards.[23]

Other areas of municipal housing policy proved equally contentious. Under the 1923 Housing Act Conservatives opted to pass central subsidies to private builders, rather than allow the Housing Committee to deal directly with its waiting list of 6,200. Shortages also dictated experimentation with prefabricated construction, but Conservatives insisted that half of these houses should be offered for sale. As the Conservative Housing Committee chairman recalled, 'there was still a very large reactionary section on the Council at that time'.[24] Yet it is for its achievements under William Crane's energetic chairmanship that the Housing Committee was to become well known. In total between 1920 and 1939, the corporation constructed approximately one new house for every sixteen inhabitants. Almost half were built under the 1924 Wheatley Act, and the city had one of the highest per capita completion rates in Britain, which contrasted favourably with other Conservative controlled authorities.[25] This later commitment to rented public-sector provision can be judged nicely against the government's own abandonment of general-needs subsidy in 1933, when Nottingham's Housing Committee proposed to build some 1,500 unsubsidised dwellings. Local Conservative minimalists argued that if costs had fallen sufficiently to allow such construction at affordable rents, then corporation intervention in the housing market was unjustified. Even so, in council the proposals were passed 'without demur'. Indeed a clear majority of members, actively or passively, supported the Housing Committee's progressive objectives. As one senior Conservative alderman confided, 'there was a time when I regarded Alderman Crane as a fanatic and visionary', but now he thought 'the committee were doing sound, valuable and useful service'. Indeed one Labour left-winger jibed that he 'was at a loss to understand why Mr Crane is in the Tory Party'.[26]

There were, however, limits to this policy consensus, for within the Tory ranks there remained a highly vocal minority which objected strongly to the municipalisation of the city's housing stock. Intervention was seen at best as a temporary expedient, and certainly not 'to house people who could, in the main, provide suitable accommodation for themselves'. Crane and the Housing Committee, however, subscribed to different criteria, qualitatively and quantitatively. In adhering to the tenets of the garden-city movement the city acquired a national reputation for its low-density suburban housing. Partly this was a response to a shortage of city-centre sites, partly because Crane (despite considerable opposition) thought flats and tenements 'un-English', but primarily because the committee saw its civic objective as one of laying down permanent standards for a better future.[27] The fact that only 1.5 per cent locally (3.8 per cent nationally) of houses surveyed in 1935 were 'overcrowded' indicates the extent of progress. Yet not all indicators were positive. Nottingham, for example, still had the third highest infant mortality rate of large British cities in 1939, despite the demolition and replacement of over 3,600 slum houses.[28] However, in 1939 the governing Conservative party twice refused to endorse Housing Committee requests to clear a further 1,350 slum properties. Critics argued for repair rather than demolition, and to the chagrin of Labour, and of Crane, senior Conservatives observed that many of the condemned properties were indeed 'beautiful houses', both 'pleasant and suitable for the people living in them'.[29]

In reality, this retreat centred primarily on the anticipated £½ million cost of the project. City rates had risen by 1s 4*d* in the pound in 1938, prompting the immediate formation of an independent ratepayer party (the Nottingham Citizen's Association) which was tacitly supported by several prominent Tory councillors. The Conservative leadership sought to curtail spending by increasing the powers of the Finance Committee, and passing to it the duties of the General Purposes Committee. Conservative disquiet found two other immediate targets: capital spending on housing, and the principles of shared committee patronage.[30] The Conservatives highlighted the fact that the largest spending committees (other than Housing) – Education, General Works and Highways, Public Assistance, Watch and Health – were all chaired by Labour members. This was a red herring; it ignored both the scale of committee remits and the fact that the Conservatives always retained a vetoing majority on all committees and in full council. Yet it provided sufficient incentive, in a year when the inter-party agreement was to be renewed, for many Conservative councillors to call for a end to formalised co-operation. The reaction against expenditure also provides an important measure of past achievement in municipal provision. To characterise this as attributable wholly to Labour influence would be inappropriate. Basic agreement over immediate objectives had provided a changing foundation for local consensus, which was not based on the political negative of accommodating Labour's growing strength. It was this new agreement which was under threat in 1939 until the war provided a core agenda around which party factions could reunite.

As Cecil Armitage, the new Conservative leader recalled, a temporary concordat was quickly reinstated to ensure 'during the difficult time of war a fair representation on the Council ... and to get a united war effort'.[31] The agreement expired in November 1944. In the interim, the operation of a formal electoral truce and basic agreement over civic priorities cauterised many former political sores. Yet two notable issues, reconstruction and member autonomy, provoked significant disagreement although – paradoxically – both in their separate ways cemented post-war consensus. The city's Reconstruction Committee, chaired by Crane, reported in October 1943 and called for civic 'energy and far-sightedness'. It offered an overview of future municipal objectives and planning requirements, particularly the needs of the next twenty years. Although commended by the press for its vision, a number of Tory members publicly belittled the 'purely utopian' idealism of this immature 'little committee' in its attempts to 'bluff and rush' the corporation into 'great capital expenditure'. It was wholly reminiscent, Crane complained, of objections raised after the Great War when 'senior members of that Council felt the Corporation would be ruined if the Housing Committee were allowed to proceed ... until force of public opinion compelled them to give way'.[32] After some debate members agreed in principle to an expansive package to improve the local infrastructure, purchase what building land remained in Nottingham, and, as a corollary, to seek an extension to the city's boundaries.

Free-marketeers bitterly opposed the corporation's attempts to monopolise landownership, some packages of which were compulsorily purchased from speculative builders. Land shortages also revived calls for the substitution of flats and terraces in place of the garden-city approach. The most sustained criticisms, however, came not from the Tory right but from an 'Independent' alliance of former Labour members and Liberals, who campaigned vigorously against certain key aspects of the reconstruction package (particularly the inner-ring-road proposals made in the late 1940s and early 1950s) as part of a broader attack on the Conservative–Labour caucus.[33] Initially, however, protests centred on an extended dispute over group discipline, rooted in the expulsion of three Labour councillors and their subsequent exclusion from committee work. It took four years of increasingly bitter wrangling to secure the reinstatement of the three: Armitage finally conceded that the 'clamour' being generated was publicly undermining the 'great work' achieved by wartime co-operation.[34] The party leaders also agreed to renew and expand the now expired temporary inter-party power-sharing agreement. This was a recognition that a majority in both parties again broadly concurred on the governing fundamental priorities of housing provision and civic regeneration. Built in were measures to accommodate minor parties and independent members, with a provision for external arbitration to interpret the concordat's 'true spirit' should a dispute arise. When Labour was returned at the 1945 municipal elections with a large controlling majority, they honoured the agreement, and it was renewed for a further six years in 1951 (when the council was Tory-controlled). Thus, in the decade after 1945, each committee had a chair or vice-chair from each of the major parties, allocated proportionally to party strength.[35]

The key local election issue in 1945, nationally and locally, was housing. While fewer than 500 houses had been destroyed locally, the war years simultaneously saw rapid population growth, a fall in average family size and a significantly higher than average rise in marriage rates. As a result, between 1939 and 1951 the number of households rose by around 15,000, and despite increasingly stringent criteria, by VE Day there were already almost 7,000 names on the city's housing waiting list. Twelve months later this total had risen to 10,500 and it finally peaked at 12,500 in 1951. At the same time some 2,875 condemned properties still had to be cleared, while a 1942 survey had estimated that large areas of the city's housing stock was obsolete. This was a problem largely ignored until the 1960s.[36]

Labour promised a zealous concentration on municipal construction while Conservative rhetoric laid greater emphasis on broader deregulation and economic prudence. In practice, both parties agreed to concentrate corporation resources on housing, and between 1945 and 1955 the city's housing net loan indebtedness trebled from £6.1 million to £18.4 million, greater than the investment expenditure on all other services combined (a pattern running contrary to inter-war trends). Yet initial progress was slow, both absolutely and by comparison with other cities, although places such as Coventry and Plymouth, with much more severe war damage, were given priority resources. By the end of 1946 only 179 permanent corporation dwellings had been completed, largely because of severe labour shortages.[37] The Housing Committee's reluctant response was to purchase some 2,100 steel prefabricated houses, although when the contractors fell seriously behind schedule even this initiative was cancelled.[38] Ministry officials continued to promote various systems by offering special grants and extra allocations, one of which was the then under-utilised 'No Fines' option. With local builders fully employed on traditional schemes (where low productivity remained a perennial concern) the prompt, economic completion of projects employing 'No Fines' technology persuaded the corporation to negotiate a series of major contracts to build two-thirds of the new 7,000-unit Clifton Estate. The corporation bought the 944-acre Clifton site, then outside the city boundary, in 1946. Attempts to obtain planning permission were thwarted both locally and centrally, and this threw city planning into crisis. By 1948 Nottingham had sufficient land to build only a further 3,500 houses. A public enquiry was convened in 1949 to arbitrate between largely pre-determined and competing interests. The Ministry of Agriculture opposed the Clifton project (as did the NFU and other rural-interest groups) because of the loss of productive farmland, while the Coal Board was enthusiastic because the alternatives meant sacrificing coal-bearing areas.[39] The County Council was also hostile, although it signified that it would support the scheme if the city abandoned its boundary extension application, so that the additional rates revenue would accrue to the county. Both political parties had openly backed the application as agreed policy. City representatives were, therefore, wholly taken aback to find four Tory city councillors appearing against them at the enquiry, arguing for alternative sites and a policy of high-density city-centre provision. Crane contemptuously branded the four 'traitors', and later called on 'everyone who really wants houses to be built to vote solidly' for a motion of censure subsequently moved by Labour, which passed easily.[40]

Labour accused the Clifton rebels of placing personal and sectional interests before those of the city. Given the robust and well-established party system, the overt politicisation of certain key issues was perhaps hardly surprising: the parties did, after all, represent different classes and ideologies. Yet it was a feature of the period that such disputes were normally short-lived, and that compromise – an essential ingredient for consensus – prevailed. 'Dispensing with political differences where the interests of the city were concerned' was, according to a senior Conservative alderman, founded on the distribution of patronage 'without question or dispute, on an equitable party basis'.[41] The traditional, and at times competing, ethos of loyalty to one's committee ran parallel to that of party allegiance: as one bewildered Labour committee vice-chair complained, when facing orchestrated criticism against alleged extravagances during a trip to inspect the Paris abattoir system: 'I am sure that all right-minded members of this council of all Parties will deplore this [criticism] with me. I completely fail to understand how this can be made a Party matter in view of my statement that this was a committee decision.'[42]

Compromise also found its modifying form in political pragmatism. Nottingham's Labour group had a commitment to, and preference for, municipal provision, but unlike many councils in the Midlands post-1945, it nevertheless consistently endorsed the maximum allocation of new starts to private enterprise from the city's annual quota. There was little support within the Labour group for radical initiatives to which Conservatives could be expected to take exception. Between 1945 and 1950 the Labour group resisted local pressure from trade unions and constituency activists to implement a direct building scheme for council housing construction. Group officers, the city executive and full-time Labour officials used their positions to squash contact with left-wing groupings, and counter and isolate radical opinion within their own party. Within this remit fell the city's Trades Council (NTC). Once the bastion of moderate opinion, the NTC had been infiltrated by a small but vociferous and active minority of left-wingers who were viewed with considerable distrust by the leadership of the Labour Party. Relations between the NTC and the Labour group became strained, and on the advice of the TUC the NTC ceased affiliation to the Party. In 1953, after several years of mutual antipathy, consultative ties between the two bodies were temporarily broken off.[43]

In both major parties attitudes to matters of discipline, custom and committee loyalty were changing. For example, in 1945 Labour members of the Education Committee had either publicly supported or abstained when a proposal for a much needed extension to the College of Arts came before the full council. The proposed extension violated party policy by (at least in theory) deflecting resources from the housing campaign. Six years later, similar objections were raised when considering a report favouring the construction of a new technical college (part of the Reconstruction Committee's recommendations). Where the Labour chair of the Education Committee previously had continued to exert his independence of opinion, now he bowed to group pressure and, without warning, moved to withdraw the proposal. Conservatives, infuriated, deplored the lack of usual prior co-operative consultation on agenda issues. Yet they themselves had earlier the same night exploited a legal loophole to debar certain Labour members from voting on the central issue of housing rents.

Labour continued to press for a reduction in committee autonomy, and in effect to strengthen party control. However, the 1951 and 1952 municipal election results provided the greatest stimulus for increased group authority. In 1951 the Conservative majority was cut from nine to two, and in 1952 each party returned thirty-four members. Maximising voting potential meant exerting greater party discipline, even in areas traditionally considered to be outside party jurisdiction. In several highly-charged debates in 1951, the Conservative Sheriff broke with custom to cast his vote decisively in chamber. In turn Labour instructed its nominee, Lord Mayor George Wigman, to do likewise. He steadfastly refused to comply – an action which cost him the group leadership after his year of civic office. In 1952 the Conservative mayor likewise refused to exercise his casting vote. This meant that neither party had a majority, but both claimed leadership of the council which, under the terms of the inter-party agreement, would mean each should have a majority on each committee. Senior members from each group then met to see if a 'reasonable solution by negotiation' could be found.[44] When this failed, Joseph Littlefair, the Conservative group leader, invoked the agreement's arbitration clause. According to the local press, this marked the personification of consensual civic practice:

> Nottingham, where the parties have always scrupulously honoured agreements governing a number of matters that might otherwise give rise to endless bitterness and bickering, could well act as a role model to the country. The latest example of the way Nottingham deals with these ticklish situations is a triumph for reasonableness and decency in local government … – an attitude of 'city before party' amongst the members on all occasions, and, in particular, of a readiness to compromise when party lines really clash.[45]

Indeed, in resolving a tricky impasse, the concordat functioned according to its historic design, settling not only a dispute over patronage, but the very control of the corporation (awarded to Labour). Both parties rejected coalition leadership in favour of party-determined government.

A lack of 'reasonableness' was becoming apparent elsewhere in council activity. In late 1951 and 1952, the Conservative-controlled Fire Brigades Committee opted to take a persistently authoritarian line in the aftermath of a national fire-fighters' dispute: it was, they maintained, 'a struggle between authority and discipline on the one hand and utter disregard for law and order on the other'.[46] By contrast the government, other employing authorities and, increasingly, Nottingham's Labour group urged restraint and conciliation. Repeated attempts to impose disciplinary measures were blocked by a temporary, if fluctuating, Labour majority in full council. Indeed, as it rebounded to and from committee, so central and antipathetic became the dispute that at one point Labour offered to relinquish its claim for council leadership in exchange for control of the Fire Brigades Committee – an offer rejected by Conservatives.

Industrial relations might be thought a natural arena for doctrinaire disagreement, and a similar unwillingness to compromise erupted over housing policy. First the parties disagreed over rents, with Labour perhaps surprisingly advocating a differential policy in preference to universal increases. Second, a more fundamentally, they disagreed over policy. Post-war consensus had essentially been re-forged with primacy accorded to corporation provision. However, the increased role envisaged by the incoming Conservative government for private development – readily accepted by the Housing Committee – went, to Labour eyes, beyond any pragmatic accommodation, especially given the numbers on the housing waiting list.[47] The Conservative group soon provided greater grist to Labour's mill in seeking to prevent the city developing its sites at Wollaton and Glapton (adjacent to Clifton). Here they argued that Wollaton, because it was situated in a residential area, should be handed to the private sector, and that the benefits of socially mixed neighbourhoods justified speculative provision at Glapton. This was a move bitterly opposed by Labour for more than twelve months. The parties again split openly in 1954 over the first major post-war slum clearance project at Denman Street. This was part of a larger, although by national standards modest, five-year programme involving 2,650 dwellings. Rejecting the recommendations of the Medical Officer of Health for wholesale demolition, a Conservative majority opted both to clear and to improve. In Labour's view this was perpetuating 'slum conditions at the expense of the City and to the advantage of those landlords who will benefit by the Corporation acquiring their houses at market value'.[48]

Labour had appointed Tommy Ives as a full-time group and party secretary. Ives was left-of-centre and proved a constant irritant to the Conservatives, partly because of his undoubted organisational dynamism, but partly because his professional status infringed the Tory amateur ideal of local government. Primarily, however, this 'new phase in which political conflict [became] more acidulated and corrosive' centred on two issues: the failure of the two parties to agree ward boundary revisions, and an intemperate dispute over civic patronage. The town clerk, who was commissioned to produce a compromise solution to the boundaries problem, noted that both parties simply remained 'at arm's length', and that an 'undertone of bitterness' permeated all discussions as both sides sought to redraw the map to their own political advantage. However, it was the decision by a local Labour branch to oppose the retiring Sheriff, Bill Cox, at the next elections that provoked Tory claims of 'Bevanite' or 'Semi-Communist' domination.[49] The inter-party agreement stipulated an unopposed return for retiring civic officers, but the Labour group was unable to enforce this provision against branch hostility: Cox was a former Labour councillor, one of the wartime rebels, who had now crossed to the Tory benches. Moreover, those clauses of the agreement covering committee appointments were also not functioning correctly. The deaths of a number of committee chairs of long standing generated considerable friction over replacements, with Labour at one stage threatening to resign all posts; the tradition of promotion by seniority and custom had fallen victim to increased inter-party animosity. It was in this atmosphere that, despite initial reluctance, the Labour group publicly endorsed constituency and branch demands to renegotiate the agreement, which was due to expire at the end of 1956. As a result, in 1957 Labour took all the committee chairs amid Littlefair's claim that 'democracy … will become a mockery. The wild men of the Socialist Party are in control.'[50]

The most immediate casualty was Crane, chair of the Housing Committee for almost forty years. Even the Labour activists hesitated to depose him, and instead combined the committee with the Estates Committee to displace him. This arrangement soon collapsed. Abandoned too was the protection previously afforded to aldermen. Appointments were henceforth to be allocated strictly according to relative party strength. Not surprisingly, however, personal ambitions decreed that electoral truces for civic office nominees were retained, while Labour also finally offered committee vice-chairmanships to their opponents (a practice not uncommon elsewhere).

It was in this atmosphere of political hostility that two issues thrust Nottingham centre-stage nationally. The first was the party's pioneering proposal to construct a new civic theatre, rooted loosely in the 1943 Reconstruction report and the war and post-war enthusiasm for cultural enterprise. The passing of the worst of the housing shortages stimulated interest in the project, which finally became Labour policy in 1956. To a Conservative leadership of reputedly less than catholic tastes, the philosophy of an innovative municipal theatre proved anathema, and there was disagreement over the degree of rates subsidy warranted for cultural and entertainments provision. This was an intense, ill-tempered and polarised debate between the champions of voluntarism and those of municipalisation.[51] Thus 1961 saw an incoming Conservative administration first contemplate turning the partially completed new theatre into a car park, then attempting unsuccessfully to give the site to a private theatre group in exchange for a cancellation of the project's liabilities.[52]

The decision by the Labour-controlled Watch Committee to suspend the city's chief constable, Athelstan Popkess, provoked even greater civic and national controversy. Popkess had wanted to establish a corps of traffic wardens. This, and other initiatives, was rejected, and he allegedly retaliated by instigating criminal investigations to sully 'the reputations of leading Labour Party members' – details of which were leaked mysteriously to the press the day before the municipal elections. The town clerk demanded Popkess submit a report to the Watch Committee, and his failure so to do prompted the suspension. Local Conservatives and the Home Office demanded his immediate reinstatement by those now dubbed the new 'Wardens of Tammany Hall' – Labour's governing inner circle. It was, they said, one further example of 'Socialist Dictatorship', an epithet born locally with the adoption of single-party rule, but then broadly associated with the arrogation of rigid disciplinary codes and powers by certain Labour council caucuses.[53] Labour's cause was hampered by both a hostile press and the attempt to block public debate or scrutiny of their reasons for suspending Popkess. Subsequent police investigations found little substance to any allegation of corrupt practice, but local reaction was hostile to the Labour group and in 1960 Labour lost contests for nine of the eleven it currently held, with swings against the party approaching three times the national average.[54]

The Popkess affair marked the nadir of post-war inter-party relations. A new Labour leadership determined on a more consensual brand of city politics, and policy became less visionary and more cautionary. Early precedents were set over housing rents. In 1960 the Labour group reluctantly accepted that cuts in central grants and rising repair bills made rent rises inevitable. When, in 1963, the Conservatives introduced a controversial means-tested rebate scheme to remove Exchequer and rate fund subsidies from tenants considered able to pay a full economic rent, Labour members were divided. They were unsure whether to be 'courageous enough to say that we shall scrap' the Conservative arrangements or merely 'introduce a more equitable scheme'. Finally, the group opted to refrain from issuing any election manifesto, particularly on the rents question.[55] In fact, it had already decided to abolish the new scheme. A preoccupation with efficiency and the rates, and a return to the classical nexus of value for money in local government, became the hallmark of post-Popkess Labour administrations, drawing praise from the Chamber of Commerce as Nottingham's rates poundage remained amongst the lowest of county boroughs in the country.[56]

By the mid-1960s inter-party relations were again 'close', with a 'comfortable atmosphere' prevailing. It was under these consensual circumstances that inertia was transformed into vigorous action on the housing front. Although the waiting list hit a post-war low of 4,300 in 1964, little progress had been made in slum clearance. Estimates in 1965 suggested that some 12,500 unfit houses still remained, predominantly in the St Ann's and Meadows areas which, at current demolition rates, would take twenty-eight years to clear. The corporation finally embarked on a greatly enhanced clearance programme which, in 1970 saw a record 2,036 houses demolished, compared with a yearly average between 1955 and 1968 of only 330.[57]

As part of the local government reorganisation of 1974 Nottingham lost its county borough status and became a district council. In the process it lost control of a number of services to the county council. The transition was accompanied by a political dispute which revealed that 'the old custom of reasonably friendly and amateur government in local affairs was on its way out'. In the face of Conservative demands for 'a democratic start for the new Council', on which Labour had a 44–10 majority, they were excluded from the all-important Policy Committee.[58]

Political agreement in Nottingham, as a working alliance between modernising Tory paternalist and municipal socialism, pre-dated national consensus, although it joined the main stream on reconstruction after 1940. By the late 1950s agreement was shattered as the Playhouse and Popkess affairs clearly demonstrate. Despite some mending of fences in the 1960s, Labour's rejection of Conservative pleas for representation on the principal policy-making body of the new district council demonstrated that politics, like national ones, were a long way along the road towards post-1979 conviction politics.

Notes

1 R. Lowe, 'The Second World War, consensus and the foundation of the Welfare State', *Twentieth Century British History*, I (1990), pp. 152–82; P. Addison, *The Road to 1945: British Politics and the Second World War* (1982 edn), ch. 1.

2 D. Tanner, *Political Change and the Labour Party 1900–1918* (Cambridge, 1990), p. 296. For a useful overview critical of Tanner's generalisations re local and regional politics, see K. Laybourn, 'The rise of Labour and the decline of Liberalism: the state of the debate', *History*, 80 (1995), pp. 209–26.

3 *Nottingham Daily Express*, 24 October, 1 November 1912.

4 By post-1918 standards, five of these wards were winnable. The best performance in 1912 was in Bridge where, in a straight contest with Liberals, Labour took 41.6 per cent of the vote; *Nottingham Daily Express*, 3 November 1913.

5 *NG*, 24 May 1910, 5 March 1912; L. F. Wilson, 'The State and housing of the English working class with special reference to Nottingham, 1845–1914' (University of California, Ph.D. thesis, 1970), pp. 255–9, 268–81; R. Smith, P. Whysall and C. Beuvrin, 'Local authority inertia in housing improvement 1890–1914: a Nottingham study', *Town Planning Review*, 57 (1986), pp. 409–11, 420–1.

6 P. Boobbyer (MOH), 'Notes on the local housing situation', 21 January 1921, reprinted in Nottingham City Council (NCC), *Annual Report of the Health Committee* (1928), pp. 114–15; NCC Housing Committee Minutes, 1915–18 *passim*; NCC Report of the Housing Committee, 10 October 1919.

7 NCC Housing Committee Minutes, 17 September, 4 October 1918, 10 December 1920; NCC Economic Committee Minutes, 8 July 1921; NAO CA ENQ/1920/136.

8 NCC Housing Committee Report, 26 November 1918; NCC Minutes, 2 December 1918; *Nottingham Journal and Express*, 29 November, 3 December 1918, 23, 29 September 1919. See also R. Smith and P. Whysall, 'The Addison Act and the local authority response: housing policy formation and implementation in Nottingham 1917–1922', *Town Planning Review*, 61 (1990), pp. 194–6.

9 NCC Housing Committee Minutes, 26 September 1919, 29 March 1922; *NJ*, 7 October 1919; *NG* 13, 23 April 1920, 4 January 1921.

10 Tanner, *Political Change*, chs. 4 and 13, especially pp. 124–7, 386–90; T. Adams, 'Labour and the erosion of local peculiarity', *Journal of Regional and Local Studies*, 10 (1990), p. 27.

11 NLSL L.33 Nottingham and District Annual Trades Council Reports, 1917–20; *NJ*, 30 January 1920; P. Wyncoll, *The Nottingham Labour Movement 1880–1939* (1985), pp. 165–77, 184; B. Waites, *A Class Society at War: England 1914–18* (1987), p. 221; J. Holford, *Reshaping Labour: Organisation, Work and Politics – Edinburgh in the Great War and After* (1988), pp. 154–63.

12 *NJ*, 3 November 1919.

13 *NG*, 2 November 1921, cited in Wyncoll, *Nottingham Labour*, p. 193.

14 See, for example, *NJ*, 29 October, 2 November 1920.

15 *NG*, 10 November 1920.

16 *NG*, 8 November 1920. This edition also contains the text of the inter-party agreement.

17 *NG*, 8 November 1920.

18 *NJ*, 13, 17 September 1926, 21 October 1927; *NG*, 16 September 1926.

19 *NJ*, 21 November 1927, 15 December 1932, 2 November 1934; *Guardian Journal* (hereafter *GJ*) 15, 18 August 1961; T. Driberg, *Reynolds News*, 5 July 1959; *EP*, 30 November 1934.

20 *NJ*, 18 October 1920, 2 November 1923, 28 October, 3 November 1925, 1 November 1926; *NG*, 2 November 1922, 1 November 1927.

21 *NJ*, 20 October 1930, 29 October 1930; C. Cook, 'Liberals, Labour and local elections', in G. Peele and C. Cook (eds.), *The Politics of Reappraisal, 1919–1939* (1975), pp. 181–2.

22 P. R. Shorter, 'Election politics and political change in the East Midlands of England' (University of Cambridge, Ph.D. thesis, 1975), p. 142.

23 *NG*, 2 November 1928, 2 November 1929, 10 December 1932; *NJ*, 24 October, 2 November 1928, 7 November, 1, 2 December 1932.

24 *Fifth Report from Select Committee on Estimates* (PP 1945–6), Minutes of Evidence, p. 173.

25 *Ibid.*, p. 172; NCC Annual Reports of the General Works and Highways Committee (1920–40); NCC Epitome of Accounts, 1949; R. Smith and P. Whysall, 'The origins and development of local authority housing in Nottingham, 1890–1960', in S. Lowe and D. Hughes (eds.), *A New Century of Social Housing* (Leicester, 1991), pp. 36–7; J. H. Jennings, 'Geographical implications of the municipal housing programme in England and Wales', *Urban Studies*, 8 (1971), p. 124; J. Darke, 'Local political attitudes and council housing', *Urban Studies*, 8 (1971) p.163.

26 *NG*, 28 February, 6 March 1934, 7 February 1939.

27 *NG*, 21 September 1937; *EP*, 26 May 1937; Gray, *Settlement*, p. 101; R. Unwin, 'Introduction' to T. C. Howitt, *A Review of the Progress of the Housing Schemes in Nottingham under the Various Housing and Town Planning Acts* (Nottingham, 1928).

28 NCC Housing Committee Report, 8 May 1936; Jennings, 'Municipal housing', p. 129; S. Merrett, *State Housing in Britain* (1979), p. 59; NCC Annual Report of the Health Committee (1938).

29 *NG*, 1 August 1939; *NJ*, 29 July 1939.

30 *NG*, 4–7 April, 2 May 1938.

31 *NJ*, 8 December 1942.

32 NCC Report of the Reconstruction Committee on Post-War Development in the City of Nottingham, 9 September 1943; *NJ*, 4, 5 October 1943.

33 *NJ*, 2 January, 5 June 1945; *NG*, 19, 22 November 1943; N. J. Hayes, 'Nottingham 1945–66: party responses to changing political, social and cultural expectations' (Open University, Ph.D. thesis, 1992), pp. 67–72.

34 *NJ*, 5 December 1944.

35 Copies of the post-war inter-party agreements are reproduced in N. J. Hayes, *Consensus and Controversy: City Politics in Nottingham 1945–66* (Liverpool, 1996), appendix 1.

36 Hayes, 'Nottingham 1945–66', pp. 53–5.

37 NCC Epitome of accounts: year ending 31 March 1949 & 1955 (Nottingham), tables 8 and 10; NCC Reports of the Housing Committee, February–September 1945; Ministry of Health, *Housing Returns: Appendix B*, January 1947; *Select Committee*, pp. 148–9, 160–71.

38 *NJ*, 5 June 1945, 5 February 1946; NCC Housing Minutes, September 1946–September 1948, passim.

39 PRO HLG 107/136, Ministry of Town & Country Planning, Inter-Department Planning minutes, 18 August 1948.

40 *NG*, 15, 26 July 1949.

41 *EP*, 14 October 1948; *NJ*, 15 October 1948.

42 *NJ*, 8 November 1949.

43 Letter from Councillor Coffey (Secretary of the City Party Executive) to Tom O'Brien, MP, 28 November 1952, in author's possession; Hayes, *Consensus and Controversy*, ch. 5; R. Stevens, '"Disruptive elements?": The influence of the Communist Party in Nottingham and District Trades Council, 1929–1951', *Labour History Review*, 58 (1993), pp. 22–37.

44 Letter from J. Littlefair to E. Purser (Labour Group leader), 14 May 1952, in author's possession.

45 *NG*, 30 May 1952.

46 *NJ*, 8 January 1952; Hayes, 'Nottingham 1945–66', pp. 130–40.

47 *NJ*, 5 January 1951; NCC Housing Committee Minutes, 23 January 1952.

48 NAO LPC, Box 7, Nottingham Labour Group, Policy Sub-Committee Report on Housing in the Denman Street Areas, September 1954; *Slum Clearance*, Cmd 9593 (1955).

49 *GJ*, 30, 31 March, 30 April, 13 May, 10 June 1954; Letter from T. J. Owen to E. Purser, 4 February 1954: copy in author's possession.

50 A. Howard, *New Statesman*, 21 August 1964; W. Thornhill, 'Agreements between local political parties in local government matters', *Political Studies*, 5 (1957), pp. 85–8; B. Keith-Lucas and P. G. Richards, *A History of Local Government in the Twentieth Century* (1978), pp. 67–8; *GJ*, 28 July 1959.

51 *GJ*, 4 February 1958, 18 November 1961.

52 N. J. Hayes, 'Municipal subsidy and Tory minimalism: building the Nottingham Playhouse 1942–1963', *Midland History*, 19 (1994), pp. 128–46.

53 *GJ*, 28 July 1959; G. Block, *Party Politics in Local Government* (1962); N. J. Hayes, 'Tammany Hall resurrected? Images of Labour Caucus Rule in Nottingham, 1956–60', *TTS*, 68 (1993), pp. 136–44.

54 Hayes, *Consensus and Controversy*, ch. 7.

55 Nottingham Labour Group, Notes on Discussion of Electoral Policy, March 1963, in author's possession.

56 Hayes, 'Nottingham 1945–66', pp. 494–505.

57 City of Nottingham, Nottingham Position Statement, May 1974, pp. 3–9; Central Housing Advisory Committee, *Our Older Homes: a Call for Action* (1966), table 1; Modern Records Centre, University of Warwick, MSS 9/3/21/23, Jim Cattermole, East Midlands Labour Party Organiser's Report, 26 January 1966. Interview with Eric Foster, 12 January 1989: notes in author's possession.

58 *GJ*, 19 July 1973.

20

ECONOMY, INDUSTRY AND EMPLOYMENT

S. D. Chapman

At the beginning of the twentieth century the traditional textile industries continued to lead the city's economy (table 20.1). I. & R. Morley, which celebrated its centenary in 1899, was the most substantial firm, employing over 3,000 people in seven factories in the area, over 400 at the Fletcher Gate warehouse, and about 4,000 framework knitters and ancillaries in villages across the county. In the vanguard of the lace industry were several merchant–manufacturers, Simon May & Co., Thomas Adams & Co., and Richard Birkin & Co. Similarly, the traditional brewing industry had generated several large firms, and with these may be linked two major tobacco manufacturers, one of which (Players) was still in its relative infancy. The collieries were mostly at a distance from the city centre, but by their relatively heavy demands for labour contributed to local prosperity. The 'new industries' of the 'second industrial revolution' (engineering, chemicals, etc.) were not as prominent or numerous as far-sighted prognostication of twentieth-century changes might have divined. Jardines aside, textile engineering was weak considering Nottingham's long commitment to hosiery, lace and cotton spinning. Such losses were more than compensated by the rise of three great enterprises, Boots Pure Drug Co., Imperial Tobacco Co. (Players) and Raleigh Cycle Co. The enterprise of all three firms was to sustain the local economy through the difficult years of decline in the traditional industries (table 20.2).

Table 20.1 **Nottingham's major companies (by value), *c*.1900**

Company	*Sector*	*Capital (£)*
I. & R. Morley	hosiery	*c*.2,000,000
Boots	chain stores and manufacturing	1,155,000
Stanton Ironworks, Ilkeston	coal and iron	915,000
James Shipstone & Sons	brewing	651,000
Humber, Beeston	cycles	500,000
Hardy's Kimberley Brewery	brewing	450,000
Nottingham Brewery Ltd	brewing	440,000
Home Brewery Co.	brewing	400,000
Simon May & Co.	lace merchants and manufacturers	400,000
New Hucknall Colliery Co.	coal mining	365,000
William Hollins & Co.	spinners, weavers and clothing manufacturers	350,000
Grand Clothing Hall	men's clothing	350,000
Thomas Adams & Co.	lace merchants and manufacturers	332,000
W. H. Hutchinson & Sons Ltd	brewing	315,000
Joseph Burton & Sons Ltd	grocers	300,000
Burton Brewery Co.	brewing	290,000
Digby Colliery Co.	coal mining	275,000
Bestwood Coal & Iron Co.	coal mining	270,000
Burroughs Adding Machines	adding machines	250,000
Nottingham Suburban Railway Co.	transport	250,000
Richard Birkin & Co.	lace manufacturers	218,000
Linby Colliery Co.	coal mining	200,000
John Player & Sons	tobacco	200,000
John Jardine & Co.	lace machine builders	?200,000+
R. J. Dexter	cigar manufacturers	160,000
Trent Navigation Co.	transport	157,760
Armitage Bros.	grocers	150,000
M. Jacoby & Co.	lace merchants and manufacturers	150,000
W. E. & F. Dobson	lace manufacturers	150,000
Daft & Skevington (Sampson's Factory, Lenton)	lace manufacturers	150,000
Manlove Alliott & Co.	engineering	150,000
Turney Bros.	leather	123,600
Raleigh Cycle Co.	cycles	121,000
Nottingham Manufacturing Co.	hosiery	120,000
Goddard, Massey & Co.	engineers and ironfounders	120,000
Wollaton Colliery Co.	coal mining	105,000
Anglo-Scotian Mills, Beeston	lace manufacturers	100,000
Ed. Cope & Co.	lace manufacturers	100,000
Griffin & Spalding	departmental store	100,000
J. Pidcock & Co.	malt and corn merchants	100,000

Source: *Allen's Nottingham Red Book* (1990–03), section on Local Joint Stock Companies, with additions (I. & R. Morley, Stanton, Simon May, Jardine, Birkin, fire of 13 January 1902, Daft & Skevington, Wollaton Colliery Co.).

Table 20.2 **Nottingham's top forty companies, *c*.1900**

Textiles and leather	13
Coal, iron, engineering	12
Brewing and malt trade	7
Retailing	4
Tobacco	2
Transport	2
Total	40

Source: As table 20.1.

On the other hand, some industries, including hosiery and lace, were traditionally composed of large numbers of small firms, few of which employed more than a hundred or so people. At the beginning of the century there were around 400 hosiery factories in the East Midlands employing about 40,000 people in all.[1] Data relating to small-scale enterprise is not always available in such detail. In addition, for centuries Nottingham entrepreneurs have set up businesses outside the borough boundaries which should not be excluded from an analysis of the city's economy simply on that account. Table 20.1 includes several firms which were either in the immediate locality (satellite towns such as Beeston) or situated on the coalfield. It suggests that most of Nottingham's leading firms were incorporated by the turn of the century, but this should not mislead us as to the nature of their leadership. Some of the largest firms were still essentially family firms. I. & R. Morley was owned and run by the Morley family, headed by Lord Hollenden, a grandson of the Nottingham founders. Jesse Boot was still the supreme autocrat of Boots. Indeed, most firms were 'family firms' at the beginning of the century, and this situation changed only slowly.

Textiles

In 1900 Nottingham's world-famous lace industry was at the peak of its prestige and size, and its importance in the local, national and international economy. Fashion dictated that every house, from mansion to terraced two-up and two-down, must have its lace-draped curtains, tablecloths, and bedcovers, and that women's clothing – bodices, sleeves and skirts – should exhibit yards of lace edging. There was a substantial export trade to the United States, Latin America and elsewhere, and the demand seemed insatiable. The main *textile* exporters were focused on Wood Street (London), Manchester, Glasgow and Leeds, but as Nottingham held undisputed sway in lace the world's buyers jostled one another in the Lace Market. The long-established leaders of the industry – Thos. Adams & Co., Birkin, Vickers & Hine, Simon May & Co. – were joined every year by new entrepreneurs who crowded into cramped 'standings' (rented space) in suburban factories. Most of the manufacturing was done in the satellite 'villages', including Beeston, Long Eaton and Ilkeston, much of whose prosperity was built on the industry. When Nottingham became a city in 1897 it was truly 'the City of Lace'.[2]

Two clouds lay on the horizon. One was that John Jardine & Co., the Basford lace-machine builders, were busy exporting Levers machines to Europe, America, and other competitor countries. The firm advertised that they supplied complete factories and arranged the finance with which to build them. Manlove, Alliott & Co. of Radford were eager to supply dyeing equipment and other ancillary engineering supplies. The Levers machine represented the apogee of engineering excellence; it was built to run indefinitely with minimum maintenance.[3] While the demand for lace continued buoyant nobody showed any great anxiety, but even minor contractions of the market spelt trouble for many small producers. The other cloud resulted from the paucity of technical education in the city. The School of Design had only patchy support from the producers, most of whose small masters failed to recognise its value. The Textile Department of University College Nottingham was not established until 1920 and even then suffered from desultory support. In the long run the artisan tradition, although the foundation on which Nottingham industrial achievements were built, proved insufficient to meet American, German and (later) Italian and Japanese competition in the twentieth century.

The First World War brought a dramatic change of fashion and in the course of the 1920s and 1930s the lace industry was reduced to a shadow of its former glory. Homes were cleared of clutter in favour of space, light and clear lines, while women emancipated themselves with lightweight, relaxing, and simple dress lines. Wearing lace now became a sign of middle age. Firms in the industry struggled, and half went bankrupt in the early 1920s. Others pulled out in despair. The number of Levers machines in operation fell from 2,600 in 1910 to around 850 in 1937, while the number of firms declined from 220 to 85 in the same period. The experience of Simon May & Co. is instructive. The firm's capital climbed rapidly from £74,000 in 1885 to £420,000 in 1912, but in the early 1920s profits disappeared and the firm fought desperately to make good its post-war losses in Bolshevik Russia.[4]

Nottingham's other traditional industry, hosiery and knitwear, should have fared much better, for here the post-war shift in fashion offered splendid opportunities to many firms. As women's hemlines rose there was an unprecedented demand for hose while a new emphasis on informality and the outdoors pushed knitted outerwear to new heights of popularity. Growing prosperity (particularly in southern England) enabled more and more people to afford underwear and lingerie. While manufacturing in cotton and wool contracted between the wars, hosiery and knitwear enjoyed renewed growth. For a variety of reasons Nottingham was slow to spot the new opportunities. For three generations the town's entrepreneurial talent had expected major openings to be in lace rather than hosiery, because the fashion end of textiles has always yielded the greatest profit margins, and the plain underwear and hose worn by both sexes through the Victorian years offered little scope for creativity in product or design. Hine, Mundella & Co., the Nottingham Manufacturing Company, had never been particularly profitable, and other well-known innovators such as Paget of Loughborough and Matthew Townsend of Leicester went bankrupt.

When the tide of fashion began to turn towards the end of the nineteenth century, most of the initiatives were seized by Loughborough and Leicester manufacturers, and for some years Nottingham entrepreneurs failed to respond. Probably the most prosperous hosiery firms between the wars were J.B. Lewis & Son (Meridian) and George Spencer & Co. (Vedonis) who secured the British licence for production of the American 'interlock' fabric manufacture. The Meridian Works on Haydn Road, built in the early 1920s, are still in production, now as the flagship of the Courtaulds Clothing Group. Marathon Works (H. L. Beales) on Radford Boulevard were probably the city's earliest Marks & Spencer contractor.[5] In the 1930s some of the most enterprising developments came from German Jews who migrated into the region, often with encouragement from Marks & Spencer. The most successful of these firms were Charnos at Ilkeston (Charles Noskwith) and Mansfield Hosiery Mills (Djanogly brothers). In the post-war years Charnos grew to be a major producer of hosiery and lingerie, while Djanoglys became the principal suppliers of knitted outerwear to Marks & Spencer.[6]

Notwithstanding these modest initiatives, the main player in the Nottingham hosiery industry, I. & R. Morley, was conservative and defensive rather than entrepreneurial. Morleys' Chairman, Lord Hollenden, was the leading light in the Wholesale Textile Association, a City of London-based warehouse group formed to compel the many thousands of retail hosiers and drapers to deal only with them and not directly with the manufacturers. In the 1930s the WTA issued dire warnings to various chain stores, but after the Second World War contract selling triumphed. In 1950 Morleys still had the biggest capital in the hosiery industry (£1.6 million), but in the mid-1960s it collapsed completely, a sad reminder of the inevitable fate of conservative manufacturers in a fashion industry.[7]

Surprisingly, Nottingham's most striking success in textiles in the first half of the twentieth century was in a sector in which it had no tradition or reputation: ready-made clothing. The initiative began in 1890 when William Hollins & Co. of Pleasley Vale (Mansfield) extended from spinning cottons and merino for hosiers to producing a wool and cotton mixture which they called 'Viyella' yarn. Hollins commissioned weavers to make Viyella into fabrics, which was sold direct to bespoke shirt-makers for making men's shirts and nightshirts. Giving a cloth a branded proprietary name was something new in the trade at the time, and its promotion by advertising and a sales force calling on retailers was equally novel. Hollins had the advantage over its neighbours and traditional customers, the hosiery manufacturers, of already being a substantial concern with the resources to launch direct into wholesaling on its own account. The refusal of the largest ready-made clothiers to use a branded fabric compelled Hollins to employ three or four small making-up firms, then to start its own garments department at its Radford Mill in 1903. When this proved inadequate, a completely new steel and glass factory was built on Castle Boulevard in 1919 and extended in 1933. Viyella House was a well-known Nottingham landmark which at its peak employed hundreds of people. The late twentieth-century decline of the textile industry has led to the closure of all Hollins' concerns in the region, but the recently refurbished building proudly survives, a monument to this enterprise.[8]

Boots

Much of the prosperity of Nottingham in the twentieth century derived from the enterprise of three outstanding firms, Boots, Players and Raleigh. Measured by the size of capital invested all three were, on a national or international scale, not huge employers at the turn of the century, but all were to show vigorous growth in the first half of the century. Boots was the most successful of all, and is still the largest employer in the city.

Jesse Boot was a herbalist who inherited a tiny shop in Goose Gate, one of the poorest shopping districts of the town, surrounded by terraces of back-to-back houses and close to the Lace Market. The Thompsonian system of plant cures which his father and he pursued in the town had limited potential. In 1877 the young Boot launched out into cut-price patent medicines, running a series of advertisements in the *Nottingham Daily Express* financed by one of his neighbours. The promotion created a sensation in the town and was an immediate commercial success. Boot moved to larger premises in Goose Gate, diversified into other cut-price lines, and extended his advertising to eye-catching window displays, endless bill-posting, more newspaper space, and even to brass bands. Further success encouraged him to duplicate the Goose Gate-style shop in other parts of Nottingham and in nearby towns including Sheffield, Derby, Lincoln, and Burton-on-Trent. From the outset Boot manufactured many of the preparations he sold over the counter, and he soon had to rent factory space to keep up with the expansion of his retail chain.[9]

Two almost fortuitous developments further shaped the growth of his business. A legal test case in 1879, *Pharmaceutical Society* v. *The London and Provincial Supply Association*, decided that the Pharmacy Act of 1868 permitted companies to employ qualified pharmacists. In 1884 Boot took advantage of this development to install a qualified man in his new Goose Gate branch, and a fully-equipped dispensary became a feature of all his shops. The following year, when overwork compelled Boot to take a holiday, he met and married Florence Rowe, the daughter of a St Helier (Jersey) stationer. Mrs Boot, like Jesse, had been brought up to retail enterprise and was determined to develop her own business. Boot reluctantly acceded to pressure, allowing her space in the corners or on the upper floors of his shops to sell stationery, fancy goods, pictures, books, gifts and a variety of similar lines. In 1900 Florence's 'No. 2 Dept', as it was long known, accounted for practically a quarter of the turnover.

Thus by the turn of the century the Boots retail system was already well established and thereafter it was simply a matter, as far as Jesse Boot was concerned, of opening new branches. Usually Boot started a new branch from scratch, but occasionally he would buy up an existing business or even a small chain of chemists'

Plate 54 **Boot & Co. Ltd, 16–20 Goose Gate**. Jesse Boot's first purpose-built shop was designed by local architect Richard Charles Sutton and opened in 1883. Sutton designed large display windows, which was what Boot needed following the success of the advertising campaigns he began in 1877. Boot had previously worked from 6 Goose Gate, the herbalist's shop started by his father in c.1850. John Boot died in 1860 but the business was carried on by his widow Mary, and from 1863 (when he left school at the age of thirteen) by Jesse, who went into partnership with his mother when he reached twenty-one. Shortly after moving to the premises shown here Jesse Boot established the business as Boot & Co. Ltd, with himself as both Chairman and Managing Director

shops. The big plum was Day's Metropolitan and Day's Southern Drug Co., an acquisition of sixty shops which gave Boot access to London and the south in 1900. His retail empire multiplied from 181 shops and a turnover of £600,000 in 1900 to 618 shops and £7.6 million turnover in 1920. The shops steadily increased in size as well as number so that a few in large towns began to take on the appearance of department stores, particularly as Florence added her libraries and tea shops to them. The Pelham Street branch in Nottingham (1903) was one of the earliest and grandest.

Chronic arthritis forced Boot to retire in 1920. Since he believed his only son (John Campbell Boot) to be a spendthrift, he sold the controlling interest to an American, Louis K. Liggett, who ran the Rexall private chemists' co-operative in the USA. The Boot family and some of the investors were aghast at the sale, but events proved it to be a good move. With failing health, Boot had been losing his grip on the business for some years, and the new owners were able to cut out some of the dead wood and restore profitable growth. A new system of government by committee, expense control and retail administration by Territorial General Managers was inaugurated. Young executives were sent to the United States to study some of the most recent innovations in retailing. John Boot became vice-chairman and specialised in retail properties. He took up his father's drive for more retail outlets, and in 1933 he was able proudly to announce Boots' thousandth shop. At the same time he tried to move Boots up-market by discarding some of the gimmicks and showmanship of Jesse Boot's years. The resumed growth of the retail empire stimulated manufacturing and the streets around the Midland Station became crowded with buildings of all kinds converted into Boots' factories and warehouses. A search for more space and better-designed plant started in 1927 and in 1930 the first building was opened on a large landfill site near the Trent at Beeston, which was soon followed by the famous Owen Williams steel and glass model factory. The subsequent build-up of factories and functions on the Beeston site and at other locations is shown in table 20.3.

The growing prosperity and improved status of Boots in the 1920s was strongly associated with John Boot's leadership and his determination not to be eclipsed by Liggett's men. Sir Jesse Boot, recently created Lord Trent, died in 1931 and most of his 'old guard' retired or died about this time. A dramatic decline in Liggett's fortunes in the American depression gave John Boot, now the 2nd Lord Trent, an opportunity to seize control. Drug Inc., a large US conglomerate that had acquired L. K. Liggett Co., compelled Liggett to sell Boots when his American retail chain became insolvent. The first and strongest bidder was the Philip Hill Group which already owned Beechams, Timothy Whites and Taylors, and several proprietary medicines. This deal was blocked by the Treasury for rather dubious reasons connected with exchange control, whereupon Trent stepped in with a financial consortium headed by the Midland Bank and won control. This 'repatriation' of ownership was a personal triumph for Trent and gave him complete and unquestioned authority within the firm for the next twenty-one years, until ill-health forced him to retire.

Astonishing as it may seem to modern business analysts, in all Trent's activities, profit was never the significant motive; 'his great idea always was prestige at all costs', his Finance Director (John Greenwood) wrote in his hagiography. Prestige meant more shops and more prime locations, up-market brands and prizes at agricultural shows (ostensibly to support the Farms and Gardens Department), and branches in corners of the Empire to nurture his imperial pride. He was less interested in manufacturing, which consequently continued to be the Cinderella of the business. Trent's substantial achievement was to win public acceptance of Boots as shops for good value rather than just cheap goods or cut-price offers. But he left a great many problems for his successors, of which poor profitability was the most obvious and immediate concern.[10] Solutions were quickly found. A financial genius called Arthur Cockfield (now Lord Cockfield) was brought in as Finance Director and soon became Managing Director. He commissioned a firm of chartered accountants, Peat, Marwick & Co., to analyse the company's performance and their 1966 report spelt out the elements of future strategy. Some progress was made in Cockfield's time, but differences with the new Chairman (Willoughby Norman, who had married one of Trent's daughters and liked to be thought of as 'the third Mr Boot') led to his resignation.

Table 20.3 **The growth of Boots' manufacturing facilities in Britain, 1930–80**

Factory	*Site*	*Product(s)*
Pharmaceutical		
D.1 (1930–32)	Beeston	soap
D.10 (1933)	Beeston	'wets': internal liquids, creams, toiletries, household and external liquids and sterile products
D.6 (1937–78)	Beeston	'dries': medicated confectionery, powders
D.95 (1975–78)	Beeston	tablets
A.6 (1948)	Airdrie	cosmetics and toiletries
B.2 (1971)	Basingstoke	medical products (Crookes)
C.1 (1980–83)	Cramlington (Co. Durham)	Brufen
Chemical		
Various buildings	Beeston	Ibuprofen, agrochemicals and saccharin
E.16, E.60	Nottingham (Island Street)	insulin, alkaloids and speciality chemicals (multi-purpose plants)
Printing	Nottingham (Station Stret)	a wide range of printed matter, e.g. containers, wrappings, advertisements

Source: Records of the Boots Company PLC.

The most promising development in the 1960s and early 1970s was on the manufacturing side. A relatively small research team headed by Dr Gordon Hobday identified the anti-inflammatory drug marketed as 'Brufen' and profits of manufacturing (as distinct to retailing) climbed to 40 per cent of turnover in 1977–78. Boots reaped a poor reward for this breakthrough because they had no international marketing network and were locked into an agreement with the American pharmaceutical company, Upjohn. Hobday, by now Managing Director, recognised the problem and tried to merge with Glaxo, a move blocked by the Monopolies Commission. Consequently the 1970s and 1980s were spent building up an overseas marketing organisation, particularly targeting the USA and Europe. The growing complexity of Boots led in 1970 to the establishment of a new style of organisation featuring unprecedented devolution to subsidiary companies.[11] Today the chain of retail branches is once again the main source of the company's profits after the pharmaceutical division and its international marketing organisation was sold early in 1995.

Players' Cigarettes

John Player, the son of a Saffron Walden solicitor, moved to Nottingham at the age of twenty and opened a retail store in Beast-Market Hill to sell seeds and agricultural manures to country farmers. Tobacco was at first a sideline to please his customers, but in a few years it absorbed the whole business. Perhaps his most astute move was to marry his next-door neighbour, a wealthy widow ten years his senior. It was most probably her money which helped to put him ahead of a score of other tobacconists in the town.[12]

When John Player began to sell tobacco it was sold loose from jars, weighed and handed over in small screws of plain paper, rather like a sweet bag, but he soon realised that customer allegiance to a particular type of tobacco was strong and he began to pre-pack. He soon prospered and in 1877 Player purchased as a going concern the tobacco manufactory of William Wright, which had been established in the Broad Marsh in 1823 and already employed 150 workers. At this time Nottingham boasted nineteen firms engaged in tobacco processing, although there was no bonded warehouse for any kind of goods.

John Player and his two sons succeeded even as relatively late arrivals and as an inland firm, in winning a position of market leadership exceeded only by Wills of Bristol. The basic reason why is suggested in table 20.4. In their early years Wills were valued at nearly twelve times as much as Players and employed two and a half times the labour force, but the Nottingham firm spent four times the market leader on advertising. Brand promotion evidently paid off, particularly as the habit of cigarette smoking overtook pipe smoking. Players' share of UK cigarette sales rose from 9 per cent in 1905 to 24 per cent in 1920, and the indications are that this share continued to rise until at least the late 1930s.

Plate 55 **John Player & Sons, Broad Marsh, 1880, ex-Wright & Sons, 1874.** In 1877 Player took over Wrights' factory, established in 1823. Player expanded the packaging of cigarettes, for convenience of selling and identity of product, but as business prospered expansion was essential and from 1881 he began to develop the site in Radford with which the firm was associated for much of the twentieth century

With the purchase of the Broad Marsh Factory and with rapidly growing experience of the trade, the Player genius for advertising and marketing first showed itself. A plain packet of tobacco containing a particular blend was obviously a ripe vehicle for a name and for that name to be printed on the packet. The first brand name to be registered was Gold Leaf, although in 1877, when he first began manufacture under his own name, John Player registered his first actual trade mark, the familiar drawing of Nottingham Castle. 'Gold Leaf' was evidently an immediate success, for a Player price list of 1881 shows a dozen other varieties of branded packet tobaccos had already appeared. From the simple black-only print on the paper pack it was a short and logical step to introduce colour, and the Gold Leaf packet of 1885 was a work of art, printed in nine colours with an overall design resembling the Picasso dove in gold on the reverse. All cigarette packets were originally of the soft cup variety and naturally very flimsy, and subsequently a small piece of plain card was inserted as a stiffener. The cigarette card, still known as 'stiffeners' in the trade, was born and soon was destined to become an art form in its own right. The manufacturer quickly recognised these as a major incentive to brand loyalty. The most famous Player trade mark was the sailor's head. In 1883 John Player was attracted to a painting of a bearded sailor produced thirty years earlier by an artist called Wright of Clapham when uniform had just been introduced by the Royal Navy. The portrait was being used by a small tobacco company, Parkins of Chester, to advertise their 'Jack's Glory' brand. John Player immediately bought and registered the painting as a trademark.

Table 20.4 **Size of the main components of the Imperial Tobacco Company**

	Capital (1901) (£m)	*Payroll (1900)*	*Advertising (1898) per annum (£)*	*Travellers (1897)*
Wills	7.0	3,000	5,000	30
Players	0.6	1,200	20,000	10

Source: B. W. E. Alford, *W. D. & H. O. Wills and the Development of the U.K. Tobacco Industry* (1973), pp. 213, 215, 263, 293.

From the acquisition of the Wright business in 1877, Player's marketing and advertising methods were so successful that he was able to purchase thirty acres of land in an undeveloped area of Radford. On this site he built the three blocks which became No. 1 Factory along a square fronting to Radford Boulevard. As he was not yet ready to make full use of this new factory, Player rented 'standings' to small lace makers and finishers. In April 1884 production was transferred to the new site but the whole factory was not occupied by Players until 1902.[13]

John Player died of liver cancer in 1884 at the age of forty-five, and for the next nine years the business was continued by family friends and senior employees. It was an interregnum during which his two sons, John Dane Player (1864–1950) and William Goodacre Player (1866–1959), were educated at Nottingham High School and groomed to succeed their father. When the business was incorporated in 1895 the sons became joint managing directors. Six years later, when the prosperity and independence of the British tobacco industry was threatened by the powerful American Tobacco Co., while retail chains like Salmon & Gluckstein were making inroads on manufacturer's resale price maintenance, thirteen leading firms federated to form the Imperial Tobacco Company. J. D. Player was one of the original directors of the combine and was also appointed advertising manager to the parent company. W. G. Player became a director following the first board meeting. According to the company's historian, Imperial Tobacco 'leaned heavily on the advertising skills of Messrs J. D. and W. G. Player', but this did not prevent Players' brands competing with those of other members of the group. Nor did it dilute the quality of the Nottingham firm's advertising.

Before the end of the century, Players' payroll reached 1,000, making it the largest employer in Nottingham. The firm expanded rapidly between the two world wars, when cigarette smoking reached a peak of popularity. The 2,500 employees in 1914 grew to 5,000 by 1928 and to 7,500 by 1939. Three more factories and a bonded warehouse were built in Radford. Confidence continued to grow after the war and by the late 1950s Players' cigarette sales finally overtook those of Wills, which they had closely trailed for twenty years. By this date the mood was changing. In 1962 the Royal College of Physicians Report on Smoking and Health showed a clear correlation between smoking, lung cancer and early mortality. It proved to be the first of a sequence of authoritative medical reports which the powerful tobacco lobby was unable to refute and from which it could not deflect public attention. However, continuing confidence in the future was expressed with the building of the Horizon factory on a forty-acre landfill site close to Clifton Bridge. The factory, said to be the most modern in the world when it opened in 1971, initially employed 1,000 people on each of two shifts.

The tide could not be turned. After the most difficult decade in its history,The Imperial Group was compelled in 1981 to reorganise and to make drastic economies. Five factories were closed, 3,000 workers made redundant, and a massive £35 million investment undertaken to raise productivity. The changes were too late. In 1986 the Group was taken over by the Hanson Trust and the accumulated acquisitions sold off in the course of the next few months.

The effective advertising that raised Players above its rivals both within and outside the Group has lent it some resilience during adversity. In recent years the John Player name has, through sponsorship, come to be associated with sporting images in motor racing, motor-cycle racing, tennis, rugby, and cricket, though such promotions are now banned by government regulation. Hanson has further streamlined its operation and, as a result of further mechanisation, reduced the labour force. Nottingham has been fortunate that most of the losses have occurred elsewhere in the organisation, especially in Bristol, Liverpool and Glasgow. In 1994 60 per cent of Imperial's 2,450 payroll were employed in the city and all the cigarettes and hand-rolled tobaccos are made at the Horizon factory.[14]

Raleigh Cycles

The cycling boom of the 1880s saw scores of workshops with a handful of craftsmen turning out two or three hand-made bicycles a week. In Nottingham one such was started by three young men, Woodhead, Angois and Ellis, in Raleigh Street in 1886. The difference between this firm and the many that failed or were absorbed by rivals was that the founders made an unusually well-designed and reliably constructed machine. As a result they attracted the attention of Frank Bowden, a lawyer who had made his fortune in Hong Kong finance. Bowden's health was apparently damaged by his labours in the Far East but cycling proved to be an effective restorative, and he became a passionate enthusiast for the new recreation. He committed all his entrepreneurial talent and financial connections to the Raleigh Street concern and in 1889 launched the Raleigh Cycle Co. with a capital of £20,000. The new enterprise made twelve models, and so successful was the company that in 1891 it was decided to increase its capital to £100,000, which was soon to make it one of the top forty companies in Nottingham. Increased production was initially undertaken in an old

Plate 56 **Raleigh Bicycles**. The superiority of Raleigh bicycles had to be demonstrated to the world, or so Frank Bowden passionately believed. Raleigh riders entered for every sporting event in Europe and America, winning records and carrying off the prizes. Bowden persuaded the world champion A.A. Zimmerman to ride a Raleigh, bringing prestige as well as profits and prosperity to the company. Bowden and his lieutenants were themselves always eager to test new ideas by riding their bicycles around both town and country

lace factory, but as the new firm prospered in the early 1890s a purpose-built factory was erected on five acres at Faraday Road, Lenton. It opened in 1896. By the turn of the century, the Raleigh cycle works were producing nearly 10,000 machines a year, with buoyant sales in both the domestic and export markets.

The Edwardian age saw the cycling craze wane, and markets had to be won by hard work. Bowden concentrated on raising productivity by investing in automatic tools and other machinery to produce standardised interchangeable parts. He introduced hire purchase, and he set up depots in all large towns. Important export markets were built up on the European Continent and in India, China, and other countries. While a sequence of small rivals collapsed, Raleigh raised output to 30,000 machines in 1907 and to 50,000 in 1912. During the First World War Bowden took on munition work as well as contracts for the forces, and his payroll rose from 2,000 to 5,000. Cycle output reached almost 100,000 in 1920 and extensions were added to the Lenton works. By this time the factory was the largest cycle works in the world. The period also saw some diversification into motor cycles and, at different times, two light cars.

The inter-war years were difficult decades for most British businesses, but Raleigh fared better than many. Practically every working man owned a bike and cycling became a popular pastime for all, giving unprecedented access on uncluttered roads to the countryside. Sir Harold Bowden continued his father's policy of investing in increased productivity, and was able to bring down the price of a standard bicycle from £14 in 1921 to £4 19*s* 6*d* in 1932. The same year Raleigh bought up Humber Cycles of Coventry, which had begun its life nearly fifty years earlier in Beeston, and production was concentrated in Nottingham. Output climbed to 400,000 cycles in 1936 and nearly half a million in 1938. Further attempts to enter the motor car and motor accessories market were less successful, and were finally abandoned just before the Second World War.

The early post-war years were golden ones for Raleigh. Full employment and post-war restocking generated unprecedented demand in the home market while foreign competitors were struggling to return to normal. The company kept its name in the public eye by sponsoring Reg Harris, who dominated cycle racing in the 1940s and 1950s; 'Reg Harris rides a Raleigh' was the great advertising line of the time. Output passed the million mark in 1951. Two major acquisitions followed: Triumph of Coventry in 1954 and BSA of Birmingham in 1957. Extensions brought the factory site to sixty acres, but by the time the new buildings were opened the post-war boom had spent itself.

A shift of consumer preference towards the motor cycle and motor car, and stiffer competition in overseas markets, were only part of Raleigh's problems in the 1960s. The Bowdens, father and son, were dead, and a new generation of directors was more cautious about innovation. The company lacked the instant response to opportunity that had been the hallmark of its first half-century. Already in the 1950s Raleigh cycles were beginning to look somewhat middle-aged, particularly to the young, as Tour de France style *derailleur* gears became more fashionable than

Sturmey-Archer three-speed hubs. Raleigh's success with the moped (motorised cycle) proved to be ephemeral and their motor-scooter (the Roma, modelled on the Italian Vespa) was a flop. The unisex Moulton safety bike was finally adopted seven years after Raleigh had turned down Moulton, who went off to establish his own very successful company. The Raleigh 'Chopper' (1970), an adolescent's cycle aimed at the American market, attracted attention but did not generate massive sales. Possibly the most imaginative development was the acquisition of the little Carlton racing-cycle works at Worksop, which took Raleigh into the hand-made sector of the market in the 1960s, and into prams and children's toys in the 1970s.

Faced with intensifying competition, the British cycle manufacturers, like so much of British industry, attempted to solve their problems by merging their interests. By the late 1950s Raleigh had only one major national rival, the British Cycle Corporation (BCC), whose brand names included Phillips, Hercules, Norman and Sun. BCC was the cycle division of Tube Investments (TI) and in 1960 the two operations were merged by TI buying all the shares in Raleigh and, having done so, handing over BCC to the Raleigh management. The BCC factories were absorbed in Raleigh and the range of brand names steadily reduced. Raleigh's official history is silent on the point but, if this merger was like others of the period, the amount of management time spent on rationalisation diverted attention from innovation and chasing market opportunity in a period of critical change.

Raleigh was a vertically integrated plant which manufactured and assembled every single component. This practice became untenable in the 1970s as competitors increasingly bought in components from Taiwan, India, and other Far-Eastern countries, particularly parts such as spokes and brake cables which could be mass-produced by unskilled labour. Change was resisted for a decade, partly because Lord Plowden and the TI board feared that large redundancies would disaffect labour through the entire TI Group of companies, and partly because of the fortuitous circumstance that the oil boom generated a large demand for cycles in oil-rich Nigeria. Exports to that market rose to 17 per cent of the entire Raleigh output. The bubble finally burst in 1980 as the pound sterling rose to an unprecedented $2.40 and export markets dried up.

More recent years have seen the conglomerates assembled in the 1960s dismantled to create less cumbersome and more streamlined business organisations. After losing £100 million the TI Group sold Raleigh in 1987 to a group of British and American businessmen calling themselves Derby International. The group has specific interests in the cycle industry, also owning Gazelle in Holland and Kalkaf in Germany. The new management has turned the company around, focusing their main research and development work on mountain bikes, the first of which was produced by Raleigh in 1985. Recent innovations have been the introduction of front and rear suspensions for these bikes, bonding techniques (adhesives) to obviate the use of high-temperature welding, and materials for extra lightness and rigidity. The plant now features robotics and laser machines for cutting tubes. In 1994 1,250 workers were producing 750,000 units a year, 60 per cent being mountain bikes. Raleigh continues to be the quality manufacturing company it has always endeavoured to be, and has returned to the vanguard of innovation and productivity in the cycle industry.[15]

Textiles: strategies of a declining industry

The decline of the Lancashire cotton industry and the West Riding woollen and worsted industries has been a feature of the British economy since 1920. Because of the historical importance of these two sectors of the textile industry, there has been a widespread tendency to think of hosiery and knitwear as a minor and peripheral activity. This was never strictly true, but the forty years after the Second World War saw the East Midlands specialism easily outstrip its northern rivals, and continue to be relatively prosperous. In 1984 employment in the industry (90,100) was only slightly less than it had been in 1924 (97,500), and it was larger than cotton and silk (32,500) and wool and worsted (41,900) collectively. This was broadly the consequence of major shifts in fashion which favoured women's hosiery, knitted outerwear, leisure wear, swimwear and lingerie. By 1970 it was estimated that as much as half of all the apparel worn in the world was made of knitted (as distinct to woven) fabrics, and the period was clearly one of major opportunity for local producers both in domestic and overseas markets.[16]

Despite these opportunities some firms faced severe challenges and a few major enterprises failed. The shift from fully-fashioned stockings to seamless legwear ('tights') plunged several old-established houses which had specialised in quality hose, notably I. & R. Morley, into financial difficulties. Some firms which had concentrated on building up a brand name to sell to small retailers were in trouble as the number of drapers tumbled from 40,000 in 1900 to 11,000 in 1946 and then practically disappeared in the 1960s. New technology favoured concentration in fewer firms: in 1948 a knitter looking after seamless hose machines could produce 100 dozen pairs a week, by 1982 productivity had multiplied twenty times to 2,000 dozen pairs a week. There were however some strong incentives for growth. In particular, the variety chain stores (Marks & Spencer, Littlewoods, British Home Stores, Woolworths, and others) continued to offer unprecedented opportunities to firms that could match their exacting specifications and meet tight delivery dates. Several firms in the Nottingham area, most notably Mansfield Hosiery Mills (later Nottingham Manufacturing Company after a 'reverse take-over') and Marathon (John Benles), prospered on the Marks & Spencer connection for a generation or more. Others including Meridian, Charnos and the Albert Martin Group maintained a contract (i.e. chain store) as well as branded (small retailer and departmental store) business for many years, although it was not always easy to serve two masters.

These changes were relatively gradual and took place within a buoyant industry, so that most firms adjusted to them. The first really traumatic alteration occurred in the later 1960s when, to guarantee outlets for its synthetic yarns, Courtaulds bought up numbers of leading firms. Unwilling to be left out, Coats Paton and the Dawson

Group (Scotland) followed suit. Marks & Spencer, anxious to maintain competitive sources of supply, encouraged some of its main suppliers to retain their independence. At the time it seemed as if an industry that had been dominated by small family firms for three centuries was being turned into three or four huge vertically integrated conglomerates. In fact, about two-thirds of the firms remained independent, but the general outcome was to divert hosiery firms from major economic issues such as productivity, markets, and industrial relations to fending off the predators or dealing with new directors in Coventry or Glasgow who had no experience of hosiery and knitwear. When companies were taken over the old family leadership invariably disappeared with their handsome capital gains, leaving the next in rank to wrestle with distant management; a few managers soldiered on for several years but many others went off to serve independent rivals or to establish their own firms. Leadership might have been expected to pass to the next lower stratum of authority in the Midlands factories, had there been one qualified to assume control. In the small firms what passed for middle management was all too often inadequately educated, untrained, introspective, and so inured to the authority of the hereditary family leadership that when much of it suddenly disappeared there was little local drive left in the business. Consequently it took the new management the better part of a decade (broadly the 1970s) to sort out their acquisitions. The period of takeovers exposed the limitations of the traditional family kind of leadership and the lack of specific experience among the new owners. In fact the main – perhaps the only – beneficiaries of the takeover period were the independent firms who remained under the Marks & Spencer umbrella and took advantage of the dislocation of old rivals.

By the late 1970s two other major problems were affecting the hosiery and knitwear industries. The rapid expansion of what is often called the 'Pacific Rim' industrial countries (Hong Kong, Singapore, Taiwan and Korea) began to undermine the competitiveness of local firms. The MFA (Multi-Fibre Agreement between forty trading nations, originating in 1974) formally regulated the import of textiles from the Far East by placing quotas on imports from particular countries. Since the 1960s Hong Kong has been much more than a low-cost producer of clothing. In that decade it invested in production in Singapore, Taiwan and Macao, in the 1970s in Sri Lanka, the Philippines, Indonesia and Mauritius, and in the 1980s in mainland China, so maintaining low costs and providing new quota allowances for access to the British market. Since British producers could not beat Third World labour costs, the only solution was to manufacture overseas or, more precisely, to delegate labour-intensive functions to cheap labour areas, reserving home production for design, finishing, and up-market designer products. This strategy of 'globalisation' has secured the survival of larger firms (which had the capital and credit to finance it) but invariably at the cost of domestic employment. Courtaulds' payroll, to take a prominent example, fell from 80,000 in 1981 to 20,000 in 1994 while UK-based manufacturing slipped from 80 per cent to 40 per cent.

The other major challenge has been the growing diversification and sophistication of fashions and consumer taste in the European market. In the post-war decades the bulk suppliers of the variety chain stores prospered on long runs of standard items, especially in underwear (men's and women's), hosiery, foundation garments and sweaters. This changed in the 1980s as both sexes were tempted into buying numerous varieties of underwear and knitted tops, rapidly superseding the conventional habits of the previous two or three generations. To meet the new demand Marks & Spencer, among other chain stores, dropped many of their traditional suppliers, including Marathon. Meridian, by now absorbed in Courtaulds Clothing, survived the crisis under a new generation of managers who had the skill and financial resources to keep in step with the major retailers.

The industry itself has been rather less vocal about a further problem, that of competition from textile producers in Italy, Germany, France and other European Community countries. It is easy to protest about 'unfair' competition from the Far East, but drawing attention to the greater resilience of European textile producers brings into question the enterprise and competitiveness of British industry. In the 1960s and early 1970s neither Courtaulds nor Coats Patons had direct experience of the fashion end of the industry; both were simply bulk producers of yarns. A handful of firms rightly saw that the future lay in the fashion-conscious end of the industry. Charnos of Ilkeston was one of the earliest, advancing from hosiery into lingerie from 1959.[17] Another success story is David Parker's Sherwood Group which makes bras and lingerie in Long Eaton with lace from Guy Birkin's factories in Nottingham, Long Eaton and Borrowash. They are now the largest supplier of bras to the UK private label sector while Courtaulds are the most substantial supplier to Marks & Spencer, making Birkins Nottingham's largest lace manufacturers.[18]

So far as small firms are concerned, the most promising development has been the regeneration of the Lace Market area as a centre for fashion clothing.[19] While it is scarcely possible to compete with the Far East in cheap mass-produced textiles, the rapid movements and high mark-ups of fashion clothing continue to make this sector very profitable where firms are designer-led. Nottingham's outstanding success story in this area is Paul Smith, who opened his first boutique in Byard Lane in 1970 and became a manufacturer at the end of the decade. He now provides work for about thirty-five different factories within an eighty-mile radius of Nottingham, and exports to thirty-eight countries, particularly to Japan and the Far East, employing 270 people in his own warehouse and several times that number through contractors in the area. Smith was recently made an honorary freeman of the City.

Smaller firms have characteristically lacked the resources to launch new fashion lines and, to help them, the Nottingham Fashion Centre was opened in 1984. But HATRA (the Hosiery and Allied Trades Research Association) has been forced to close down after nearly half a century in Nottingham (1949–93), while the Knitting Industries Federation has migrated to Leicester with a much-reduced staff. More firms would have gone under without the continued support of Marks & Spencer which, although buying £300 million a year through Hong Kong, continues to source most of its clothing in Britain and Continental Europe. In the present world trading position, it seems inevitable that only fashion-conscious quick-response producers are likely to survive, and then only by delegating their labour-intensive operations to Third World manufacturers.

Restructuring of the Nottingham economy

During the course of the twentieth century there have been numerous other changes in Nottingham's industrial economy. Some of the great names of yesterday have disappeared completely. Moses Mellor & Son, once the leading hosiery machine builders, migrated to Leicester as early as 1910. Turney Brothers' huge leather works at Trent Bridge, built grandly by Sir John Turney, survives only as a prestige apartment block.[20] Shipstones' Brewery at New Basford, the last within the city boundary, was shut down amid much lament in 1990, and the Home Brewery Head Office at Daybrook (designed by Cecil Howitt and built 1937–38) is currently under threat following closure of the brewery by the owners, Scottish and Newcastle Breweries. Collieries near to the town, including Clifton, were gradually worked out, and the closure of Gedling in 1992 marked the end of an era. Pharmaceutical research has been lost to German industry, while in Toray of Bulwell the Japanese are now the leading fabric providers in the city. So who are the major employers today? In table 20.5 an attempt has been made to identify the forty top employers to compare with the leaders at the beginning of the century listed in tables 20.1 and 20.2. The table is based on a list of the top 100 employers, measured by turnover and payroll size, published by the Nottinghamshire Chamber of Commerce & Industry. The list is not ideal because it excludes firms said to be based outside the county, producing some anomalies; thus Raleigh Cycles are included because TI sold it off, but John Player & Sons is not listed because the firm remains at present a constituent of the Hanson Group. Electricity is in the list, but not gas. To compensate for these omissions Players, Courtaulds Textiles, Stanton, Royal Ordnance, Plessey and Charnos have been added and all forty firms summarised as categories of industrial activity in table 20.6.

Taken together, tables 20.5 and 20.6 suggest several conclusions about industrial employment towards the end of the century. The first must be that Boots is overwhelmingly the largest employer, not only with the large payrolls of its core-group activities in health care and retailing, but also in new acquisitions and developments. The major development in recent years is evidently in the area of food manufacture, drink and tobacco, although Northern Foods, the largest company in this category, is dwarfed by Boots. Another inference is that textiles have proved to be remarkably resilient with several firms (Sherwood Group, Courtaulds, Charnos) appearing as major employers. Firms in the category of metals, engineering and electronics (Plessey, Royal Ordnance, Stanton, Sapa) appear to have little in common unless we wish to call them twentieth-century science-based enterprises, or (in the cast of ROF and Stanton) old firms resurrected by new technology.

Table 20.5 **The top forty companies in the Nottingham area, 1995**

Company	*Product(s)*	*Turnover (£m)*	*Payroll*
Boots Company PLC	health care	4,167	80,099
Imperial Tobacco (Players)	cigarettes	(3,736)	1,490
(2,450)			
Boots the Chemist Ltd	retailing	(2,806)	(46,273)
East Midlands Electricity	power supply	1,445	7,590
Courtaulds Textiles	clothing group	427	(15,500)
Halfords Ltd (Boots)	retailing	356	(8,946)
Convenience Foods Ltd	food	303	6,264
Bass Leisure Activities	food and drink	277	(7,423)
Northern Foods Ltd	food	223	4,818
Sherwood Group PLC	textile manufacturing	153	3,385
Melton Medes Ltd	holding company	120	2,998
A. G. Stanley Ltd (Boots)	retailing	112	(2,222)
Stanton PLC, Ilkeston	iron pipes	109	1,290
Derby Holdings Ltd	holding company	103	1,733
MCD (UK) Ltd	carpet distributors	102	649
Boots Opticians Ltd	health care	102	(2,792)
Plessey, Beeston	telecommunications		2,000
MCD Group Ltd	carpet distribution	93	560
Crookes Healthcare Ltd	health care	92	190
Boots Properties PLC	property development	86	n.d.
Sapa Holdings Ltd	aluminium	84	1,102
Children's World Ltd	retailing	(84)	(1,969)
Charnos PLC, Ilkeston	hosiery and lingerie	34 (84)	900
(3,000)			
Bowyers (Wiltshire) Ltd	food	(82)	(1,404)
Raleigh Industries Ltd	cycles	82	1,335
Royal Ordnance	armaments	80+	750
Melham Holdings Ltd	holding company	77	814
Sandicliffe Garage Ltd	retailing	67	477
CCN Group Ltd	management services	65	1,250
East Midlands Electricity (Installation Services)	power supply	64	1,963
George Akins (Holdings) Ltd	holding company	56	278
Vision Express (UK) Ltd	health care	(56)	(1,116)
Sherwood Group (Trading) Ltd	textiles	52	1,273
Nottingham Group Holdings PLC	printing and stationery	47	483
Hooley's Garage Ltd	retailing	46	214
Hyperama PLC	wholesale cash and carry	44	96
Nottingham Group Ltd	printing, etc	44	479
A. R. Daunt & Co. Ltd	wholesale tobacco	43	123
Toray Textiles (Europe) Ltd	textiles	(43)	320
Paul Smith	fashionware	25 (85)	270

Source: Nottinghamshire Chambers of Commerce and Industry's list of the top hundred companies, with additions (see text).

Notes: Much of the turnover and payroll data refer to business and employment outside the Nottingham area, for instance most of the business of Boots the Chemists is in shops dispersed throughout the UK. In such cases, the data is shown in brackets, with figures on turnover and payroll in the Nottingham area, where available, stated first.

Table 20.6 **Industrial sectors of Nottingham's top forty companies, 1995**

Textiles (including carpet distribution)	8
Retailing, wholesaling and distribution	7
Food, drink and tobacco	6
Metals, engineering and electronics	5
Health care	4
Power generation	2
Holding companies (undisclosed activities)	4
Property and management services	2
Printing	2
Total	40

Source: As table 20.6.

Nottingham's record in science-based industries is not encouraging. Until very recently local employers showed little interest in pure or applied science-based research, while for many years University College languished as a poor relation to better-sponsored competitors in Birmingham, Manchester, and Sheffield.[21] The one outstanding science-based firm, Ericsons at Beeston (now Plessey–GEC) was originally a product of Swedish enterprise, while the Royal Ordnance Factory in the Meadows grew out of Cammell Laird's search for skills and sanctuary from enemy attack on its shipbuilding site at Birkenhead (Merseyside). Boots did not enter pharmaceutical research until after the Second World War, and sold out to a German concern in 1995. Textile machine-building was largely abandoned to the Germans and Americans in the earlier decades of this century, and later it was left to the Japanese Toray Company to show how to bring textile plants at Bulwell and Mansfield into profit. Critical appraisal might suggest that Nottingham has retained its prosperity more by good fortune of inward migration than by the farsightedness of local enterprise.

While there has been no single growth to rival the giants founded last century, a wide variety of small and small-to-middling firms have shown commendable enterprise. They have been greatly encouraged by the early and strong growth of industrial trading estates. The exemplar was Sir Ernest Jardine, head of the leading firm of lace machine-builders, who created the Colwick Industrial Estate from 340 acres of farmland by the Trent in 1923. Since then the city council has been active in providing new industrial estates, especially through land rehabitation, for instance at Blenheim (west of Bulwell) and Queen's Drive, both on old colliery sites. Traditionally small manufacturers rented 'standings' in lace and hosiery factories built by speculators for the purpose, and this practice continues to the extent that numerous textile firms now occupy the Victorian warehouses in the Lace Market area of the city, as well as many others on various trading estates round the city. An annual publication, *The Nottinghamshire Textiles and Clothing Industry Register*, identifies 470 firms in the county, with more than half the employment in and about the city. Small science-based enterprises are now catered for at Highfields 'Science Park' where there are forty-three firms, mainly in electronics.[22]

Employment in Nottingham today

The most authoritative source for the current structure of employment comes from the Department of Trade and Industry's census of employment. The most recent census was taken in 1991 and the results for Nottingham and the two adjacent districts of Broxtowe (Beeston) and Gedling (including Carlton and Arnold) are summarised in tables 20.7 and 20.8. The figures are rounded to the nearest hundred, and indeed must be taken as orders of magnitude rather than precise payroll data. Perhaps the most significant feature of the situation represented in the tables is that manufacturing now represents only 19.6 per cent of employment in Nottingham itself, a situation which more or less mirrors the national position where 18.2 per cent are in manufacturing. The largest employment sector is now health, educational and community services, including government and police, whose 52,000 payroll represents 32.2 per cent of employment in the city. Distribution, hotels and catering come second with a 35,000 payroll (21.7 per cent), though this is exaggerated by 3,000 employed in Boots' distribution operation. Banking and business services now employ 20,600 or 12.7 per cent of the city's employed population, a number which reflects Nottingham's importance as a major commercial centre.

Table 20.7 **Structure of employment in Nottingham and the adjacent districts, Broxtowe and Gedling, 1991**

		Nottingham	*Broxtowe*	*Gedling*
1	Agriculture and horticulture	0	100	200
2	Energy and water supplies	2,100	800	2,600
3	Manufacture of metals, mineral products and chemicals	6,800	1,300	700
4	Metal goods, engineering and vehicle industries	12,200	5,000	1,900
5	Textiles, food, drink, tobacco, furniture, paper and printing	19,500	3,600	4,300
6	Construction	8,500	1,000	1,700
7	Distribution, hotels and catering	35,000	6,700	5,700
8	Transport and communications	7,600	1,700	600
9	Banking and business services	20,600	1,900	1,300
10	Hospitals, education, police, government and other community services	52,000	6,100	7,800
Totals		164,300	28,200	26,800

Source: 1991 Census of Employment.

Table 20.8 **Structure of employment in manufacturing, Nottingham, Broxtowe and Gedling, 1991**

Category 5 (part)	*Nottingham*	*Broxtowe*	*Gedling*
Hosiery, knitwear, and other textile manufacture	3,800	600	0
Clothing and footwear	4,300	500	1,000
Printing, paper, and publishing	4,900	400	900
Furniture and timber	1,100	500	900
Food and drink	2,400	1,100	600
Tobacco	1,400		
Categories 3 and 7 (part)			
Pharmaceutical products	5,900	0	0
(Distribution of such products	3,000)	0	0
Others	800	1,300	700
Category 4 (part)			
Hand tools and finished metal goods	400	200	100
Mining machinery	100	0	
Other mechanical engineering	5,600	800	1,200
Telecommunications equipment	100	0	0
Other electrical and electronic	1,600	3,600	500
Pedal cycles	1,500	0	0
Other vehicles	1,000	400	0

Source: As table 20.7.

The manufacturing sector data are slightly distorted because so many factories are situated in the satellite towns (Beeston, Carlton, Long Eaton, Ilkeston, etc.). Manufacturing employment in Broxtowe at 8,600 is 30.6 per cent of the Borough's total while that at Gedling, 6,200, is 23.1 per cent. However, the actual numbers are together much smaller than those of Nottingham (table 20.7). Even the addition of Long Eaton (with its important lingerie and furniture-making industries) and Ilkeston (with Stanton ironworks and Charnos) would not outweigh the balance. In other words, Nottingham continues to be the largest centre for employment, but its industrial base, like that nationally, now represents no more than one-fifth of all employment opportunities.

The other major dimension of economic change has been the shift towards a more service-based local economy. Nottingham has always been a regional centre, providing marketing and professional services for people from many miles around, but in the last twenty or thirty years the growth of retail shopping malls and out-of-town

Plate 57 **Head Office of the Nottingham and Notts. Joint Stock Bank in Thurland Street, *c.*1919**. The clerks include a Miss Goddard, who had joined the bank staff in 1915 at the age of fourteen. By 1918 there were two women clerks, both employed because of the wartime shortage of young male clerks. The hall, designed by local architect Watson Fothergill, can still be seen today

centres has generated more employment, often, no doubt, at the expense of facilities in surrounding villages and small towns. This centralisation has also benefited Boots, the city's largest employer, as company chemists have grown at the expense of private retail chemists. Employment in government service has significantly increased with the migration of the Inland Revenue from London to Nottingham. But perhaps the greatest increase in the service sector is at the city's two universities, where student numbers more than doubled between 1985 and 1995. The influx of students not only benefits the town by augmentation of consumer expenditure; many of them stay on in the area after graduation, offering advanced skills to industry and trade employers. The University of Nottingham now employs 4,000 people (2,100 academics and research staff) while Nottingham Trent University has 2,670 people (965 academic and research) on its two sites. The Queen's Medical Centre employs 5,700 and not only provides health care, but is also a major research enterprise employing considerable numbers of scientists and technicians.

Table 20.9 **Sample of trade union memberships in Nottingham**

Amalgamated Society of Lace Makers and Auxiliary Workers			
1939	1,440	1959	1,208
1971	1,213		
Amalgamated Engineering Union			
1930	2,000	1946	10,000
1951	8,500		
Nottingham Hosiery Finishers' Association			
1934	1,350	1939	1,500
1951	2,708	1959	2,573
1969	3,200		
Nottingham Hosiery Workers' Society			
1919	5,100	1921	7,400
1933	2,000	1939	2,000
1942	1,666	1945	3,544
National Union of Hosiery and Knitwear Workers, Nottingham District			
1947	4,652	1951	6,068
1969	8,202	1973	10,068
National Union of Hosiery and Knitwear Workers, Nottingham Finishers' District			
1969	3,364	1973	3,536
Nottingham Typographical Society			
1927	715	1936	842
1943	939	1952	1,133
National Union of Printers, Bookbinders and Paper Workers, Nottingham Branch			
1931	821	1939	1,200
1945	900	1949	1,300
1952	1,500		
National Union of General and Municipal Workers, Nottingham Branches			
1934	1,865	1939	3,652
Nottingham Co-operative Society employees			
1937	2,200	1951	3,000
Nottingham and District Trades Council, affiliated branches and societies			
1950	152	1956	185
1960	180	1965	206
1995	104		

Sources: The table is neither an exhaustive nor a representative list of unions, and the information has been gathered from a range of sources including trade union annual reports, branch minutes, and correspondence files, and from the annual reports of the Nottingham Trades Council. See also R. Stevens, *'Fighting on the Byways': John James Charlesworth, 1900–93* (Nottingham, 1993).

Organised labour in Nottingham (*Richard Stevens*)

A proportion of Nottingham's work-force have been members of trade unions throughout the twentieth century. Complete membership statistics do not exist, but table 20.9 provides evidence from some of the major industries and the number of affiliated branches to the Trades Council.

Textiles

Organisation by trade of workers in the hosiery industry was hampered by the diverse nature of the manufacturing process. The Nottingham Hosiery Workers' Society sought to organise the knitting side of the industry, and was one of the five constituent unions that merged to form the National Union of Hosiery and Knitwear Workers (NUHKW) in 1945. A number of small, specialist unions covered the finishing side of the industry. The largest was the Nottingham Hosiery Finishers' Association (NHFA). All the local unions had amalgamated with the NUHKW by the end of the 1970s.

Attitudes among hosiery employers towards trade unionism were mixed, but in general the relations between employers and unions in Nottingham have been amicable. The level of unionisation varied from firm to firm, but where union organisation was most complete, shop collectors or stewards and shop committees were established in all departments. The collectors and committees had direct responsibility for immediate negotiations with management. The late Harold Gibson, formerly general secretary of the NUHKW, recalled that 'it was a piece-rate industry. A lot of the work of the full-time officials, local officers and members of the Union, the collectors and the other branch members in the factories, was arguments about piece-rates and methods of work'. If agreement could not be reached on the shop floor, the full-time officials of the union or unions concerned were called in to lead the negotiations. As Harold Gibson put it, the shop and works committees 'would negotiate, but if they'd got a problem and they couldn't solve it, they'd ask a full-time officer to come along, or sometimes, if it was a new line or a new system, they would tend to ask the officer to come in with them to help them, hoping the officer would have some experience of this type of change elsewhere'. In the hosiery unions, contacts between activists and leading officials were often close, and responses to problems also could be swift. Rex Breedon, a steward in the NHFA, recalled of the Association's general secretary between 1947 and 1969, John ('Jack', 'Johnny') Charlesworth, 'I've called him [on the telephone] many a time: "Johnny, I've got some trouble on." "Alright, I'll be down. Give me an hour." And he'd be down within the hour. And he hadn't got a car, he'd go on bus, or bike. He'd be there'. Nevertheless, shop stewards conducted the lion's share of routine negotiations: 'In Johnny's day, the shop stewards went in for a rise, they didn't wait every year. When lines were changed they wanted to change the piece-rates … . They did the negotiating for it throughout the year. And Johnny would only go in if they called him in … if it looked a bit like they were coming up against a brick wall.'[23]

In the lace industry the chief union, the Lace Makers' Society, catered mainly for the 'aristocrats' of the lace trade, the twisthands, and maintained a high level of organisation in the workplace. Shop floor representatives were elected by their fellow twisthands and were called 'responsible members'. These men represented their members' interests in negotiations and disputes with employers, but they were also responsible for maintaining discipline among the members in matters concerning the collection of dues, levels of overtime, and working practices in general. If their authority was challenged, or they were unable to resolve disputes, the executive council of the Society stepped in. The 'auxiliaries' in the lace trade, including large numbers of females, were less well organised and generally joined the Auxiliary Society of Female Laceworkers, which amalgamated in 1933 with the Auxiliary Society of Male Workers and the Lace Makers' Society.[24]

Players

At Players there was a close relationship between union branch structure and workplace representation. The main union at Players was the Tobacco Workers' Union (TWU) and union organisation at Players was helped by a somewhat paternalist outlook on the part of management, which tolerated both trade unionism and political radicalism among its employees. On the other hand, paternalism could also undermine militancy. In the late 1950s and early 1960s the company paid an annual bonus to its employees. The extra money was, of course, very welcome, but according to a former TWU activist, Len Squires, 'it hung over like a "Sword of Damocles", because anyone who stepped out of line was in danger of having some of the bonus withdrawn'. Indeed, this is what happened to members who came out on strike in 1960 over the introduction of new machinery and manning levels.[25]

Until 1948 the TWU was organised in just one large branch covering the entire Players complex in Radford. Following wartime expansion to a membership of over 4,000 (out of a work-force of some 7,000), the branch was reorganised into a district comprising five separate branches, each roughly based on one of the factories of the Players complex in Radford. The district had a full-time secretary, and a district committee consisting of representatives of each branch. In the factories, stewards were elected to represent workers in each shop or department. These men and women were responsible for the collection of dues, the distribution and collection of ballot papers, and negotiations with management concerning shop-floor disputes, and this structure made the union an accessible organisation for ordinary members.[26]

Other industries

Among the most well-known of all shop floor representatives have been the shop stewards in the engineering industry. With a number of large-scale enterprises such as Raleigh, the Royal Ordnance Factory, Blackburns, Jardines, Ericsons at Beeston and the Royal Ordnance Depot at Chilwell, the city and its suburbs were well represented in light engineering. The Amalgamated Engineering Union (AEU) was the single most important union and represented workers at Raleigh and the Royal Ordnance Factory. Due to the vital importance of the munitions industry in wartime, shop-floor representation was expanded greatly during both world wars, although it fell back somewhat under the strain of mass unemployment during the inter-war period. At its most extensive, shop stewards were elected to represent every aspect in every department of a given firm. These would then form a joint shop stewards' committee led by a convenor. The AEU was not the only union representing workers in the engineering industry; others included the Transport and General Workers' Union (TGWU) and the National Union of General and Municipal Workers (NUGMW), which elected stewards who sat on the joint works committee. Stewards were directly answerable to their members, and thus had to represent the wishes of at least the majority. Since the 1950s hostile commentators have often presented stewards as militant, ultra-left-wing trouble-makers. Many stewards undoubtedly were ideologically committed, but unless they reflected the views of their members they faced a loss of confidence and support.[27]

The printing industry included the production of two local 'dailies' and two evening newspapers until 1953, though there was just one by 1983. Other large-scale print works included Formans, Howitts, Boots, and Derrys. Trade unionism in the printing industry was a complex affair, with several separate unions involved in organising print workers during much of this century. A slow process of amalgamation, spanning some three decades has resulted finally in the establishment of the Graphical, Paper and Media Union, which caters for all print workers. Workplace organisation centred on the 'chapel' system, and this was most advanced among the more skilled sections of the work-force, such as compositors and bookbinders. Each union with sufficient membership in a firm would form its members into a chapel. In large firms, one or more chapels based on different departments would be formed. A chapel would elect a 'father of the chapel' (or, in the case of female print workers, a 'mother of the chapel'): in effect, a senior shop steward or convenor. The father/mother and committee were responsible for all immediate, day-to-day negotiations with management; the collection of union dues; the discipline of the membership; maintaining vigilance in regard to potential demarcation disputes with other unions; and, occasionally, the distribution and collection of ballot papers, and the dispensing of various union benefit payments. Chapels were established in the more densely-unionised, larger firms long before 1914, but it was not until the 1940s and early 1950s that the system was extended to cover the great majority of firms and to include less skilled workers.[28]

Industrial relations

Strikes were comparatively rare in 'moderate' Nottingham, but unions of predominantly skilled workers sought to restrict entry into the trade in order to maintain 'scarcity value' labour. The most effective way of doing this was to control the numbers of apprentices and trainees employed by each firm. Therefore, '100 per cent membership' or a 'closed shop' was the ideal aim of all unions but few, if any unions, ever managed to secure closed-shop conditions in every workplace in the city. Some managed a closed shop for specific sections of their memberships, but much depended on the attitude of the employer. Male lace twisthands vigorously maintained closed shops in the firms where the Lace Makers' Society organised employees. The Society's twisthands refused to work with non-Society twisthands, which forced employers to dismiss the offender or insist that he joined the Society. In the hosiery-finishing industry, skilled journeymen such as trimmers, bleachers, scourers and dyers also managed to obtain closed shops in the majority of the establishments where their respective unions had members. In engineering, sheet-metal workers maintained closed shops at Metropolitan Meters in Hyson Green. The various unions at the Royal Ordnance Factory in the Meadows enjoyed virtually 100 per cent unionisation by the end of the Second World War. In printing, the more skilled occupational groups maintained closed shops. Perhaps the most effective closed shop was that which existed in the Nottingham Co-operative Society, which insisted on union membership as a condition of employment, and the major beneficiary of this was the National Union of Distributive and Allied Workers, which merged with the Shop Assistants' Union in 1947 to form the Union of Shop, Distributive and Allied Workers (USDAW). Outside the Co-operative movement the USDAW faced often very different and far more difficult situations. Boots gave every encouragement to trade-union recruitment short of making membership a condition of employment, but other companies, such as F. W. Woolworth, were implacably hostile to trade unionism.[29]

Even before 1914 the city council had accepted the insertion of a 'Fair Wages Clause' into its conditions of employment, which helped to ensure, at least in theory, that trade union rates and conditions were adhered to. Thus trade unions benefited in two main ways as the council became increasingly important as an employer of labour: local government employees were more likely to join their respective unions; and outside employers, if so inclined, had less opportunity to undercut the local trade-union rates. During the 1920s and 1930s NTC expended much effort trying to persuade the corporation to provide work schemes for the unemployed, and every opportunity was seized to raise the issue of 'direct labour', particularly in connection with the new housing developments at Aspley and elsewhere, and with the municipal gas undertaking.[30] In 1933 NTC launched what was to become a long-term and sustained effort to persuade the city council to adopt a forty-hour week for all its employees without loss of pay. This was to try to increase the levels of both employment and 'direct labour' within the city. Initially, NTC received a favourable response from the council. However, when the council put the case to the Annual Conference of Municipal Corporations, it was rejected and the corporation subsequently refused to implement the measure on the grounds of cost, although NTC continued its campaign until 1938.[31]

In addition, attempts were made to secure closed-shop conditions among local corporation employees in the city. In 1936 NTC, along with twelve interested unions, urged the Labour group on the city council to request 'that notices be exhibited in Corporation Departments intimating that the City Council desires that all its

Plate 58 **The General Strike, 4–12 May 1926**. Although 2,200 volunteers were enrolled as special constables the regular Nottingham police force managed to contain the activities of the strikers. Transport was the major problem. Some private bus operators tried to maintain their services but their vehicles were usually overturned by the strikers. The bus shown here on Parliament Street in front of the Theatre Royal appears to have been immobilised by tampering with the engine (note how the engine cover to the right has been lifted up). A normal corporation service was restored on 14 May, when the Transport Committee agreed to reinstate all sacked employees. On the right-hand side of this picture can be seen the statue of Samuel Morley (1809–86), industrialist, philanthropist and MP, erected in 1888. The marble statue, which had become a traffic hazard, was removed in 1927. After a public protest the corporation decided to re-erect it in the Arboretum, but in the process it fell off the back of a lorry and was smashed. A new bust of Morley (by Joseph Else) was commissioned, which is now in the entrance to the Arboretum

workmen [*sic*] should be members of the appropriate trade union for their respective class of work'. The council agreed to this proposal, demonstrating perhaps an acknowledgement that densely unionised work-forces were sometimes more disciplined and, consequently, collective bargaining was more easily facilitated. Spontaneous, militant action such as 'lightning' or 'wild cat' strikes were less likely to occur, and negotiations could be conducted within an existing, proven framework. Even so, a closed shop was not established, and when in 1946 the Trades Council asked the city council to make union membership a condition of employment, their request was turned down by the (now Labour-dominated) council, which claimed that for local authorities to do so would be illegal.[32]

The introduction of new processes in printing, hosiery, and many other industries since the Second World War, has greatly undermined the status of various skilled groups and increased the difficulties of maintaining closed shops. Furthermore, the Employment Act (1982) has provided for compensation from public funds for employees dismissed as a result of closed-shop agreements.

Notes

1 S. C. Wallwork, 'A review of the statistics for growth of the British hosiery industry 1844–1984', *Textile History*, XXII (1991), p. 91.

2 A. Sims, 'The organisation of the lace market and lace marketing' (typescript, 1953); NAO Adams MSS, M 10751/3.

3 *Nottingham Illustrated* (1895), pp. 40–2; *Jardines Monthly Register*, 1892–95.

4 D. E. Varley, *A History of the Midland Counties Lace Manufacturers Association* (Long Eaton, 1959), p. 101; N. H. Cuthbert, *The Lace Makers' Society* (Nottingham, 1960). Records of Simon May Ltd, partners' private memo books. The company also traded in other (non-textile) commodities (e.g. cigars) and some of its great success was no doubt due to this early diversification.

5 NAO J. B. Lewis & Co. records. Vedonis records (in private hands).

6 Information from Mr R. Noskwith (Charnos) and Sir Harry Djanogly.

7 J. Millington and S. D. Chapman (eds.), *Four Centuries of Machine Knitting* (Leicester, 1989), pp. 34–5.

8 S. D. Chapman, 'Innovating entrepreneurs in British ready-made clothing industry', *Textile History*, XXIV (1995); F. A. Wells, *Hollins and Viyella: a Study in Business History* (Newton Abbot, 1968), especially chs. 6–7.

9 S. D. Chapman, *Jesse Boot of Boots the Chemists* (1974).

10 *Ibid.*, ch. 7; J. E. Greenwood, *A Cap for Boots. An Autobiography* (1977); J. M. Keyworth, *Cabbages and Things ... with a Memoir on Philip Ernest Hill* (privately published, 1990).

11 Reminiscences of Lord Cockfield, Sir Gordon Hobday, W. R. Norman, and other retired executives.

12 *Dictionary of Business Biography*, IV (1985), article on John Player and his two sons.

13 S. A. Mason, 'Tobacco and lace: the growth of John Player and Sons, 1881–1903', *TTS*, 85 (1981), pp. 102–10.

14 B. W. E. Alford, *W. D. & H. O. Wills and the Development of the U.K. Tobacco Industry, 1786–1965* (1978); Maurice Corina, *Trust in Tobacco: the Anglo-American Struggle for Power* (1975); Imperial Tobacco Co. Ltd, *The Imperial Story* (1990). NAO John Player & Sons records, especially DDPL 6/3/1–20, monthly summary of sales 1908–74. Information from the Company.

15 G. H. Bowden, *The Story of the Raleigh Cycle* (1975). Information from Ian Phillips (former Managing Director of Raleigh) and from the Company.

16 S. D. Chapman, 'Mergers and takeovers in the hosiery industry', *Business History*, XXX (1988), pp. 219–39.

17 S. D. Chapman, 'Hosiery and knitwear in the 20th century', in D. T. Jenkins and N. B. Harte (eds.), *The Cambridge History of Western Textiles* (forthcoming), ch 30.

18 Information from Guy Birkin Ltd.

19 Louise Crewe, S. Longford and P. Totterdill, *The Notts. Fashion Sector* (Nottingham University, Department of Geography, 1994).

20 T. S. Nutting, 'Hosiery machine building industry' (University of Nottingham, M.Phil. thesis, 1995); *Nottingham Illustrated: Its Trade, Art and Commerce* (Brighton, 1891), pp. 33–5.

21 A. C. Wood, *A History of University College, Nottingham 1881–1948* (1953).

22 Brazier, *New Geography*, ch. 5; Crewe, *Notts. Fashion Sector*; L. Crewe, *The Notts. Textile and Clothing Sector: a State of the Industry Report* (Nottingham, 1994).

23 Interviews with Harold Gibson, 2 June 1992, Rex Breedon, 8 March 1993, and Marian Hunt, 21 June 1993. The most recent work on aspects of hosiery trade unionism in the Nottingham area is R. Stevens, *'Fighting on the byways', John James Charlesworth, 1900–93* (Nottingham, 1993).

24 Cuthbert, *Lace Makers' Society*; Stevens, *Fighting*, pp. 75–6, 101.

25 Interview with Len Squires, 23 October 1991.

26 *Ibid.*; interview with Kath Charlesworth, 6 April 1992; NUMD Tobacco Workers' Union (TWU) Nottingham Branch Minutes, 1925–34; TWU No. 4 (Nottingham) District Committee Minutes, 1948, 1952; TWU Nottingham Nos. 1,2,3,5, and 6 Branches, and Joint Branches and Shop Stewards' Meetings, Minutes, 1948; TWU No. 4 District, miscellaneous correspondence, 1948–52; TWU Annual Delegate Meeting *Reports*, 1948 and 1949; TWU *Annual Reports*, 1929, 1932–35, 1946, 1949–51; TWU *Rules*, 1947.

27 K. Coates and T. Topham, *Trade Unions in Britain* (Nottingham, 1980), ch. 5; NLSL, Nottingham Trades Council *Annual Report*, 1959.

28 National Society of Operative Printers and Assistants, Nottingham Branch Minutes, 1913–32; National Union of Printers, Bookbinders and Paper Workers (NUPBPW) Nottingham Branch Minutes, 1925–52; Nottingham Typographical Society (NTS) Minutes, 1920–60; NLSL, NTS *Annual Reports* 1929–52; interviews with Alf Teeboon, 18 May 1992, Terry Brady, 3 July 1992, and Joe Foster, 14 July 1992; correspondence, Lol Quail to R. Stevens, 6 July 1992, and Lewis Abery to R. Stevens, 5 August 1992; C. J. Bundock, *The Story of the NUPBPW* (Oxford, 1959); A. E. Musson, *The Typographical Association* (Oxford, 1954).

29 NUMD, Amalgamated Society of Lace Makers and Auxiliary Workers (ASOLMAW) EC Minutes, 1921–71; Nottingham Hosiery Finishers' Association (NHFA) Minutes, 1931–33, 1936–60; National Union of General and Municipal Workers, Nottingham Branch (NUGMW) Midland and East Coast DC and EC Minutes, 1931–52; NUPBPW Nottingham Branch Minutes, 1925–52; NTS Minutes, 1920–60; *East Midlands District Bulletin*, 1946–49; F. W. Leeman, *Co-operation in Nottingham* (Nottingham, 1963); *Hats Off to the People* (Nottingham, 1951).

30 NUMD NTC Minutes, 1925–32.

31 NUMD NTC Minutes, 1933–38.

32 NUMD NTC Minutes, 1928–31, 1936; NLSL NTC *Year Books* 1929–31, 1937, 1947; *NG* 19 September 1946.

21

FAMILY LIFE IN THE TWENTIETH CENTURY

Julie O'Neill

There is a common belief that in the past families were different. Certainly they were different in size: the average Nottingham household was 4.33 people in 1911 but only 2.37 in 1991. But were they different in nature? Research has consistently refuted widely held beliefs such as those relating to the supposed importance in the past of extended families.[1] In fact, the family is continually changing to reflect society, and this exploration of family life in twentieth-century Nottingham will not attempt to discover a golden past and compare the city family of the late twentieth century unfavourably with its mythical predecessors; rather, it will focus on selected themes which reflect family preoccupations at different times during the past one hundred years.

Survival

A baby born in Nottingham in 1900 could expect to live for less than fifty years. Although short by both biblical and current standards, life expectancy had improved considerably since the 1840s when the mean age at death was 22.3 years. By 1990, the improvement was such that men could expect to live to 73.2 years and women to 78.7. In the 1840s those living in the town's richest ward (Park) could expect to live for eleven years longer than those in the poorest (Byron).[2] That such differentials in longevity between rich and poor persist 150 years later is clear from standardised mortality rates for 1986–90, which vary from 77 per 1,000 in Wollaton ward to 187 per 1,000 in Forest ward.[3]

The improvement in life expectancy through the century is mainly due to a reduction in infant mortality (figure 21.1). In 1895 the infant mortality rate was 189 per 1,000 births, representing one-third of all deaths in Nottingham. Many babies

Figure 21.1 **Infant mortality rates, 1901–94**

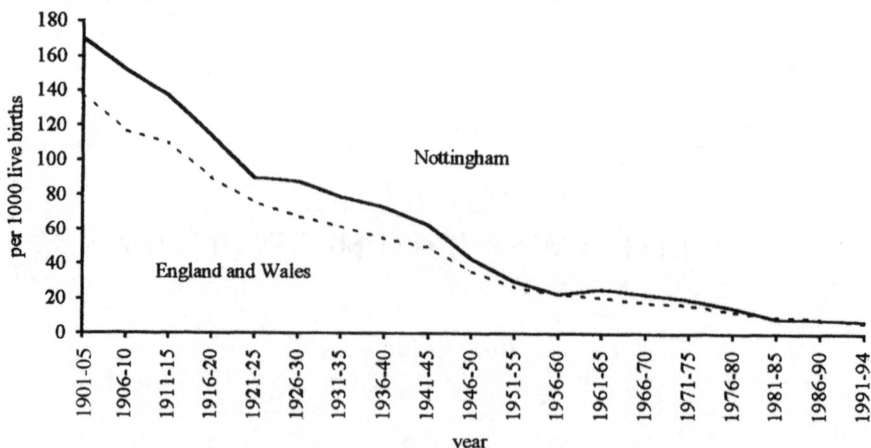

Sources: Annual Abstracts of Statistics; A. H. Halsey (ed.), *British Social Trends since 1900: a guide to the changing social structure of Britain* (Basingstoke, 1988); City of Nottingham, Medical Officer of Health, *Annual Reports;* Nottingham Health Authority Annual Reports.

died not necessarily because of their poor physical condition, but often because unhygienic methods of feeding resulted in dehydrating illnesses such as diarrhoea. The establishment of Mothers and Babies Welcomes from 1908 and Child Welfare Clinics from the 1920s played an important part in reducing infant mortality rates, but as figure 21.1 shows the level remained considerably higher than the national average until the 1950s.[4] By 1993 it had declined to 7.3 per 1,000 live births, a tiny fraction of its 1900 level, but in spite of this improvement inequalities in life chances for babies born in the city remain. Those born to families in economically disadvantaged areas of the city are twice as likely to have a low birth weight and five times more likely to die before the age of one than those in the most advantaged areas.[5]

One reason for the slow rate of improvement in the city's child mortality rates in the first half of the century may have been the poor conditions in which many people still lived, since the modernisation of the housing stock and its amenities was a protracted process. General improvements in housing and public health were more effective in enhancing life chances, especially for mothers and children, than was personal health care. Until the late 1940s the medical profession played very little part in the lives of most families. Many working men and women had free access to a doctor through their workplace, a sick club or, after 1912, through the National Health Insurance scheme, but free health care was not generally available to non-working women and their children until the National Health Service began in 1946. Until then midwives were usually called upon to help in childbirth, but doctors would only be contacted in times of serious illness, and then only if the family could afford it. People generally relied on traditional cures for common ills – vinegar and brown paper for headaches, mustard plasters for coughs and colds, castor oil, aniseed and liquorice, brimstone and treacle for regularity. Herbal medicines were also common and folk wisdom about their use widespread amongst both men and women. 'We always had dried dock leaves and stinking nanny hanging up in the attic for making poultices, for abscesses and boils, and rue tea for keeping the blood clear and nettle soup if anyone was sick.' One father, remembered for his rheumatism cures, 'was always making medicines, rubbing oils, pills, potions, cough medicines. There was always something boiling on the fire and jugs of herbs – camomile, raspberry leaves – brewing on the hearth.' For more serious complaints, advice was sought from herbalists or chemists who had their own concoctions; one local chemist was especially well known for his 'Gasman's Brew' for bronchitis.[6]

Eating

Getting enough to eat was the main preoccupation of many families. In the Edwardian era, while the affluent family living in the Park might be guided by books on household management and etiquette, which advised fashionable hostesses that a dinner party should consist of not less than eight courses – soup, fish, entrée, joint of meat, game, sweet, hors d'oeuvre, ice – the labourer's family in the Marsh areas lived predominantly on bread, dripping and weak tea supplemented by potatoes, cabbage and bacon. Ironically, as a result of food rationing, price control and advice on food values during the First World War, the poor were probably better fed than in the preceding years. After the war the concern for healthy eating continued, but the practices of the affluent and the poor again diverged. Those in regular employment benefited from increasing wages and were able to eat more fruit, vegetables and newly-introduced roughage breakfast foods, while others struggled to keep pace with the spiralling costs of bread, milk and other basic foods.

In the inter-war years, while affluent Nottingham families dined on expensive cuts of meat and luxury fruit and vegetables delivered by Burton's on Smithy Row or Skinner & Rook on Clumber Street, poorer families ate cow heel, pig's head, chap and trotters, sheep's head, fish 'head and shoulders' (heads and tails of fish) and 'speck jocks' (bruised fruit). They shopped at markets, bought sixpenny parcels of left-over meat from Wilcocks on Sneinton Road, or queued at the Shambles under the Exchange where 'you could get as much meat as you could carry for a bob on a Saturday night'. After 'soaky' (bread soaked in a basin of tea with milk and sugar added) for breakfast, children might be sent on a shopping trip to get 'two penn'orth' of bacon bits from Parr's on Mansfield Road, bits of cheese for free from Alcock's, 'two penn'orth' of dripping and a handful of pork scratchings from Wagner's and tripe parings from Sanderson's on Hockley, 'two penn'orth' of 'fish flaps' (cuttings from fish) from Palmers on Southwell Road, meat trimmings from Thoroughgood's on Cheapside, pastry cuttings, yesterday's stale bread and cake from Lloyds on Pepper Street, broken biscuits and biscuit crumbs, and the supreme luxury of 'dusty allsorts' (remains at the bottom of sweet jars) from a sweet shop.

Mothers were noted for achieving small economic miracles with limited means. Pigs' heads were specially valued; jelly could be made out of the ears, stew from the brains and pasties from the rest of the meat. A dinner for ten could be made out of a breast of lamb and 'three penn'orth' of pot herbs (celery, carrots, parsnips, turnips, onions). Bone and bean stew was the staple diet for many. On richer days, a threepenny or sixpenny wrap-up consisting of chops and pieces of liver and sausage would go a long way towards feeding a family. Those whose income was a little more secure could look forward to regular treats. In one family there was always a 'tup-penny' piece of salmon for 'dad' on Sunday; another could look forward to faggots on Friday and tripe and onions on Saturday every week.[7]

Pawnshops were an essential part of many families' battles to keep hunger and creditors at bay. There were fifty-one pawnshops in the city between the wars, and five even in the affluent 1960s. Many people preferred to pawn their Sunday suits and wedding rings rather than submit to the indignity of going to 'The Shakey' – the poor law guardians' office on Shakespeare Street – where, after interrogation, an applicant for relief might receive 'a voucher to go to Marsden's at the top of King Street for a loaf of bread, a quarter pound of margarine, a quarter of cheese, half of sugar'.[8] Although pawnshops never completely died out, rights to a range of welfare benefits have ensured that Monday-morning queues in the 1990s are no longer outside Whiting's on Sneinton Road or Williamson's in Lenton, but outside post offices as those receiving benefit wait to cash their giros from the 'Social' (the Department of Social Security).

House and home

During the inter-war years living conditions improved for most city residents, partly as a result of the corporation's slum-clearance schemes. One of the areas cleared in the 1920s was Red Lion Street, known locally as 'The Marsh', from which almost 1,500 people were moved. With its back-to-back houses, courts and alleys, pubs and lodging-houses, vagrants and prostitutes, The Marsh had a reputation which ensured that most outsiders avoided it. Former residents recall that the lodging-houses, with men sitting outside all day drinking, particularly contributed to the area's seedy appearance. A notice on the wall outside Flint's lodging-house advised '4d. a night, bring your own flea powder'. Occupants of the back-to-back houses shared tub toilets down the street which were emptied by 'muck majors with the ten o'clock horses'. Inside the houses were rats and mice, but people remember most vividly the bugs – crickets over the walls, flea-infested straw mattresses and 'black clocks' (cockroaches). Children remember the stench as they swept the black clocks off the walls and crushed them underfoot. On bed legs, mothers either spread Vaseline, or stood them in jam jars of Lysol to prevent the cockroaches from crawling over their sleeping children or settling under the ridges of iron bedsteads. Families had to be sure to have their furniture fumigated before moving to a new home.[9]

Moving from the slums to a new council house, from Coalpit Lane to Skipton Circus, or from The Marsh to Sneinton, was described by one child of the time as

> like moving from Hell to Heaven … . When we got to Cardale Road, all I did was go round the house looking in wonder. I couldn't believe the electric light. And the gas stove, I didn't know what that was. An iron bath and the toilet, a proper toilet, I had to flush it every time I saw it. And the big cast iron boiler for the washing and a back garden for hanging the clothes out.'

Not everyone, however, welcomed the chance to move to a new house. One mother refused to go to a house with a bath, fearing that while she was busy with her lace-work downstairs, one of the children might drown in the bath upstairs. Instead she chose to move to another bathless, but cheaper, house.[10] Others found the new estates less satisfactory than they had anticipated. Life on new estates like Clifton reflected the 'suburban ideal emphasising domesticity and privacy, the family rather than the community', with material improvement being acquired at the cost 'of a certain social sterility and a sense of lifelessness that persists to this day'.[11]

A very different life-style was enjoyed in other parts of the city, notably in the grand houses in The Park, Mapperley or around the Arboretum. The daughter of a senior member of the corporation staff recalled her father travelling to work in his pony and trap from his home in the Arboretum area while mother organised home life downstairs, with the help of the resident maid. The experience of the daughter of a lace factory owner who lived in Mapperley Park was similar. With two maids and a gardener, home is mostly remembered for its social events – fine parties at Christmas, its billiard room and croquet and badminton on the lawns in summer.[12] Many of the city's richest inhabitants retreated to mansions in the surrounding villages from their former homes in The Park and commuted to Nottingham by motor car.

While the inter-war period brought poverty to many families as industrial decline, strikes in the mining industry and the national depression took its toll on the local economy, for others it was a time of prosperity. Employees in the new industries, the railways, the police force or local authority had a regular income and benefited from the growth in production and falling prices of consumer goods between the wars. Many were able to buy their own home on one of the new private housing estates at Wollaton, or beyond the city boundaries in Beeston, West Bridgford, Carlton and Arnold. On land formerly belonging to Wollaton Hall, new houses cost £490 – £40 down and 14*s* 6*d* per week for twenty years – a bargain for those with a regular income and an employer who would help by providing the deposit repayable from weekly wages. But perhaps the biggest house bargain of the inter-war years was a small builder's purchase of Lord Trent's former home in The Park. Reputed to have cost £6,000 to build, 'St Heliers' was sold at auction in 1932 for £7.[13]

In her new home, the suburban housewife, helped by the introduction of household gadgets bought on the 'never-never' (weekly or monthly payments), kept house with less effort than earlier generations. Whereas her mother used coal and wood fires for cooking and for heating the clothes-washing boiler, and wore a coarse hessian

Plate 59 **Lewis Court, 1934**. The courts and alleys of the Marshes are remembered for their cramped and unhygienic living conditions. But they are also remembered for their neighbourliness, and this picture shows residents sharing dustbins, washing-lines and doorstep life. One of the criticisms made of redevelopment and rehousing from the 1930s to the 1970s was the loss of community

apron as she scrubbed the outside step and blackleaded the grate, the daughter cooked on a gas or electric oven, washed clothes in an electric boiler, vacuum-cleaned with her Hoover and polished the linoleum with an O Cedar mop. Flush toilets and toilet-rolls replaced earth closets and newspaper (usually the *Evening Post*). The suburban housewife was able to afford this life-style long before her council estate contemporary, but both women's lives were eventually transformed by their new living conditions. With fewer children, more household equipment and better housing, women acquired a new primary role as 'home-maker', and home became a private place to which the family retreated together.

Family preoccupation with the home re-emerged from the 1960s when house ownership expanded, new housing estates mushroomed around the city, and inner-city areas were redeveloped. Considerable concern was expressed about the effect of redevelopment on community spirit. Petitions were organised against the destruction of St Ann's but eventually 10,000 houses were demolished, to be replaced by 3,500. A quarter of the former inhabitants were rehoused in the area; others moved elsewhere in the city. While some welcomed their new location others, missing the companionship of St Ann's and burdened by higher rents on the new estates, returned to live in cheaper properties in the city centre. Some voiced sadness tinged with anger about the development which had changed the nature of St Ann's. From an area teeming with life and a multiplicity of shops, it had become a boring council estate with a small, characterless shopping precinct:

> When we were a slum, people came into the area to buy bread on a Sunday, and to work from Monday to Friday and down for all kinds of knees-up on a Saturday night. We had life … . Now we've been redeveloped no-one comes into the area any more to work, shop or sing and dance … . Not only the face of the neighbourhood changed but the body and spirit of the people.[14]

A former community leader of St Ann's asked rhetorically: 'where in this new world we have built is the warmth, colour, character and easy community spirit we used to have?'[15]

Much the same was true of the Meadows: in the words of one commentator, 'the community, which before demolition still seemed natural and coherent no longer matters when the physical structures have been removed … . The emphasis on the domestic interests (with all its consequent goods) draws people away from old associations … debt and discontent are left.'[16]

The St Ann's development, like that of the Meadows which followed, consisted mainly of terraced houses and small gardens. The designs of both estates with their many narrow lanes were criticised as burglars' and muggers' paradises.

A child's life

For the first half of the century work dominated the lives of most children. They may have been freed from working in chimneys, mines and factories, and provided with a basic education, but most families depended on their help with household tasks, looking after younger siblings, or contributing to the family income. Boys were more likely to have a paid job outside the house than their sisters. They chopped wood, fetched water, ran errands and blackleaded their neighbours' grates. They looked after barrows at the cattle market, collected jam jars and rags to sell, made deliveries from shops and ran errands. One boy delivered coal for his mother's coal-dealing business during the week and on Saturday used a handcart 'to push tripe out from Huntingdon Street to Tom Sanderson's shops … . I had to go to each shop with a bath of tripe and trotters. Used to take me till 2 o'clock on a Saturday, and I got paid sixpence for it.'[17] Girls were more likely to be found in the home, helping with the housework and minding younger children.

Young children often shouldered considerable responsibilities, particularly the oldest child. In the 1930s one mother left home at 6.00 a.m. to walk from Sneinton to her work in Aspley, leaving her eight-year-old daughter to get the younger children up, breakfasted and off to school. After school she was again in charge of house, meals and children until mother returned at 9.00 p.m. The burdens on one-parent families were even heavier. A twelve-year-old boy who became the breadwinner when his father died in the First World War 'used to go out and play marbles and come back with 1*d*. or ½*d*. which would help us buy food … he'd play marbles and sell the ones he'd won and give the money to mother'.[18]

Life for those in the city's Children's Homes in the 1920s and 1930s was just as hard:

> Every morning, you'd make the beds, spread the bread and dripping for breakfast, make the cocoa. Then somebody lit the kitchen fire, somebody else lit the dining room fire, someone else dressed the smaller ones and saw that everyone was ready for school. The older children had to look after the younger ones. When you came home from school at dinner-time you'd got jobs to do then. One had to peel the potatoes in the outside shed … others had to rub the knives forks and spoons up and down to get them shiny. We set the table with an oilcloth and knives and forks. We served, cleared the table, washed the pots. At nighttime when we came from school, the older ones blackpolished the shoes … the girls used to have to darn their long black stockings … . We used to make the beds every day and on a Saturday we used to strip the beds and fold the dirty linen to go to the laundry … . And the floors were polished with big tins of Ronuk. We used to put the Ronuk on, on your hands and knees, leave it a bit to dry and get your dusters and buff it up till you could see your face in it. While you were doing that someone was scrubbing the yard out, scrubbing the drains out with disinfectant and the outside toilet at the bottom of the yard. And the yard itself was scrubbed. The sweep swept the chimney but every week one of the children would have to clean the flues. And we used to have to chop the wood and fetch the coal in … . I only remember work. I never remember being young enough not to work.[19]

While some children never had time to play, others recall their play vividly. Children from middle-class families typically played at home. A child from the Arboretum recalled that from her nursery, where she was attended by a resident maid, she watched passers-by in the street. Sometimes she was allowed to play hide-and-seek or ball in the Arboretum, where the park-keeper promised her mother that he would keep an eye on her.[20] Working-class children from Sneinton found the rocks and caves in The Mounts an attraction. Some might even venture as far as Colwick Woods but usually they played on the streets near their homes. Playing tricks on others, spirit rapping or tying door-knockers together, and tin lurky, were favourite games. Children might have some toys, such as marbles, snobs, hoops, diabolos, or even a shillycock and battledore, but most made what they could for themselves. Old washing lines and ropes from orange boxes were used for skipping ropes and for swinging around lampposts, tin trays made excellent sledges, pegs and scraps of cloth made little dolls. Few Edwardian children were as fortunate as the lace manufacturer's daughter who was given 6*d* every week and taken to Willoughby's on Milton Street to choose her toys.[21] Poorer children would be drawn to Cohen's Penny Bazaar on Hockley.

During the inter-war years the ways in which many children spent their spare time changed. Whereas the courts, yards and streets were the focus of communal activity for both children and adults, those who moved to new council estates on the edge of town or to the new private-housed suburbs found more space and freedom inside the house. One child recalled that after her father bought a house in West Bridgford, spare time was spent at home with the family instead of on the streets with her friends; they played ludo, snakes and ladders, tiddly-winks, read a lot, had regular singsongs around the piano and gathered around the newly-acquired radio.[22]

In the early years of the century, it was common for parents and children of all classes to spend Sundays together. Families walked for miles to visit relatives, the surrounding countryside, or to window-shop in town in the afternoon. Richer families might take a tram to the edge of town and walk in the Lambley Dumbles, near the river at Attenborough or further afield in Clifton Grove where tea would be taken at Rose Cottage; they might even take a trip by train to Southwell and visit the Minster.[23] Before the First World War families might also enjoy a night out in town on other days of the week, but there was a class differentiation in the kinds of venue they might frequent. The Theatre Royal with its Shakespeare, opera and other theatre pieces attracted a largely middle-class clientele while a working-class family was more likely to go to a variety show at the Empire or the Hippodrome or a thriller at The Grand in Hyson Green. But by the 1930s, cinemas had replaced variety theatres as the most popular form of entertainment for adults and children of all social classes; Alan Sillitoe recalled that in the 1930s: 'The pictures were a solace and a consolation, and it was a poor week if I didn't get the few pennies necessary to take myself to a matinee or Saturday afternoon.'[24] For other children, too, 'Going to the pictures' was the highlight of the week:

> We used to go to the cinema – the Dale, or the Fleapit [Palace] at the bottom of Sneinton Road, or the Rio or the Cavendish. The Cavendish was about the favourite. We used to go twice a week cos the programmes used to change in the week. We used to go with our parents and we used to go to the Tuppenny Rush on a Saturday afternoon. It played a big part in our lives, the cinema. If we hadn't got money, we used to take bottles back, anything to get a few coppers to go to the pictures. You used to get tuppence on a bottle. Or you'd do a few errands to scrounge enough to go to pictures.[25]

Charities, churches and businesses ensured that even the poorest children enjoyed outings and other entertainments. There were Sunday School trips, cheap camping holidays run by scouts or boys' clubs, and parties and holidays provided by Pearson's Open Air fund. At Christmas, Sneinton children were well served: Solari's provided gifts, the Salvation Army gave a party and the Hippodrome put on a film show. Even political parties contributed, handing out blue and yellow streamers at election time. The Tories held an end-of-election party to which one child from each house in Sneinton was invited.[26]

After the Second World War there was a new enthusiasm for family life. Parents tended to spend more of their recreation time with their children on picnics, trips to the seaside, window-shopping, visiting relatives, bicycle rides or – for an increasing number – trips by car. However, in the late 1950s, a generational division over recreation began to emerge. Perhaps the Queen's Coronation in 1953 marked the beginning of this divide for, as one child of the time recalled, there was no street party where she lived in St Ann's as 'all the grown ups were in our house with their eyes glued to the television'.[27] Family outings gave way to a pattern in which parents watched television while their children went out to play on the streets again.

Meanwhile another revolution was taking place amongst older children, the newly-invented teenagers, who were creating a new and separate culture of their own. In Nottingham, as throughout Britain, the arrival of 'Rock 'n' Roll' in 1956 defined the new generation more surely than the Festival of Britain in 1951 or the Coronation. Rejecting their parents' values and abandoning adult-run organisations such as Scouts, Guides and church-based clubs which had been so popular in the inter-war years, they favoured 'hanging out' on street corners or at 'caffs' such as the Moo Cow on Carrington Street, reputedly the first with a juke-box. Even at the Palais, where jitterbugging to quick-step music had once been banned, sedate afternoon tea-dances to the Peter Fielding or Wylie Price Orchestras for adults of mature years gave way to teenagers and rock and roll.[28]

In the 1990s, patterns of children's play reflect new opportunities created by changing technology, as well as concerns about their safety. Children no longer generally play on the streets where strangers and traffic are regarded as dangerous, nor do they often go to the cinema. Instead they are more likely to watch television or play with a computer and video games in their bedrooms. Older brothers and sisters may frequent Rock City, Ritzy or another of the city's many clubs which attract young people from miles around. Meanwhile, many parents watch television and videos or enjoy child-free social lives at pubs, clubs, restaurants, cinemas or bingo halls. For a small number of children, however, the practical demands of family life continue to dominate, as they shoulder the responsibility of being the main or only carer for a sick or disabled parent.[29]

Women at work

In the first half of the century it was generally accepted that the woman's place was in the home. Although women filled men's occupational shoes while the country was engaged in two world wars, neither event was a turning-point in their long-term employment opportunities. Peace brought a return to the home, or to traditional women's work.[30] Among the middle classes wives rarely worked outside the home. Typically they took responsibility for organising the housework, which the servants undertook, while they spent their spare time on voluntary activities such as church work, the Mothers' Union, the Red Cross or St John's, or socialising with women of

Plate 60 **Street play in the Meadows 1976**. Children playing in the streets of the Meadows prior to redevelopment. The dangers posed by traffic and fear of strangers are such that the sounds of children playing street games are heard less often in the 1990s

their own class, playing bridge or other card games at home. However, it was not uncommon, even from the later Victorian years, for daughters to be sent to learn a trade, presumably as an insurance against dependence on parents in the event of failing to find a husband. Geoffrey Trease recalled that his mother, the daughter of a doctor, had become one of Mrs Watson's 'young ladies' at her high-class dress and milliner's shop in the 1890s. This experience was shared by the daughter of a lace factory owner before 1914, who declared that 'Nell must be put to a trade because we do not know what is going to happen and she must be able to make her own living.'[31]

Among working-class women the position was slightly different. A Board of Trade enquiry estimated that 24.1 per cent of married or widowed women were working in *c.*1908, and traditionally about two-fifths of Nottingham's work-force has been female.[32] However, these gross figures hide some significant discrepancies. Until the Second World War Boots, Players and Raleigh refused to employ married women, but the situation was different in the textile trades, particularly for work in the home as outworkers. Mothers seaming stockings or finishing lace were a familiar part of the home life for generations of Nottingham families. One woman recalled of the 1920s:

> My grandfather was under the impression that his money was enough to keep the family. He thought the women were there to do the cooking and the cleaning and had enough to do looking after the children and the home. He didn't know my grand-

> mother did lace-work to make ends meet. We used to hide it before he came home … but once, I shall never forget, he came home early one afternoon when we were doing this lace-work. And he was in such a rage that he threw all this lace-work on to the street … . That's how it was with my grand-dad … he was the breadwinner and that was it.[33]

Another woman, who continued to work for Simon Mays & Co. after she married in the 1930s, gave up factory work in favour of packing handkerchiefs at home: as she explained, 'when you was married you didn't go out to work – your place was in the home'.[34] These attitudes endured into the 1940s as the views of a photographer's wife suggest: 'if you had children you never expected to go out to work at all. You looked after the children … . Women did not usually go out to work after they were married, not unless there was a reason for it – perhaps the husband had died or was unable to work.'[35] On the other hand, some women who would have gone out to work were prevented from doing so by practical constraints. One young mother in the 1930s was thwarted by her own mother who, aware of the double burden of housework and employment, refused to look after the baby. 'You had the baby, you look after it; your husband married you, let him keep you … we'll have her while yer get yer housework done – or your jobs what you've got to do – but not to go out to work, and then come home and do your work.'[36]

Plate 61 **Women lace workers, *c.*1914**. For generations the lace industry provided married women with the opportunity to continue working while raising a family. The bag lady (second from the right) would arrange the distribution and collection of factory-made lace to these women finishers working as home (as outworkers) before the First World War

Figure 21.2 **Women in the labour force, 1911–91**

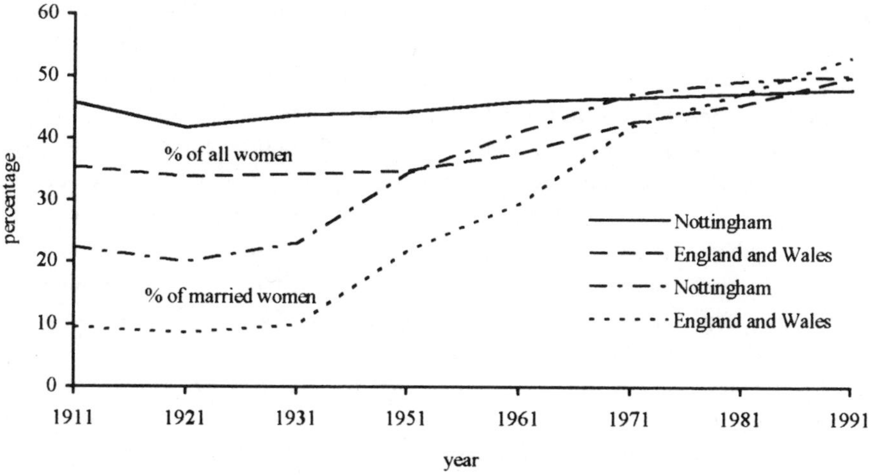

Sources: Decennial Census returns.

After 1945, when the demand for labour in national reconstruction ran at record levels, the idea of women as a permanent part of the work-force began to gain favour. Married women were able to share in important new opportunities when the national bans on them working as teachers or civil servants were lifted after 1945, and the bans operated by the larger Nottingham employers were never resumed. Consequently, employment opportunities for women increased in the 1960s as long-term structural changes helped to transform the economy from a manufacturing to a service base, while in the 1970s changes in legislation relating to equal pay and rights, and maternity provisions, encouraged women to work as well as to bring up children. In these circumstances it is hardly surprising to find that married women returned to work in ever-increasing numbers.

As figure 21.2 shows, women have traditionally formed a large proportion of Nottingham's work-force, notably in the textile trades. In 1911, 43.2 per cent of Nottingham's work-force was female, 45.7 per cent of women aged fifteen or over was in paid employment, and 71 per cent of the 30,500 work-force in textiles was female.[37] Employment opportunities continued to be available even when the textile trades faltered, because Players and Boots both employed a substantial number of unmarried women. Since the 1960s the number of women in employment has grown steadily, although from a higher base than in other areas of the country. Similarly the proportion of married women in the work-force grew from 22 per cent in 1911 to 50 per cent in 1991, again mirroring national trends. However, the loss of female employment opportunities as the textile and tobacco trades have declined was reflected in the 1991 census when rates of female participation in the work-force were shown to have fallen below the national average. Women's unemployment, at 11 per cent, was almost double the national average.[38]

In recent years working outside the home has become not only acceptable for married women, but desirable and even essential. From the 1960s the increasing trend towards home-ownership was an important element in the desire and need of married women to contribute to the family economy. More recently rising house prices and declining access to affordable rented accommodation have served to make many families dependent on a second income. In addition, economic decline from the late 1970s disproportionately affected full-time jobs in traditional men's work in Nottingham's industries, and led to an unemployment rate of 19.9 per cent in 1991, almost double the national average. As the local economy has shifted away from full-time male employment towards part-time temporary female work, dependence on women's earnings has increased. However, the social security benefit system, and the low level of wages paid to women, ensure that most do not find it worthwhile considering becoming the breadwinner while their partners become house-husbands. In any case, although large numbers of women have traditionally been part of the work-force, there is little evidence that men in Nottingham have taken a share in the unpaid work in the home caring either for children or for elderly relatives. One woman gave as her reasons for leaving a part-time cleaning job in the 1990s: 'I'm a slave to them at home [her husband and two teenage sons]. I'm *** if I'm going to go out to work and be a slave to someone else, then come home and clear up after these as well.' For most married women who work part-time, the picture in the 1990s continues to be one of low pay and intermittent work.[39]

Families in a multi-cultural city

The city's present ethnic and cultural diversity derives mainly from arrivals during and after the Second World War. In 1931, immigrants represented 1.6 per cent of the total population. In 1991 the immigrant population was almost 8 per cent, and more than half were from the New Commonwealth, notably the Caribbean, India and Pakistan (table 18.5).

Arrival in a new land can be disappointing if the country does not live up to expectations. A Jamaican, who arrived in 1953, described how he found a room in St Ann's, where Irish, Poles, Ukrainians and other immigrants had settled before him and where the accommodation and standard of hygiene were inferior to anything he had experienced in his homeland. Like other Jamaicans of the time, he was subject to racial prejudice when searching for work, and he suffered a further disappointment when, unable to get a position in his skilled trade in the city, he took a labouring job with a wage considerably lower than he had received at home. He recalled that the words which came to mind were not those of the patriotic songs he had learned about the Motherland when in Jamaica, but those of an English poet who had written

> England is a pleasant place for those that reach on high
> But England is a cruel place for poor folks such as I.[40]

Most post-Second-World-War immigrants have differed in race and often also in religion from the indigenous population. These differences have, arguably, acted against dispersal amongst the wider population. The 1991 census showed that the city's 10.8 per cent ethnic minority population, whether immigrant or local born, is concentrated in inner city areas. Such concentration is sometimes regarded as a measure of deprivation, although it may equally be that members of ethnic or cultural minority groups prefer the convenience or the security of living near friends, places of worship, speciality food shops, clubs and other organisations which serve their community.[41] Until the 1960s, St Ann's was noted for its range of shops reflecting the cosmopolitan nature of the community, with shops offering German, Polish and Italian specialities. Today shops, services and clubs specialising in serving minorities can be found in Radford, Lenton, Hyson Green and Sneinton.

Bringing up a family in a foreign country is a difficult task for parents who wish to pass on their own cultural traditions to their children. Italian immigrants in the 1950s commented that their children had attended an Italian nursery, spoke Italian and had been brought up in the Italian tradition but had nevertheless grown up to identify themselves as English. Nottingham was their home and England was their country.[42] More recent immigrants have experienced similar problems in conveying homeland traditions to their children. The lack of religious practice, moral guidance, strict discipline and a comprehensible approach to education are often commented upon and compared unfavourably with experience in the homeland. Possibly of greatest concern to immigrants is their fear that family traditions of mutual support between generations will be undermined if their children adopt British values.[43] One woman from Guyana commented that although she loved Nottingham, she missed her extended family:

> For instance, I remember when I was pregnant ... my relative from about 70 miles away she said to me 'Cousin, I going to come and move in with you nearer your time.' And she'd come and move in with me and she do all the washing, looking after, you know. That is how we live. Every member of your family looks after you, your children. Here people as soon as they grow up they go and live as far away as they can from their parents. So that parents when they are old – who's to look after them?[44]

One reflection of such concerns is that some parents send their children back to the homeland, often to their grandparents, to be raised amidst approved influences. Most children, however, grow up in their parents' adopted land amid the influences of the new culture. As much as parents might want to pass on 'back home' philosophies to their children, some of the children doubt that homeland traditions can survive among the generation born in Britain.[45]

Many migrants intended to remain a few years and then return to their homeland, but few have done so. A Jamaican who arrived in the 1950s commented that after so long it would be difficult to uproot from his friends. An Italian who arrived in the 1960s took steps to return home, even buying property there for that purpose, but in the end abandoned the plans when he and his wife realised that their ties to children and grandchildren were greater than their ties to their homeland. Another Italian, who decided to return home after seventeen years in England, was frustrated by the bureaucracy, nepotism and corruption which confronted him on arrival, and found himself thinking fondly of the relative order in Nottingham. 'It took me two weeks to find out I was in the wrong place. I was Italian but I was a foreigner over there ... and when I reached Nottingham ... I feel as if I'm home.'[46]

Such an affectionate view of city life is not necessarily shared by other immigrants and their local-born descendants. Although there is a great variation in the affluence and life-style of members of the city's ethnic groups, poverty, poor health and poor employment prospects remain major concerns, with unemployment disproportionately high among young black and Asian people. Racial discrimination in job allocation continues to cause unrest and dissatisfaction, and under such circumstances it is hardly surprising that some parents from ethnic minority groups are worried about the long-term prospects for their children.[47]

The demise of family and community?

In the mid-1990s the heritage of some of the changes which have affected family life in Nottingham during the century are evident. Improvements in the general level of health, welfare and social security provision have ensured that ill-clad, barefoot children are no longer regularly seen on the streets. Smaller families and the common ownership of washing-machines, refrigerators and other household equipment have freed married women from a lifetime dominated by child-bearing and housework, and enabled them to combine their domestic role with participation in the paid work-force. Large institutions, once thought appropriate to house orphans, the mentally ill or impaired, the elderly and the disabled, have been closed in favour of smaller, more personal units. The multi-cultural population is a reminder of the varieties of family life which coexist within the city. Sadly, there is also evidence that some citizens are failed by both family and State as the State has withdrawn from some of its responsibilities and families are unable, or unwilling, to pick up the pieces. In the 1980s recession the city witnessed the return of street beggars, as tramps were joined by vagrant alcoholics, drug-users, the mentally ill and the homeless. In 1929 a city charity noted the large increase in the number of vagrants and beggars, particularly in the number of men under the age of forty, and expressed concern that unemployment was forcing self-respecting and hard-working people into vagrancy.[48] More than sixty years later, at another time of high unemployment, reports continue to be concerned with the homeless. In 1991, 2,664 ho1meless families were recognised as eligible for rehousing; in 1992 a report by Shelter, the charity for the homeless, noted that young people represented 40 per cent of applicants for their service, and a study in 1994 estimated that there were about 2,150 single homeless people in the city.[49]

As reasons have been sought for the changes of the 1990s, attention has focused on the role of the family. At the beginning of the twentieth century, there was already a firmly established belief that the family was in decline. At that time, blame was attributed to the growth of industrial society in the nineteenth century, which had led to a separation of home and work and to an increasing number of women working outside the home.[50] In the last decade of the century, the demise of the family is again a dominant concern with attention focusing on the decline of marriage, family size, increasing divorce, illegitimacy and one-parent families. However, as table 18.4 shows, the nuclear family remains the most common form of family life. National statistics show that 90 per cent of people marry at some time in their lives and 78 per cent of children are brought up in a family unit with two parents, even if both are not necessarily their own natural parents. However, in national terms Nottingham does have a higher than average number of cohabiting couples, lone parents and single people.[51]

Concerns about family decline also focus on the supposed breakdown of the extended family and consequences for the care of growing numbers of elderly people, regardless of the historical evidence that the extended family has never been common in Britain.[52] In fact, although the elderly form an increasing percentage of the population, a smaller proportion lives in institutional care than at the beginning of the twentieth century, while much the same proportion live with their children. In 1906, 6 per cent of Nottingham's elderly lived in poor law institutions, but by 1991 only 4.7 per cent of the city's pensioners lived in residential care while 8 per cent lived with their children. The view that modern families do not care for their elderly is also challenged by evidence that the family, with very little help from the State or the local authority, continues to be the predominant source of care for the elderly outside residential homes.[53]

Changing state policies and deteriorating economic conditions have been blamed, both nationally and locally, for the deteriorating quality of family life in the 1980s and 1990s. At grass-roots level many long-time Nottingham residents believe that the greatest change to affect family life during the century has been the decline of neighbourliness. Some link its demise to the slum clearances of the 1920s and 1930s when inhabitants, formerly pressed together in inner-city slums, were dispatched to distant council estates where each family was separated from its neighbour by a fence and garden. Others see increasing materialism or the isolating influence of television since the 1950s as responsible. Yet others blame the increasing diversity of the population whether in the form of the mixture of social classes in the All Saints area, or the mixture of cultures and races in St Ann's or Sneinton where the common bond of living in the same neighbourhood is outweighed by cultural and language differences.[54] Whatever the perceived cause, there is a common belief that neighbourliness no longer exists.

> It's marvellous how we've advanced over the years but in some ways the old days were better. People were more helpful and friendly. If anything were wrong you

> knew who you could fetch and they'd all help with no thoughts of payment at all .... You knew everyone. It was a caring neighbourhood. [The Bottoms 1920s–30s] Anyone would help you. There was lots of love, no feeling of jealousy at all. We were all in the same boat.[55]

Another person recalled:

> It might have been a deprived area [St Ann's 1950s–60s] but the people were marvellous. They were always ready to help one another and nothing was too much trouble for them. There wasn't much money about but we were happy. And it was safe to walk the streets without being set upon by thugs and hooligans.[56]

These views are shared by members of the older generation, whether local-born or immigrants to the city. A Jamaican immigrant who served in the RAF during the war then settled in the city in the 1950s commented, 'The biggest change I've seen in Nottingham is – once upon a time you could walk down the street night and day without interference or fear but you can't do that today. You didn't have to lock your doors .... Nottingham was a very nice place to live.'[57]

A Jamaican woman added – 'Houses is better, better conditions ... everything is different ... [but] this vandalise thing we have now, breaking in houses and burglary'.[58]

The decline of the listening ear and consolation of friends or neighbours may explain the growth of self-help groups, telephone advice lines and private counsellors in the city.[59] Such growth may also be related to the withdrawal of the State from many aspects of family support. In the mid-years of the century, it seemed that so many of the tasks fundamental to family life were being removed from the home to outside institutions, that the family would be divested entirely of its practical roles and left only to cater for the emotional needs of its members. In the last twenty years of the century the State has returned a variety of tasks to 'the community' – and in the 1990s individual families have had to shoulder once more the financial and practical commitments of caring for their own members. 'Community care' in reality usually means family care, but as one authority has cogently pointed out, 'family care' generally means care by women, or more likely, one woman.[60]

At the end of the twentieth century we are witnessing not the demise of the family but a retreat to the family as the state and community opt out of formerly accepted communal roles. This was a view reflected in the words of a mourner at a Nottingham funeral who, on casting an eye over those attending, pronounced: 'Over ninety years on this earth and that's what it amounts to .... In the end it's only the family that bothers to come. And it's the family that 'as to pick up the bill.'[61] As elsewhere, suggestions that the family is in decline are as inappropriate in the 1990s as they were at the beginning of the century.

Notes

1 Decennial Censuses 1911 and 1991; M. Anderson, 'What's new about the modern family?', *The Family*, 31 (1983), pp. 2–16.

2 Family Policy Studies Centre, *Fact Sheet 6: Children* (Family Policy Studies Centre, 1988); OPCS, *Population Trends*, 78 (Winter 1994), table 12; A. Rogers, *This was their world* (1972), pp. 45–6.

3 Standardised mortality rates 1986–90 for all ages based on Nottingham Health Authority = 100. Nottingham City = 118. Chief Executive's Department – City of Nottingham, *Poverty in Nottingham* (Nottingham, 1994), table 11. See also ch. 18 in this book.

4 *Annual Health Report for 1895* (Nottingham, 1895); *Annual Health Report for the City of Nottingham 1900* (Nottingham, 1900), p. 21; P. Boobbyer, *Summary of Nottingham City Health Reports 1916–28* (Nottingham, n.d.), pp. 6, 36–7.

5 S. Wilson, *Aiming for Health in the Year 2000* (Nottingham Health District, 1995), p. 70; City of Nottingham, *Poverty*, Technical Appendix, table 13: *Health Profile*: Nottingham City (Nottingham Health Authority, 1992).

6 Interviews Nottinghamshire County Council Oral History Collection, Local Studies Library (NLSL) A8, A13, A23, A33, A58; Interviews Centenary of Nottingham History Collection (CN) CN3, CN7.

7 NLSL A8, A54, A94; CN4, CN14.

8 R. Smith, *Burn Off Your Rusts* (video, East Midlands Branch, Town Planning Institute, 1985); CN37.

9 Gray, *Nottingham*, p. 97; CN8, CN17, CN31.

10 CN17; CN38.

11 R. Silburn, *People in their Places, One Hundred Years of Nottingham Life* (Nottingham, 1981), p. 33.

12 NLSL A47a; NLSL A60; K. Brand, *The Park Estate* (Nottingham, 1985) p. 31.

13 Gray, *Nottingham*, p. 98; *EP*, 16 June 1932.

14 R. Gosling, *Personal Copy* (1980), pp. 195 and 219.

15 *Ibid.*, pp. 194–5, 218–25.

16 J. Seabrook, *What Went Wrong? Working People and the Ideals of the Labour Movement* (1978), pp. 35–6. Other studies of the St Ann's redevelopment argue along similar lines: K. Coates and R. Silburn, *Beyond the Bulldozer* (Nottingham, 1980), ch. V.

17 NLSL A8, A43, A54, A63, A94.

18 NLSL A33, CN3.

19 CN10.

20 NLSL A47a.

21 NLSL A56.

22 CN1.

23 NLSL A47, A56, A94; CN3, 1932.

24 A. Sillitoe, *Life Without Armour* (1995), p. 25; *Kelly's Directory*, 1932.

25 CN3.

26 CN3, CN5, CN21, CN28.

27 CN32.

28 CN36, CN39; 'The Palais' – in *The Way We Were*, Channel 4 TV, 1992.

29 J. Church and C. Summerfield, *Social Focus on Children* (1994), p. 53; Carers National Association, *Facts About Carers Leaflet* (1995).

30 L. Martin, *Never Let Anyone Draw the Blinds* (1989), pp. 40–1; J. O'Neill, 'Nottingham people in the First World War', in D. Marcombe (ed.), *Nottingham and the Great War* (Nottingham, 1985); H. Smith (ed.), *War and Social Change*, (Manchester, 1986), pp. 208–29.

31 NLSL A47a, A60, A60a; G. Trease, *A Whiff of Burnt Boats* (1971), p. 9.

32 Board of Trade, *Enquiry Into the Cost of Living of the Working Classes* PP Cd 3864 (1908); K. Coates and R. Silburn, *Poverty: the Forgotten Englishman* (1970), p. 50.

33 CN30.

34 Mrs H. b.1915 quoted in S. Taylor, 'The effect of marriage on job possibilities for women', *Oral*

History, 5/2 (1977), p. 54.

35 NLSL A75.

36 Ms E. Hickling quoted in S. Taylor, 'The effect of marriage', p. 55.

37 Decennial Census 1911.

38 R. Price and G. S. Bain, 'The labour force' in A. H. Halsey (ed.), *British Social Trends Since 1900* (1988), p. 172; 1911 Decennial Census.

39 J. Lewis, *Women in Britain Since 1945* (Oxford, 1992), pp. 3, 69, 78, 88–9; interview MD (private collection).

40 CNB1, CNB5, CNB6, CNB7.

41 Nottinghamshire County Council, *Disadvantage in Nottinghamshire: County Deprived Area Study* (NCC, 1983).

42 CNB2, CNB3.

43 Javed Choudry and Mrs Nighat Bibi quoted in R. Malik and S. Gregory *Living with two cultures* (Meadows Community Arts, n.d.), pp. 18–19; CNB1, CNB4, CNB5.

44 CNB4.

45 NLSL B61.

46 CNB1, CNB2, CNB3.

47 Wilson, *Aiming for Health in the Year 2000*, p. 20; City of Nottingham 1991 *Census – Ethnic Group Information for Nottingham City* (Nottingham, 1993); J. Wickenden, *Colour in Britain* (1958) p. 9; F. Bayliss and J. Coates, 'West Indians at work in Nottingham', *Race*, 7/2 (Oct 1965); J. Habbuck and S. Carter, *Half a Job?* A report on job discrimination against young blacks in Nottingham (CRE, 1980); NLSL B4, B61.

48 Nottingham Council of Social Service, *Charity Organisation Society Annual Report 1929*.

49 Shelter – Nottinghamshire Homeless Action, *Housing and Homelessness Facts and Figures* (Shelter, Nottingham, 1992); D. Whynes and J. Giggs, 'The Health of the Nottingham Homeless', *Public Health*, 106/4 (1992) pp. 307–14; J. Vincent, P. Trinder, I. Hack, *Single Homelessness – Towards a Strategy for Nottingham* (Nottingham Hostels Liaison Group, 1994).

50 J. Harriss, *The Family* (1992), p. 40.

51 OPCS, *Birth Statistics* (1992); CSO, *Social Trends 25* (HMSO, 1995), pp. 34–8; The Times 1 March, 10 April, 13 June 1995; M. Henwood, *Inside the family* (Family Policy Studies Centre, 1987), p. 4; CSO, *Social Trends 25* (1995) tables 2.4 and 2.10.

52 Anderson, 'What is new about the modern family?'

53 Derived from *1991 Census Area Profile – Nottingham* (Department of Planning and Economic Development, Nottinghamshire County Council, 1993); M. P. Hall, *The Social Services of Modern England* (6th edn, 1963), p. 287; OPCS, *General Household Survey* 1992 (1994), table 36, p. 28.

54 CN interviews; Smith, *Burn off your rusts*.

55 CN8.

56 *EP*, 7 May 1994.

57 CNB5.

58 CNB6.

59 Ninety-three self-help groups listed in *Directory of Self-Help Groups in Nottingham and District 1994/5* (Nottingham Council of Voluntary Service, 1994).

60 E. Wilson, 'Women, the "community" and "family"', in A. Walker (ed.), *Community Care, the Family, the State and Social Policy* (1982).

61 J. H., personal communication, 1993.

22

LEISURE

Jeff Hill

In the autumn of 1933, the writer and social documentarist J. B. Priestley made a detour in the planned itinerary of his English journey in order to visit Nottingham. He and his fellow passengers on the bus journey from Leicester were heading for the Goose Fair which in the 1930s, as today, was for Nottingham people 'one of the highlights of the year. They even speak of Goose Fair weather, that definite autumnal nip in the air … its as much a centre of interest in school as Christmas … if there was not a school holiday the kids would take it anyway.'[1] Priestley observed that a good many people had enjoyed themselves at the fair but he argued that it was not a genuine popular festival of spontaneous pleasure made by the people, but a gross form of entertainment provided for them by 'an assembly of devices, chiefly mechanical, contrived to attract the largest number of pennies in the shortest possible time'. In Nottingham, as elsewhere, there had been a powerful development of commercial leisure, and this had helped to sustain the city's reputation as the most frivolous of provincial towns. Priestley's objection, expressed in relation to Goose Fair and to a football match between Notts County and Nottingham Forest, was that the commodification of entertainment was destroying the creativity of recreation and replacing it with a culture of easy gratification 'for' the people rather than 'of' them.[2]

In the twentieth century leisure time, leisure space and leisure funding have transformed the life-styles of almost everyone. Working hours have been reduced, the Saturday half-day has been transformed into the weekend, and annual paid holidays have become a right rather than a reluctantly granted concession. Larger homes and smaller families have offered house-room to leisure activities, particularly the great new invention of the twentieth century, the ubiquitous television. Higher living standards have enabled people to pay for a range and regularity of leisure to make best use of the time which has become available. In this chapter we ask how these changes have affected leisure activities, but the subject is now so vast that it has been necessary to limit the perspective to three areas, and then only to deal with these at best partially. First we shall look at the growth of a leisure industry, the provision in return for payment of leisure activities which so concerned Priestley in the 1930s; second, we shall examine the voluntary sector to see whether Priestley was right in his assumption that commercialism was destroying voluntary recreations; and third, we shall look at the role of the municipality as a provider of leisure facilities.

The commercialisation of leisure

J. B. Priestley's opinion that Goose Fair was a particularly 'cheap, nasty and sordid example' of commercial leisure provision was particularly ironic given the timing of his visit. The Fair was not held during the First World War, and when in 1919 the corporation proposed to make the suspension permanent it was forced to beat a hasty retreat in the face of hostile popular opinion.[3] Goose Fair may have been a commercial event, but it was held in great affection locally. When the new Council House was built and the market-place remodelled in the 1920s the corporation carefully steered around the question of abolition, preferring relocation. The Fair was held in the market-place for the last time in 1927, and successfully transferred to the Forest in 1928, where it remains.[4]

Popular opinion insisted that the Fair should be retained, and for Priestley the local Derby between Nottingham Forest and Notts County which he attended in 1933 was another symbol of the way in which leisure was being commercialised, in this case through professional sport.[5] Football clubs had first sought paying spectators to help pay their expenses, but the professional game fed on an exponential growth in spectator numbers from the 1890s onwards. In the twentieth century Nottingham's two professional clubs were modest achievers for over seventy years until Forest emerged as a leading national club following the Cup Final victory over Luton Town in 1959.[6] Neither club is or has been wealthy. Both have existed on a narrow basis of capital, aided for many years by the draconian system of industrial relations that applied in professional football until the 1960s, whereby players were held to relatively modest wage-ceilings and engaged on contracts which effectively tied them to the club. In terms of the commercialisation of sport, instead of seeing the clubs as businesses manufacturing a ready-made product for mass consumption, we should perhaps view them as dependent on their community of spectators. Gate money was the major source of finance until at least the 1970s, and spectator loyalty and affection provided the support on which their very existence rested.[7] It was this special relationship between a football club and its followers that explains its durability and the place it has in the life of the city. Neither club could have contemplated uprooting their operation elsewhere, even when times were bad, as other commercial undertakings might routinely do in order to continue in business. The possibility of groundsharing found little or no support.

In recent years Forest have escaped from the rather low-key operation which saw the club in the Second and Third Divisions between 1911 and 1957. Under the mercurial Brian Clough, who was appointed manager in 1975, and with the support of his assistant Peter Taylor from 1976, Forest were promoted to the First Division where they won the Championship in 1978 and went on to win the European Championship in both 1979 and 1980. Other domestic honours followed, as the club became a major player in the Premier League, with a rebuilt ground capable of hosting international matches.[8] The transformation has occurred since the club adopted limited-liability status in the 1980s – the last top-level football club to abandon the idea of it being a club for members. Notts County adopted limited-liability status as long ago as the 1890s, and the team won the Cup in 1894, but despite occasional forays into the higher reaches of English football – the club was briefly top of the First Division in 1983 – they have not in recent times been able to match the success of Forest. Today, reflecting the business work of the modern football team, both clubs have commercial managers.

A similar picture of small-scale commercialism emerges in relationship to the development of Nottinghamshire County Cricket Club. Notts. was one of the first of the leading county cricket clubs to promote professionalism in the 1870s and, in contrast to many other counties, it generally employed a high proportion of paid players in its teams. Yet the club's activities could only ever be described as semi-commercial, because maintaining an ethos was equally important.[9] Even before 1914 county cricket at Trent Bridge attracted large crowds, especially for matches against other counties in the 'big six' group,[10] or the international fixtures against Australia which began in 1899, but the club was run by and for its mainly middle- and upper-class membership. Through the later 1920s and 1930s Notts. enjoyed considerable playing success, winning the County Championship in 1929 with a team including players of the calibre of George Gunn, Larwood, Voce and Staples, but financial losses were a regular occurrence. In 1931 the club had total indebtedness of almost £4,500 and although the England–Australia Test Match of 1934 brought some relief the club was again in debt in 1935.[11] The pursuit of commercial profit through cricket was secondary to the maintenance of a *club* ethos at Trent Bridge, and an upper-class ethos symbolised by the captain Arthur Carr. Although Carr was a skilled practitioner who captained England in the 1920s, this was not always the case with amateur captains. Even in the 1960s the club captaincy was always entrusted to a gentleman of the right social standing, despite the presence in the team of internationally-renowned, but working-class, professionals. The irony is that in the 1850s William Clarke's All-England XI had introduced commercial cricket under the direction of relatively humble farmers and artisans with an entrepreneurial cast of mind.

The full commercial exploitation of cricket had to await the revolution introduced by Kerry Packer in the 1970s. The club had shown a more business like attitude towards the task of winning the county championship when it engaged Sir Garfield Sobers as its first overseas paid professional in 1968, and immediately gave him the captaincy. He was replaced in 1975 by the South African Clive Rice who, together with the New Zealander Sir Richard Hadlee, led the team to an unprecedented series of triumphs in the years from 1978, including the county championship in 1981 and 1987, and all the major cup competitions between 1987 and 1991.

Sport illustrates some aspects of the commercial development of popular recreations, but cinema provides an example of capitalist entertainment in a more mature stage of its growth. In the inter-war years there was still nothing like the facility for home entertainment which has developed since 1945. As the powerful resistance to organised leisure which had been a feature of the First World War gradually receded, people flooded into the town in search of entertainment, and the cinema was one of the main beneficiaries. Cinema, which initially overlapped with and eventually superseded music hall, was well established as a popular form of entertainment even before 1914. In 1906 the King's Theatre and the Empire, on South Sherwood Street, were offering motion-picture shows: the King's a complete twice-nightly programme of 'animated pictures', and the Empire a mixed programme of live acts,

Plate 62 **Elite Picture Theatre, Parliament Street, 1921 (drawing from the souvenir brochure)**. The Elite, designed by Adamson & Kinns (of London) was 'the last word in amusement houses' when it opened on 22 August 1921. Besides a 1,600-seat cinema this beautiful palace of white faience offered the choice of three large cafés, a ballroom and a pair of shops. The 'noble array of niched emblematic and legendary figures', which graces the top of the building, has always been much admired. The cinema closed on 12 April 1977 and flirted with bingo. Now, after alterations, it has more shops, offices and an external restaurant

which included Fred Karno's 'latest and greatest creation' alongside film of King Edward VII reviewing veterans at Derby.[12] By 1913 there were seven picture-houses in the city, showing a variety of films and seeking to outbid each other in standards of comfort and size. The King's had by now become the Scala, a new building on Market Street 'fitted up in the latest style', with all its pictures passed by the National Film Censor (the British Board of Film Censors set up in 1912); the Regent in Mansfield Road proclaimed itself to be the 'finest appointed hall in the city and absolutely the best pictures'.[13] This was popular mass entertainment: prices at the Mechanics Hall ranged from 4*d* to 1*s*, with children admitted for half price. This was well within the reach of the ordinary working-class family, although the price range ensured that social segregation was maintained.

The inter-war period saw a major boom in cinema-going. Between the early 1920s and the 1930s the number of cinemas grew from twenty-six to about sixty, many of them in the palatial style adopted for the Astoria at Lenton or the Futurist on Valley Road.[14] In the 1930s and 1940s a broad range of films was on offer, but most were American despite the protection afforded the British film industry after 1928. On a typical weekend in the 1930s Nottingham cinema-goers could see American stars such as Janet Gaynor, Franchot Tone, Joan Crawford and Clark Gable, or British exports such as Madeleine Carroll and Cary Grant. British films starring Robert Donat, Fay Compton and Jack Hulbert were also much to the fore.[15] Although the fare on offer was 'gendered' in the sense of there being specifically 'women's films' (Dolly Haas in 'Girls will be Boys' was one example), cinema does appear to have been a pastime genuinely open to all. It avoided the masculine bias of older entertainments such as pubs and football which carried male sociability out of the workplace and into 'spare time', a concept it is difficult to apply to many women, especially married women.

The period from the 1930s to the mid-1950s was the heyday of cinema entertainment. It presented a stark contrast with the late 1950s when new leisure pursuits began to displace the cinema. The last picture shows were screened in some much-loved theatres, including the Commodore at Aspley. 'Up the Junction' marked the closure of the Capitol in Radford.[16] Since the 1950s cinemas have attempted to consolidate their position by concentrating the product in a few centrally-located venues. In the early 1970s the multi-screen arrangement arrived at the Odeon on Angel Row and the Savoy on Derby Road, both old-established cinemas. In the 1980s a larger version was built at the Showcase complex, a new suburban site in Lenton offering numerous parking spaces. Ironically this offered the cinema some hope of competing with the ubiquitous television, at least among the middle class, with access to personal transport and the resources to pay the admission fees.

The images and ideas disseminated in the cinema meant that from an early stage it became the focus of concern over public morals. As such it attracted the attention of both official and private bodies interested in the spiritual well-being of the public. When the first 'talkie' was screened in 1929, the *Nottingham Journal* described the film, 'Lucky Boy', as 'not too aggressively American' compared with previous imports.[17] It was always difficult for guardians of public taste to be neutral over films, especially in a national context where things American were often regarded with distaste. Councillor Dutton encapsulated this attitude in 1946: 'I am not convinced that the overwhelming flood of stuff from Hollywood has been to the benefit of our youngsters. I would like to see 50 to 75 per cent of the rubbish that comes from America put off completely.'[18] One issue, over which these concerns converged, was the question of Sunday opening. Controversy persisted from the 1930s until the early 1960s because the issue seemed to reflect a clash between the commercial and the traditional in popular culture. It erupted in 1939 when the Watch Committee, taking advantage of the Sunday Entertainments Act, proposed that cinemas be allowed to open from 7.45 p.m. on Sunday evenings. This initiative was prompted by fears of crime, especially among juveniles, which was reported to have risen by 400 per cent over the previous decade. According to the police, crime rates were particularly high on a Sunday, presumably perpetrated by bored young people, but the trend was less obvious in towns where Sunday opening had been allowed. Not everyone was convinced. Councillor W.R. Blandy argued that films adversely affected the morals of young people, while another member of the council suggested that Sunday opening would simply encourage youths to stay out late and require more police to control 'crowds of juveniles in the Market Square'.[19]

The Sunday question also represented a clash between a new secular form of popular culture and an older notion of social community based on the churches and chapels. Both the nonconformists and the established churches opposed cinema opening on the day of rest. 'It should be the aim of church people to preserve the sanctity and peace of Sunday', proclaimed T. Shipside when opening the Nottingham West Circuit Methodist bazaar in March 1939, and he was supported by Bishop Talbot in opposing Sunday cinema-going. In the end it was the exigencies of wartime that brought a relaxation of attitudes. Following representations to the council by the army in 1940 Sunday opening was accepted for the duration of the war as a means of entertaining troops stationed in and around Nottingham.[20] After the war, the question was put to a local referendum, and in the summer of 1947 Nottingham voted 28,177 to 12,068 in favour.[21]

The Sunday-opening issue illustrated the threat posed by the cinema and other commercial forms of entertainment to the churches. It revealed the relative decline of church-based voluntary recreations that had developed during the course of the nineteenth century. The Conservative MP for Nottingham Central, J.K. Cordeaux, claimed in 1961 – in an attack on the film *Saturday Night and Sunday Morning* – that 'most of our young people spend their weekends in natural and healthy recreation and social contacts', but in post-war Nottingham these activities were less likely than in the past to be committed to church or chapel.[22]

Voluntary organisations

Before 1914, despite the growth of commercial recreations, voluntary recreation and leisure probably accounted for the majority of non-work activity and this continued to be the case after 1918. Among the mass of clubs and associations, those with a religious orientation were especially prominent, which is not surprising given Nottingham's strong nonconformist tradition. Chapels promoted a vigorous programme of social activities: looking back on the post-1918 period, one person commented that 'all social life for younger people was the church or chapel. That was the social side of life.'[23] Something of the flavour of this culture can be gleaned from the many commemorative histories written to celebrate the contribution of the churches and chapels to community life. The Derby Road Methodist Church opened just a few months before the outbreak of war in 1914. During the inter-war years its members organised a complete range of cultural activities including a Sunday School, a guild, a women's meeting, a choir, a benevolent society and a Thursday evening fellowship.[24] Similarly, in Arkwright Street, the Bridgeway Hall Mission, opened in 1927, sought to be a lively, attractive social centre where celebrity concerts and films were held in the 1930s. A specific appeal was made to the young and, in the years following the Second World War, to the immigrant population of this part of the city.[25] The Bridgeway Mission represents an interesting example of the attempt by the churches to respond not only to alternative recreational forms but to the changing social geography of the city. The once-powerful Arkwright Street Methodist chapel had, by the 1920s, fallen on hard times as its wealthier patrons had moved to the newer middle-class suburbs developing in West Bridgford. Bridgeway Hall was a conscious attempt to fashion a religious culture aimed at the less well-off residents of the Meadows. The Methodist chapel at Sherwood attempted the same for the rather better-off residents of the area. The Young Leaguers Union, which started in 1905 to support the National Children's Home, held concerts and organised rambles and card parties; in the 1920s it had eighty regular members. For more than a decade after 1918 the Sherwood Methodists ran their own scout troop, a drama group, a girls' club, a camp-fire gathering, and cricket, tennis and badminton teams. However, it was proving difficult by the 1960s to recruit the leaders needed to keep these activities going, an experience common also to the Salvation Army.[26]

Other denominations also maintained a creative and essentially local culture. In the later 1920s Addison Street Congregational Church launched a fund-raising campaign to build a larger hall to accommodate all those interested in attending its musical and dramatic events.[27] The Albion Congregational Church on Sneinton Road was particularly lively, with a boys' brigade, life boys, girl guides, Brownies, a choir, an adventurers' club and an over-60s group for men. During the Second World War, however, its activities were disrupted when the schoolroom was taken over as a British restaurant.[28] The war brought various disadvantages, particularly the black-out, rationing and bomb damage, as well as the requisitioning of premises. It would be wrong to imply that rapid decline set in for religious-based leisure after 1945, but the attempt to counter alternative attractions in the consumer leisure boom of the 1950s and 1960s was a difficult and, in the end, losing battle. The passive and privatised pleasures of the television drained away much of the dedication to corporate activity on which church culture had depended.[29] Many of the commemorative histories produced in the years after 1945 look back to earlier days as being almost a golden age when conditions for chapel-led recreation were much more favourable.

The physical expansion of the city in the first thirty years of the twentieth century placed a distance between the rich and the poor which was also reflected in chapel-based culture. The most successful chapels had been those like the Derby Road Baptists who could rely on independent sources of finance to underpin their activities. When the better-off members began to move away in the late 1940s attendances and finances declined. In the predominantly working-class districts such as Radford and Hyson Green autonomous chapel recreation became much more difficult. The Hyson Green Baptist Church on Palin Street, an impressive Gothic structure seating 500 when it opened in 1883 was, by the late 1920s, greatly changed. 'The task', noted its historian in 1928, 'has become increasingly difficult.'[30]

Although some denominations, notably the Salvation Army, had a specific mission to the poor, in general churches and chapels strove to encompass a broad social range, to bring in 'all walks of life' as Ralph Bristow, former Bandmaster of the Salvation Army in Nottingham, has described it. By contrast, there were other voluntary organisations whose purpose was to enrich predominantly the material and spiritual life of the working class. Various branches of the labour and trade-union movement had this as a cardinal aim. The city had its share of politically-based popular culture which promoted educational as well as sporting and other outdoor activities. By contrast with Continental Europe, the Labour movement in Britain invested relatively little time and energy in creating an 'alternative' culture, although the more left-wing elements such as the Independent Labour Party (ILP) and the Communist Party encouraged cultural activity as part of their political strategy. In the 1920s and 1930s the ILP organised whist drives, bazaars, cricket matches, tennis competitions, dramatic events and rambling, alongside its overtly political work.[31] Similarly the Nottingham Trades Council promoted an educational and cultural scheme in the 1930s for unemployed workers; it included a football team.[32]

Another small group of activists, based around the Communist Party, organised weekend camps at venues such as Lambley Dumbles, where in fine weather in the 1930s a turn-out of some fifty people might be expected for a weekend of rambling, music, camp-fire cooking and, of course, socialist talk. In many of these activities there was probably a strong emphasis on youth and, as in church activities, an easier mixing of the sexes than would have been found on the terraces of the football grounds. One former political activist, recalling the cultural and social events of this time, concluded that by comparison with the more militant and energetic left-wing groups the Labour Party itself seemed to have a rather 'middle-aged' mentality.[33] Of course, the aim of these groups was to bring social and cultural fellowship to the aid of the political and industrial struggle. The one organisation which, nationally, played a leading role in orchestrating such activities and which exercised an important influence over their development in Nottingham – as it did over the city itself – was the Co-operative movement.

By the inter-war years the Co-op was a well-established retail organisation. However, its original mutualist and communitarian aims were still intact and could be financed from accumulated profits. It nurtured an important series of summer schools and travel initiatives, especially for activities in the labour movement, many of them linked to the Women's Co-operative Guild. The Co-op's Educational Committee, founded in 1920 to provide training for members who had been in the armed services, promoted a wide range of cultural events including choral singing, lantern lectures and carnivals. Children were particularly well catered for: the Women's Guild organised teas and musical events for poor children as well as ethical educational sessions on subjects such as child-rearing. As work progressed in the 1920s and 1930s the Workers' Educational Association (WEA) and the Labour Party were drawn in. In 1938 a children's fancy-dress carnival featured prizes for the winning costumes and music from the West Bridgford Co-operative Orchestra.[34] In the 1930s the recreational programme included outings to Penzance, and to Southampton to see the new liner *Queen Mary*. These cultural activities came to a climax after the Second World War with the establishment of the George Street–Broad Street Arts Centre – ironically in former nonconformist chapels – where cinema, theatre and camera clubs were popular in the 1950s.[35] These developments reflected concern in the Co-operative movement to keep alive the idea of a collective alternative to capitalist commercialism.

Politically-inspired recreation, although different from and in many ways opposed to other forms of voluntary leisure, none-the-less had one thing in common with them: it tended to be addressed to an *indigenous* population. The ethnic minorities had to look to their own devices. There had, of course, long been an Irish presence with its own distinctive cultural organisations, and this still continues today.[36] Since 1945 other ethnic groups have arrived in the city in sufficient numbers to establish their own organisations. By 1951 there were more than 5,000 European-born residents in Nottingham, mainly from Eastern Europe and particularly Poland.[37] These newcomers implanted their own cultural associations, often investing them with a religious and political purpose. In the case of the Poles – Roman Catholics, like the Irish – their social clubs served to perpetuate wartime camaraderie with regular dinners and reunions, and to provide a focus of continuing opposition to the Communist regime in the homeland. The Ukrainians similarly presented a hostile front to the Soviet Union. In the late 1950s they resisted the Home Office's efforts to register them as Russians, and in 1967 they organised a protest against the visit to Britain of the Soviet leader A. N. Kosygin. Since the 600 or so Lithuanians, Latvians and Estonians living in Nottingham believed themselves to be under a Soviet death threat, it is not surprising that immigrant social life emphasised ethnic and national identities, manifested in the folk-song and dance festivals organised by the Ukrainian community, or the regular 'Miss Polonia' beauty contests and theatrical events of the Polish community at their social centre in Pelham Road.[38] A dual identity developed, so that when in September 1963 the new Ukrainian Assembly Hall was opened in Bentinck Road the theme of the keynote speech was: 'We intend to make our children good Ukrainians and therefore good citizens of this country.'[39]

From the 1950s New Commonwealth and Pakistan immigrants and their families rapidly came to outnumber the European-born residents of Nottingham. Like their predecessors from Ireland and Eastern Europe they experienced prejudice on the part of the indigenous population, although judging from the events of August 1958 racial tension was of a more severe nature than previous ethnic hostility. In the aftermath of these riots the city acquired a reputation for racial tolerance. Whether this was deserved is another matter: the Commonwealth Unity weeks of the 1960s and the positive attempts made by the Education Committee to achieve racial understanding by retaining mixed inner-city schooling do not appear to have eased the feelings of rejection held by many in the black and Asian communities.[40] Immigrants from the Indian sub-continent were perhaps less offended by their reception than those from the West Indies, whose prior sense of Britishness had been much stronger and for whom, therefore, the sense of disappointment was all the more acute. This was coupled with a belief in both the West Indian and the Pakistani communities that residence in Britain was to be temporary.[41]

Taken together these features help to account for the characteristic detachment developed by the black community in its recreational life. If there had been a sexual division of leisure in much working-class recreation during the course of the twentieth century, there has undoubtedly been a racial division of leisure since the 1950s. A number of organisations were created to cater specifically for the interests of immigrant groups. Initially these usually had practical functions such as giving advice on welfare, employment and educational opportunities, but they subsequently developed a cultural side. The West Indian Students' Association (WISA) had a music and drama group, and in the late 1960s sponsored the Caribbean Artists Movement.[42] The Pakistan Friends League, established in 1963, sought to emphasise the separateness of the community in linguistic, cultural and religious ways, 'so that we may maintain our identity as Pakistanis'.[43] The Meadows Muslim Centre became a focal point for the Asian Community, and the Marcus Garvey Centre in Lenton served a similar function for the African Caribbean community. One black woman's views on this community life are interesting:

> I think there's quite a strong community spirit in Nottingham. You get used to a set group of people that you've been around for years. Myself being a Rasta woman and being part of an informal group of Rasta women that have been together over the years, I really value that.[44]

Recently the contribution of women to this community life has been stressed: the ANISA project, for example, has played an important role in training Asian women as crèche and play-scheme workers, and even in sport 'there has been female netball teams for years but it hasn't been acknowledged as much as the men's football'.[45]

Sport bridges the ethnic divide, but other leisure patterns have contrasted significantly with those of the white population. In 1961 the *Evening Post* carried an article on the problems of party-going: 'Saturday night and Sunday morning is party time for many of Nottingham's 6,000 coloured community, who like to relax that way after a hard day's work. But too often the police get invited too – by angry neighbours.' Eric Irons, a leading member of the West Indian community, responded that 'we are naturally noisy people. It is a way of life.'[46] The spontaneous and informal recreation of party-going has introduced a lively addition to Nottingham's leisure patterns but it has also produced friction, notably the tensions aroused in the Hyson Green flats during the late 1970s and early 1980s, where 'blues' parties lasting for three or four nights were organised on a commercial basis, by the owners of powerful sound systems who took short-term sub-lets on flats and charged for admission. The parties created both racial and generational tension, but one black youth-worker claimed that young blacks had been driven out of the city centre by a combination of cost and surveillance: 'they were creating their own culture to suit their own needs because in many cases their needs weren't being met anywhere else ... you have to see the blues within that context'.[47]

Plate 63 **The Boots Company outing to the British Empire Exhibition, 1924**. One of the most popular of the welfare initiatives of Jesse and Florence Boot was the staff outing. Initially trips were made to local beauty spots and to the seaside, but they gradually became more ambitious. On 6 August 1894 a special train took staff to Castleton; in July 1908 two specially chartered trains took employees to the Franco-British Exhibition of Science, Arts and Industries in London; and here in 1924 staff are seen leaving for the British Empire Exhibition. The excursion needed eight special trains from the Victoria Station to take approximately 5,500 staff to Wembley

Companies and leisure facilities

By contrast with the United States where civic 'boosterism' often turned on the involvement of local industrialists in sport and recreational activities, Britain seems to have derived much less from this kind of corporate patronage. Yet most major cities have their company sports and recreational clubs, especially those based on leading businesses whose owners perceived a link between recreational provision and the productivity levels of their work-force. The link was reflected in Jesse Boot's early social excursions with his employees to the nearby countryside in the 1890s, and it blossomed into the welfare activities inaugurated by Florence Boot for women workers at the Island works before 1914, and the sports grounds provided at Plaisaunce, Boot's house by the Trent, for male and female employees.[48] Education for leisure was another idea from Boots, expressed in the Boots Day Continuation School, a joint venture between the firm and the city council. The council provided teaching staff, books and equipment for a school which had grown to around 700 pupils by the early 1930s. Alongside staple subjects such as English, needlework, arithmetic and technical drawing, the curriculum made generous provision for gymnastics, country dancing, drama and hobbies classes. Obviously there was an element here of inculcating 'approved' pastimes in young minds, as well as a more obvious attempt to instil work discipline – each pupil's progress was reported to the firm and promotions could be determined by school reports. At the same time a genuinely recreational experience, albeit of a rather gendered nature, was being offered to many young people.[49]

Other firms encouraged similar developments, if rather less systematically than Boots. *Players Post*, the house magazine of John Player and Company, provides glimpses of the social activities pursued under the aegis of the firm, including drama groups, a flying club, sports events at the recreation ground on Aspley Lane, and flower shows. The Players Rifle Club, formed in 1919, was one of the earliest in Nottingham. The company also sponsored national events in golf, horse-racing and hovercrafting, but most famously in the late 1960s, the John Player Sunday League in cricket.[50] The company placed special importance on keeping their elderly retired employees together through social functions. A Pensioners' Club formed in 1967 with a membership of seventy-five included bingo, dominoes, cards, and occasional excursions. It was so popular that within a few months membership had risen to 1,600 and the clubhouse was overrun.[51]

Raleigh formed an athletics club in 1924, and the firm matched the members' penny-a-week subscriptions. Football, hockey, cricket and tennis teams played at its sports ground on Coach Lane, Wollaton, until well after the Second World War.[52]

Yet welfare capitalism of this sort was not necessarily a panacea. At Players, according to one of its more articulate workers, it produced only alienation:

> Factories may differ, but those working in them are all suffering from the same industrial malaise. We are second fiddles to machines … .Mechanisation … has led to jobs

> that are both dull and monotonous … .There is never a sense of fulfilment … .The company bends over backwards to make amends for the lethargy that the factory has produced in the worker. Recreational facilities abound; but the number of people using them is small in percentage. Perhaps others, like me, resent the gradual envelopment of recreation by the umbrella of factory life.[53]

The corporation as leisure provider

Leisure can never be seen as purely a commercial product, as the range and vitality of voluntary recreation clearly shows. It also overlooks the increasing role played during the twentieth century by the municipality, which necessarily has motives both of commerce and of civic pride.[54] As a provider of leisure facilities, the corporation had been active since the 1850s, and by the 1930s its role in leisure activity had broadened into a number of new areas. Parks, allotments, swimming-baths, tennis courts, recreation grounds and golf courses were added to the stock of civic amenities, and the corporation continued to provide allotments. Among the main beneficiaries of the corporation's activities by the inter-war years were the city's children. The council developed an understandable pride in its sporting and cultural programme in the educational curriculum, which brought the enjoyment (and, doubtless, suffering) of organised games and cultural activities to schoolchildren for the first time. Education Committee Annual Reports reveal a wide and ambitious programme of activities. Thus in 1935 note was made of the fifty violin classes organised by elementary schools out of school hours, of the work of school choirs and especially the annual music festival each October, of the folk-dance festival in the spring, of the special series of orchestral concerts given, of swimming, sports and camping activities, of evening play centres and the coaching of boys in boxing techniques by city policemen.[55]

Even so, there were limiting factors, one of which was caused by geography. Nottingham's response to section 11 of the 1944 Education Act, which required local authorities to estimate their immediate and future plans for both primary and secondary provision, noted that 'in acquiring sites for new schools every endeavour will be made to provide adequate playing fields'. This was more easily said than done. At the end of the war thirty-six schools had available to them the use of only ten parks, playing fields and recreation grounds for sport. Moreover, because of the built-up nature of the city the playing fields were in almost all cases located towards the outskirts.[56] The Education Committee's report of 1960 acknowledged that the problem was ongoing: 'unfortunately many schools still have to use public parks for games'. The committee praised the unselfish contribution of the teachers who had given their free time to coach games: 'many hours of enjoyment have been given to the girls and boys who have joined in hockey, netball, tennis, rounders, cricket, association and rugby football, athletics, cross-country running, swimming and other outdoor pursuits, thanks to the work of these teachers'.[57] School sports were a source of some pride to the city council and the work of twenty-seven schools had featured strongly in the week of celebrations that marked the quincentenary of the 1449 charter.[58]

In the events of 1949 the city council had played an important role in fostering a sense of identity, and subsequent initiatives were inspired by a desire to address the recreational needs of the entire community. They were typified in the late 1960s and 1970s by the creation of leisure centres as focal points of community life, pursuing the aim of 'sport for all'. These were not always successful. The policy of siting them alongside schools in suburban locations, while helping to overcome the problem of school games, created a problem of access for those without cars, and in the 1970s a class bias grew up in the use of such facilities. To counter this trend the corporation turned once again to the needs of the inner city, exemplified in schemes such as the restoration of the Victoria Baths at Sneinton as a community centre.[59] Similarly, in the area of entertainment, the two icons of civic provision – the Playhouse and the Royal Centre – aim to cater for the widest possible audience through subsidised ticket prices, which allow access to many shows for all but the very poorest.

In a city of Nottingham's size the range of recreational activity is necessarily very wide and is provided by commercial and municipal activities, business paternalism and generally by the voluntary enthusiasms of ordinary people. During the course of the twentieth century commercial and municipal provision has grown in importance as the voluntary sector – particularly perhaps the Church – has been partially eclipsed. In this chapter it has been possible only to dip into recreational life. Major sporting achievements connected with the city and its people have necessarily been glossed, including the ice-skating triumphs of Torvill and Dean in the 1980s and the recent success of one of Britain's few professional ice-hockey teams, the Nottingham Panthers.[60] Equally, nothing has been said of the thousands of amateur sports clubs which compete in and around the town, some with their own facilities and others using municipal accommodation in the city's parks. Nor have we discussed that vast band of individual sportsmen and women, the fishermen, the joggers and the annual Robin Hood Marathon competitors. Again, little space has been found for the professional and the amateur in public performance, from the Playhouse as Britain's leading repertory theatre under John Neville's direction in the 1960s, and the Royal Centre hosting the highest quality performances in the entertainment world in the final decades of the century, to the Lace Market and Co-operative Arts Theatres. Nor have we discussed the public house, still as popular – albeit in a transformed state – in the late twentieth century as it was in the nineteenth, from the omnipresent Trip to Jerusalem through the well-known city-centre pubs such as The Salutation and The Bell, to the numerous establishments throughout the suburbs. Among other entertainments the Palais de Dance – opened in 1925 and described as 'one of the finest buildings of its kind in the provinces'[61] – both before and after the Second World War, Rock City and the 1990s night-club scene reflect modern leisure interests. Goose Fair is as popular as ever, and the city has a range of museums as well as a thriving tourist industry and heritage movement. While many people may in the late twentieth century prefer to take their entertainment at home with the television, the video and the home computer, those willing to venture out into what is now a regional centre will have cause to agree with J. B. Priestley that the city's reputation for enjoying itself is not misplaced. The commercialisation of leisure which Priestley so detested has not destroyed the capacity for enjoyment.[62]

Notes

1 Recollections of B. G., a Nottingham primary school teacher *c.*1960–90, January 1996.

2 J. B. Priestley, *English Journey* (1977 edn), pp. 131–43.

3 *EP*, 12–20 February, 3 March 1919.

4 *EP*, 18 October 1928.

5 Priestley, *English Journey*, p. 138.

6 K. Warsop (assisted by P. Wain), *The Magpies: the Story of Notts County Football Club* (Buckingham, 1994); *Notts County Centenary Handbook, 1862–1962* (n.d.); A. J. Turner (ed.), *The Hundred Years Story of the Nottingham Forest F.C.* (n.d., *c.*1964), p. 81.

7 The Forest Supporters' Club has been active in fund-raising. See R. Taylor, *Football and its Fans: Supporter and their Relations with the Game, 1885–1985* (Leicester, 1992), p. 36.

8 P. Attaway, *Nottingham Forest: a Complete Record 1865–1991* (Derby, 1991); T. Francis, *Clough: a biography* (1987); B. Clough with J. Sadler, *Clough: the Autobiography* (1994).

9 K. Sandiford and W. Vamplew, 'The peculiar economics of English cricket before 1914', *British Journal of Sport History*, 3 (1986), pp. 311–26.

10 Lancashire, Yorkshire, Middlesex, Surrey and Kent were the other members of the Big Six. P. Wynne-Thomas, *'Give me Arthur': a Biography of Arthur Shrewsbury* (1985).

11 P. Wynne-Thomas, *The History of Nottinghamshire County Cricket Club* (1992), pp. 171, 183.

12 *NG*, 2, 4 July 1906.

13 *NG*, 2, 4 April 1913.

14 A. Southern and S. Winfield (eds.), *At a Cinema Near You: a History of Cinema in Nottingham* (Nottingham, n.d.).

15 *EP*, 23 March 1935.

16 *EP*, 8 June 1968.

17 *NJ*, 24 June 1929.

18 *EP*, 3 December 1946.

19 *EP*, 31 March, 4 April 1939.

20 *NJ*, 22, 23 February 1940. Similarly Goose Fair continued in a 'reduced' format through the war although without the traditional coconuts, brandy snap and gingerbread: P. Wilkes, *The Great Nottingham Goose Fair* (Burton on Trent, 1989), pp. 43–4.

21 *NJ*, 19 July 1947.

22 *EP*, 4 February 1961.

23 NLSL Nottingham Oral History Project, a/14/a–b/21.

24 A. E. Lee, *A History and Record of the Activities of the Methodist Church, Derby Road, Lenton, Nottingham, 1851–1951* (Nottingham, n.d.).

25 Bridgeway Hall Methodist Mission, *Souvenir Brochure, 1864–1964* (Nottingham, n.d.), pp. 12, 25–6.

26 A. H. Colgrave, *Sherwood Methodist Church, 1835–1981* (Nottingham, n.d.), pp. 20–1, 25, 31–3, 40, 45. Information on the Salvation Army from Ralph Bristow, interviewed by Sue Clayton 27 July, 1 December 1994.

27 Addison Street Congregational Church, *Money-Raising Scheme, 1929* (NLSL pamphlet).

28 *Annual Report of the Albion Congregational Church, Nottingham, 1941–2* (NLSL pamphlet).

29 R. Swift, *Lively People: Methodism in Nottingham 1740–1979* (Nottingham, 1982), p. 164; interview with Ralph Bristow, 1 December 1994.

30 Hyson Green Baptist Church, Palin Street, Nottingham, *Centenary and Jubilee Celebrations, 1828–1928* (Nottingham, n.d.)

31 S. G. Jones, *Sport, Politics and the Working Class: Organised Labour and Sport in Inter-War Britain* (Manchester, 1988); NUMD Acc. 233/3b, 49, 85, 87, 106, ILP Executive Committee Minutes, 4 October, 2 December 1927, 13, 25 May, 10 August 1928.

32 NUMD Tr.M., 32/12, Nottingham and District Trades Council Records, 23 January 1935.

33 NLSL Interviews, a/46/a–c/2.

34 *The Wheatsheaf*, March 1914, 1915, January 1917, March 1938.

35 F. W. Leeman, *Co-operation in Nottingham: a History of One Hundred Years of Nottingham Co-Operative Society Ltd.* (Nottingham, 1963), pp. 131–4; Gray, *Settlement*, p. 107.

36 *NG*, 30 April 1964.

37 Brazier, *New Geography*, p. 86.

38 *EP*, 25 April, 28 May 1958, 15 October 1959, 7 April 1964, 5 February 1967.

39 *EP*, 9 September 1963.

40 Nottingham West Indian Students' Association (WISA), *Handbook* (Nottingham, n.d. [*c.*1968]).

41 D. Lawrence, *Black Migrants, White Natives: a Study of Race Relations in Nottingham* (Cambridge, 1974), chs. 2, 3 and 7; S. Thomas, P. Banjako, A. Louis (eds.), *A Retrospective View: Black Women in Nottingham* (Nottingham, 1994).

42 WISA *Handbook*.

43 NLSL Pakistan Friends League, *Report and Accounts, December 1968*.

44 Thomas, *Retrospective View*.

45 *Ibid.*, R. Malik and S. Gregory (eds.), *Living with Two Cultures: Experiences and Expectations of the Pakistani Community in the Meadows Area of Nottingham* (Nottingham, n.d.), p. 37.

46 *EP*, 6 June 1961.

47 Quoted in J. E. Kingscott, 'Oral history in libraries, with special reference to the Nottinghamshire Oral History Collection and the Hyson Green Project' (Loughborough University, MA thesis, 1988), p. 96.

48 C. Weir, *Jesse Boot of Nottingham* (Nottingham, 1994), pp. 46–52.

49 F. W. Coe, 'Boots Day Continuation School Nottingham', Nottingham and District Branch, Institute of Handicraft Teachers, Nottingham Annual Conference 1933.

50 *Players Post*, nos. 2, 4 (1967), 10, 15 (1968); NLSL Interviews, a/106/a/1.

51 *Players Post*, nos. 2, 4 (1967), 13 (1968).

52 NLSL Interviews, a/40/a/1.

53 R. Fraser (ed.), *Work: Twenty Personal Accounts* (1968), pp. 13, 16, 18. Women apparently coped much better than men because of their ability 'to turn their minds from the futility of factory life' (p. 14), by 'chattering all day long about their homes, who's in the family way and anything else unconnected with work'. See also ch. 21.

54 S. G. Jones, *Workers at Play: a Social and Economic History of Leisure, 1918–1939* (1986).

55 NAO CA/ED, 1/4/1, *EC, Annual Report Year Ended 31 July 1935*.

56 NAO CA/ED, 5/6/1, *EC, Development Plan for Primary and Secondary Education* (n.d., *c.*1945).

57 NAO CA/ED, 1/4/26, *EC, Annual Report Year Ended 31 August 1960*.

58 NAO CATC, 10/119/60/34/33, Nottingham Quincentenary Week, 1949, *Secondary Schools Sports Souvenir Programme*.

59 Brazier, *New Geography*, p. 100.

60 C. Hilton, *Torvill and Dean: the Full Story* (Oxford, 1994). The National Watersports Centre at Holme Pierrepont is internationally recognised as a Nottingham facility.

61 Nottingham City Council, *Guidebook* (1939), p. 3.

62 Priestley, *English Journey*, p. 131.

23

EDUCATION

Brian H. Tolley

The Education Act of 1902 introduced a unified system of educational administration to England and Wales. The school boards were abolished and the councils of the counties and county boroughs became the new local education authorities with responsibility for elementary, secondary and higher education as well as ancillary services. In Nottingham, where the corporation had, since 1889, exercised a responsibility for the development of technical instruction, it was a welcome step forward. It brought to an end what had often been seen as the excessive expenditure of an ambitious School Board, charged solely to provide elementary education but restlessly seeking to extend its activities into new areas and able to finance this by a precept upon the rates. The corporation was now able, through its Education Committee, to exercise control over all educational development in the city. It could determine its own priorities and could balance the need to promote education against other pressing demands on its financial resources. The provision of schools, the support services which they required, the development of further education and even the maintenance of the University College and School of Art, were now subject to close scrutiny by local politicians aware of the danger of being thought profligate with the money they raised from the rates.[1] In this chapter we trace the changes in education which have taken place in Nottingham since 1902, and examine some of the policies which have produced the structure which exists today.

The work of the Education Committee

The new Nottingham Education Committee inherited 13,000 elementary school places in sixty-four school departments and 2,473 places in the fourteen school departments provided by the Church of England and Roman Catholic Church respectively. The denominational bodies were generally in favour of the new situation, which provided a real lifeline for the maintenance of their schools.[2] For the Education Committee, however, the fact that many of these schools were in a poor state of repair, requiring urgent action to bring them up to a standard acceptable to the Board of Education, presented a major problem. The growth of population after 1903, and the consequent increase in the demand for school places, was such that the Education Committee could ill-afford to close dilapidated premises. It had to resort to providing temporary school accommodation for children in the Meadows, Carrington, Hucknall Road and Gregory Boulevard areas as existing schools were demolished or extensive alterations were undertaken. In 1907 the city was short of more than 2,300 elementary school places and the Board of Education had begun to admonish the Education Committee for its failure to remedy the deficiency other than by using temporary accommodation. Plans to build a new elementary school in the Meadows were vetoed by the corporation on the grounds of cost and a project to construct a school on Haydn Road suffered the same fate in 1909.[3] Threats to stop the payment of the block grants to Nottingham led to more prevarication on the part of the Education Committee, which was under pressure from the corporation to delay as long as possible such expensive projects. An elementary school was eventually built on Haydn Road (1911), but not before more threats had been issued by the Board of Education, alarmed to discover that the city was also dragging its feet in the provision of schools for Basford and Sneinton Dale.[4]

The failure to build new schools and to enlarge existing premises led to serious overcrowding and inefficient teaching. Children of all abilities and standards of attainment were brought together in the senior departments of schools, to await the day on which they might leave full-time education. At Berridge Road School in 1911, 109 boys were being taught in a room designed to accommodate sixty pupils. In thirty-eight school departments, pupils in Standards IV, V, and VI were being taught together by one teacher.[5] Firmly convinced that the majority of pupils in elementary schools were anxious to leave as soon as possible, the Education Committee emphasised the need to restrict the curriculum to basic subjects and to adopt the most formal teaching methods to achieve maximum impact.[6] At a time when the inspectorate was encouraging elementary school teachers to experiment, the attitude of the Education Committee can only be described as regressive.

When the corporation became responsible for secondary education after 1902 it was assumed that the Board of Education would accede to requests to recognise the four old higher grade schools in Nottingham as efficient secondary schools. The Board's model for a secondary school was that of the traditional grammar or public school, its curriculum essentially academic rather than vocational. Such schools taught predominantly middle-class pupils and offered only a small number of places to boys and girls from working-class backgrounds who were scholarship holders.[7] By contrast, the ethos of the old higher-grade schools was quite different. These schools were rooted in the elementary system and the majority of boys and girls attending them came from public elementary schools. Under these circumstances it is hardly surprising that the Education Committee's request to create four municipal secondary schools was rejected, and in 1905 only High Pavement and Mundella were recognised as coeducational secondary schools. The more advanced pupils of People's College, and eight teachers, were transferred to High Pavement. People's College, like Huntingdon Street School, then reverted to being an ordinary elementary school. The Education Committee accused the Board of precipitate action and of discouraging 'the demand of the people for increased educational facilities', but it was unable to reverse the decision.[8]

For a few boys and girls, Nottingham Boys' High School and the High School for Girls provided a secondary education to which, with scholarships, they had access, and the University College offered advanced 'secondary' education until the age of entry was raised to sixteen in 1911. For most children the general qualifying examination which they took at the age of eleven determined whether they would stay in the elementary school system or move to one of the two secondary schools.[9] Both institutions quickly established a reputation for academic excellence and a growing number of their pupils achieved distinctions, going on to university, college, and the established professions.

Under the aegis of the School Board, Nottingham had been provided with a comprehensive range of evening schools. Some, based in the ordinary elementary schools, offered courses in basic literacy and numeracy to young people who had left day school early and were anxious to improve their employment prospects. Others were in the higher-grade schools, where the instruction offered was often a preparation for the examinations of the Department of Science and Art. This type of evening work was regarded as 'secondary education' by those whose circumstances had prevented them from staying long enough at day school to take the higher-grade school course. The five technical and commercial centres established by the Board and offering instruction in subjects with a bearing on local trades and commercial occupations proved equally popular.[10] The Board had also co-operated with the Recreative Evening School Association to provide evening classes for young people whose needs were more social than educational. A mixture of learning together and engaging in communal activities such as drama, play-reading, singing and dancing, provided an alternative to the drab home environment in which many of them lived.

The Education Committee had less success with the more structured evening work it introduced in the continuation classes held in schools like Carrington and St Ann's Well Road. Much the same situation arose at the revived technical and commercial centres and by 1910 only the one at People's College survived. The fall in attendance at the more advanced evening classes was due to the development of better day-school opportunities, the lack of motivation which prevailed during periods of trade recession, and the unpopularity of courses which entailed regular homework and examinations. It was also due to the indifference of many employers towards this form of continuation education. Few industrialists showed any real interest in the work of the Education Committee and ideas for the development of a system of evening professional and trade schools like the French *écoles practique d'industrie et de commerce* or the German *handelschulen*, optimistically discussed by the committee in 1906, were stillborn.[11] Only when employers like John Player & Sons, Jardines and Jesse Boot demonstrated genuine interest in continuation schools for their young employees did the development of this type of educational institution become a reality.[12]

Crowding children of all ages and abilities into the upper parts of the ordinary elementary schools made it imperative to distinguish between those pupils who were simply waiting to leave school as soon as possible and those who might benefit from extending their schooling if parental support was forthcoming. Huntingdon Street and Queen's Walk Schools had retained something of their former character, and their popularity was such that parents in many parts of the city were anxious to transfer their children to them. The term 'intermediate' began to be used to describe both schools which, by 1914, were concentrating solely upon upper-standard work, and after 1918 Trent Bridge, Haydn Road and Morley Street Schools were also converted into intermediate establishments.[13]

Schooling continued during the First World War. Pupils at the Berridge School collected money for good causes connected with the war, and girls knitted mufflers and mittens for soldiers at the front. However, in 1917 the buildings were turned into a military hospital and the pupils dispersed to other schools. They returned in 1919.[14]

The 1918 Education Act

One of the pillars of post-First World War reconstruction, the Education Act of 1918, laid on the local authorities the duty to provide for the progressive development of education in their areas. A large number of very able children were being denied access to a secondary-school education in Nottingham because the Board of Education continued to oppose the creation of more secondary schools. The decision was taken to concentrate resources on the introduction of several selective central schools by converting existing elementary schools for this purpose. These would provide an alternative to High Pavement and Mundella, by taking pupils – chosen for their ability – out of the ordinary elementary schools. The fact that 30 per cent of the boys and girls who won places at High Pavement and 60 per cent at Mundella left before the age of sixteen reinforced the conviction of W.J. Abel, clerk to the Education Committee, that there was a need for the new selective central schools with a curriculum markedly biased towards careers in industry and commerce. Clarendon Street, People's College, Trent Bridge, and Huntingdon Street Schools were chosen.[15]

Pupils were selected for the central schools by means of an annual general examination at the age of eleven which was taken by all children in the city's elementary schools.[16] All the indications were that the central schools would quickly establish themselves and gain the support of employers who were anxious to recruit able young people straight from school with skills and competencies that could be used immediately in the workplace. In the event, this experiment in post-elementary selective education was short-lived. It was overtaken by the new pressure to reorganise the whole field of elementary education which followed the publication of the Hadow Report in 1926, and by the appointment in 1924 of Nottingham's first Director of Education, A. H. Whipple, who had his own ideas about the way in which the educational system in the city should be developed. Whipple had developed a philosophy of education which opposed the separation of children into academic and non-academic bands, the former competing for places in the secondary schools, the latter drifting through the upper standards of the elementary schools until it was time for them to leave with few, if any, qualifications. He came to Nottingham just at the time when the Labour Party was proclaiming its determination to extend educational opportunity, and even the Conservatives were concerned to meet the reasonable aspirations of the working classes for a better education, not merely because this might win votes but also because here was a chance to influence minds in such a way that it might contribute to the stability of the established order.[17]

Whipple seized the opportunity to undertake a complete reorganisation of the school system. The political climate in the city reflected national trends, and

Plate 64 **Minver Crescent, Aspley, 1934**. This aerial view of one of the inter-war council housing estates shows the garden-city planning structure in action, and the spaciousness of the layout by comparison with some of the inner-city slums the new residents had once endured. In the centre is the 'family of schools' promoted by the first Director of Education, A. H. Whipple, with the secondary school appropriately named after Alderman William Crane, chairman of the city's housing committee for forty years

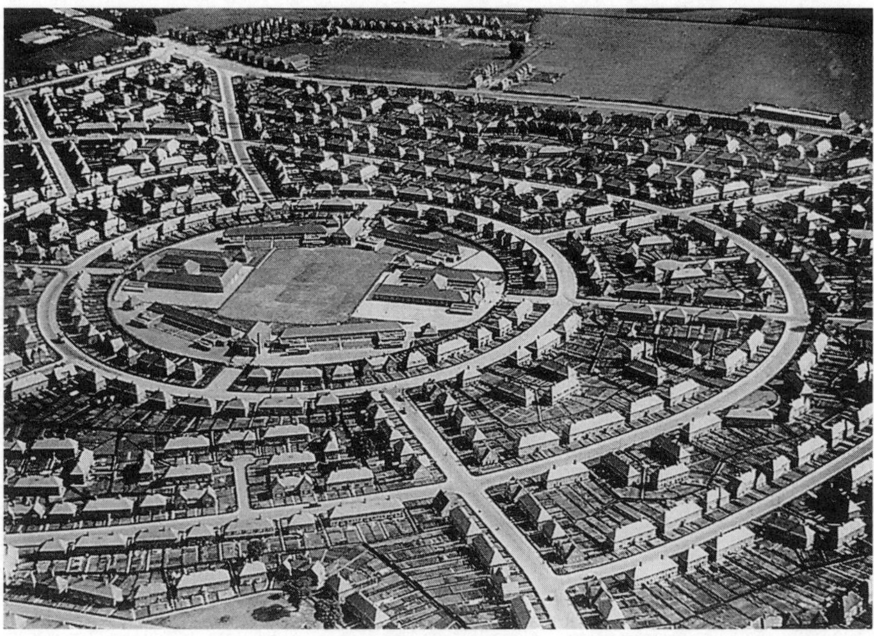

the Education Committee was generally backed by a more supportive city council. Whipple proposed the introduction of new senior schools which would be non-selective and which would form the upper part of a hierarchy of schools, including infant and junior schools, organised in such a way that together they served a particular district of Nottingham. When the Education Committee was convinced that it could provide sufficient school accommodation for the 12,000 pupils in the senior departments of the Nottingham elementary schools, Whipple was able to put his scheme into operation.[18] He was aided by the fact that between 1919 and 1924 the corporation had built model housing estates and these had to be provided with schools. For Whipple this was an opportunity not only to experiment with the reorganised school system, but also to make the 'families' of schools a focal point for the estates, helping to weld together communities which had been uprooted from their homes in other parts of the city.

Under Whipple's scheme the existing selective central schools were to be phased out and Nottingham was divided into sixteen districts. Ideally, each would contain two non-selective senior schools, one for boys and one for girls. The senior schools were to be served by a cluster of feeder schools located within walking distance of the pupils' homes. Where possible modifications to the buildings of existing schools would enable them to fit their new role as senior departments with additions such as laboratories, domestic science rooms, gymnasiums, and assembly halls. New schools were built to fill gaps wherever they were needed, including Haywood School (1930) to serve the Sherwood District, Cottesmore Senior Schools for Boys and Girls (1932) to serve the Lenton Boulevard district, Pierrepont Senior Girls' School (1933) to serve the Gordon Road Housing Estate, and the Morley Senior Schools (1933) to serve the Wells Road district. The William Crane Schools at Aspley took pride of place as an example of a purpose-built complex of schools at the centre of a large new housing estate. The infants, junior, and senior departments were all separated by gardens and attractive recreational areas. In accordance with the prevailing conviction that children should be exposed to as much fresh air as possible, seventeen of the new schools built between 1924 and 1933 were designed on open-air lines. Classrooms had south-facing French windows opening wide on to the playground.[19]

By 1933, when the William Crane Schools were fully operational, most of the reorganisation of the schools' system, including the building of new schools to serve the other housing estates around the city, had been completed. Whipple's scheme assumed that staff in the infants, junior and senior schools which served a particular district, would communicate with each other to co-ordinate their work and ensure that children naturally progressed through each stage of their education. He was particularly anxious that although the senior schools would offer a good all-round education from the age of eleven, they should emphasise practical work in science, art, domestic subjects, and handicraft.[20]

The aim to make the senior schools the focus for community development had two strands. In the first instance, Whipple recognised a demand for amenities out of school hours for those young people, 'the lost sheep of the future, the rebels to constituted authority' who, in the normal course of events, would never consider joining an organisation of any kind. These young people, unlike their counterparts who attended the secondary schools, were 'not shackled by homework' and in their leisure time they needed to be provided with some educational activity, preferably in a familiar environment where friendships could be maintained. The second strand was to concentrate upon adults who, particularly on the new housing estates, needed companionship and assistance in building their communities. Evening Institutes offering courses designed to appeal to adults were located in the senior schools which became the venue for social gatherings, dances, amateur dramatic and operatic functions, and a variety of other recreational activities organised by clubs and societies. The benefits were enormous. There was a greater respect for the fabric of the schools than in other parts of the city, local delinquency rates fell, and whole families identified the schools as centres of both educational and social life.[21] The successful development of the joint use of the educational facilities provided in the new housing areas was a major landmark in the inter-war years.

By the time Whipple retired in 1938 he had enjoyed considerable success in re-establishing Nottingham's reputation as a city with a progressive education authority. Confident in the ability of its principal officer to determine the main lines of policy, the committee had endeavoured, despite the financial constraints imposed by central government, to expand a whole range of educational facilities on offer. The schools meals service, for example, had grown rapidly. In 1910 only about 10,000 meals were provided annually, but by 1938 the figure was nearly 344,000 for day schools, a figure which excluded the very large number of meals provided for children in nursery classes and special departments. The activities of the Juvenile Employment Bureau had been extended. Nottingham had been one of the few authorities to set up such a body as part of the educational service in 1923, and under Whipple the Bureau had continued to ease the transition from school to adult employment for many young people. The school medical service had also been expanded with new clinics and health centres in various parts of the city.[22]

The Second World War

It fell to F. E. Stephenson, Director of Education 1938–56, to seek to maintain the school system in Nottingham, together with other vital educational services during the Second World War. Plans for the mass evacuation of the 20,173 pupils within the Nottingham evacuation zone were never fully implemented, and in the air raids during 1940–42 children retreated quickly to shelters erected close to their schools.[23] The main problem was how to provide schooling for the large number of children whose schools had been closed or had been requisitioned for war purposes. In January 1940 only nineteen Nottingham schools were fully open out of a total of 120. A shift system was introduced in various parts of Nottingham and some 10,000 children were taught either in the mornings or in the afternoons. The general standard of education was maintained as teachers struggled valiantly to compensate for the dislocation caused by the war and an increasing number of their colleagues were drawn into military service. While children drank their orange juice and cod-liver oil, engaged in waste-paper collections, did their best to increase egg production by keeping chickens in playground coops, and 'dug for victory' on their school allotments, their teachers maintained as much of the normal educational provision as possible.[24]

The urgent need for trained manpower during the war obliged Stephenson to undertake a major review of all technical education being provided in the city, including the large number of technical courses offered by University College. Three secondary technical schools were established from September 1941: the Secondary School for Art and Crafts, which was effectively a junior department of the College of Art in Waverley Street; the People's College, specifically intended to meet the needs of the building industry; and a Secondary School for the Textile Trades in temporary accommodation provided in the University College on Shakespeare Street. Entry to the three technical schools, at the age of thirteen, was determined by the results of examinations set by the schools themselves. Each institution established, through its advisory committees, a good relationship with the industries with which it was associated, but they were all phased out by the early 1960s as a result of post-war changes in secondary education.[25]

The 1950s and 1960s

In the Development Plan which the Education Committee was obliged to produce immediately after the war, priority was given to building schools to serve the needs of the housing estates around the city, and to ensure primary-school provision for every child below the age of eleven. The process of building up the new primary-school sector went ahead as quickly as resources allowed. By 1966 there were 125 primary schools in the city with four special nursery schools and twenty-two nursery classes attached to infants' departments. Oversized classes were slowly eliminated as existing buildings were modified, new buildings were completed, and the supply of teachers improved. The opening of the purpose-built College of Education at Clifton in 1960 successfully increased the supply of primary school teachers. Many young men and women did their teaching practice in Nottingham schools and stayed on, once qualified, to begin their professional careers in the city. The curriculum of the primary schools was widened to include new subjects, including French, and experiments in teaching methodology were encouraged. Special education came under the control of the primary education subcommittee of the main Education Committee and during the post-war years considerable progress was made in developing existing facilities for children with physical and mental handicaps, as well as building new schools, including the Ewing School for the Deaf, opened in 1960.[26]

Stephenson was not convinced that Pamphlet No.1, 'The Nation's Schools' issued by the new Ministry of Education in 1946, could be applied in Nottingham.

The pamphlet categorised secondary schools into grammar, technical and modern. Stephenson accepted the concept of a select few children being given an academic education in the traditional grammar school, and he believed that for the foreseeable future the three technical schools in the city had a distinct role to play, but he dismissed the 'modern' secondary school as lacking credibility. He believed it would become synonymous with inferiority, and be regarded as catering for pupils of a lower mental calibre. As a result, after the war priority was initially given to the renovation and expansion of the existing provision rather than to creating a new hierarchy of schools. An acknowledged deficiency in grammar-school places was rectified with the building of three new ones which, with the continued use of places reserved for Nottingham children at the two High Schools, raised the percentage of pupils attending this type of school from about 13 per cent of the 11–16 age group to more than 15 per cent, a figure which was deemed appropriate for the size of the city.[27] It took fifteen years to complete the programme, and even then it did not entirely overcome the shortage of grammar-school places, given the post-war bulge in the school population.

Plate 65 **'Constructional play for a toddler group'**. From the section on 'Day Nurseries', in the Medical Officer of Health's Annual Report for 1952. At that date the city had nine nurseries with 135 approved places for children to the age of two, and 205 places for those aged two to five

The bulk of the secondary-school population continued to be served by the non-selective senior schools (designated 'secondary') which developed their curriculum and organisation with little interference from the Education Committee. Some made better progress than others. A few in the older parts of the city, often in the least adaptable buildings, were seriously affected when many of their most able pupils left as a result of families being rehoused. Often they were left with a residue of boys and girls whose parents were not well disposed towards extending the education of their children.[28] The reputation these schools acquired seemed to bear out the misgivings which Stephenson had held in 1946 that such institutions would be relegated to an inferior status. In contrast, other Nottingham secondary schools grew in stature and popularity as they developed their curriculum and encouraged their pupils to stay on beyond the statutory leaving age, transferring in some cases either to the grammar schools or to People's College or Clarendon College, the two further education institutions in the city. It was the success of these secondary schools in combining academic studies for those pupils whose aptitude lay in this direction, with technical and practical courses for other pupils who showed more inclination to develop their interests in these fields, that led Stephenson to proceed with the introduction of the bilateral school to Nottingham.

These schools included a band of selected pupils taking a five-year course leading to GCE at O level, as well as other pupils who would leave school at fifteen without necessarily acquiring any formal qualifications. Twelve secondary schools took their first selected pupils in September 1957. For Stephenson and his successor, W. G. Jackson, who became Director of Education in 1958, the development of the bilateral schools was seen as a means of overcoming the deficiency in grammar-school places in the city.[29] It also offered one solution to the problem of coping with the margin of error increasingly identified in trying to establish academic potential at eleven plus. By 1971, as a result of new schools coming into the system, closures and amalgamations, all twenty-two secondary schools in Nottingham (excluding the grammar schools) were coeducational or single-sex bilaterals, including three voluntary-aided Roman Catholic schools.

The decision was also taken to experiment with comprehensive education on the largely self-contained Clifton housing estate, and in 1958 Fairham was opened to provide a secondary education for all boys living there. Some 30 per cent of the 250 boys who were the first completely non-selective cohort of pupils, remained at school for the full course of five years leading to GCE at O level. Their performance in 1964 was comparable with that attained by pupils in other parts of the city where the bilaterals and grammar schools existed side by side. Nevertheless, although the Labour group on the corporation had pledged itself in 1957 to abolishing the selection process in favour of comprehensive education, it was reluctant to base policy-making on these first encouraging results from Fairham.[30] It was not until the issue of Circular 10/65 by the Labour Government that the Education Committee declared its intention to work towards a comprehensive system for the whole city. This would be based upon the conversion of the bilateral schools into non-selective secondary schools for the 11–16 age range. There would then be a co-ordinated scheme of full- and part-time courses for young people over sixteen in the Colleges of Further Education and the grammar schools which were to become sixth-form colleges. The reorganisation was to be evolutionary, and only when adequate buildings had been provided and teacher supply guaranteed would the changes be imposed.

The comprehensive system and new challenges

A change of political control of the City Council in 1967 made little difference to the policy of gradual implementation; the Conservatives, while promising to protect the best schools, nevertheless accepted the broad principle of eventually reorganising along comprehensive lines.[31] However, in 1970 it was decided to retain the bilateral schools indefinitely and to examine the possibility of creating a new sixth-form college to which pupils from these schools might transfer. The grammar schools were to be left intact.[32] Almost immediately, another change in the political control of the City Council resurrected the 1966 scheme for non-selective schools and sixth-form colleges, although it provoked considerable opposition on the grounds of the lack of consultation and the speed with which the Education Committee proposed to move.[33] Parents' groups joined forces with teachers and politicians to seek to modify particular parts of the programme, to reject the closure of certain schools, and to preserve what were perceived to be well-proven parts of the old system of education in the city. When Margaret Thatcher as Secretary of State for Education approved the Nottingham scheme in June 1973 most of the impediments in the way of reorganisation were removed. Bilborough, Forest Fields and High Pavement grammar schools became sixth-form colleges and nineteen secondary schools in the city admitted their first comprehensive intake in September that year.

In 1974 local government reorganisation saw the control of education pass out of the city's hands into those of the county. By then, apart from those boys and girls who attended the High Schools (which had also changed from direct grant to independent status) or one of the other remaining private schools in Nottingham, all secondary pupils were being educated in comprehensive schools. Each served a prescribed catchment area with its own recognised 'family' of primary schools from which children transferred at the age of eleven. Each sought to establish its own identity and to develop a curriculum which encompassed the traditional academic disciplines, instruction in practical subjects, games, and physical education. Many of the facilities used during the day by school pupils were available for use by adults in the evenings and at weekends. The wheel had turned full circle and Whipple's concept of the educative and social role of the school had been rediscovered.

This was particularly important at a time when the exodus of middle-class families to the suburbs and dormitory villages was having a marked effect upon the composition of the school population. Some areas suffered from the type of social deprivation identified and highlighted by the Plowden Committee, and lack of interest in education among parents in these areas was a constant concern of the Education

Committee. The problem was compounded by the tendency for children to change schools frequently. Each year in the inner city one child in four changed schools: in suburban areas the figure was one in twelve. Sometimes this was the result of slum-clearance projects which threw families into disarray, but it was also occasioned by the disintegration of family life and the emergence of new social trends which emphasised individual freedom at the expense of traditional family ties.[34]

The arrival of large numbers of immigrant families from the West Indies and from India and Pakistan presented the Education Committee with a new challenge. In 1964 the number of new Commonwealth immigrant births in Nottingham rose to nearly 10 per cent of the total and it was necessary to plan for the impact this would have on the demand for school places.[35] The task of striking a balance between the maintenance of educational standards for local children and the application of successful measures for the educational and social integration of those immigrant children was one of the most difficult problems facing the Education Committee. The attempts to assimilate these new arrivals into the British way of life concentrated initially upon the development of extensive programmes for teaching English as a foreign language. Specialist groups of primary teachers began to work across primary schools in the city, teaching English to pupils who had little or no access to the normal school curriculum. In 1976 a Language Centre was established which was attended by secondary-aged bilingual children for part of each week.[36] The focus of much of the language teaching increasingly took account of multiculturalism, and there was a shift away from assimilation and towards promoting the values of a pluralist society. John Fox, Director of Education 1982–91, was particularly concerned to ensure that the Education Authority implemented a multicultural policy for all schools, not just those recruiting from ethnic minority families.

The 1980s saw changes in the education of children with special needs in accordance with legislation passed in 1981. Progress towards integrating special needs pupils was slow, but by 1990 there was a well-founded strategy for integrating them into mainstream schools.[37]

The changing economic and social structure of Nottingham and the concomitant problems found in many parts of the inner city, made it imperative for the Education Committee to commit resources to the further development of other services such as adult education, youth work and careers guidance.[38] This latter service became particularly important from the 1970s when the downturn in the economy, the introduction of new technology which eliminated many of the basic jobs done by school-leavers, and the tendency for more women to return to work after childbirth, conspired to create a major problem for school-leavers seeking employment.

Further and higher education

When the City of Nottingham took over responsibility for elementary and secondary education in 1902 it already had long experience of maintaining two institutions of higher education, the University College and the School of Art, both of which had been supported with money from the rates and the Residue Grant. The University College was almost wholly supported by the civic authority, and at a time when other university institutions – Birmingham (1900), Manchester and Liverpool (1903) – were receiving charters conferring full university status and the right to award degrees, it lacked the financial support which these universities received from local industrial benefactors. Its dependency on the corporation was confirmed in the Charter of Incorporation of 1903. Efforts to widen the appeal of the college to serve regional interests and generate support from outside the city failed, and no prominent academic who might have achieved some success in promoting the work of the college in science and technology during these early years stayed long enough to be effective. Most left for other universities, or found places in industry.[39]

Until the end of the First World War, the survival of University College as a university institution remained in the balance because of its precarious financial position. The situation was saved as a result of the munificence of Jesse Boot, who made the first of many generous donations to the college in 1920 when he gave £50,000 to establish a Chair of Chemistry. In 1921 Boot gave the Highfields Estate to become a new, out-of-town campus, and by the time building work was completed in 1928 he had invested – excluding his gift of the land itself – some £438,000 in the project. Arts and science departments moved from Shakespeare Street to the new Trent Building at Highfields in 1928, and were soon followed by the existing departments of civil and mechanical engineering, and a new department of electrical engineering.[40]

Boot died in 1931 and in subsequent years great efforts were made to provide financial security for University College by raising more money through endowments and enlisting the financial support of neighbouring local authorities in the East Midlands.[41] Actively encouraged by the University Grants Committee, there was also an attempt to change the constitution of the institution in such a way that the stranglehold of the corporation might be removed. In 1938 a supplemental charter was obtained which broadened the regional basis of support and provided broader academic representation on the college council. The Second World War proved to be a turning-point in its fortunes, since the contribution which the universities had made to the war effort, and the recognition that in the period of reconstruction there would be a great need for university-trained personnel in all walks of life, led to the demand for more universities. Nottingham was favourably placed to join the mainstream of these developments, and in 1948 a charter was granted conferring full university status.

Under Bertrand Hallward, the energetic and visionary first Vice-Chancellor, the acquisition of more land around the original Highfields Park proceeded at a rapid rate. New buildings were erected including, in 1956, the Portland Building, which included dining facilities, an art gallery, and concourse lounges. It became the focal point for the community of staff and scholars that Hallward was seeking to build. All these developments were funded by the University Grants Committee. In 1953 the University received the first of a series of gifts from the Cripps family of Roade,

Northampton, in this case of £300,000 to establish two chairs. These gifts encouraged the Boots Company and Rolls Royce to endow others. The Cripps family also donated £375,000 for the building of a new hall of residence which opened in 1959, at which point there were five halls housing more than 40 per cent of the total student population. Another eight were built by 1964–65. Government funding for major new science and engineering projects produced Basil Spence's 'Technopolis', with its science library and Tower Block. Medicine was added in 1970, the first new medical school in the United Kingdom since 1893.[42] A large number of new degree courses across a wide spectrum of disciplines was introduced as student numbers grew from 1,700 in 1947 to about 7,500 in the late 1980s, although due to cuts in government expenditure the growth in teaching and research was increasingly dependent upon income from industry and commerce, which reached over £20 million a year by 1990, and £40 million in 1995. The continued munificence of the Cripps family also led to several important projects on the main campus, including a Student Health Centre, a Sports Hall, and a new Computer Centre. The University Grants Committee provided the financial support necessary to build the central University Library for the Arts and Social Sciences, opened in 1973.

The School of Art and Design was, in 1902, like University College, managed by a committee of the corporation. The School continued to function along lines which differentiated between fine-art instruction, including painting and sculpture, for middle-class students, and more practical teaching of drawing and draughtsmanship to artisan students who were hoping to become designers in one of the staple trades of the town. After 1918 Joseph Else, its Principal, began a campaign to attract local industrialists to take an interest in the School. In 1934 it became the College of Art and Crafts, and the College was soon recognised as the centre for architectural training in the East Midlands. Other initiatives included the teaching of fine art to WEA classes, courses in advertising, commercial art, and photography. During the Second World War the college was encouraged to develop the most advanced work in art and design, for which it would be the regional centre, and to loosen its commitment to training for Nottingham's staple trades.[43] The transition was accomplished by the 1960s, although by 1970 its diploma and degree courses were taught under the auspices of the newly-created Trent Polytechnic, of which it had become a constituent faculty.

The origins of the Polytechnic lay in the decision taken in the closing stages of the Second World War to cease the technical instruction given in the University College and to create a new independent Technical College in Shakespeare Street, with its own staff and equipment. The Nottingham District Technical College came into being in August 1945 with 1,995 full- and part-time students being enrolled for courses during its first year.[44] During the 1950s the College increasingly taught higher-level courses including London external degrees, and its expansion was greatly assisted from the end of the decade by the construction of new premises, notably the Newton and Maudsley Buildings.

By the mid-1960s there was a comprehensive portfolio of full- and part- time London external degree courses in the natural and social sciences, technology and building, and general arts. The successful teaching of these courses led to recognition by the newly-created Council for National Academic Awards (CNAA) and to the validation of its degree programmes. In June 1970 the former Regional College of Technology became Trent Polytechnic, jointly funded by the city, Nottinghamshire and Derbyshire Education Authorities, and central government. Ronald Hedley was appointed director, and although it was intended that the Polytechnic would concentrate upon science, technology and other specifically vocational subjects in art and design, it began to absorb an increasing number of students in disciplines from the arts and social sciences. Nurtured by the CNAA, new degree courses were introduced across all departments. There was no doubt in Hedley's mind that the Polytechnic was 'a new type of university conceived as such in official thinking', and he was convinced that it would eventually be equal in status to the older institution in the city.[45] A forecast reduction in teacher training provided the impetus and opportunity for the amalgamation of the Polytechnic with the College of Education at Clifton in 1974. New buildings such as the School of Science, were erected on a green-field site and valuable land earmarked for expansion in the city was used for other purposes.[46]

During the 1980s the Polytechnic, partly protected from government restraints on spending by the three local authorities, continued to grow rapidly and through the success of its degree courses achieved increasing autonomy from CNAA. In 1989 it was removed from local authority control and in 1991 the Government decided that the binary divide in higher education between universities and other institutions of higher education should be abolished. Common funding for teaching and research and degree-awarding powers enabled the institution to achieve university status in November 1992 as the Nottingham Trent University. With over 50 per cent of its 15,300 students coming from outside the East Midlands, it was a national as well as a local institution and in 1993–94 its claim of quality teaching across a wide range of courses was recognised in the allocation of the largest teaching budget (£25 million) of all 128 higher education institutions.[47] Research, consultancy and the provision of external degrees at home and abroad were also becoming an increasingly important part of Trent's work.

The City of Nottingham thus entered the 1990s with two universities, both of which owed their foundation to the local authority. Although each institution has a quite separate and distinctive ethos their presence confers prestige upon the city. As the decade moves to a close and Nottingham becomes a unitary authority when the structure of local government changes yet again, the corporation will once more assume some responsibility for schools and educational services. However, the control it once exercised over every stage of educational provision cannot be restored. The Colleges of Further Education and the Sixth Form Colleges have their own central government funding body. Schools like the City Technology College in Sherwood, and the greater freedom to control their own school budgets given to governors under the local management of schools system, will inevitably mean that whatever new body is created to administer education in Nottingham, its powers will never equal those once wielded by the old Nottingham Education Committee.

Notes

1 *EC* Minutes, August 1909. Report on the costs of Education. In 1909 the committee reported that Nottingham was spending less on education than towns of comparable size.
2 D. Wardle, 'The work of the Nottingham School Board' (University of Nottingham, M.Ed. thesis, 1961), p. 106; H. M. Jenkins, *Church Schools in Nottinghamshire* (Nottingham, 1954), p. 182.
3 *EC* Minutes, March 1908, January 1909.
4 *EC* Minutes, March 1911.
5 *EC* Minutes, 1907/1908. Elementary Schools. Organisation and Accommodation; HMI Report, *The Training of Older Children in Nottingham* (1911).
6 *EC* Annual Report, 1914.
7 B. Simon, *Education and the Labour Movement, 1870–1920* (1965), p. 242; see also: *Report of the Consultative Committee on Secondary Education with Special Reference to Grammar Schools and Technical High Schools* [The Spens Report] (1938), p. 72: the regulations for secondary schools of 1904 'were based wholly on the tradition of the Grammar Schools and the Public schools'.
8 O. Banks, *Parity and Prestige in English Education* (1955), p. 62; B. H. Tolley, 'Technical education in the East Midlands: a study in educational administration and history' (University of Nottingham, Ph.D. thesis, 1979), ch. VII, p. 368.
9 A. C. Wood, *A History of the University College, Nottingham. 1881–1948* (Oxford, 1953), p. 59; *EC* Annual Report, 1906/1907.
10 Tolley, 'Technical education in the East Midlands', pp. 370–2. The School Board and the Nottingham Trades Council were at one in advocating the development of the 'secondary evening school' as compensatory education for the working man, forced by circumstances to abort full-time education at an early stage.
11 *EC* Annual Reports, 1909/1910, 1906/1907. The committee discussed seeking the co-operation of 'merchants, manufacturers and workmen' in order to introduce a system of evening Professional and Trade Schools on the continental pattern.
12 *EC* Annual Report, 1914/1915.
13 *EC* Minutes, 1907/1908. Elementary Schools, Organisation and Accommodation; Buildings Sub-Committee, 18 July 1923; log Books of Trent Bridge Boys' and Girls' Schools, Notts.
14 S. Zaleski, *Berridge: the Schools' First One Hundred Years* (Nottingham, 1984).
15 *EC* General Purposes Sub-Committee. Outline Suggestions. W. J. Abel. February 1919, and Report of the Buildings Sub-Committee, 14 July 1920.
16 *EC* Annual Reports, 1925–28.
17 A. H. Whipple, *Education up to Fifteen Years. What is and what might be* (Nottingham, 1939); Simon, *The Politics of Educational Reform* (1974), p. 123.
18 Whipple, *Education up to Fifteen*, Introduction.
19 A. H. Whipple, *City of Nottingham: William Crane School* (Nottingham, 1935).
20 Whipple, *Education in Nottingham 1924–1933*, pp. 6, 61–2.
21 Whipple, *Education up to Fifteen*, pp. 189, 201.
22 Whipple, *Education in Nottingham*, p. 125.
23 *EC* Annual Report, 1939/1940, Minutes 14 December 1939; P. R. Holloway, 'Evacuation and education' (University of Nottingham, M.Ed. Dissertation, 1982), p. 14.
24 *EC* Minutes, 20 January 1940; Annual Report, 1940/1941. Forty-six schools in Nottingham had allotments in 1941 covering more than 13.9 acres in total.
25 C. A. Jones, *A History of the Nottingham School of Design* (Nottingham, 1993), p. 77; Annual Report of the Castle Museum and College of Art. 1939/1940, p. 642; and 1940/1941, p. 441; *Nottingham Chamber of Commerce*, Minutes of Council Meetings, 29 March 1943, 2 August 1944; *EC* Annual Reports, 1960 and 1961. See also *Guardian Journal*, 2 November 1964.
26 City of Nottingham Development Plan for Primary and Secondary Education, July 1946, pp. 4, 25–8.
27 *Ibid.*, pp. 2–3.
28 *Ibid.*, p. 2; *EC* Annual Reports, 1965–69.

29 *EC* Annual Reports, 1957, 1958. The intention was to raise the proportion of pupils taking GCE courses from 14 per cent to 30 per cent.

30 Edwards, p. 431; *Times Education Supplement*, 13 November 1964.

31 *Guardian Journal*, 19 May 1967.

32 *Guardian Journal*, 25 November 1970, 25, 26 November 1970, and for a profile of Oliver Barnett, ex-headmaster of Forest Fields Grammar School and a leading campaigner to protect the Nottingham grammar schools, 15 January 1973.

33 *EC* Comprehensive Education in Nottingham, September 1972.

34 *EC* Annual Reports, 1969–73. See also *Comprehensive Education in Nottingham* (1972).

35 Edwards, p. 428.

36 I am grateful to Andrew Craig, co-ordinator of Nottinghamshire Education Authority's Ethnic Minority Projects, for information upon this subject.

37 For the information concerning special educational needs, I am indebted to Denise McBrinn of the Nottinghamshire Pupil and Community Services Department.

38 For information concerning the Careers Service, I am indebted to Noel Harrower, former Principal Careers Officer for Nottingham.

39 Tolley, 'Technical education', pp. 560–4.

40 S. D. Chapman, *Jesse Boot of Boots the Chemist* (1974), pp. 162–4; Wood, *University College*, p. 93.

41 *Ibid.*, pp. 121–3.

42 S. Ablett, 'The Medical School of the University of Nottingham' (University of Nottingham, Ph.D. thesis, 1992), pp. 50–60.

43 Jones, *A History of the Nottingham School of Design*, pp. 57–61, 87.

44 Nottingham Regional Technical College, *Prospectus*, 1945/1946.

45 R. Hedley, *Nottingham Regional College of Technology. Accommodation Problems and Outline Proposals for Long Term Development* (January 1967); NAO CA/ED/13F/2/1/7/1, *Guardian Journal*, 3 August 1971.

46 *Guardian*, 13 January 1976; *EP*, 24 April, 16 July 1976.

47 *Times Higher Education Supplement*, 29 December 1989; *EP*, 11 November 1992, 25 May 1993; Nottingham Trent University, Annual Report, 1992/1993. See also *Mission Statement of the Nottingham Trent University*, Annual Report, 1992/1993.

Conclusion: Nottingham today

John Beckett and Colin Griffin

The City of Nottingham is today a thriving commercial and industrial centre, quite different from the tiny settlement which first came to play a significant regional role in the tenth century. In the medieval town it was a struggle to reach the River Trent across the meandering flood plain beneath the Castle Rock and St Mary's Hill. For 700 years the compact little settlement which grew out of the Saxon *burh* and the Norman borough created following the building of the castle hardly changed. A town wall was built and then taken down. Houses and other buildings were erected and demolished. A community never much exceeding 3,000 or 4,000 people lived out their everyday lives amidst the squabbles documented in the borough court rolls, periodic outbreaks of plague and other epidemics, and with an enduring capacity to adapt to whatever circumstances might throw up, as demonstrated by events during the Reformation and Civil Wars.

The past 300 years have seen far more 'change' than the previous 700. Once population started to increase, and the town began to industrialise, a new urban world came into being. It was not simply a question of pushing back the physical frontiers, although this was effectively achieved with the enclosure of the open fields and the boundary extensions of 1877, 1932 and 1951. More significantly, it was about an internal restructuring of urban space as the pre-industrial town was transformed into a modern industrial city. Until the eighteenth century most people lived and worked in the centre of the town, with the sites of highest status closest to the market-place. The seventeenth- and eighteenth-century rebuilding produced a fine townscape with many impressive houses. Towards the end of the eighteenth century, as population grew and social conditions deteriorated, the middle classes began to relocate on the western edge of the town. In the 1840s they moved into the Wellington Circus area, and in the 1850s into the Park. Meanwhile the working classes crowded into the centre of the old town or, in the case of some of the better-off lace workers, into the surrounding industrial villages. After enclosure the lower middle classes moved on to the Sandfield, and the working classes on to the Clay Field and the former meadows, although many remained in the slums of the Broad and Narrow Marshes and other central areas.

In the second half of the nineteenth century the process of segregation speeded up. As industrialists sought prime sites in the middle of the town – typified by the massive lace warehousing of the 1850s and beyond – the horse tram, the railway and later, the electric tram, enabled the middle classes to move further from the centre. Nottingham did not develop any major industrial zones, but the social differentiation of local society became increasingly apparent with The Park and Mapperley Park (developed towards the end of the century) as the major high-status areas, and working-class areas scattered around the rest of the town, often cheek-by-jowl with industrial premises.

During the twentieth century these changes have proceeded apace. Since the 1920s, and particularly with the advent of mass car ownership, many middle-class families have moved further afield, either to private estates within the town boundaries such as Wollaton, or to the adjoining but administratively distinct suburbs such as Beeston and West Bridgford, or to dormitory villages like Burton Joyce and Ruddington. Numerous working-class families moved into council property built by the corporation on green field sites beyond the old urban core, and serviced by trolley-bus and later motor-bus routes. Since the 1980s many council tenants have become private householders by purchasing their properties. The city centre, now largely bereft of residents, has in turn become the commercial heart of the city, symbolised by the fact that the major shopping centres, the Victoria and Broad Marsh malls, are on what were in the nineteenth century heavily overbuilt areas of poor quality working-class housing. With the loss of population has come the demolition or reuse of buildings. The city centre today has three Anglican churches, the same three that were there before the great expansion of population began: St Mary's, St Nicholas's and St Peter's. The nineteenth-century Anglican churches have all been demolished. Most of the nonconformist chapels have either been demolished, or converted to other uses, among them the High Pavement Unitarian Chapel, rebuilt in 1876 and now the city's lace museum. Hardly a pupil is taught within the confines of the old town. Once, partly because of the quality of its water, Nottingham was famed for its ales; now, through rationalisation and takeovers, the city's capacity for brewing has virtually disappeared. Once, the town had one daily paper, three expensive weeklies and 'a host of weekly papers price 1*d* … . With all these "organs of public opinion" we ought to manage.'[1] Today the only daily paper, the *Evening Post*, is printed in Derby.

Yet for all these changes, Nottingham today is as much of a regional centre as it was in 920, with a more recently cultivated image as 'Queen of the Midlands' and commercial interests which spread throughout the East Midlands. The market-place, the commercial heart of the old town, is today, as it has been for the past 900 or so years, still the meeting-place and focal point of the city, and although the garden image was lost in the great expansion of the late eighteenth and early nineteenth centuries, there are still a handful of serene and peaceful spots where the old town can be recreated in the imagination. The post-enclosure Arboretum and recreational walks remain as much-appreciated symbols of positive Victorian attitudes towards open spaces. Changing attitudes since the 1960s towards conservation and alternative use, rather than wholesale destruction and renewal, mean that at the heart of

Plate 66 **Punks in the Old Market Square, 1984**. A group of punks, sporting the current fashions in clothing and hairstyles, meeting in the market-place, just as mods, rockers, Teddy Boys, and generations of other young people have done in the past.

the city are buildings and areas which bring to mind the historic past, while the city's museums remind us of its long heritage, whether in the caves, the lace trade, or along the canal, to mention only a few. But the city cannot stand still. The recent move towards out-of-town retail sites such as Castle Marina suggests that even its commercial heart may not survive in its present form. Urban regeneration is as necessary as ever and continues, as the millennium approaches, through the investment of City Challenge capital in the renovation of St Ann's and Sneinton, and the commitment of city planners, business leaders, and academic institutions to develop a hi-tech industrial and commercial base appropriate to the twenty-first-century city.[2] Whether the people of Nottingham will feel more secure, content and free, in this post-modern city must remain, if the twentieth century experience is anything to go by, an open question.

In the 1830s Nottingham was a radical town, and people travelling away from home were likely to be asked whether all was quiet. Travellers at the end of the twentieth century can be sure that wherever they roam across the globe mention of the city's name will bring a response which suggests an association with a mythical medieval renegade by the name of Robin Hood. As we have tried to show in the preceding pages, Nottingham has rather more to its past than a folk hero, a castle and a wicked sheriff: although perhaps the same tradition was being kept alive when Brian Clough's Nottingham Forest twice robbed the rich clubs of Europe to bring the European Cup to what at the end of the 1970s was a rather humble city ground. A century ago Wylie and Potter Briscoe wrote that 'amid the unresting roll of our modern machinery and the din of today's business we may hear, if we only listen, the voices of a venerable past'.[3] The machinery may not roll in quite the way it did in 1893 when these words were written, but we hope that this book will help to raise awareness of the city's rich and varied history over the past 1,000 years.

Notes

1 NAO M.23,788, 6 January 1860.

2 R. N. E. Blake, 'The City Challenge: planning by partnership in Nottingham's inner area', *Trent Geographer* (1993), pp. 13–30; *The Guardian*, 4 January 1996, for a report on Nottingham as the UK's first 'technology region'.

3 W. H. Wylie and J. Potter Briscoe, *History of Nottingham* (1893).

Select bibliography

This bibliography covers the main printed primary and secondary sources used in the text. No attempt has been made to list the numerous primary sources referenced in the endnotes, and also excluded are general works, City Council reports (annual and occasional), newspapers, directories, and ephemeral literature. A full bibliography of writings on Nottinghamshire, including Nottingham, will be found in M. Brook (ed.), Nottinghamshire: a bibliography of historical writing on the country (TSRS, 42, 1997). *All items are published in London unless otherwise indicated.*

Printed primary sources

Anon., 'Copy [by Dr Charles Deering] of a Ms Account of Nottingham [1641]', *TTS*, 2 (1898).

Bailey, T., *Annals of Nottinghamshire: History of the County of Nottingham including the Borough* (4 vols., Nottingham, 1853).

Bailey, T. B., *In Memory of Thomas Hancock, Civil Engineer to Nottingham Water Works Company, 1782–1805* (Nottingham, 1898).

Barnett, A., *The Poor Laws and their Administration being an Enquiry into the Causes of English Pauperism and the Failure of Measures Intended for its Relief* (London, 1833).

Blackner, J., *The History of Nottingham* (Nottingham, 1815).

Blagg, T. M. and F. A. Wadsworth, *Abstracts of Nottinghamshire Marriage Licences*, vol. 1 (1930).

Boulton, H. E. (ed.), *The Sherwood Forest Book*, (*TSRS*, 23, 1967).

Campbell, A. (ed.), *The Chronicle of Æthelweard* (1962).

Copnall, H. H. (ed.), *Nottinghamshire County Records of the Seventeenth Century* (Nottingham, 1915).

Cox, T., *Magna Britannia or Topographical, Ecclesiastical and Natural History of Nottinghamshire* (1720).

Cropper, H. S., *The Freemen of Nottingham and their Estates* (Nottingham, 1880).

Deering, C., *Nottinghamia Vetus Et Nova or an Historical Account of the Ancient and Present State of the Town of Nottingham* (Nottingham, 1751).

English, Asmodeus, *Revelations of Life in Nottingham* (Nottingham, 1860).

Farley, A. (ed.), *Domesday Book seu liber censualis Wilhelmi primi regis Angliae* (2 vols. 1783–1816).

Felkin, W., 'Statistics of the labouring classes and paupers of Nottingham', *Journal of the Royal Statistical Society*, II (1839).

— *History of the Machine-Wrought Hosiery and Lace Manufactures* (1867).

Field, H. (ed.), *The Date Book of Remarkable and Memorable Events connected with Nottingham, 850–1884* (Nottingham, 1884).

Foulds, T. (ed.), *Thurgarton Priory Cartulary* (Stamford, 1994).

Full Report of the Speech delivered by Mr Bailey at a Meeting of the Nottingham Town Council February 19, 1838, on the subject of the Repeal of the Corn Laws (1838).

Gilbert, A., *Recollections of Old Nottingham* (2nd edn, Nottingham, 1904).
Goodman, J. B. (ed.), *Victorian Cabinet Maker: the memoirs of James Hopkinson, 1819–1894* (1968).
Guilford E. L., 'Extracts from the records of the Borough of Nottingham', *TTS*, 26 (1922).
— 'Extracts from the records of the Borough of Nottingham', *TTS*, 27 (1923).
Henson, G., *History of the Framework Knitters* (1831).
Henstock, A. (ed.), *The Diary of Abigail Gawthern of Nottingham 1751–1810* (*TSRS*, 33, 1980).
Hine, T. C., *Nottingham: its Castle: Supplement* (Nottingham, 1879).
Historical Manuscripts Commission, *Report on the Manuscripts of Lord Middleton preserved at Wollaton Hall* (1911).
Holdsworth, C. J. (ed.), *Rufford Charters*, I (*TSRS*, 24, 1972).
Laird, F. C., *Topographical Description of Nottinghamshire* (1810).
MacRitchie, Revd William, *Diary of a Tour through Great Britain in 1795* (1897).
Moritz, C. P., *Journeys of a German in England in 1782* (1965).
Orange, J., *History and Antiquities of Nottingham* (2 vols., 1840).
Robertson, A. J. (ed.), *Anglo-Saxon Charters* (Cambridge, 1956).
Roworth, W., *Observations on the Administration of the New Poor Law in Nottingham* (Nottingham, 1840).
Royal Charters Granted to the Burgesses of Nottingham, AD 1155–1712 (Nottingham, 1890).
Sanders, Robert, *Complete English Traveller* (1772).
Sawyer, P. H., *Anglo-Saxon Charters: an Annotated Handlist and Bibliography* (1968).
Seaton, Edward, *A Report on the Sanitary Condition of the Borough of Nottingham* (Nottingham, 1873).
Seddon, P. R. (ed.), *Letters of John Holles, 1587–1637* (*TSRS*, 31–2, 1975–86).
Smith, T. H., *Hints to the Churchwardens, Overseers and Rate Payers of St Mary's Parish, Nottingham* (Nottingham, 1834).
Standish, J. (ed.), *Abstracts of the Inquisitions Post Mortem Relating to Nottinghamshire* (*TSRS*, 3–4, 1904–14).
Stevenson, W. *et al.* (eds.), *Records of the Borough of Nottingham*, I–IX (Nottingham, 1882–1956).
Stevenson, W. H., 'A description of Nottinghamshire in the seventeenth century', *TTS*, 11 (1907).
Stevenson, W. H. (ed.), *Asser's Life of King Alfred* (Oxford, 1959).
Stevenson, W. H. and A. Stapleton, *The Religious Foundations of Old Nottingham* (Nottingham, 1895).
Strangers Guide to Nottingham (2nd edn, 1827).
Tarbotton, M. O., 'Recent sanitary operations and town improvements', *Allen's Illustrated Hand-Book of Nottingham* (Nottingham, 1866).
— *A Short History of the Old Trent Bridge with a Descriptive Account of the New Bridge, Nottingham* (Nottingham, 1871).
Thomis, M. I. (ed.), *Luddism in Nottinghamshire* (*TSRS*, 26, 1972).
Thompson, A. H. (ed.), 'The Chantry Certificate Rolls for the County of Nottingham', *TTS*, 18 (1914).
Thoroton, R., *The Antiquities of Nottinghamshire* (1677).
Throsby, J. (ed.), *The Antiquities of Nottinghamshire*, II (1790).
Toulmin-Smith, L. (ed.), *Itinerary of John Leland, 1534–43* (1907).
Tourist's Picturesque Guide to Nottingham (Nottingham, 1871).
Train, K. S. S. (ed.), *Lists of the Clergy of Central Nottinghamshire* (*TSRS*, 15, part II, 1954).
Wadsworth, F. A., 'An assessment for St. Mary's Church, Nottingham, 1637',
TTS, 33 (1929).
Walker, V. W. (trans.), and D. Gray (ed.), *Newstead Priory Cartulary, 1344 and other archives* (Nottingham, 1940).
Webster, W. F. (ed.), *Nottinghamshire Hearth Tax 1664, 1674* (*TSRS*, 37, 1988).
Whitelock, D., D. C. Douglas and S. I. Tucker (eds.), *The Anglo-Saxon Chronicle: a Revised Translation* (1965).
Williams, A. and R. W. H. Erskine (eds.), *The Nottinghamshire Domesday* (1990).
Wood, A. C. (ed.), *Memorials of the Holles Family, 1493–1656* (Camden Society, 3rd series, 55, 1937).
— 'Nottinghamshire by G. M. Woodward', *TTS*, 61 (1957).
Wylie, W. H., *Old and New Nottingham* (1853).

Secondary sources

Allen, C. *et al.*, 'A Bronze Age burial site at Clifton, Nottinghamshire', *TTS*, 98 (1994).

Alvey, R. C., 'A cesspit excavation at 26–28 High Pavement, Nottingham', *TTS*, 77 (1973).

[Anon.], *Centenary: Vickers & Hine Ltd 1818–1918* (Nottingham,1918).

Armytage, W. H., *A. J. Mundella 1825–97* (1951).

Aspin, C. and S. D. Chapman, *James Hargreaves and the Spinning Jenny* (Helmshore, 1964).

Attaway, P., *Nottingham Forest: a Complete Record 1865–1991* (Derby, 1991).

Barley, M., *The Chiefest Grain* (Nottingham, 1993).

Barley, M. W., 'Notes on the Anglo-Saxon Pottery from Kingston on Soar', *TTS*, 61 (1957).

— 'Nottingham town wall', *TTS*, 69 (1965).

— 'Town defences in England and Wales after 1066', in M. W. Barley (ed.), *The Plans and Topography of Medieval Towns in England and Wales* (CBA, Research Report 14, 1976).

— *The English Farmhouse and Cottage*, (Gloucester, 1987).

Barley, M. W. and F. I. Straw, 'Nottingham', in M. D. Lobel (ed.), *Historic Towns*, I (1969).

Barnes, F. A., 'Lenton Priory after the Dissolution; its buildings and fairgrounds', *TTS*, 91 (1987).

Barnes, F. A., *Priory Demesne to University Campus* (Nottingham, 1993).

Baylay, A. M. Y., 'Southwell, Pavement probably Pre-Norman', *TTS*, 5 (1901).

Beats, L., 'The East Midlands Association 1642–44', *Midland History*, IV (1978).

Beckett, J. V.,'The Church of England and the working class in nineteenth-century Nottingham: the building of St Stephen's, Hyson Green', *TTS*, 92 (1988).

Beckett, J. V. and K. Brand, 'Enclosure, improvement and the rise of "New Nottingham" 1845–67', *TTS*, 98 (1994).

Bennett, M., 'Nottingham Justices of the Peace and the Social Order', *NH*, 47 (1991).

— 'The King's Gambit: Charles I and Nottingham in the summer of 1642', *TTS*, 96 (1992).

Best, S., 'Unfit for human habitation', *Sneinton Magazine*, 14 (1984).

— 'The destruction of Denison's Mill', *Sneinton Magazine*, 23 (1986).

— 'How the racecourse came to Colwick', *Sneinton Magazine*, 46 (1993).

— 'Mission accomplished: the early years of St Christopher's Church', *Sneinton Magazine*, 49 (1993–94).

— 'Sneinton School Board's brief life', *Sneinton Magazine*, 50, 51 (1994).

— 'Minnitt's Folly', *Nottingham Civic Society Newsletter*, 96–100 (1995–96).

Bosworth, A., 'Nineteenth-century churches in Nottingham', *NH*, 46 (1991).

— '"Grandeur and Trumpery": the creation of the Roman Catholic diocese of Nottingham, 1850', *NH*, 47 (1991).

Bosworth, Anne, 'Aspects of middle class life: the Park Estate, Nottingham, 1841–1881', *Journal of Regional and Local Studies*, 5 (1985).

Bowden, G. H., *The Story of the Raleigh Cycle* (1975).

Brand, K., 'The Park Estate, Nottingham: the development of a nineteenth-century fashionable suburb', *TTS*, 88 (1984).

Brand, K., *The Park Estate* (Nottingham, 1985).

— 'Temporary accommodation', *Nottingham Civic Society Newsletter*, 93 (1994).

— *The Shire Hall and Old County Gaol* (Nottingham, n.d.).

— *Thomas Chambers Hine, 1813–99* (Nottingham, n.d.).

Brand, Ken, *An Introduction to Mapperley Park* (2nd edn, Nottingham Civic Society, 1996).

Brazier, S. *et al.*, *A New Geography of Nottingham* (2nd edn, Nottingham, 1988).

Brocklesby, R., 'How they lived: William Robinson, sr., Nottingham Hosier', *NH*, 11 (1973).

Bryson, Emrys, *Portrait of Nottingham* (1974).

Butler, R. M., 'The common lands of the Borough of Nottingham', *TTS*, 54 (1950).

Cameron, A., 'William de Amyas and the community of Nottingham, 1308–50', *TTS*, 75 (1971).

Cannell, D. M., *George Green: Mathematician and Physicist 1793–1841* (1993).

Carpenter, B., *Some Account of the Original Introduction of Presbyterianism in Nottingham* (Nottingham, 1865).

Chambers, J. D., 'Nottingham in the early nineteenth century', *TTS*, 45 (1941).
– *Modern Nottingham in the Making* (Nottingham, 1945).
– 'Memoir of a Nottingham lace merchant, William Cripps 1798–1884', *Bulletin of the Business History Society* (June 1950).
– *A Century of Nottingham History* (Nottingham, 1951).
– *The People of Nottingham, 1851–1951* (Nottingham, 1951).
– 'Population change in a provincial Town, Nottingham 1700–1800', in L. S. Pressnell (ed.), *Studies in the Industrial Revolution* (1960).
– *Nottinghamshire in the Eighteenth Century* (2nd edn, 1966).
Chapman, S. D., 'The evangelical revival and education in Nottingham', *TTS*, 66 (1962).
– 'Working-class housing in Nottingham during the Industrial Revolution', *TTS*, 67 (1963).
– 'The genesis of the British hosiery industry, 1600–1750', *Textile History*, 3 (1972).
– *Jesse Boot of Boots the Chemists* (1974).
– 'Enterprise and innovation in the British hosiery industry 1750–1850', *Textile History* V (1974).
– 'Mergers and takeovers in the hosiery industry', *Business History*, XXX (1988).
– 'The Robinson Mills: proto-industrial precedents', *Industrial Archaeology Review*, XV (1992).
– 'The innovating entrepreneurs in the British ready-made clothing industry', *Textile History*, XXIV (1993).
Charles, F. W., 'Severns: a fifteenth century timber framed building ...', *TTS*, 74 (1970).
Charsley, T. J., T. J. Rathbone and D. J. Lowe, *Nottingham: a Geological Background for Planning and Development* (British Geological Survey, 1990).
Cheetham, F. W., *Medieval English Alabaster Carvings in the Castle Museum Nottingham* (Nottingham, 1973).
Church, R. A., 'James Orange and the allotment system in Nottingham', *TTS*, 64 (1960).
– *Economic and Social Change in a Midland Town: Victorian Nottingham, 1815–1900* (1966).
Church, R. A. and S. D. Chapman, 'Gravenor Henson and the making of the English working class', in E. L. Jones and G. E. Mingay (eds)., *Land, Labour and Population in the Industrial Revolution* (1966).
Clarke, A. B., 'Notes on the Mayors of Nottingham, 1660–1715', *TTS*, 41 (1938).
Clay, P. and J. H. Richards, *Official Record of the Celebration of the Diamond Jubilee of Her Majesty Queen Victoria, June 1897* (Nottingham, 1898).
Clough, B. with J. Sadler, *Clough: The Autobiography* (1994).
Coates, K. and R. Silburn, *Poverty, Deprivation and Morale in a Nottingham Community: St Ann's* (Nottingham, 1967).
– *Beyond the Bulldozer* (Nottingham, 1980).
Colvin, H. M., *History of the King's Works*, I (1963).
Coope, R. T. and J. Y. Corbett (eds.), *Bromley House, 1752–1991* (Nottingham, 1991).
Cornwall, J. (ed.), *The County Community under Henry VIII* (Rutland Record Series, I, 1980).
Cossons, A., *The Turnpike Roads of Nottinghamshire* (2nd edn Nottingham, 1994).
Crewe, L., 'Skills, work and training: the employment experience of the Vietnamese community in Nottingham', *EMG*, 15 (1992).
Crewe, L., S. Longford and P. Totterdill, *The Notts. Fashion Sector* (Nottingham University, Department of Geography, 1994).
Crook, D., 'Moothallgate and the venue of the Nottinghamshire County Court in the thirteenth century', *TTS*, 88 (1984).
Cummins, M., *Nottingham Cathedral* (3rd edn, Nottingham, 1994).
Cummins, W. A., 'A Graig Lwyd stone axe rough-out from Holme Pierrepont, Nottinghamshire', *TTS*, 82 (1978).
Cummins, W. A. and A. J. Rundle, 'The geological environment of the dug-out canoes from Holme Pierrepont, Nottinghamshire', *Mercian Geologist*, 3 (1969).
Curtis, Revd J., *A Topographical History of Nottinghamshire* (1843).
Cuthbert, N., *The Lace Makers' Society* (Nottingham, 1960).
Daniels, C., 'Excavations on the site of the Roman Villa at Southwell, 1959', *TTS*, 70 (1966).

Daniels, S. And S. Rycroft, 'Mapping the modern city: Alan Sillitoe's Nottingham novels', *Transactions of the Institute of British Geographers*, 18 (1993).
Davies, G., *A Touch of Colwick* (Chorley, 1994).
Douglass, S. P., A. G. MacCormick, and S. N. Mastoris, 'The Old Flying Horse, Nottingham: a structural and documentary survey', *TTS*, 91 (1987).
Drage, C., 'Nottingham Castle: a place full Royal', *TTS*, 93 (1989).
Dunster, S., 'An independent life: Nottingham Widows, 1590–1650', *TTS*, 95 (1991).
Edwards, K. C., 'A new bridge over the River Trent', *EMG*, 9 (1958).
— 'The Park Estate, Nottingham', in M. A. Simpson and T. H. Lloyd (eds.), *Middle Class Housing in Britain* (Newton Abbot, 1977).
Edwards, K. C. (ed.), *Nottingham and its Region* (Nottingham, 1966).
Elsdon, S. M., 'Iron Age and Roman sites at Red Hill, Ratcliffe-on-Soar, Nottinghamshire', *TTS*, 89 (1982).
— *Iron Age Pottery in the East Midlands* (Nottingham, 1993).
Epstein, J., 'Some organisational and cultural aspects of the Chartist movement in Nottingham', in J. Epstein and D. Thompson (eds.), *The Chartist Experience: studies in Working-Class Radicalism and Culture 1830–60* (1982).
Erickson, C., *British Industrialists: Steel and Hosiery 1850–1950* (Cambridge, 1959).
Evans, R., 'Music in St Mary's Church, Nottingham', *NH*, 38 (1982).
Evans, R., 'Theatre music in Nottingham, 1760–1800', *TTS*, 88 (1984).
Foster, V. and B. Taylor, *Railways in and around Nottingham* (Huddersfield, 1991).
Foulds, T., 'The foundation of Lenton Priory and a reconstruction of its lost Cartulary', *TTS*, 92 (1988).
— 'The siege of Nottingham castle in 1194', *TTS*, 95 (1991).
Foulds, T., J. Hughes and M. Jones, 'The Nottingham borough court rolls: the reign of Henry VI (1422–55)', *TTS*, 87 (1993).
Francis, T., *Clough: a Biography* (1987).
Fraser, D., 'The Nottingham Press, 1800–1850', *TTS*, 67 (1963).
— 'Nottingham and the Corn Laws', *TTS*, 70 (1966).
Fry, T., *The History of Sherwood: a Nottingham Suburb* (1989).
Garrison, L. (ed.), *The Black Presence in Nottingham* (Nottingham, 1993).
Garton, D., 'Dunston's Clump and the brickwork plan field systems at Babworth, Nottinghamshire', *TTS*, 91 (1987).
Giggs, J. A., 'Fringe expansion and suburbanisation around Nottingham: a metropolitan area approach', *EMG*, 5 (1970).
— 'Traffic reorganisation in the central core of Nottingham', *EMG*, 5 (1973).
— 'Schizophrenia and ecological structure in Nottingham', in N. D. McGlashan and J. R. Blunden (eds.), *Geographical Aspects of Health* (1983).
— 'Mental disorder and ecological structure in Nottingham', *Social Science and Medicine*, 23 (1986).
— 'Drug abuse and urban ecological structure: the Nottingham case', in R. W. Thomas (ed.), *Spatial Epidemiology* (1990).
Giggs, J. A. and D. K. Whynes, 'Homeless people in Nottingham', *EMG*, 11 (1988).
Giggs, J. A. *et al.*, 'Class A drug users: prevalence and characteristics in Nottingham', *British Journal of Addiction*, 84 (1989).
Gill, H., 'Notes on the domestic architecture of Old Nottingham', *TTS*, 11 (1907).
— 'Nottingham in the eighteenth century, especially with reference to domestic architecture', *TTS*, 16 (1912).
— 'Notes on the Carmelite friary at Nottingham', *TTS*, 26 (1922).
Gillott, S., 'Bestwood: a Sherwood Forest Park in the seventeenth century', *TTS*, 89 (1985).
Girouard, M., *Robert Smythson and the Elizabethan Country House* (Yale, 1983).
Godfrey, J. T., *The History of the Parish and Priory of Lenton* (1884).
Godfrey, J. T. and J. Ward, *A History of Friar Lane Baptist Church* (Nottingham, 1903).
— *The Homes and Haunts of Henry Kirk White* (Nottingham, 1908).

Gosling, R., *Personal Copy* (1980).

Gover, J. E. B., A. Mawer and F. M. Stenton, T*he Place-Names of Nottinghamshire* (Cambridge, 1940).

Granger, J., *History of the Nottingham Mechanics' Institution 1837–1887* (Nottingham, 1912).

Gray, D., *Nottingham: Settlement to City* (Nottingham, 1953).

— *Nottingham through 500 Years* (2nd edn, Nottingham, 1960).

Greaterix, N., 'The Robinson Enterprises at Papplewick, Nottinghamshire', *Industrial Archaeology Review*, IX (1986–7).

Greenwood, J. E., *A Cap for Boots. An Autobiography* (1977).

Grieg, P., 'The layout of Lenton fairground, 1516', *TTS*, 96 (1992).

Griffin, A. R., *Mining in the East Midlands 1550–1947* (1971).

— 'Thomas North: mining entrepreneur extraordinary', *TTS*, 76 (1972).

Griffin, C. P., 'Chartism and opposition to the New Poor Law in Nottinghamshire', *Midland History*, 2 (1974).

— '"Three days down the pit and three days play": underemployment in the East Midlands coalfields between the wars', *International Review of Social History*, 39 (1993).

Guilbert, G., K. Fearn and G. Woodhouse, 'Archaeological evaluation of crop-marks near Holme Pierrepont, Nottinghamshire 1922: an interim report', *TTS*, 98 (1994).

Guilford, E. L., *A History of Abel Collin's Charity, Nottingham* (Nottingham, 1915).

Gurnham, R., *A History of the Trade Union Movement in the Hosiery and Knitwear Industry* (Leicester, 1976).

Hall, R. A., 'The Five Boroughs of the Danelaw', *Anglo-Saxon England*, 18 (1989).

Hamilton, A., *Nottingham City of Caves* (Nottingham, n.d.).

Hammond, P. J., 'The collection and disposal of Nottingham's night-soil', *NH*, 34 (1985).

Harrison, F. M. W., 'Nonconformity and the corporation of Nottingham', *Baptist Quarterly*, 21 (1965–6).

— *The Nottinghamshire Baptists* (1978).

Haslam, J., 'The Second Burh of Nottingham', *Landscape History*, 9 (1987).

Hayes, N. J., 'Tammany Hall resurrected' Images of Labour Caucus Rule in Nottingham, 1956–60', *TTS*, 68 (1993).

— 'Municipal subsidy and Tory minimalism: building the Nottingham Playhouse, 1942–1963', *Midland History*, 19 (1994).

— *Consensus and Controversy: City Politics in Nottingham 1945–66* (Liverpool, 1996).

Heath, J., 'Leisure provision in Victorian Nottingham', *NH*, 28 (1982).

Henstock, A., 'County House, High Pavement, Nottingham: A Georgian and Regency town house', *TTS*, 78 (1974).

— 'Late medieval building contracts for the Nottingham area', *TTS*, 88 (1984).

— 'A road traffic census of Nottingham in 1819', *TTS*, 90 (1986).

— *Tracing the History of Your House* (Nottingham, 1988).

Hildyard, M. T. H., 'Some letters of Robert and Mary Thoroton and others', *TTS*, 57 (1953).

Hilton, C., *Torvill and Dean: the Full Story* (Oxford, 1994).

Hodder, E., *Life of Samuel Morley* (1889).

Holmes, D. E., 'A craftsman in iron: Francis Foulgham, Ironsmith, and the Newdigate family', *NH*, 24 (1980).

Holt, J. C., *Robin Hood* (revised edn, 1989).

Honeyman, K., *Origins of Enterprise: Business Leadership in the Industrial Revolution* (Manchester, 1982).

Hosford, D. H., *Nottingham, Nobles and the North* (Hamden, 1976).

Hudson, J. W., *A History of Adult Education* (1851).

Husain, M. S., 'The increase and distribution of New Commonwealth immigrants in Greater Nottingham', *EMG*, 6 (1975).

Hutchinson, J. (ed.), *Lucy Hutchinson: Memoirs of Colonel Hutchinson* (1908).

Hutchinson, L., *Memoirs of the Life of Colonel Hutchinson* (1806).

Iliffe, R. and W. Baguley, *Victorian Nottingham: a Story in Pictures* (20 vols., Nottingham, 1970–83).

Jackson, W. G., *Nottingham – A Sketch of Its History and Industries* (Nottingham, 1933).
Jacob, F. H., *A History of the General Hospital near Nottingham* (Bristol, 1951).
Jenkins, H. M., *Church Schools in Nottinghamshire* (Nottingham, 1954).
Jennings, S. B., 'The 1669 Ecclesiastical Returns for Nottinghamshire: a reassessment of the strength of Protestant Nonconformity', *TTS*, 99 (1995).
Johnson, R., 'Seventeenth century ironworks at Bulwell and Kirkby', *TTS*, 64 (1960).
Jones, Carol A., *A History of Nottingham School of Design* (Nottingham, 1993).
Knight, D., 'Excavations of an Iron Age settlement at Gamston, Nottinghamshire', *TTS*, 96 (1992).
Knight, D. and A. J. Howard, *Archaeology and Alluvium in the Trent Valley: an Archaeological Assessment of the Floodplain and Gravel Terraces* (Nottingham, 1995).
Lamplugh, G. W. and B. Smith, *The Water Supply of Nottinghamshire from Underground Sources* (1914).
Lawrence, D., *Black Migrants, White Natives: a Study of Race Relations in Nottingham* (Cambridge, 1974).
Lawrence, D. H., *Nottingham and the Mining Country in Selected Essays* (1929).
Laxton, B., 'Nottinghamshire houses dated by dendrochronology', *TTS*, 99, (1995).
Leeman, F. W., *Co-Operation in Nottingham* (Nottingham, 1963).
Leighton-Boyce, J. A. S. L., *Smiths the Bankers 1658–1958* (1958).
High Pavement Chapel Biographical Catalogue of Portraits (Nottingham, 1932).
Lester, J. F. M., *Dear St Catherine's* (1929).
Lingwood, Lemmon, *The Illustrated Handbook to Nottingham* (Norwich, 1906).
Longford, S., 'Women's mobility deprivation: a case study of Strelley, Nottingham', *EMG*, 15 (1993).
Lowe, D. and J. Richards, *The City of Lace* (1982).
Lucas, J. and B. Haynes, *The Trent Bridge Battery* (Glasgow, 1985).
Lyon, R., *1843–1968. The Nottingham College of Art and Design* (Nottingham, 1968).
MacCormick, A., 'Prehistoric bronzes in Nottingham City Museums', unpublished report, Brewhouse Yard Museum (1992).
MacCormick, A. G. *et al.*, 'Three dug-out canoes and a wheel from Holme Pierrepont, Notts. ', *TTS*, 72 (1968).
Mackreth, D. F., 'Nottingham, Broxtowe', *East Midland Archaeological Bulletin*, 8 (1965).
McLynn, F. J., 'Nottingham and the Jacobite Rising of 1745', *TTS*, 83 (1979).
Macmillan, A. W., 'Bronze Age metalwork', Handlist 1, University of Nottingham Museum (1976).
McVay, D., *Notts County Football Club* (Nottingham, 1988).
Madeley, R., 'The geography of health in Greater Nottingham', *EMG*, 9 (1986).
Manning, Ian, *Images of Nottingham* (Derby, 1994).
Marshall, R., *A History of Nottingham City Transport, 1897–1959* (Nottingham, 1960).
Mason, S. A., 'Tobacco and lace: the growth of John Player and Sons, 1881–1903', *TTS*, 85 (1981).
— *Nottingham Lace, 1760s–1950s* (Ilkeston, 1994).
Mastoris, S., 'The reeves and bailiffs of the town of Nottingham before 1284', *TTS*, 87 (1983).
Mastoris, S., 'Regulating the Nottingham markets: new evidence from a thirteenth-century manuscript', *TTS*, 90 (1986).
Mastoris, S. N., 'The boundary between the English and French Boroughs of medieval Nottingham', *TTS*, 85 (1981).
— 'A tax assessment of 1504 and the topography of early Tudor Nottingham', *TTS*, 89 (1985).
Mastoris, S. N. (ed.), *History in the Making: Recent Historical Research in Nottingham and Nottinghamshire 1986* (Nottingham, 1987).
May, J., 'Some bronze implements from Nottinghamshire', *TTS*, 66 (1962).
Meller, H. E. (ed.), *Nottingham in the Eighteen Eighties* (Nottingham, 1971).
Mellors R., *In and About Nottinghamshire* (1890).
— *Radford and Hyson Green then and now* (Nottingham, 1913).
— *Old Nottingham Suburbs then and now* (Nottingham, 1914).
— *Men of Nottingham and Nottinghamshire* (2nd edn, 1924).
— *The Gardens, Parks and Walks of Nottingham and District* (Nottingham, 1926).
Millington, J. and S. Chapman, *Four Centuries of Machine Knitting* (Leicester, 1989).

Murphy, P., 'Irish settlement in Nottingham in the early nineteenth century', *TTS*, 98 (1994).

Musty, J. and A. G. MacCormick, 'An early Iron Age wheel from Holme Pierrepont, Notts. ', *Antiquaries Journal*, 53 (1973).

Nailor, A. V., 'A group of tenth-century pottery from Nottingham', *Medieval Ceramics*, 7 (1983).

Notts. County Centenary Handbook, 1862–1962 (n.d.).

O'Brien, C., 'Land and settlement in Nottinghamshire and lowland Derbyshire', *East Midland Archaeological Bulletin*, 12 (Supplement, 1978).

Oldfield, G., 'The fields within the town: the story of Nottingham's Lammas Lands', *NH*, 19 (1977).

— *The Heymann Family of West Bridgford* (typescript, Nottingham, 1983).

— 'The Nottingham Lace Market', *Textile History*, XV (1984).

— 'Municipal elections in nineteenth-century Nottingham', *NH*, 40 (1988).

— 'The Nottingham Borough Boundary Extension of 1877', *TTS*, 94 (1990).

— 'Bendigo – a local hero?', *NH*, 44 (1990).

— *The Lace Market, Nottingham* (Nottingham, Civic Society, n.d.).

O'Neill, J., 'Nottingham people in the First World War', in D. Marcombe (ed.), *Nottingham and the Great War* (Nottingham, 1985).

Oswald, A. and R. G. Hughes, 'Nottingham and Derbyshire stoneware, *Trans. English Ceramic Circle*, 9, part 2 (1974).

Owen, C. C., 'The early history of the Upper Trent Navigation', *Transport History*, 1 (1968).

Paton, J. L., *John Brown Paton: a Biography* (1913).

Pevsner, N. and E. Williamson, *The Buildings of England: Nottinghamshire* (2nd edn, 1979).

Phillips, C. W., 'Some recent finds from the Trent near Nottingham', *Antiquaries Journal*, 21 (1941).

Ponsford, M. W., 'Nottingham town wall: Park Row excavations 1967', *TTS*, 75 (1971).

Ponsford, M. W., and A. Carter, 'Nottingham town wall: Park Row excavations 1967 and 1968', *TTS*, 75 (1971).

Posnansky, M., 'The Lower and Middle Palaeolithic industries of the English East Midlands', *Proceedings of the Prehistoric Society*, 29 (1963).

Preston Morley, P. and H. Pegg, *A Revised Survey of the Seventeenth Century Tokens of Nottinghamshire* (1983).

Revill, S., 'A sixteenth century map of the River Trent near Shelford', *TTS*, 75 (1971).

Roberts, D. E., 'Controversies on lighting in Nottingham', *Local Historian*, 11 (1975).

— *Nottingham Gas Undertaking 1818–1949* (Nottingham, 1977).

Robertson, G. C. (ed.), *The Stretton Manuscripts* (Nottingham, 1910).

Roffe, D. R., 'Introduction to the Nottinghamshire Domesday', in *Nottinghamshire Domesday* (1990).

Rogers, A., 'Parish boundaries and urban history: two case studies', *Journal of the British Archaeological Association*, 3rd series, 35 (1972).

— 'Religion in Nottingham in the nineteenth century', in J. F. Phillips (ed.), *Town and Village in the Nineteenth Century* (Nottingham, 1972).

— 'The 1851 Religious Census Returns for the City of Nottingham', *TTS*, 76 (1972).

Rowley, J. J., 'Drink and the public house in Nottingham, 1830–60', *TTS*, 79 (1975).

Russell-Gebbett, J. P., 'High Pavement: Britain's first organised science school', *History of Education Society Bulletin*, 43 (1989).

— 'High Pavement School Science 1885–1905: struggle and survival, Part I', *History of Education Society Bulletin*, 52 (1993), and 'Part II', 53 (1994).

Salisbury, C. R., 'The excavation of Hemington Fields', *Current Archaeology*, 145 (1995).

Salisbury, C. R., P. J. Whitley, C. D. Litton and J. L. Fox, 'Flandrian courses of the River Trent at Colwick, Nottingham', *Mercian Geologist*, 9 (1984).

Scoffham, E., *A Vision of the City: the Architecture of T. C. Howitt* (Nottinghamshire County Council, 1992).

Seabrook, J., *What Went Wrong' Working People and the Ideals of the Labour Movement* (1978).

Seddon, P. R., 'Colonel Hutchinson and the disputes between the Nottinghamshire Parliamentarians, 1643–45: new evidence analysed', *TTS*, 98 (1994).

Shipman, J., *Excavations at Nottingham General Hospital* (1899).

Silburn, R., *People in their Places, One Hundred Years of Nottingham Life* (Nottingham, 1981).

Sillitoe, A., *Saturday Night and Sunday Morning* (1958).

— *Life Without Armour* (1995).

Simpson, A., *Stacking the Decks: a Study in Racial Inequality in Council Housing in Nottingham* (Nottingham, 1981).

Smith, C., 'The landscape and natural history of Iron Age settlement on the Trent gravels', in B. Cunliffe and T. Rowley (eds.), *Lowland Iron Age Communities in Europe* (Oxford, 1978).

Smith, R., 'The relief of urban poverty outside the Poor Law, 1800–1850: a study of Nottingham', *Midland History*, 2 (1974).

— 'Towards the mature industrial city 1800–1880: the development of All Saints Parish, Nottingham', *Midland History*, XIV (1989).

— 'Population movements and the development of working class suburbs 1801–1851: the case of Nottingham', *Local Population Studies*, 47 (1991).

Smith, R. and D. Shaw, *The Changing Character of Inner Nottingham 1800–1983* (Nottingham, 1983).

Smith, R. and P. Whysall, 'The Addison Act and the local authority response: housing policy formation and implementation in Nottingham 1917–1922', *Town Planning Review*, 61 (1990).

— 'The origins and development of local authority housing in Nottingham 1890–1960', in S. Lowe and D. Hughes (eds.), *A New Century of Social Housing* (Leicester, 1991).

Smith, R., P. Whysall and C. Beuvrin, 'Local authority inertia in housing improvement 1890–1914', *Town Planning Review*, 57 (1986).

Smith, R. S., 'A Woad Growing Project at Wollaton in the 1580s', *TTS*, 65 (1961).

— 'Glassmaking at Wollaton in the early seventeenth century', *TTS*, 66 (1962).

— *Sir Francis Willoughby of Wollaton Hall* (Nottingham, 1988).

— *Early Coal Mining Around Nottingham, 1500–1650* (Nottingham, 1989).

Snell, Lord, *Men, Movements and Myself* (1938).

Southern, A. and S. Winfield (eds.), *At a Cinema Near You: a History of Cinema in Nottingham* (Nottingham, n.d.)

Stafford, P., *The East Midlands in the Early Middle Ages* (Leicester, 1985).

Stapleton, A., *The Churches and Monasteries of Old and New Nottingham* (Nottingham, 1903).

Stevens, R., *'Fighting on the Byways', John James Charlesworth, 1900–93* (Nottingham, 1993).

— '"Disruptive Elements": the influence of the Communist Party in Nottingham and District Trades Council, 1929–1951', *Labour History Review*, 58 (1993).

Stevenson, W., 'Art sculpture in alabaster', *TTS*, 2 (1907).

— 'Topographical and other early notes about Nottingham', *TTS*, 22 (1918).

— 'Land tenures in Nottinghamshire', in J. P. Briscoe (ed.), *Old Nottinghamshire* (1881).

Stevenson, W. and A. Stapleton, *Some Account of the Religious Institutions of Old Nottingham* (Nottingham, 1895).

Sutherland, J. (ed.), *Memoirs of the Life of Colonel Hutchinson* (Oxford, 1973).

Sutton, J. F., *Nottingham Cricket Matches from 1771 to 1853* (Nottingham, 1853),

Sutton, R. C., 'Radford Grove or Folly', *TTS*, 17 (1913).

Swift, R. C., *Lively People: Methodism in Nottingham 1740–1979* (Nottingham, 1979).

Swinnerton, H., 'The story of early man in Nottinghamshire', *TTS*, 54 (1950).

Syer, G., 'A Visit to Nottingham in 1828', *NH*, 53 (1994).

Taylor, F. W., *The History of Nottingham Bluecoat School, 1706–1956* (Nottingham, 1956).

Taylor, R., *Football and its Fans: Supporters and their Relations with the Game, 1885–1985* (Leicester, 1992).

Taylor, S., 'The effect of marriage on job possibilities for women', *Oral History*, 5/2 (1977).

Teeboon, A., 'The Nottingham and Nottinghamshire Hospital Saturday Fund, 1873–1948', *TTS*, 84 (1980).

Thomas, A. W., *A History of Nottingham High School, 1513–1953* (Nottingham, 1957).

Thomas, C. J., 'The growth of Nottingham's residential area since 1919', *EMG*, (1971).

Thomas, F. M., *I. & R. Morley. A Record of a Hundred Years* (1900).

Thomis, M., *Old Nottingham* (Newton Abbot, 1968).

– 'The politics of Nottingham Enclosure', *TTS*, 71 (1967).
– *Politics and Society in Nottingham, 1785–1835* (Oxford, 1969).
– 'Gravenor Henson: the man and the myth', *TTS*, 75 (1971).
– 'The Nottingham Captain: a portrait of Jeremiah Brandreth, the Rebel', *NH*, 14 (1974).
Thomis, M. I., R. A. Preston and J. Wigley, 'Nottingham and the Reform Bill Riots of 1831: new perspectives', *TTS*, 77 (1973).
Tolley, B. H., 'Nottingham University, 1881–1911: the formative years', in *One Hundred Years of Nottingham Life: the Centenary Lectures Delivered at the University of Nottingham* (1981).
– 'University College, Nottingham, and the Nottingham Education Bill of 1901', *Journal of the History of Education*, 10, 4 (1981).
Trease, G., *Nottingham: a Biography* (1970).
Truman, N., *Nottingham and its Churches, 1449–1949* (Gloucester, 1949).
Turner, A. J. (ed.), *The Hundred Years Story of the Nottingham Forest F.C.* (n.d., *c*.1964).
Varley, D. E., *A History of the Midland Counties Lace Manufacturers Association* (Long Eaton, 1959).
– 'John Heathcoat (1783–1861) founder of the machine-made lace industry', *Textile History*, I (1968).
Victoria County History, *Nottinghamshire*, I (1906), II (1910).
Walker, M., 'The Nottingham cholera epidemic of 1832', *TTS*, 95 (1991).
Wallwork, S. C., 'A review of the statistics of the growth of the British hosiery industry 1844–1984', *Textile History*, XXII (1991).
Waltham, A. C., 'The sandstone caves of Nottingham', *Mercian Geologist*, 13 (1992).
– 'The sand mines of Nottingham', *Bulletin of the Peak District Mines Historical Society*, 12 (1994).
Wardle, D., *Education and Society in Nineteenth-Century Nottingham* (Cambridge, 1971).
Warren, J. C., 'John Blackner', *TTS*, 30 (1926).
Warsop, K. (assisted by P. Wain), *The Magpies: the Story of Notts. County Football Club* (Buckingham, 1994).
Watkin, J., 'An Iron Age shield from Ratcliffe-on-Soar', *Current Archaeology*, 141 (1994).
Watts, M. R., *Religion in Victorian Nottinghamshire: the Religious Census of 1851* (Nottingham, 1988).
Weir, C., 'The growth of an inner-urban housing development: Forest Fields, Nottingham, 1883–1914', *TTS*, 89 (1985).
– *Jesse Boot of Nottingham* (Nottingham, 1994).
Weller, J. C., *Say to the Wind: a Study of the Revival of Religion in Nottingham 1780–1850* (Nottingham, 1957).
Wells, F. A., *British Hosiery Industry* (1935).
– *Hollins and Viyella: a Study in Business History* (Newton Abbot, 1968).
Wells, R., *Riot and Political Disaffection in Nottinghamshire in the Age of Revolutions, 1776–1803* (Nottingham, 1984).
Whynes, D. and J. Giggs, 'The health of the Nottingham homeless', *Public Health*, 106/4 (1992).
Wilkes, P., *The Great Nottingham Goose Fair* (Burton-on-Trent, 1989).
Wilkins-Jones, F. M., 'The Firs, Old Basford: relic of an 18th century textile complex', *NH*, 18 (1976).
Winn, S., 'Psychiatric disorders in Nottingham: a comparison of diagnostic and age groups', *EMG*, 9 (1986).
Wood, A. C., *The History of Nottinghamshire* (Nottingham, 1937).
– 'The Duke of Kingston's Regiment of Light Horse', *TTS*, 49 (1945).
– 'The history of trade and transport on the River Trent', *TTS*, 54 (1950).
– *A History of University College, Nottingham. 1881–1948* (Oxford, 1953).
– 'Nottingham 1835–1865', *TTS*, 59 (1955).
– 'Nottingham Parliamentary Elections 1869–1900', *TTS*, 60 (1956).
Wylie, W. H. and J. Potter Briscoe, *A Popular History of Nottingham* (Nottingham, 1893).
Wyncoll, P., *Nottingham Chartism* (Nottingham, 1966).
– 'The First International in Nottingham', *Marxism Today*, December 1968.
– *The Nottingham Labour Movement 1880–1939* (1985).
Wynne-Thomas, P., *'Give me Arthur': a Biography of Arthur Shrewsbury* (1985).
– *Trent Bridge* (1987).

Young, C. S. B., 'Excavations in Nottingham', *TTS*, 74 (1970).
— 'Excavations in Nottingham', *TTS*, 75 (1971).
— 'Excavations in Nottingham', *TTS*, 76 (1972).
— 'Excavations in Nottingham', *TTS*, 78 (1974).
— *Discovering Rescue Archaeology in Nottingham* (Nottingham, 1982).

Theses and dissertations

Ablett, S., 'The Medical School of the University of Nottingham: origins and development' (University of Nottingham, Ph.D. thesis, 1992).
Amos, D., 'Food and health in nineteenth century Nottingham' (University of Nottingham, MA dissertation, 1994).
Arblaster, B., 'Health services in Nottingham and the provision for women, 1860–1940' (University of Nottingham, MA dissertation, 1985).
Atkinson, J. D., 'Working-class attitudes to education in Nottingham, 1836–1870' (University of Nottingham, Ph.D. thesis, 1976).
Bailey, E. P., 'Leenside: the Churches and the making of a Nottingham slum' (University of Nottingham, MA thesis, 1993).
Becket, E. M., 'The development of education in Nottingham in the nineteenth and early twentieth centuries' (University of Nottingham, MA thesis, 1922).
Bennett, M., 'The Royalist War Effort in the North Midlands, 1642–6' (Loughborough University, Ph.D. thesis, 1986).
Bradbury, J., 'An investigation of the spatial distribution of crime in Greater Nottingham' (University of Nottingham, Ph.D. thesis, 1981).
Chapman, S. D., 'William Felkin, 1795–1874' (University of Nottingham, MA thesis, 1960).
Cutting, D., 'The Nottingham Parliamentary Election of 1865' (University of Nottingham, M. Phil. thesis, 1972).
Donbavand, R. M., 'The social geography of Victorian Nottingham, 1851–1871' (University of Nottingham, Ph.D. thesis, 1982).
Evans, R., 'Music in eighteenth-century Nottingham' (Loughborough University, MA thesis, 1983).
Ferguson, N. A., 'Working class housing in Bristol and Nottingham 1868–1919' (University of Oregon, Ph.D. thesis, 1971).
Foster, S., 'Nottingham Chartism and the Press, 1838–1848' (University of Nottingham, MA thesis, 1985).
Fry, Terry, 'The General Lunatic Asylum, Nottingham, 1812–1902' (University of Nottingham, Advanced Certificate in Local History dissertation, 1994).
Harrison, F. M. W., 'The life and thought of the Baptists of Nottinghamshire' (University of Nottingham, M. Phil. thesis, 1972).
Hayes, N. J., 'Unemployment, employment and industry in Nottingham, 1930–39' (Open University, BA dissertation, 1986).
— 'Nottingham 1945–66: party responses to changing political, social and cultural expectations' (Open University, Ph.D. thesis, 1992).
Holloway, P. R., 'Evacuation and education' (University of Nottingham, M. Ed. thesis, 1982).
Jennings, S., 'Bunny and Bradmore 1640–1690, change and continuity in an age of revolutions' (University of Nottingham, MA thesis, 1991).
Kingscott, J. E., 'Oral history in libraries with special reference to the Nottinghamshire Oral History Collection and the Hyson Green Project' (Loughborough University, MA thesis, 1988).
Lewis, P. M., 'The evolution of the hand stocking frame 1750–1815' (University of Nottingham, M. Phil. thesis, 1985).
Lloyd, P., 'Politics and personnel of politics in Nottingham 1642–1688' (University of Nottingham, M. Phil. thesis, 1983).

Maude, S. M., 'Population, mobility and urban growth: a study of migration in the nineteenth century with particular reference to Nottingham' (University of Nottingham, M.Phil. thesis, 1974).

Moses, J. H., 'Elections and electioneering in the constituencies of Nottinghamshire, 1702–1832' (University of Nottingham, Ph.D. thesis, 1965).

Myers, A., 'The organisation and structural dimensions of Hunter–Gatherer Lithic Technology' (University of Sheffield, Ph.D. thesis, 1986).

Neel, S., 'Anglo-Saxon settlement in the East Midlands' (University of Nottingham, Ph.D. thesis, 1995).

Nutting, T. S., 'History of the British knitting machine building industry' (University of Nottingham, M.Phil. thesis, 1994).

Oldfield, G., 'The Municipal Boundary Extension of Nottingham, 1877–1952' (University of Nottingham, MA thesis, 1989).

Posnansky, M., 'Some considerations of the Pleistocene chronology and prehistory of part of the East Midlands' (University of Nottingham, Ph.D. thesis, 1956).

Pottle, M. C., 'Loyalty and patriotism in Nottingham, 1792–1816' (University of Oxford, D.Phil. thesis, 1988).

Roffe, D. R., 'Nottinghamshire and the North; a Domesday Study' (University of Leicester, Ph.D. thesis, 1987).

Russenberger, L., 'The Villa Estate in nineteenth century England' (University of Chicago, Ph.D. thesis, 1988).

Severn, J., 'Church building in Nottingham 1660–1851' (University of Nottingham, MA thesis, 1991).

Shorter, P. R., 'Election politics and political change in the East Midlands of England' (University of Cambridge, Ph.D. thesis, 1975).

Smith, R., 'The social structure of Nottingham and adjacent districts in the mid-nineteenth century' (University of Nottingham, Ph.D. thesis, 1968).

Straw, F. I., 'An analysis of the town plan of Nottingham: a study in historical geography' (University of Nottingham, MA thesis, 1967).

Thomas, C. J., 'Geographical aspects of the growth of the residential area of Greater Nottingham in the 20th Century' (University of Nottingham, Ph.D. thesis, 1968).

Tolley, B. H., 'Technical education in the East Midlands. A study in educational administration and history' (University of Nottingham, Ph.D. thesis, 1979).

Tong, Liza Anne, 'A local study of Carrington, Nottingham: industrial village to disappearing suburb, 1830–1930' (University of Nottingham, MA dissertation, 1995).

Vernon, C. V., 'The poems and letters of Henry Kirke White' (University of Nottingham, Ph.D. thesis, 1980).

Vine, P. M., 'Analysis of the Distribution of Selected Neolithic and Bronze Age artifacts in central England' (University of Nottingham, Ph.D. thesis, 1987).

Wardle, D., 'The work of the Nottingham School Board' (University of Nottingham, M.Ed. thesis, 1961).

Williams, D. H., 'The contribution of the Church of England to education in Nottingham during the nineteenth century' (University of Nottingham, MA thesis, 1991).

Williams, H., 'The lives and works of Nottingham Artists, 1750–1914' (University of Nottingham, Ph.D. thesis, 1981).

Wilson, L. F., 'The State and the housing of the English working class with special reference to Nottingham, 1845–1914' (University of California, Berkeley, Ph.D. thesis, 1970).

Wood, P., 'Political developments in Nottingham, 1868 to 1885' (University of Nottingham, MA thesis, 1989).

Index

Note: Page references in *italics* refer to figures, those in **bold** refer to tables

List of subscribers

Andrew Abbott
Mrs S. Aldred
Barry and Zofia Alexander
David G. Allen
Mrs D. M. Amos
R. W. Arberry

D. E. Bagley
James Bagshaw
E. P. Bailey
Mrs M. A. Bailey
Simon Bailey
Miss Eileen M. Ball
Mr K. T. Ball
Revd John Banks
Mr Ray Banks
Arthur and Joasia Barton
Gary and Adele Bates
Timothy Beals
Miss V. M. Beecham
Anthony Beecroft
David Beecroft
Beeston and District Civic Society
Mr B. W. Beilby
Bibliographical Services, Nottinghamshire County Council
Mr Eric Binns
Graham Black
Mrs Audrey Bland
Mrs J. M. Bonser
Mrs M. J. Booth
Jean and John Boseley
Alfred S. Bowley
Mrs Barbara Bradley
Bramcote and District Probus Club
Joan Bray
Ralph and Joy Bristow
John Brock
Brocklewood Junior School, Nottingham
Michael Brook
The Revd John Brown and Mrs Patricia Brown
Stuart Burnett
Mr L. Burton
Mr R. E. Butler
Mrs L. Buxton

John Cadman
Andrew J. Cameron LL.B.
Miss D. M. Cannell
E. F. Cantle
Mr M. B. Carter
Mr R. M. Carter
Mr Alec Casterton
Peter Anthony Casterton
Professor L. J. Challis
Mrs Sheila A. Chambers
R. E. Charmbury
Mr Bryan Chorm and Miss Janet Clarke
Claremont Primary School, Nottingham
Councillor Alan Clark
Mr R. C. Clark
Mr P. F. Clarke
Mr Robin C. Claytor
Mr S. R. Cockbill
Professor Edward C. Cocking
Mr E. R. Coddington
Mrs Kathleen Coles
Mrs Margaret J. Connors
Mr Gary Cooke
Mrs R. H. Cooper
Mrs Rita Cooper
Dr Simon Corcoran
Sir Neil Cossons O.B.E.
Professor A. D. Cox
Richard Cox
Maxwell A. J. B. Craven
Crossdale Drive Primary School, Keyworth
Mrs Anita K. Csiba
Ian and Councillor Georgina Jane Culley

Mr F. Danby
Dr P. R. Danby
Mr and Mrs P. Darlison
J. Davies
John Davies
Mr M. J. Davies
Dr John H. Davis
Mrs K. H. Davis
Mr and Mrs H. Dawson
N. J. Dawson
Mr J. E. Dear
Mr Frank Dennett M.B.E.
Department of Continuing Education, University of Nottingham
Barry and Anne Donlan
Mr K. Donlan

LIST OF SUBSCRIBERS

Mr T. G. B. Donlan
K. E. Drage
Peter Richard Duke

Mr Peter Ellis
Mrs S. M. Elsdon
D. M. Elson
Mrs M. Exley

Peter Featherby
Mrs P. J. Fisher
Mary Foley
A. P. Ford
A. J. Fox
Miss J. M. Fox
Malcolm Fox
Mr and Mrs A. France
Mr A. Francis
Mrs C. M. French
John and Sheila Frisby
Douglas Froggatt
Mr T. J. Fry
Mrs Grace E. A. Fyles

Mrs F. M. Gardiner
Mr A. P. Garner
Mr K. R. Gent
Mrs Judith Gifford
Mr H. B. Gillett
Mr Graham Godfrey
Mr K. Goodman
A. A. Goodwin
Mr M. D. Grant
Peter Graves
Ian C. Gray
Valerie and John Gray
Dr A. D. Green
Canon Fred Green
Professor and Mrs A. D. M. Greenfield
Professor Alan R. Griffin
Mr E. A. Grummitt
John and Janet Gurnhill

Mr and Mrs I. F. Hall
A. N. R. Hamilton
Martine Hamilton-Knight
Mr M. H. F. Hammond
Mr and Mrs R. Hammond
Mr P. Hands
Mr J. E. Harlow
Alma Harris
Mr H. A. Harrison
Mrs Marion Harrison
Noel Harrower
John Hewitt F.C.A.
David Hey
Mr J. B. Hibbitt
Mr B. Hickling
J. A. Hicks
Mr R. Hill
Peter Hoare
Mrs Derrica Hodgson M.A.
P. J. Holland
Ann and Neville Hoskins
Mr P. T. Howarth
Mr R. A. Hudson
Tom Huggon
Chris Hughes
Dr Jill Hughes

Huntingdon Primary School, Nottingham
Mrs S. D. Husbands
Mr M. Hutchings
S. J. Hyde

D. R. Jackson
Mr M. J. Jackson
Mrs Abida Y. Jacques
Robert C. James
Miss Fiona C. Jelley
Revd Stuart Jennings
Jesse Gray Primary School, Nottingham
Ivan H. Jones
Mrs Maureen Jones
Professor Michael Jones
Philip E. Jones

Mr R. R. Kershaw
Miss Kathleen Killingback
Miss J. U. Killup
Joan King
Geoff and Judy Kingscott
Gavin Kinsley
Mr S. A. B. Kipping
Richard Kirk
Ms M. A. Knowles

Mr and Mrs R. A. Latham
Mr E. J. Lawrence
Hugh McD. Lawson
Kenneth and Margaret Lawson
Miss S. M. Leeds
John R. Lester
Mr David Lister
Mr and Mrs D. Little
J. H. Littlewood
Patricia A. Lloyd
The Local History Press
Local Studies Library, Nottingham
John William Lock
Brian Loughbrough
Mr Peter Lowery

J. M. McMeeking
S. Manley
Mr R. W. Manson
Mr Stephen C. A. Marks
Stanley Marsden
Mr Paul R. Marshall
Mr D. E. Martin
Mr G. Mason
Andrew Geoffrey Mein
J. Miller
Mr T. M. Milner
Dr Anne Mitson
Mr S. C. Moore
Nigel and Mary Morley
Dr G. M. Morris
Mr J. Morton
Sarah Morton
Mount C. of E. Primary School, Newark
Miss F. N. Mulholland
Mrs E. Mumford
Neil Munroe
G. Murfet
Mrs J. Murray

P. A. Neaverson
Newark Archaeological and Local History Society

D. A. Newham
Maureen Newton
Andrew Nicholson
J. E. and Mrs J. M. Nicholson
T. J. Norman
Nottingham High School
Nottingham Subscription Library
Nottingham Trent University
Nottingham Trent University Clifton Campus Library

Marcus Oakland
Mr Brian Odam
Peter and Catherine O'Malley
Orchard Primary and Nursery School, Nottingham
A. V. Oscroft

Mr R. Parkinson
Mr J. D. Parry
Mr N. S. Parsons
Sylvia E. Parsons
Denis R. Pearson
Barbara and Robin Phillips
Miss D. F. Phillips
G. F. Pike
Brian G. Pilcher
Brian Playle
Mr J. Plumb
Mr Roy Plumb
Charles Pogson
Mr David Potts
Mr M. E. Pugson
Mr Richard H. Pykett

John Radmall
Rob Raynham
Mr R. E. Redgate
Caroline E. Rees
Councillor John Riley
Miss A. S. Robertson
Mrs Barbara Robinson
Beryl Robinson
John N. Robinson
Mr P. Robinson
Mr D. W. Roe
Peter W. Roper
Sandra Rose
Mr G. G. Rothwell
Revd P. Rowley
Ruddington Local History and Amenity Society
Miss Dorothy Rutland

St Margaret Clitherow Catholic Primary School, Nottingham
Ms Jean M. Sallis
Mrs P. M. Sansome
Mr J. H. Saunders
Dave Savage
Mr B. T. Scothon
Mrs Joan Sears
John Severn
Ian Charles Shapeero
Bill Shaw
Mr M. A. Shaw
The Shepherd School, Nottingham
Margaret and David Sibley
Professor and Mrs H. Siefken
D. W. Sissons
Dr David Smith
J. H. Smith
Mr M. Smith
Mrs Priscilla Smith
Robert Smith
Mr R. W. Smith
Mrs P. M. Snellgrove
The Society of the Lacemakers of Calais
Josephine Spray
Mr and Mrs M. J. Stacey
Sydney Stares
Barry Start
Mr George Stevens
Mrs J. Stevenson
Mrs F. A. Stokes
Mr W. Storer
Dr Brian Sugden
Mr F. E. W. Swann
John S. Swinscoe

Mrs J. E. Targett
Chris Taylor
Mr David Graham Taylor
Robert Taylor
R. Penniston Taylor
Mr Bryan Temple
Hugh Thompson
Alan Thurlby
David Tilly
Mr J. H. Treece
Alan Trench
Pamela and Gordon Tunnicliffe
Mrs G. A. Turland

V. M. van der Lande
Mr J. Vass
J. F. Veale
C. M. Voisey

Mrs Eileen Wade
Mrs Maisie Waggott
Mrs Marjorie Wainwright
P. B. Waite
P. Wakefield
Tony and Janet Waltham
Michael Walton
Christine M. Ward
Mr M. Webster
Lady White
Ted and Gillian White
Dr John K. Whittle
John Douglas Whitworth
David M. Wilde
D. J. Willey M. A.
Canon D. H. Williams
Mr E. C. Wilmshurst
Mr J. V. and Mrs R. A. Wilson
Charles Woolsey
Mr John W. A. Worley
Professor Chris Wrigley
Dr D. L. Wykes

Mr Cheong-Ho Yi
Mrs Beryl Young